JUN 0 6 2007

WITHDRAWN

D1116493

The Administration of Physical Education, Sport, and Leisure Programs

Printed Materials Collection
IOWA CITY IOWA

sixth edition

The Administration of Physical Education, Sport, and Leisure Programs

Kenneth G. Tillman
Trenton State College

Edward F. Voltmer

Arthur A. Esslinger

Betty Foster McCue
University of Oregon

796.06
A238t
1995

Allyn and Bacon
Boston • London • Toronto • Sydney • Tokyo • Singapore

NC WESLEYAN COLLEGE LIBRARY
ROCKY MOUNT, NC 27804

Senior Series Editor: Suzy Spivey
Vice President, Social Sciences: Susan Badger
Series Editorial Assistant: Lisa Davidson
Manufacturing Buyer: Aloka Rathnam
Marketing Manager: Anne Harvey
Editorial-Production Service: Electronic Publishing Services Inc.
Cover Administrator: Suzanne Harbison

Copyright © 1996, 1979, 1967, 1958, 1949, 1938 by Allyn & Bacon
A Simon & Schuster Company
Needham Heights, Massachusetts   02194

All rights reserved. No part of the material protected by this copyright notice may be reproduced or utilized in any form or by any means, electronic or mechanical, including photocopying, recording, or by any information storage and retrieval system, without written permission from the copyright owner.

Library of Congress Cataloging-in-Publication Data

The Administration of physical education, sport, and leisure programs
/ Kenneth G. Tillman . . . [et al.]. — 6th ed.
        p.   cm.
    Rev. ed. of: The organization and administration of physical
education / Edward F. Voltmer . . . [et al.]. 5th ed. c1979.
    Includes bibliographical references and index.
    ISBN 0-205-18646-7
    1. Physical education and training—Administration.   I. Tillman,
Kenneth G.   II. Organization and administration of physical education.
GV343.5.A36   1995
796'.06'9--dc20   95-13893
                                                                CIP

Printed in the United States of America

10 9 8 7 6 5 4 3 2 1   99 98 97 96 95

NC WESLEYAN COLLEGE LIBRARY
ROCKY MOUNT, NC 27804

Dedication

The first edition of this book was published in 1938. It was followed by editions in 1949, 1958, 1967, and 1979. Dr. Edward F. Voltmer and Dr. Arthur A. Esslinger, authors of the first four editions, were pioneers in the field of physical education administration. They were instrumental in formulating administrative theory in physical education. Dr. Betty Foster McCue, my co-author of the fifth edition, was a fine administrator who continued the leadership Drs. Voltmer and Esslinger provided through this textbook. These three authors, who were leaders in the physical education profession for many years, communicated the principles of physical education administration to thousands of students and professors while carrying out their administrative responsibilities at a number of different universities. It seems appropriate to dedicate the sixth edition, to Dr. Edward F. Voltmer, Dr. Arthur A. Esslinger, and Dr. Betty Foster McCue. They have contributed much to the physical education profession and to the people who were privileged to know them.

Contents

Preface

A challenging task in any revision is to maintain the integrity of previous editions and to translate changes that have occurred during the interim into a practical format for students. These objectives guided my efforts as I researched the material for this book and ultimately put it in textbook format. Because it has been 15 years since the fifth edition, a major restructuring, updating, and refining of the administrative material was needed. There have been significant changes in the physical education profession and in administrative theory during the past 15 years. These changes are reflected in the presentation of each chapter.

The earlier editions of this book were written primarily for students planning careers in education. There has been an explosion in career opportunities for physical education students in nonteaching professions such as leisure, sports, and health promotion, and this edition has been designed for these students as well as students in educational programs. The book is structured to be pertinent for students preparing to administer nonteaching or teaching programs. It can also be used effectively in a class that includes both teaching and nonteaching physical education majors.

The format of this edition includes three distinct parts. Part I includes five chapters that present administrative and management concepts. Part II covers management responsibilities in the areas of public relations, liability, facilities, financial management and budgeting, the purchase, care, and security of equipment, and evaluation. Parts I and II are relevant to students preparing for either teaching or nonteaching administrative positions. Part III includes chapters that pertain to specific career fields such as teaching of physical education, the teaching of health education, administering intramural or athletic programs, and the management of leisure and health promotion programs. These chapters can be used individually if all of these programs are not included in the administrative course for which this text is being used.

Chapter 17 is an entirely new chapter and presents comprehensive information about the administration of leisure and health promotion programs. Included is information about careers in the fitness industry, sports medicine, recreation, dance, and sports. Special programs such as outdoor education, orienteering, outward bound, and adventure education are other career fields presented in this chapter.

The relationship of physical education to health education, intramurals, and athletics has changed dramatically since the early editions of this text. This sixth edition presents the current status of each of these programs with the attendant problems and issues that confront each one. Although it is recognized that health education is a discipline separate from physical education, health education maintains an important presence in this edition. There are still states that have joint certification in health education and physical education and educational administrators, particularly in secondary schools and smaller higher education institutions, continue to have administrative responsibility for both programs.

Appendixes A and B remain outstanding features of this text. Appendix A provides thorough coverage of methods of organizing competition and Appendix B presents athletic field and court layouts. Appendix C, which includes curriculum guidelines to supplement the information in the physical education and health education program chapters, is an added feature.

An activity teaching approach can be used to present the administrative principles included in this edition. A series of activities are included at the end of each chapter. Suggested simulations provide the opportunity for students to experience administrative duties and the performance tasks give students the opportunity for further hands-on involvement with administrative responsibilities. An up-to-date, expanded reference list at the end of each chapter further strengthens this edition.

Updated coverage of Title IX and the impact of the American Disabilities Act of 1990 and the preceding federal legislation is included throughout the book. Each chapter has been rewritten to capture current practices in the field and to reflect on societal influences on programs and administrative procedures and policies. Technological advances are incorporated throughout the book and it is organized to move smoothly from topic to topic, with administrative relationships clearly defined.

This edition presents administration in a comprehensive way without getting mired in extraneous details. It is easy to read and understand, and the material is carefully arranged in a logical sequence. Administrative concepts are clearly articulated with easy-to-understand terminology and the information is presented in a straightforward manner that fits well with a variety of teaching styles.

I wish to thank many people who provided assistance and support during the writing of this edition. First of all, I want to thank my good friend Dr. David Camaione, professor of exercise science at the University of Connecticut, for suggestions and ideas that made it possible to incorporate leisure and health promotion programs as an integral part of this book. Many colleagues at Trenton State College shared ideas and information. They include Dr. Roosevelt Butler and Dr. Joao Neves from the School of Business, Dr. Daniel Schmidt and Dr. Phyllis Cooper from Physical Education, Dr. Joseph Herzstein and Dr. Donald Brown from Health Education, Dr. Frank Romano and Dr. Donald Wright from Educational Administration, Mrs. Jeanne Cortina from the Student Life Office, Dr. Ann Shenkle from Special Education, Mr. Joseph Camillone, Athletic Trainer, and Mr. Tom Isaac, Athletic

Equipment Manager. I am also indebted to many librarians at the Roscoe L. West Library for their assistance and encouragement. I would also like to thank the reviewers of this edition: Debra E. Westermann, College of Great Falls; Agneta Sibrava, Arkansas State University; J. Walter Lisk, University of South Carolina at Aiken; Leon E. Griffin, University of New Mexico; and Daniel P. Stewart, Flagler College.

Finally, it would not have been possible to complete this project without the support of my wife, Dee. She kept me on track when my computer skills needed refining and found a way to put the charts and tables found in this book on the computer.

Special Acknowledgments

Edward F. Voltmer

Edward F. Voltmer (1897–1964) began his teaching career in country schools in Iowa after his graduation from high school. He enlisted in the U.S. Navy during World War I, where he was a medical corpsman and marched with John Philip Sousa's band. He then went to the University of Iowa, where he earned nine varsity letters (three each in football, basketball, and baseball) and received his bachelor's degree in 1923. After teaching in Okmulgee, Oklahoma, following his graduation, he returned to the University of Iowa, where he earned his M.S. degree in 1927. He then taught and coached at Arizona State Teachers College (now University of Northern Arizona), where he established the Department of Health and Physical Education. In 1932 he received his Ph.D. from the University of Iowa. He was on the faculty at the University of Iowa for the next four years, where he coached the tennis team and taught in the physical education program. Albion College in Michigan selected him to head their Department of Health and Physical Education in 1936. He continued in this position until 1943 and also coached the basketball, tennis, and golf teams at the college. The following year he managed a Service Club in Coffeeville, Kansas, and then joined the army, where he directed a physical reconditioning program for wounded servicemen at Percy Jones Hospital in Battle Creek, Michigan, before returning to Albion College as a professor of physical education in 1946. In 1947 he accepted a position at Drake University in Des Moines, Iowa, where he was head of the Department of Health, Physical Education, and Recreation and coached golf until his death in 1964. He was active in many organizations, coauthored the Handbook for Athletes with his brother, Dr. C.D. Voltmer, and published numerous articles. He and his wife, Ruby, had three daughters.

Arthur A. Esslinger

Arthur A. Esslinger (1905–1973) received his B.S. in physical education in 1931 and his M.S. in education in 1932 from the University of Illinois. He received his Ph.D. in physical education from the University of Iowa in 1938. He served on the faculty at Bradley University from 1931 to 1938 and Stanford University from 1938 to 1943. From 1943 to 1946 he filled several capacities for the armed forces, where he served as special consultant to both the secretary of war and the surgeon general of the army and was chief of the physical reconditioning branch and director of physical training for the Army Service Forces. He was director of physical education at Springfield College from 1946 to 1953. He then assumed the position of dean of the School of Health, Physical Education, and Recreation at the University of Oregon, which he held for 18 years until 1971. On retiring as dean, he continued to teach and advise graduate students. At the time of his death in 1973, he had been appointed as professor and director of graduate studies in the School of Health, Physical Education, and Recreation at the State University of New York at Buffalo. He was active in numerous professional organizations and served as president of both the American Academy of Physical Education and the American Association for Health, Physical Education, and Recreation, now AAHPERD. He received many awards, including the highest award of AAHPERD, the Luther Halsey Gulick Award. He wrote a number of publications, including several manuals he wrote for the army, where he founded a modern physical training program based on concepts from physiology, psychology, and physical education. He served on the Board of Directors of Little League Baseball from its inception until his death and he was on the Board of Directors of the YMCA. He and his wife, Mary, had one daughter.

Betty Foster McCue

Betty Foster McCue (born 1916) received her B.S. in physical education from the University of Pittsburgh in 1942. She then worked for four years at YMCAs in Warren, Ohio, and Denver, Colorado. After completing her M.S. at MacMurray College in 1947, she remained there for two years as an instructor before moving to Iowa State University, where she received her Ph.D. in 1952. She spent two years as an associate professor at the University of Nebraska before being appointed professor and chair of the Department of Physical Education for Women, first at Oberlin College from 1955 to 1965 and then at Duke University from 1965 to 1968. During this period, she also taught summer school at the Universities of North Dakota, Colorado, Iowa, and Utah. In her free time she enjoyed camping, bicycling, canoeing, and traveling. In 1968, she moved to the University of Oregon, where she was appointed associate dean of the College of Health, Physical Education, and Recreation in 1972. She married Arthur Slater-Hammel in 1977 and retired from the University of Oregon the following year. She is author of Physical Education Activities for Women (Macmillan, 1969) and served on the editorial board of the Journal of Physical Education and Recreation. She was also advisory board chairperson of Quest. She was active in professional organizations and was chair of AAHPER (now AAHPERD) professional preparation panel for three years and a board member for the National Association of Physical Education for College Women and the North American Society for Sport History. Dr. McCue maintained a strong interest in international physical education throughout her career and was a representative at the International Association of Sports for Girls and Women Conferences in Paris and Tokyo and presented a paper at an Asian Seminar at the Wingate Institute in Israel.

Professional achievement is only one dimension of these physical educators. They were caring individuals whose outstanding personal attributes formed the foundation for the impressive contributions they made to the profession that meant so much to them. It was also these outstanding personal characteristics that made them special to family, friends, colleagues, and generations of students.

I

Administrative and Management Concepts

1

Fundamentals and Importance
of Administration

Administration or Management?

The terms *administration* and *management* are often used interchangeably to refer to the direction and control of the affairs of a business, institution, or government entity. Similarly, the words *administrator* and *manager* both describe one who has executive responsibility and maintains control or direction over some organization or part of the organization. Both of these terms are used in this context throughout this book. The terms *management* and *managers* are more prevalent in business; in education, the terms *administration* and *administrator* are more common.

There are different levels of administration or management. People in the top levels are more likely to be called administrators, with middle- and lower-level personnel called managers. This distinction is based on the degree of responsibility, not on the value or worth of the person carrying out the responsibility. Many levels of administrative responsibility are given to people in the physical education, leisure, and sport fields. For this reason, a book of this type is important for anyone preparing for a position in these professions.

Importance of Administration

An organization is a group of people working together in a planned and coordinated manner to achieve a designated purpose. Each of us is involved in a variety of organizations that provide opportunities and services not available to individuals working independently. Skillful administration is essential to the success of the organization. Purposes of organizations differ significantly and range from developing and selling goods to providing services. The primary purpose of physical education, leisure, and sport organizations is to provide services. Organizations vary widely in size, composition, resources, division of work, and structure of the administration. Each organization develops objectives to guide its endeavors. The objectives of an educational institution differ from the objectives of a profit-oriented health promotion organization and the objectives of both differ from the objectives of a nonprofit organization that provides services for older adults. The common denominator is that the success of each is based on the effectiveness of the organization.

Organizations are a key ingredient in the development of modern cultures. Throughout history, organizations have been critical not only for improved living conditions, but even for survival. Organizational principles apply in a similar manner to the success and survival of educational, leisure, and sport programs. Why do some fitness centers fail? Why are some school physical education programs not supported by the communities they serve? Why do some intercollegiate and interscholastic athletic programs deviate from acceptable educational practices? The answers to these questions can often be found in the failure of organizational procedures and the lack of effective administrative leadership.

Organizations do not automatically function smoothly and efficiently. Their success depends largely on a specialized type of leadership known as administration or management. Administrators are responsible for coordinating the resources of an organization to achieve its goals. Many skills are required of an effective administrator. Interpersonal skills are paramount for success as an administrator. Gone are the days of the autocratic administrator who arbitrarily makes decisions without involving other members of the organization. Ability to communicate is the basis for establishing and attaining organizational objectives. Employee satisfaction, which has been found to be a critical element for success in business, is equally important for success in nonbusiness endeavors.

It is true that what can be accomplished depends on the facilities, equipment, personnel, and other situational variables. However, a good administrator will have a substantially better product or program than an ineffective administrator. Likewise, over a period of time a skilled administrator will be more successful in bringing about improvements in facilities, equipment, personnel, community support, and financial resources. Outstanding facilities and resources do not automatically result in model programs, nor do inadequacies in these areas doom organizations to mediocrity. It has been demonstrated repeatedly that an administrator makes a difference by appropriately using the skills of staff members and using administrative techniques to overcome both real and perceived deficiencies.

Attainment of objectives depends on the administrator being familiar with legislation and professional practices and standards. This information must be incorporated into the objectives, which are established in a cooperative fashion. Including the best practices and keeping in view the standards pertinent to the organization leads to high-quality programs. In addition, an administrator's success is determined by the level of involvement of the organization's members. Teamwork is the hallmark of a good organization. Teamwork becomes more difficult as the size of the organization increases. Problems often arise when people do not work together harmoniously. Jealousies, frictions, and confrontations often challenge the administrator. Skill in overcoming these types of problems and channeling individual efforts into group cohesion leads to a level of morale that characterizes exemplary programs.

Justification for Studying Administration

In virtually all programs of professional preparation in leisure studies, physical education, and sports, courses in administration are required. Administrative theory has evolved into an academic discipline with important application to these fields. Administrative courses have come to be regarded as essential for professional preparation for several reasons. In the first place, even entry-level positions in physical education, sports, and leisure programs entail administrative responsibility. The nature of these programs demands that professionals have administrative skills in order to function effectively. Examples are the teacher who ability-groups a class, the coach who arranges a practice schedule, the aerobics instructor who publicizes an innovative aerobics class, and the intramural coordinator who organizes teams for competitive equality.

Regardless of experience, whether a first-year employee or a 20-year staff member, work in an organization will be under the direction of an administrator. The size of the organization determines the levels of administration and the person to whom one reports. In any case, it is important to know how to operate within the organization and under the direction of an administrator. Being familiar with the administrative pattern of the organization provides insights into the work environment. This leads to being a more effective employee. Understanding the complexities of administration also increases the opportunity to provide positive input. The relationship of the administrator and staff person largely determines the success and satisfaction of the work experience.

Many graduates in these fields eventually gravitate to administrative positions. These assignments cannot be undertaken and discharged successfully unless the individual has had professional preparation for them. It is possible for a person to be a successful teacher, instructor, or coach and yet be totally unprepared to move to a higher administrative level. Administration is a large, involved field of specialization with its own philosophy, principles, and techniques; these must be acquired before one can become a skilled administrator. The rapid development of special courses, certification programs, and administrative programs in executive development and management indicates the growth and importance of this field of study.

The following chapters detail specific administrative responsibilities to prepare professionals in physical education, health education, leisure studies, and sport for assuming administrative positions.

The Task of Administration

As the leader of an organization, the administrator should accomplish the goals for which the organization was created and for which it exists. Whether in the field of leisure, athletics, or instructional physical education, the responsibility of the administrator is to attain the objectives that have been established. However, the accomplishment of the objectives of the various programs represents only part of the administrator's task. There is also responsibility for the people associated with the administrator in the organization. Their commitment and effort on behalf of the organization's objectives must be secured.

Administrators sometimes think that if their staff members have high morale and satisfaction with their jobs that production will take care of itself. This is too simplistic. It is important to have good attitudes and high morale on a staff but this does not automatically result in the necessary level of motivation to perform at an optimum level. Accompanying these characteristics must be a commitment on the part of all staff members to the organization's objectives. This translates into staff members' continuing to develop their talents through graduate study, in-service programs, and keeping up-to-date by reading professional journals and books and attending conferences and conventions. This is a major task for all administrators who desire their organization to reach long-term objectives.

Motivation is a complex factor that must be carefully considered by every administrator. Different types of motivation are needed for different types of positions and people differ in the ways in which they are influenced by motivational approaches. A major challenge of an administrator is to motivate staff to perform at their highest level of ability and to synchronize personal objectives with the objectives of the organization. This is why communication skills are considered to be one of the four essential skills of an administrator (see the following section). An administrator must be an effective communicator in order to spell out the means by which the organizational objectives will be attained and to obtain the enthusiastic cooperation of the staff. The ability to motivate is one of the most important administrative tasks, and well-planned and carefully targeted communication is the key to motivation.

It is also possible for the administrator to put a great deal of pressure on subordinates to increase their output and to ignore human relations within the group. Research studies have shown that technically competent, job-centered, insensitive, and tough administrators may achieve impressive production records for a year or two. However, the results of this approach are invariably lowered morale, dissent, lack of motivation, low productivity, and high personnel turnover. The professional sports world provides graphic examples of this principle. Certain football coaches and baseball managers are hired for short-term results. Their teams often improve dramatically for the first few years, but then there is a major collapse or at least a steady reversion to their former level of play and the coach is fired, only to resurface with some other team whose owner is desperate for a winning season.

Essential Skills of Administration

Many competencies are critically important for the administrator. These skills must be present if an organization is to achieve high performance through maximum use of its human, financial, and material resources. Numerous proficiencies comprise each of the essential skills described in this book.

Communication Skill

Communication skill is the ability to send and receive information, ideas, emotions, and feelings. Through communication, information is exchanged and shared and people influence the attitudes, behaviors, and understandings of others. This skill has become more and more important as the dictatorial administrative approach has been found ineffective. The key to reaching organizational objectives is to be able to communicate effectively with staff, colleagues at different administrative levels, program participants, and members of the community.

Different types of communication skills must be used. Both verbal and nonverbal communication are important. Verbal communication includes both spoken and written exchange. Modern technology has exploded the range of verbal communication. Faxes and e-mail now compete with memos, letters, newsletters, and posters for communicating thoughts and messages. Nonverbal actions such as gestures and body language also transmit information that an administrator should comprehend and be able to use. Pictures, cartoons, and diagrams are other nonverbal techniques that are used.

Technical Skill

Technical skill is the ability to apply the processes, methods, procedures, and techniques that are necessary to accomplish or comprehend the specific kind of work done in an organization.

The technical skills required in sport, leisure studies, health education, and physical education include budget making, equipment purchase and care, planning and maintenance of facilities, scheduling athletic contests, publicizing activities and events, establishing policies, developing programs, supervising instruction, managing an office, evaluating programs, and enforcing safety procedures.

Conceptual Skill

Conceptual skill includes the ability to think abstractly. Ideas are conceived and applied to the organization. This is the ability to see the big picture and view the organization as a whole. It is important to understand the operation of the organization within its environment and to anticipate changes that will take place.

Conceptual skill is a special ability that keeps an organization in the forefront. This skill permits a person to be a leader, not just a managerial overseer. New trends are viewed within the context of the overall organization and changes are based on one's analytical and diagnostic capacities.

Interpersonal Skill

Interpersonal skill is the ability to interact with other people effectively. It includes the ability to work well with others and to motivate, lead, and understand needs and interests. The essential skill of communication is certainly a part of this skill.

This skill involves understanding other people and being able to work effectively with them. It signifies skill in human relations and requires a realistic understanding of self. Satisfactory staff involvement and contributions result when interpersonal skills are highly developed.

The term *essential* means that an administrator must develop all four of the skills in this section in order to be successful. This is a challenging task for anyone interested in a career in administration.

Key Administrative Concepts

It is not possible to understand administration unless one knows the meaning of authority, power, delegation, responsibility, and accountability. These concepts are significant not only for administrators but for all staff members. These concepts are interrelated and an effective administrator applies them in a judicious manner for the benefit of the organization.

Authority

Authority is the right given to a person to act in certain ways to carry out tasks of the organization. It is the power given to a person because of the office he or she holds. The authority given to a person should be spelled out in the job description of the position and should be commensurate with the responsibility.

For public education and for public institutions of higher education, the source of authority is the state. For the public schools, the local board of education is the agent of the state. The board of education grants authority to the superintendent, who in turn delegates the necessary authority to the principal of a school. From the principal comes the authority to the chairpersons, athletic director, and others who have a designated responsibility such as being the liaison with community groups using the gymnasium. For private institutions of higher education, the state grants them authority via a charter. From then on, the line of authority goes from the board of trustees to the president, the dean, and then to departmental chairpersons. Directors of privately owned health clubs and fitness centers receive their authority from the owners. A person administering a city recreation program receives authority from that government entity.

When a person accepts a position as chairperson, director, or dean of a department, division, or college, the authority attached to that position falls to him or her. The same principle applies to a person who accepts a position as athletic director, director of a fitness center, or coach. The authority of the position should be clearly stated.

Power

Power is ability to command or control others. Some power comes from the authority given to a person because of the position he or she holds. For example, the manager of a health spa who can hire and fire employees is able to control and affect the behavior of others.

Power is an important part of leadership, which is a central characteristic of a successful administrator. It is usually not enough just to have the power of the position. Effective leaders are respected for their abilities, skills, accomplishments, and expertise. This increases their power base.

Another component leading to power is the difficult-to-define characteristic called charisma. Great administrators usually have this characteristic in abundance. Their personality gains respect and trust and wins support from those in their organization. Many successful coaches are known for this characteristic. Their technical skills are probably no better than those of many other coaches but their charisma motivates their athletes and assistants to perform beyond expectations.

Delegation

Delegation is the shifting of authority to another person. Administrative duties tend to overwhelm people who do not know how or are afraid to give authority to other staff people. It is important to specify the tasks to be done and to give the person the authority to carry out the duties involved.

Delegation enables an administrator to get more work done. Another strong reason for delegation is that it involves more staff in the affairs of the organization. This is also a good technique for developing a skilled staff by giving them the opportunity to learn new and challenging tasks. The organization also benefits by making use of the specialized skills of its employees.

Responsibility

Responsibility is the obligation to carry out assigned tasks in an acceptable way. When accepting a position or job, the administrator accepts responsibility for the duties involved.

An administrator may delegate authority to one or more colleagues for a specific assignment or for a designated facet of a program. However, the administrator is still held responsible by superiors for all the activities. The administrator cannot evade responsibility if a staff member inadequately handles the assignment. A good example is a physical education chairperson who assigns a staff member responsibility to organize a comprehensive high school intramural program, which the principal had scheduled to be accomplished by the end of the year. If, at the end of the year, an intramural program is not in place, the chairperson is responsible.

An important consideration in regard to responsibility is that authority and power must be commensurate with the level of responsibility. The responsibility for running a YMCA walking program does not require nearly the authority—and power—that organizing a 10-kilometer run to raise $5,000 for a new weight room does.

The power and authority of a position must match the responsibility. Whether accepting an administrative position or assigning responsibility to someone else, an administrator must remember that responsibility without commensurate authority is impossible.

Accountability

Accountability is the responsibility to successfully perform a task or duty. Administrators are responsible to someone for their actions. In the private and nonprofit spheres it is the business or agency, respectively. Accountability is now receiving equal emphasis in education, with states and parents, as well as the local educational authority, demanding accountability. People who accept administrative responsibility are accountable for their actions.

Comparison of Administrative and Nonadministrative Positions

Ordinarily new graduates devote the majority of their time to nonadministrative tasks. In education, they teach. In recreation, they organize and supervise activities under the direction of someone else. In a tennis and racquetball club, they assign court times, give lessons, and arrange for member services such as babysitting and equipment repair. As has been indicated earlier in this chapter, all of these positions require administrative skills, but the majority of the time is spent with other types of responsibilities. Eventually, the opportunity to assume more administrative duties arises and the employee must decide whether to enter administration, to which he or she must devote more time and energy. He or she must evaluate all aspects of this type of service because administration has its disadvantages as well as its advantages.

In a position in which at least half of the responsibilities are administrative, the individual should understand the following limitations:

Administration is more time-consuming than teaching or low-level management. The administrator is never finished because the responsibilities are so numerous that it is rare that there is nothing more to do. The administrator is concerned with every operational aspect and is obliged to see that everything functions smoothly.

Administration is involved with countless details. The person who abhors details should not consider being an administrator. In a large organization, the administrator may be able to delegate many details to other staff members, but this is not ordinarily possible in most school and leisure positions.

Because of the heavy demands on the administrator's time, there are fewer opportunities for stimulating exchanges with students and other program participants. For many people, such relationships are one of the most rewarding aspects of their profession.

The responsibilities of the administrator are great. This person is responsible for the achievements and failures of the department, program, or club. In addition, the problems staff members are unable to handle finally come to the administrator for solution. Tension and pressure are part of an administrator's life.

If a person enjoys teaching, research, or writing, it must be recognized that administrative responsibilities will probably make it necessary to curtail these activities. The extent to which this is necessary depends on the percentage of total workload one devotes to administration.

At times the administrator must make decisions that affect others adversely. It is inevitable that promotions, merit salary increases, tenure, and long-term contracts must be denied to some staff members who do not deserve them. These actions usually result in disappointment, criticism, and at times embitterment on the part of those concerned. Staff members may have to be disciplined, an unpleasant experience. There is no way to avoid such problems.

The administrator must relate to all staff members in such a way that each serves with maximum effectiveness. This requires tact and diplomacy. The administrator must adjust to the idiosyncrasies of associates. Some excellent teachers and staff members may be unreasonable and demanding. Tolerance and patience are usually necessary to handle such people. Conflicts result in changes in the personal associations that are possible with staff members.

Administration is often a lonely assignment. The need for a professional relationship with all staff members means that the administrator must not be partial to any of them. If a preference is shown for some staff members, socially as well as professionally, others will feel discriminated against.

Conflict is an inevitable part of administration. Some inexperienced administrators labor under the delusion that the frictions and disturbances that occur are due to faulty administration. However, conflict is inextricably wound up in the life of any organization. The administrator must face strife and resolve the difficulties to allow the work of the organization to proceed.

Stress is a part of any administrative position. Anyone who wants to be an administrator must be able to handle the stress that comes with the job. This is necessary for personal health and for the efficient functioning of the organization.

This is an imposing list of administrative challenges that a person must be willing to accept. Fortunately, there are many rewarding and pleasant aspects of an administrative career. They include the following:

Ordinarily, the administrator receives an excellent salary, usually higher than that of any member of the teaching or nonadministrative staff. This is in recognition of the importance of the leadership role.

In the noneducation field, there is greater job security for a person in an administrative position. They are less likely to be released or transferred. For some people, this is an important consideration.

One of the greatest satisfactions of the administrator is the opportunity to help young staff members grow and develop into professional leaders. Through guidance, direction, and supervision the administrator can play an important role in their future success. The administrator must provide the climate in which staff members advance; otherwise, the organization will not succeed.

An administrator is more likely to be called on to speak for the profession. There will be invitations to speak at conventions and conferences and to present workshops.

Although time is limited, administrators are in a good position to generate ideas and to share information with leaders in the profession that will stimulate research and writing.

Administrators are in a good position to bring about program innovations and to influence the philosophy and principles of their profession.

The nature of their position gives them clout when expressing ideas or interacting with others. This extends beyond their own department or organization.

Administrators have the opportunity to be involved with many community activities. An administrator develops leadership skills that are desired by community organizations.

Ample opportunities are available in administrative positions to develop mental, social, and professional skills. Many people thrive on searching for solutions to difficult problems and using their talents for the benefit of organizations they represent. It is exciting to make improvements and serve others. Satisfying personal achievements are a positive aspect of being an administrator.

The satisfaction of achieving the objectives of the organization is a very rewarding feature of the administrator's work. The administrator is able to make a larger contribution to these purposes than any other staff member because their power and authority to influence is far greater than that of a teacher or staff member.

Duties of Administrators in the Physical Education, Health Education, Leisure, and Sport Fields

The duties of administrators in these fields are extensive and, in many cases, complex. Duties are people-oriented and are characterized by a wide range of responsibilities. Extensive involvement with facilities and equipment is a variable with which administrators in many other fields do not contend as much. Diversity of responsibilities makes these positions challenging and interesting, but this diversity also requires a broad range of technical skills and knowledge. A person cannot have a narrow focus but must take a broad view and consider interrelationships between the different aspects of the programs typically included in these fields.

Size of the organization certainly affects the responsibilities of an administrator in the physical education, health, leisure, and sport professions. In smaller organizations, the administrative aspects of the position are not usually as varied and time-consuming as they are in a larger organization. Also, administrators in smaller institutions usually have non-administrative tasks. In physical education, they may include teaching or coaching responsibilities. Still, there is a striking similarity in the administrative duties regardless of the educational level or organizational complexity.

The administrative duties are encompassed in the following categories:

Public relations

Liability and safety

Facilities

Budget and finance

Purchase and care of equipment

Evaluation

Personnel administration

Office management

Program objectives

Program administration

1. School physical education programs
2. Intramural programs
3. Interschool athletics
4. School health education programs
5. Leisure and health promotion programs

Each of the above duties is considered in detail in subsequent chapters.

Class Activities

Simulation 1

Situation   The administrator of a fitness center has a staff of 14 with programs including weight control, low-impact aerobics, racquetball, swimming, and tennis.

Divide the class into groups of five or six. Have each group develop five administrative scenarios that would probably occur in the fitness center. Design a scenario depicting each of the key administrative concepts of authority, power, delegation, responsibility, and accountability.

Simulation 2

Situation   The position of director of the Ewingville High School health and physical education department is open. Members of the department have been asked to draft the portion of the job description that highlights the four essential skills of administration that will be required of applicants for the position. The essential skills are communication, technical, conceptual, and interpersonal.

Members of the class act as department members and write the job description. Four groups can be formed, with each group drafting the description for one of the essential skills or groups can write a description covering each of the skills and the class can develop a composite after they are written.

Performance Tasks

1. Debate the pros and cons of being an administrator.
2. Describe the value studying administrative theory has for a student majoring in one discipline included in this book.
3. Survey several nonphysical education administration books and describe the importance of administration for health, physical education, sport, and leisure programs.
4. Attend a school board meeting and evaluate how well the meeting was run and how effective the administration was in presenting agenda items.
5. Meet with three administrators, one of whom is in the physical education, sport, and leisure field, and find out what they feel are their most important duties.
6. Observe an administrator for two or more hours. Describe how each of the following skills were used:

   a. Communication skills
   b. Technical skills
   c. Conceptual skills
   d. Interpersonal skills

7. Interview three administrators who were formerly teachers. Ask them to compare the advantages and disadvantages of teaching and administration.
8. Write a position paper advocating employing administrators who have background experience in the physical education, sport, or leisure fields.
9. Interview two administrators and ask them to explain what they feel are the most important skills of an administrator.
10. Write an administrative duty that would be envisioned for each of the ten categories listed at the end of this chapter. Make a composite list for each category. Refer to these lists when the categories are covered in later chapters.

References

Barker, Larry L., and Deborah A. Barker, *Communication*, 6th ed. Englewood Cliffs, NJ: Prentice Hall, 1992.

Boone, Louis, and David Kurtz, *Contemporary Business*. New York: Dryden Press, 1994.

Conn, James H., "The Litigation Connection—Perspectives of Risk Control for the 1990s." *Journal of Physical Education, Recreation and Dance,* February 1993, 64:15, 61.

Devito, Joseph A., *Essentials of Human Communication*. New York: HarperCollins Publishing, 1992.

Hellriegel, Don, and John W. Slocum, Jr., *Management,* 6th ed. Reading, MA: Addison-Wesley, 1992.

Kreitner, Robert, *Management*, 6th ed. Boston: Houghton Mifflin, 1995.

Leith, Larry, *Coaches Guide to Sport Administration*. Champaign, IL: Human Kinetics, 1990.

Lynn, Susan, "Establishing a Management System." *Florida JOPERD,* Spring 1993, 31:35–56.

Pederson, Larry, and Lee Dexter, "Busting Bureaucracy from the Bottom Up." *Parks and Recreation,* October 1993, 28:37–40.

Stoner, James A.F., *Management,* 5th ed. Englewood Cliffs, NJ: Prentice Hall, 1992.

Truemper, Ross, "Leadership Qualities: Motivation, Persistence Key Factors for Successful Athletic Administrator." *Interscholastic Athletic Administration,* Fall 1993, 20:16–17.

Wichmann, Larry, "Beat the Clock: Seven Days to Better Time Management." *Men's Fitness,* April 1993, 9:81.

2

Application of Administrative Theory

Leadership

Administrative theory has little value if it isn't used effectively by the administrator. Leadership skills determine the level of success of an organization or business. Leadership can be described as the ability to influence group members to set and attain objectives. It entails much more than being able to plan, budget, staff, and carry out other technical managerial skills. It is true that effective leaders are able to use the power of their positions to generate employee effort. However, this is not enough of a basis for successful leadership. A leader provides a climate within the department or organization that brings about desired outcomes through individual or group efforts. Motivation is an important ingredient imparted by a good leader. Staff who are inspired to excel and to make their business, department, or club a model for quality are the outcomes of effective leadership.

Another example of good leadership is the establishment of an environment that encourages leadership by many organization members. Leadership is not the sole prerogative of the high-level or even middle-level administrators. An organization becomes powerful when many different members assume leadership roles. For example, a departmental committee or a community task force in a nonprofit organization requires leadership from a member or members of the organization. It is impossible for one administrator to always be the leader, even for small physical education departments or community centers.

Leadership is a complex phenomenon. The ability to relate in a positive fashion to staff is important, but being well-liked is not sufficient. The key is to get action that will attain the desired objectives. *Charisma* is a term often used when referring to good leaders. The sports world provides vivid examples of charismatic leaders. Coaches who motivate teams to perform beyond their apparent abilities and players who assume leadership roles to bring about significant team achievement are described in our media daily. Successful leaders in the movement science professions also have this type of charisma, which inspires group loyalty, promotes excitement, generates effort for a common objective, and results in a stellar service, program, or product.

It would be nice if we could identify the traits that result in charismatic, successful leaders. Unfortunately, there isn't a set of traits that distinguish good and poor leaders. Leaders come in all sizes and shapes. Different situations and different people require different types of leadership and different leaders. A skilled administrator can use different approaches in varying situations. Flexibility is a prime requisite for leaders, certainly for leaders who must lead in many different situations.

In this chapter, important skills of administrators are presented. These are pertinent skills for anyone who assumes a leadership role.

Objectives

In order to proceed quickly and efficiently toward any objective, it is essential to know the objective. Nothing is more important for administrators to know than the objectives they are expected to achieve. Certain human and material resources have been provided with which the administrator is expected to accomplish various objectives. These objectives give direction to the efforts of the administrator and staff and provide the basis for evaluating the success of the department, agency, business, or group.

Objectives are set for administrators, staff, participants, and program. The ultimate reason for objectives is to attain the purpose or purposes of the organization. In education the purpose revolves around knowledge, appreciations, understandings, and life skills. Private health clubs have a profit motive and recreation programs are targeted on providing services to their constituents. The purpose of a health program might be stated in terms of improving the health of the people who participate. It becomes obvious that objectives are necessary to reach overall organizational purposes that are broader in scope. Attainment of incremental and focused objectives leads to successfully reaching the purpose for which the organization exists. For example, in a health club the purpose might be to provide financial return on an investment. However, specific objectives are needed. They might include the following: Provide diversified fitness programs that are appropriate for all strata of members, as documented by research studies during the last five years; develop a public relations vehicle that will increase membership by 15% in one year; and design an environmental setting that will be satisfying to participants as evidenced by a 90% approval rating on a membership survey.

Once an organization has clearly stated its purpose or mission, it is important to develop specific objectives at all levels that will lead to the attainment of the purpose. This is why physical education curriculum guides indicate the educational purpose of the school and then specify the objectives of physical education that will contribute to the school's educational purpose. There are also specific objectives for the different activities included in the physical education program. These objectives should, in turn, ultimately contribute to the school's educational purpose.

In our profession, a variety of terms such as *objective, purpose, goal,* and *mission* are used. In some instances, they are used interchangeably. However, *mission* is usually used in a broader context than is *objective. Mission* is interpreted as a broad goal that has been established to designate the purpose of the organization. From this definition, it is possible to see that *goal* and *purpose* also have long-range, broad meanings. Objectives are characterized by a relatively short time span and specific, measurable accomplishments. They represent the desirable end results of some activity. *Aim* and *target* are other terms used to indicate direction and to bring about change through a planned program.

Purposes and objectives of physical education, health education, intramurals, athletics, and leisure and health promotion programs are presented in the chapters devoted to these programs in Part III of this book, which is titled *Program Administration.*

Characteristics of an Administrator

Of all the people in an organization, the administrator is the most influential. The top administrator bears the responsibility for all organizational operations. Other administrators have responsibility for designated programmatic or departmental functions. The leader's effectiveness is based on the premise that two dimensions of leader behavior are significant in administration: task-oriented behavior and people-oriented behavior. This premise is supported in Chapter 1, where the essential skills of administration are discussed. Two of the essential skills are conceptual and technical competence, which are task-oriented. The other two, communication and interpersonal ability, are salient attributes of people-oriented behavior.

The manner in which a leader perceives his or her role is based on personal philosophy. The word *philosophy* has been defined in many ways. In its simplest definition, it is the logical investigation of the truth and theories of existence, behavior, and knowledge. In a fuller definition, philosophy is a science that investigates the facts, principles, and problems of reality in an attempt to describe, analyze, and evaluate them.

Importance of a Philosophy

The philosophy of the administrator is of crucial importance. It is a significant factor in determining the procedures that are followed and the type of program that is created and supported. It serves as a signpost to guide the administrator's steps. All administrators become involved in philosophical problems. They cannot be successful unless they can formulate a valid philosophical foundation for their actions.

Every administrator has a philosophy, whether or not he or she realizes it, and decisions are based on the beliefs and values that constitute this philosophy. One's philosophy is the result of all past experiences. It may be mature or immature, consistent or inconsistent, logical or illogical, rational or irrational.

Sources of Philosophy

The philosophy of physical education, leisure studies, health education, and sport administrators develops out of at least three factors, namely a philosophy of life, a philosophy of education, and a philosophy of the profession. Other considerations may be involved, but the administrative philosophy of the executive in these fields is strongly affected by each of these aspects.

Philosophy of Life

It would be impossible to have a philosophy of administration entirely dissociated from one's philosophy of life. Life purposes and ideals, the values an individual holds, and reactions to people and their response are all part of one's personal philosophy, which inevitably exerts a powerful influence on philosophy of administration.

A philosophy of life relates significantly to the manner in which an individual works with subordinates. Administrators have power. It comes from two sources: the office (formal) and the manner in which the administrator relates to staff members (informal). Formal power or authority is delegated and vested in the office regardless of the person who happens to fill it. Informal power or influence is earned or achieved regardless of the office held. It depends on the personality and character of the administrator and the manner in which the individual works with staff members.

It is apparent that the administrator who supplements the formal authority of position with the informal power or influence earned through personal leadership is the better executive. Experience has demonstrated that the administrator must earn the respect and cooperation of subordinates. To rely solely on the authority vested in the office is to court certain failure.

The administrator's relationship with students and program participants in the leisure field is governed largely by a philosophy of life. Associations with superiors, with colleagues and with staff members, and responsibilities for budget, equipment, facilities, office management, and public relations must not be regarded as more important than relationships with students and participants. Otherwise, the administrator becomes virtually inaccessible to them. If the students and participants are regarded as having the highest priority, program success is much more likely.

A proper point of view for a physical education administrator is expressed in the following statements:

The student is the most important person in our business.

The student is not dependent on us—we are dependent on the student.

The student is not an interruption of our business—the student is the purpose of it.

The student does us a favor when he or she calls—we are not doing a favor by serving the student.

The student is part of our business, not an outsider.

The student deserves the most courteous and attentive treatment we can give.

The student brings us wants; it is our job to fill them.

The student is the lifeblood of any school.

This same philosophy is equally important for the administrator in the leisure, health education, and sport fields.

Philosophy of Education

A philosophy of education is of crucial importance to the educational or leisure program administrator. His or her beliefs concerning the objectives and mission of education govern his or her attitudes and decisions regarding program matters. Executives' thoughts and actions in the physical education, health education, and leisure studies profession receive their purpose and direction from a philosophy of education.

Philosophy of the Profession

An administrator's professional philosophy grows out of her or his life and educational philosophy. The approach and the programs of health education, physical education, and leisure activities differ from other educational programs but the ultimate goal of providing a developmental experience that will benefit the person involved is the same. The administrator's professional philosophy undergirds thoughts and actions concerning such matters as outcomes, standards, methods, and curriculum. A professional philosophy enables the administrator to evaluate accomplishments based on professional standards. It gives direction to actions and keeps one on the track.

Even though there isn't a single set of skills or personal traits that ensure success in an administrative capacity, there are a number of personal attributes that are important for an administrator to have or develop. First and foremost is an interest in and concern for others. Staff members need to know that their efforts are appreciated and that their ideas are valued. It is important that recognition be given for accomplishments and that encouragement be extended for both personal and professional growth.

It has previously been emphasized that interpersonal skills and communicative abilities are essential for an administrator. Delegation of authority provides the climate in which staff can develop their own leadership skills and contribute more to the organization.

An administrator should be open to change and to look to the future. Staying in the vanguard of movements in their profession engenders staff enthusiasm and allows programs to meet changing needs. This can be an important element in staff motivation, which is another important skill for an administrator to possess. An administrator who is respected by professionals both in and out of her professional field acts as a catalyst for organizational pride, which is another valuable motivational incentive.

Consistency in carrying out administrative responsibilities also rates high with staff members, as does being part of the decision-making process. The administrator who can tap into the human resources of a staff and use the wide range of talents that are invariably present will have a better organization and a happier and more productive staff. This is just one example where creative skills of an administrator will be used. Creativity is a characteristic that serves an administrator well. It is just as important for an administrator to be creative as it is for a teacher to be creative. Creative administrators find positive ways to overcome insufficient funding and less-than-perfect facilities and still provide outstanding programs. Even more importantly, creativity is needed for handling personnel problems and interacting with the public. Creative ideas lead to excitement for staff, participants, and members of the community.

The creative administrator is an imaginative person who considers every possible alternative and then shapes a variety of different ideas to satisfy current needs and meet future projections. Creativity is the base on which conceptual skill evolves. It allows the administrator to envision future developments in the profession and within society and then foresee innovative ways to capitalize on the changes taking place. Such an administrator encourages creative staff members by providing a receptive climate for ideas, plans, and suggestions that are new, deviate from the norm, and may even fail. Staff members thrive on this type of administrative leadership.

Effective problem solving through staff involvement and decision-making techniques that meaningfully incorporate staff input are techniques used by effective administrators. Appropriate supervisory and management styles are other important requirements of an administrator.

Carrying Out Responsibilities

Administration is a process, not an end in itself. It is the process by which an organization strives to achieve its objectives. The more efficient the administrative process, the more likely it is that the objectives will be achieved.

Two different concepts can be used to describe the processes of administration. One conceptual approach is to consider the tasks that confront the leader. The following questions can form the basis from which to work:

What is the purpose of the group? (the objectives)

How will the purpose be achieved? (policies, rules, and procedures to be used)

What resources are necessary for the operation? (personnel, facilities, equipment)

How will members be organized? (allocation of people to jobs)

What timelines will guide progress?

How and when will progress be evaluated?

A second and more common approach to studying the theory of administration is to identify the processes by using descriptive terminology. There are variations used by different writers; some use a four-part process that includes planning, leading, controlling, and organizing. A seven-part process consisting of planning, organizing, staffing, directing, coordinating, reporting, and budgeting provides an easy-to-follow delineation of responsibilities and has been found to be particularly pertinent for the physical education and leisure fields.

Planning

Planning is deciding in advance what is to be done. Objectives are identified and alternate ways of reaching the objectives are considered. It is a method or technique of looking ahead to devise a basis for a course of action. It is an intellectual activity involving facts, ideas, and objectives. Knowledge, logical thinking, and good judgment rather than hunches must be involved in planning if it is to be effective.

Organizing

Organizing is the process of arranging and distributing jurisdiction, work, and resources among an organization's members, enabling them to reach the organization's objectives effectively and with as little wasted effort, time, and money as possible. A structure is created, establishing relationships among staff members that will best meet the goals of the organization. Organizing involves designing a structure, determining staff relationships, and allocating resources.

Such factors as the grouping of activities, departmentalization, delegating of work, arranging of tasks, and the use of committees and administrative staff are included in the organizing process.

Staffing

Staffing is employing appropriate personnel to accomplish the tasks that have been identified as necessary for the success of the organization. Consideration must be given to items such as the number of staff required, the particular talents needed, and the manner in which the members of the staff will interact with each other. The operational efficiency of a department, club, fitness center or other grouping in this field depends largely on how well members of the staff work together.

Directing

Direction initiates action. Guidance is provided to involve staff in decision making and to encourage individual efforts. The starting and stopping parameters of a task are spelled out, members of the group are given the power to act, and leadership is provided to begin a task. The key is to be able to achieve objectives through cohesive efforts of individuals, who often have divergent views, ideas, experiential backgrounds, and work ethics.

Direction is important because when it is done effectively it enhances the chances of a successful operation. When it is done poorly, it threatens the progress and success of the enterprise. The manner in which direction is conducted has a marked effect on the behavior of those being directed. Both the quantity and quality of their performance depends on their reaction to the directions they receive.

Coordinating

The problems of coordination multiply as the size and complexity of the organization increase. The close and constant contact of individuals in a small department simplifies the organizational setup, promotes communication among staff members, and facilitates supervision and control. Although all of these factors make coordination easier, it would be incorrect to assume that the administrator of a physical education department in a small high school or the manager of a small racquetball club need not be concerned with coordination. Keep in mind that even two people involved with a common task need to coordinate their efforts.

Reporting

Administrators in the physical education, leisure activity, health education, and sport fields are usually middle-management leaders. They are not only responsible for the operation of their unit or department and the welfare of staff and participants in the program, but they must also answer to presidents, principals, owners, or boards of directors or school boards who are responsible for the broader institutional or business function. The administrator, therefore, must report in two directions: downward and upward. The ability to give a clear, concise, and accurate report of the status of the department or particular aspects of it is an important element of effective administration.

Budgeting

The budgeting process includes planning a budget to meet program requirements, updating and maintaining budget records, and monitoring the accounting system. Budget plans for expenditures must, of course, be reconciled with available resources. As competition for the available funds increases, skill in budgetary matters assumes ever more importance for the administrator.

In many ways, the budget controls the activities of the organization. The budget affects all of the programs, projects, and services that are provided and is used for planning and controlling the use of financial resources.

The Organizational Environment

Historically, administrative theory has developed from a position that stressed the importance of particular traits a successful leader should possess to the current functional approach. This latter approach holds that administration is primarily concerned with interpersonal relationships that develop the most effective use of the human and material resources of the organization. Everyday experiences show that effective administration is the result not of a unique solution to a problem but of a relationship among the elements involved. The elements are as follows:

Internal environment (situation within the organization)

External environment (forces outside the organization)

Technology (computers, sophisticated equipment)

Political structures (government groups)

Workforce (faculty or equivalent in leisure activities)

Administration (leader)

Functional administration is consistent with the concept that administration is a dynamic process and, thus, it should be recognized that there isn't one particular type of individual who has the ability to succeed in all circumstances. Leaders may use different techniques yet be equally successful in similar situations. Effective leadership occurs when all factors work in harmony to maximize achievement and staff self-satisfaction. To attain the ultimate objective of the organization, it is necessary to complete a number of substeps. The administrator must recognize that effectiveness is concerned not only with the completion of particular short-term tasks, but also with the continued well-being of all the people in the organization.

Internal Environment

The internal environment is the immediate surroundings of the school, business, or recreational facility. Included are faculty, staff, employees, officers of the organization, school boards, and boards of directors. Formal interactions occur in this environment. Examples include committee meetings, team teaching, professional discussions, guest speakers, and other professional endeavors where people work together to achieve a common goal of the organization. A set of values evolves in the internal environment that may be considered the culture of the organization. The stronger the culture of the organization, the clearer the purposes, policies, and procedures of the organization.

External Environment

The external environment encompasses forces outside the internal environment. This includes community members and local, state or province, and national government units and agencies. Economic and sociocultural factors are also part of this external environment, which has an impact on the way that an organization functions. The significance of the external environment is that its many components often have conflicting objectives. Because no organization operates within a vacuum, the external environment is an important consideration for any administrator. For an organization to be effective, it must be able to exist harmoniously within the wider sphere of the general society.

For example, a physical education department chairperson is often required to make decisions that affect all or most of the external elements. It is not an easy task, and the more sensitive he or she is to the various pressures and the influence on the achievement of the departmental objectives, the better he or she is prepared to make a reasoned decision. This relationship does not preclude opportunities for a physical education chairperson and faculty to initiate change within the school, or indeed society at large. However, the astute administrator must be conscious of the changing attitudes and values of the external environment.

Technology

The sophistication of equipment now available has had a significant impact on the organizational environment within which physical education, leisure, and sport administrators now function. Chapter 5 covers the impact of the computer on these fields. Other technology is also giving administrators new tools to carry out their tasks and provide innovative programs. Facilities and sport and fitness equipment are rapidly changing with current technological developments. Indoor climbing walls, adjustable floors in swimming pools, cardiovascular printouts during exercise, and computerized exercise equipment are examples of the technology that now affects programming in the physical education and leisure professions.

Political Considerations

Legislation is the most obvious example of the way in which politics are a part of the environment of the organization. Regulations and laws are passed that must be followed. They can change the nature of programs and determine resources that are available. Administrators must not only be aware of legislation but must also get a reading of political trends and move into the political arena to gain support and protect their turf.

Workforce

In a physical education or health education department, the workforce is made up of the departmental faculty members. In the fitness center of a pharmaceutical company, the workforce would include the activity instructors, personal fitness staff, and other employees who work with participants in the center programs. Although it is important for staff of the departments or centers to get along together and to enjoy working with one another, this is not the real reason for their participation in the organization. Ideally, they have been chosen for their ability to provide professional competencies to accomplish the tasks consistent with the objectives of the organization.

Administrators should attempt to develop esprit de corps among the staff, but high morale may not necessarily lead to high productivity. High morale may be related to social groupings, which have little to do with the departmental objectives. Such a basis for group cohesiveness could be the result of reaction against the way a leader perceives administrative procedures. This negative reaction is usually to the detriment of the organization.

Morale that is most effective is that which is related to the achievement of the organization's mission (purpose). This means that the organization's objectives and the personal objectives of organization members must be closely interrelated. Good leadership creates a climate that allows members to fulfill their own ambitions and at the same time work for departmental objectives.

Administrator

The leader is a critical cog in the organizational environment. The important role and key responsibilities of this person is covered in detail in an earlier section of this chapter, Characteristics of an Administrator.

Structure of the Organization

Formal and Informal Structure

An organization is a collection of people with different responsibilities working together for a common purpose. This format results in the accomplishment of tasks that exceed what individuals working alone could accomplish. Organizations have a particular form depending on how authority and responsibility are assigned and the way in which lines of communication are established. An organization has two types of structure: the formal structure and the informal structure.

Formal structure is the formal roles that members occupy; it establishes the authority of one role over another. This structure is relatively constant even when personnel change. A formal structure establishes working relations by clarifying tasks and letting the staff know what is expected of them in their positions. This structure includes regulations, procedures, and job standards that have been established for each position. The formal structure also institutes the relationships among different positions and provides the parameters within which employees assist and cooperate with each other in reaching organizational objectives. The formal structure provides the framework within which specialized skills can be applied and honed for optimum benefit of the organization. This aspect of an organization aids administrators in evaluating performance because designated responsibility accompanies the positions that are part of the formal structure. Information that comes to the administrator from this source is a critical tool in problem solving and decision making.

The larger and more complex the organization, the more need there is for an extensive formal structure. On the other hand, small departments and businesses generally place more reliance on a simple formal structure with informal relationships.

The informal structure develops from the human relationships and communication networks that evolve naturally and spontaneously as members are brought together under the formal framework. The emphasis is on personal and social interactions. Although the formal organization can design the roles of a chairperson, manager, exercise therapist, or teacher, it must be remembered that these roles are filled by individuals who have abilities, personalities, interests, and goals of their own. Therefore, friendships are formed and lines of informal communication and rapport are established within the formal structure. The formal structure increases in size as the organization grows. Groups in the informal structure tend to remain small because they are grounded in personal relationships. Informal groupings can either contribute to an organization or detract from it. The wise administrator is aware of the presence and importance of informal structures and encourages them by creating a nurturing environment that leads to support for the objectives of the formal structure. Creative ideas, practical solutions to problems, and unity of purpose are examples of the positive impact of the informal framework of an organization.

Ideally, the formal and informal structures are synonymous, but rarely are the two systems perfectly matched. It is important to guard against the formation of unhealthy cliques and subgroups. Pressure can be exerted on staff members to conform to the philosophy of the leaders of the subgroups rather than to the organizational philosophy. Informal groups can also cause conflicts among individuals and block program improvements and change.

One might ask whether it is wise for a leader to become closely associated with the informal organization. The degree to which the administrator socializes with staff members on the job requires careful deliberation in terms of real and perceived relationships. Real or imagined favoritism must not be perceived by the staff. Therefore, must the leader or administrator be aware of but detached from the informal structure? If the leader becomes too involved with parts of the informal organization, do other members feel reluctant to discuss matters openly? If this was the case, the administrator could lose an important avenue of feedback or positive contributions from staff members. Thus, the administrator must determine how involved he or she can become in the informal structure.

Both the formal and the informal structures are important and must be understood by the administrator. The effectiveness of an organization depends in large measure on the appropriateness of the formal structure and the compatibility of the informal organization.

Organization Chart

The organization chart is sometimes referred to as the table of organization or the chain of command. It is actually a diagram that shows the reporting relationships of the various subunits within an organization. Each subunit has a designated responsibility that is captured in the diagram. The diagram also shows the different tasks within the organization. For instance, in a secondary school physical education chart, the various parts of the instructional program, such as adapted physical education, dance, and team sports, might be indicated as well as the intramural program and athletic program if these two programs are administered by the physical education department.

Lines of authority for organizational positions can also be shown on an organization chart. The charts can range from a general outline of the different administrative components of an educational institution, nonprofit service organization, or health promotion business to a detailed listing of each subdivision of the organizations. Organization charts shown in Figures 2-1, 2-2, 2-3, 2-4, and 2-5 provide examples of the way in which organizational interrelationships and designated lines of responsibility can be diagrammed. Organization charts can take different formats. A common criticism is that they indicate the relative value of a person or position rather than communicating differentiated duties, the reporting relationship, and position responsibilities. (They are sometimes depicted in a circular manner so as to show that every person is important.) They can be schematic in nature or be extremely detailed to represent every person in an organization. Names are sometimes used on organization charts, but it is best to establish an organization chart based on responsibilities.

Line, Staff, and Functional Relationships

An organization chart shows two types of relationships: line relationships and staff relationships. Line positions are usually shown by solid lines and staff positions by broken lines on a chart. Functional relationships are not obvious on a chart but are present when individuals in staff positions have authority normally reserved for staff in line positions. This will be examined further as line, staff, and functional relationships are explained.

Line Positions

People in line positions have direct responsibility to achieve the objectives of an organization. They appear in the vertical part of an organization chart and have a direct link with the person to whom they report and to the people who report to them. Responsibility is closely attached to the objectives and procedures of the position they hold. They are specifically responsible for the services, end products, or participant achievements designated in their job descriptions.

Staff Positions

In small schools, leisure organizations, and businesses, most positions are line positions. However, as organizational size increases, staff positions become part of the organization. The role of those assuming staff positions is to provide advice and support for those in line positions. This support may take the form of technical assistance, interpretation of laws and regulations, and help in implementing new programs or analyzing program outcomes. Staff positions appear on organization charts in a horizontal position and often serve several line positions. An example of a staff person in a school system is a special services employee who gives advice and assistance to the principals, and the administrators of health education, physical education, and other disciplines and is also available to teachers who are implementing a program for disadvantaged children.

Functional Authority

In some situations, people in staff positions have authority over those in line positions. This is referred to as functional authority. This authority is only for the phase of responsibility given to the staff person. The person in the line position is still in the direct chain of command and has responsibility for attaining the objectives of the line position. An example is

NC WESLEYAN COLLEGE LIBRARY
ROCKY MOUNT, NC 27804

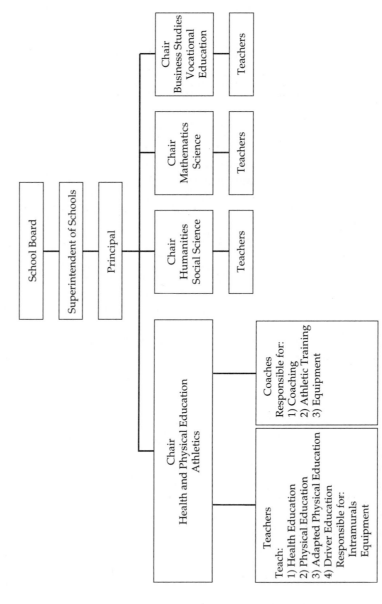

FIGURE 2-1. Organization Chart of a Small High School Health, Physical Education, and Athletic Department

NC WESLEYAN COLLEGE LIBRARY
ROCKY MOUNT, NC 27804

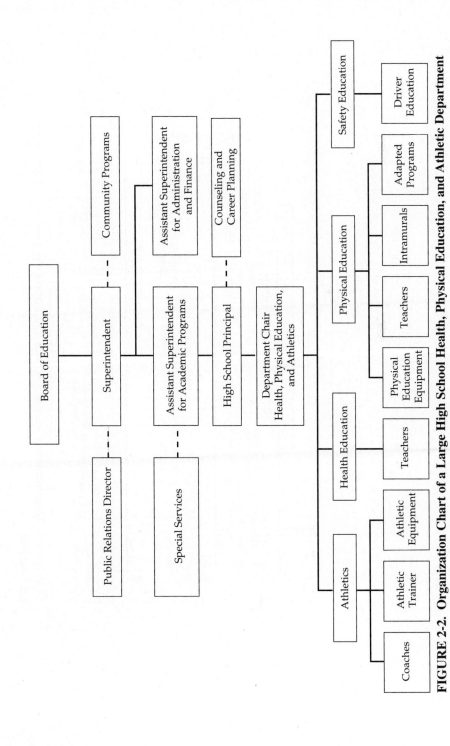

FIGURE 2-2. Organization Chart of a Large High School Health, Physical Education, and Athletic Department

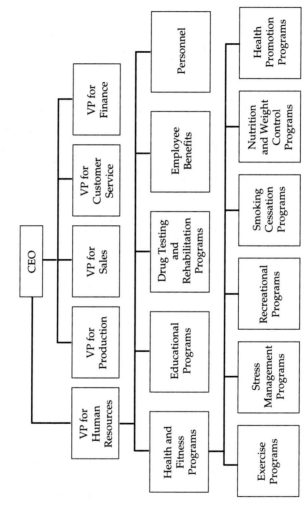

FIGURE 2-3. Organization Chart of a Health and Fitness Program in a Manufacturing Company

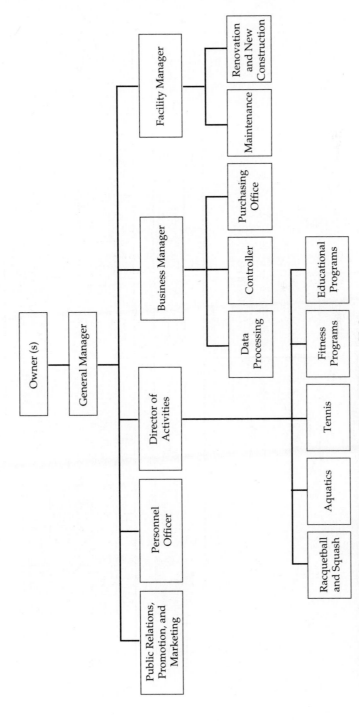

FIGURE 2-4. Organization Chart of a Private Sector Fitness Club

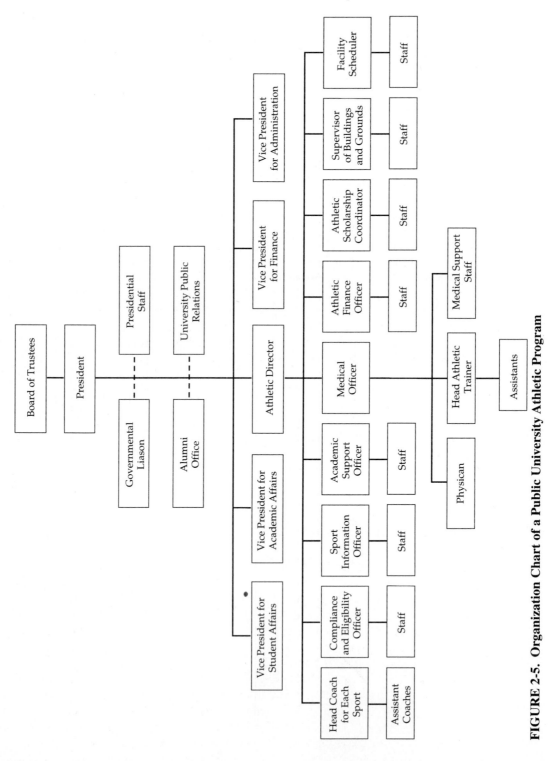

FIGURE 2-5. Organization Chart of a Public University Athletic Program

the staff position of affirmative action officer. If a person in a line position fails to follow the affirmative action plan while hiring a new employee, the affirmative action officer is responsible for negating any job offers and requiring the person in the line position to reinstitute the search and follow acceptable affirmative action procedures.

Types of Administration

Early studies of administration developed categories for administrative styles. The categories were based on the leaders' conception of the power and authority they possess and how they use it. It was assumed that administrators could be put into groups according to the way they handled their administrative responsibilities. It was also thought that administrators could be characterized by a specific administrative style. However, administrators are just as complex as the administrative process itself. They are usually a composite of several styles and effective administrators change their style according to a number of variables. The variables include staff experience, cohesiveness, knowledge, and leadership skills. Other variables are the time available, the nature of the task, and the situational environment within which the task occurs. In reality, most administrators use a combination of styles even when responding to a single administrative duty.

There has been a significant change in approach by administrators during the last few decades. This change has been expedited by the view that administration is a joint task of the administrator and staff members, whether they be faculty members or workers on an assembly line. Greater support is obtained when staff members are part of the decision-making process. Better use is also made of the skills and knowledge of individuals in the organization. This contributes to better functioning of the organization and a more pleasant environment in which to work.

Types of administration can best be viewed as being on a continuum. This continuum ranges from complete freedom for the staff to the other extreme, where the administrator makes all the decisions without input from staff or, in many cases, even considering their feelings. The continuum looks like the following:

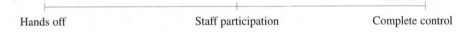

Hands off   Staff participation   Complete control

A leader who uses the hands-off approach is referred to as a laissez-faire administrator. This person is really not an executive at all, making little use of the formal power of the position and expending no effort to obtain informal power. This type fails to exert leadership and never takes a stand. Staff members can basically do what they want. Complete abdication of authority and direction characterizes a person at this end of the continuum. The consequence of this type of leadership is an attitude of hopelessness and very low morale on the part of staff members.

The leader who demands full control of every situation is classified as an autocratic administrator. This type of administrator relies solely on the formal power of the position and is arbitrary, inconsiderate, and coercive. The use of close and continuous supervision together with tight and inflexible control over individual and group behavior are other ways this administrator operates. Staff members are expected to do everything they are told to do and do it unquestioningly simply because they are employed by the organization. This administrator is not interested in the opinions of subordinates and never solicits their suggestions.

Administrators of this type are rarely successful in a democratic society. Staff members have a smoldering resentment, lack of morale, and loss of initiative and enthusiasm. Staff turnover is high. The abuse of power that characterizes such an administrator causes more administrative failures than any other single factor.

There is an autocratic type of administrator who is called a benevolent dictator. This person is friendly, approachable, and understanding, looks after the needs of staff members and wants to know their problems. Interest is manifested in each individual and excellent work is praised by this type of administrator. Morale and productivity under such an administrator are usually excellent at first. The negative aspect of this type of executive leadership is the loss of initiative and creativity on the part of staff members. So much reliance is placed on the administrator's judgment and wisdom that staff members lose their independence and incentive to contribute. Also, because such an administrator is assumed to have more wisdom and more experience than staff members, the important decisions and policies are made solely by the administrator without taking advantage of staff experience and insight.

The administrative style that is most successful is the participatory style. Administrator and staff are involved together. In some situations, the administrator needs to move toward the autocratic end of the continuum and at other times he or she relaxes control over the decision-making process. A leader who believes in the participatory administrative style is sometimes referred to as a democratic administrator. This type of administrator makes the fullest possible use of the formal power of the position and the informal power of personal leadership. The democratic administrator respects the skills and personalities of subordinates and, by relating to each staff member, obtains maximum contribution to the objectives of the organization. This type of administrator solicits the opinions of staff members and involves them in decision making. Group participation is encouraged and freedom to act prevails. Regular staff meetings are scheduled and effective communication is provided. Staff members are an integral part of a program evaluation process.

Administrators find that they operate along the full length of the continuum even though it should always be the administrator's objective to make the fullest use of each individual's talents on behalf of the organization. It is necessary at times to take action without conferring with staff members. Nevertheless, participatory administration provides greater opportunities for people in the organization to contribute more fully in decision making and the implementation of decisions and therefore gives them greater commitment to the organization and its objectives.

Application of Regulations and Laws

An effective administrator must be conversant with all regulations and laws that pertain to programs and administrative duties in her or his area of responsibility. This includes regulations passed by local government or, if a school, by the local board of education. There are also many state or province laws, standards, and regulations that must be followed. Finally, there are federal or national laws and mandates that establish parameters within which programs can be developed and that determine how schools, nonprofit organizations, and businesses can function.

Some type of regulation, if not a law, affects every area of administrative responsibility in physical education, health education, leisure activities, health education, and sports. Equipment used in programs must meet standards that guarantee minimum levels of safety. Budgets are developed following governmental guidelines, particularly if public institutions are involved. Financial procedures must be consistent with governmental requirements. New construction and renovations are carefully controlled by building codes. Fire department regulations and safety procedures are mandated when facilities are used for either regular or special programs.

Educational programs must function within the many laws and regulations that have been established at all three levels of government. Nonprofit and profit programs also have restrictions applied to their operation. In addition to government regulations, there are often other standards established by professional organizations, industries, and special interest groups. Administrators must understand these regulations and follow them carefully when carrying out their administrative responsibilities.

Personnel decisions require strict adherence to the law. The type of questions that can be asked during an interview, the wording of job vacancy announcements, and conditions of employment are examples of situations that require that the administrator carefully scrutinize pertinent laws and follow approved procedures.

A number of the regulations and laws relate directly to the problem of liability and the administrator's responsibility. This reason alone makes it critically important that administrators study laws and regulations that pertain to all aspects of administrative responsibility. Being up to date in this area also requires that the administrator be a member of professional organizations in her or his field and read current literature that not only describes but also interprets pertinent regulations and laws.

It is impossible to cover all regulations that affect an administrator in physical education, leisure activities, and sport because there are variations from community to community. However, there are three laws that have a significant impact in the United States. They are described here because they are applicable to several later chapters.

Title IX

> No person in the United States shall, on the basis of sex, be excluded from participation in, be denied the benefits of, or be subject to discrimination under any education program or activity receiving federal financial assistance.
>
> *Title IX of the Education Amendments, 1972.*

Title IX has had a significant impact on educational programs. Although it was enacted in 1972, compliance was not required in schools, colleges, and universities until 1978. Many institutions came into compliance but there was resistance on the part of individuals, groups, and institutions. In 1984, the Supreme Court ruled in *Grove City College v. Bell* that the law applied only to programs that received direct federal aid. Because few athletic programs received such aid, Title IX was no longer considered relevant for athletic programs. The impetus that had been generated to implement Title IX in athletics was slowed as a result of this verdict. However, the Civil Rights Restoration Act of 1988 negated the *Grove City* decision by stipulating that an institution receiving federal funding must not discriminate in any program.

Title IX has been responsible for impressive advances for girls and women in athletics. The increase in number of teams, number of sports, and the number of participants at all levels of competition has been phenomenal since the original legislation in 1972. Expanded opportunities to participate in athletics and public acceptance that athletic competition is a positive experience for girls are two other important outcomes. Because of this attitude and the participation of more girls and women in school and university teams, Title IX has also indirectly been a major factor in increased opportunities for athletic participation in noneducational settings such as sport clubs and recreation programs for all ages. Unfortunately, equity has still not arrived for girls and women. There are still more athletic opportunities for boys and men, and inequities are found in many other aspects of the programs. Practice time, budget, travel arrangements, scholarship assistance at colleges and universities, game and practice facilities, level of coaching, locker room and athletic training facilities, equipment, publicity, and game schedules fail to meet the equity test in too many institutions (Fox, 1992b, p. 34).

Physical education instructional programs have changed significantly as a result of Title IX. The biggest change has been the movement from single-sex to coeducational classes. Although Title IX mandates coeducational classes, this does not mean that all classes must be taught coeducationally. For example, ability grouping or student selection may result in single-sex classes. Unfortunately, the change to coeducational classes was often made for the sake of expediency rather than for concern for quality programs. The easiest way to implement coeducational classes was to make them totally elective without regard for skill levels or differences in student ability. This has resulted in watered-down programs with wide variances of skills in the classes. Too often, this type of a program does not meet the needs of either the highly skilled student or the student with a low level of motor ability. Many classes would be much better if they were based on ability grouping, which is acceptable under Title IX. Programs should be developed that best meet the needs of all students on an equal basis. Title IX also requires that instructional facilities and equipment used for physical education classes meet the same standard for both sexes. It is not acceptable for the smaller gymnasium to be the girls' gym! Chapter 12 contains additional information about Title IX as it relates to physical education instructional programs.

Staff policy must also be consistent with Title IX. Hiring procedures must not discriminate against either sex and job stipulations such as number of classes that are taught and nonteaching assignments must be consistent. Pay for extra duties, including coaching, must be the same for both sexes. Comparable office space, staff locker rooms, and teaching resources are to be provided for all faculty.

Many states have laws covering sex discrimination. The administrator must be familiar with these laws also because the more stringent law takes precedence.

It behooves administrators to be knowledgeable about Title IX and to implement policies and procedures that fulfill the spirit as well as the letter of the law. It is important that all student programs and conditions for the staff be equitable for both sexes.

Public Law 94-142, the Education for All Handicapped Children Act

This legislation was signed into law on November 29, 1975. Special education in this law is defined as "specially designed instruction, at no cost to parents or guardians, to meet the unique needs of a handicapped child, including classroom instruction [and] instruction in physical education." It provides that there shall be appropriate and fair procedures followed to supply education for handicapped students. An individualized education plan (IEP) is required for each child.

Mainstreaming is a term that refers to the practice of placing disabled children into regular classes on a full or part-time basis. The term *mainstreaming* is not used in P.L. 94-142 and the legislation is not a provision for mainstreaming, nor does it mandate that all disabled children be educated in regular classes. The law does specify that the disabled child is to be educated in the least restrictive educational environment. In many situations, attending regular classes has been found to be the least restrictive educational environment for disabled students and mainstreaming, in these cases, is the appropriate educational format. Inclusion of disabled children in appropriate physical education classes is an objective of physical education administrators and teachers.

The administrator in health and physical education must follow the provisions of Public Law 94-142 when designing curriculum and implementing physical education programs. Carefully written IEPs for each disabled student in the physical education program make it possible for all students to have high-quality health and physical education programs.

Public Law 94-142 is important legislation for health and physical education programs. Administrators must know not only the law itself but the interpretations of the law that apply to health and physical education instructional programs. Staff should be involved in writing IEPs to provide meaningful health and physical education experiences, based on the principle of inclusion, for each student and to make health and physical education an integral part of each child's total educational experience. This is more important than compliance from a legal standpoint.

Public Law 94-142 was amended in 1990 by Public Law 101-476, Individuals with Disabilities Education Act, which made some changes in the law and reaffirmed the earlier legislation. Notice that the term *handicapped* has been replaced with the term *disabled* in the new law. Additional information about the impact of Public Law 94-142 and Public Law 101-476 on physical education instructional programs is included in Chapter 12.

Affirmative Action

One of the most important responsibilities of an administrator is to employ qualified staff members. There are many laws that protect applicants from employment discrimination. These laws must be followed carefully to prevent litigation. More importantly, a better faculty or staff will result when hiring is determined by ability rather than by friendship, race, gender, or age. The Civil Rights Act of 1964 and the Equal Employment Opportunity Act of 1972 guarantee the right of employment to individuals without regard to color, gender, national origin, race, or religion. Later legislation has extended this same right to the disabled and people between the age of 40 and 70.

Affirmative action programs are required of many businesses and educational institutions to ensure that employment practices are consistent with laws that prohibit discrimination in employment. These programs are designed to increase employment opportunities for groups of people, such as women and minorities, who are underrepresented in the workforce. They are also designed to eliminate discrimination at different levels in the work force. Too often, management and administrative roles are not accessible to minority groups. For example, most high-level administrative positions in athletics are filled by white males. Although Title IX was intended to prevent sex discrimination, since its passage the percentage of women coaching women's sports has actually decreased (Acosta and Carpenter, 1992).

Affirmative action programs are based on the proportionality principle. It must be determined whether minority representation at all levels and positions is proportionate to the numbers of the minorities in the relevant labor market. If not, affirmative action plans must be followed to reach this goal. These plans must spell out specific programs, the time frame of the program, and the specific objectives that have been set.

Several steps must be implemented. A staff analysis to determine minority representation and an analysis of the labor pool will provide guidelines for an affirmative action plan to ensure equal opportunities for all groups. The advertisement of positions and wording of job descriptions must be stated in a manner that encourages applications from qualified individuals and gives equal consideration of all qualified applicants. Finally, the interview process must not discriminate against qualified applicants. Interview questions must be pertinent for determining a person's ability to handle the responsibilities of the position.

Affirmative action extends beyond the employment phase and includes discrimination or other unequal treatment in the workplace. Promotion opportunities, educational and training provisions, firing or discharging employees, layoffs, pay scales for comparable work, performance appraisals, and work conditions must be nondiscriminatory. Sexual harassment is another practice that is prohibited under Title VII of the Civil Rights Act of 1964. This applies to all aspects of the work environment as well as in administrative processes such as hiring, promoting, and discharging an employee.

Class Activities

Simulation 1

Situation   A staff member has proposed that the school program be revamped so instructors teach only their favorite classes.

Administrators are usually a composite of several administrative styles and change their styles according to the situation. Administrative styles range from the autocratic to the laissez-faire. Prepare a skit dramatizing three administrative styles for the situation described above. Show how an administrator would use autocratic (complete control), staff participation, and laissez-faire (hands-off) approaches. Discuss the strengths and weaknesses of each approach.

Simulation 2

Situation   There will be a $10,000 budget cut for the next fiscal year.

Divide the class into three groups and have each group select one person in their group to be the administrator. Have three envelopes, each containing a card with either hands off, complete control, or staff participation written on it. Have the groups select an envelope and then simulate the specified administrative style when deciding how to implement the $10,000 budget cut.

Simulation 3

Situation   A typical day in an athletic director's life includes tasks that require assuming many different responsibilities. Typical tasks during a week include the following:

1. The following athletic contests will be held:

    a. Home conference swim meet Friday and Saturday.

    b. 2 boys' and 2 girls' basketball games; home games on Tuesday and away games on Friday.

    c. One wrestling meet at home Wednesday.

    d. One ice hockey game on a neutral rink Monday.

2. Weekly coaches' meeting.
3. Budget requests are due in the principal's office on Thursday.
4. Report must be prepared for school board meeting next week.
5. Parents call about lack of playing time for their daughter.
6. You are asked to speak at the Rotary Club.
7. Correspondence.
8. Telephone calls.
9. The state coaches' convention will be held in two weeks.
10. Four coaches' positions are still open for the spring season, which begins in one month.
11. Fundraising plans are needed for next year's athletic banquets.
12. Evaluation forms must be completed within two weeks for all winter sport coaches.
13. A newspaper has called for a comment about the unsporting conduct of your school's students at last week's basketball game.
14. Lockers must be assigned for spring sports athletes.
15. A time must be scheduled for your weekly tennis game with three faculty members.

You are the athletic director. Prioritize the above tasks and schedule your time from Monday through Saturday on a weekly calendar form to accomplish the tasks.

Performance Tasks

1. Use the situation described in Simulation 3. Categorize the athletic director's tasks according to the following seven processes (some tasks will require more than one process):

    Planning

    Organizing

    Staffing

    Directing

    Coordinating

    Reporting

    Budgeting

2. Interview a school administrator in your home district or a local district to find out the difference between the formal and informal power of the position.
3. Observe how a physical education administrator in your discipline is involved in each of the following processes: planning, organizing, staffing, directing, coordinating, reporting, and budgeting. Evaluate the administrator's effectiveness.
4. Design a flow chart depicting the following:

   a. A K–12 school district organization chart
   b. The national structure of the American Alliance for Health, Physical Education, Recreation, and Dance (AAHPERD)
   c. An organizational plan for a high school department of health, physical education, athletics, and driver education
   d. A wellness center or sport club

5. Categorize the type of administration found in your high school. Compare its effectiveness with other types of administration you have observed in noneducational settings.
6. Provide specific examples of how Title IX of the Educational Amendments of 1972 and Public Law 94-142 have changed programs in the health, physical education, sports, and leisure fields.
7. Analyze the different kinds of effects that the external and internal environments have on an administrator.
8. Write your professional philosophy. Discuss with a classmate the factors that have been most influential in structuring your philosophy.

References

Acosta, Vivian, and Linda Jean Carpenter, "As the Years Go By—Coaching Opportunities in the 1990s." *Journal of Physical Education, Recreation and Dance,* March 1992, 63:36–41.

Block, Martin, "Americans with Disabilities Act: Its Impact on Youth Sports." *Journal of Physical Education, Recreation and Dance,* January 1995, 66:28–32.

Brandt, Ellen, "Coed Sports." *Physician and Sportsmedicine,* September 1991, 19:121–124.

Crase, Darrell, "The Minority Connection: African-Americans in Administrative Leadership Positions." *Physical Educator,* Winter 1994, 51:15–20.

Durrant, Sue M., "Title IX—Its Power and Its Limitations." *Journal of Physical Education, Recreation and Dance,* March 1992, 63:60–64.

Ensman, Richard G., "Everybody Wins: Guides for Working with Young Employees." *Dance Teacher Now,* February 1994, 16:37–40.

Fox, Connie, "Title IX and Athletic Administration." *Journal of Physical Education, Recreation and Dance,* March 1992a, 63:48–52.

Fox, Connie, "Title IX at Twenty." *Journal of Physical Education, Recreation and Dance,* March 1992b, 63:33–35.

Kamlesh, Mathur, and Daniel Solow, *Management Science: The Art of Decision Making.* Englewood Cliffs, NJ: Prentice Hall, 1994.

Kjeldsen, Erik, "The Manager's Role in the Development and Maintenance of Ethical Behavior in the Sport Organization." *Journal of Sport Management,* May 1992, 6:99–113.

Kurato, Donald F., and Richard M. Hodgetts, *Entrepreneurship: A Contemporary Approach,* 3rd ed. New York: Dryden Press, 1995.

Lirgg, Cathy D., "Effects of Same-Sex Versus Coeducational Physical Education on the Self-Perceptions of Middle and High School Students." *Research Quarterly for Exercise and Sport,* September 1993, 64:324–334.

Mechikoff, Robert A., and Steven Estes. *History and Philosophy of Sport and Physical Education.* Madison: Brown and Benchmark, 1993.

Miller, Lori, et al., "The Impact of Americans with Disabilities Act of 1990." *Clinical Kinesiology,* Fall 1993, 47:63–70.

O'Brien, Dianne B., and James O. Overley, "The Americans with Disabilities Act: Historical Background and Implications for Physical Education and Recreation." *Journal of Legal Aspects of Sport,* Spring 1994, 4:29–36.

Soucie, Daniel, "Effective Managerial Leadership in Sport Organizations." *Journal of Sport Management,* January 1994, 8:1–13.

Wilde, T. Jess, "Title IX: Gathering Momentum." *Journal of Legal Aspects of Sport,* Fall 1993, 3:71–87.

Wong, Glenn, and Carol Barr, "Title IX Wields a Mightier Sword." *Athletic Business,* May 1992, 16:16–17.

3

Administrator-Staff Dynamics

The Human Element

Administration involves three major aspects: the interpersonal, the technical, and the conceptual. The interpersonal dimension of administration is focused on managing the people in the organization. Positive interactions and interrelationships keyed on organizational goals are the outcomes for an administrator who is skilled in this area. The technical aspect involves such considerations as budget making, purchase and care of equipment, construction and maintenance of facilities, office management, curriculum construction, and other responsibilities that require technical knowledge and skill. An administrator is expected either to have the technical skills that are required for the position or to attain them through in-service study, formal courses, or a mentoring program. The conceptual aspect of administration is the ability to conceive ideas and to visualize abstract relationships. It is important to be able to view a department, club, or other organization as a whole and to have an understanding of how individual or group actions affect others and the objectives of the organization.

Of these three phases of administration, administration of the interpersonal component in an organization is generally considered the most important and the most difficult. The success of an organization is ultimately determined by the people who do the teaching or other tasks. How well these responsibilities are accomplished determines the degree of success attained.

Basically, the administrator's job consists of getting tasks completed for, with, and through people. The most important skill to learn is the management of people, not the administration of things. Although conceptual skills are critically important, allowing an administrator to grasp trends and perceive innovative changes, productive action on these concepts cannot occur without interpersonal skills. The objective of an administrator is to relate to staff members in such a way that 100 percent effort is obtained from 100 percent of the people 100 percent of the time. Although this objective is idealistic, it serves as a guideline for the conscientious administrator. Trying to reach this objective is a challenging prospect for even a few months, but it is the administrator's obligation to strive for this objective throughout his or her tenure.

Making maximum use of human skills and developing each individual's potential are the hallmarks of a successful administrator. They lead to satisfied faculty members and employees and enable an organization to attain its objectives. Successful administrators must have good interpersonal skills in order to apply their technical and conceptual skills effectively.

Understanding Human Nature

Because the behavior of people is at the very heart of the administrative process, it follows that the administrator must understand human beings. People are very complex and a genuine understanding of them is invaluable in getting cooperative efforts to accomplish the organization's purposes. Some administrators develop an excellent insight into human nature by broad and varied experience with people, but even this is not a substitute for an academic preparation in the behavioral sciences. For the administrator, a strong background in psychology and sociology is as important as an adequate preparation in technical courses such as anatomy, physiology, management, and budgeting. Realistic perceptions of people and the differences among age groups are valuable attributes. The study of administration must be grounded in the study of people.

In the last half of the twentieth century, an explosion of knowledge and technology has occurred in the behavioral sciences. A vast amount of research that has profound implications for physical education, health education, sport, and leisure administrators has become available. It is important that administrators become familiar with this literature.

Motivation

One of the administrator's most important responsibilities is to motivate all staff members to expend their best efforts. An individual who gives less than his or her best effort weakens the organization. It has been repeatedly demonstrated in athletic competition that teams of motivated players, each of whom gives maximum effort, often defeat opposing teams that are superior in skill but not highly motivated. By the same token, an organization is weaker and less successful in its operations when any member gives less than optimal performance.

Similarly, the administrator is often held responsible when a high level of motivation does not exist among the staff members. At times, the factors affecting motivation may be beyond the power of the administrator to remedy. Inadequate facilities and equipment, an insufficient number of staff members, low salaries, few promotions, and low status within the institution are factors that may diminish motivation. These are factors that the administrator is often unable to correct. However, there is no doubt that the administrator is the leading factor affecting the motivation of staff members.

To accomplish a highly motivated, cooperative attitude on the part of the staff, the administrator must harness effectively all the major motivational forces available. Some of the major motivational forces are the basic needs or interests that are universally characteristic of people. Maslow developed a hierarchy of human needs, which he ranked in order of importance: physiological needs (food, shelter, clothing), safety needs, then social (belongingness), esteem (self-respect), and finally self-actualization (self-fulfillment) (Maslow, 1943, pp. 370–396).

A number of behavioral scientists have supported the thesis that human needs or interests are organized in a hierarchy, with the physiological needs for survival at the base. At progressively higher levels are the needs for belongingness, esteem, and self-actualization. This is probably too simple an explanation of motivation. Different people and different cultures may react in different ways to Maslow's hierarchy of human needs and varying needs may affect a person's behavior at any one time. It is important for the administrator to be aware of the types of needs that are present and strive to provide a work environment that satisfies these needs, whether they appear in a certain order or in combination with each other. A skillful administrator in the fields of physical education, health education, leisure, and sports has a grand opportunity to enable each faculty and staff member to function at the highest level (self-actualization).

The mistake countless administrators make is to assume that their staff members are motivated solely by money. There is no question that money is a powerful motivator of human beings. It is a prerequisite for meeting the survival needs. It contributes to the satisfaction of the higher-level needs. However, it is not the only motivator. The administrator can achieve maximum motivation only by tapping all the motives that yield favorable attitudes. The leader who relies primarily on the economic motives of buying an individual's time and then telling the person precisely what to do, how to do it, and at what level to produce is disregarding what behavioral science has learned about human behavior.

The Organizational Climate

The environment within which one works is extremely important to each person. These surroundings include attitudes, work conditions, colleagues, offices, and buildings. Another important part of the climate is the relationship of the faculty and staff members with the administrator. This factor has significant implications for the motivation of the people in the organization. For this reason, it is an extremely important responsibility of an administrator to create the proper climate between the different levels of authority in the organization.

Motivational Theories

Douglas McGregor, in *The Human Side of Enterprise* (1960) suggested that there are two styles of motivational leadership. The first, which he called Theory X, takes the view that employees find work distasteful and will avoid work if at all possible. In this theory, employees want direction and must be forced or threatened in order to work.

The second theory, called Theory Y, assumes that people enjoy working and that they will accept responsibility and be able to direct themselves. A further extension of this theory is that people are interested in their organization and want to apply their talents to do a good job.

Quality circles   The business world has contributed this concept, which affects managerial styles in many fields, including physical education, health education, athletics, and leisure programs. The quality circles developed in Japan were characterized by small groups working together to solve problems and implement solutions. In the fields of physical education, health education, leisure, and sports they are used to include teachers, coaches, and staff in the decision-making process. They are participatory management at its best. Concepts from quality circles have extensively influenced management procedures in other countries (Evans and Lindsay, 1993).

Total quality management (TQM)   Although TQM is a business phenomenon, it is being carefully examined by educational and nonprofit organizations, where many of the principles apply. It is designed to build quality into goods and services through a deep commitment to quality by every member of the organization. Teamwork is emphasized and employees are empowered to make their maximum contribution to the organization. Employee participation is a key management principle that is applicable to management in the physical education, leisure, and sport fields (Evans and Lindsay, 1993).

Theory Z   This concept was created by William G. Ouchi in his book Theory Z: How American Business Can Meet the Japanese Challenge (1981). It incorporates elements from Japanese management and modifies some parts of the traditional American way of managing. Plunkett and Attner describe Theory Z as "the management view that mutual responsibility, loyalty, and regard between companies and their employees yields higher productivity and well-being for all" (Plunkett and Attner, 1994, p. 821).

These examples of management theories show that there are many types of management styles and that there has been a steady move in the direction of participation and involvement by employees. Theory X and Theory Y administrators represent extremes and the majority of administrators are somewhere between them. Different situations and different faculty and staff require that the management approaches be varied in order to best motivate the workers to accomplish organizational objectives. These approaches may vary, but the most success accrues when ideas are shared and all employees are included in the management process.

Other Variables Related to Motivation

In addition to identifying and nurturing the right motives to affect human behavior there are other factors involved in motivation. The manner in which organizational decision making is done is significantly related to motivation. The effectiveness of communication within the organization is another important consideration. The leadership processes used by the administrator have a strong influence on motivation. It is important to take into consideration differences of interests, values, cultural background, attitudes, and personal skills. Some individuals are highly motivated by a good salary, job security, and comfortable working conditions. Other people place a higher priority on challenges, acceptance of ideas, or opportunity for advancement.

Both extrinsic and intrinsic rewards are needed for job satisfaction. Extrinsic rewards such as promotions, compensation, benefits, recognition, and work environment are obviously motivational factors to be considered. Equally important are the intrinsic rewards that come from satisfying and enjoyable work. The feeling of self-worth, the knowledge that you have made a difference, and personal enjoyment attained through work are intrinsic motivational outcomes that accrue from the efforts and planning of a skilled administrator.

It is important for an administrator to consider the following principles when striving for a work environment that will motivate people with varying needs and goals:

Work should provide personal satisfaction.

Administrators should take a personal interest in the work of each staff member. They must be conversant in all aspects of their organization, even though they cannot be expected to be experts in all areas.

Departmental or organizational efforts should be joint ventures between staff and administration. Information must be shared with staff members so that they become a part of the organization and take an active, enthusiastic approach.

Establish pleasant working conditions that are conducive to reaching the objectives of the organization. Provide employees with sufficient resources to carry out their responsibilities.

Staff members should be permitted to make job-related decisions. This contributes to the need for achievement. A good workplace enables each person to be an achiever.

Spell out responsibilities clearly so that each person knows what is expected from her or him. Give staff the authority they need to accomplish duties.

Provide for challenges and achievement and build in opportunities for advancement. Advancement can take different forms, such as increased responsibility or more challenging duties, even if circumstances don't permit advancement through change of position.

Treat everybody fairly and consistently. This doesn't mean that everyone will be dealt with in the same manner, but all situations must be handled fairly.

Give recognition for work well done. This recognition should include personal praise as well as public recognition of significant achievements. Praise in public and reprimand in private is a good policy to follow.

People are motivated by pride in their school, department, club, team, or organization. This pride comes from significant achievements, an enjoyable work environment, and community recognition of outstanding performance.

Leadership Processes

The administrator, more than anyone else, affects the human relations in any organization. He or she is intimately involved with motivation, communication, personnel, daily operations, and the decision-making process, and thus is in a key position to affect the human resources of an organization. This is not to say that there are not other factors that may enter the picture; there are other elements over which the chairperson has no control.

Some administrators are job-centered; others are employee-centered. Administrators who are job-centered are primarily interested in the productivity of their staff. Those who are employee-centered are interested in both their employees and their productivity. They identify with them and trust their colleagues, who reciprocate by having confidence and trust in them.

Mutual trust and confidence are indispensable ingredients in the relationship between the administrator and staff members. A leader who does not have a genuine concern for the worker's welfare and does not treat employees fairly is extremely damaging to morale.

Staff members also have little confidence in administrators who have little upward influence. Research has shown that it is important for the administrator to have substantial influence with his or her own superior. Staff members look to their chairperson to obtain salary increases, promotions, improved facilities, adequate equipment and supplies, and better working conditions for them. When their administrator cannot deliver the needed resources, they lose confidence. This is particularly true when other departmental chairpersons and directors have more success than their own.

Staff members do not expect to get a fair break when their chairperson is incompetent. This is particularly true when the chairperson is not conversant in the technical aspects of the work. No one expects the administrator to be expert with every detail of every job but staff members expect their leader to be technically competent. If this is not the case, they lose confidence in their leader.

Staff members cannot hope to be treated fairly by their leader when they have reason to doubt his or her integrity. If the administrator is devious, insincere, selfish, vain, arrogant, unscrupulous, or disloyal, colleagues will soon find out. No matter how technically competent or whatever assets the administrator might have, if staff members cannot trust their administrator, the climate in the organization will not be healthy.

Communication

Communication is an essential process of administration. An organization cannot function without it. An administrator's decisions are meaningless unless they can be communicated to others. As a matter of fact, most administrative decisions depend on data transmitted by others in the organization to the administrator. The breakdown in communications has caused serious problems in countless organizations.

Communication is an intricate process. Numerous factors are involved from the time a communication is initiated until the transmitter receives feedback. The sender must use either verbal or nonverbal mechanisms that accurately convey the intended message and the mode used to send the message must be appropriate. Appropriateness is determined by the speed with which a reply is needed, the complexity of the message, resources that are available, relationship with the receiver or receivers, the number of people involved, confidentiality issues, and the impact that is desired from the communication.

Most tasks of an administrator require the use of communication. The range of communication is extensive. There are situations in which communication is straightforward and designed for informational purposes. At the other extreme are complex, sophisticated messages that require extensive back-and-forth interaction, which may require the use of more than one type of communication. In any type of communication, the key is clarity. Much is lost in the transmission from person to person and, as a result, care must to taken to be sure the message conveys its intent accurately.

Communication requires more than sending a message. An administrator must also be a good listener and receive messages, whether they are replies to an administrator-introduced communication or staff-initiated messages. Unfortunately, too often administrators do not develop their listening skills as effectively as they do their sending techniques.

Channels of Communication

Many means of communicating are available. The most direct is face-to-face communication. In small departments and organizations, this type predominates. It provides an opportunity for exchange between the sender and receiver, which makes it possible to clarify meanings and receive immediate feedback. When people do not meet face-to-face, some type of indirect communication is needed. The use of an intermediary is one possibility, although significant loss occurs when a message is passed through one or more people. It does maintain the personal touch and may lead to clarification by discussing the message with the intermediary.

There are many ways to reach out with written communication. Memos and letters have been joined by technological advances such as facsimiles, word processing systems, voice mail, and e-mail. Properly used, they can all be effective. In larger organizations it is often necessary, because of the time element, to use less direct communication techniques.

Meetings, properly organized and functioning efficiently, are also excellent communication vehicles. Administrators can also use video and teleconferencing formats to disseminate information and keep staff members informed. Of course, the telephone is an indispensable tool of the administrator. It has many of the advantages of face-to-face communication and overcomes time and distance obstacles. The cellular telephone expands the usefulness of the telephone for the administrator.

Blockages

Blockages in communication occur at a number of points in the system. The administrator often causes the problem when he or she forgets to communicate or sends incomplete, inaccurate, or contradictory messages. Some are unwilling to share information with their colleagues. In this latter case, staff members become bitter and frustrated when they are denied information to which they are entitled and that staff members in other departments receive. It is unfortunate that some administrators are indifferent to situations of this type. There is no patented solution when staff members are faced with this predicament. The first step should be to initiate dialogue with the administrator in a nonconfrontational manner. One or two staff members should discuss the advantages of participatory administration and make the point that accurate information received in a timely fashion permits staff members to make their greatest contribution. Every effort should be made to resolve differences within the administrative unit in a professional way. If this fails, the staff must make a professional judgment as to whether it is best to accept an undesirable situation or take the problem to the administrator's superior.

Receivers themselves may block communication. They may be distracted or hostile, or they may choose to ignore or carelessly receive messages. The administrator must be reminded that people generally retain approximately 10 percent of what they hear, 20–30 percent of what they see, and 50 percent of what they do. Face-to-face dialogue with the administrator is often needed. Sometimes the crux of the problem is simply a lack of feedback. Feedback is essential to effective communication. This serves as the basis for changes and adjustments that can emanate from effective communication. At the very least, some mechanism is needed to inform the sender that a message has been received.

Flow of Information

It is important that information flow in all directions. This means that there must be information going downward, upward, and sideward. The downward communication is from the administrator to the faculty or staff members. Upward communication is an important way for an administrator to obtain information from staff members. Often overlooked is sideward communication, which involves peers and those working at the same level of the organization, whether it be faculty members in a university or activity directors in a YMCA. (See Figure 3-1.)

Upward communication is facilitated when the climate of the organization encourages it. All staff members should feel a responsibility for initiating upward or sideward communication that is pertinent and accurate. The administrator needs such information, particularly in larger organizations, to know what is going on. The administrator may be unaware that some facilities need repair or that certain equipment is defective or inadequate. Such problems should be reported immediately so that corrective action may be taken. As the administrator's decisions are being implemented, he or she must know how they are working out. Some actions may be creating unnecessary difficulties for staff members or they may be unreasonable or unfair. Upward communication provides the best way for staff to bring

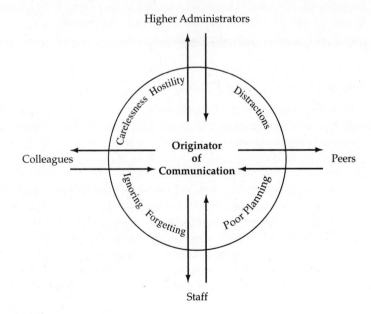

FIGURE 3-1. Flow of Information with Potential Blockages

such matters to the administrator's attention. Unless these problems are resolved, the consequences might prove detrimental to the organization. Not only is inefficiency encouraged but faculty morale is undermined.

Sideward communication serves a number of purposes. It facilitates cooperation among those who have different responsibilities. For example, in a high school physical education department it is important that the person directing the adaptive program work closely with those teaching in the instructional program because some students will be mainstreamed into these classes. A high level of coordination is needed for facility use, and this comes from effective sideward communication. This communication also leads to joint problem solving and combined efforts in departmental activities and projects.

Decision Making

Decision making is another administrative process that has important implications for the human relations in an organization. Many authorities regard it as the most important administrator activity because it is involved in all of the other processes of administration such as planning, organizing, controlling, directing, coordinating, and evaluating. Every administrator wants to make sound decisions and implement those decisions effectively. In fact, this is what administration is all about. Thus, decision making is recognized as the heart of organization and the process of administration.

A multitude of decisions are made in every organization. These decisions may be categorized as personal and organizational. Personal decisions are those that every staff member makes in discharging duties. In education, they relate to such matters as what will be taught, what teaching styles will be used, what teaching aids will be used, how pupil progress will be evaluated, and what discipline will be used. Organizational decisions, on the other hand, relate to the operations of the entire organization and generally are of concern to all members of the department.

The Decision-Making Process

A number of steps must be followed in decision making. The amount of time devoted to each step and the research and study involved in each step are determined by the complexity of the problem for which a decision is needed.

Steps in the decision-making process are as follows:

1. Investigate the situation and concisely define the problem.
2. Identify objectives that will lead to the elimination of the problem.
3. Identify barriers or hurdles that must be surmounted.
4. Search and analyze alternate solutions to the problem.
5. Select the best alternative to solve the problem.
6. Implement the alternative that has been chosen.
7. Evaluate the results and make needed adjustments.

It is helpful to list and categorize information at each step of the process.

Faculty Participation in Departmental Decision Making

Administrative policy in all fields is moving toward including members of the organization more extensively in the decision-making process. In educational circles, the principle that all who might be affected by a decision should share in making it has wide acceptance. No aspect of the decision-making process is more widely misunderstood and improperly implemented. One interpretation is that all concerned faculty members should participate fully in the discussion and then finally make the decision by a formal vote. Another view is that after full discussion of the matter by the concerned faculty members, the administrator would then make the final decision. A third point of view holds that all faculty members should discuss the problem and then be delegated by the administrator to make some of the decisions, with the administrator reserving the right to make the remainder of the decisions. Finally, there is the procedure whereby the administrator makes the decision without referring the matter to staff members.

The principle that all personnel who might be affected by a decision should share in making it is subject to a variety of interpretations. The term *share* causes the confusion. It is the consensus that all affected by a decision should participate in discussing it. There are two main advantages to such a procedure. The first is that such discussion provides maximum input in regard to the decision. Staff members provide a larger number of ways of looking at a problem, a larger number of suggestions for a solution, and a larger number of criticisms of each proposed plan. The administrator would be remiss in not making full use of the talents of the members of his or her staff. Vital information or the best idea for solving the problem could come from an unexpected source.

The second advantage of allowing those affected by a decision to participate in the process is that staff members will implement the decision better when they have had such an opportunity. In connection with this point, Likert (1967, p. 212) says:

> Without question, wise decisions are important and necessary to the success of an enterprise, but it is equally true that no decision is any better than the motivation used in carrying it out. An excellent decision poorly executed because of hostile or apathetic motivation is no better in its consequences for the organization than a poor decision. It is well to keep in mind the formula: Results achieved = quality of the decision × motivation to implement the decision. If either term in the right half of the equation is low, the action performed will be unsatisfactory.

Giving concerned staff members an opportunity to discuss the issue and to express their convictions and concerns definitely constitutes sharing in the decision-making process. However, to some the term *share* goes beyond this point. They believe that the decisions should be made by a vote of those concerned. They conceive this as democratic administration.

The authority for making organizational decisions belongs to the organizational administrator. It has been delegated by a superior. If the administrator wants to delegate this authority to the faculty, he or she may do so. However, this act does not remove the responsibility for the results of the decision from the administrator. Decisions that might well be made by faculty members because they are directly involved with implementation include such matters as curriculum, purchase and use of audiovisual and other instructional aids, teaching methods, classroom discipline, and evaluation of student performance.

In the last decade, students have become increasingly involved in the decision-making process. As consumers of education, this seems a right and natural function for students.

They are directly affected by decisions that are made and they are able to share unique insights into the effects of these decisions. They take their responsibilities conscientiously and they have contributed fresh and worthwhile ideas to the educational scene.

Class Activities

Simulation 1

Situation   You are in your first year as chairperson of a high school physical education department of ten members. Your principal has asked you to design a communication system for your department.

Present this document to the members of your department for suggestions before submitting it to your principal.

Simulation 2

Situation   You are director of a fitness center, an athletic program, or a physical education program (select one). Staff morale was low under your predecessor.

Write guidelines for your organization to improve morale and thereby upgrade program quality.

Simulation 3

Situation   Participation has drastically decreased in elective physical education classes that require vigorous effort on the part of the students.

To resolve this problem, show the approaches that would be used by different motivational leadership styles. Simulate a meeting with the physical education faculty by the following:

A Theory X administrator

A Theory Y administrator

A Theory Z administrator

An administrator using the quality circle concept

An administrator emphasizing TQM

Performance Tasks

1. Investigate the channels of communication in a department, school building, school district, or business organization. Analyze the effectiveness of the communication channels and suggest improvements.
2. Interview a school principal to find out what she or he feels are the most important qualities a principal should have to motivate subordinates.
3. Develop a motivational plan that you feel will improve the teaching and learning climate in your university classes.
4. Interview several teachers and ask them to list the qualities they feel an administrator must have in order to be motivational.

5. Observe teachers, coaches, or employees in leisure programs and determine whether staff participation plays a major role in the organization's decision-making process.
6. Establish guidelines that you would recommend for an administrator in order to involve staff in the decision-making process.

References

Daft, Richard, *Management*, 3rd ed. New York: Dryden Press, 1994.

Evans, James R., and William M. Lindsay, *The Management and Control of Quality.* St. Paul: West Publishing, 1993.

Fandt, Patricia M., *Management Skills: Practice and Experience.* Minneapolis/St. Paul: West Publishing, 1994.

Garrison, Ray H., *Managerial Accounting: Concepts for Planning, Control, Decision Making,* 7th ed. Homewood, IL: Irwin, 1993.

Gold, R. Richard, and Arren DeLuca, "TQM in P and R." *Parks and Recreation,* September 1993, 28:86–91.

Griffin, Ricky W., *Management,* 4th ed. Boston: Houghton Mifflin, 1993.

Koch, Susan J., and Debra J. Jordan, "We Can Work It Out—Resolving Staff Conflicts." *Camping Magazine,* July/August 1993, 65:21–25.

Likert, Rensis, *New Patterns of Management.* New York: McGraw-Hill, 1967.

McGregor, Douglas, *The Human Side of Enterprise.* New York: McGraw-Hill, 1960.

Maslow, Abraham, "A Theory of Human Motivation." *Psychological Review,* 50, 1943.

Mawson, L. Marlene, "Total Quality Management: Perspectives for Sport Management." *Journal of Sport Management,* May 1993, 7:101–106.

Plunkett, Warren R., and Raymond Attner, *Introduction to Management,* 5th ed. Belmont: Wadsworth Publishing Company, 1994.

Schermerhorn, John R., Jr., *Management for Productivity,* 4th ed. New York: Wiley, 1993.

Schmiedeler, John, and Patrick Schmiedeler, "Athletic Programs: Students' Needs, Growth, Satisfaction Focus of Total Quality Management." *Interscholastic Athletic Administration,* Fall 1993, 20:9–11.

Weekes, Evelyn N., *Total Quality Management: An Approach to Outcomes Assessment in Education.* Guthrie, OK: Midwest Publications, 1992.

Whetten, David A., and Kim S. Cameron, *Developing Management Skills: Gaining Power and Influence.* New York: HarperCollins, 1993.

4

Physical Education, Health Education, and Leisure Staff

Significance of Staff

The single most important function performed by an administrator is hiring competent people who have excellent personal characteristics. This is an awesome responsibility, but skill in finding and employing outstanding people ultimately determines the level of success of any organization. Staffing is a multistage process. It begins with the search for high-quality candidates for positions, continues through the screening, interview, and hiring process, and culminates in a program designed to further the professional development of the employees from the day they begin work until they leave the school or company. The importance of this task requires that an administrator be well-prepared. It entails a significant expenditure of time, careful planning, and the following of procedures that are designed to find the best-qualified candidate for each opening.

It is a truism that a program will not advance beyond the vision of those who administrate it, but no school or other organization can be greater than its staff. Every program relies on staff members for efficient operation. Any organization that selects staff members on the basis of friendship or politics rather than on qualifications can only fulfill its objectives in a mediocre way.

The staffing principles in this chapter apply to positions in educational and noneducational settings. Many college and university students are in programs that prepare them for jobs in corporate fitness, health promotion, and leisure fields. The process used to staff these positions requires the same intensity and thoroughness that is used to fill teaching positions. Desired personal characteristics of employees and techniques used to incorporate new employees into the workplace are pertinent for both teaching and nonteaching positions.

Before 1925, well-trained people in the field of physical education were comparatively scarce. Except for a brief decline during the Depression, the supply of men graduating from college with majors in the field rose gradually from 1925 to 1941, then dwindled to just a few during World War II. From 1946 to 1952, the number increased rapidly, after which there was a noticeable decline followed by a slight rise in 1956. Calls from the armed forces during the Korean and Vietnamese conflicts temporarily removed from teaching some of the graduates during the late 1950s and 1960s. However, the supply of men with bachelor's degrees adequately met the demand during these years. Declining student enrollment during the 1970s resulted in an oversupply of male physical educators in most areas. Women with bachelor's degrees in physical education have a different history. For many years, there was a shortage of female physical educators. Not until the pupil decline starting in the mid-1970s were there sufficient female teachers to meet the demand and eventually create a surplus. An oversupply of both women and men in physical education remained during the 1980s and into the 1990s. This has resulted in many students changing their career goals and moving into programs such as health promotion and sport management, where career opportunities have been increasing. Although teachers have been in plentiful supply, this period was characterized by a severe shortage of coaches in secondary schools. Many students who want to coach have moved into other fields that make it possible for them to coach part-time.

Although there has been a decreased demand for physical educators, it should be pointed out that many school districts would be understaffed if they had optimal physical education programs. In many situations, this is a matter of economics, but it becomes obvious that the physical education profession must sell the public on the value of physical education for every student. The American Alliance for Health, Physical Education, Recreation, and Dance is working diligently to promote legislation that will result in daily physical education for all elementary and secondary students. Administrators and teachers must energetically support this effort, which will not only contribute to the well-being of youth but will certainly generate many more positions for physical educators. The goal must be comprehensive physical education programs for all students. This, together with programs for the out-of-school population (including workplace programs and exercise and activity programs for retired people), will result in a dramatic increase in job opportunities.

The supply of women and men with graduate preparation was inadequate in the late 1940s. The steady growth of graduate education has resulted in an impressive number of physical education teachers who now have at least a master's degree. By 1976, there was already an oversupply of men with doctoral degrees. As a result of Title IX of the Education Amendments of 1972 and the implementation of affirmative action plans in the early and mid-1970s, many education positions that had been closed to women and other minority groups were opened. This resulted in a significant increase in the number of women and minorities pursuing master's and doctoral degrees and thereby educationally qualifying for administrative and higher education positions in physical education. Unfortunately, even 20 years after this legislation, women and minorities are still underrepresented in administrative positions in physical education and athletics. This is also true of coaching positions (Fox, 1992; Acosta and Carpenter, 1992).

Because requirements for physical education majors vary widely from state to state and from school to school, it does not follow that all those who receive degrees are equally prepared. The number of semester or quarter hours that are required and the specific courses that are included in a major differ significantly from school to school. Also, the type and quality of instruction differs considerably. Out of this varied preparation come graduates with varying qualifications. However, the administrator who really wants a well-prepared physical education faculty can have such a staff. It costs little more to hire good instructors than to hire poor or even average ones. It is a matter of knowing good qualifications, obtaining the best possible applicants, and being able to determine which of the candidates has the best qualifications for the position. These principles apply to positions in other fields also.

Qualifications

There are many important characteristics that an administrator must consider when selecting a physical education or health education instructor or a staff person in the leisure field. Obviously, technical skills are extremely important. These requirements must be clearly stated in the job description. If gymnastics is a part of the teaching load, then competency in this area is required. If administrative or coaching responsibilities are a part of the position, administrative or coaching skills of the applicant must be carefully evaluated. If the position includes developing personalized exercise programs, then the candidate must demonstrate this ability and have approved certification.

There are many other qualities, often more difficult to measure, that must also be considered. Of key importance is the ability of the person to relate positively to others. Does the candidate enjoy working with people? Does the person applying for a teaching position enjoy young people and have a commitment to the teaching process? Will the candidate continue to develop as a professional and strive to overcome weaknesses that might be present? Does the person have the ability to stimulate and motivate others? Will the candidate command respect? Answers to these types of questions must be carefully sought in order to obtain high-quality staff members.

Personal Characteristics

It is easier to evaluate technical skills of applicants than it is to evaluate personal traits. Technical skills are observable and can be demonstrated. Performance standards are likely to be available and for some activities such as swimming, performance is objectively determined through certification programs. Still, it is imperative that the administrator select candidates who have desirable personal characteristics. The application and interview process must be designed to obtain accurate information about a number of characteristics. Even though administrators differ in the priority they place on an individual's characteristics, each of the following should be evaluated thoroughly:

Personality   This is a complex area because each person has a unique personality and different aspects of one's personality are typically exhibited in different situations. In non-technical terms, personality can be viewed as an individual's way of behaving, experiencing, and thinking. These characteristics are of prime importance in determining whether a person should be selected for a position. For example, the close relationship that develops between the student and physical education teacher or coach makes it critical for the physical education teacher or coach to have exemplary personality characteristics. If a coach verbally expressed to the team members the value of following rules and then circumvents rules, the principle that the coach has been teaching is discredited.

Emotional stability is also an important personality attribute for the physical education teacher–coach. The pressures involved and the impact that this person has on students demands that a proper personal perspective be maintained. Self-control, acceptance of disappointments and criticisms, adaptation to changing situations, patience, an even temperament, and ability not to worry about trivial things are examples of qualities that professionals in the health and physical education, leisure, and sport fields need.

A person can be highly proficient in teaching skills, but it is the personality characteristics that determine effectiveness in reaching objectives in the interpersonal realm. The kind of a person one is ultimately comes through when teaching or interacting with other people. Beliefs are more effectively communicated through actions than through words.

Honesty/Integrity   Fairness and truthfulness are critical attributes. They are the cornerstones of trust and make it possible for a person to be a role model for students. A person who has integrity adheres to ethical principles.

Communication Skills   Teachers of all disciplines must be able to communicate effectively, both orally and in writing. However, in physical education, communication skills are even more important. Physical educators often need to communicate with parents and other members of the community, especially when carrying out coaching and intramural responsibilities, presenting a sports night program, or being involved in other school programs. Professionals in the leisure fields have the same need for communication skills. They interact with participants and community groups, so clear and concise communication is a requisite. Health educators need well-honed communication skills when dealing with controversial health-related topics.

Health and Physical Fitness   This is a particularly important attribute for physical educators. The physical demands placed on a person teaching physical education are great and increase when after-school interscholastic and intramural responsibilities are included. Maintaining enthusiasm and handling the pressures associated with teaching physical education requires a satisfactory level of mental and physical health and fitness. The stamina to demonstrate, spot effectively, and teach physical skills requires a high level of health and physical fitness if the students are to learn in a safe climate.

One of the objectives of physical education programs is to develop physical fitness. The example set by the physical education teacher is an important influence on students. This is another reason why physical fitness and health are important qualifications.

Intellectual Capacity   A teacher or leisure professional must have better-than-average intelligence. This is important for educators if they are going to develop as teachers and apply the principles of learning to their discipline. Mastery of traditional teaching techniques and implementation of new teaching approaches require above-average intellectual ability.

Creativity   To make a program come alive, staff members must be creative. Meeting individual needs requires a creative person. Creativity enables professionals to keep participants motivated by generating excitement through variety and new challenges. Skillfully adjusting to changing conditions and different populations is also an attribute of a creative person.

Flexibility   Professionals in both educational and noneducational settings must be adaptable. For instance, acceptance of student differences and varying moods requires physical educators to be flexible. Capitalizing on learning situations that develop suddenly or change from year to year places a premium on teacher flexibility. The spark of interest that surfaces when a student is motivated by something he or she has read, seen on television, or perhaps been shown by an older sister or brother provides an optimum learning opportunity that can be used by the flexible teacher. The teacher's approach to each student must vary in response to the personality of each student and to changes in the learning environment.

Enthusiasm   How often would a person return to an aerobic class in a fitness center or get involved in a program at a sport club if the leader was not enthusiastic? If a teacher exhibits fervor for an activity, this attitude carries over to the students. An enthusiastic teacher establishes an enjoyable climate for learning. The quality of enthusiasm is one of the most valuable motivating characteristics a person can have.

Caring   This means accepting each student or participant as a person and having sincere interest in them. Caring permits the leader to nurture even those with strange and impulsive actions. The caring teacher shows students that he or she thinks that they are important. Feelings of self-worth are important for personal development.

Leadership Ability   It is valuable for a staff member to be able to lead. He or she may lead in a class situation or within an administrative context, where leadership skills are needed to influence and direct others toward the objectives of the organization. When considering new staff, seek candidates who will be able to develop the skills they need for leadership roles.

Other Considerations

There are considerations in addition to personal characteristics that must be evaluated when employing staff members. Professional involvement, experience, certifications, and academic preparation are some of the areas that must be examined.

Professional Involvement   A person just entering the field should not be expected to have had the same level of professional involvement as an experienced applicant. However, even students applying for their first position should have been actively involved in professional organizations during their university studies, both within their college or university and in state, regional, and national organizations, which invariably provide opportunities for student participation. An experienced applicant should be active in professional organizations. This indicates interest in the profession, shows commitment, and is one way of determining whether the person is knowledgeable about current issues and innovations. Experienced applicants see professional involvement as a means of enhancing personal development and supporting their profession.

Leadership roles and participation in nonprofessional organizations are other good indications of the background employees should have. Skill in interacting with other people, evidence of leadership ability, and a range of interests are all important characteristics that can be exhibited by this type of participation.

Experience   Appropriate experience is important in the development of a physical education teacher. Supervision is important during the formative years in order for the teacher or prospective teacher to profit from mistakes and failures. Experience can be counterproductive when the same errors are repeated. What one does about failure is the important factor. The true value of experience from the viewpoint of improving teachers is that it leads to better performances.

Experiences should be varied. The multifaceted nature of the physical education profession puts a premium on diversified skills and abilities. The student preparing to teach should strive to gain as many experiences as possible. Participating in sports, teaching skills to varied ages groups, leading aerobic lessons, and working as camp counselors are examples of ways to gain experience. The full-time teacher continues to develop by participating in different aspects of the physical education field. In terms of experience, repetition of the same thing soon yields a rapidly diminishing return.

Experience serves as a testing device for those who select and evaluate teachers. Improvement through experience provides a mechanism for determining which ones are strong and capable of developing their skills to a higher level. It furnishes a practical means of selecting the good instructors while giving all a chance to improve. Many good teachers have the essentials at the start, and experience helps to develop and clarify their strengths.

Experience has the same value in the nonteaching fields. It is important to have as wide a variety of experiences as possible and to have good supervision in order to rectify mistakes and build on failures. Experience permits a person to raise the level of competency and expand the scope of areas in which proficiency is attained.

Certification   Standards are established in many facets of the physical education, leisure, and sport fields. This has led to certification programs that can be used to gauge a person's qualification to perform certain tasks. For example, the American College of Sports Medicine has several certifications for people who are involved in health and fitness and cardiovascular rehabilitative exercise programs. The administrator of a health club that offers these programs should require appropriate certification for staff who are being considered to work in any of their exercise programs. There are also certifications for aquatic programs and some states have coaching certifications. Even if certifications are not required, they strengthen candidates' applications.

Academic Preparation   Good professional preparation is of prime importance for success. Given equivalent personality qualifications, the person with a thorough preparation is much more valuable than the one with poor professional preparation. Experience is of significant value, but it does not compensate for a weak professional preparation.

Certification requirements for teaching vary from state to state. An administrator should look beyond minimum requirements when considering applicants. Review the nature of the courses that have been taken, the breadth and depth of the courses, and those that best match the position that is available. The challenge is to determine which applicants have the strongest academic background.

Courses   There are several categories into which courses are grouped for students preparing to teach physical education. The first category is general education. This curricular area is the foundation on which each student builds the remainder of his or her program. Communication skills, social sciences, natural sciences, physical sciences, and humanities give students a broad perspective, which is an important characteristic for a teacher. The trend has been to design interdisciplinary courses and to include nonwestern culture and gender studies in these courses.

The second category to be included in teaching programs is professional education. This includes both theoretical and practical components, with a strong emphasis on teaching methodology. Teaching experience early in a student's program and expanded time spent in schools characterize this category of a student's academic program.

Major courses are the third category of courses that are included in a student's program of study. College and university programs include many different courses specific to the field of physical education and encompass the study of history, philosophy, physiology, evaluation, curriculum, administration, human movement, and motor learning. Activity courses are another important part of this category. They provide a skill base for the student preparing to be a physical education teacher. Teaching methods are also included in these courses. A wide variety of activities, ranging from team and individual sports to adventure program activities such as mountain climbing, are offered in activity courses. It is important that physical education candidates have the needed skill background for the courses they will be teaching.

Because certification programs in many states include joint certification in health and physical education, it is also important that the student majoring in physical education have a strong background in health. An administrator should know the requirements and be prepared to evaluate a student's preparation to teach health on the basis of an in-depth program of health education, not simply on minimum certification standards.

The major courses for a student preparing to teach health education or to work in some other health profession include courses in wellness, human growth and development, drug use and abuse, diseases, environmental health issues, nutrition, stress, body systems, consumer health, accident prevention, and safety. Community health, school health, administration, curriculum, health care systems, and evaluation are other courses that should be part of a health major's program. In addition, method courses are extremely important because of the sensitive nature of many health topics. The health student should also have a strong background in biology and chemistry.

The program for a nonteaching physical education major encompasses courses that provide specific preparation for the nonteaching career. This might be in health promotion, corporate fitness, athletic training, physical therapy, sport management, or some other related field. The administrator hiring in these fields must make sure undergraduate courses have provided the information and skills necessary to handle the responsibilities of the position. For example, business courses are important for a student who is being considered for a management position in corporate fitness. Practical experiences in the form of internships are as important for these fields as are teaching experiences for the student preparing to be a teacher. Internships should be an integral part of nonteaching major programs.

Specialization Some physical education departments have established areas of emphasis in their undergraduate programs that permit students to specialize in one aspect of physical education. A student's program can place an emphasis on aquatics, team sports, gymnastics, adaptive physical education, sociological aspects of sport, or some other area of the curriculum where a core of courses is offered. The advantage to this approach is that the student can become highly skilled in the area of specialization. The disadvantage is that most physical education positions in elementary and secondary schools require ability in a range of activities. There is also a concern that some students do not obtain the solid, broad foundation needed for future specialization and development as a physical educator. Students should strive to have a broad skill base and develop competency in as many sport skills as possible. It is also valuable to develop special skills in one or two of these sports. If this can't be achieved within the context of the physical education curriculum, more advanced skills can be attained through experience on a school athletic or intramural team, classes taken privately, participation with a community sport group, or playing regularly in a sport club setting.

Caliber of professional programs The caliber of the physical education graduate is influenced significantly by the quality of the preparation program, which is determined by a number of factors. Of major importance are the standards for admission and retention of the student. Screening of applicants on motor ability, intellectual competence, and activity background in high school should be a minimal standard for admittance to a professional preparation program. Satisfactory scholarship and performance standards should be required for retention in a program.

The quality of the teaching staff is another vitally important consideration. In certain institutions, highly trained specialists are available to teach each professional course. There is a great difference between what students get out of courses taught by well-prepared teachers and what they learn in courses taught by instructors who have only a superficial background in the area. Unfortunately, in some institutions the professional courses are taught by staff members who lack the background and mastery of the subject matter. This applies equally to activities and classroom courses.

Another critical factor is the pride the department takes in the quality of its graduates. It is important for physical education, health education, and leisure studies departments to be proud of the reputation gained by graduating superior students. All faculty members should be dedicated to developing high-quality preparation programs and expend every effort to accomplish this objective.

The final consideration is the matter of sufficient resources and higher administrative support for a superior operation. Such factors as the adequacy of the equipment, facilities, library, and number of faculty members is an important consideration. If the number is inadequate, staff members are forced to teach courses where they have little expertise and either they are overloaded with additional classes or their classes are too large for effective teaching.

Advanced study With the abundance of physical education teachers, there is no justification for school districts, higher education institutions, or other organizations to employ physical educators who have only minimal qualifications. Most colleges and universities require a doctorate or its equivalent for employment or tenure. There are also a number of states that require a master's degree or at least a designated number of graduate hours before permanent certification is given; some school districts have similar requirements before employing or tenuring a faculty member. An undergraduate degree should be only the starting point for professionals in the physical education and leisure studies fields. Administrators who are evaluating applicants should consider advanced study, whether it be formal course work or in-service programs.

The Staffing Process

The staffing process begins with the determination of need. The next step is to obtain approval to initiate the search. Careful determination of the job description precedes the search process, which ultimately results in interviewing the best candidates. Even after making an offer and having it accepted, the staffing process should continue with a program to acclimate the new person to the organization.

Planning Needs

The administrator should evaluate departmental needs and, based on these needs, write a justification for either creating a new position or filling a vacant position. Staff members should be involved in this process. The goal is to accurately reflect departmental or organizational needs and then initiate a search to fill the position. In most cases, a justification must be submitted to the person who makes allocations for positions in order to obtain approval to proceed with the hiring process. The evaluation of departmental needs serves another important purpose because it involves analysis of changing needs and perhaps changing directions in the department. These determine the job description that is written so the new staff member is qualified to carry out the current mission of the department and the organization or institution.

Many staff members have multiple roles. This magnifies staffing difficulties because multiple skills are needed and weighting must be given to the various responsibilities. Perhaps the combination that causes the most problems is when a person will be teaching physical education and coaching. Too often, the coaching aspect of the position determines the person who will be hired. Teaching ability and commitment to teaching should be the first criteria used when selecting the person to fill this dual role. Physical education programs suffer when staff members teach only in order to coach. Candidates must be hired who are qualified to teach and coach and who consider both responsibilities to be worthy of their full effort.

Recruitment of Applicants

It is important to have a pool of qualified applicants from which to select the best candidates. A comprehensive job description should be written to solicit candidates who have the appropriate qualifications. The job description should include the title of the position, a list of the specific duties involved, competencies that are desired, educational and experience requirements, certifications needed, salary range, and any other requirements for the position. It should be stated that the employer is an equal opportunity employer. Job announcements should also incorporate information about the school or organization and describe special features of the community in order to make the position appealing. The goal is to recruit highly qualified applicants. Included with the job description should be specific information about how to apply for the position and the deadline for applying. It is important for the applicant to know how an application can be obtained and what other information should be submitted.

Any health requirements and physical capabilities that are part of the job description must relate to the ability required to successfully handle responsibilities of the job. Drug testing is another controversial area where legal advice should be obtained before it is included as a requirement in a job announcement.

Job announcements should be distributed widely. College and university placement offices should be notified. Advertisements placed in newspapers and professional publications have proven to be effective. It is especially important to place ads in sources that will reach racial and ethnic minorities. Informing colleagues of openings and attending professional conferences and conventions to meet candidates are good recruitment techniques. Job fairs hosted by colleges and universities should also be considered. For difficult-to-fill positions, commercial placement organizations are another source of applicants. Good applicants can also be located within a school system or organization. Lateral or upward moves by current employees can be advantageous to both the individual and the organization.

Criteria and Sources of Information for Selection of Staff

The formation of a search committee should take place concurrently with discussion of departmental needs and the writing of the job description. In smaller departments, all staff members may compose the search committee. In other situations, members can be appointed by the administrator, who should select staff members who will provide broad representation and be knowledgeable about the requirements of the position.

A file should be set up for each applicant and each person should be notified when his or her file is complete. A separate file also makes it easy to answer questions from an applicant who calls to check on the status of her or his application. Careful records must be kept so that affirmative action records will be accurate. It is professional courtesy to keep applicants informed during the selection process and to inform them immediately when they are no longer being considered.

As many sources of information as possible should be used to evaluate applicants for a position. The first step is to do an initial screening, which includes an evaluation of the candidate's written application and other supporting documentation to determine whether the candidate meets the requirements of the position. This initial screening can be done by a designated person or persons or by the entire search committee. The search committee will then evaluate the remainder of the applicants who meet the requirements of the position and determine who will be invited for an interview. Organizations and schools usually have a policy for the number of candidates who will be invited for an interview. Three to five candidates are typically interviewed and then the search committee sends its recommendation to the administrator, who has the authority to accept or reject the recommendation. Sometimes three candidates are recommended and the administrator can select any of the three. The exact role of the administrator in the selection process is determined by institutional policy. The governing body of a business or educational institution has ultimate authority for hiring staff members unless this authority has been delegated to someone else, usually the chief executive officer.

When the search committee is evaluating the applications that have been received for the position, the following sources of information are commonly used:

Cover letter. The cover letter that accompanies the application is a good source of information. How well does the person express herself or himself? Why does the person want the job? What specials skills does the person have?

Application. Applications provide extensive background information about candidates. Educational information, experiences, interests, and recognitions that have been received are on most applications. There are sometimes open-ended questions about a person's philosophy of life or philosophy of education. Questions are sometimes designed to determine writing skills and ability to express ideas.

Résumé. A résumé provides a brief synopsis of a person's background and highlights special achievements and skills.

College transcripts. Most employing officers are interested in examining transcripts of candidates. They provide insights that may prove helpful. Indications of strengths and weaknesses may be revealed. The academic ability of the candidates does have significance.

It should be pointed out that the institution attended by the candidate is an important consideration. Some colleges and universities are high-quality institutions and their physical education graduates are superbly prepared. Physical education departments in such institutions make every effort to eliminate weak candidates. Although professional preparation is only one criterion to be assessed in employing new staff members, its quality can be readily evaluated by determining the institution where the preparation was obtained.

University activities The extent of participation in various activities provides valuable information. Leadership responsibilities are listed and it is possible to get an indication of the candidate's interests.

Record of participation in sports This is a particularly important consideration where coaching is involved.

Statement of philosophy of physical education The philosophy of candidates is invariably requested. Ordinarily, it is determined in the personal interview. At times, a written statement is requested.

Professional activities Information about professional activities is very important. Active membership in professional organizations and regular attendance at conventions and conferences indicates interest in the profession and personal development.

Written examinations Many states use the results of one or more of the National Teacher Examinations for certification purposes. These tests evaluate the candidate's general professional background and knowledge in the field of physical education.

Performance of physical education skills Although a high level of skill doesn't mean that a person will be a successful teacher, the ability to perform sport skills is a valuable characteristic for a physical education teacher to have. If it isn't possible to observe the sport skills of an applicant, this information can be gleaned from the application, which will usually indicate the extent of sport participation on a recreational or varsity sport level.

Reference letters   Reference letters are usually involved in the selection of new teachers. They may be assets or liabilities. When they accurately portray the weaknesses as well as strengths of the candidates, they are invaluable. When weaknesses and undesirable characteristics are not mentioned where they exist, a letter of recommendation has little validity. Some administrators, in order to get rid of a weak or undesirable staff member, have overstated these staff members' qualifications in letters of recommendation.

In this situation, the reputation of the writer is of major importance. The integrity of many individuals is so well-established that complete reliance may be placed on their recommendations. The same confidence cannot be felt in a recommendation if the writer's integrity is unknown. In this latter case, one's confidence in a written recommendation is improved when the author holds a responsible position in an institution that has a professional program of recognized standing.

The Family Educational Rights and Privacy Act of 1974 provides that students over the age of 18 may not be denied the opportunity to review and inspect their education records. This includes their references, unless they waive this right. This has made it even more important to know the person who has written the recommendation. Follow-up telephone calls and personal discussions are highly recommended.

The crucial importance of the character of candidates has been pointed out. The best way to assess this quality is from information supplied by individuals who have been closely acquainted with the candidate. This information can be obtained via a letter of recommendation or a discussion (in person or by telephone). Of all the qualifications that must be evaluated fully and accurately, none compares to character.

The search committee evaluates all the information that has been submitted by each candidate. The first step is to determine how the technical skills of the applicants mesh with the job requirements. Only applicants who are qualified to assume the duties listed in the job description can be considered. The top applicants in this category are then evaluated on their personal characteristics and how well they will fit into the department. It is important that new staff members contribute positively to staff relationships and that their philosophy be consistent with the philosophy of the organization. It is not desirable that all staff members should be from the same mold and, in fact, every effort should be made to have diversity among staff members. Divergence of opinion and different types of personalities add strength to a staff and are critical factors in establishing relationships with the heterogeneous student population.

The applicants who meet the criteria for the open position and are ranked highest by the search committee are invited for interviews after their references have been checked. It is good to make telephone calls to references that have been provided by the candidates and also to other people who have worked with or known the candidates. Because only a few people are invited for an interview, it is imperative that the search committee carefully consider all records and recommendations that have been submitted by each candidate.

The Interview

The search committee is responsible for structuring the interview of each candidate. In fairness to all candidates, their visits should be organized similarly. It is usually best to have one member of the search committee handle all logistic details during the candidate's visit. All members of the department should be involved in the interview process and an opportunity should be provided for nondepartmental members to participate. As many viewpoints should be obtained as possible.

The Personal Interview   The personal interview is undoubtedly the most important of all procedures used to select new staff members. It is unusual to select a candidate without an interview. Preliminary interviews are sometimes conducted at conferences or conventions, but finalists for a position should come to the community where the job will be for a final interview before being hired.

The interview should be carefully planned. It is designed to evaluate such factors as manner and appearance, poise, personality, verbal expression, professional philosophy, recreational interests, professional attitudes, aspirations, and ability to interact with other people. The candidate should be encouraged to ask questions about any matter of concern and should be interviewed by small and large groups. In addition to the formal interviews, impressions may be obtained at lunch and dinner meetings or during participation in recreational activities.

The same or similar questions should be asked to each candidate, and the questions should be based on the job that is available. The candidate should be informed that notes will be taken and, after the interview is completed, the notes should be reviewed and rewritten. Accurate information forms the basis for selecting one candidate over the other. There are some questions that may not be asked because they are discriminatory. Examples of unacceptable topics on which to ask questions are as follows:

Height or weight

Religion

Race or color

Marital status

Child care plans or number of children

Age

Birthplace

Sexual preference

Family health status

Disabilities

Questions asked during the interview must be targeted on the position for which the person is being interviewed.

Observation While Teaching   It is desirable to observe the candidates teach during their interviews. Arrangements should be made to teach one or two classes. If this isn't possible, a demonstration lesson should be presented to the search committee and interested faculty members. Recommendations relating specifically to the candidates' teaching success should be obtained from their previous places of employment in addition to observing the teaching they do during their interview. An alternate procedure for first year teachers is for the administrator or members of the search committee to visit classes during the applicant's student teaching experience. Recommendations of the public school teacher who has been observing the candidate's student-teaching performance should also be carefully studied.

On the Job

Orientation A critical component of the staffing process is to blend new staff members into the department or organization. A planned orientation program is needed for this purpose. Orientation includes both formal and informal activities. It is preferable to have an orientation booklet that includes information new staff members need to know. The department curriculum guide should be reviewed with new staff and all policies and procedures carefully explained. Although duties are covered in the interview process, it is important to cover these duties again during the orientation. Nonteaching and teaching duties must be thoroughly explained. One part of the formal orientation program should cover logistic matters such as how to obtain keys, where various offices are located, how to request secretarial services, and how staff communicate equipment and maintenance needs.

One of the best orientation procedures is to assign a mentor to each new staff member. The mentor is available to assist the new staff member whenever a question or need arises. Mentoring is a key facet of the informal part of the orientation process, which will continue throughout the first year in the position. Departmental and committee meetings can also be used effectively in the orientation process. All staff members should help to acclimate new staff members to the workplace by including them in departmental activities and offering them support.

Teaching Load Sound administration requires thorough consideration of the amount of work assigned to each staff member. The number of daily classes taught by elementary physical education teachers varies with the length of the class period. At the lower elementary grades, teachers often teach six to eight classes per day. These classes are usually 25–35 minutes in length. In the upper elementary grades, the class periods are normally lengthened and the teachers teach five or six classes per day. Some elementary physical education teachers have an additional assigned duty for one class period if the gymnasium serves as a lunchroom.

Teaching loads in secondary schools are reasonably well-standardized, although the number of class periods taught per day varies according to the length of each period. Most teachers teach five or six periods per day and have one planning period plus a lunch period. Additional time may be allotted for consultations and conferences with students, responsibilities with student organizations, and other assigned duties. Collective bargaining agreements specify teaching load as well as salaries and other working conditions. If there is union representation, it is imperative that the administrator work closely with the union, which may be the local or state education association, and follow the teaching load agreements that are included in the teachers' contract.

Departmental chairpersons in the secondary schools who do not have full-time administrative positions usually do not have a full teaching load, so that they can handle their administrative responsibilities. A similar arrangement is made for athletic directors who are part of the physical education department. In many school systems, the chairperson and athletic director who have teaching responsibilities also receive extra compensation for their administrative duties.

It should be recognized that teaching load involves more than the number of classes taught per day. Conferences with students, grading papers, and various clerical duties such as recording physical fitness test scores and preparation are all involved. All these factors are related to the total number of students taught by each teacher, which should not exceed 180 per day. A teacher can have a heavier teaching load than a colleague even though the latter may teach one more class per day. An administrator must consider the total number of students taught by each teacher, the number of different preparations, the level of course difficulty, and the type of students being taught when computing teaching load.

On the higher education level, 12 hours per week of undergraduate academic teaching is a common standard. At research institutions, six and nine hours of teaching per week is more common. At some colleges and universities, 15–18 hours of physical activity classes per week is typical. No standard work load exists for administrators in institutions of higher education. In addition to their administrative assignments, most teach one or two classes per semester and, at smaller institutions, a few coach. An administrator must spend whatever time it takes on administrative duties to make the department run efficiently. She or he must do that whether it requires 10 or 60 hours a week.

Proper class size depends on such factors as space and equipment available, type of activity, degree of classification of pupils for activity, and grade level. Although there are many modifying factors, certain general conclusions regarding class size may prove valuable. Generally, a class of 25 or 30 is not too large to provide an excellent teaching situation. When teaching high-risk activities or activities that require high levels of skill, classes should be smaller. In adaptive classes, one to five students might be the norm depending on the degree and type of disability. Larger classes are feasible when students are ability-grouped, so grouping of students at different skill levels within the class is not needed. If team-teaching or a differentiated staffing plan is implemented, larger classes are possible as long as there is sufficient equipment and space. The use of teacher-interns, paraprofessionals, student teachers, and teaching assistants as part of a differentiated staffing plan not only makes teaching larger classes practicable, but it also makes it possible to vary large- and small-group instruction according to the activity and the specific skills being taught. Incorporation of clerical and equipment personnel into the differentiated staffing equation provides more time for teachers to spend on actual teaching responsibilities.

In-service   As part of the staffing process, an administrator needs to provide in-service opportunities to encourage new staff development. Provision should be made for attendance at workshops, conferences, and conventions. The chance to share special skills or other expertise with colleagues is also a valuable in-service experience. One of the best in-service techniques is to include new staff in professional organizations.   Formal study should be the foundation of any in-service program. Graduate study for an advanced degree, specialized courses, and certification programs are examples of formal study that accelerate staff development.

Evaluation of Staff

Education administrators are obligated to assess the teaching effectiveness of their staff members. Their supervisory responsibilities require that they know the strengths and weaknesses of every one of their teachers. The same responsibility rests with administrators of non-school programs. Such knowledge is essential in order to schedule personnel most advantageously and to give them help and guidance where needed. In addition, such data are needed for decisions on continuing employment, tenure, promotions, and salary increases.

The evaluation of teaching effectiveness is a difficult task. A great deal of research in regard to teaching effectiveness has been done, but the results are inconclusive. Much effort has gone into the determination of qualities, traits, or behavioral characteristics that distinguish the effective from the ineffective teacher. These many investigations have failed to come up with any criterion or constellation of criteria that can be used to evaluate all teachers objectively. It is possible to measure teacher–student interaction, and several scales have been designed for this purpose. It is also possible to observe different styles of teaching that are used. A decision must be made as to whether an instructor will be evaluated on teacher actions or on student outcomes. Most administrators use a combination of these two approaches and, despite the problems involved, determine teacher effectiveness. This must be a cooperative effort between the teacher and the administrator. Teachers must know how their performance will be evaluated and the criteria that will be used. The goal is to improve teaching effectiveness through the evaluation process.

Many administrators evaluate staff effectiveness by determining the extent to which the departmental objectives are being achieved. If evidence is available that student performance on standard tests for the various physical education objectives has attained a satisfactory level, the administrator is justified in believing that the staff as a whole has met the most important criteria. Of course, this does not mean that there isn't room for even higher attainments. It is quite likely that even better performance might be obtained. Likewise, some staff members are probably more effective in accomplishing objectives than others. Consequently, the administrator must constantly evaluate the performance of every staff member.

The increased emphasis on accountability has made it even more important for the administrator to assess accurately the performance of staff members. Performance criteria must be clearly designated to permit the administrator to precisely evaluate staff members on the basis of their ability as teachers. Competency-based criteria should form the basis of staff evaluation. The criteria should be established for each school so that staff members are aware of the performance standards that will be used to evaluate their teaching ability. Most states, many institutions of higher education, and many teacher education organizations establish performance criteria that can serve as a basis for a physical education department's competency requirements.

The best procedure for an administrator to use when evaluating staff members is to actually observe them in action. Several classes should be viewed to get a true picture. Videotape can also be an effective technique. It has the added advantage of allowing the administrator and the teacher who taught the class to view the session jointly. This procedure tends to contribute more to teacher development and improvement and is not as likely to cause teacher resentment.

The administrator receives information about staff members from a variety of other sources. From parents, students, other faculty members, and citizens in the community may come unsolicited reports that reflect on the performance of the teacher. Students may share information about their instructors; often, some of this comes back to the administrator. Legitimate student feedback is valuable. Student evaluations, anonymously submitted on a regular basis for all faculty, are helpful to the administrator and can assist the teacher in pinpointing weaknesses. In nonschool situations, it is important to obtain evaluations from program participants.

In normal associations in and about the department, the administrator gains many impressions of colleagues. Such factors as personal appearance, punctuality, thoroughness, attention to detail, cooperativeness, and professional attitude are revealed to the observer.

It is important that the staff member receive a copy of the evaluation, whether it is an informal unstructured report of a class visit or a more extensive evaluation. Staff appraisal should be keyed to staff improvement.

Self-evaluation is too often overlooked as an evaluation technique in physical education. It is highly cherished by coaches who view films of their teams' performances over and over in order to gain insight for future improvements. Self-evaluation of teaching performance in the physical education class setting also leads to improvement. The teacher having responsibility for carrying out a specific assignment must be significantly involved in the evaluation process if improved performance is to be achieved.

Criteria of an Effective Staff

Some of the criteria of an effective staff are as follows:

An adequate number of staff members are available to cover all assignments without being overloaded or without classes being too large.

Staff members meet the recognized standards of professional preparation.

Specialists are available for all positions requiring specialized preparation.

Each staff member has a mastery of the subject matter for which she or he is responsible.

Each staff member satisfactorily meets the needs of students through physical education.

Staff morale is high. Staff members are loyal to each other and the department.

The staff is enthusiastic and dedicated to the success of students.

The staff members are respected by other faculty members; they command admiration and respect in the community.

The staff members are progressive: they keep abreast of the literature and research, they belong to the appropriate professional organizations, and they regularly attend professional meetings.

Each staff member is conversant in the various methods of presenting the subject to students and is consistently successful in the methods used.

Staff members use appropriate evaluative procedures.

Student interest and participation are enthusiastic. Absences, excuses, and disciplinary problems are minimal.

Class Activities

Simulation 1

Situation   Your high school has an opening for a physical education teacher and is ready to begin the interview process. This person will be expected to teach several different activities, coach the tennis team, and be advisor for one student club.

Divide the class into three groups.

Group 1: Establish the procedure that will be followed during the interview.

Group 2: Write questions that will be asked during the interview in the order in which they will be asked.

Group 3: Develop a rating scale for evaluating the applicants during the interview.

Complete the simulation by having five or six students serve as interview teams and interview individuals in the class, who represent candidates applying for the position. Follow the procedure that was established by Group One and use the questions and rating scale of Groups Two and Three.

Simulation 2

Situation   A health club is being opened in your community and the owner is interviewing people for the position as personnel director.

Have one member of the class be the owner, who will interview several applicants. The remainder of the class will critique the answers given by the applicants. The owner will ask two questions:

What personal qualities do you expect the people you hire to have?

How will you recruit the best possible candidates for the positions?

Performance Tasks

1. Research various journals and books to find desired characteristics of physical education teachers. Rank the top ten characteristics. (The same procedure can be followed with coaches, health education teachers, and personnel in the leisure professions.)
2. Write an article for your state association journal or newsletter describing the qualities you would look for if hiring a physical education teacher.
3. Survey students in other disciplines to find out what qualifications they feel physical education teachers should have.
4. Interview two administrators and two teachers or leisure program employees. Find out what professional and civic activities these people feel experienced applicants for a position should have on their résumés.
5. Establish a procedure that could be followed to obtain highly qualified physical educators to teach in the school where you are the administrator.
6. Meet with parents of children twelve and under and ask them what qualities they want teachers and coaches of their children to have.
7. Design evaluation instruments that would be good to measure the teaching effectiveness of health and physical education teachers, coaches, and personnel in leisure and health promotion programs.

References

Acosta, Vivian, and Linda Jean Carpenter, "As the Years Go By—Coaching Opportunities in the 1990s." *Journal of Physical Education, Recreation and Dance,* 1992, 63:36–41.

Ballinger, Debra, "Becoming An Effective Physical Educator." *Physical Educator,* Late Winter 1993, 50:13–19.

Fox, Connie, "Title IX and Athletic Administration." *Journal of Physical Education, Recreation and Dance,* March 1992, 63:48–52.

Graber, Kim C., "Studentship in Preservice Teacher Education: A Qualitative Study of Undergraduate Students in Physical Education." *Research Quarterly for Sport and Exercise,* March 1991, 62:41–51.

Graham, George, Christine Hopple, and Mark Manross, "Novice and Experienced Children's Physical Education Teachers: Insights into Their Situational Decision Making." *Journal of Teaching in Physical Education,* January 1993, 12:197–214.

Huang, Han S., "Future Trends in Physical Education Professional Preparation Curricula." *Journal of the International Council for Health, Physical Education and Recreation,* Fall 1993, 30:43–46.

Locke, Lawrence F., "Implications for Professional Preparation and Practice." *Quest,* February 1994, 46:120–122.

Sawyer, Thomas H., "The Physically Illiterate Physical Educator: What Can Be Done?" *Journal of Physical Education, Recreation and Dance,* January 1992, 63:7–8.

Schirick, Ed, "Risk Management—Preventing Lawsuits Concerning Employment Practices." *Camping,* November/December 1993, 66:5–6.

Siedentop, Daryl, *Developing Teaching Skills in Physical Education.* Mountain View, CA: Mayfield Publishers, 1991.

Staffo, Donald, "Clarifying Physical Education, Coach Responsibilities: A Self-Analysis Guide for Those in Dual Roles." *Physical Educator,* Late Winter 1992, 49:52–56.

Stroot, Sandra, "In the Beginning: The Induction of Physical Educators." *Journal of Teaching in Physical Education,* July 1993, 12:375–385.

Watkins, Jim, "Athletic Administration: Pre-Season Meeting with All Coaches Provides Information, Creates Enthusiasm." *Interschool Athletic Administration,* Spring 1994, 20:18–19.

Williamson, Kay M., "A Qualitative Study on the Socialization of Beginning Physical Education Teacher Educators." *Research Quarterly for Exercise and Sport,* June 1993, 64:188–201.

5

Office Management in the Computer Age

Dramatic changes have taken place in office management with the advent of computers. New technology is emerging at a pace that would have been impossible to envision even a few years ago. It is imperative that administrators in physical education, health education, sport, and the leisure fields make use of this technology with the same vigor found in business and industry. Improved technology makes it possible to complete office responsibilities faster and more accurately. Even more importantly, the administrator is able to increase efficiency and improve productivity, which in education translate into improved instructional programs. In the leisure field, more time can be spent on providing high-quality programs and reaching out to people for whom the programs are designed.

Office Automation

Office automation is the merging of computer and communication technology with traditional office practices. Included in the goals of office automation are the reduction of paperwork, better analysis of data, simplification of tasks, support for administrative duties, improved communication, and reduced time needed for managerial responsibilities. Although the sophistication of the technology used varies considerably with the department, school, or organization, automation must keep pace with changes and technological systems must be upgraded as finances and training for personnel become available.

Mainframe computers are the largest, fastest, and most expensive computers. They are found primarily in large companies, corporations, and organizations, including educational institutions. Some physical education departments, primarily those located in large universities, have access to mainframe computers. Minicomputers are smaller versions of a mainframe and are cheaper and slower. They are more likely to be found in research laboratories, small businesses, and universities. Mainframes and minicomputers permit users to share access to the computer through stations called terminals. Microcomputers or personal computers are most commonly used in the physical education, health promotion, and sport fields. The user has complete control over how this equipment will be used.

Software is the program used in a computer; it provides instructions that the computer follows. Administrators should select software carefully to make sure it can carry out the office functions that are needed. Some software has been written specifically for physical education and athletic functions. An administrator must be aware of the software that is available and select the software that is best for the tasks to be performed.

Office automation includes a number of functions that improve departmental and organizational efficiency.

Word Processing

This is the most common use of microcomputers in an office. Word-processing capabilities have made the typewriter obsolete for all but a few tasks. It is the cornerstone of office automation because it can do much more than put printed material on paper. It enables you to create, edit, print, and save any kind of office document. Material of perfect quality is produced with a good printer and users can easily revise and reorganize any document. Much time is saved by seeing what has been written on the screen and then making changes before printing. Correspondence, reports, publicity information, and the many other communications that originate in a physical education, health club, or similar office are effectively prepared and printed by word processing. Information can be easily recalled and merging features make it possible to rapidly print individual letters. The ability to store reports and other information for future use is another valuable feature for an administrator.

Database

A database is a collection of data organized in such a way that it can be retrieved in an orderly manner according to categories or classes. Administrators need many different types of information. For example, physical education directors need information about students. Student records can be stored and retrieved by name, grade in school, age, height, test scores, address, or other categories. Databases are developed around the kind of information the administrator needs; this information can then be retrieved according to the different categories or combinations of categories that are on the database. Another computer database would be for class schedules. A file on facilities that are available for teaching stations could be developed and used in conjunction with a student course preference file to speed up the process of determining how many sections of each activity are needed and how many would fit into the available facilities.

Spreadsheets

Spreadsheets are rows and columns in which data are entered for analysis. These worksheets are extensively used for budgeting, equipment recordkeeping, and even for calculating grades. Spreadsheets allow the storing of numbers and the manipulation of these numbers. Spreadsheet programs recompute automatically the entire spreadsheet when an entry is changed. They also make it possible to see what the results would be if various changes are made. For example, an administrator can find out what the effect on the equipment budget would be if the higher of two bids is accepted.

Graphics

Graphics are not used as extensively as word processing, spreadsheets, and databases but graphics are useful when preparing reports and presenting information to staff and the public. Graphic software can be used to depict ideas and to present information through graphs, cartoons, drawings, and other images.

Communication

This is a rapidly growing use of microcomputers. Networking with other people via the computer opens up all kinds of opportunities for administrators and staff members in the physical education, health education, athletics, and leisure fields. There can be local networking, which allows rapid communication within an office or building. A broader type of networking is to connect computers via telephone lines to information services and electronic bulletin boards. A modem is needed to convert the material from the computer into a form that can be transmitted over telephone lines and retrieved by another computer. This system makes it possible to send and receive information on national and even international networks. Databases can be accessed for information about administrative issues, problems, or responsibilities.

Electronic mail (e-mail) offers an easy way to send and receive messages within a building, to different locations within a community, and to different offices on a campus. Messages can also be sent throughout the state or country or around the world. It is possible to save electronic mail in electronic notebooks and it is easy to forward and reply to mail that is received. Incoming and outgoing mail can also be printed if the information can best be used in this format.

Computer conferencing is another way in which computers are used for communication. Several people can communicate at the same time about an issue of mutual concern or interest. The conference can take place at one time or over a period of time if there is a need to have time to react to proposals that are presented while conferencing.

Facsimile (fax) machine use has exploded and administrators in physical education and leisure service organizations should have ready access to fax machines. There are many situations in which an administrator needs to transmit information immediately. This type of communication costs less than a telephone call and is more accurate because exact duplicates of documents can be sent. Facsimile transmission is equally effective with handwritten memos, typed letters, drawings, or complex documents.

It is obvious that computers can be used in every phase of an administrator's responsibility. Public relations, budget making, class scheduling, staffing, or any other duty can be more speedily accomplished with computers. More importantly, the computer makes it possible to carry out duties more effectively. Not every administrator can have a fully automated office, but the goal should be to incorporate computers as extensively as resources permit. A plan for automation should be in place. Automation plans should be updated on a regular basis and these plans should include strategy for upgrading equipment because technological advances occur constantly. New technology will continue to shape office procedures in the future.

Office Management

Every administrator needs to understand the essentials of efficient office management, whether the office is fully automated or has only one computer used for word processing. This need is obvious in large departments where secretaries, clerks, and receptionists provide a variety of services for the public and department personnel. However, the same functions must be performed in a one-person department, where no secretary and little office equipment is available. Regardless of the size of the department, correspondence must be carried on, reports rendered, materials duplicated, equipment ordered, records filed, and records maintained. Whether the department is large or small, the internal requirements are the same. The only difference is that in the small department the administrator must do more things; in the large department the various duties are delegated to others to perform.

An effective office operation is important to the success of the department. The work of the administrator and the staff members is assisted materially by office personnel. Faculty members are relieved of a variety of duties that can be better performed by office employees. Services to students and the general public are improved. Communications are enhanced. As a consequence, better public relations are engendered. Interestingly, advanced office technology has the effect of placing more office responsibilities on staff members. It has made it imperative that staff members become competent in the use of office technology as more office tasks are expected of each employee with less support staff. Development of staff skills in the use of technology is an important administrative consideration.

There are proper and improper ways of performing all the tasks in an office. Doing them correctly saves both time and money. The efficient operation of a department requires sound office procedures. Such procedures have been tested and proved in business and industry and can be readily adapted to school and leisure situations. An administrator must make use of proven procedures.

Office Unit Orientation

Administrative offices should be centrally located so as to be accessible to all who have business with the director or staff members. In elementary and secondary schools, the office is almost invariably located near the entrance to the gymnasium, inside the gymnasium, or even in the locker room. Staff offices should be located adjacent to the administrative office. A small office is appropriate in the locker room for supervision and interaction with students between classes but teachers should have their office for planning and preparation away from the locker room and near the administrator's office.

Office Facilities

The office facilities needed depend on the size of the organization and the functions it serves. Although needs vary, a desirable physical education office arrangement should include the following facilities:

A waiting and reception room for visitors, students, participants, and others who have personal or business matters to discuss with the administrator. It should be large enough to accommodate the largest number of visitors who are likely to occupy it at any time. This space should be separated from the other office facilities.

A service area where students, participants, and the general public may be assisted. This could be located at one side of the main office. With a window and counter space, this area can serve as an information center and a place where students can adjust their registration for classes or activities. Ordinarily, such matters can be handled by a member of the office staff.

A work station, where the members of the clerical staff perform their services. With the advent of the computer, the design of this area has changed dramatically. Desks, chairs, and computer tables are designed and arranged for the comfort of the people who work in this area. Lighting is of the background type rather than direct lighting, which was fine when typewriters were used. Filing cabinets and other office equipment such as paper cutters, work tables, and electric staplers are found in this work station. This area is a repository for department records and often staff mailboxes are located here. An important function of the office staff is to duplicate materials. This can be done in this area, but it is advantageous to have a separate area for the photocopy machine. A small room where office supplies can be secured should be located in or adjacent to this room. The administrator should strive to obtain optimum working conditions in the office. It is impossible for the personnel to achieve maximum output where noise, confusion, and distraction prevail. Unnecessary traffic and distraction must be eliminated.

A private office for the administrator. It is advantageous for the administrator to have an office in which he or she can hold private conferences and concentrate and develop the plans vital to the organization. Another advantage of the private office is that visitors and conversations in the office do not distract office workers.

A conference room adjacent to the main office is a desirable facility. It should be used for staff and committee meetings and for meetings with guests.

Office Functions and Practices

The size of the office usually varies with the size of the institution or business and the extensiveness of the program. In some small schools, the physical education administrator is fortunate to have an office. In other small schools, the office is often shared with several other staff members. The office staff, if any, usually consists of a part-time secretary or volunteer student secretary or clerk. At the other extreme are physical education administrators in large colleges and universities, who have several secretaries and a receptionist, all housed in commodious offices with the latest equipment.

Regardless of the size of the office staff and facilities, there are many functions common to practically all offices. These are answering and placing telephone calls, receiving visitors, answering correspondence, filing, duplicating materials, keeping appointments and meeting obligations, and providing services to staff members. Each of these functions will be discussed briefly.

Answering and Placing Telephone Calls

In larger offices, telephone calls are placed and answered by a secretary or receptionist. The administrator without office assistance must perform this function. It is important in this situation to have an answering machine to take calls when in conference or out of the office. Increasingly, offices are being equipped with voice mail, which measurably improves office efficiency. This telephone communication system makes it possible to leave and retrieve messages. The telephone is answered automatically with a personal greeting and messages are accepted and stored in the voice mailbox. Messages can be played back at any time and messages can be sent and received from any phone. It is also possible to be notified of new messages through pagers or telephones. Calls must be returned as soon as possible. Standard telephone technique and courtesy should be observed in all cases. Favorable or unfavorable impressions of the department are readily created by the manner in which telephone calls are received. The proper procedures do not accidently occur—they must be taught and insisted on by the administrator.

The individual answering the telephone must be as friendly and as cordial as if the caller were a visitor in the office. Good public relations are created by courtesy and helpfulness. Sincerity of purpose and desire to serve people is the key to good telephone relationships. Because emotions are readily reflected in one's voice, care must be exercised not to show anger or brusqueness. When it is necessary to give a negative answer, the caller must be treated courteously.

The telephone should be answered promptly. The department or organization should be identified immediately. The name of the person answering the call is often given (as in "department of physical education, Ms. Kai speaking." A simple "Hello" or "Yes" is not a sufficient greeting when answering telephone calls in a business office.

A pencil and telephone pad should be available to take messages or record telephone calls that are to be returned. Proper procedure should be followed and courtesy extended to the caller whether the phone is answered by a secretary, the administrator, or another staff member. If the administrator is not available, the secretary may be able to provide the desired information. The secretary should understand the procedure to follow regarding interruptions when the administrator is occupied. When the administrator leaves the office, the secretary should know where he or she can be located and when he or she expects to return. When the administrator is out of the office, a form similar to the one in Figure 5-1 should be used to indicate that a call has been received. If the person called is not in, the secretary should always offer to take a message. It is helpful to get the name of the caller. If the caller's name has not been given, such questions as "May I have her call you?" or "Mr. Pollack is not in. May I take a message?" are in order.

```
┌─────────────────────────────────────────────┐
│                                               │
│   Date _____ 19 _____ Name _____    │
│                                               │
│   While you were out, there was a telephone call. │
│                                               │
│   Time _____ o'clock      │
│                                               │
│   From _____          │
│                                               │
│   Of_____            │
│                                               │
│   Message_____            │
│                                               │
│   Telephone number is: _____        │
│                                               │
│   Signed _____             │
│                                               │
└─────────────────────────────────────────────┘
```

FIGURE 5-1. Form for Recording Phone Calls

The office telephone is primarily for business use. Unless it is against policy, it is permissible to make a brief, local personal call, but this privilege should not be abused. Lengthy personal calls should not be permitted. Business calls always have priority over personal calls.

Receiving Visitors

Every member of the clerical staff should be well-versed in the common courtesies of greeting visitors. Needless to say, all visitors should be made welcome. They should be greeted cordially and every effort should be made to meet their needs. If the visitor has no appointment, the purpose of the visit should be determined. In some instances, the office staff member may be able to supply the desired information. If it is necessary to wait to see the administrator, the visitor should be comfortably seated and offered something to read. If the administrator is not available, either an appointment should be arranged or an effort made to have someone else provide the assistance the visitor desires. Visitors with appointments should be met at the scheduled time. A courteous procedure should be worked out whereby the secretary interrupts unnecessarily long interviews, especially when other visitors are waiting. When there are no other visitors, the administrator might wrap up the visit by summarizing what has been discussed and asking whether there are other matters to be considered.

Answering Correspondence

One of the quickest ways for an administrator to gain a poor reputation is to be careless about answering correspondence. Some administrators have a policy of answering every letter within 24 hours after it has been received. Although this may not be possible in all cases, it is a sound practice to answer correspondence promptly. The answer should be prompt and complete. All questions and letters should be answered carefully and in proper written form with good grammar.

Many letters the administrator receives can be answered better by some other member of the department. A form is usually used, requesting the appropriate action by the staff member. Many routine letters can be answered directly by the secretary. This will save the valuable time of the administrator. In larger institutions, many letters of the same type are often received. These may be answered by a standard form reply.

It is standard procedure to spellcheck on the computer and to proofread all outgoing letters to detect mistakes. The address should be checked for accuracy. The letter should be saved on the computer or a copy made and filed with related correspondence.

In many small schools, administrators have no secretarial help whatsoever and must handle their own correspondence. If the administrator is unable to use the computer, the only recourse is to write letters longhand. The opposite extreme is the availability of a full-time or part-time secretary to take shorthand. Between these extremes are schools in which dictating machines are used. These machines have several advantages. Administrators can take them home and dictate letters at night or over the weekend. Administrators who have part-time secretaries can dictate at any time and have the completed tapes available for the time the secretary has available for this work. If the administrator is constantly interrupted during dictation to a secretary or has difficulty composing a letter, much secretarial time can be saved by using a dictating machine.

Filing

An effective filing system is essential to any office. This includes filing materials in filing cabinets and saving information by setting up topical files on the computer and storing the information on computer disks. Less manual filing is necessary as greater use is made of computers and their storage capabilities. All correspondence, records, budgets, and reports must be filed in such a way that they can be located quickly. It is not difficult to locate recently filed material, but on occasions several years may elapse before it is needed. Reference to filed material is constantly necessary; when it cannot be located, delay, inefficiency, and sometimes embarrassment result. The filing system should be standardized and coded so the information is easily accessed by different personnel.

There are many filing systems, but in schools the alphabetical system is used almost invariably. The material to be filed is classified according to name, subject, or a combination of name and subject. Large offices usually use both a name and a subject file, but the majority use the combination system.

The name file refers to names of people or organizations with whom correspondence or business is carried out. In this system, a folder is made for each name or corespondent if there is sufficient material to justify starting a folder. From three to ten papers justify starting a folder. A lesser amount is filed in a miscellaneous folder. A miscellaneous folder is made for each letter of the alphabet and is located behind the last name folder under each alphabetical letter.

Subject filing refers to filing the material according to subject matter. The subject headings must be specific, significant, and technically correct. Nouns are generally used to refer to the subject. Subheadings are used in subject filing. A miscellaneous folder is also used in subject filing. The papers within each subject folder are arranged by date, with the latest date on top.

A subject file is necessary in any physical education office because of the nature of its operation. Items such as budgets, schedules, contracts, equipment orders, records, and reports must be filed according to subject. Because there are many more items to be filed under subjects than under names, most physical education offices should have subject files that are subdivided by name.

In setting up a filing system for a medium-size secondary school, the first step should be to segregate the total program into specific subjects, such as physical education, intramural sports, health education, and interscholastic sports. Each drawer of a four-drawer filing cabinet would refer to a specific area, with the subareas listed in alphabetical order.

The physical education drawer could be subdivided into the following areas:

Annual reports.   A folder for each annual report should be included.

Budget.   A folder for the annual budget for each of the past five years should be maintained.

Committees.   A folder for each committee should be filed.

Correspondence.   Folders should be arranged alphabetically under this heading. All originals and copies of communications should be filed in the appropriate folder.

Departmental policies.   The departmental policy file should be included in a folder. If desirable, a number of folders might be used, with each including the policies in different areas.

Equipment.   A folder should be included listing the equipment. New equipment on order should also be noted.

Financial matters.   Duplicate copies of all requisitions and duplicate vouchers submitted for payment can be filed under this heading.

Service program.   A folder for each activity taught should be available. This might include lesson plans, rules, syllabi, examinations, and teaching aids, such as clippings from newspapers and magazines. In addition, a folder for the program and schedule for each year for the past three years should be included.

Student help.   Records for all part-time student help should be kept in this folder.

Student records.   A folder for each student should be available. This should include medical examination records and correspondence with physician, parents, and others. Excuses and the anecdotal record of student achievement and conduct can also be filed in this folder. These might be filed in a separate drawer. Content and availability to the student must conform to school policy.

Test data.   Complete data on physical fitness and other tests should be filed in folders according to the school year in which they apply.

The intramural sports drawer could be subdivided as follows:

Eligibility rules.   The eligibility rules for participating in various activities should be included.

Intramural activities.   A folder for each sport in the program should be available. These folders should include rules governing that activity. In addition, they might include past records and schedules.

Officials.   With the names, addresses, telephone numbers, and qualifications of all officials in the program should be available.

Participation records.   A complete record of the results of all competition should be maintained.

Programs.   A folder should be available that contains the details of each year's program for a period of five years. The details should cover such items as the participants and teams in each sport and the results of all the competition.

Publicity.   A folder should be retained that has all the posters, announcements, news stories, and other publicity materials.

Schedules.   This folder should contain schedules for all intramural activities for the current year.

Past records and season reports. This information should be in another folder.

The health education drawer might be arranged as follows:

Administrative policies.   A folder under this heading should be included for each of the following areas: communicable disease control, emergency care and injuries, excuses, health of school personnel, and scheduling.

Health services.   A folder under this subject heading should be included for each of the following areas: health examination and follow-up, screening, counseling, communicable disease control, and cleanliness of the school.

Health instruction.   A separate folder under this subject heading should be available for each of the following areas: personal health, weight control, vision and hearing, dental health, communicable and noncommunicable disease, first aid and safety, family life education, nutrition, exercise, rest and recreation, health services and products, community health, drug education, mental health and personal adjustment, addictions, and any other topics that are included in the instructional program.

Healthful school living.   A separate folder under this subject heading should be included for each of the following areas: school lunch, seating, heating, lighting, ventilation, swimming pool sanitation, and locker and shower room sanitation.

The interscholastic sports drawer might be subdivided as follows:

Budget.   A folder should be filed for the interscholastic athletic budget for each year for the past five years.

Contracts.   A folder is desirable for each sport that involves contracts.

Eligibility lists.   For each sport, a folder should be available that contains eligibility lists.

Equipment lists.   A folder for each sport should be available that contains data concerning equipment. These data should include an equipment inventory plus a listing of new equipment that has been ordered.

Game reports.   A folder for each sport should be included that contains game reports for all games. The game reports should include such data as attendance, weather, opponent, score, and gate receipts for home contests.

Officials.   All data relating to officials should be filed under this heading in folders arranged according to sports.

Schedules.   Schedules for all sports in the current year should be included in a folder. Folders for previous years should also be maintained. In some schools, a folder for future schedules is needed.

Sports.   A folder for each interscholastic sport should be maintained. Included in such a folder should be squad personnel, current records, practice plans, scouting reports, coaching aids, and the like.

Transportation.   A folder should be developed for each sport. Every folder should contain all arrangements for travel by the respective team.

Duplicating Materials

A constant need exists in an office to have materials duplicated. In addition to the requirements in instructional classes for examinations, reading lists, syllabi, instructional materials, and outlines, intramural directors require numerous copies of rules and schedules, and staff members need many copies of materials. Administrators also need to have various materials duplicated, such as departmental regulations, announcements, minutes of committee meetings, and instructions to staff members and students.

In many institutions, materials are photocopied in the central office. However, when the volume justifies it, it is advantageous for departments to own photocopying or printing equipment. It is advisable to restrict the use of this equipment to authorized personnel only. On staffs where little if any office help is available, staff members are responsible for reproducing their own materials.

Keeping Appointments and Meeting Obligations

On many occasions physical education administrators must make appointments to speak to people or to perform some task by a certain stipulated time. To meet these obligations, the administrator must have an infallible reminder system. The administrator simply cannot afford to miss or to be late for an appointment or forget details.

The administrator needs a pocket appointment book. This should include all the notations that are on the desk calendar. Administrators often make appointments when away from the office and also need to know of office appointments when elsewhere.

A secretary, when available, should also maintain a desk calendar and see that the calendar and those of the administrator are accurate, identical, and up to date. To remind one's employer of a task to be done, the secretary should place the file on the administrator's desk. If it is obvious that the administrator has overlooked a call or appointment, the secretary should remind him or her of it. It is a sound practice to spend the first few minutes each morning with the secretary, discussing the daily schedule. Some secretaries place a typed schedule of the administrator's appointments on the desk every morning. When leaving the office at the end of the day, the administrator should check the calendar to see whether there are any early appointments for the following day.

The establishment of regular office hours facilitates the making and keeping of appointments. When staff members, students, tradespeople, and others know what the regular office hours are, they can usually arrange to see the administrator at a mutually convenient time. The administrator must keep the secretary informed concerning any changes in office hours, especially when he or she will be absent or late.

Faculty members should also have regular office hours when they are available for conferences or meetings with students, colleagues, and anyone else who wishes to see them.

These office hours should be posted and adhered to. The office personnel should be aware of these office hours in order to be helpful to those who wish to contact staff members.

When the need to perform a task arises, many administrators try to take care of it immediately. If the administrator is free for an immediate appointment or can make a telephone call, write a letter, or prepare a report at once, rather than defer it, there is no possibility of forgetting it. If the matter cannot be immediately disposed of, it should be noted on a calendar or notepad. Calendars are essential in any office to ensure that appointments are kept and obligations met. The administrator needs a desk calendar with 15- or 30-minute time designations. All appointments and obligations should be noted on the calendar.

It is a mistake for the administrator to rely on memory for the conduct of daily affairs. It has been said that the shortest pencil is better than the longest memory. Everything that cannot be taken care of immediately should be written down.

A very helpful office device that may be combined with a desk calendar is the office tickler. The tickler carries reminders for certain routine activities. Every department has many duties that recur each year. These can be indicated on the office tickler in advance. The tickler file usually consists of a box of 3" × 5" memorandum cards. A tabbed guide for each month and 31 tabbed guides for each day of each month are needed. Each activity that is to be performed at a future date is noted on the appropriate card. The cards are filed according to dates. The tickler file should be checked every morning. Certain items that occur frequently throughout the year can be handled by a single card. Thus, if the payroll must be completed on the last day of each month, the same card may be used each month, rather than making twelve separate entries.

In larger offices, secretaries make the necessary arrangements for committee meetings. Working out a convenient time and place for a number of people to meet is often a time-consuming process.

Providing Services to Staff Members

A major function of the education office is to provide services to staff members. The most important of these is the use of word processing to produce examinations, reading lists, course outlines, reports, speeches, and letters. In many secondary schools, such assistance is not available and staff members either do their own work or get along without it. Neither alternative is desirable. The time of staff members is often too limited to produce these materials, but these materials are essential to staff performance. Fortunately, computers have made it much easier for staff members to produce their own materials and many prefer to do at least some of their own word processing.

Secretaries may also assist staff members by arranging appointments, gathering travel information, maintaining student personnel records, recording test data, contacting students, and arranging for meetings. The more staff members can be relieved of these essential details, the more time will be available for them to perform their teaching, supervisory, and advisory functions.

The next three sections describe office management for different sized high schools. Although they are written about high schools, the principles of office management are equally pertinent to businesses and organizations of different sizes. The smaller the organization, the more detail work must done by the administrator and usually, but not always, less sophisticated equipment is available.

Office Management in a Small High School

The heavy load of the administrator in a small school makes good organization and efficient methods of office management essential. The administrator should have one period set aside every day for the conduct of departmental affairs. If such time is not provided, the administrator must use a free period or time before or after school.

Whatever assistance the administrator has may come from students. Fortunately, it is sometimes possible to obtain senior students interested in office work who will volunteer their services to gain experience or who will do this work as part of an internship. It is not difficult to find students who can use word processors. The administrator may have to use several students to accomplish all the necessary duties. In this way, the duties that require special skill can be reserved for the period when the student with that skill is available.

It is relatively easy to teach student clerks how to use the telephone, receive visitors, file materials, use the photocopy machine, maintain records, and perform the essential housekeeping duties of the office. They can render invaluable service if they are used wisely. They must be given recognition for their services, and care must be exercised not to exploit them.

In the small high school office, equipment is usually limited. The minimum items in any office should consist of the following:

One desk for each teacher

Desk tools (paper cutter, scissors, ruler, paste, pens, pencils, paper, stapler, and clips)

Calendar and memorandum pads

A large work table for student assistants

Extra chairs for guests

A four- or five-drawer filing cabinet with lock

Several card files of different sizes

Bookshelves

Magazine stand

Access to a photocopy machine

A telephone, computer, printer, and work station are important items. If this equipment is not available in the physical education office, access to a telephone and a computer within the school must be obtained.

Office Management in a Medium-Sized High School

In a medium-sized high school, the physical education administrator has the same duties as the administrator in the small school. However, she or he is much more likely to be allocated time for administrative duties. The administrator may be relieved of one or two teaching periods per day for this purpose. More office equipment is usually available and the administrator usually has more people to whom to delegate various duties. It might be possible to use the principal's clerical staff for dictation, word processing, and photocopying.

Student assistants are still needed. For part-time and student secretarial help, specific job descriptions are helpful. If they are given written instructions and policies concerning their responsibilities, they will be much less likely to make mistakes.

At least one, but preferably two or three computers with work stations should be available. A telephone is also needed.

Office Management in a Large Institution

In a large school where clerical personnel are available, the role of the administrator is that of office manager. All the activities carried on in the office are his or her responsibility. The duties of the different individuals are assigned and supervised by the administrator.

A standard procedure in large offices is to develop a job description for each member of the clerical staff. This lets the employee know specifically what is expected and that he or she is held responsible for demonstrating competence in these responsibilities. This does not mean that employees cannot assume other duties in the office as circumstances require. A smoothly operating office includes a staff that is willing to help wherever needed.

In a large office, a definite organizational structure might be necessary for the office personnel. Responsibility must be vested in some individual—usually the most experienced or the highest-ranking member. The administrator does not have the time to attend to the details of managing the office. The assignment of duties, distribution of work, and supervision of the work of all office personnel should be delegated to this head person.

The administrator is responsible for the development and maintenance of high morale and esprit de corps among the office personnel. This is accomplished by creating pleasant working conditions, by establishing reasonable standards of accomplishment, and by providing suitable working tools and friendly, helpful supervision.

In large schools, communication within the office and among the staff can be complex. The accepted practice is to use written interstaff memoranda. Special forms are available for this purpose. These memoranda save time and have the advantage of fixing responsibility. In addition, they reduce the risk of misunderstanding and error.

Figure 5-2 is an example of a form that facilitates communication within a larger organization. It also saves the administrator's time.

The major items of office equipment for a large organization include the following:

Several computers, printers, and work stations

One typewriter for completing forms

Photocopy machine

Filing cabinets

Dictation machine and transcriber

Calculator with printer

Staplers (including electric stapler)

Bookshelves

Paper cutter and pencil sharpener

Three-hole punch

Collator

```
┌─────────────────────────────────────────────────────────────┐
│                                                               │
│           Division of Health and Physical Education           │
│                                                               │
│    FROM:     Jane Abbott, Chairperson   DATE: _____   │
│                                                               │
│    TO: _____  Brown          For your files    _____  │
│        _____  Flemming       For your information _____   │
│                              Please route to  _____   │
│        _____  Ford           Please see me     _____  │
│        _____  Jones          Please call me    _____  │
│        _____  Henry          Please handle     _____  │
│        _____  Hirsch         Please draft reply for: _____  │
│                                 My signature  _____    │
│        _____  Morgan            Your signature  _____    │
│        _____  Pastor                                          │
│        _____  Rogers                                          │
│        _____  Smith                                           │
│        _____  White                                           │
│        _____  Wilson                                          │
│                                                               │
└─────────────────────────────────────────────────────────────┘
```

FIGURE 5-2. Form for Interoffice Communication

Centralized Stenographic Services

Some organizations centralize their stenographic services in what is often called a stenographic pool. Work is given to the pool and it is done in the order in which it is received. Services commonly include word processing, transcribing, photocopying, filing, and completing forms. For small and medium-sized departments, this can be a cost-effective way of providing high-quality stenographic services.

The Secretary*

An important asset many administrators overlook in planning their work is a capable secretary. By working with an intelligent secretary, delegating all the responsibility that the secretary is capable of assuming, and leaving many time-consuming routine matters in the secretary's hands, the administrator is able to devote much more time to creative work. The wise administrator, then, should know what a good secretary is and how to make the best use of the secretary's abilities. Intelligence, personality, and character are the three general personal qualifications of a good secretary.

Intelligence should be practical and analytical, not merely abstract. The secretary should be able to comprehend any situation and make a reasonable decision about it, using sound logic to back up judgment. Intelligence must include a capacity for detail and an ability to deal with the almost endless routine matters that arise in any administrator's office. If this intelligence is to function to the best advantage for the secretary and the administrator, behind it

---

* The authors are indebted to Eleanor Metheny, Emeritus Professor, University of Southern California, for material in this section.

must be a genuine interest and pride in the activities, well-being, and progress of the department. If the secretary is desultory and detached regarding the duties and performs them mechanically, he or she will not be an asset. An administrator whose secretary is dedicated to the position and takes a deep personal interest in the success of the department is indeed fortunate.

The personality of the secretary is of critical importance. This person constantly encounters students, staff members, other faculty, and visitors, and it is vital that a favorable impression be created. Because the administrator spends a significant amount of his or her working hours in the company of the secretary, their personalities must be compatible. The pleasant, cheerful, and sensible secretary is not only easier to work with than the temperamental one but usually accomplishes much more in the same amount of time.

The caller's first impression of the administrator comes from the front office, where he or she is received by the secretary. The secretary must be cordial, alert, and tactful. By manner and appearance, the secretary should convey the impression of the well-run office where all demands are given courteous attention. Needing patience, good humor, and diplomacy in dealing with those who come to the office, the secretary must also exercise discrimination in determining which of them have legitimate business with the employer and which do not.

Telephone voice and manner should be as pleasant as office personality. The secretary should be able to convey to the person who calls that he or she is talking to a capable and willing person who, in most cases, can supply the information needed without troubling the administrator about it. The belligerent "who wants to talk to him?" attitude is rude and inexcusable.

The secretary who really becomes a part of the organization must be extremely adaptable and willing to do whatever must be done, no matter how far it may seem to fall out of his or her sphere of activity. The position exists as a service to the administrator, and is never limited to the mere mechanics of letter writing.

To be worthy of the name, the secretary must be absolutely reliable in all situations so that the employer may trust this person completely. The secretary's loyalty must be absolutely unquestionable. In the course of a day's work, a secretary sees and hears confidential information and must never gossip under any circumstances about office information, however trivial. The necessity for personal integrity is obvious.

The education of the good secretary should be more than a matter of shorthand, word processing, filing, and office practice, although these are essential. Most important is the correct use of the English language, both written and spoken. Because the secretary composes numerous letters that go out over the signature of the employer, the secretary should use correct style and form in order to make letters convincing. He or she should know the essentials of order and have a systematic way of getting work done in the quickest, best possible way. The person in this job should sense task priorities.

It is desirable but not essential that the secretary have some preparation in the field the employer is administering. If this is not possible, the secretary should acquire at an early date a very real interest in that field and keep reasonably well-informed about it. This not only adds to enjoyment of the work but increases the secretary's value to the employer.

Having hired a secretary, many administrators seem to feel that their responsibility is ended. If the administrator takes that attitude, he or she will soon have not a capable secretary, but just another person working in the office. As soon as the secretary begins working, the administrator should see to it that all possible information concerning the work to be done is available for the secretary. In any organization, there is almost endless red tape in which the secretary becomes entangled in the course of a day; the workings of much of this are eventually learned by trial and error. However, a knowledge of the regulations saves endless time and trouble. Do not expect the new secretary to immediately assume charge of all the routine matters that arise, but gradually delegate all the responsibility the secretary is able to handle. This is the point at which some administrators fail. They cannot bear to see authority to act on matters, however trivial, placed in hands other than their own. Remember that this person is an intelligent adult; having been given responsibility, this person can be trusted with it. The secretary's judgment soon may be almost as good as the administrator's in situations covered by departmental policies.

Much has been written of loyalty of the secretary to the employer, but much more might be written about the loyalty of the employer to the secretary. This person is intelligent and capable of handling the job, and should be backed up by the employer in any reasonable situation, not made the scapegoat for mistakes that occur in the office. Humiliating the secretary in order to inflate one's ego before important callers is an inexcusable but not uncommon practice. Mutual loyalty and respect help to create an office morale that makes the secretary feel an integral part of the organization: He or she is working not *for* but *with* a wise and understanding person, not for a salary but for the good of the profession. This feeling makes the person a real asset to the employer.

Class Activities

Simulation 1

Situation   A new high school is being built in a community of 50,000 people. Each department is asked to explain its needs.

Divide the class into groups representing the physical education department and have them design what they feel would be the best physical education office plan for the new facility.

Simulation 2

Situation   A new computer system is being installed in all offices in a high school.

Have the class determine the functions that a computer must perform for health, physical education, and athletic programs. Write a report and present a verbal summary of the report for the high school principal.

Performance Tasks

1. Describe the typical physical education office. Does the typical office contribute to or detract from effective teaching?
2. Compare a fitness or health club office with the office typically found in a secondary school. Why is there usually a dramatic difference?
3. Interview two office managers in a business in the community and a physical education or athletic administrator. Compare the ways the offices are run.
4. Design an office that would contribute to staff morale and increase teaching effectiveness.
5. Visit a school and describe the physical education office procedure in the school. Cover the strong and weak points.

6. Interview a secretary and ask for suggestions as to how administrators can have well-organized and efficient offices.
7. Interview an elementary school office secretary, a secondary school secretary, a college secretary, and a business secretary. Compare the differences in their responsibilities. Find out what their relationship is to administrators and staff. What changes would they recommend to improve office efficiency?

References

Brownell, Greg, *Computers and Teaching*, 2nd ed. St. Paul, MN: West Publishing, 1992.

Donnelly, Joseph E. (Ed.), *Using Microcomputers in Physical Education and Sport Sciences.* Champaign, IL: Human Kinetics, 1987.

Gray, Bill, "Computerizing Marketing and Sports Information Offices: In-House Publishing." *Athletic Administration,* February 1994, 29:12–13.

Hill, Charles W., and Gareth R. Jones, *Strategic Management*, 3rd ed. Boston: Houghton Mifflin, 1995.

Johnson, Tanya, "Counting on Computers." *Athletic Management,* August/September 1993, 5:46–48.

Key, James, "Reaching Out with Internet." *Journal of Physical Education Recreation and Dance,* February 1994, 65:21–24.

Keys, Jessica, *Infotrends: The Competitive Use of Information Technology.* New York: McGraw-Hill, 1992.

Ladd, Garry G., "Computer Managed Instruction in Physical Fitness and Weight Training." *National Strength and Conditioning Association Journal,* July/August 1993, 15:70–71.

Mohnsen, Bonnie, "Using Computers—Helping Physical Education Administrators." *Journal of Physical Education, Recreation and Dance,* January 1991, 62:40–44.

II

Management Responsibilities

C h a p t e r

6

Public Relations

Principles of Public Relations

The present concept of public relations has emerged from the term *publicity*. Public relations is much broader than publicity. Although publicity is a major tool, public relations is concerned with *all* the impressions people receive rather than those obtained only through the various publicity media. It is a management function that determines people's attitudes and understandings and, based on this information, executes a plan to obtain understanding and support from the targeted people. Public relations is characterized by a multiplicity of approaches. One approach, even an exceptionally good one, will become inadequate over a period of time. A specific approach may be satisfactory for one issue, but a successful organization requires ongoing acceptance by the public. Public relations must be not only multifaceted, but also continuous. There is no such thing as an off season for public relations!

The message provided through a public relations program must be clear and precise and project the desired image and idea. Proper recognition must be given to the importance of public relations in every organization. An administrator needs many skills, but there is no skill more important than the ability to effectively promote the organization and gain acceptance of the service or product of the organization. This is not a responsibility that can be delegated. It is a responsibility that must be shared. Every person in the organization, including the administrator, is involved in public relations whether she or he intends to be or not. The key is for administrators to recognize the importance of this responsibility and to provide the leadership necessary for an effective program. This includes sufficient funding, staff training, and a comprehensive *written* plan. A specific individual who has special public relations skills may be given responsibility to create and administer the public relations program, but the greatest possible success comes when staff members believe in the worth of the organization and impart this attitude to everyone they meet.

The comprehensive nature of public relations starts with the contacts and relationships that personnel in the organization have with other people. Public relations also includes information transmitted by newspapers, radio, television, telephone, reports, newsletters, letters, and any other way that an organization communicates to others. It also involves the impression made when a person comes into the school, health club, or aerobic class. The principles of public relations are the same for educational and noneducational enterprises; only the techniques differ. Noneducational businesses traditionally place more emphasis on public relations than do many educational institutions. There is a lesson in this for the educational administrator. Even if there is insufficient money for grandiose public relation tactics, a successful public relations strategy can be developed and implemented. The key is to have a carefully designed plan and to prepare every faculty and staff member to be a contributing part of this plan.

Human Relations Versus Publicity

It is helpful for the administrator to recognize that there are two broad aspects of public relations: human relations and publicity. The most important aspect is human relations, which involves personal relationships with people. It has been established that the most effective public relations is carried on through person-to-person communication.

Publicity, on the other hand, is the use of various methods to disseminate information and to influence public opinion in the direction of intelligent group action and support. The ultimate purpose of publicity should be to create a favorable image and understanding of the organization and its program.

Purposes of Public Relations

Public relations is the vehicle used to inform and to influence. This applies to all endeavors. The message that is given to inform varies with the organization and its objectives. The goal is to promote goodwill with people who are part of the organization or who are needed for support. Financial support is often considered first when speaking of support, but personal involvement and active participation are equally important for organizations. For example, a community center needs volunteers to support programs, participate as board members, and encourage people to be part of the center's activities. Communication is the foundation on which effective public relations is built.

People must be influenced to act in ways that promote the organization and gain acceptance for its goals, products, and programs. Successful public relations goes beyond acceptance to playing an active part in some aspect of the organization that will enable it to function more effectively. In a physical education department, this may mean becoming a member of a curriculum study committee, voting for a bond issue to build an addition to the gymnasium, or attending a physical education demonstration night at an elementary school to become aware of the physical education programs provided in the school district. In a fitness center, good public relations is translated into increased membership and expanded participation in programs.

Responsibility for Public Relations

The ultimate responsibility for a public relations program rests with the administrator in charge. As has been emphasized, this is an extremely important function of the administrator. However, every person in the organization is responsible for public relations.

The responsibility for public relations involves two aspects: human relations and publicity. In the human relations phase, all those affiliated with the organization—instructors, teachers, administrators, custodians, and office personnel—are agents of public relations. Students and other participants are also public relations agents. They represent a vitally important public and are the recipients of the program. After their involvement in the program they can become powerful agents. Whether they become supporters or detractors of physical education depends on their experiences in it. Inevitably, all these agents, including the administrator, are involved in public relations in their every contact—every word and action—with other people. Because these contacts have significant implications for the organization, the administrator must be concerned with them and do everything possible to ensure that the overall result will be favorable.

The administrator can best discharge responsibility for public relations by understanding the factors that create favorable and unfavorable impressions and experiences. It is therefore important to cultivate, promote, and encourage the favorable conditions and to eliminate the unfavorable ones. The administrator must develop a sensitivity about the image of the organization and work unceasingly to improve that image.

Because everyone connected with an organization is a human relations agent, it follows that the total public relations program must be a team effort. Because a single agent can do more damage to public relations than can be overcome by all the remaining members, the administrator must give constant and careful attention to the impressions each colleague is creating. This is also part of the total staff effort and staff members should encourage each other to be good role models and spokespeople.

In addition to the key role in the human relations of a department, the administrator also has the ultimate responsibility for all the publicity that is produced. Through the various publicity media, it is possible to communicate with people who cannot be reached personally.

Planning and Organizing the Public Relations Program

A number of factors must be considered in establishing a public relations program. These factors depend on the size of the organization and the status of the current program. The funding that is available and the decision to hire public relations specialists full- or part-time are variables that influence the configuration of a public relations program. The most important considerations involved in planning and organizing a public relations program are discussed below.

The specific objectives of the program should be based on the institutional or business mission statement. Because everybody in the organization is part of any public relations program, it is critical that objectives emanate from all the staff. A feeling of ownership by all is important. In large organizations or schools, representatives of constituent groups may develop a set of objectives, but these objectives should be discussed and approved by all members of the staff. Unless there is unity and support for the program by all staff members, there is not much point in initiating such a program.

The past and present policies and procedures must be evaluated in terms of the effects that they have had on the public relations of the organization or a department or unit thereof. Data should be collected from as many groups as possible regarding their reactions to these policies and procedures. In a physical education setting, these groups include students, parents, alumni, faculty, school administrators, and other people who use departmental facilities. Factors that produce misunderstanding and resentment must be eliminated.

If possible, one person should be designated to have responsibility for implementing the public relations program. This is more likely in a business organization, a large university athletic program, or for an entire school system. If a full-time position is not possible, a well-qualified person should be designated to undertake this assignment. In some physical education departments, the department chairperson assumes this responsibility. There are specific duties that must be regularly performed and others that occur at irregular intervals. When one individual is responsible for these duties, they are more likely to be done promptly and efficiently. Often, everyone's responsibility becomes no one's responsibility. An important function such as public relations must have someone designated to coordinate efforts.

The efforts of a health education or a physical education department must be integrated with the school or school system public relations program. This same principle applies to leisure and health promotion programs that are part of a larger umbrella structure.

The facts to be emphasized in public relations should be determined so the program has a focus. The focus must be based on facts that have been obtained from constituents. Surveys and polls are helpful in this regard. The decisions concerning the emphasis and direction of a program should incorporate the viewpoints of all staff members. This is also true when special features are planned for publicity purposes or when an extraordinary event is planned to highlight some aspect of a program.

A multifaceted media approach should be used for disseminating information. Some people can best be reached via print media, others by radio, and still others by a combination. The use of a variety of communication techniques enables organizations to reach more people and reach them most effectively. The exception to a multiple-media approach would be if a designated group of people has been targeted and one media form has been found to be best in reaching that group of people.

Evaluation of the effectiveness of the public relations program should be conducted on a regular basis. Such an evaluation is necessary to guide future efforts and to assess what has been accomplished.

The public relations program plans and policies should be available in writing. Printing a booklet that all members will have is a good idea for helping staff members become familiar with the public relations plan. It should be developed by staff members and should serve as a guide for all members of the department or organization. It is important for everyone to know the overall public relations objectives and to understand the role and responsibilities of each person. A written program is an important instrument for every public relations program.

Multiple Publics

There isn't just one public. Formerly, the idea was held that a school or department had inter-actions with a "public." We know now that there are many publics differing in size, orga-nization, interests, communication skills, educational level, and unity. Every religious, polit-ical, service, ethnic, social, and professional organization constitutes a public. A public does not necessarily have to be an organization. Publics are also based on gender, occupation, income level, and other classifications that give people similar outlooks. Each public in a community must be considered when developing a public relations plan. In addition, it should be remembered that every individual is a member of several publics.

This concept of publics is important in public relations because the approach to a spe-cific group depends on its nature and interests. A successful approach to one group may prove ineffective with other groups. One of the lessons that specialists in public relations have learned is that different communication techniques must be planned for specific groups—one plan doesn't fit all!

Communication Skills

The value of communication skills for an administrator was emphasized in an earlier chap-ter. These skills are equally important for every person in an organization who comes in con-tact with another person outside the organization. In the fields of physical education, leisure, health education, and sports, face-to-face communication is commonly used. This increas-es the need for good verbal communication. Effective communication skills based on cor-rect use of English can be considered to be the essential foundation of a public relations program. Communication, whether in oral or written form, with any public or a member of a public has either a positive or negative impact. It is through communication that most impressions are made about an organization or department. Staff members must evaluate their use of both verbal and nonverbal communication. Actions can easily give a message that differs from a written or verbal statement. Think of the basketball coach who talks about sporting behavior but who berates officials during a game. Most nonverbal negative mes-sages are more subtle but they can be equally disastrous for a public relations program.

Feedback is a valuable outcome of good communication. Administrators must address the listening component of communication when setting up public relations programs. Com-munication is so important that administrators would be well-advised to provide in-service programs to develop these skills. This is also one of the reasons that communication skills are an important consideration in evaluating job applicants. Communication, whether in a tele-phone conversation, a speech, a note to a parent, a report on the progress of a person in a car-diac rehabilitation program, or a newsletter, sends either a positive or negative message based on the quality of expression and correctness of language use as much as on the contents.

Public Relations in Physical Education

Purposes

The purposes of public relations in physical education are consistent with the purposes of pub-lic relations in the entire field of education. Inasmuch as the public schools are supported by taxation, an obligation exists on their part to give an accounting of their activities to the public.

These schools belong to the people. The public invests heavily in education and citizens are entitled to know what is being accomplished with their money. In addition to discharging this responsibility to the public, the schools find it necessary to keep people informed about their activities in order to obtain the kind of support needed to maintain high-quality programs. The cost of public schools is the largest item in municipal budgets, but as long as public confidence and support are maintained this expense will be embraced by the community.

The attitude of the public toward education is the determining factor in the support that is provided. This factor alone is enough of a reason to have public relations programs that are well-planned and executed. It is important that people understand education and buy into the importance of schools in preparing students to be productive members of society. When this describes members of a community, the schools in that community are financially supported and the people take an active interest in education.

Still another purpose of public relations in education and physical education is to rectify mistakes, clear up misunderstandings, and eradicate negative and antagonistic attitudes. These conditions always exist in the general public, and they are powerful deterrents to goodwill. It is particularly important that every person receive accurate information and be influenced in a positive manner by public relations. Too often, the leaders of attacks on the schools are people who are misinformed or don't have all the facts.

There are many specific reasons for public relations in physical education:

It can clear up common misconceptions about physical education.

It lets people know the value of a good physical education program.

It keeps the public informed of changes in the program.

It lets people know about the many outreach programs in physical education.

It informs people in the community about the programs available to them.

It helps to develop and keep good morale in the physical education department when programs are recognized and respected.

It informs people of activities and events.

It establishes the feeling of joint partnership in the physical education programs.

It can generate support for programs.

It can ensure that the public knows the cost-effectiveness of the physical education program.

It helps gain support for bond issues and other projects that improve the quality of programs and services.

It gives people confidence in the program.

It generates feedback that can be used to improve the programs in the department.

It keeps the lines of communication open between the department and the public.

Need and Importance

It has been pointed out that public agencies have an obligation to report periodically to the community. It has also been emphasized that continued public support depends heavily on an effective public relations program. There must be mutual understanding between the public agency and the people who are served. This occurs when a continuous system of communication is in place and the other principles of good public relations are followed.

Of all areas of public schools, physical education, particularly, must bring about a harmonious relationship among parents, teachers, school administrators, and other citizens in the community. This need stems from the fact that physical education is often misunderstood and the philosophy, activities, and methods in physical education are steadily evolving. Too often, adults are either not aware of present programs or they do not understand and appreciate current curricula. Most people react in terms of their own experience and, for some, this experience might not reflect what is occurring in present programs.

Far too few physical educators concern themselves with reporting and interpreting physical education to the public and school administrators. Having a good program is the most important public relations tool for physical education. However, just having a good program is not enough by itself. The challenge for a public relations program is to communicate this fact to the many publics from whom support is needed and to shape a favorable attitude toward physical education. This attitude translates into financial support. During difficult economic times, school budgets must often be reduced. Too often, physical education programs feel the pain of such cuts more than other programs if good public relations programs are not in place and physical educators have not been active in speaking out about current programs and the value of physical education.

When school costs are increasing so enormously, all items in the educational budget are been scrutinized with great care. Any program that cannot be justified in terms of its benefit for students will have difficulty in surviving. Physical educators must justify their existence. Unfortunately, physical education facilities are the most expensive classrooms in our schools. They take up a significant percentage of the total space in both elementary and secondary schools. School administrators, school boards, parents, and the general public must be persuaded that the funds expended for physical education pay rich dividends. When these groups understand what physical education can contribute to students in terms of health, vitality, physical fitness, citizenship, sporting attitudes, and happiness, adequate support results. Parents pay for what they want for their children. Think of the huge sums parents spend for their children in nonschool programs in dance, swimming, ice skating, martial arts, and many other sport activities. They want what is best and unstintingly support what they are convinced is desirable. But they must be convinced!

Principles

Six principles that constitute a sound basis for an effective public relations program in physical education are discussed in this section.

The public relations program must be based on truth. All facts, data, and interpretations that are reported to the public must be presented impersonally, unselfishly, and honestly. By the very nature of public relations, any misrepresentation will inevitably create adverse public opinion.

The best foundation for good public relations is a sound program. The most elaborate public relations program cannot cover the basic defects of a poor program. It should never attempt to do so. The first step in successful public relations is a physical education program that is making a genuine contribution to the lives of students. A limited, poorly taught program can have no other result than bad public relations. A good physical education program is the base on which an effective public relations program can be developed. Many issues and problems may occur that result in a confrontational environment for a physical education department. However, if a high-quality program is in place, these difficulties are kept in proper perspective and public confidence in physical education returns.

In this connection, it should be pointed out that the program can be far from ideal and still develop good public relations. In schools that have limited facilities, equipment, time allotment, and large classes, the physical educator is not expected to accomplish what could be done under ideal circumstances. The criterion, however, is how effective is the program *under the circumstances?* In any given situation, a superior teacher will produce better results than a poor or mediocre teacher. Many physical educators have obtained improved facilities, equipment, and time allotment because of the excellent public relations developed for a program that was as good as it could be under unfavorable circumstances.

The public relations program should be continuous. Unfortunately, too few physical educators have any definite public relations plans for their departments. What few programs do exist are usually of the campaign type, which are not as effective in molding public opinion as is a continuous program. The common practice has been to neglect the public relations program until an emergency arises and then to conduct an intensive campaign to secure public support. Although this procedure has some value, it so resembles propaganda that the public develops a more suspicious, defensive attitude than it would if it were supplied regularly with information. Campaigns are more successful if the public has been educated by a continuous program of public relations.

Public relations is a two-way process between the community and the schools. The concept of public relations wherein everything originates within the schools and flows to the public is limited. The public can provide more than mere financial support, as important as that is. The trend is toward genuine cooperation in planning and working for good schools, with the public giving as well as receiving the ideas. Mutual understanding and teamwork between the community and the school give laypeople greater confidence in their schools. In addition, parents gain a better understanding of the role of the home, the community, and the school in the whole program of education.

A physical education advisory committee can be an effective component of the two-way interaction between the different publics and the physical education department. In some communities, such committees exist for many of the school areas. Committees are considered to be school board committees. It has been found to be most effective when members serve two- or three-year terms to give continuity to the committee. It is also best to limit the number of consecutive terms that a member can serve on the committee so that different members of the community can get involved and generate an infusion of new ideas each year. Volunteers to serve on the committee are solicited each year and the superintendent of schools and director of physical education recommend new members for the committee to the board of education. After the members are approved, the president of the board of education sends a letter inviting them to become members of the advisory committee. The membership normally consists of from 15 to 30 members, depending on the size of the community, with one-third being school personnel. The public members are chosen to represent different occupational, geographical, ethnic, and socioeconomic groups throughout the school system. The school people should also represent a cross-section of school personnel (recent employees and long-time staff members, elementary and secondary teachers, and administrators). One school board member is usually assigned to be an ex-officio member of each committee. The physical education administrator is the secretary of the physical education committee and provides leadership and direction. The chairperson is elected by the group.

Each year the physical education advisory committee is informed of the work of past committees and the needs and problems of the physical education programs in all the schools. Suggestions and ideas are received from members of the committee and problems are discussed, study groups formed, resolutions passed, and the minutes provided for the superintendent, who transmits the committee's resolutions and recommendations to the school board.

A knowledge of what the public thinks about the schools is essential. The more school personnel know about the level of understanding and attitudes of the public, the more intelligent and effective is the public relations program. Thus, schools have been making increasing use of surveys and opinion polls. The advantages of knowing the areas of ignorance and misinformation in the community, the prevailing opinions and attitudes on educational matters, the views of particular groups, and the obstacles to be overcome are obvious.

This principle has particular implications for physical education. Because of ongoing changes in philosophy, objectives, programs, procedures, and evaluative techniques in the field, many members of the community do not have accurate knowledge about physical education or what constitutes a good program.

The effective public relations program involves all school personnel. Schools could learn some valuable lessons from business organizations regarding the orientation of all personnel in their public relations responsibilities. The most successful stores devote much effort in training all staff members to work successfully with people, yet in most schools there is an assumption that everyone will automatically practice good public relations. Good public relations do not happen in the normal course of events; they are the result of a well-planned program, intelligently and continuously executed. The quality of the public relations program is commensurate with the effort put into it.

Relatively few physical education departments have a planned, comprehensive public relations program. Only rarely is this subject discussed in staff meetings or included in departmental policies. Seldom is an organized effort made to familiarize the teaching staff with desirable public relations procedures. Even though there is abundant evidence to the contrary, the presumption apparently exists that the teaching personnel always practice good human relationships. Nonteaching personnel such as the student aides, secretaries, custodians, and equipment room attendants are also important from this standpoint, yet few efforts are made to ensure that they treat students, faculty, and the general public in a courteous, dignified, and friendly manner. A brusque secretary, a dirty or unshaven custodian, or an inconsiderate equipment room clerk can damage the reputation of the physical education department.

Nevertheless, the overall impression of the public toward physical education depends much more on dedicated, superior teachers than on any other consideration. The impressions received by students from their teachers are gained over a much longer period of time, and these impressions are more intimate, dynamic, and vital. They relate to matters of much more crucial concern to students. The favorable public image created by the teacher may be adversely affected by discourteous secretaries or custodians; on the other hand, the finest possible impressions created by nonteaching personnel cannot begin to compensate for an incompetent, selfish, disinterested teacher.

Key Publics

Many publics are critically important to the physical education profession. They must be carefully considered in public relations programs. These publics include students, parents, other teachers, school administrators, school board members, media personnel, and representatives of related governmental and social agencies. Each of these groups will be considered in greater detail.

Students   The most important group from the standpoint of public relations is the student body. There are two reasons for this situation. In the first place, student reactions to physical education powerfully affect the opinions and attitudes of parents, other members of the family, and friends. Each pupil is a daily reporter on what happens in physical education. What the student thinks and says about school work and teachers is extremely important. If happy and successful in their relationships, they are boosters for the program. No more effective approach could be made to parents. Even parents who had negative attitudes toward physical education become ardent supporters when their children's reports are enthusiastic and favorable. The instances are legion where parents, convinced of the importance of physical education for their children, have used their influence to bring about improved facilities, equipment, class size, and time allotment. The correlation between *pupil approval* and *public approval* of physical education is very high.

The second reason why students represent such an important group is that they are tomorrow's public. They eventually become the parents, doctors, lawyers, businesspeople, school administrators, members of congress, politicians, public officials, college presidents, and school board members. Their attitudes toward physical education are conditioned largely by their own school experiences. People who strongly support physical education and others who are bitterly prejudiced against it are found in every community. Some physical educators share the credit for the friends and supporters who have been created; others are responsible for the enemies.

Unfortunately, much harm has been done to physical education in various states and communities by people who are antagonistic to it. Some of these people obtain positions of power and influence, which they use to the detriment of physical education. Behind the defeats and setbacks physical education has suffered is the failure of one or more physical educators. Every student who is slighted, neglected, humiliated, or otherwise mistreated during his or her experiences in physical education has been adversely affected. On graduation from school, if the sum total of impressions is negative, the student can hardly be expected to be an enthusiastic supporter.

Parents   The importance of this public has already been emphasized. It has also been pointed out that educators can obtain the support of parents by providing them with an excellent program while they are in school and by contributing positively to the health, fitness, skill development, social adjustment, and recreational competencies of their children. Additional ways of increasing the understanding and appreciation of parents are also available to the physical educator and should be used.

Parents can be informed about physical education via reports, open house programs, visits to school, invitations to participate in lessons, parent–teacher meetings, demonstrations ranging from planned performances to presentations of typical lessons, meaningful report cards, and the many types of publicity that can be used to keep the entire community aware of physical education objectives and programs. All publicity should be based on information that is important for the people to know and is of interest to them. For example, parents are always interested in having the achievements of their children recognized through pictures and press releases.

Publicity emphasis should be placed on the value of physical education and its contribution to the well-being and education of students. The message that physical education provides physical, social, mental, and emotional benefits for each student must be conveyed to parents along with information about changes in programs that have and are taking place to attain these benefits. The contributions physical education makes in the physical realm must be highlighted along with evidence to show that physical education is an integral part of a child's educational experience. In other words, parents should be educated to know the objectives of physical education and the means by which they are being attained. They should know what constitutes a high-quality physical education program.

The major interest of parents in physical education revolves around their sons and daughters. If a child is not making satisfactory progress, parents want to know why and what might be done to remedy the situation. They are interested in the content of their children's classes and the value that each activity has for them. They might have questions about the teaching procedures and methods of evaluation that are used, so information on these topics should be provided on a regular basis. Of course, the health and physical fitness of their girls and boys is a matter of vital concern to all parents.

What parents want to know about physical education corresponds closely with the information physical education administrators seek to include in a comprehensive public relations program. The following items, based on the parents' interest as well as information that enhances their understanding of physical education, are suggested as being of most value for shaping a public relations program:

Progress and achievement of their children

Program of activities

Health and physical fitness levels of their children

Methods of instruction

Objectives of physical education

Need for physical education

Behavior of pupils in physical education

Physical skill development

Social influence

Information about the teachers of physical education

Intramural programs

Physical education facilities

Other Teaching Personnel   Another important public for physical education is the other teachers in the school system. Good public relations with this group pays valuable dividends. When they comprehend the nature and purposes of the program and are sympathetic, they are helpful in interpreting it to students, parents, and the general public. In their advising and counseling functions, they can be helpful to both the students and the physical education department. Also, if they are favorably disposed toward physical education, they are unlikely to vote for school policies and regulations that are unfavorable to it.

Physical educators can win the support of the other teachers in a number of ways. The most important step toward this end is the development of an educationally respectable program—one that merits a place in the schools. Teachers usually obtain from their students a fairly accurate impression of the physical education program. An excellent program will gain their respect. Other teachers admire physical educators who are educators—who exert a wholesome influence on their students. They lose respect for physical education when questionable practices that teach youth undesirable lessons are tolerated.

Physical educators must also fulfill their role as teachers. They should attend faculty meetings, PTA meetings, and other school functions. They should demonstrate interest in all school activities and avoid conveying the impression that they are a group set apart from the other faculty. The more they associate with other teachers professionally and socially, the better their public relations are with this important group.

School Administrators and School Board Members   This is a small but very important public. The status of physical education in a school or a city system can be drastically affected by this group. When the people involved become convinced that physical education merits an increased time allotment, more teachers, or an additional gymnasium or swimming pool, these improvements are strongly supported.

Physical educators can win the support of their principals and superintendents if they become part of the team in trying to accomplish the purposes of the school. School administrators want loyalty and cooperation from their teachers. They do not want teachers who are working toward objectives that have little relation to those of the school system.

School administrators and school board members are sensitive to public opinion. The best way to win their support is to have favorable information come to their attention from students, parents, other teachers, and the media. The combination of a good program and good public relations usually produces the desired results. It is also helpful if the physical educators conduct an effective program of evaluation with which they can demonstrate objectively how the children in the program have developed. An annual report that cites and substantiates the progress and present status of the program justifies needs and explains problems is invaluable in interpreting the program to this particular public.

Members of the Press, Radio, and Television   The importance of these publicity media emphasizes the necessity to work cooperatively with their representatives. The publicity they can disseminate is invaluable, and the only cost is the time and preparation required to cooperate. Physical educators should take full advantage of this opportunity and assist the representatives of these media in every way possible. This includes providing accurate, easy-to-use information about programs, staff, and activities. Another important consideration is to treat all individuals impartially. The surest way to damage public relations with members of the press, radio, and television is to show preference to one group.

Representatives of Government and Social Agencies   Good public relations should exist between physical educators in the schools and those in other agencies in the community, such as the Jewish community centers, the YMCA, YWCA, boys' and girls' clubs, senior citizen centers, neighborhood centers, and the municipal recreation department. It is mutually advantageous for all to work cooperatively with each other. Facilities, equipment, and personnel may be shared on occasions. Programs may be cooperatively arranged. Most important of all, understanding each other's programs provides broad-based support for all of the programs. For example, if physical education in the school is under attack, the personnel of other community agencies can be of invaluable assistance.

The Teacher's Role

In the daily interaction of pupil and teacher, the most lasting and vital public relations are undoubtedly built. Certainly teachers have the most contact with pupils and work more directly and intimately with them than do nonteaching personnel. Consequently, the intrinsic value of teacher–pupil relationships is a major factor in the school's public relations.

Physical education teachers have exceptional opportunities to contribute to the wholesome development of their pupils. The activities are exciting and challenging, and students are enthusiastic about them. The goals—health, physical fitness, skills, wholesome recreation, and social adjustment—are vitally important and desired by parents and pupils alike. With these advantages, physical education teachers are strategically situated to develop outstanding public relations.

Unfortunately, these opportunities are often ignored. Not at all uncommon in physical education are undesirable teaching practices and procedures. Among the faculty members who may irrevocably damage the department's public relations are the following:

The teacher who tosses out a ball and tells the students to play

The teacher who offers the same activities year after year without progression or change

The teacher who ignores the weak and inept to concentrate on the superior performers

The teacher who never teaches systematically

The teacher who exploits physical education classes to locate and develop varsity performers

The teacher who is sarcastic, abusive, disparaging, and impatient

The teacher who concentrates on only one objective of physical education to the exclusion of others

The teacher who is untidy or slovenly in appearance

The teacher who shows dislike or bias toward students because of their physical or mental disabilities, or their racial, social, or religious backgrounds

The teacher who is lazy, weak, or a poor disciplinarian

Such teachers have a devastating effect on public relations. Students, parents, other teachers, school administrators, board members, and the general public have nothing but scorn and disrespect for them.

Studies show the characteristics that students most esteem in their teachers are the following:

They like a teacher to be fair and firm, with no favoritism to any pupil or group. They resent teacher bias. Often, teachers are judged unfair because of an inadequate understanding of their motives. Teachers should be alert in discovering and remedying misconceptions that occur.

They like a teacher to be sincere. It is impossible to teach successfully what one fails to practice. Courtesy cannot result if the teacher is discourteous. Good sporting behavior cannot be expected if the teacher or coach endorses an illegal play or unsporting tactic. Pupils quickly discover whether a teacher sincerely believes in and practices such virtues as honesty, courtesy, loyalty, good sporting behavior, and charity.

They like a teacher who is interested in them. They resent being ignored or brushed off. The informal relationships in physical education provide an ideal setting for students to talk with their teachers about their daily work, studies, future problems, or hobbies. Physical educators can be effective counselors if they are willing to take the time to talk to their students.

They like teachers who make learning interesting. They prefer teachers who are motivational, who are patient and give them additional assistance, and who help them evaluate their progress. They like teachers who are considerate of the opinions of students and who make learning a joint endeavor.

They like teachers who know their subject. They quickly discover the teacher who is poorly prepared, and they soon lose respect for this type of teacher.

Some physical education teachers confine their public relations efforts to the classroom. They hold themselves aloof from the community and its organizations and groups. This is unfortunate from a public relations standpoint because part of the teacher's responsibility is to inform the community about the quality of the physical education program. A community likes teachers, particularly physical education teachers, who have so many skills to share, to participate in community activities. The people want teachers to fit in, to observe their customs and traditions. In reality, a teacher's private life is not his or her own. Teachers, especially those new in a community, should be sensitive to the behavior codes that differentiate one community from another. They should not be enslaved to local customs, but they should respect prevalent traditions within the limits of good taste and good sense.

There is also an obligation on the part of all citizens to participate in community enterprises, and every teacher should do so. In many communities, physical education teachers are encouraged to engage in youth activities that relate to their field. Youth organizations, service clubs, religious organizations, civic and fraternal groups, and many other community organizations offer opportunities for physical educators to broaden their community contacts.

Physical education teachers have been unflatteringly stereotyped over the years. They are too often envisioned as overdeveloped muscularly, attired in sweat clothes, inarticulate, lacking in social skills, and uninterested in scholarly and cultural attainments. By their actions, physical educators must invalidate these stereotypes. They must be aware of these erroneous perceptions and make a strenuous effort to eradicate them.

In summary, the role of the physical education teacher in the public relations program is to be an outstanding teacher and to establish good relationships in the community. The value of tact, courtesy, and friendliness toward all with whom he or she comes into contact cannot be overestimated and dedication to the students is essential.

Other Factors Affecting Student Attitudes toward Physical Education

It is erroneous to assume that unfavorable student attitudes are produced only by teachers. Administrative procedures, regulations, and policies sometimes result in negative reactions from students. Administrators must consider students' views, ideas, and desires when determining attendance regulations, uniform requirements, the grading system, and content of the physical education program. The quality of the program is important, together with the choices that are provided for the students. Finally, an adequate amount of good equipment is important.

Unfortunately, many institutions do not have the resources—chiefly facilities—for an adequate physical education program. Faculty members face serious obstacles in their efforts to develop favorable attitudes among their students when the teaching stations are unattractive, inadequate in size, and poorly lighted, ventilated, and maintained. Overcrowded, dirty, unsanitary, and inadequately lighted, heated, and ventilated locker and shower rooms also detract from a student's desire to participate in physical education. The importance of good services provided by the equipment room should also be recognized.

Conducting a physical education program that will gain the support and endorsement of the students requires careful attention to a multitude of factors. It is unrealistic to expect favorable reactions from all of the students all the time but this is a desirable objective. By applying what we know about student reactions to physical education programs, we can attain the approval of the great majority.

Publicity Techniques and Media

Publicity is an integral part of public relations. It provides an opportunity to communicate with an audience that cannot be reached personally. Many more people can be reached via the various publicity media than through person-to-person contact. The favorable opinions of this much wider audience are of crucial importance to physical education.

The major publicity media include newspapers, radio, television, videos, slides, graphics and pictorial materials, public addresses, demonstrations, open houses and tours, school publications, bulletin boards, and annual reports to parents. So many media are available that it is difficult to select which ones to use.

The obvious criterion for determining what media to use is that it should be the best one available for the specific purpose. The particular public or publics for whom the information is primarily intended is another important factor. Expense, time, ease of preparation, and availability are other considerations.

The Newspaper   The local newspaper is a powerful factor in molding public opinion. As it reaches practically everyone in the community, it becomes an invaluable means of informing people about physical education. Because of the public's interest in its schools, newspapers are very liberal with space for school news. The only cost for this is the time required to cooperate with the press. Physical educators should take full advantage of this opportunity and assist the representatives of the local papers in every way possible. They should furnish the journalists with news regarding physical education in the school and undertake to learn what constitutes news, what are news values, and how news stories are prepared. Such a background is highly desirable, for most physical educators often find it necessary to write news stories. In only the larger institutions is there a separate publicity writer whose sole duties are to assemble and prepare news stories. In the majority of schools, the person in charge of physical education must prepare the material and either place it in the hands of those responsible for school publicity or give it directly to the newspapers. It is a mistake to depend entirely on the visits of the reporter in order to get physical education news into the local papers. When the physical education director prepares stories, they fall into one of three different types. *News stories* are reports of the events as soon as they are over. They must contain the six basic elements of all newspaper leads: who did what, when, where, why, and how. *Advance stories* are notices given out in advance of events, stating in future tense the basic elements. The more important the events, the greater the number of advance stories. *Feature stories* are those in which the writer explains, interprets, describes, and develops in popular form some interesting subject for the purpose of informing, entertaining, or giving practical guidance. The feature story generalizes over many events and a long time, whereas news and advance stories usually treat one event at a specific time.

When preparing and submitting news stories, the physical educator needs to be familiar with the requirements of the newspaper. Each paper has policies that writers must follow when submitting a story. There are certain key points to keep in mind for any newspaper:

Be factual, accurate, and concise.

Provide a clear copy that can be easily read.

Meet the deadline that is required.

Provide stories that have broad-based interest in the community.

Properly mark any pictures that accompany the story.

Remember that there is a difference between a story and an editorial.

Use correct grammar in writing.

Structure the story to require as little rewriting as possible.

Write in the third person.

Avoid using an excessive number of superlatives.

It is important to have a good working relationship with the press in your community. This means that trust must be present; you shouldn't have hidden agendas when giving information to a newspaper writer. Get to know members of the press, and be aware of the type of stories and the information they need. Remember that you are operating on a two-way street, so assistance that you give will be returned to you in the form of newspaper coverage for your program. Be reasonable with your requests and strive to understand the pressures under which a newspaper reporter operates. This means you should be willing to talk about negative as well as positive issues. Finally, be accessible, honest, fair, and appreciative.

Radio and Television   Radio and television are powerful media because of the large numbers of people they reach. They can be effectively used to interpret physical education and to provide the public with essential information. Local radio and cable television stations often welcome programs from the schools and are usually cooperative in making their facilities available. Programming on cable television is an exciting way to keep the community informed about physical education programs and activities.

All commercial radio and television stations are required to devote a certain amount of time to public service announcements. Physical education has the opportunity, along with other school activities, to participate. This is usually done through the educational institution or professional organization rather than on a departmental basis. A public service announcement about the value of physical education over national television can assist all physical education programs. In addition, information and announcements may be broadcast by means of spot announcements and newscasts over local stations. Many of the same materials prepared for newspapers can be used on a newscast if they are rewritten.

Public television is another good resource, particularly for college and university physical education departments. Courses can be offered through this medium and programs can include physical educators speaking in their area of expertise. It is also sometimes possible to include unique physical education activities, such as an exercise program for older adults, in public television programming.

When physical educators have opportunities to present programs over radio or television, they should seek technical assistance. Ordinarily, the person with this responsibility for the school system or the university renders this assistance. Radio and television personnel are also available for this purpose.

Videos and Slides   These visual aids are increasingly used by schools to present ideas, activities, and needs. The public has few opportunities to observe the work of the schools, and these media are usually more effective than verbal descriptions.

The rapid advancement of video technology has made videotapes an economical, user-friendly means of communicating with the public. The ease of use and economy of producing videotapes has made this the visual medium of choice for presenting information about a program or activity. It is also an effective way to explain physical education to the public and to gain support for departmental endeavors such as a facilities renovation or restructuring of the curriculum.

Slides are also used effectively to present a message or inform the public. Slide presentations can be either pictures or graphics or a combination. They are relatively inexpensive to produce and are particularly valuable when used in conjunction with a talk on some phase of the school activities.

Other Graphic and Pictorial Materials   Photographs, charts, graphs, and diagrams are included in this category. The Chinese proverb "A picture is worth a thousand words" emphasizes the importance of these media.

Photographs tell a story and arouse interest. If they are well-chosen, they interpret, dramatize, inform, and explain. They can be used in newspapers and reports, bulletin boards, exhibits, and window displays. For best results, photographs should have a good background, show action, and involve small groups only.

Charts, graphs, and diagrams are valuable in presenting various types of statistical data. Data on budget, school growth, and participation in school activities, as well as comparisons of various types, are much more effectively portrayed by these visual aids than by words.

Public Speaking   Physical educators have frequent opportunities to speak before groups. They receive invitations to address PTA groups, service and fraternal clubs, and social and civic organizations. All such invitations should be accepted because they present opportunities for developing good public relations. It goes without saying, however, that the effect of an address depends on how well it is presented.

The fact that an invitation to speak has been extended indicates that the group has an interest in what the physical educator has to say. Nevertheless, much careful preparation is needed. There are, of course, people who can give an excellent address with little preparation, but they are the exception to the rule. In general, the quality of the speech corresponds to the amount of time devoted to its preparation.

Mastery of subject matter and interest in it are two prerequisites to effective speaking that the physical education teacher should possess. Sincerity and enthusiasm are other essentials. Speech authorities urge that speakers make an outline of the major points they wish to cover rather than write the speech out in detail and memorize it. Reading a speech is also considered poor practice. Another common mistake is to try to cover too much in one talk. Practice in delivering the speech is recommended.

Student Publications   The student newspaper, the school annual, and the student handbook are important communications media that can be used to advantage by the physical educator. These projects are vital to the students, who are grateful for whatever assistance and cooperation they receive from the faculty. Student reporters should be treated courteously and extended all the assistance they require. Student publications can be of great help in giving the students, including those working on them, an understanding of physical education.

Annual Reports   Many school systems publish an annual report that describes the status, progress, activities, and needs of the schools. In the yearly report to the school administrators and the school board, the physical education administrator should present a fair and honest summary of what has been accomplished in the department and indicate what its important needs are. The presentation is made stronger when the administrator can provide objective evidence rather than personal opinion to support recommendations. For example, if one can present *objective* data that show that local children do not compare favorably with other children or with recommended standards, the report is much more likely to secure helpful action.

Demonstrations   Demonstrations are extensively used by physical educators to promote understanding and support. Correctly used, these media provide an unusually effective means of interpreting physical education to parents and the general public. It is easy to get the public to attend, and it is not difficult to create the understandings that lead to favorable public opinion. In addition to the public relations value, demonstrations are of exceptional educational value to students and teachers.

Demonstrations are placed before the public on special occasions such as parent–teacher conference night, open-house night, field and play days, or whenever such demonstrations are warranted. They should be regular occasions rather than a device to use only when physical education is in trouble. As an integral part of the physical education program, they deserve the time, space, and personnel required for their proper execution.

Demonstrations should represent the regular program to the public. They should involve all or as many students as can be used rather than only the outstanding performers. Preparation for the demonstration should not interfere appreciably with the regular program of instruction. The primary purpose is to *inform* the public, not to entertain it. Physical education has outgrown the practice of spending weeks preparing for an exhibition that does not represent the physical education program. Experience has shown that this approach damaged public relations rather than improved them. The demonstration should endeavor to present a representative cross-section of the program and, at the same time, interpret it to observers.

Public Relations by National, District, and State Organizations

The national, district, and state physical education organizations such as the American Alliance for Health, Physical Education, Recreation, and Dance (AAHPERD), Eastern and Southwest Districts of AAHPERD, the National Association for Sport and Physical Education, and Iowa AAHPERD initiate and carry out a definite public relations plan. In fact, this is one of their major functions. They supplement the work of local physical educators and perform certain services on the national, regional, and state levels that could not be done by individual teachers. The total public relations effort requires an effective program not only on the local level but also on the wider state, district, and national levels.

The public relations functions of AAHPERD are directed by a professionally trained person assisted by other paid personnel and by the national officers. On the district level, the public relations effort is spearheaded by the officers and a designated person or persons or a special committee of the district association. State association officers and appointed or elected individuals conduct public relations programs for the various states.

The public relations functions of the national, regional, and state organizations are impressive. Programs at the regional and state level vary from region to region and state to state. The programs at the national level change with the times and the ideas of the officers. One of the landmark public relations efforts was the Physical Education Public Information (PEPI) project of AAHPERD. This project was effective in promoting physical education from the local level to the national level and led to a heightened consciousness on the part of the membership of the need and value of comprehensive public relations programs. The Jump Rope for Heart project is another program that has been an outstanding vehicle to gain recognition for physical education and to involve students of all ages in the jump rope activity. It has also generated significant sums of money for physical education at the state and national level.

The National Association for Sport and Physical Education (NASPE) is an outstanding example of a national organization that uses a variety of approaches to support, strengthen, and advance sport and physical education. They have established a network of volunteers who keep abreast of the latest issues and needs in the fields of sport and physical education and establish priorities and goals. NASPE has a strong advocacy program that ranges from legislative lobbying to campaigns to inform the public about the importance of high-quality physical education programs. They also publish a steady flow of public relations materials that can be used by their membership. Examples are the pamphlet *101 Ways to Promote Physical Activity and Sport* and the publication *Sport and Physical Education Advocacy Kit* (SPEAK).

Some of the other things national, district, and state organizations do to further the public understanding and support of physical education include the following:

Disseminate and suggest public relations ideas and methods to members of the organization in the field

Prepare and disseminate material for release to newspapers, radio and television programs, and speakers

Establish cooperative relationships and mutual understanding with related national organizations such as the American Medical Association, Parent–Teachers Association, American Public Health Association, National Recreation Association, and the President's Council on Physical Fitness and Sports

Publicize conventions, meetings, and speeches

Gather and pass on to members information regarding the newest developments and best practices in physical education

Study all bills that come before Congress and state legislatures to ascertain their possible effect on physical education

Take the lead in developing the strategy to be used in promoting certain bills and opposing those detrimental to physical education

Promote an international relations program

Provide a plan and means of getting physical education literature published in educational and other periodicals serving professional groups

Prepare films, books, and brochures that interpret physical education

Conduct a research program to gather data on important needs and problems

Conduct national and regional conferences on specific areas of physical education, such as facilities, teacher education, and athletics, to solve problems and upgrade the profession

Public Relations in Interscholastic and Intercollegiate Athletics

Basically, all that has been stated in regard to physical education public relations applies with equal force to interschool athletics. Every contact, impression, or relationship people have with the athletic program of an institution molds public opinion positively or negatively. Because of the powerful interest in athletics and the public's tendency to overemphasize winning teams, it is particularly important to cultivate as much goodwill as possible by effective public relations. In addition, good public relations increase attendance at contests and gain support for the athletic program.

There is a distinction between the public relations programs found in intercollegiate athletic programs at large universities, where these programs are major businesses that generate and spend huge sums of money, and interscholastic programs and intercollegiate programs operating within the traditional educational setting. The information in this section is more oriented to the second type of program. The major athletic programs have a full-time public relations staff, provide significant financial resources, and orient their total public relations program to sell athletics as a product that will provide funding for the program. Much of their exposure comes from television, bowl games, and national championships. The public relations programs of these institutions have more in common with those of businesses than with those of educational institutions.

Newspaper, Radio, and Television Personnel

An extremely important consideration is the relationship of the athletic director and coach with sportswriters, publishers, and representatives of radio and television. Publicity through these various media, if translated into dollar value, would be infinitely more than an athletic department could afford to pay, but usually the only cost of this publicity is the time and effort required to cooperate with the personnel.

It is important to be honest with all members of the media. If a coach or athletic director is not in a position to speak about some issue or a player, the reason should be explained. It is good to establish trust with members of the media, which allows the sharing of confidences under parameters that are understood and accepted by both parties. The coach should not use the media for his or her personal publicity or to obtain an unfair advantage for the team. If this is done, there will be a loss of respect for the coach and team, who thereby lose a powerful source of support. No athletic director or coach can afford to alienate the media.

In communities with more than one newspaper, the coach must be impartial to the representatives of each. Much rivalry naturally exists between papers, and the coach may lose the support of all the papers by showing partiality to one. The same situation applies to relationships with representatives of the different radio and television stations in the community.

It is poor economy to be restrictive with complimentary tickets for a newspaper, radio, and television personnel. When they come to cover a contest, special conveniences should be provided for their representatives. Good seats are essential. If a press box is available, it should be equipped so that the writers and broadcasters get the game information first, either by telephone from the field or by messenger. The press box should be equipped with telephones to the outside. School representatives should be in the press box to provide assistance and supply pertinent information. Complete statistics should be provided at halftime and immediately after the game. Refreshments should be available before and during the game. In short, every effort should be made to anticipate the needs of these people and assist them in doing their jobs.

Alumni and Parents

Weekly letters to alumni, supporters, faculty, parents, and other interested groups are an effective public relations tool, as are preseason and postseason newsletters with team brochures. End-of-season statistics are also important in keeping supporters of the program informed and interested in the team. Regularly scheduled meetings with coaches of in-season sports allows people to obtain firsthand information about the teams and the season. Periodic letters to parents are another good public relations technique. All of these methods are of value in transmitting correct information to interested groups, and if they are done well, supporters are gained. Much of the antagonism toward coaches and teams is the result of misinformation or the lack of information.

Other Faculty Members

The support of faculty members for the interscholastic and intercollegiate athletic program is invaluable, and the cooperation of most of them can be easily gained if the athletic director and coaches demonstrate interest in and support of the purposes of the school. If every effort is made to conduct the athletic program on an educational basis, most of the faculty will be supportive. Faculty members resent pressure from coaches to grant unwarranted concessions to athletes. They dislike overemphasis on winning, with the concomitant poor sporting behavior, excessive demands on the time of students, and debasement of academic standards. Other faculty members admire and support coaches who attend faculty meetings and other staff functions, who consider themselves a part of the school team and cooperate with school policies and purposes, and who are always more concerned about the welfare, character, and ideals of their athletes than anything else.

Booster Clubs

Booster clubs are a great source of support and revenue for athletic programs. They must be properly organized and approved by the governing body of the institution. Control of the booster club must remain with the educational institution, and adherence to the rules and regulations of the institution and the athletic governing bodies is mandatory. Some institutions have one booster club encompassing all sports and others have sport-specific booster clubs. A booster club should have a constitution and by-laws to guide its operation and to spell out its goals. It must be clear that booster clubs can function in an advisory capacity, but all decisions concerning policy and personnel for athletic programs are the responsibility of the school administration.

Booster clubs raise money in many ways to provide financial support for the athletic program. Money is used for a variety of purposes, including student awards, recognition banquets, uniforms and equipment for teams, and other athletic costs not covered by the school budget. They can also spearhead fundraising for capital improvements of athletic facilities. At universities with athletic scholarship programs, booster clubs raise money to finance these scholarships.

Booster club members also support athletic programs by attending contests and taking an interest in the performance of the athletes. They may also assist the athletic director at contests and use special skills such as promotional expertise for the benefit of the athletic program.

Opponents

Contrary to the opinion of some coaches and rabid fans, opposing teams represent a public with whom good relations are essential. Fundamentally, mutual respect and good conduct should apply in all relations with teams from other institutions. Visiting teams should receive courteous, hospitable treatment and every consideration should be shown to them as guests. Some of the courtesies to be shown to visiting teams include the following:

Provide official hosts on arrival of the team. These representatives of the athletic department should try to provide for every need of the visitors.

Provide satisfactory dressing and showering facilities.

Encourage exemplary behavior of fans of the home team.

Avoid "trash talk" during contests.

Require good sporting conduct by players and coaches before, during, and after the contest.

Recognize an outstanding play or performance by a visiting team member.

Write letters of commendation for outstanding qualities exhibited by a visiting team.

Unfortunately, athletic contests sometimes include various kinds of unsporting conduct, including fights among players and fans. To combat this situation, some high schools have successfully initiated students exchanges for a school day before a contest. A special program designed to put athletics in proper perspective and to provide for student interaction is planned for the students who spend a day at their opponent's school. An entirely different atmosphere results at the contest that follows when students know each other and find that an athletic contest with friends can be as challenging and more fun than with enemies.

Athletic Publicity

Publicity for school athletics should stress the educational purposes and true values of these activities. Many undesirable practices and pressures persist in athletics because the public has not been educated to understand the educational values of athletic participation. Indicative of the appeal of athletics is the important position they hold in our schools and the interest the public has in every aspect of the athletic programs. The amount of space devoted to high school and college/university athletic programs and contests in newspapers establishes beyond a doubt the prominent position school athletics hold in the United States. Due in part to this passion for athletics, many undesirable practices are found, such as excessive emphasis, disregard for sound educational practices, and illegal financial payments to star players. An athletic publicity program should be designed to keep athletics in proper perspective as an important part of the school's educational program.

Athletic publicity is an important vehicle to promote support for a school's athletic program. This includes accounts of athletic contests, stories about teams, expectations for each sport season, year-end summaries, and feature stories about athletes. The human interest stories about individual athletes can be a good way of pointing out the many values of athletic participation and show how this participation is an important educational experience. Incidents involving sporting behavior, teamwork, sacrifice, courage, loyalty, integrity, leadership, and self-discipline effectively show the public the benefits of athletics.

As has been pointed out, athletic publicity in large universities with high-powered programs is the responsibility of a specialist in public relations who has a full-time staff. In smaller institutions and in many high schools, this function may be handled in a variety of ways. Sometimes, one person has this responsibility on a full-time or part-time basis. Those who have this duty on a part-time basis may be faculty members, coaches, or a person who is not otherwise affiliated with the school. Often, the athletic director assumes this responsibility or coaches provide the publicity for their teams. Students may also be assigned to handle athletic publicity. It is important that one person have overall responsibility for athletic publicity if efforts are to be appropriately coordinated and all teams are to be properly represented in publicity efforts. It is also important that this person report to the athletic director so that publicity consistently reflects the school's position that athletics are an educational experience.

Some of the important publicity techniques that can be used to promote athletics are as follows:

Community newspaper articles and game coverage

School newspaper articles and game coverage

Radio and television announcements and game coverage

Posters

Souvenir programs by community organizations

Windshield and bumper stickers

Direct mail and circulars of information

School yearbooks

School and departmental catalogues and bulletins

Talks by coaches and athletic administrators

Billboards

Advertisements in newspapers, on the radio, and in community publications

Flyers distributed in the school and throughout the community

Telephone campaigns and postcard mailings

Inclusion of athletic information by community businesses (such as schedules printed on placemats in restaurants or on grocery bags at local stores)

Promotional activities such as admitting former letter winners free to a game or giving a free admittance with the purchase of one ticket

Free admission for youth teams in soccer, football, or another sport to a designated game

Special prices for purchase of season tickets

Special activity such as a faculty vs. students free-throw contest at the halftime of a basketball game

Promotional gifts to every person who attends a game (such as pencils or pens with schedules printed on them or a miniature football or a plastic mug in the shape of the team mascot)

It is important to print a brochure about each team and give this to all sportswriters and sportscasters in the area. This brochure contains pertinent publicity material about the team. The names of all squad members, with data concerning year in school, height, weight, experience, position, and prior records of each, are given. The previous season's record, offensive and defensive information, and the outlook for the present season are indicated. The names, experience, and achievements of the coaching staff are also included. Other information usually included is the schedule, school colors, nicknames, seating capacity of home facility if pertinent, and information about the school. This brochure can be given to alumni, booster club members, and parents to further advance support of each team.

Coach's Role

Every coach fills an important role in the public relations program of an athletic department. The way they handle their coaching duties determines, to a large extent, the benefits that their athletes receive. Athletes look up to their coaches and their attitudes toward competition are molded by their coach. They will develop a healthy attitude toward athletics if they have respect for their coach. Athletes who enjoy their sport and speak positively about their experience on a team are the best spokespeople for athletics.

A coach is instrumental in shaping both the playing style and the attitude of players on the team that she or he coaches. A team that plays to its potential and follows the principles of good sporting behavior represents the school and the community well. Coaches have an extensive amount of influence in the community. The conduct and the personal characteristics of a coach go a long way toward shaping the opinion of people in the community about the worth of athletics. No aspect of an athletic public relations program is more important than the coach.

Radio and Television

Radio has been an extremely important medium for athletic publicity. It helps maintain interest in teams throughout their season and serves to increase the number of people who follow them. Radio is a viable public relations tool for high schools and small colleges as well as for universities with major athletic programs.

Television is used successfully by universities with high-caliber teams as a means of financing athletic programs. Along with the financial benefits come significant public relations benefits. There is no better or more effective means of gaining publicity than appearing on national television. This publicity results in significant increased financial support for the athletic program and the university and is an important factor in recruiting athletes. Although they don't have the same impact, public television and cable television are possibilities for high schools and smaller universities and this possibility should be aggressively pursued and included in the public relations plan of these institutions.

Public Relations in Health Promotion and Other Leisure Fields

Principles

The principles of public relations that are described for physical education and athletic programs apply to health promotion and leisure fields also. Having a quality program is the most important factor in any public relations plan. High integrity and a comprehensive publicity program carried out on a year-round basis are other important principles. As with any program, the key ingredient for program success is the support and involvement of all staff members.

Purposes

Businesses and nonprofit organizations must generate money in order to exist. Therefore, the ultimate purpose of a public relations program is to sell services and programs that provide funding for the business or organization. Other purposes are similar to those in physical education and athletics. It is important to inform people of the value of a program. This might be the physiological benefits from an aerobics class at a fitness center or the personal enjoyment that results from participating in a travel program sponsored by a senior citizens' organization.

The purpose of public relations is to convince potential customers of the quality, enjoyability, and other benefits of programs. The special features of programming, equipment, and facilities are highlighted in publicity. The background and unique skills of staff members are explained as part of a public relations program to serve as encouragement for people to participate. The purpose is to overcome psychological and logistic obstacles that prevent people from becoming participants.

Forms of Publicity

Many forms of publicity work best to reach out to the targeted populations. The type of publicity varies according to the organization and to the specific program being publicized. An organization that programs for diverse ages needs to use many more approaches than an organization that appeals primarily to one age group. Another difference is that noneducational organizations place more emphasis on paid advertising than do schools and universities. The type of publicity used is limited only by the imagination of the person in charge of publicity and the financial resources available. Of course, results obtained by using different methods determine which publicity procedures will continue to be used.

Examples of forms of publicity that are used in the field include the following:

Paid advertising in newspapers and on the radio

Feature articles about interesting programs and other newsworthy information (an effective way to get free advertising in the newspaper)

Bulk mailings

Flyers that are distributed as widely as possible

Annual reports

Telephone solicitation

Special demonstrations that arouse public interest

Open houses at the organization's facilities

Free, short-term introductory programs

Special offers that constitute a savings over a regular membership or normal program fee

Speeches to civic organizations

Participation in community activities

Billboards

Word-of-mouth from members and participants

Regular reports to newspapers and radio stations about programs and starting dates (an effective form of free advertising)

Marketing Strategy

To be successful, it is necessary to have a good marketing strategy. This is part of the public relations plan that every organization must have. The strategy must have the support of everyone in the organization, from the board of directors and chief executive officer to those who carry out the plan. Of course, it is important to have one person responsible for coordinating the public relations efforts.

The first step is to research the needs of the community and make sure there is a market for the product or service. Structure your service to be compatible with the market. Advertising should target the populations that will be most receptive to what your organization has to offer. Sell the community on the value of your service and much free advertising will follow. By arranging special events, having special promotions, including community leaders on your board, and giving awards to people in the community, an organization can quickly gain acceptance by the community.

A good marketing strategy includes the establishment of a fair and reasonable cost for program offerings. The surroundings must be attractive and appeal to the clientele that has been targeted. The facility should provide for ease of access and have plenty of safe parking in close proximity.

The most important marketing strategy of all is a good staff and a good program. A good program will sell itself. Finally, even an outstanding program will not be a leader forever if it stays the same. Be innovative, make changes, and stay ahead of the competition.

Class Activities

Simulation 1

Situation   There seems to be a growing desire in the community to reduce the amount of physical education provided for the students at all grade levels. The director of physical education has formed a committee of physical education teachers to consider this issue.

Form the class into committees. Each committee will design a comprehensive public relations program to gain community support for physical education.

Simulation 2

Situation   A privately owned racquetball and tennis club will open in six months.

As the public relations officer for the club, develop a promotional program to sell season memberships.

Performance Tasks

1. Distinguish the basic differences between publicity and public relations by giving an example of each.
2. Compare the public relations effort in the school you attended with the public relations approach of a major corporation in your community.
3. Find five examples of promotional techniques that have been used to publicize some aspect of physical education. Evaluate each technique.
4. Clip out and analyze all articles about athletics, physical education, and other aspects of elementary and secondary schools for seven consecutive days from one newspaper. Summarize your findings.
5. Write an article about a fictional coach who creates a negative image for athletics and the school.
6. Select examples of public relations efforts by AAHPERD and state professional organizations. Evaluate their effectiveness.
7. Examine three business advertisements and rephrase them to promote physical education, health education, sport, or leisure programs.
8. Write a letter for a physical education department to send to the parents of students in the program.
9. Make a bulletin board (or poster) promoting some aspect of your future career.
10. Find pictures or make a drawing that depicts five different public relations techniques that can be used to sell the value of physical activity.

References

Aldrich, Kenneth R., "Balance, Not Dominance—The Three Rs Are Not Enough." *Journal of Physical Education, Recreation and Dance,* March 1994, 65:57–60.

Dwyer, Thomas, *Simply Public Relations: Public Relations Made Challenging, Complete and Concise.* Stillwater, OK: New Forums Press, 1992.

Giles-Brown, Elizabeth, "Teach Administrators Why Physical Education Is Important." *Strategies,* June 1993, 6:23–25.

Helitzer, Melvin, *Sports Publicity, Promotion and Public Relations: The Dream Job.* Athens, GA: University Sports Press, 1992.

Mogel, Leonard, *Making It in Public Relations.* New York: Macmillan, 1993.

National Association for Sport and Physical Education, *Sport and Physical Education Advocacy Kit (SPEAK).* Reston, VA: AAHPERD, 1994.

Ritson, Robert, "Reform in Education: Becoming Political Advocates." *Journal of Physical Education, Recreation and Dance,* January 1994, 65:4.

Rubarth, Lisa, "Twenty Years After Title IX: Women in Sports Media." *Journal of Physical Education, Recreation and Dance,* March 1992, 63:53–55.

Wragg, David W., *The Public Relations Handbook.* Cambridge, MA: Blackwell Publishing, 1992.

7

Liability and Safety Considerations

Administrative Responsibility for Safety

Safety is the responsibility of every person involved in providing programs for students, athletes, and adult consumers. It doesn't matter whether the programs are provided for physical education, athletic, or leisure use, safety must have the highest priority for anyone who teaches, coaches, supervises, or provides other services in these programs. Although everyone must be knowledgeable about safety and follow strict safety standards, the ultimate responsibility for operating a safe program rests with the administrator in charge. It is mandatory that the administrator consider safety in all aspects of program administration and management.

There are two major reasons why so much emphasis is placed on safety by administrators and staff of physical education, athletic, and leisure programs. The first reason is the nature of activities included in these programs. These activities are associated with rapid movement, sudden and explosive starts and turns, physical exertion, the use of many different instruments for hitting objects, high-velocity projectiles that are thrown or caught, the freedom to improvise, falling, and body contact. The essence of these activities requires that safety procedures be followed. The second factor is the litigious society within which programs exist. Litigation has become a way of life and the chance of legal action resulting from an injury, imagined or real, is greater now than at any time in history.

Legal issues cannot be treated in a casual manner and each person entering the profession must know the most relevant and current information about safety procedures. Many injuries are reported by students who participate in physical education and athletic programs and a larger percentage of these injuries lead to litigation each year. The frequency of pupil accidents has several implications for teachers and coaches. It is imperative that they know the legal parameters within which they function. These are determined by statutory enactments at the state and federal level. Judicial decisions also establish precedents that must be followed carefully. A decision in one locality that comes through the court system may have a far-reaching impact on programs nationally.

Each administrator and staff person is individually responsible for personal acts of negligence. State laws vary considerably with regard to immunity and the legal responsibilities of school districts, colleges and universities, and private and governmental employers. With jury awards of a million dollars and more commonplace, employees must be familiar with all facets of the law as it applies to their position.

Administrators strive to develop and administer programs that focus primarily on the well-being of all participants. This desire creates a delicate balancing act between offering vigorous activities, adventure programs, and other demanding ventures and watering down programs for fear of litigation. The easy way out is to offer a bland program with minimal challenges and risks. The preferred approach, of course, is to have stimulating programs that put a premium on the development of personal skills within an environment designed for participant safety. It is the administrator's responsibility to conduct the program in a way that precludes legal action against staff members, administrators, owners, institutions, organizations, and businesses. This can be accomplished by eliminating the common basis for legal action: negligent behavior. This is a difficult assignment for the administrator, but it is the primary objective.

Once the administrator knows the legal framework within which the program functions, all staff members must be informed of their duties and responsibilities based on policies, procedures, and guidelines developed to prevent injuries due to negligent action or inaction on the part of the staff. Policies and procedures should include appropriate ways of administering, teaching, and supervising all areas of a program. This includes such things as supervision techniques, curriculum, methodology, instructional and support environment, discipline, organization, and first aid.

Tort

A tort is a wrongful act that results in an injury to the person, property, or reputation of another person and for which that person may seek compensation through legal action. The primary focus in physical education, athletics, and leisure programs is on civil action to provide restitution for a wrong that was committed to another person. These wrongs are unintentional acts that turn out to be harmful and are based on behavior that is asserted to be negligent. In other words, a tort is an activity or behavior that strays from what would be considered normal conduct. The administrator needs to understand the principles of negligence and the defenses against negligence and know how to provide programs that will not be jeopardized by negligent actions.

Negligence

Negligence is the failure to act in a manner that would be expected of a reasonably prudent person in a similar situation or under comparable circumstances. It is an unintentional act and is not premeditated, but the action (commission) or lack of action (omission) results in an injury or harm to another person. Negligence is said to occur when a person does not act as a reasonably prudent and careful person would act. Negligence refers to civil, not criminal, actions and is the basis for civil lawsuits when an injury or loss results.

The theory of negligence was established on the principle that those who are harmed as the result of others' carelessness or failure to carry out responsibilities properly must be compensated. The harm must result from a wrong or fault that violates the standard of conduct expected of a member of a civilized society.

In a free society, anyone can be sued and people in the fields of physical education, athletics, and leisure studies are vulnerable to litigation due to the nature of their activities and the number of injuries that occur in these fields. It is up to the courts to determine whether negligence occurred. For this reason, administrators place a heavy emphasis on safety and liability and staff members must be safety-conscious and carry out their responsibilities in a manner that meets the standards of the profession. A teacher's career may be ended, a health club bankrupted, or an athletic program devastated by a negligent act.

Of course, the most important concern is for the well-being of the participants. A negligent action can result in an injury that will seriously affect a person's health and future life. Concern about negligence is a major issue for instructors and administrators. It is imperative that they understand what constitutes negligence and perform their duties in a way that meets the standards expected of professionals performing their duties.

"Negligence depends upon the existence of four essential elements. To recover damages in court actions for negligence, all four elements must be present. They include:

1. A duty or obligation, recognized by law, requiring a person to conform to a certain standard of conduct for the protection of others against unreasonable risk.
2. A failure on a person's part to conform to the required standard of conduct; a breach of duty.
3. A reasonably close causal connection between the conduct and the resulting injury; proximate or legal cause.
4. Actual loss or damage; a legally recognizable injury." (Hart and Ritson, 1993, p. 2)

All four of these elements of negligence must be present in order for a plaintiff to recover damages.

Duty

It must be shown that the individual (defendant) had a duty to the person (plaintiff) who was injured. In a teaching or coaching situation, the teacher or coach has responsibility for the safety and well-being of the people in the class or on the team. Duty is seldom an issue when the injured party is a member of the class or team. The person in charge of supervising a health club, instructing a community dance group, or providing commercial facilities for tennis players has a similar duty to provide a safe environment for these participants.

Breach of Duty

The defendant must be shown to have used unreasonable conduct in carrying out responsibility to the injured person. The standard of care provided must be that which could be expected of a professional person in a similar situation. The defendant's conduct will be compared with the actions that would be expected of a reasonably prudent person. The actions of the defendant and the situation under which these actions are carried out are both evaluated in determining whether he or she acted appropriately. The "ordinary care" clause is interpreted differently according to factors such as skill and age of participants, the nature of the activity, and the surroundings. What may be deemed ordinary care in one case may under different surroundings and circumstances be considered negligence.

Foreseeability is also an important consideration in evaluating breach of duty. The question asked is whether there should have been reasonable anticipation that harm or injury would be likely to result from the acts or omissions. The teacher or coach is measured against the standards exhibited by proficient teachers and coaches in similar situations. It must be shown that the person should have anticipated that an accident or injury was likely to occur in that situation.

Causal Connection

It must be shown that the breach of duty actually caused the injury. It does not matter what kind of negligent action might have been taken if this action did not result in the injury. There must be a direct relationship between the action or inaction of the defendant and the injury that occurred. In determining causal connection, it is not whether the defendant's conduct in whole or in part was lawful, unlawful, intentional, unintentional, negligent, or nonnegligent. Causal connection is a neutral issue, blind to right and wrong. The only pertinent factor is whether the act or failure to act on the part of the defendant resulted in the injury.

The causal connection is often called proximate cause. This means that there is an unbroken chain between the cause and the injury. This unbroken chain must be present in order for a defendant to be found liable.

Damage Issue

It must be shown that an actual loss, harm, or injury did occur. It is not enough to show that a duty existed and that this duty was breached. If an injury or other damage did not actually result from the actions of the defendant, there is no case.

Defenses Against Negligence

Common defenses used to counteract actions of negligence include elements of negligence not proven, assumption of risk, contributory negligence, last clear chance, comparative negligence, governmental immunity, act of God, and certain technical legal aspects.

Elements of Negligence Not Proven

This is the best defense. If it can be shown that the defendant did not have a duty to the plaintiff or that this duty was carried out as would be expected of a prudent and reasonable professional person functioning in the same role, or that the act was not the proximate cause of the injury, or that, in fact, an injury did not happen, the defendant cannot be found negligent. As has been stated, all four of these elements must be present.

Assumption of Risk

The assumption of risk defense is based on the legal theory of *volenti non fit injuria*—no harm is done to one who consents. It is founded on the knowledge of the injured, either actual or inferred from other acts or conditions, of the risks involved and on the individual's consent to take a chance that injury may occur. It is assumed that the plaintiff is aware of the danger in a given situation and willingly accepts this risk.

Various types of risks are inherent in certain activities and people engaging in these activities are expected to have a thorough knowledge and understanding of these risks. The participant is then said to have assumed these risks by engaging in the activity. The voluntary assumption of risk—either express or implied—must be adjusted in consideration of age and capacity of the individual to cope with the risks involved. When an *in loco parentis* relationship exists, an adult must not allow a child to become involved in unreasonable or considerable risk.

Assumption of risk applies only to the normal hazards of the activity and may not include defective equipment, dangerous areas, or acts of negligent conduct.

A number of states have eliminated this doctrine as a separate doctrine, and it is commonly used as a factor in comparative negligence rather than as a separate entity. The strict requirement that a person must be completely aware of any risk that is involved has resulted in many changes in athletic, physical education, and leisure programs. The dangers involved in using certain pieces of equipment must be clearly marked for all users of the equipment to read. Most interscholastic and intercollegiate athletic programs provide participants with comprehensive statements detailing the possible injuries, up to and including death, that can result from participation in specific sports. Students sign these statements to indicate that they are aware of the risks. It is common practice in physical education and leisure programs to use a variety of communication techniques to be sure that participants are aware of possible dangers in risk activities and to put the responsibility on them to knowingly accept the risk.

Contributory Negligence

In a state that accepts contributory negligence as a defense, any negligence on the part of the plaintiff bars this person from recovering any damages. Contributory negligence refers to situations in which the plaintiff in some way contributes to his or her own harm. The defendant attempts to show that the plaintiff was negligent and thereby contributed to the injury. Although the defendant's conduct might have been the substantial cause of the injury, no damages may be collected. It should be pointed out that contributory negligence on the part of children is difficult to establish. Courts have held that small children cannot be expected to act as adults would.

Fewer and fewer states still recognize contributory negligence as a defense. Hart and Ritson state that "the majority of jurisdictions have slowly moved away from this concept and have offset the drastic consequences of contributory negligence by developing and implementing the concept of last clear chance and comparative negligence" (Hart and Ritson, 1993, p. 16).

Last Clear Chance

As stated by Hart and Ritson, last clear chance is a modification of the harsh rule of contributory negligence. "It allows a plaintiff who is guilty of contributory negligence to recover damages if it is shown that the defendant had the last clear opportunity to avoid the harm or injury" (Hart and Ritson, 1993, p. 16).

Comparative Negligence

Most jurisdictions have moved away from contributory negligence to comparative negligence. An assessment is made of the varying degrees of negligence on the part of the defendant and the plaintiff and a settlement is apportioned accordingly. For example, if the settlement is for $100,000 and the jury finds that the negligence of the defendant was 75 percent of the fault and the negligence of the plaintiff was 25 percent of the fault, the plaintiff would receive $75,000.

Some states have modified their approach to comparative negligence and allow recovery only if the negligence of the plaintiff was minor when compared with that of the defendant. Others apportion the amount according to fault as long as the plaintiff isn't more than 50% at fault. If plaintiffs are more than 50 percent at fault, they receive nothing.

Governmental Immunity

The doctrine of governmental immunity is often referred to as the doctrine of sovereign immunity or the doctrine of nonliability. Technically, sovereign immunity is the immunity of the state; governmental immunity encompasses subdivisions of the state such as municipalities. Simply stated, it prevents legal action for damages against the government and its political subdivisions. Public educational institutions have long been considered to fall under the blanket of governmental immunity.

There has been a steady movement away from governmental immunity in many states. Hart and Ritson state:

> The legislative and judicial trend among the states has been away from immunity as witnessed by the number of states which have abrogated the doctrine either totally or in part. A review of state statutes and case law indicates the overwhelming majority of states have either judicially or statutorily abolished or limited both sovereign and governmental immunity through enactment of tort claims acts and by authorization to procure liability insurance.
>
> *Hart and Ritson, 1993, p. 12*

Even if a jurisdiction retains governmental immunity, a distinction is made between governmental and proprietary (operated for profit) functions; activities that are proprietary can be held liable for negligence. It is not as easy as it might appear to distinguish between proprietary and governmental functions with regard to educational institutions. The courts in some instances have held that regardless of the nature of the activity, public educational entities, because of their governmental nature, are powerless to enter into a proprietary function. Other courts have held that they are liable when conducting proprietary functions. Generally, however, most courts have held that the activities and functions of school districts do not automatically become proprietary, with the resulting loss of immunity, simply because the activity yields some revenue or profit.

Charging admission to athletic contests, leasing school facilities, selling student projects, and certain fundraising activities are functions that could be considered either governmental or proprietary. Courts do not draw a consistent line between governmental and proprietary functions.

Governmental immunity is also restricted in some jurisdictions according to the type of duties employees perform; there may also be statutory exceptions to immunity. It is important that administrators be thoroughly aware of the status of governmental immunity and other defenses against negligence in the jurisdiction in which they operate.

Act of God

An act of God is an unforeseen happening that is beyond the control of the responsible person. An example would be a sudden bolt of lightning that struck without any indication that a storm was approaching. This defense is being used much less frequently and more emphasis is placed on the prudent actions taken by the person in charge to anticipate happenings that can be considered acts of God.

Save-Harmless Legislation

When states, by either legislative or judicial process, partially or totally abrogate governmental immunity, there is usually an accompanying statue or provision that deals with the vulnerability of the individual employee. Collectively, these enactments and statutory provisions are called save-harmless legislation. Although worded in different ways, the intent of save-harmless legislation is to provide financial protection for employees of governmental agencies who are charged with negligence in the discharge of duties within the scope of their employment.

Save-harmless legislation requires districts to defend and pay any judgments executed against employees. This legislation covers only acts performed within the scope of their employment and usually it does not cover such things as gross negligence and deliberate and malicious conduct.

It is important that personnel in private enterprises have liability insurance. Usually the owner or the board of directors buys liability insurance under an umbrella policy to cover employees. The administrator should make this coverage a high priority and be certain employees are fully covered. People working with nonprofit organizations and public recreation groups should know what coverage they have before they begin working and if the coverage is insufficient, purchase personal liability insurance.

Educators should be aware of the status of governmental immunity, save-harmless legislation, and liability insurance provisions in the states in which they work. In some of the states where governmental immunity is still recognized, liability insurance is not necessary. School districts may not even be allowed to purchase liability insurance because immunity from being sued exists in the state. This situation is more of an exception than a practice as increasing numbers of states have abrogated or at least modified the doctrine of governmental immunity.

It is generally held that a statute authorizing the purchase of liability insurance does not waive governmental immunity that still exists in the state, at least not beyond the limits of the policy coverage. Because personal liability for negligence always exists even in the presence of school district coverage, individual teachers, coaches, and administrators should thoroughly investigate the liability coverage they have and purchase personal liability insurance if it is needed. Many private carriers handle this kind of insurance and the insurance programs provided by professional organizations usually provide coverage tailored for people in the professions at a reasonable rate.

Risk Management

Legal liability is an important issue for administrators in physical education, health education, athletics, and the leisure fields. Administrators and their faculty, coaches, and staff members must be knowledgeable about all facets of liability. This includes understanding what constitutes negligence and comprehending the impact of negligent actions on programs, participants, and those who deliver the services. However, the administrator has a much more complex responsibility in managing legal liability issues. Knowledge and understanding are important, but the administrator must ensure that the best possible safety procedures are incorporated into the instruction, supervision, and operation of the programs. This means that the administrator must have a comprehensive risk management program in place.

An administrator's first step in developing a risk management program is to identify the risks present in the program. The next step is to estimate the extent of the risks, taking into consideration both the severity or seriousness of injuries that may happen and the frequency or likelihood that an injury will occur. The third step in a risk management program is to assess the approaches that can be taken to reduce risk. The final step is to implement risk reduction procedures and policies. These steps are taken to make programs safe and still provide quality programs that will not be burdened with liability claims and financial judgments.

Staff members as well as administrators should be familiar with the areas where negligence is most likely to occur in physical education, athletic, and leisure programs. Staff members, managers, and administrators should work together to develop a risk management program that places a high priority on prevention techniques. Important features of risk management programs are included in this section of the chapter.

Supervision

Supervisory deficiencies produce large numbers of legal actions for negligence in athletics, physical education, and leisure programs. A cardinal principle of supervision requires that active supervision be exercised over the group or area of responsibility and that supervisors never absent themselves when they are supervising. It is also important that the entire group of participants be able to be supervised from a single vantage point. Proper supervision also implies a duty to protect those who are being supervised from negligently injuring themselves by engaging in activities for which they are not properly suited or that might be inherently dangerous.

Proper supervision requires that both general and specific supervision be present. General supervision is a broad overview of the class, team, or activity area. All participants should be in view and the supervisor should make sure that they are participating in appropriate activities. During general supervision, the instructor should observe to make certain that activities are proper and that participants are following safety guidelines and procedures that are in effect for the location or type of activity. General supervision also includes enforcing rules and regulations, stopping inappropriate actions, and seeing that a safe environment is present. Specific supervision entails working with one or a few participants at a time. The supervisor may be helping a person learn a new or more difficult skill, be giving feedback, or be enforcing a rule that a student or a group of students has failed to follow. Specific supervision requires more hands-on activity on the part of the supervisor and focuses on subdivisions of the total group. It must be remembered that responsibility for general supervision does not cease when giving specific supervision. An important skill for a coach or instructor is the ability to provide assistance for one athlete or student and still know what all the other members of the group are doing.

Appropriate supervision requires the following:

The supervisor must *always* be present. A supervisor can never step out of the supervisory area for even a few minutes.

The supervisor must be actively involved in supervision. Simply being present is not enough. Doing paperwork, reading a newspaper, or talking to a visitor does not constitute supervision even if in close proximity to students or others being supervised. Supervision includes monitoring the activities of all participants, enforcing rules, and seeing that a safe environment is maintained.

The supervisor must always be with students who are doing difficult skills or trying a skill for the first time but, at the same time, the supervisor must keep all students in view.

The supervisor must know the capabilities of the participants and keep records that chronicle skill levels and health problems. A physician's statement authorizing the return to activity after a participant has been out with a serious illness or injury must be required.

The supervisor must emphasize safety regulations and procedures on a regular basis.

The supervisor must inform participants of safety procedures through posted signs and course syllabi.

The supervisor must eliminate potential dangers as part of the planning process.

The supervisor must develop competencies that are needed to supervise different activities properly.

The supervisor must be qualified to supervise. It is important to know who is permitted to have a supervising function in a school situation. Do the school district or state regulations permit teacher aides or student teachers to serve in the role? Are certifications such as CPR required?

The supervisor must know the emergency procedures to be followed in case an accident occurs.

The supervisor must be certified to give first aid.

Instruction

There are many expectations of a person who is instructing others. The courts have held that there is a certain level of performance that can be expected of a teacher. The instruction must be proper and complete and appropriate teaching methodology must be used. Any risk to the participants must be minimized. It is expected that an educational program will meet high educational standards and be conducted in a safe manner.

Instructional guidelines include the following:

The selection of activities for a program must be appropriate for the age and skill levels of the participants. An evaluation of existing activity offerings should be made regularly to make certain the courses are satisfactory.

The curriculum must be approved by the Board of Education at the secondary level and the appropriate governing body at the college and university level. Teachers should teach only approved activities that are in the curriculum. There should be a good selection of activities.

Teaching procedures should be consistent with procedures that are commonly accepted by the profession.

Teaching progressions are followed in all situations. It must be shown that students have the background and experience necessary to participate at the level at which they are being taught.

Students should be grouped by age, size, experience, strength, and physical capacity when this is needed in order to safely participate in an activity. Teachers are expected to be aware of individual differences and teach accordingly.

Teachers should know the health status and physical capabilities of the students.

Lesson plans should be detailed and careful records kept to document the student's physical education experience.

Provide all necessary protective equipment and implement measures to ensure that safe procedures are followed.

Never force a student to perform a skill.

Classes should be organized suitably and correct teaching procedures should be used.

The teaching methodology must be consistent with accepted professional standards. Instructions should be appropriate and sufficiently detailed so the students understand them.

Provide safety instructions on a regular basis. Include warnings about safety risks that are involved.

Employ only qualified teachers. Penetrating questions will be asked in court about the qualifications of the teacher. Certification, experience, and qualifications to teach the activity where the injury occurred will be investigated.

Teachers must attend workshops, participate in in-service programs, read professional literature, and generally make certain they maintain their teaching skills at a high level and follow accepted teaching methodology.

Grounds, Facilities, and Equipment

Physical education, athletic, and leisure programs have expanded rapidly. Students and participants in leisure programs have an inherent right to expect that these programs will be conducted in safe environments with properly designed and maintained equipment. To depart from the standard of care that is expected of a reasonable and prudent person in ensuring safe environments and proper equipment is to invite injury and litigation. No one is expected to assume the risk of unsafe equipment, insecure locker rooms, or fields and courts that have not been periodically inspected.

Equipment has come under close scrutiny by the courts. Equipment must be safe for the age and skill level of the person who uses it and it must be designed with safety in mind. It is important that only safe equipment be purchased and used. Administrators, coaches, teachers, and others involved in programs using equipment are expected to have expertise in selecting safe equipment and knowing how to use it suitably. The same principle applies to the use of facilities.

There are a number of factors that are important to keep in mind when including grounds, facilities, and equipment in a risk management plan.

Equipment, grounds, and facilities should be checked on a regular basis. This is a joint responsibility of the administrator and all those who are using them.

Equipment should be appropriate for the activity for which it is being used.

Safety equipment should be provided for all activities that require such equipment. For example, eye guards are needed for racquetball. Equipment must be not only provided but used!

Facilities must be used in a safe manner. A safe facility can be turned into an unsafe environment because of the way a game is designed, courts are laid out, or traffic through the area is routed.

Facilities, grounds, and equipment must all be maintained in good condition.

Grounds should be inspected daily for holes, uneven areas, and debris. Any dangerous material found on the grounds should be removed immediately.

Unsafe grounds should not be used, even if an activity has to be canceled, until they are safe.

Equipment and facility areas should be secured when not in use. Even if students are not supposed to be in a certain area or use equipment, they are attracted to do so by the nature of the equipment and the facility setting. Using unauthorized equipment or participating in an unsupervised activity can have serious consequences if someone is injured.

Protective equipment must fit properly and meet established safety standards. Good examples are football helmets and lacrosse helmets that must meet the standards of the National Operating Committee on Standards for Athletic Equipment (NOCSAE; see Chapter 10).

Warning notices relating to equipment, facilities, and their use must be prominently displayed.

Purchase high-quality equipment and do not use equipment that is worn or broken unless it has been repaired.

Have facilities thoroughly checked on a regular basis. Professional companies are available for this purpose. Keep all inspection records on file.

Teach students to check the equipment they are using and have them check the equipment each time they use it.

Buy from reputable companies that supply products that meet safety specifications.

First Aid and Medical Assistance

Coaches, recreation specialists, physical educators, and others who are involved with activity programs should have had courses that prepare them to understand the injuries that occur in their sports or program activities. They should also be prepared to provide first aid when injuries occur. They must never attempt to diagnose or treat an injury.

It is important to have a written plan for handling medical problems that occur in athletics, physical education, or leisure programs. Coaches and teachers should know emergency procedures that are to be followed and apply immediate first aid when circumstances warrant. They must be certified in first aid and CPR. First-aid equipment must be readily available for each teaching station and for all athletic practices and contests. Head, neck, and back injuries should all be considered serious and approved first-aid procedures must be followed. Emergency telephone numbers should be posted near telephones for immediate access in case of an emergency.

Every school should employ athletic trainers for athletic programs. This policy will result in the best possible care for injured participants and the athletic trainer will be able to develop and coordinate comprehensive injury prevention programs. Having a certified trainer is a valuable aid in preventing allegations of inadequate or improper care following an athletic injury. (See Chapter 17 for detailed information about athletic trainers.)

Consent forms for emergency care are recommended for all students and should be kept on file at the school. It is particularly important for athletes; it might be advisable to have a copy of this form accompany the team during contests away from home. These forms authorize school personnel to seek emergency medical treatment for a student in the absence of her or his parents. Due to malpractice litigation, physicians may refuse or substantially delay treatment if they do not have this type of authorization. See Figure 7-1.

When an injury occurs, an accident report form should be completed and kept on file. It is important that this form include only facts and not include opinions about what caused the injury or what steps could have been taken to prevent the accident from occurring. The accident report form will be used in court if a lawsuit is filed and the case goes to trial. These reports are valuable for the implementation and administration of a safety program in the school as well as providing important information in the event of a lawsuit. In light of substantial delays that often occur between the time of an accident and subsequent legal action, accident report forms should be filed while the event is fresh in the minds of all involved, including witnesses. See Figure 7-2.

CONSENT FOR EMERGENCY CARE

STUDENT: _____

Be it known that I, the undersigned parent or guardian of the student above-named, do hereby give and grant to any medical doctor or hospital my consent and authorization to render such aid, treatment, or care to said student as, in the judgment of said doctor or hospital, may be required, on an emergency basis, in the event said student should be injured or become ill while participating in an interscholastic activity sponsored or sanctioned by the   (state high school athletic association), of which   (name of high school)   is a member.

It is hereby understood that the consent and authorization hereby given and granted are continuing and are intended by me to extend throughout the current school year.

    Dated this _____ day of _____ , 19____ ,

    at _____(city)_____ , _____(state)_____ .

WITNESS:_____   _____

                                                     (Parent or Guardian)

FIGURE 7-1. Consent for Emergency Care

Transportation of Students

Only school transportation should be used to transport students. The use of private cars is a hazardous undertaking and should be avoided. If teachers or coaches drive a school bus or van, they must meet the school requirements to perform this function and they should follow all safety procedures with the vehicle. The vehicle should be checked thoroughly before beginning a trip and a code of student conduct when riding in a school vehicle should be enforced at all times.

If a person is required to use a personal vehicle, the vehicle must have sufficient insurance and the insurance must cover both the employee and students when the vehicle is used for this purpose. It is especially important that the car be in top running order and all safety features be checked before it is used for this purpose. Under no circumstances should another person be allowed to drive the car of the teacher or coach. Also, students and other volunteers should not be permitted to drive vehicles transporting students for school-sponsored activities in secondary schools. Colleges and universities often have students drive athletic vans. Students should be approved to do this and be given specific training. Student drivers should be used only after establishing an institutional policy covering this practice. It is important that insurance coverage remain in effect when vehicles are driven by students and other legal ramifications should be investigated before a decision is made to let college students drive school vehicles.

Part A. Information on ALL Accidents

1. Name: _____ Home Address: _____

2. School: _____ Sex: M □ F □: Age: _____ Grade or Classification: ___

3. Time accident occurred: Hour _____ A.M.: _____ P.M. Date: _____

4. Place of Accident: School Building □ School Grounds □ To or from School □ Home □ Elsewhere □

			DESCRIPTION OF THE ACCIDENT
5. NATURE OF INJURY	Abrasion _____ Amputation _____ Asphyxiation _____ Bite _____ Bruise _____ Burn _____ Concussion _____ Cut _____ Dislocation _____ Other (specify) _____	Fracture _____ Laceration _____ Poisoning _____ Puncture _____ Scalds _____ Scratches _____ Shock _____ Sprain _____	How did accident happen? What was student doing? Where was student? Specify any tool, machine or equipment involved. _____ _____ _____ _____ _____ _____ _____ _____ _____ _____
PART OF BODY INJURED	Abdomen _____ Ankle _____ Arm _____ Back _____ Chest _____ Ear _____ Elbow _____ Eye _____ Face _____ Finger _____ Other (specify) _____	Foot _____ Hand _____ Head _____ Knee _____ Leg _____ Mouth _____ Nose _____ Scalp _____ Tooth _____ Wrist _____	_____ _____ _____ _____ _____ _____ _____ _____ _____ _____ _____

6. Degree of Injury: Death □ Permanent Impairment □ Temporary Disability □ Nondisabling □

7. Total number of days lost from school: _____ (To be filled in when student returns to school)

Part B. Additional Information on School Jurisdiction Accidents

8. Teacher in charge when accident occurred (Enter name): _____

Present at scene of accident: No: _____ Yes: _____

9. IMMEDIATE ACTION TAKEN

First-aid Treatment _____ By (Name): _____

Sent to School Nurse _____ By (Name): _____

Sent Home _____ By (Name): _____

Sent to Physician _____ By (Name): _____

Physician's Name: _____

Sent to Hospital _____ By (Name): _____

Name of Hospital: _____

10. Was a parent or other individual notified? No: ___ Yes: ___ When: _____ How: _____

Name of individual notified: _____

By whom? (Enter name): _____

11. Witnesses: 1. Name: _____ Address: _____

2. Name: _____ Address: _____

12. LOCATION	Specify Activity	Specify Activity	Remarks
	Athletic field _____ Auditorium _____ Cafeteria _____ Classroom _____ Corridor _____ Dressing room _____ Gymnasium _____ Home Econ. _____ Laboratories _____	Locker _____ Pool _____ Sch. Grounds _____ _____ Shop _____ Showers _____ Stairs _____ Toilets and Washrooms _____ Other (specify) _____	_____ _____ _____ _____ _____ _____ _____ _____ _____

Signed: Principal: _____ Teacher: _____

FIGURE 7-2. Standard Student Accident Report Form (*Source:* National Safety Council)

Permission Forms, Waivers, and Releases

Permission Forms

These forms are used primarily as a mechanism to inform parents or guardians about an activity that will take place and to request permission for their child to participate. These forms are a good device to keep parents and guardians aware of activities in which their children can be involved, but they do not absolve the school of any legal liability. It is a good policy to require permission forms to be completed, as they serve to gain the support of parents for activities and, most importantly, if a problem does develop it is easy to verify that the parents were knowledgeable about the activity in which their child was participating.

Waivers and Releases

Participants in athletics and other programs are often requested to sign waiver or release forms, which the school or organization uses in hopes that these forms will give protection against the chance of litigation. These forms are considered a type of contract in which people waive their right to sue responsible employees, the school district, or the organization sponsoring the activity. It should be recognized that a parent or guardian cannot sign away the right of a minor and minors may not legally enter into a contract. So even though a parent or other adult may sign away their right to sue, a minor still has the right to sue even though a waiver or release form was signed.

Waiver or release forms should be written by legal counsel for proper language and structure. It is important to spell out in detail the dangers of the activity and to provide warnings about the risks involved in participating in the activity. The responsibilities of the participant should also be stated, together with an explanation of the risks they assume.

Waiver or release forms do have value, but they do not absolve an administrator, teacher, or coach of responsibility to the participant once such a document is signed. It is a good administrative policy to have waivers signed. They can be used effectively in defending against a lawsuit, as they show that the participant was aware of the dangers that were involved and entered into the activity with this knowledge. Properly written waivers are valuable in showing that the person who signed the waiver was properly warned and knowingly assumed risk when participating in the activity. They inform parents and participants and provide a record of parental permission for the minor to participate. A signed waiver form is also a way of indicating that safety is a responsibility that is shared with the participant.

Figure 7-3 is a sample release form that incorporates warning information, assumption of risk, agreement to hold harmless, and the agreement on the part of the participant to obey instructions.

Class Activities

Simulation 1

Situation A student sustained a broken finger when hit by a soccer ball during a physical education class. The parents of the student are suing the teacher, the principal, and the board of education.

SAMPLE RELEASE FORM

(Both the applicant student and parent or guardian must read carefully and sign.)
SPORT (Check applicable spaces):

☐ Football ☐ Basketball ☐ Track
☐ Volleyball ☐ Wrestling ☐ Baseball
☐ Cross-Country ☐ Gymnastics ☐ Softball
☐ Soccer ☐ Swimming ☐ Tennis
☐ Golf

STUDENT

I am aware that playing or practicing to play/participate in any sport can be a dangerous activity involving MANY RISKS OF INJURY. I understand that the dangers and risks of playing or practicing to play/participate in the above-checked sport(s) include, but are not limited to, death, serious neck and spinal injuries that may result in complete or partial paralysis, brain damage, serious injury to virtually all internal organs, serious injury to virtually all bones, joints, ligaments, muscles, tendons, and other aspects of the skeletal system, and serious injury or impairment to other aspects of my body, general health, and well-being. I understand that the dangers of playing or practicing to play/participate in the above-checked sport(s) may result not only in serious injury, but in serious impairment of my future abilities to earn a living, to engage in other business, social and recreational activities, and generally to enjoy life.

Because of the dangers of participating in the above-checked sports(s), I recognize the importance of following coaches' instructions regarding playing techniques, training, other team rules, etc., and agree to obey such instructions.

In consideration of _____ High School permitting me to try out for the above checked sport(s) and to engage in all activities related to the team(s), including but not limited to trying out, practicing, or playing/ participating in that sport(s), I hereby assume all the risks associated with participation and agree to hold _____ _____ High School of _____ School District, (city, state), collectively and individually, its employees, agents, representatives, medical personnel, coaches, and volunteers, including managers and trainers, harmless from any and all liability, actions, causes of actions, debts, claims, or demands of any kind and nature whatsoever that may arise by or in connection with my participation in any activities related to the _____ High School athletic team(s) checked above. The terms hereof shall serve as a release and assumption of risk for my heirs, estate, executor, administrator, assignees, and for all members of my family.

I specifically acknowledge that FOOTBALL, WRESTLING, GYMNASTICS, and BASEBALL are VIOLENT CONTACT SPORTS involving even greater risk of injury than other sports.

Date _____ Student Signature _____

PARENT/GUARDIAN

I, _____ , am the parent/legal guardian of _____ (student). I have read the above warning and release and understand its terms. I understand that all sports can involve MANY RISKS OF INJURY, including but not limited to the risks outlined above.

In consideration of _____ High School permitting my child to try out for the above-checked sports(s) and to engage in all activities related to the team(s), including but not limited to trying out, practicing, or playing/ participating in that sport(s), I hereby agree to hold _____ High School of _____ School District (city, state), collectively and individually, its employees, agents, representatives, medical personnel, coaches, and volunteers, including managers and trainers, harmless from any and all liability, actions, causes of actions, debts, claims, or demands of any kind and nature whatsoever that may arise by or in connection with participation of my child/ward in any activities related to the _____ High School athletic team(s) checked above. The terms hereof shall serve as a release and assumption of risk for my heirs, estate, executor, administrator, assignees, and for all members of my family.

I specifically acknowledge that FOOTBALL, WRESTLING, GYMNASTICS, and BASEBALL are VIOLENT CONTACT SPORTS involving even greater risk of injury than other sports.

Date _____ Parent/Legal Guardian Signature _____

FIGURE 7-3. Sample Release Form (Reprinted with permission of the National Federation of State High School Associations)

One group of students will write a description of how the injury occurred and act as the judge and jury for a mock trial. The remainder of the class will be divided into two additional groups. One group will be composed of the plaintiff, with witnesses and attorneys. The second group will be composed of the defendant, with defense witnesses and attorneys. Each group will review the description of how the injury occurred and build their case to present in court.

A mock trial will be held, with the plaintiff charging negligence and the defendant presenting defenses against this charge.

Simulation 2

Situation The athletic director of a medium-sized high school is meeting with the school's coaches before the start of the school year. On the agenda is a discussion of liability and safety considerations for coaches.

Write and present a speech to be given by the athletic director. (If desired, general principles relating to liability can be covered by a few students and other students can develop safety guidelines for specific sports.)

Performance Tasks

1. Design a checklist to be used in a school district to determine that facilities and equipment are safe to use.
2. Investigate four negligence cases that have been brought against health clubs, physical education programs, or athletic programs. Compare types of alleged negligence in each case.
3. Examine safety guidelines found in the curriculum guides of five school districts. What similarities do you find?
4. Review three articles on liability in physical education or athletics. What key issues are covered in the articles?
5. Write a statement for a defendant's lawyer to make for a teacher who has followed all the proper supervisory procedures during an activity in which a student was injured.
6. Visit a civil courtroom and observe the procedures that are followed during a court case.
7. Develop procedural guidelines for teachers to follow to prevent negligence from occurring when teaching movement activities.

References

Adams, Sam H., "Duty to Properly Instruct." *Journal of Physical Education, Recreation and Dance,* February 1993, 64:22–23.

Anderson, Matthew A., and Gary R. Gray, "Risk Management Behaviors in NCAA Division III Athletic Programs." *Journal of Legal Aspects of Sport,* Spring 1994, 4:78–84.

Athletic Administrators Reference Manual, Kansas City, MO: National Interscholastic Athletic Administrators Association (updated annually).

"A Checklist for Accident Report Forms." *Strategies,* November/December 1993, 7:15–17.

Cohen, Andrew, "Triple Indemnity." *Athletic Business,* January 1995, 19:16–18.

Cotten, Doyice J., "Risk Management—A Tool for Reducing Exposure to Legal Liability." *Journal of Physical Education, Recreation and Dance,* February 1993, 64:58–61.

Dougherty, Neil J. (Ed.), *Principles of Safety in Physical Education and Sport*, 2nd ed. Reston, VA: AAHPERD, 1994.

Dougherty, Neil J., David Auxter, Alan S. Goldberger, and Gregg S. Heinzmann, *Sport, Physical Activity and the Law.* Champaign, IL: Human Kinetics, 1994.

Drowatzky, John N., *Legal Issues in Sport and Physical Education Management* (Monograph). Champaign, IL: Stipes Publishing, 1993.

Gilbert, Ronald R., *Aquatic Injuries: Evaluation and Strategy.* Washington, DC: Atla Press, 1990.

Gray, Gary, "Safety Tips From the Expert Witness." *Journal of Physical Education, Recreation and Dance,* January 1995, 66:18–21.

Gray, Gary R., and Scott E. Crowell, "Risk Management Behaviors in Division I Athletic Programs." *Journal of Legal Aspects of Sport,* Fall 1993, 3:64–70.

Hart, James E., and Robert J. Ritson, *Liability and Safety in Physical Education and Sport.* Reston, VA: AAHPERD, 1993.

Herbert, David, "Emergency Response for Foreseeable Injuries Is Legally Required." *Strength and Conditioning,* February 1994, 16:32–33.

Koehler, Robert, *Law: Sport Activity and Risk Management*, 3rd ed. Champaign, IL: Stipes Publishing, 1991.

Kozlowski, James C., "Standard for Sports Participation Debated: Recklessness or Negligence?" *Parks and Recreation,* October 1993, 28:22–25.

Lea, Melissa, and Edward Longhman, "Crew, Compliance, Touchdowns and Torts: The Growth of the Modern Athletics Department, Its Legal Needs and Modes for Satisfying Them." *Athletic Administration,* October 1993, 28:48–51.

Lincoln, Sharon M., "Sports Injury Risk Management and the Keys to Safety—Coalition of Americans to Protect Sports (CAPS)." *Journal of Physical Education, Recreation and Dance,* September 1992, 63:40–42.

Merriman, John, "Supervision in Sport and Physical Activity." *Journal of Physical Education, Recreation and Dance,* February 1993, 64:20–22.

Mullen, Bernard J., Stephen Hardy, and William A. Sutton, *Sport Marketing.* Champaign, IL: Human Kinetics, 1993.

Nelson, Roger, "Gender Equity and the Courts." *Scholastic Coach,* November 1993, 63:5–8.

Van der Smissen, Betty, *Legal Liability and Risk Management for Public and Private Entities: Sport and Physical Education, Leisure Services, Recreation and Parks, Camping and Adventure Activities* (3 Volumes). Cincinnati: Anderson Publishing Company, 1990.

Young, Kevin, "Violence, Risk, and Liability in Male Sports Culture." *Sociology of Sport Journal,* December 1993, 10:373–376.

Wong, Glenn W., and Burke Magnus, "Informed Consent." *Athletic Business,* December 1993, 17:10.

8

Facilities

The Planning Process

The administrator of physical education, athletics, leisure, and health promotion programs finds that construction, maintenance, and use of facilities is a major area of responsibility. It is an area that often doesn't receive as much emphasis as it should in educational programs, considering the impact facilities have on programs and the funding that is required to construct new facilities, maintain current facilities, and make needed renovations. The problem is exacerbated by the fact that major building programs don't occur on a regular basis, yet administrators are expected to be prepared to explain the school's facility needs on short notice and also to be knowledgeable about the latest materials, types of construction, and current trends in facility design for physical education, health education, athletics, and leisure programs.

This points out the need for a comprehensive facility master plan. This plan should be updated regularly and should be reviewed on a yearly basis to determine renovations that can be made to upgrade the facilities. These plans should identify facility needs as far into the future as possible and establish priorities for facilities. Seldom does an administrator have funding available for all renovations and new construction at one time. It is important that facilities be improved on a regular basis and as program needs change. It is short-sighted to wait until program pressure requires that major changes in facilities be made. The cost is usually greater and, too often, an institution must get along with inadequate facilities for a long time before funding can be arranged and construction completed.

It should be remembered that physical education facilities in educational institutions can be expected to have a lifetime of 50 or more years. It therefore becomes even more important that facilities be planned carefully, upgraded on a regular basis, and maintained in the best possible condition. In the leisure and health promotion fields, facilities are probably even more important because the financial success of leisure programs is highly dependent on the attractiveness and the user friendliness of the facilities. Private health clubs and fitness centers must appeal to customers and provide surroundings that will bring in new members and keep current members.

Inadequate Facilities

A number of factors have led to the construction of inadequate facilities. One of the most significant is the practice of copying a gymnasium or other facility that is in another community or to simply replicate a facility that was built 10 or 15 years earlier, mistakes and good points alike. These practices are too often used in schools because they are temporarily less troublesome than making a survey of local conditions, studying trends and innovations in building construction, and evaluating the effect of different types of construction on the physical education, intramural, and interschool programs and the educational goals of the community before beginning to build.

In some situations, those in authority are unwilling to seek and use the advice of informed staff members, and in other circumstances physical education people are unable to advise judiciously when consulted. Lack of planning is another factor that leads to inadequate facilities. When decisions are made in a hurry, it is impossible to design a facility that serves rather than limits the programs that will use the facility. Escalating construction costs are sometimes not taken into consideration; miscalculation of expenses can necessitate severe construction modifications. Too often this results in a facility that is inadequate for the use for which it was intended.

Flexibility

Flexibility is the key word in facility design. The days of having only a rectangular basketball court that also serves volleyball and badminton are gone. Special use areas must be carefully considered and worked into the overall design of the facility. It is important that the facility be built to accommodate programs that will change over the life of the building. This is one of the reasons that large open spaces are often incorporated into buildings. This space can be altered in different configurations as programs change. This type of space can be used for different activities on a given day.

The need for flexibility has been highlighted by the change in educational philosophy from formal, structured programs to programs that encompass varied activities. This type of program requires extensive building adaptability and has made many current buildings obsolete. Future needs are also carefully considered by the leisure industry when designing and constructing facilities. For a multipurpose facility, the same flexibility principles apply. For single-purpose facilities such as tennis or fitness centers, the space is designed exclusively for that purpose. However, the wise planner still designs a building that will be adaptable should interest in tennis increase or decline or different types of fitness activities be desired by the public. Future expansion or modifications of service areas should also be incorporated into a building plan if it is to have a satisfactory level of flexibility.

Essentials of Good Planning

Wise and efficient planning and construction of a physical education, athletic, or leisure activity facility prevents many administrative, financial, and functional difficulties. For example, decreasing or eliminating permanent seating increases the amount of space that is available for activity or support services, well-placed activity rooms make supervision easier, areas that are open to view and attractively designed appeal to participants, reduction of unnecessary corridor space saves money, properly placed drinking fountains and lavatories make the building a more efficient service unit, properly sloped floors in locker rooms are easier to keep clean, sloping roofs shed water much better than flat ones, natural light and solar energy can provide significant savings, and cement locker bases make the cleaning of the locker room easier. Any effort spent in planning will pay large dividends in the future to those who are responsible for the facility.

It is not satisfactory to leave all matters of arrangement to the architect, who may not be a specialist in construction of this type. This is particularly true when a physical education and athletic facility is being built as part of an elementary or high school educational complex. Architects have been much maligned for physical education construction errors and inadequacies. This is usually unfair because reputable architects request information to guide them in planning the facility. The fault usually lies with the physical education, leisure, or athletic staff members who do not plan sufficiently for the facility or fail to adequately communicate their needs to the architect. Architects want to know the educational goals, the activities to be included, the number of teaching stations needed, and other pertinent information that will assist them in designing a functional building. Problems occur when sufficient guidance is not provided. This sometimes happens when the school board, board of trustees or regents, board of directors, or appointed administrative officers do not establish a construction plan that permits sufficient input from the physical education faculty or designated committee. Unfortunately, the fault sometimes lies with the physical education faculty, athletic staff, or leisure personnel, who fail to thoroughly determine needs and do not provide information in sufficient depth to guide the architect. It is erroneous to assume that architects and engineers are in a position to keep abreast of all new concepts, designs, and materials for physical education facilities. They share this responsibility with those who will use the facility.

Planning for a Building

It is the responsibility of the administrator to make sure that adequate planning is done for the new facility. Due to the magnitude of this task, all staff members should be involved.

Program needs and requirements must be projected for the life of the building. Facility maintenance requirements and costs for the future use of the building must be carefully considered during the planning phase. The building plan should include a detailed list of the various areas required—gymnasiums, special activity areas, classrooms, conference rooms, swimming pool, offices, locker and shower rooms, and storage facilities—with their dimensions and desirable features indicated. Fitness clubs and leisure centers must also specify service area needs such as reception centers and lounge accommodations. For athletics, home and visiting locker rooms, a training room, and officials' rooms for both women and men must be included.

A building (planning) committee must be in place far in advance of the beginning of construction or renovation. A minimum of one year for planning is needed; two years is recommended. This committee is usually chaired by the administrator for the unit that will use the facility. If the facility is to be used for physical education, the director of physical education will chair; if it is an athletic facility, the athletic director should chair; and if it is an addition to a fitness center, the manager of that facility should chair the committee. If construction encompasses an entire school or several different kinds of activities, these people may be members of an overall building committee, with responsibility for a subcommittee that would make recommendations for their special area. In small schools or leisure programs, all staff members may be on the building committee. If it is a large school or organization, representatives from the various programs that will use the facility should be selected for the committee. Regardless of who is on the committee, every staff member and faculty member should be given the opportunity to provide input and react to building plans as they proceed from initial concept to the final construction phase. Incorporating community involvement and gaining the support of interest groups and political bodies is another significant task of the planning committee.

The planning process is of critical importance. As a first step, the need for a new facility must be clearly established. The need must be based on such factors as philosophy, goals of the school or organization, interests of students or other users of the facility, community use, and future projections. For public buildings, the community must be involved in the planning and the facility that is being planned must be integrated carefully into the school, organization, or campus master plan. Funding is another important facet of the planning process. The amount of money available is an important consideration in the planning process. Sources of funding differ. It might be from a bond issue, fundraising, or from investment sources, depending on whether it is a public or private facility. The building must fit within the available funding range. In some situations, facility needs are determined first and then funding sources are investigated to provide the resources that are needed. Funding is an important part of each step of the planning process. Typically, adjustments must be made in the construction plans, based on the available finances.

It is important that the administrator and all members of the building committee be familiar with current literature relating to the specific facility being planned and be thoroughly knowledgeable about trends and important features that must be included in such facilities. Facility innovations occur at a rapid pace and it is important that the latest information be obtained from sources throughout the building industry. Members of the committee should visit exemplary facilities, preferably accompanied by the architect, with the aim of getting ideas for the best facility for the available funds. It is also a common practice to employ a consultant to assist and guide the committee during the planning process. On large projects, a consultant is sometimes used as a liaison between the committee and the architect. A well-informed and well-prepared committee is instrumental in getting the best possible facility.

It is important to select an architect who is experienced with constructing the type of facility being planned. There may be hiring guidelines established by the school, university, or organization for selecting an architect and, of course, these must be followed. At a minimum, the architect's professional status should be determined, examples of previously designed buildings should be inspected, areas of specialization analyzed, and references from previous clients required. It is also important to determine the architect's interest and desire to design the facility being planned. The architect should be excited about the project and be the type of person who will make the project a cooperative venture. The architect should also have a strong supporting staff. Specialized skills are needed during the various steps of the architectural process and it is important that the architectural firm have employees with diverse specialties.

Steps in Constructing a Building

Although the architect is responsible for meeting codes and regulations when designing a building, the building committee should also be aware of the requirements that will influence the type of building and its configuration. Full accommodation for people with disabilities is required under the Americans with Disabilities Act of 1990 (P.L. 101-336). Buildings must be accessible to those with disabilities; they must be able to use the facilities without artificially imposed barriers. This law also has important implications for existing buildings when renovations take place. The needs of the disabled must be considered from the standpoint of access, service areas of a building, spectator seating, and use of the facilities included in the building. Federal, state, and local regulations all must be followed when constructing a facility. Each community has building codes, with which the architect must be familiar. The health and fire departments in a community are just two examples of areas that have specific codes that are determining factors in the construction of a building.

Environmental factors also shape building plans. The site that is selected must meet environmental requirements, which are established at various governmental levels. The building, once constructed, must also meet environmental standards. Two other areas that are of prime importance for the building committee and the architect to consider are the functionality of the building and the aesthetic qualities. Too often, these two factors have been regarded as being in opposition to each other. They are both extremely important and a skilled architect, guided by the building committee, will design a building that is both aesthetically appealing and highly functional.

There are several steps in construction planning and at each step the building committee must be actively involved.

Planning Stage. This is probably the most important part of the entire building process. The committee members must give the architect extensive and detailed information about the programs that will be conducted in the facility, together with unique and special needs. Input should be provided about the type of facility that each facet of the program needs.

Schematic Design. In this phase, the architect presents a design incorporating the program needs into a facility plan. The committee should carefully review the plan to make certain it meets the established program needs and come to an agreement with the architect about the type of building or renovation to be built.

Design Development.   The architect prepares models and provides information about materials to be used in the building. The engineering systems to be used in the building are part of the information that the committee must examine at this stage. The conception of the building, together with cost estimates, is provided to guide the committee in making decisions to approve or modify.

Construction Documents.   At this time the architect prepares working drawings and specifications on which bids will be solicited. It is important that the committee has given appropriate guidance to the architect up to this point so these documents accurately reflect the needs of the school or organization and the wishes of the building committee. Adjusted cost estimates are also probable at this time as more detailed drawings are developed. The committee may find it necessary to accept changes because of cost projections at this stage as well as at the design development stage.

Construction.   The committee must work closely with the architect while the facility is under construction. Usually, the chairperson of the committee is a key person in monitoring the construction with the architect. Sometimes a consultant is hired for this purpose.

Teaching Stations

A teaching station is any room or space where a person can instruct a group of students or participants in a health promotion or leisure program. It is a space where a learning environment is established for a group of people; the definition can be expanded to include areas where a team practices or people work out under supervision. A significant amount of space is required for physical education activity programs. As a result, it is expensive to construct an adequate number of teaching stations; for this reason, many facilities are inadequate for the physical education, leisure, and athletic programs offered in some localities. Sometimes, these programs must be reduced or eliminated entirely. Thus, facilities can have a grave impact on the number and kind of programs that can be offered.

The total number of teaching stations required for a school depends on the following factors:

Number of students
Number of days per week the program is required
Number of years program is required
Class size
Nature of the program
Number of periods in the school day
The climate in the area
The requirements of the intramural and interschool programs

The number of teaching stations required in a school for the instructional program can readily be determined by the following formula:

$$\frac{N \times p}{P \times n} = \text{Teaching stations}$$

N = Total number of students enrolled at the institution
p = Number of required class meetings per week
P = Total number of periods per week that each teaching station is available
n = Number of students per class

As an example, 12 teaching stations would be needed if a high school had a student enrollment of 2,400 students, each student had physical education five days per week, the average class size was 30, and there were 35 periods per week when each teaching station was available.

$$\frac{N \times p}{P \times n} = \frac{2,400 \times 5}{35 \times 30} = \frac{12,000}{1,050} = 11.4$$

It should be remembered that this formula does not provide for future growth when current enrollment figures are used, nor does it accurately depict intramural activity or interscholastic athletic needs. The formula provides the minimum number of teaching stations that are needed. More will be needed if specialized teaching stations such as a fencing room and gymnastic areas are not used for all class periods during the week. Scheduling flexibility also necessitates more than the absolute minimum number of teaching stations. Outdoor teaching stations should not be included in the calculations unless the school is located in a geographical area where outdoor stations can be used year-round. In a majority of schools in the country, outdoor teaching stations cannot be used during the winter months. If the outdoor facilities can be used throughout the year, a smaller number of indoor teaching stations is sufficient.

Sufficient space must be provided for intramural and interscholastic programs during the peak after-school and evening hours. The scope of the program determines the number of stations needed to provide practice and game facilities for athletics and areas for intramural activities. A location is needed for each activity that will use the facility during the highest usage period.

Indoor Physical Education Facilities

The trend in the construction of indoor physical education facilities is to provide a large area that can be used for a variety of activities. Synthetic surfaces, improved acoustic engineering, new lighting features, technological advances in movable and retractable bleachers and equipment, electronically controlled apparatus, and advanced computerization of heating, ventilation, and air conditioning systems have been important factors in this trend. It has been found best to have specialized teaching stations for activities such as combatives, gymnastics, dance, adaptive programs, and fencing. The flexibility of a large central activities area makes it possible for even these types of activities to be included in a multipurpose design if this is desired. Swimming pools, bowling lanes, four-wall handball, squash, paddleball, and weight training are examples of teaching stations that must be designed as a separate entity. Flexibility and multipurpose use are key considerations in facility designs for facilities that will meet changing needs during the life of the building and provide the best return for the money.

New facilities are designed to serve varying groups and to keep equipment readily available for different classes and programs. Built-in media equipment enables instructors to use videos, music, and other audiovisual teaching aids with a minimum amount of wasted teacher or class time. Teachers and coaches can quickly configure different-sized areas by electronically moving bleachers or partitions or by using illuminated game lines.

Field House–Arena–Activity Center

These are all terms used to describe buildings characterized by a large, central, multipurpose activity area. Multiple markings on the floor, removable floors, easily moveable and retractable equipment and bleachers, versatile lighting and sound equipment, and easy access with specialized equipment make it possible to use facilities such as these for classes, intramurals, athletics, recreation, conferences, special events, and a variety of community functions. The desired size of the facility is determined by the number of classes and the kinds of activities for which it will be used.

This kind of facility has become an excellent option as new construction techniques have made it possible to encapsulate larger and larger areas. Accompanying technology has provided optimal lighting, heating, air conditioning, and ventilation in these large open areas; even more importantly, it is feasible to speedily move and store equipment according to the purpose for which the area is being used. The fact that a large area can be speedily changed into different-sized units further enhances the value of this type of construction. A large open area lends itself to changing programs and user interests over the life of the building.

The Main Gymnasium

Some facilities are designed using the main gymnasium concept. The number and kind of teaching stations needed determine the size of the gymnasium. Consideration must also be given to the number of seats needed for spectator events. This type of building does not provide the flexibility found in buildings that have large central activity areas. However, the incorporation of synthetic surfaces, folding bleachers, swing-up basketball backboards, and similar innovations permits much more flexibility and can make this type of construction satisfactory for a physical education, athletic, or leisure program.

Courts for badminton and volleyball are invariably laid out in the main gymnasium in addition to those for basketball. It is desirable to plan for sufficient courts to handle a class of appropriate size. An instructor can handle 36 students adequately on three volleyball courts. If there are only two courts for 24 students it is obvious that the instructional cost is appreciably greater.

It may be necessary to conduct fencing, dancing, wrestling, and gymnastics in the main gymnasium. However, separate areas for these activities are preferable. This is particularly true of gymnastics and wrestling, which require specialized equipment that must be moved before and after class. If separate rooms are not provided for these activities, easily accessible storage space for the equipment must be provided in the main gymnasium.

There is a difference of opinion in the profession about the need for folding partitions to divide a large area into two or more separate teaching stations. For some activities and in some teaching situations, partitions are valuable. The improvement in acoustical engineering, the use of the gymnasium for activities requiring many different dimensions, and the fact that there is no longer a "girls' side" and "boys' side" of the gymnasium have made partitions less important. Nets can be used effectively as partitions and provide desired safety by preventing loose equipment from going into other teaching stations. If folding partitions are used, they should extend from floor to ceiling and move on an overhead track. The partitions should be electrically operated with an automatic shutoff feature if anyone or anything contacts the moving partition. They should be recessed when closed and should be insulated in order to prevent sound transmission between teaching stations. The doors should be sturdy enough that balls may be thrown against them by students practicing various skills.

It was a common practice in past years to construct a combination gymnasium–cafeteria or gymnasium–auditorium in elementary schools. High schools and even some leisure facilities have attempted to use the gymnasium as both an activity area and an auditorium. This practice never works out satisfactorily, as conflicts in the use of the facility inevitable occur. Combination usage appears attractive from the standpoint of short-term economy, but over a period of years more satisfactory results are obtained from a separate gymnasium.

Auxiliary Gymnasium

A large number of high schools and colleges and universities find it necessary to construct an auxiliary gymnasium when they construct only a main gymnasium. This is a multipurpose area and can be used for a variety of activities such as fencing, dancing, calisthenics, games of low organization, tumbling, badminton, and volleyball. Such a facility is often used for intramural and recreational activities when the main gymnasium is occupied by the varsity squads.

In a recreational or commercial facility, the type of auxiliary gymnasium needed is determined by the type of programs offered and the specific interests of the members. Client demand may dictate that the gymnasium be a single-purpose facility.

Wrestling Room

This room should be a minimum of 50' × 100' to accommodate two mats of 42' × 42' plus additional matted area for practice. The floor under the mat should be resilient to extend the life of the mats and to cushion impact. The walls should be matted to a height of six to eight feet high and there should be no protrusions into the room. Proper ventilation and lighting are of prime importance, as is having the area zoned for heating purposes. The ceiling should be a minimum of 12' high and be covered with an acoustic material. The room should be brightly painted and have a space set aside outside of the matted area for a recessed drinking fountain and a place for supplies. Direct access through double doors should be provided to the area where wrestling meets will be held if bleachers are not available in the wrestling area.

Gymnastic Room

This activity probably requires more equipment than any other phase of a physical education or athletic program. It is highly desirable to have a permanent area available for gymnastics so equipment does not have to be repeatedly put up and taken down. Not only does a permanent facility save time, but the longevity of the equipment and the safety of the participants increase when equipment can be left in one position and does not have to be moved and adjusted.

Gymnastic equipment appeals to anyone who sees it. From a liability standpoint, it is important that rooms containing gymnastic equipment can be easily and effectively secured when the equipment is not being used under supervised conditions.

If possible, bleachers should be available in the gymnastic area so the equipment does not have to be moved for competition. The equipment should be placed so that it is possible to have women's and men's teams practice simultaneously and even have gymnastic meets scheduled at the same time if this is desired.

Dance Studio

It is difficult to develop a first-class dance program without a specialized dance facility. The studio should be approximately 60' × 100' for class purposes and in most high school situations it will be used for all forms of dance. At universities, it may be possible to have one area for modern and ballet and another for folk and social dance. A ceiling height of 24' should be provided if a facility is to be used for modern and ballet. The floor for all forms of dance should be resilient, nonslippery, and constructed for easy cleaning. Maple floors are good for dance activities but should never be placed directly on a concrete base; greater resilience is essential. If possible, seating, preferably in a theater-type setting, should be incorporated into the dance studio. Specialized equipment such as mirrors, ballet barres, lighting for performances, and sound equipment should be designed expressly for the dance studio.

Other Specialized Areas

Available funds and activities emphasized in a particular community often determine whether other specialized areas will be included in a facility. The administrator should use faculty and community experts, recommendations from the literature, and the standards and rules established by the governing bodies of the sports for which the specialized facility is being designed.

Storage

Storage space must be planned just as thoroughly as teaching stations because faculty effectiveness is influenced significantly by the size, location, and organization of storage areas. As a rule, it is good to plan for 20 percent more storage space than is actually needed at the time a building is constructed. A central storage area for small equipment is recommended for tight control and efficiency in issuing equipment. If possible, the design should be such that the room will accommodate one or more people to issue equipment for classes and to perform equipment repair and maintenance. Larger storage rooms should be located adjacent to teaching stations that have specialized equipment that must be stored after class or at the end of each day. Much teacher and student time is wasted when storage areas are inadequate or poorly planned.

Activity Area Locations in a Building

Accessibility for students, clients, and community members must be considered in the design of an activity facility. The facility should be an integral part of the school or fitness center design and yet be placed so it can be used without disrupting other parts of the program. Specialized areas should be available without opening the entire facility or school building.

Activity areas in colleges and universities are moving into residence halls and even academic buildings. This practice makes physical activity an integral part of a student's life and provides easily accessible activity space throughout the day and into the night. This is a good example of the relationship between facilities and programming.

The deciding factor in the location of many elementary and secondary schools is the accessibility to outdoor physical education and recreational facilities. In recent years, the trend has been for school districts and community recreation departments to work out arrangements for joint use of facilities. Such arrangements have resulted in many more physical education areas than would otherwise have been possible. Likewise, the school facilities are available for use by recreation departments during the after-school hours. These buildings are usually designed with the physical education facilities in one wing or at one end of the building. Such joint planning benefits everyone in the community. Parking space must also be considered when athletic events catering to spectators are to be scheduled in the facilities.

Room Dimensions

The size, shape, and height of rooms vary according to the purposes for which they are used; consequently, it is not possible to determine the optimum dimensions without knowing the local conditions that affect them. Too large a room is proportionately more expensive in terms of the service it can render per unit cost. A room does need to be large enough to service all activities for which it is to be used and to handle the largest number of people who will use the facility at one time. An idle, enclosed space represents an unwarranted financial burden. Then, too, more teaching stations can be provided if the enclosed space is broken into smaller units. Odd-shaped, many-sided rooms with projections are costly to construct and are limited in their uses; consequently, they should be eliminated as much as possible in planning.

Each room should have sufficiently high ceiling to accommodate the activities that are to take place in it. Any additional height is unnecessary and costly, and any reduction in desirable height cramps the activity program. The recommended standards for gymnasium ceiling heights are 20' for elementary schools (if the gymnasium is to be used by the recreation department the ceiling height should be raised to 24') and 24' for junior and senior high schools. Locker, shower, and classrooms need not be more than 10–12' high.

Traffic Control

One of the most common mistakes in gymnasium construction is the failure to make adequate provision for the circulation of the people who will use the facilities. The main objectives in planning for traffic patterns are as follows:

Providing ease of access to all parts of the building

Reducing congestion and speeding traffic flow

Keeping travel distances to a minimum

Providing ease of supervision

Making it possible to restrict travel to parts of the facility that are being used

Minimizing disturbances to other building users

Increasing safety

Reducing stress level

Providing for joining with future additions

In planning for traffic control, a flow chart should be prepared to show the movement of all the different people who will be involved with the facility. Although students will be the main users, consideration must also be given to spectators at athletic contests and intramural events, as well as to various groups of the recreation department who will use the facilities in the evenings and during the summer months. In addition, consideration must be given to personnel who deliver supplies and equipment. A similar flow chart should be used when planning traffic patterns for sport buildings, commercially operated facilities, and health promotion clubs.

Materials and Construction

The available funds and materials, the use to which the facility is to be put, the attitude of the community toward types of construction and materials, and the workforce largely determine the quality and type of material and construction used in each unit in the building. If funds are ample and the community wants to use them, there can be great freedom of choice in materials and construction. However, most communities must build economically and they consequently wish to select serviceable, reasonably priced materials and put them together in a comparatively inexpensive but substantial manner. In economizing, it is best to use materials of a good standard grade; it is false economy to use cheap materials. All materials must meet fire and health code standards. Safety is of prime importance when selecting materials and determining the type of construction that will be used. Durability, appropriateness for the designated purpose, and aesthetic qualities are other important considerations.

Indoor Surface Materials

Most physical education facilities have several types of floor surfaces. The activity areas are usually high-grade maple or a synthetic surface; the classrooms hardwood, tile, or carpet; locker rooms tile, concrete, or synthetic carpeting; the dance studio maple; and the offices carpet, hardwood, or tile. Cost is a determining factor for many schools. Many other factors should also be considered, particularly when deciding on the surface for the activity area. Initial cost must be compared with the anticipated life of the material. Maintenance, durability, acoustic quality, attractiveness, and adaptability to multiple use are also critical considerations. Material should be carefully analyzed before a decision is made.

Synthetic surfaces are being used extensively in new construction. The versatility of this type of surface makes it very appealing. It can be used for many different sports as well as for other student activities. The two most common types are polyvinyl chloride (PVC), which is usually manufactured in wide strips and applied to concrete flooring with adhesive, and polyurethanes, which can be obtained in strips or poured in place. There is a wide variance in the quality of synthetic surfaces manufactured by different companies. Before deciding on a specific product, it is imperative that the school thoroughly investigate the performance of the synthetic surface it wants to use. Will it maintain its present characteristics over a period of years? Can it be easily maintained? Does it have satisfactory resiliency and will it be safe for participants? Will the company provide the necessary service and is the company capable of backing up the guarantee?

Synthetic surfaces are an important development in physical education construction. However, high-grade maple remains an excellent floor surface for many schools. This type of flooring has stood the test of time and hard use. Maple is a dense, strong, heavy, remarkably hard, and exceptionally durable wood. It is free from slivering and splintering, extremely resilient, and polishes under friction, thus increasing its wear resistance. Because of its close grain, it is very sanitary. Standard lengths are preferable to the special long lengths. The long lengths are much more expensive, without compensating benefits.

Walls

Concerning the walls of the gymnasium, a number of factors should be considered:

It is decidedly advantageous to have the walls smooth up to 12' in order to have them serve as rebounding surfaces for balls.

No wall should constitute a hazard because of its rough or uneven surface.

The lower portion of the walls should be able to take hard usage and should be resistant to marking and scarring.

The lower walls should be finished with materials that can easily be cleaned without affecting the finish.

Light-colored walls reflect light better and provide a more cheerful atmosphere.

Fastenings for equipment and apparatus should be placed in the wall before the finished surface is applied.

There should be no projections from the walls into the playing area. Roll-away bleachers should be recessed. Drinking fountains should not be located in the gymnasium area.

Above the 12' level, acoustic materials should be emphasized.

A dead air space between the inner and outer walls provides insulation against sound, cold, and heat.

Ceilings

Ceiling materials vary considerably according to the room. For offices, standard classrooms, and high gymnasium rooms, acoustic tile is recommended. If apparatus is to be fastened to the ceiling, all necessary clamps and fasteners should be installed before the ceiling is finished. To prevent condensation of moisture, ceilings should be insulated. Light-colored ceilings have the same general lighting advantages as light walls.

Ceilings should be out of reach of thrown balls and other objects in activity areas. In many arenas, they have retractable equipment attached to them. An open look, with beams and roof visible, can be attractively presented and many times is better than a false ceiling.

Doors

Wood, glass, reinforced wire, iron, and steel are used in doors found in physical education, athletic, and leisure use buildings. The specific purpose of the door dictates the material to be used. Building codes also determine not only the material to be used but also the type of door to be used.

Other significant points to consider in selecting and installing satisfactory doors are these:

All exit doors must open outward and be equipped with panic bars, so egress is always possible in case of an emergency.

Doors must be accessible for disabled people and meet the standards established in P.L. 101-336, the Americans with Disabilities Act.

Fire doors must meet all pertinent fire codes.

Large doors should be provided to building areas where large numbers of people will enter and exit in a short period of time.

Doors should be designed to handle the moving of large equipment and materials.

Doors should be strategically located to facilitate the circulation of traffic within the building.

Doors should be of high-quality material so they work smoothly and quietly.

Strong, efficient locks should be provided for doors that must be kept secured.

Water-resistant doors must be used when they are exposed to the outside elements or to damp areas such as swimming pools and shower rooms.

Lighting

Lighting for physical education, sport, leisure programs, and fitness centers is provided by both natural (windows and skylights) and artificial means. Natural lights are good for offices, reception areas, conference rooms, classrooms, and hallways. It is recommended that activity areas where ball skills are used be illuminated by artificial light to control glare and the level of light provided. Locker rooms should also include artificial lights for reasons of security, the danger of window breakage, and temperature control.

When natural light is used, it must be combined with artificial lighting. The intensity of artificial light can be regulated by adjusting the intensity of the source and by placing fixtures and reflectors correctly. Semidirect light causes less glare and eyestrain and is ideal for activities such as weight training and tennis. The quantity of light needed is determined by the activity and by the level of competition. A satisfactory quantity of light for general physical education is 50 footcandles; for more exact vision, greater intensity is desirable with high-level sport activities requiring 70 or 80 footcandles or more. A footcandle is a measurement of illumination equivalent to that produced by a standard candle at a distance of one foot.

There are basically three types of lighting used in physical education and similar facilities. The properties of each should be investigated in order to determine the best type for each building and each part of the building. Incandescent, fluorescent, and high-density discharge lamps each have features that make them appropriate for different areas of a building.

Incandescent   Incandescent lights have low initial cost and excellent color. However, they have low efficiencies, a short life, and high operating costs.

Fluorescent   Fluorescent light has a long life, provides low brightness and low operating temperatures, and is more efficient than incandescent bulbs. They have a higher initial cost and require an auxiliary piece of equipment called a ballast.

High-Density Discharge   There are three kinds of high-density discharge lamps: mercury vapor, metal halide, and high-pressure sodium lamps. Mercury vapor lights are seldom used today because of their low efficiency and poor color properties. Metal halide and high-pressure sodium lamps have many of the same characteristics, with long life, high efficiencies, and low operating costs. High-pressure sodium lamps outperform metal halide lamps in each of these categories but their color properties are poor, whereas metal halide lamps have good color properties. They both have high initial costs, require auxiliaries, have glare potential, and have startup and restrike requirements.

Careful consideration should be given to energy conservation when choosing a lighting system. Key-operated switches, light control by rows from different switches, dimming capabilities, and a master control to turn off unneeded lights are examples of features that should be incorporated into a lighting system. The most important conservation feature is to select the most energy-efficient lamps for the lighting needed. A number of energy programs are being developed privately and by state and federal governments. For example, the Green Lights Program, sponsored by the Environmental Protection Agency, promotes energy conservation, pollution reduction, and lower electric bills through the use of more efficient lighting. Administrators should investigate each of these programs and implement those that are feasible.

Emergency light must be provided throughout the building. This is particularly important in areas such as the swimming pool and areas where large crowds gather.

Heating, Cooling, and Ventilation

The comfort level of a building is important if the building is to properly serve the people who use the facility. On a commercial level, people will not use a building if it does not have good climate control. In a school, room temperatures must be maintained at a level that is conducive to learning. Physical education facilities have special needs. The air temperature needs vary according to the use of different parts of the building. For example, a swimming pool needs a warmer air temperature than does a racquetball court. There are different needs in a locker room than on a basketball court.

It is best to have a system that encompasses heating, cooling, and ventilation rather than having separate systems. The system should be computerized to make it possible to keep room temperatures, ventilation, and humidity at the desired levels even during changing indoor and outdoor conditions. Ventilation is extremely important to remove odors, keep the air fresh, and maintain proper humidity levels. Ventilation aims to produce a minimum of four changes of air per hour without creating drafts.

Noise must be kept to a minimum and drafts of air should not be felt by those in the facility. Temperature levels should be able to be controlled according to the use of each part of the building. The heating, cooling, and ventilation system is one of the most important parts of a building. The type of system that is best for the building must be carefully and thoroughly researched during the planning stage. Energy conservation is an important consideration because significant sums of money will be saved yearly by an energy efficient system.

Plumbing

In selecting plumbing equipment, it is wise to purchase good standard materials from a reliable dealer. Durability, strength, simplicity of design, and a good finish are the marks of satisfactory equipment.

All pipes for water, heat, gas, or other purposes and all sewage and drain pipes should be laid before the walls and the foundation are built. Care should be taken to mend the damp-proofing in the event that pipes are laid after the walls are in. The cleaning problem is simplified, the appearance is improved, and the danger of accident is reduced if pipes are enclosed in the walls. Those factors sufficiently outweigh the increased cost of installation and the greater difficulty of getting at pipe when something goes wrong, so that enclosing in the walls is recommended if provision is made for access when necessary.

Specific suggestions for each of the following service units are presented under the unit concerned.

Heating   Sufficient radiation should be provided to furnish adequate heat on cold days—about 60°F for activity rooms, about 70°F for locker rooms, and about 80°F for the shower and swimming pool rooms.

Proportionately fewer heating units are needed to heat large rooms than to heat small ones because as rooms get larger, the volume increases more rapidly than the area of exposed outer surface through which heat passes.

Heat pipes should be insulated to conserve heat, to prevent burns, and to prevent overheating of some rooms and halls. Heat sources should be distributed so that they provide a comparatively even temperature throughout the room.

Showers   Sufficient showers to care for the peak load should be provided. The recommended ratio for class purposes is one shower per four students. Placing a post shower with multiple heads in the center of the room has many advantages over wall showers. This plan also permits use of shower barriers rather than solid walls around the room, and affords easy supervision.

Shower heads should be designed to permit water to be discharged diagonally downward so that those who use them can avoid getting their heads wet. An in-wall liquid soap dispensing system is recommended, although a bar soap procedure with recessed soap dishes is preferred by many.

Individual control of showers is advocated. Although central control is more economical, individual control under supervision is not particularly expensive and is much more satisfactory to the shower takers. For economy purposes, a master control can be used to shut off the water when showers are not in use. The shower heads should be stationary, be easy to maintain and replace, and provide a satisfactory spray. They should be self-cleaning and nonclogging.

The recommended light for a shower room is 20 footcandles. Shower facilities must be included for the disabled.

Drying Rooms   The drying room should be located between the shower and locker rooms, with entrances to each. It should be approximately the same size as the shower room. The floor and the walls (up to 6') should be similar to those in the shower rooms. Towel racks adequate to accommodate the peak load should be installed. Foot drying ledges, approximately 18" high and 12" wide, should be built around the wall. They should be constructed of the same material as the wall, be enclosed, and have rounded edges.

Lavatories   Lavatories should be near the toilet room. White porcelain finish is preferable. Paper towels and liquid soap should be provided near the lavatories. Faucets that turn off automatically when left on are practical.

Toilets   Enough toilets to take care of peak load classes should be provided—approximately one urinal for twenty boys, one stool for fifteen girls, and one stool for twenty boys. Toilets that flush readily with a small amount of water are best.

Cuspidors   Cuspidors that flush easily with a little water are practical; the foot flush type is preferable. At least one cuspidor should be placed near activity areas, recessed in the wall with bars to keep balls out of it. This is essential because some players must expectorate during activity periods, and if a proper place is not provided, they will use the floor or wall. The finish should be a different color from that of the drinking fountain.

Drinking Fountains   Drinking fountains should be located near the main activity areas and in the locker room. Drinking of water should be encouraged by providing a convenient supply; consequently, additional fountains may be necessary. Refrigerated water should be provided.

Locker Rooms   The locker room should be large enough to provide 20 square feet for each occupant during the peak load. The recommended standard for lighting is 30 footcandles. The recommended temperature is 70°F. Adequate ventilation and acoustic treatment are vitally important.

Locker rooms should be designed with supervision in mind. Large locker rooms for classes, with team rooms and smaller rooms that can be used for visiting teams, should be included in a physical education facility design. Visiting teams should have the privacy of a separate dressing room.

Cement bases or pedestal-mounted dressing benches should be provided for lockers. Aisles 5' wide should be provided between lockers on pedestals. Thirty inches should be allowed between lockers and floor-mounted benches when cement bases are used.

Forced air ventilation through lockers is highly desirable. Rooms should be designed so there aren't hidden areas that prevent proper supervision.

Team Rooms   Full-length lockers large enough to permit storage of practice equipment should be available for all squad members. Providing open lockers with a small box in which to secure valuables is a recent trend, especially for sports such as football and ice hockey that have large amounts of equipment.

It is desirable to locate lockers around walls in order to leave center area open for squad meetings if a separate meeting room is not provided. The team room should be available to squads in season. A bulletin board and a chalkboard should be installed. The training room should be adjacent to the team room.

Custodial Facilities   Custodial closets should be located appropriately to facilitate custodial operations. A storage area for custodial supplies is necessary. A service sink in or adjacent to the custodial closets is also a necessity.

Locker Unit

Lockers and baskets vary greatly in size, materials used in construction, and methods of handling. The wire type allows closets to dry much better than the metal louver type, but admits more dust and presents more security problems. Larger, full-length (60–72") lockers are more convenient and adequate than the smaller 12" × 12" × 36" type but are also more expensive. The problem, then, is to provide the combination of lockers and baskets that most adequately meets the needs of the various groups concerned without entailing too great expense.

It is generally agreed that varsity athletes should have individual lockers in the locker room. Full-length lockers are recommended, but if funds do not permit them, half-length lockers can be used (although storage areas must then be provided for some sports). A system of spacious open lockers with boxes in which to secure valuables is becoming more prevalent, especially at the college and university level. Each locker should have a good, strong lock on it. The master-key–combination type is recommended.

A combination of storage lockers and full-length (dressing) lockers is best for most schools. Full-length lockers are provided to care for peak load. The peak load includes class members, recreational activity people, and intramural competitors who need lockers during the same period of time. Sufficient storage (box) lockers must be available for each student who uses the locker room. Storage lockers range in size but a common size is 12" × 12", with depth the same as the full-length locker. Most systems incorporate 5, 6, or 7 storage lockers per dressing locker, which may be full- or half-length. Students store their equipment in a storage locker when not in class and then transfer their lock to a dressing locker to secure their street clothes and unused equipment while in class. Baskets are sometimes used in place of storage lockers, particularly if an attendant is available to issue the baskets.

Health clubs and other commercially operated centers place a greater emphasis on appearance of their lockers to create an appropriate image for their clients. Attractive wood lockers are available, as are open hanging areas for clothes with metal or wooden boxes in which to secure valuables. The choice of locker is determined by the desired image, ease of use, and security needs.

Literature from locker manufacturers should be examined carefully to make certain lockers meet desired construction standards. Metal and finish quality and assembly techniques are extremely important. Different sizes and unique features provided by different locker manufacturers should be evaluated in light of the particular locker needs. Bright-colored lockers should be used in an overall plan to bring warmth and life to locker rooms.

The following locker room accessories are desirable:

Benches for all lockers: either long benches fastened to the floor by steel posts or benches mounted on concrete pedestals with lockers installed on them

A bulletin board near the entrance to the locker room or rooms

Hair dryers, electrical outlets, and mirrors for all locker rooms

Apparatus

Apparatus such as gymnastic equipment, climbing equipment, batting cages, and volleyball standards should be selected on the basis of its prospective usefulness in furthering a good activity program. Rugged, simple, standard pieces should be chosen. Even though the original cost may be greater, the difference will be compensated for in reduced repair bills and maintenance costs. Because shipping costs for heavy pieces are relatively high, it may be more economical to purchase from some dealer close at hand.

Mobile pieces that can be fastened to the floor or wall are recommended. They should be designed to swing back and attach to the wall, be raised to the ceiling, or rolled off on wheels to an apparatus storage room when not in use, leaving the main floor available for other activities. Mats and smaller pieces of equipment that require no fastening should be stored out of the way on a platform on wheels or in boxes on wheels that make them easy to move.

Elementary School Gymnasium

Special factors should be considered when constructing an elementary school gymnasium. It should not be a combination gymnasium–cafeteria if it is to fulfill its function as a teaching facility. Providing sufficient teaching stations is just as critical at the elementary level as at the secondary level. Walls should be as uncluttered as possible and not have projections extending from them that limit their use for physical education activities. A brightly painted gymnasium presents a cheery atmosphere and establishes a good learning environment. The facility should be activity-oriented, with ropes, a cargo net, and multiple designs on the floor, and have varied pieces of equipment available. Basketball baskets should be adjustable to different heights. The gymnasium should be designed for the needs and interests of elementary school children, not a scaled-down version of a college or secondary school gymnasium.

Spectator seating is needed only if the facility is to be used for evening and weekend activities. Additional facilities are usually needed for basketball in a community and a basketball court of 50' × 84', with safety space around the perimeter, provides a good size for an elementary school gymnasium. The spectator seating should all be recessed into the wall if it is included. Storage space and an office for the physical education teacher or teachers must also be provided. Too often, these aspects of an elementary school gymnasium are overlooked or are totally inadequate.

Swimming Pool

The swimming pool is an important physical education, recreation, and health club facility. Swimming contributes to all of the commonly accepted physical education objectives and is an ideal recreational and physical fitness activity for people of all ages. Swimming is usually one of the most popular activities in the curriculum, and parents are eager to have their children learn to swim for its safety aspects as well as for the recreational opportunities it affords. The ability to swim opens the door to many other aquatic activities such as waterskiing, scuba diving, boating, canoeing, fishing, and sailing.

All of these factors justify an important place for swimming in the physical education curriculum. Many public schools have difficulty obtaining facilities to use. Most colleges and universities have swimming pools and there has been an increase in the number of high schools that have such facilities. However, few elementary schools have swimming facilities and their programs are conducted in the high school pools or in pools that belong to other agencies. School boards are now more amenable to granting approval for the construction of swimming pools, but it will be a long time before every schoolchild has access to a swimming pool. In many communities, taxpayers are unwilling to vote for construction bond issues that include the added expense of a swimming pool. Many secondary schools have been able to acquire such facilities by making them available for community use in the evenings, on weekends, and during the summer. Multiple use is the key to selling the idea of constructing a pool to the public. It is a valuable community resource and should be used for instruction, team competition, community recreational swimming, American Red Cross programs, community swim teams; it can also be rented out to groups to raise money to help pay for the maintenance of the pool.

Many health clubs and wellness centers cannot afford swimming pools. Those that do have pools find that it is a good resource that generates increased membership. Europe is far ahead in this area of providing leisure pool settings. They commonly include children's play areas, water slides, whirlpools, water spas, different pool shapes, and lounge and eating facilities in the natatorium complex. This trend can be expected to become popular in North America also.

Indoor Versus Outdoor Pool

Because outdoor pools are much less expensive than indoor ones, many communities have built outdoor swimming pools. Unfortunately, this restricts the use of the pool largely to the summer in most communities. From the standpoint of a school facility, an indoor pool is far better. Although some people are not enthusiastic about swimming indoors during the summer, the other advantages decidedly favor the construction of an indoor pool that can be used as part of the physical education program of a school system.

The dilemma of whether to build an indoor or outdoor pool has been solved in recent years by the construction of combination indoor–outdoor pools. In the most basic design, sliding doors are installed and can be opened during the summer. More sophisticated techniques are now popular and used in many locations. Sliding or removable panels, inflatable roofs that can be rolled up and stored on the side of the frame during the summer, and retractable roofs are examples of these techniques. Also, there is increasing use of plastic covers over outdoor pools in order to permit swimming for more of the year.

Preliminary Planning Considerations

Knowledge and experience must be involved in the planning of swimming pools. Throughout the country, examples of poorly designed and constructed facilities are easy to find. New concepts, materials, and processes have developed so rapidly in swimming pool construction that it would be a mistake to undertake the construction of a pool without consulting a knowledgeable individual. If the architect is not an experienced, up-to-date pool builder, an expert should be consulted. A consultant is often engaged when a large facility is being contemplated. The guidance of specialists in heating and ventilation, acoustics, plumbing, water purification, and lighting is necessary. Finally, those who will conduct programs in the pool should be involved in the planning.

In planning a new pool, the various uses that will be made of it are a prime consideration. School pools are used for more than instructing nonswimmers. They include programs for water safety instruction, the disabled, intramural and interschool competition, synchronized swimming, pageants, older adults, water polo, scuba diving, recreational swimming, and hydrotherapy. The requirements for each of these activities must be incorporated in the planning.

Every state department of health has regulations pertaining to swimming pools. Compliance with these rules is a must. These laws usually cover such factors as water circulation, filtration, water treatment practices, sanitary standards, and safety features. Industry standards should also be followed.

Design   The design of swimming pools has changed dramatically during the past decade and technological advances give every indication that pool designs will become even more impressive and sophisticated in the future. It used to be that most indoor natatoria were single, rectangular pools used for all water activities. There were a few L-, T-, and Z-shaped pools that had the advantage of providing a separate diving area and also made it possible to have a larger shallow area to accommodate beginning swimmers. Current pool design emphasizes separate pools for diving (the dotted-i design) or moveable bulkheads that make it possible to separate the pool for different uses. This makes much more efficient use of the pool space, increases safety, and provides the opportunity to support more aquatic programs.

Moveable bulkheads have proven their worth and are commonly found in swimming pools today. The same cannot be said for moveable floors, but their use can be expected to expand significantly in the future. There are several reasons why the moveable floor is gaining popularity and is being installed in more pools. One reason is the requirement by states and various competitive swimming organizations that a minimum depth of water be provided when using starting blocks for competitive events. This depth makes the pool too deep for instructional swimming classes, prevents many small children from using the pool, restricts programs for the disabled, and limits some other water activities. The moveable floor also improves pool safety and provides much more flexibility in programming by making a single-purpose pool into a multipurpose pool.

Seldom is it possible to build an instructional pool, a diving pool, a water polo pool, and a competitive pool. Moveable bulkheads and moveable floors make it possible to have all of these pools and more with only the cost of constructing one pool.

Access for the disabled is another important design consideration. Ramps and lifts are both acceptable. The available space, type of pool, and other design features must be considered when determining which type of access is best.

Pool depths for competitive swimming and diving are determined by the various competitive governing bodies. These bodies also establish standards for clear space above diving boards and diving platforms. The most stringent standard of any group that will be using the pool should be used when constructing a diving area.

The moveable bulkhead makes it possible to accommodate both meter and yard races. Some universities and swimming clubs have a pool that is a 50 meter Olympic course with a moveable bulkhead. When possible, it is a good idea to have a width of either 25 yards or 25 meters, depending on which distance is used the most in competition. This will accommodate more swimmers during practice. Eight lanes are needed for competitive purposes and this width provides good flexibility for teaching. Lanes should be a minimum of 7' wide with an additional 1.5' in the outside lanes because this contributes to smoother water for competitive swimmers.

The decks of the pool should provide sufficient space for land drills, lifesaving activities, and physical conditioning. At least 12' should be provided on each side of the pool. The width of the deck at the ends should not be less than 15'. It is a recommended standard that the total amount of deck space be equivalent to the water surface area. Governing body standards and recommendations for deck space should be used when designing the pool.

Spectator seating should be provided in a controlled area where spectators can see the nearest edge of the pool from end to end. The seating design should keep spectators away from the pool deck and water area and provide easy access. Humidity control for spectators is another feature that should be considered when planning the facility.

When designing pools, appropriate scholastic, National Collegiate Athletic Association (NCAA), National Association of Intercollegiate Athletics (NAIA), National Junior College Association (NJCA), Amateur Athletic Union (AAU), or international rule books should be consulted. This is extremely important because pool markings, standards for recessed receptacles, and construction requirements are sometimes changed by these organizations.

Location   An indoor pool can be constructed anywhere in the building but the preferred location is on the ground level. This location is not only the most economical form of construction but it also provides ready access from the outside. In the past, pools built directly underneath gymnasiums created serious problems. It is difficult to control the moisture from the pool, which can damage the gymnasium floor.

The pool should be easily accessible from both the girls' and boys' locker rooms. The pool should be located so that spectators at swimming events have direct access to the seating area. People using the pool for recreational purposes should be able to reach the appropriate locker and shower areas for the swimming pool without going through other parts of the building.

Materials   A wide variety of materials are used for the construction of the swimming pool shell. Steel, plastic, aluminum, and fiberglass are used, but concrete in various forms is used most extensively. The decks, sides, and basins of the pool are usually constructed of reinforced, form-poured concrete. Precast, prestressed concrete or concrete block can be used for the pool walls. Pneumatically applied concrete (Gunite) can also be used for the entire pool shell.

Ceramic tile is the favored swimming pool finish. The advantages of tile are that it can be readily cleaned, it is less slippery, and it is durable and attractive. Its disadvantage is its cost, although over a period of years this factor is not excessive. Abrasive tile is usually used at the ends of the pool to reduce slipping on turns in competitive swimming. The lanes, which are marked on the pool floor, are made of black tile.

A wide variety of other pool finishes are available. Rubber-based paint is the least expensive but does not have good lasting qualities. Water-resistant oil paints are much more costly but they are more serviceable. Various chemical coatings have been developed. Plaster finishes also have some good features but they are difficult to properly apply.

Circuit Breakers   Circuit breakers should be on all electrical outlets in the pool area, with no electrical outlets being located within nine feet of the water.

Ladders   Ladders should be available at each corner of the pool. They should be recessed into the side walls. Ramps or lifts must be provided for the disabled.

Coping   The coping is a slightly elevated area 12"–18" wide that extends around the entire pool. It prevents the return of water from the deck to the pool. The coping also facilitates cleaning the deck without getting dirty water in the pool.

The coping is usually made from precast concrete sections. It is essential that it not be slippery when wet.

Overflow Systems   Most state boards of health require overflow systems for sanitary reasons. They serve a useful purpose in carrying waste materials and debris off the surface of the water. They also aid in regulating water level and in reducing wave action. Recessed overflow systems also act as handholds for swimmers. Roll-out and deck-level systems, which permit the water to come over the pool wall and enter a shallow covered trench, are used in many pools. Another system is called the rim-flow system and is designed to handle almost immediately all water going over the pool walls. The recommended standard is that overflow systems extend completely around the pool. The most advanced overflow technology maintains the water at the same level in the pool by pumping water out of the gutter and back into the bottom of the pool (Goldman, 1993). This reduces wave action by keeping the water level even with the gutter.

Markings   Water depth markings should be located at critical points on the deck. They should be permanent, preferably set in tile. For swimming competition, distances should be marked in 5-yard or 5-meter increments. These markings should be permanent on both the face of the pool and the deck.

Acoustics   Noise is a problem in indoor pools unless provisions are made to counteract it. Any indoor area with smooth, hard walls and ceiling is noisy. Moisture-proof acoustic material on the ceiling and on at least two of the side walls will solve the problem.

Heating   The water temperature for instructional classes should be between 80° and 85°F, with the water for children and older adults 83°–86°F. For competitive swimming, it should range from 78° to 82°F. The air temperature should be about five degrees above the water temperature, with the relative humidity maintained between 50° and 60°. Radiant heating in the deck has proven successful in controlling air temperature. Air temperature control should be computerized.

Ventilation   Ventilation is important in order to reduce humidity and condensation. It is best provided by a mechanically operated ventilation system that brings in outside air to remove contaminants from the pool area. Ventilation should control air drafts so swimmers and spectators are not affected by the air flow. The comfort of both swimmers and spectators depends on temperature and ventilation.

Lighting   There are many advantages to completely artificial lighting. If a good system is available, uniformity of lighting is ensured: glare and shadows are eliminated and the growth of algae is inhibited. Another advantage is that the elimination of outside windows makes it easier to maintain proper air temperature, humidity, and ventilation.

Some natural lighting is available in many pools. Sunlight is desirable if the rays do not shine directly on the swimmers or spectators. This can be controlled by the proper location of windows and the use of glass block or tinted fiberglass.

The recommended standard for lighting is 50 footcandles at the surface of the water or at deck level.

Underwater Lighting   Underwater lighting is a desirable feature, although it adds to the expense of construction. Such lighting is invaluable for pageants and water shows but it also facilitates cleaning and promotes safety. Lights are not recommended at the shallow end of the pool. At the deep end the recommended location is halfway between the surface and the bottom. The sidewall lights should be 2' below the surface at the shallow end and gradually lower as pool depth increases.

Access Tunnel   An access tunnel around the outside of the pool basin, though not absolutely necessary, is a desirable feature. Such a tunnel makes it simpler to inspect and repair the plumbing and underwater lighting.

Timing Devices and Filming Capabilities   Sophisticated timing devices are installed in pools used for competitive events. Even more advanced techniques will be available in the future to research a swimmer's style of swimming and the force and power used by individual swimmers during their starts and turns. Underwater windows for filming swimmers used to be included in competitive pools. This is no longer used as extensively due to the development of underwater remote-control cameras that can pan, tilt, and zoom on swimmers. Although today most cameras are hand-held from poolside, in the future stationary mountings will be placed in pool bottoms.

Water Circulation and Treatment   The purposes of water circulation and treatment are to keep it clear, clean, and pure. The size of the filters and the capacity of the pump should be sufficient to recirculate the water four times every 24 hours so that the various processes through which the water passes can be accomplished. Filtration, pH control, alkalinity control, and disinfection are the four main types of water treatment. Appropriate treatment provides water that has maximum visibility, provides maximum protection against disease, and eliminates the factors that cause discomfort to swimmers.

Outdoor Activity Areas

A significant percentage of the physical education activities in public schools and colleges and universities takes place on outdoor facilities. Recreation programs also make extensive use of outdoor areas and other leisure programs use the outdoors to different degrees. For example, some tennis centers include both indoor and outdoor courts. Consequently, these facilities must be as carefully planned and designed as the indoor activity areas. Ordinarily, these areas in educational settings are planned as part of the total school facility and are part of the institution's master plan.

A major error in the past was the failure to provide sufficient space. Unfortunately, this mistake cannot be rectified when the area around the school is built up. To prevent such errors, school planners today are giving much more consideration to the total area available. Many standards have been proposed to serve as guides in planning outdoor facilities. These standards are useful but must be modified according to local conditions and be revised when concepts change.

A major factor that has led school boards and administrators to acquire more land for school sites is community expectations that the facilities will be available to other groups when not required for school use. The trend is definitely in the direction of joint use by the school and community. In particular, the recreation department can take advantage of outdoor play areas. In this way, the public receives maximum returns from the money expended. It is also a practice in some communities to require builders to set aside land for school purposes when an open piece of land is zoned for a housing development.

Site Selection

When sites for schools are being considered, the area to be used for athletic fields should be analyzed for its suitability. Such considerations as drainage, subsurface water conditions, accessibility, soil quality, student security, and the need for fill or rock excavation should be reviewed. Outdoor areas should be close to the locker rooms but not so close that noise interferes with indoor classes. If possible, students should not be required to cross a street to get to the activity area.

Activity Areas for Secondary Schools

Sufficient outdoor activity areas are needed to accommodate instructional classes, intramurals, and interscholastic athletics for all the students. The number of outdoor teaching stations is determined by the number of students in the school, the number of required class meetings per week, and the maximum number of students who will use outdoor facilities at any time during the school year. The number of fields needed for intramurals and interscholastic athletics is determined by the student population and the scope of the programs. Sufficient space should be provided for each intramural activity and interscholastic athletic team during the prime after-school hours. It is apparent that several outdoor athletic fields are needed. In addition, a battery of tennis courts to be used for instruction, intramurals, varsity teams, and community recreation should be provided.

Facilities for spectators must also be incorporated into outdoor field designs. The size of the community, the emphasis it places on athletics, and the extent of community and school support at athletic contests determine what spectator facilities are needed. Community use of the fields is also a factor in determining the accommodations to be made for spectators.

Junior and senior high schools need athletic fields that can accommodate football, touch football, soccer, baseball, softball, track and field, field hockey, speedball, lacrosse, and archery. A hard-surfaced area, which can be used for outdoor basketball and volleyball, is an asset. The recommended dimensions for game areas are indicated in Appendix B.

Activity Areas for Elementary Schools

Several types of activity areas are needed for elementary schools. The area should be designed so that the lower grades (K–3) can use space without conflicting with activities of students in the upper grades or having older students walk through their areas. A hard surface area with painted lines and circles should be provided for young children. An apparatus area with challenging and innovative equipment constitutes another segment of the playground. A grassy area, large enough for basic lead-up sports and movement exploration, should also be included. A larger hard surface and grassy area are needed for the upper grades for games and activities appropriate for those ages.

General Features

Drainage   This is an important consideration on unpaved areas. With adequate drainage, athletic fields dry out more rapidly after wet weather. There are two types of drainage: surface and subsurface.

Surface drainage is accomplished by grading in such a way that the middle of the activity area is slightly elevated, sloping toward the sides of the field. The recommended slope is 2 percent, i.e., 2' for every 100'. The water drains off the field into catch basins or natural water collectors. Drain tiles that convey the water to a storm sewer or other outlet are the most common type of subsurface drainage system. More complex systems are also available and are incorporated into natural turf systems such as those described later in the chapter.

Surfacing   Surfaces used for activity areas must have a number of different characteristics. The administrator needs to consider each of these characteristics when deciding on the surface to be installed in activity areas. The sport or activity that will be played on the surface determines which of these characteristics are most important.

Safe for participants

Suitable for multiple uses

Suitable for year-round use

Resilient

Durable

Easily maintained

Low-maintenance

Attractive

Nonabrasive

Reasonable initial cost

Environmentally friendly

No surface is ideal for every type of activity area. Natural turf comes the closest to being the best all-around surface. However, it does not hold up well under heavy use, it is somewhat expensive to maintain properly, and it cannot be used in wet weather. Because of these disadvantages, extensive research has been conducted to develop other surfaces that meet the varying outdoor surface needs for physical education and athletics. Two types of surfaces are needed: the court or hard surface and the field or turf surface.

Hard Surface Areas   Bituminous or blacktop surfaces are popular in public schools and colleges and universities. The common, bituminous surface has many of the advantages sought in any surfacing material. It provides a durable surface that can be used year-round. The maintenance of bituminous surface is comparatively easy and inexpensive. Such a surface can be used for many different activities. When properly installed, the surface is dust-free and drains quickly. Asphalt surfaces can be marked easily and with a high degree of permanence. Asphalt also provides a neat-appearing, no-glare surface that blends well with the landscape.

The disadvantages of bituminous surfaces are their relatively high installation costs and lack of resiliency. However, the high installation cost is offset by low maintenance costs.

Bituminous surfaces vary in firmness, finish, resiliency, and durability depending on the kinds and proportions of aggregates and other materials used in their mixture.

Asphalt can be combined with a variety of other materials to provide a reasonably resilient or extremely hard surface. The use of such materials as cork, sponge, or rubber in combination with asphalt yields a fairly resilient surface. Aggregates such as slag or granite produce an extremely hard surface when combined with asphalt.

Many different types of synthetic surfaces have been developed for physical education and athletic use. Initially, these surfaces were designed for specific activities such as tennis or track. Improvements in construction now make these surfaces multipurpose. One surface can be used for tennis, basketball, volleyball, playground activities, and street games. These surfaces have at least a 4" base with a leveling course of graded aggregate and a surface course of fine aggregate to provide a smooth, uniform plane on which to place the synthetic playing surfaces. Product specifications vary with geographic regions. When considering the installation of a synthetic surface, the quality of each commercial product must be carefully evaluated and a list of required specifications met by any contractor bidding on the job. Synthetic surfaces can also be placed over existing surfaces. This should be considered by schools that wish to upgrade current facilities.

Synthetic surfaces have many advantages. They are resilient, durable, nonabrasive, and excellent for multiple use, require little maintenance, come in a variety of colors, and are appropriate for year-round use.

Some schools and recreation departments are using 1" rubber cushions on their hard surface playgrounds, particularly under apparatus. A number of companies have developed products that are poured in place on playgrounds and serve as cushioning agents, eliminate dust and surface deterioration, and give the playground an attractive, decorative appearance. This is a valuable safety feature and is required by ordinance in some municipalities. Bark, sand, and other materials are also used under playground equipment in some communities.

Turf Surfaces   Natural turf is the most extensively used turf surface. A properly constructed turf area with appropriate maintenance provides an excellent surface for many physical education and athletic programs. The four common faults in the construction of turfed fields are the following:

Poor subsurface drainage.

Inadequate surface drainage.

Improper texture of the soil. The topsoil should be a mixture of sand and loam. The amount of clay should not exceed 15 percent.

The wrong type of grass. Expert advice should be sought before the type of grass is selected. Weather and soil conditions in different parts of the country favor certain types of grass. The assistance of the local agricultural agent or a nearby agricultural college or experimental station should be sought in order to select the best variety of grass for the fields.

Maintenance must include proper fertilization, liming, mowing, and watering. Weed and insect control, aeration, limitation on time, type, and amount of use, and regular repair of damaged areas are part of an appropriate maintenance program.

Various synthetic turfs have been marketed since the initial research in the early 1960s. This type of turf has many advantages and should be carefully considered by secondary schools as well as by higher education institutions. It is particularly valuable when outdoor space is at a premium because it can be used on a 'round-the-clock basis for many different activities, even during severe weather. There are disadvantages associated with this type of turf. There is a high initial installation cost and, although maintenance costs are less than for natural turf, it is not as maintenance-free as was first thought. Surface heat during hot weather is a problem and it has been found that the turf loses its properties over an extended period of use and must be replaced. The synthetic surfaces are steadily improving and come closer to approximating the properties of natural turf than did the early models. They are also designed to drain water through the synthetic turf and subsurface material. This advancement has negated the need to have a crowned field. Conflicting research findings have been presented relative to the rate and severity of injuries to athletes using this surface.

For some schools, synthetic turf is a valuable answer to turf problems. Each school must evaluate the advantages and disadvantages of synthetic turf to determine whether this surface would be economically feasible and would lead to a better physical education, intramural, and athletic program.

Attempts have been made to combine the best qualities of natural turf with the wearability of artificial turfs. The Prescription Athletic Turf System (PAT), developed at Purdue University, has been designed with a specialized growing medium for the turf and a carefully conceived drainage and heating system to extend the use of the turf field. The success of these fields depends on proper management and materials that are appropriate for each geographical area. Systems of this type have some excellent features.

The present and future needs of the school, the budget, the amount of space available, and the characteristics desired in a turf determine whether a synthetic, natural, or specialized turf system is best for an educational institution.

Orientation of Fields and Courts   For safety of the participants, as well as for equitable playing conditions, fields and courts should be laid out to reduce the effects of the sun's rays. In rectangular fields and courts, the flight of the ball is usually parallel to the long axis of the playing area. The direction of the sun's rays at the time of the day and year when the sport is to be played should be determined. The playing field or court should then be laid out so that its long axis is perpendicular to the sun's rays. Thus, the play on football, soccer, and rugby fields will be in a north–south direction. In baseball, the rays of the late afternoon sun should be perpendicular to a line drawn from home plate through second base.

Fencing   Most play areas should be fenced. A suitable fence for many locations consists of 11-gauge woven wire 10' high. This will protect property, provide privacy, reduce supervising problems, and keep balls and other play materials from rolling, flying, or being carried into the streets. Fencing is particularly necessary for tennis courts, softball fields, and baseball fields. Wind screens are commonly attached to fences on tennis courts. The support poles must be of sufficient strength to withstand the pressure generated by the wind blowing against the screens. Fencing can be purchased with a vinyl covering that prevents rusting, extends the life of the fence, and contributes to the aesthetics of the courts and playing fields. It is well worth the extra cost.

Lighting   Outdoor areas should be lighted for interscholastic, intercollegiate, intramural, and recreational use. Lights extend the period of time that facilities can be used. When space is at a premium, lights are particularly valuable in making it possible to use a facility for different purposes. The assistance of lighting engineers should be used whenever a project involving outdoor athletic areas is contemplated. Different types of lighting can be used and the level of illumination that is needed varies with the kind of activity and skill level of the people who will be using it. For example, a college baseball field needs better lighting than a recreational soccer field.

Softball and Baseball Fields   Softball and baseball diamonds must be oriented so that both players and spectators are bothered as little as possible by the sun. For professional games, spectators often receive more consideration than they do for school contests. The school diamonds should be laid out to favor the players, for their safety is of prime importance. For schools, it is satisfactory to have the baseline from home to first base run directly west. This will considerably reduce interference with vision by the afternoon sun. Adequate backstops should be provided to reduce lost balls and ball chasing in general and to protect spectators. The distance from home plate to the backstop and from the baselines to the fence or stands should be 30' in softball and 60' in baseball.

The construction and care of the diamond are important. The field should be basically level, although a slight slope might be needed for drainage purposes if an adequate drainage system is not installed. Specialized care is needed for both the infield and the grass areas and maintenance must be performed daily to keep the fields safe and in good playing condition.

Football Fields   The football field should be laid out and constructed carefully so that the team defending the least favored goal is handicapped as little as possible by the sun and wind. Because the prevailing winds in most sections of the country blow from the west, and because the sun shines from the west in the late fall afternoon it is often best to lay out the field north and south if possible.

When natural turf is used, the field should be crowned to facilitate drainage if an adequate underground drainage system is not in place. Grass care must include watering, proper mowing, fertilizing, weed and insect control, aeration, and controlled use of the field to give the turf time to recover from use.

Tennis Courts   For school use, a battery of from six to eight tennis courts should be a minimum. One or two courts are not adequate for class instruction.

The dimensions of the doubles court are 78' × 36'. The recommended size of the area for a court is 120' × 60'. This provides a space of 21' from the baseline to the backstop and 12' from the sideline to the edge of the court surface. Fencing 12' high should enclose the courts.

Perhaps the most satisfactory layout position for tennis courts is from northeast to southwest. However, courts as a rule are not placed at an angle, so the north–south position is most common.

Tennis court surfaces are classified as porous and nonporous. Porous surfaces permit some seepage of moisture, whereas nonporous surfaces are impervious. Porous surfaces include grass, clay, and various types of crushed materials. Most nonporous tennis courts make use of synthetic court surface preparations. These surfaces are laid on at least a 4" base and are durable enough to be used for other activities such as basketball. They are excellent surfaces in that they are resilient, do not radiate heat, eliminate glare, and are not hard on the legs and feet.

For secondary schools, colleges, and universities, porous surfaces are not practical. They require too much maintenance and cannot be used quickly enough after rainy weather. There are many regions in the United States, especially in the northern part, where hard surface courts are almost essential if tennis is to be played in the spring.

Track   The running track requires a 400-meter oval with a straightaway sufficient for 110-meter hurdles. The track should contain eight lanes, each with a minimum width of 42". The appropriate track and field rule books (National Federation of State High School Associations, NAIA, NCAA, NJCA) should be consulted for technical and competition rules before a track is constructed.

A convenient arrangement for most schools is that of placing the track around the football field. This is an economical use of space and enables spectators to use the same bleachers for both sports.

The development of all-weather tracks composed of such materials as fibrous asphalt, a rubber–sand–asphalt hot mix, a rubberized asphalt cold mix, synthetic resin material, and rubber–cork–asphalt composition was an important factor in the improvement of track surfaces. This type of track did have some disadvantages. Its resiliency changed with the weather and over a period of time it tended to become excessively hard. Heavy use had an adverse effect on it and it was necessary to control use of the surface. Further research led to the development of other synthetic surfaces that are highly successful and have rendered the traditional cinder track obsolete. The various commercial synthetic surfaces should be carefully evaluated for cost, construction specifications, durability, and maintenance requirements before choosing a surface for a specific school. There are numerous advantages of a synthetic track surface:

Resiliency contributes to the prevention of leg injuries.

The footing is always good.

Maintenance costs are significantly reduced.

Lane markings are permanent.

Condition of surface is always uniform.

Appearance of surface is enhanced.

Inclement weather does not cause cancellations or postponements of meets because of track conditions.

Rubber-soled shoes can be used as readily as spiked shoes.

The performance of athletes is not adversely affected by wet weather.

Use of the track need not be restricted to the track teams.

The surface can be used for different purposes.

Adventure Education Programs   Facilities for adventure education programs can be constructed on school grounds. In some locations it is possible to use existing trees, whereas in other cases it is necessary to build wooden structures for use in adventure activities and to attach cables and ropes to set up the challenge course. Along with staff training, outdoor adventure organizations can provide plans and guidance for constructing adventure education facilities.

Innovative Facilities

Schools, health clubs, fitness centers, colleges, and universities must all be alert to new construction ideas to provide the best possible facilities for their programs at the lowest cost. Innovative ideas have revolutionized the types of activity facilities that are now being constructed. It is impossible to give a comprehensive list of innovative ideas because once an idea proves successful it becomes a standard procedure used in future buildings. Experiments continue with many kinds of fabric structures that are used extensively to increase the amount of space that can be provided, even with limited financial resources. Convertible facilities, indoor climbing walls, synthetic ice, and mobile locker rooms are just a few of the innovative ideas that have been successful. Analysis of new and standard building materials, energy conservation techniques, use of the natural terrain, building on rooftops and underground, incorporating the newest technology in all aspects of a building, and varied building designs are examples of approaches that should be investigated to provide the best possible facilities.

Renovation of Facilities

Renovation of existing structures can create excellent facilities at considerable financial savings. Factors such as cost, problems in making buildings accessible to the disabled, portion of present building that can be salvaged, amount of space available, unique features of the current building that can be included in the renovated facility, how the renovation will fit into the master plan, contribution that the renovation will make to new and present programs, the time element, and the availability of other construction sites are factors that must be considered when evaluating the advisability of renovation. Renovation can be planned to provide additional space or to make better use of the present space. An addition to a current building is a commonly used procedure to increase available space. Installing new mechanical systems and lighting systems, automating building features, laying synthetic floors designed for multiple use, upgrading seating, windows, and aesthetic features, providing large activity modules by removing walls and other barriers, and restructuring areas for specialized use are techniques that have been used effectively in the rehabilitation of physical education facilities.

Athletic Field and Court Layouts

For detailed specifications of athletic field and court layouts for various sport and physical education activities, see Appendix B.

Class Activities

Simulation 1

Situation   A bond issue for a new indoor high school physical education–athletic facility was passed in the community where you are teaching. The architect for the project has asked to meet with the physical education faculty and coaches to receive information to guide the architectural firm in designing the facility. The high school is grades 9–12 and is projected to have 1,200 students, with a comprehensive athletic program.

Form a departmental planning committee. Establish the procedures that the planning committee will follow to obtain input from all members of the faculty. Class members will be grouped into subcommittees to generate this information. Based on the information obtained, write a report to present to the architect. In the report, include educational goals as well as the specific activities to be included in the program. Compute the number of teaching stations that will be needed and provide specific information about program needs.

Simulation 2

Situation   A new elementary school for grades K–5 is being constructed. There will be three full-time physical education teachers in the school when it is completed.

Design an indoor and outdoor facility for this elementary school.

Simulation 3

Situation   A fitness center is being planned for your community. Preliminary design information must be presented to the local planning board for approval.

Provide a preliminary drawing of the fitness center to present to the planning board. Include in the drawing the activity areas, offices, lounges, storage areas, shower and dressing rooms, entryways, and other components such as a snack area that you want for the fitness center.

Performance Tasks

1. Contact three companies that sell physical education lockers. Obtain materials from each company and select the type of locker and locker system you would recommend for a secondary school.
2. Interview two high school physical education teachers and two elementary school physical education teachers. Find out what they would change if they could have new indoor facilities for physical education.
3. Investigate the various types of lighting used for physical education and athletic facilities. Explain the strengths and weaknesses of each.
4. Visit a commercial recreation facility and select features that would be good for gymnasiums in educational settings.
5. Compare the advantages and disadvantages of a physical education facility built with a large central activity center and one built using a traditional gymnasium concept.
6. Determine the number of teaching stations that would be needed in three high schools and three elementary schools in your area if all students had daily physical education. Compare projected needs with number of teaching stations currently available.
7. Examine recent issues of *Athletic Business* for innovative features found in recently constructed physical education and athletic facilities.
8. List features you would recommend for a swimming pool in the following settings:

    a. University
    b. High school
    c. Commercial facility
    d. Community recreational facility

9. Your high school is building a new gymnasium. You have been asked to compare wooden and synthetic floors and make a recommendation to the school board. Gather material and prepare your report.
10. You are chairperson of physical education in a large urban high school where the building is 70 years old. You have been told to prepare a plan to renovate the locker rooms so they will be aesthetically pleasing and meet current needs. Prepare your plan.

References

Athletic Business (monthly magazine). Madison, WI: Athletic Business Publications.

Cohen, Andrew, "Locker Rooms: What Works, What Doesn't." *Athletic Business,* March 1993, 17:61.

Cohen, Andrew, "Locker Room Layouts." *Athletic Business,* January 1994, 18:30–32.

Flynn, Richard B. (ed.), *Facility Planning for Physical Education, Recreation, and Athletics.* Reston, VA: AAHPERD, 1993.

Gabrielsen, M. Alexander, *Swimming Pools: A Guide to Their Planning, Design, and Operation.* Champaign, IL: Human Kinetics, 1987.

Goldman, David, "Olympic Hopefuls Gain Edge with New Aquatic Facility." *Aquatics International,* November/December 1993.

Lindstrom, Chuck, "Light Up the Night." *Athletic Business,* September 1993, 17:47–48.

Maloy, Bernard, "Legal Obligations Related to Facilities." *Journal of Physical Education, Recreation and Dance,* February 1993, 64:28–30.

National Lighting Bureau, "Lighting to Win." *Scholastic Coach,* April 1994, 63:76–79.

Pate, Donald W., "Current Trends in Use, Design, Construction, and Funding of Sport Facilities." *Sport Marketing Quarterly,* December 1993, 2:9–14.

Rogers, S. Elaine, "Current Research in Areas and Facilities." *Parks and Recreation,* December 1993, 28:22–25.

Seidler, Todd, Edward T. Turner, and Larry Horine, "Promoting Active Lifestyles Through Facilities and Equipment—A Look at Children, Seniors and People with Disabilities." *Journal of Physical Education, Recreation and Dance,* January 1993, 64:39–42.

Sol, Neil, and Carl Foster (eds.), *ACSM's Health/Fitness Facility Standards and Guidelines.* Champaign, IL: Human Kinetics, 1992.

9

Financial Management and Budgeting

Importance of Financial Management

Financial management is one of the most important duties of an administrator. Finances are the ingredients that drive an organization, department, or business. Successfully controlling finances and targeting them to attain the objectives of the organization are attributes of a skilled administrator. Financial control is the base for the administrative processes described in Chapter 2. Planning, organizing, staffing, directing, coordinating, reporting, and budgeting all depend on effective financial management. The most important tool used for financial control is the budget. Other important tools are financial statements and audits.

Efficient Financial Management

Any official who receives and spends funds is expected to use sound business methods. To do otherwise reflects poorly on the official and the organization or institution she or he represents. Regardless of the size of the organization or institution or the amount of money involved, no administrator or staff person can afford to be careless or uninformed in handling public funds. Duties include the handling of money, making transactions, bookkeeping, and preparing budgets. Effective financial procedures are available and should be used.

Another reason why efficient financial management is important is because it enables administrators to obtain maximum benefit from the available revenue. Seldom are there sufficient funds to provide all the desired services for students in an educational program or participants in a health promotion program. Consequently, available resources must be used wisely. Too often, serious financial problems are caused by unbusinesslike procedures. These problems can occur regardless of the size or complexity of an organization if inadequate business procedures are followed.

It is imperative that administrators be well-prepared to assume their financial responsibilities. Academic study in financial management is important, as is working with other administrators while learning the practical aspects of this management skill. Experience is a great teacher but it can be an expensive teacher if the administrator has insufficient knowledge of financial matters and doesn't have the necessary guidance when taking over an administrative position. Colleges and universities with high-powered intercollegiate athletic programs emphasize the importance of special financial training when they employ experts to handle the business affairs of the athletic department. Also, directors of these programs are often selected for their business ability. Professional preparation programs in sport management, health promotion, and physical education administration invariably include courses to prepare students for the financial responsibilities they will encounter in their positions.

Physical education administrators have some special challenges due to the variety of programs under their jurisdiction. They have instructional programs that vary significantly. They may have responsibility for intramural programs and athletic programs. Driver education and health education programs are also the responsibility of many physical education administrators.

Computerization

Technological advances in information systems have had far-reaching effects in financial management. Even complex records are easily maintained and the administrator can obtain financial figures at any time. Reports can be rapidly generated to support departmental or organizational needs and to reply to requests for data. Another valuable outcome of computerization is the ability to keep staff informed on financial matters and to receive their input during the budget process. Also, much of the information needed when developing a budget can be accessed rapidly. For example, it is possible to have the equipment inventory computerized. Greater accuracy is possible and this information is readily available for use when determining equipment needs for the next budget.

The Budget and Financial Management

The budget is a prepared statement of estimated income and expenditures. It is quantitative and thus is usually expressed in numerical terms. It is actually an allocation of financial resources to activities of the organization. Budgets are a vital part of financial management. They project income and expenditures and link them with objectives. A budget is a guideline

TrenMos Fitness Center
Balance Sheet
March 31, 1995

Assets
Current assets:

Petty cash	$3,000
Accounts receivable (customers)	6,423
National bank	21,764
Money market investments	5,621
Inventory-food	1,112
Equipment	210,009
Supplies	4,325
Total current assets:	252,254

Liabilities and Fund Balances

Current liabilities:

Accounts payable	6,345
Deferred income–membership	1,342
Payroll tax payable	1,720
State withholding	1,627
Total current liabilities:	11,034

Fund balance:

Operating fund	174,821
Excess of revenue over expenses	66,399
Total fund balances:	241,220
Total liabilities and fund balance	252,254

FIGURE 9-1. Balance Sheet

for the use of resources; it permits the administrator to coordinate these resources with desired activities.

Financial Statements and Financial Management

A financial statement is a profile of the financial situation of an organization. The two most commonly used statements are balance sheets and income statements. The balance statement identifies the assets and liabilities of an organization or institution at a given time. Most organizations generate a balance sheet (Figure 9-1) every month.

An income statement (Figure 9-2) is used to summarize an organization's income and expenses over a period of time, often yearly. This statement shows whether a business or organization operated at a profit or loss.

Balance sheets and income statements allow comparisons from year to year and help identify trends in the financial health of an organization. They are an invaluable aid for an administrator in charting the direction of a department or organization. Many administrative

Essex Recreation Department **Income Statement** **10 Months Ending May 31, 1995**				

Revenue and support:	Prior Year Month	Current Year Month	Prior Year YTD	Current Year YTD
Gifts	0	350	870	956
Programs	7,424	6,721	56,218	58,721
Municipal taxes	6,100	8,200	61,000	82,000
Fundraisers	1,420	2,021	12,723	15,721
Total revenues and support	14,944	17,292	130,811	157,398
Operating expenses:				
Employee salaries	6,700	7,800	67,000	78,000
Employee benefits	1,340	1,560	13,400	15,600
Printing and advertising	620	570	4,700	7,780
Rentals	470	1,000	3,227	6,425
Equipment	1,000	4,000	7,620	9,200
Supplies	987	672	8,320	10,400
Telephone	112	127	1,004	1,221
Utilities	477	500	5,800	6,225
Officials	1,985	2,100	6,900	8,327
Transportation	375	400	3,300	4,120
Conferences	180	0	520	784
Food Expenses	400	320	3,124	3,720
Total operating expenses:	14,646	19,049	124,915	151,802
Revenue and support:	14,944	17,292	130,811	157,398
Operating expenses:	14,646	19,049	124,915	151,802
Net surplus:	298	−1,757	5,896	5,596

FIGURE 9-2. Income Statement

decisions are based on the financial situation of the organization. Balance sheets and income statements are two tools that provide needed financial information.

The Audit and Financial Management

Audits are formal examinations conducted to ascertain whether the financial records of an organization are accurate and follow established policies and procedures. Regular audits must be made if the budget is to function properly as an instrument of fiscal control. An audit acts as a check on the manner in which the director administers the budget and determines whether the budgetary provisions are being carried out. The audit should be made by an outside auditing firm that has no relationship to the business or organization being audited. Good financial procedure requires an external, independent annual audit.

Accounting Procedure

The proper functioning of the budget and the success of budgetary procedures depend largely on an adequate accounting system. The director should understand the accounting procedure even though this might not be a primary responsibility. It is impossible for a director to conduct department business without an accounting system. Computerized systems are used in most institutions and provide immediate access to information as well as detailed periodic reports. These reports limit the expenditures to income. Unanticipated changes in costs and income will be revealed in time to revise the budget. The director secures much of the information for drafting the budget from the accounting records. The accounting method protects the director or the coach from charges of carelessness and misuse of funds. The director can base requests for further financial assistance from the board on the information supplied by the accounting records.

The person in charge of the finances is interested in current income and expenses. Revenue is recorded on the receipts side of the budget. However, the recording of current expenditures is more complex. Copies of transactions for which funds have been spent should be kept for use during audits and in checking records. A balance sheet on which expenditures are regularly posted should be maintained in the department office so that those affected by the budget know the current balance. Completed expenditures must be regularly processed in the business office so that computer printouts accurately reflect the current financial status.

Expense Reports

Receipts should be obtained for all expenditures and attached to a report form. The use of an expense report form facilitates the accounting of expenses and is a businesslike procedure to follow. For example, a report completed after a school athletic team trip should include pertinent information about the contest such as location, date, and opponent; the mode of transportation; the number of athletes, coaches, and managers making the trip; and the cost of meals, lodging, and expenses.

Petty Cash Fund

It is an established business practice for the administrator to have a petty cash fund from which to make small purchases. Policy of the organization should specify the amount of money that can be used per purchase and the purposes for which money from this source can be used. A maximum of $50.00 is common in school settings. It is much simpler, faster, and less expensive to be able to make small purchases directly rather than going through the regular purchasing procedure. Receipts for all purchases should be obtained. When the petty cash fund is exhausted, the receipts should be submitted along with the request for an additional appropriation. Expended funds should be charged to the appropriate budget category.

The Budget

The first essential in the efficient management of any enterprise is to plan carefully in advance the income and the expenditures for a fiscal period. This is the budgeting process. A budget is merely the complete financial plan, which is based on the estimated expenditures to be made and the expected income. Budgeting originated in connection with business and government enterprises. The practice was found desirable and has since extended to most nonprofit and public service organizations, including schools.

The safest way to avoid deficits in athletics is to adopt budgets that limit the appropriations to the income and then confine the expenditures to the appropriations. The budget results in planned spending. It is the best insurance of an equitable distribution of available funds to all the activities of an organization or department. It is not unusual for athletic departments to spend too much money on one activity or program, resulting in the curtailment of other sports. The antagonism and embarrassment that may develop when this occurs could be eliminated if a budget were set up and followed. By means of the budget, the director can show where the money was spent and thus avoid any suspicion of misuse of funds. The need for increased appropriations can be shown and justified more easily and effectively with a budget than without one. Extravagant and foolish buying will be checked, and comparisons with previous years and with other institutions can be made. The budget permits an analysis of the cost of all aspects of an organization and reveals where cuts can be made, if necessary, with the least loss in the effectiveness.

Although budgets are submitted by the administrator in charge, they must be the result of combined efforts of the staff members. This bottom-up procedure provides more and better information for making budget decisions and increases staff morale and satisfaction by incorporating their thinking into decisions that ultimately affect their work. Input is thus obtained from those who best understand various segments of the program. For example, in an athletic department, coaches can best explain the needs of their respective sports. In larger administrative units, it is advisable to elect representatives to serve as a budget committee to facilitate planning for long-range as well as immediate needs. Budgets will be planned well in advance of the fiscal period for which they will be used. The fiscal year is any yearlong period. The fiscal year for most educational institutions is July 1 to June 30. Businesses are more likely to use the calendar year of January 1 to December 31 as their fiscal year, although any 12-month period can be used. Government regulations and local policy determine the time schedule administrators must follow when preparing and presenting a budget.

Procedural Steps in Budget Construction

The budgets for each business, organization, and educational institution have individual characteristics, but there are some fundamental principles that should be observed by any director who is constructing a budget. There is nothing mysterious about making one, nor is it necessary to be a business expert to do it. Any administrator can construct a satisfactory budget by carefully following a few fundamental principles. Budgets are made out annually and preparation of a new budget begins when the previous budget has been accepted. Although the principal or superintendent might have responsibility for a school budget, the athletic director and physical education director should be extensively involved with the formulation of the part of the budget that applies to their areas of responsibility.

The steps in creating a budget are collecting the necessary information, classifying the information, constructing the budget, and presenting and adopting the budget.

Collecting the Necessary Information   The budget maker collects information on expected income and projected expenditures. In estimating the income for the coming fiscal period, the director must consider carefully all the sources from which revenue may be expected. This includes such things as memberships for health clubs, participant fees for programs provided by health promotion organizations, and money generated by special activities for which fees are charged. In physical education, student fee income must be estimated based on factors that may affect enrollment and the students' desire and ability to buy student activity tickets.

The appropriation from the board of education or the board of trustees can be estimated from previous appropriations. The director is usually familiar with the board's policies and probably knows whether any changes in the appropriation are likely. If revenue is anticipated from any additional sources, the amount may be calculated on the basis of previous income from these sources.

The estimate of expenditures proceeds along similar lines. Information about departmental needs should be gathered and compiled continuously. The entire department should be encouraged to inform the director of present and future needs in order to determine where new expenditures are needed most. The director should consult staff members who are in a position to supply needed information and should keep in constant touch with suppliers and read current equipment and supply catalogues.

Classifying the Information   After the information has been gathered it should be classified. This ensures uniformity of presentation and provides for accuracy in planning. It facilitates the gathering and compiling of the data and makes it easier to review and revise estimates. The form the classification takes should resemble the form of the final budget. All the information is classified under two general heads: revenue and expenditures. Every item for which an expenditure is contemplated, even though it may amount to only a few dollars, should be reflected in the budget. These smaller items can be classified under larger headings, but the detailed information should be available if requested.

Constructing the Budget   The information that has been classified according to budget categories is now compiled into the budget format used by the organization. Income projections often must be documented with supporting information as part of constructing the budget. It is also a good policy to require written justification for all expenditures. These steps help the administrator to prepare an accurate budget and provide important data to familiarize budget reviewers with the scope and depth of departmental or organizational needs.

Presenting and Adopting the Budget   Before a budget is adopted it must be approved. The size and type of organization determine who gives approval and how many levels of approval are needed. In a small, privately owned organization, the owner may be the only person who gives approval. In larger businesses and nonprofit leisure organizations, there is usually a board of directors that gives final approval. College and university departments have their budgets scrutinized by deans, vice presidents, and the president before final action is taken by the board of trustees or board of regents. High school budgets are first approved by the principal, then by the superintendent, and, finally, by the board of education. At times, the business manager of the university or high school also must approve the budget before it goes to the board of education or board of trustees. The budget should be adopted before any purchases are made.

Administering the Budget

After a budget is adopted, it becomes the financial program of the department or organization. Should it be followed rigidly? There are some who believe that after the budget has been adopted the expenditures should be made as directed. Others believe that the budget should be reviewed again when the expenditures are actually to be made. The general practice, however, is to follow the budget figures fairly closely. Expenditures are typically 3–5% above or below appropriations.

Practically all budgets make provisions for readjustments. Emergencies are certain to occur and the budget should be elastic enough to provide for them. There are several different plans that can be followed. An emergency or contingency fund may be set aside in the original budget. If this fund is too small, the administrator may feel cramped in his or her efforts to adjust appropriations to unforeseen circumstances. If the fund is too large, it may encourage waste and carelessness and thus defeat one of the main purposes of budgeting. The most common plan is to transfer funds from one budgetary item that does not appear to need all the available money to the item on which the demand has unexpectedly increased. Such transfers, if large, must be approved by the person or persons designated by organizational policy.

Proper records should be kept so that the actual revenue and expenditures can be compared with the budget estimates. These records are invaluable to the administrator when preparing a new budget. In addition, they are of value in making necessary adjustments in the current budget. The administrator should receive monthly reports company income and expenses with the budget estimates. It is important to know whether actual income is in line with estimates. Information should always be available on the amount appropriated, the amount expended, commitments that must be paid but have not yet been received, and the remaining balance. If income is much lower than anticipated during the first half of the fiscal period, it might be necessary to reduce expenditures in the second half of the period to prevent a serious deficit.

Categories of Budgets

Three different categories of budgets are commonly used for physical education, leisure, and sport programs. The type of budget is sometimes mandated by the educational institution or organization. The administrator should be familiar with different budgeting procedures and use the strengths of each when involved in the budgeting process.

Subgroups within each budget category for physical education, leisure, and sport programs include personnel, capital outlay, equipment, maintenance and repair, and operations. In educational situations, the director has primary responsibility for the equipment, maintenance and repair, and operational aspects of the budget. Input is given for institutional budgets covering personnel and capital outlay, but, except for large universities, administrators do not have direct control over these portions of a budget.

The operational aspect of a budget includes expendable items such as balls, nets, and other equipment that is worn out in a relatively short time through normal use. Other departmental costs such as office supplies, equipment, and maintenance contracts that are expended during the fiscal year are also included in this classification. The equipment portion of the budget includes semipermanent items such as wrestling mats, gymnastic equipment, volleyball standards, weight training equipment, and timing devices that are projected to last for several years and have a significant dollar value. The exact dollar value of an equipment item to be included in this classification is determined by institutional or organizational policy.

Maintenance and repair includes items such as painting, resurfacing a floor, and repair of equipment, such as restringing tennis racquets. This category also includes replacement items in some budgets. Some aspects of this part of the budget may be included in an institutional budget rather than a department budget. Capital outlay expenditures includes all expenditures that increase the value of the school plant, such as additions to the grounds, new buildings, or fixed equipment. Installation of permanent bleachers, construction of tennis courts, and the renovation of a building for a modernized weight training facility are examples of capital outlay. The personnel section of a budget includes all staff members who are working in the unit covered by the budget.

Line-Item Budget   This is the traditional, incremental budget used for physical education and athletic programs. It is classified as a historical budget because the specific expenditure items that form this budget are based on information from previous years' budgets together with anticipated changes keyed to such things as escalating costs, increasing or decreasing student population, and new programs. Too often, these budgets include programs without seriously analyzing them to see whether they are still useful or whether resources could be used more effectively if they were reallocated. It is a simple budget to use and understand and can be constructed in a reasonable amount of time.

Planning–Programming–Budgeting–Evaluation System (PPBES)   This is a comprehensive budgeting process that has been used extensively in private business and by government agencies. This system became popular after its successful use in the United States defense department under the direction of Robert McNamara in the early 1960s. It began as a Planning–Programming–Budgeting System and has now been broadened to include an evaluation component. Many businesses and educational institutions use this budgeting process with successful outcomes.

PPBES requires the careful establishment of goals and objectives (planning). Programs are then developed to reach these goals (programming). The next step is the allocation of resources (budgeting). The final step in this budget system is the assessment of the results (evaluation). This leads to further planning and the start of the next budgetary cycle. One of the prime values of this system is that planning, programming, budgeting, and evaluation are coordinated. It is necessary to extend the planning over a period of years and each program must be compared with the others to determine how the funds can best be used to attain the goals and objectives that were established. This system provides the administrator with a means of objectively evaluating programs and determining where resources should be allocated.

Zero-Based Budget (ZBB)   This budget process became popular in the late 1970s and throughout the 1980s. It is now used extensively in business and industry. Most conventional budgets begin with the previous year's budget and build on it. Adjustments are made based on current information and experiences of the previous year. The emphasis is on any changes to be made. There is a built-in bias to continue current programs and procedures even if needs have changed or new methods are evolving. In the zero-based budget process, the budgeting unit begins at point zero and the budget must be justified in its entirety each fiscal year. Every dollar requested in the budget must be justified. In zero-based budgeting, the administrator lists all objectives for the fiscal period and then identifies the resources needed to attain the objectives. Every part of the budgetary unit starts from an equal position and the goal of this type of budget is to allocate resources where they will have the most value. A premium is placed on evaluating and prioritizing needs and specifying required resources.

There are two steps in a ZBB plan. All the activities or tasks are described and alternate ways of attaining the objectives are explained together with the consequences of not supporting the activity or task. The costs and benefits of each activity or task are also detailed as part of the first step. In the second step, each activity or task is ranked and full or partial funding is given. Properly implemented, zero-based budgets keep pace with changes and provide resources where they will be best used. Disadvantages include the extensive amount of time involved, the repetition of work each year, and the pressure placed on administrators and staff members.

Variations and combinations of the line-item, PPBES, and ZBB budget processes are also used. For example, although the budget might be a line-item budget, planning and programming procedures used in constructing the budget may be based on the PPBES and ZBB models. Also, it is difficult to accurately evaluate many objectives in the educational fields and there are intangible objectives that administrators might want to consider when making budget decisions.

The Physical Education Budget

Although in some schools the physical education budget includes interschool athletics, most schools prepare a separate budget for athletics. The public school physical education budget is much easier to prepare when athletics are separate because income does not have to be estimated and it does not involve the amount or variety of expenditures present in an interschool athletic budget. For efficient financial planning, it is usually better to prepare a separate athletic budget (Figure 9-3).

Source of Financial Support

The elementary and secondary school physical education instructional program should be financed from the school budget. In public schools, this is primarily from state and local taxes. In private schools, student tuition and other school resources are used. College and university physical education programs are also financed with institutional resources.

The intramural program is considered an integral part of the educational program and should be supported from regular school funds. Chapter 13 explains that college and university programs are often supported at least partially by sources such as student activity fees and participation fees. Even when this is the case, the cost of facilities and personnel are almost always carried in the institutional budget.

Determining Physical Education Equipment Needs

The type of budget being used determines how equipment needs are determined. The program objectives must be determined first and then a program planned to attain these objectives. As part of the planning process, the equipment needed for each activity during the fiscal year should be ascertained. The next step is to determine what equipment must be purchased. The administrator must know what equipment is on hand and the condition of the equipment. This can best be accomplished by use of a computerized perpetual inventory (Figure 9-4) and a periodic inventory (Figure 9-5). The perpetual inventory should be updated throughout the year when new items are received or put into use and when a worn-out

Budget
Shenoak School District Physical Education

Estimated Expenses

Personnel

Full-time faculty-Salary and benefits	181,724
Additional responsibilities (intramurals, clubs)	6,500

Operations

Team sport supplies	3,500
Individual sport supplies	2,760
Intramural supplies	500
Dance supplies	325
Aquatic supplies	755
Office supplies	435

Equipment

Weight-training equipment	6,485
Batting cage–Softball	1,200
Batting cage–Baseball	1,200
Computer and printer	2,683

Maintenance and repair

Team sport equipment	300
Individual sport equipment	250
Gymnasium floor refinishing	1,000

Capital outlay

Lighting of tennis courts	11,300
Locker rooms and showers under stadium	98,000

Total estimated expenses	318,917

Estimated Income

Board of education	213,317
Capital improvement bond issue	105,600
Total estimated income	318,917

FIGURE 9-3. Physical Education Budget

item is discarded. This inventory indicates when items were purchased so an approximation of the remaining life of different items can be made. The inventory information also allows the administrator to evaluate the longevity of similar items purchased from different companies and thereby acts as a guide for future purchases. The periodic inventory should be taken as close to the time of budget submission as possible and provides a complete record of the equipment and supplies for which the department is responsible. The items on a periodic inventory can be alphabetized or they can be grouped by activity or type of equipment

Perpetual Inventory Spreadsheet

Item _____

Catalog Number and Specifications	Number Ordered	Cost		Supplier and Address	Purchase Order Number	Invoice Order Number	Date Rec'd	Faculty Requesting	Date	Inventory			Total
		Unit	Total							New	Used	Discard	

FIGURE 9-4. Perpetual Inventory Spreadsheet

Periodic Inventory Spreadsheet

Page _____

Date of Inventory _____

Category of equipment _____

Item Description	1 New	2 Good	3 Fair	4 Discarded	5 Total	6 Purchased Since Last Inventory	7 Previous Inventory	8 Total	9 Lost (Difference between Columns 8 and 5)	10 Needed for Program	11 Additional Number Needed (Difference between columns 10 and 5)

FIGURE 9-5. Periodic Inventory Spreadsheet

and then alphabetized. The periodic inventory total for each item should also be updated on the perpetual inventory.

The next step is to determine the total amount and type of equipment that will be needed during the next fiscal year. If a line-item budget is being used, analysis of budgets for previous years indicates the amount of equipment normally required. This amount can be used as the starting point for determining overall requirements. Changes in the number of students, departmental policies, or the nature of the programs increase or decrease this amount. When the estimate of total equipment needed has been obtained, the amount of new equipment to be ordered is the difference between what is required and what is left over.

In making the estimate of what is needed, the administrator should be certain to order an adequate amount. It is better to err on the side of too much rather than too little equipment. This is not to suggest padding the budget, but to recommend liberal rather than conservative estimates. It is better to have a small amount of equipment left over at the end of the year than to run short.

In some elementary and secondary schools, the physical education department is given a budget for supplies (such as balls, nets, rackets, bows, arrows, and shuttlecocks) based on a certain amount per student in school. All expendable items for the department for the year must be purchased from this budget. In regard to equipment items (such as weight training mats, parallel bars, mats, and baskets), the principal is sometimes allocated a lump sum for such items annually. Priorities are established in light of all the school's educational needs and funds are allocated accordingly.

After the budget has been adopted, the equipment should be ordered. Practice varies in this regard. In some schools, the physical education administrator is free to order whatever equipment she or he prefers if total spending does not exceed the money allocated. In other schools, bids from several merchandisers must be invited. In this case the administrator must prepare specifications. See Chapter 10 for detailed information on purchasing equipment.

The expertise of staff members should be solicited before ordering new equipment. Some staff members may have had more experience with certain equipment than the administrator, and their recommendations are very helpful.

A Practical Budget

In most situations, the board of education allocates funds for the physical education program and intramural/recreational program from the general school fund. The primary responsibility is to develop the expenditure portion of the budget. Expendable supplies, office and instructional equipment, and funds for maintenance and repair should be provided for each aspect of the programs. Transportation to locations away from the school for classes must be budgeted, where applicable. The usual procedure is to estimate the cost for each activity in the program and then consolidate this information into the major categories (such as equipment, expendable supplies, transportation, and officiating for intramurals). Additional categories are needed for office supplies, student salaries, custodial assistance, and clerical work. In most high schools and in smaller colleges, these items, together with faculty salaries, are included in the institutional budget.

The High School Athletic Budget

Interscholastic athletics are usually supported in part by the institutional budget and in part by gate receipts and other sources of income. Although most schools include coaches' salaries in the regular institutional budget and provide for the maintenance and operation of the athletic facilities, many do not appropriate funds to meet all of the current expenses of the athletic program (Figure 9-6).

Ideally, interschool athletics should be financed in the same way as any other school subject. The only justification for interscholastic athletics is the significant educational experiences they provide. These experiences are so important that they merit financial support from institutional funds. These values of athletics cannot be obtained if the program must be supported by gate receipts. Gate receipts and educational outcomes are incompatible objectives. Experience has repeatedly demonstrated that athletics are conducted on a much higher plane if they derive their support from regular school funds and do not have to depend on gate receipts.

The unwillingness of many schools to finance athletics properly stems from the philosophy that only academic activities deserve such support. Athletics originated as an extracurricular activity and in some schools is still considered in that category. However, in most instances, interscholastic athletics are considered an integral part of the school curriculum and boards of education are empowered to provide financial assistance from regular school funds.

The practice of expecting interschool athletics to be largely self-supporting has led to many of the problems that have developed. The amount of gate receipts depends largely on the success of the teams. The effort to produce winning teams often results in undesirable educational practices. When the public exerts undue influence on the interschool programs, educational authorities lose control and objectionable policies are often followed. Interschool programs must have financial independence if they are to emphasize educational goals, with value to the participants as the paramount consideration.

Sources of Athletic Income

The school board should allocate funds to adequately support the entire athletic budget. The athletic budget must be carefully prepared and justifications provided to show how the money will be used to provide a high-quality program. Other sources of income are also used in many high schools. When money is obtained from these sources, it should revert to the institutional budget and not affect the amount of money available for athletics. The athletic program should not be hindered by such factors as bad weather and losing seasons, which reduce gate receipts.

Gate Receipts   Gate receipts are an important source of income for some interscholastic programs. Football and basketball are the chief income-producing sports, although even these are not operated at a profit in many schools. Other interscholastic sports rarely produce a significant profit.

Gate receipts should come predominantly from the adult public. It is an accepted policy to keep admission prices for students at a minimum; some high schools admit all students free. Students should also be given priority when it is necessary to limit attendance at athletic contests because of insufficient seating.

Budget	
Sydwood High School Athletic Department	

Estimated Expenses	
Personnel	
Coaching stipends	$78,325
Nonsecurity support (scorers, timers, ticket sellers, etc.)	14,300
Security support	9,800
Police	7,000
Officials	36,000
Transportation (private cars and school buses)	
Scouting	500
Varsity contests	6,000
JV contests	3,100
Meetings	1,000
Uniforms	10,000
Equipment	14,000
Supplies (teams)	35,000
Supplies (Medical)	2,000
Maintenance and Repair	8,500
Printing, advertisements	4,000
Office administration	2,000
Entry fees	5,200
Awards	4,000
Cleaning and laundry	3,600
Total estimated expenses	**$244,325**

Estimated Income	
School board support	$193,025
Ticket sales	16,000
Student activity fee	8,000
Concessions	7,300
Student activity passes	3,000
Fundraising	8,000
Booster club support	9,000
Total estimated income	**$244,325**

The Sydwood High School Athletic Department budget is based on the approved budgets submitted by the head coach of each sport and the athletic office costs, which include the coaching stipends for all sports and security for all contests. At Sydwood High School, the athletic trainer is a full-time faculty member whose salary in funded by the school board.

FIGURE 9-6. Athletic Budget

The philosophy that the interschool athletic program should be subsidized by the institution does not imply that gate receipts should be abolished. Gate receipts are an important source of income for some school districts and charging a fee to the public is helpful to many school administrators in maintaining crowd control. Gate receipts are not objectionable as long as they are incidental. Sufficient funds should be appropriated to ensure the adequate operation of the program. The remaining gate receipts revert to the institutional budget.

In many high schools, all athletic income goes directly into the student activity budget. This includes gate receipts and any guarantees that come from games played away from home. In this situation, the costs of equipment, travel, medical care, scouting, advertising, towels, laundry, films, officials, and other operational expenses are defrayed by the student activity budget.

The best way to increase gate receipts from high school athletics is to have well-coached, winning teams. However, there are other methods of making athletic contests more attractive to the public. A season ticket sold at a reduced rate is one of the most effective methods of increasing gate receipts. Such a plan guarantees a definite income despite poor teams and bad weather. It also provides funds early in the season when they are needed most. Adults appreciate the opportunity because it results in a saving to them. The price of a season ticket varies from 50 percent to 75 percent of the total cost of tickets to each home game. If season tickets are transferable, they are even more attractive.

In many communities, reserved seats appeal to certain spectators. Some people are willing to pay more if they are guaranteed a good seat. There are always people who are unable to arrive at the game in time to get a good seat and would not attend if reserved seats were not available.

One of the strongest attractions and most colorful features of athletic contests is the music, cheering, and pregame and halftime entertainment. Good officiating adds to everyone's enjoyment of a game. Attractive, accurate programs, a good scoreboard, and a loudspeaker system with a capable announcer are all factors that provide satisfaction to the spectators.

Other factors that contribute to the comfort and enjoyment of spectators are good seats, convenient entrances and exits, and a sufficient number of clean, readily accessible restrooms. Having good parking facilities available near the athletic field or gymnasium is an important consideration. Contests should always be started at the time advertised.

The importance of good publicity in increasing gate receipts is well-established. Publicity is discussed in detail in Chapter 6.

Student Activity Fees   Another important source of income is the student activity fee. Some high schools have adopted a student activity plan to provide support for all student activities. Under this plan, each student pays a prescribed amount and is entitled to admission to all home athletic contests and all other school functions for which there is a charge, such as school plays and concerts. In addition, the cost of the student newspaper and the school yearbook is defrayed in whole or in part. Most schools also admit students from the visiting institution to athletic contests at a reduced rate on presentation of a student activity card. Students who do not belong to the student activity association are usually admitted to home contests at a reduced fee.

The income from student body fees is usually apportioned over the various student activities. The allocation may be made by the student council, a student activity board, or a committee made up of representatives of the various activities.

Booster Clubs   Parent and community booster clubs are sometimes organized to support athletic programs. Major equipment items are purchased by these groups and they also assist in the operation of concessions, which can provide significant sums of money for the program. Booster groups sponsor end-of-the-season athletic banquets in some communities. They can be a positive force in a community, but care must be taken that the total athletic program receives support and not only certain segments. An even greater danger of booster clubs is that they can unduly influence the organization and administration of the athletic program. Administration and organization must remain the responsibility of the educational authorities. This is another reason why it is much better that the athletic program be supported entirely by the board of education.

Concessions   The income-producing possibilities of concessions are rarely appreciated in small schools and colleges. In these smaller institutions, where the financial need is the greatest, concessions are often overlooked or, if they are used, they are inefficiently operated. Professional teams and large university athletic departments have discovered that there is substantial revenue in concessions if they are properly handled.

Concessions may be handled by the school itself or by an outside concessionaire. Within the school, it may be operated by the physical education or athletic department, the athletic association, or by some student organization. When concessions are handled outside the school, the concessionaire should be selected from a round of competitive bids. In advertising bids, the detailed specifications that govern the concession should be stated and should become part of the concession contract. The concession specifications should indicate the commodities that may be sold. Standards of sanitation and methods of vending should also be explicitly stated.

The contract should provide for payment of a percentage of gross receipts; a flat-sum arrangement may be unfair to the institution or the concessionaire. Net income should not be used as the basis for determining percentages, as there is invariably the question of what costs the concessionaire includes in determining net proceeds.

For interschool athletic events that draw large crowds, the management of the concessions becomes such a large business operation that high schools and colleges have difficulty handling it effectively. In these instances, some institutions have found it advantageous to have a concessionaire handle them. Experience has shown that more income can be received from a concessionaire than from a poorly operated school concession.

Fundraisers   Many athletic programs resort to all types of fundraising activities when schools reduce their financial support. Unfortunately, many administrators and coaches find themselves spending an inordinate amount of time on fundraising to maintain athletic programs. Fundraisers range from the ever-popular swim-a-thons and run-a-thons to absurd promotions such as Jell-O wrestling. Budget difficulties in many communities have forced athletic programs to use fundraising methods to survive. The goal still must be to have athletic programs fully supported by institutional resources.

Business Support   Attempts are being made in districts with financial difficulty to get business support for athletic programs. This has been successful in some localities. Support has also been received from professional teams in some cities. These can be successful stopgap measures, but long-term financial support is critical if athletic programs are to provide educational benefits for all students who want to participate.

Pay to Play   The most recent trend in obtaining financial support for athletic programs has been to initiate pay-to-play plans in schools. Each student who wants to play on a school team pays a fee to the school. The fee charged varies enormously from a token amount to more than $100 per sport. Some states do not permit the charging of fees to play, but it is alarming to note the number of schools that charge a fee of this type to support their athletic programs. Although provisions are made for students who cannot afford the fee, it is an obstacle that excludes many students from participating in school athletics.

Procedure for Preparing the Athletic Budget

At the end of the season for each sport, a careful inventory of the equipment and supplies is made. Based on this inventory, the head coach of the sport makes out a tentative list of the equipment needed for the following year. This list and other estimated costs for the following year are reviewed by the athletic director, who might modify it in consideration of the anticipated funds. The athletic director submits a total athletic budget to the department chairperson or principal, depending on the school's table of organization. (In some large systems, the athletic director from each school submits a budget to the director of athletics for the entire school system, who prepares a district athletic budget.) The principal submits the budget to the superintendent of schools, who in turn presents the budget to the board of education for final approval.

Special Procedures in Large Cities

Interscholastic athletics in larger cities are usually coordinated by an administrator who functions from a central office, usually the superintendent's office. Methods of operation vary from city to city. When funds for athletics are provided by the board of education, gate receipts are returned to the general fund. In other situations, the receipts should be pooled and distributed as equitably as possible to all the schools. This ensures that each school has comparable financial resources; no school has an advantage over any other. Athletic equipment is purchased on a centralized basis and the quantity purchases result in significant savings.

Control of Finances

In the early days of interscholastic and intercollegiate athletics, control of finances resided in the hands of the coach or a member of the community. These people were rarely called on to account for the funds of the athletic department, and audits to check the athletic accounts were seldom used. Under these conditions, it is not surprising that a great deal of money was misused and misappropriated. Such financial practices naturally served to increase the evils of commercialization and subsidization.

Financially and educationally sound methods of handling interscholastic athletic funds have evolved. In general, the trend is for this money to be handled in the same manner as other school funds. The practice of having the treasurer or business administrator of the board of education handle all athletic funds has much to recommend it. Such a plan centralizes all financial matters and ensures a more businesslike procedure. In particular, a more accurate audit is likely to result. The recommended practice is to use a centralized accounting system whereby the responsibility for all financial accounts is centralized in one person, such as the principal or a designated business manager. A system whereby the various accounts are decentralized and handled separately leads to confusion and inefficiency.

In the centralized accounting system, all athletic funds, along with all other activity funds, are deposited with the school treasurer. Records are maintained for all deposits. When purchases are to be made, a purchase order in triplicate must be signed by the athletic director, then certified by the school treasurer. One copy is kept by the athletic director. Bills are not paid by the school treasurer until an invoice has been received from the vendor and checked by the athletic director or designee to determine that the materials received correspond with what has been ordered. At periodic intervals, at least once a month, the school treasurer submits a report to the athletic director and principal on the condition of the athletic budget.

The school treasurer should be bonded for the largest sum of money that will be in the fund during the year. The account should be audited by a qualified auditor.

Handling School Funds

Schools are often careless in their management of gate receipts. The large sums of money that often are involved should call forth all precautions to insure against loss. Another argument for the sale of tickets in advance of the game is that it prevents the accumulation of large sums of money. Theft insurance is carried by all large schools, and the game manager is usually bonded. Police protection should be provided, particularly when the funds are collected and taken from the ticket offices. Unless the amount is very small, arrangements should be made to deposit the gate receipts in a bank after the game.

It is a cardinal principle in schools as well as in business organizations that all financial transactions should be recorded in some tangible way. For this reason, receipts for all purchases are necessary. By the same token, when money is received receipts should be given and copies retained. Such receipts are essential when the accounts are audited. An accurate record of ticket sales at athletic contests must also be available. Ordinarily this is done by recording the number on the ticket roll before and after the game. These data are also necessary for the auditors.

Interschool Financial Agreements

Practically all large high schools sign contracts with each other for all interschool contests. The practice of making verbal financial agreements still persists in some high schools. Such a procedure is not businesslike and it naturally lends itself to misunderstanding and mistakes. In order to make financial agreements between schools more understandable, more explicit, and more binding, regular contracts should be signed by both schools for all contests.

Game Reports

In many schools, the athletic director is expected to provide game reports after each contest. This report includes items such as attendance (according to such categories as children, students, general admissions, and so forth), gate receipts, complimentary tickets, expenses, other income, weather conditions, and the score. These reports are a valuable record for future use, especially in the preparation of future budgets.

The College and University Athletic Budget

The athletic budgets at colleges and universities vary tremendously. At some large institutions, athletic programs are multimillion dollar businesses and the complexity of financial management rivals that of noneducational businesses. At the other extreme are college and university athletic programs that operate as a part of the total educational program of the school and receive a significant portion of their financing from the institutional budget. The huge sums of money universities receive for bowl appearances and from television contracts obscures the fact that only a small number of institutions make a sufficient amount of money to pay for the cost of their total athletic program. Athletic programs are expensive at all levels of competition and the steady escalation of costs has mandated that sound business practices be followed in the small programs as well as in the large ones.

Budgetary procedures also vary according to the size and emphasis of the athletic program. In institutions with large, high-powered programs, athletic budgets are treated as separate entities. A full-time business staff is involved in developing the budget and overseeing all financial aspects of the operation. There is usually one person who has overall responsibility for the financial management of the program. At the other end of the spectrum are athletic programs whose budgets are incorporated into the institutional budget the same as any other educational unit such as the biology department. A hopeful trend has been the greater involvement of college and university presidents in the administration of all aspects of athletic programs, including financial management. There is widespread concern about costs of athletic programs and the impact of these costs on the educational mission of colleges and universities.

Sources of Athletic Income

Income for athletics in higher education is generated in a variety of ways. Some of the ways are similar to those at the secondary level, but more sophisticated. Part of this is because colleges and universities have many more staff who devote their efforts to raising money. Gate receipts are a major source of income, with a heavy emphasis on season tickets sales and many specialized seating plans. Sky boxes have been constructed in many stadia and their rental is a lucrative source of funds.

Booster clubs members contribute huge sums to athletic programs. Incentives are usually built into plans that provide preferred seating, convenient parking, dinners with the players and coaches, awards, and different kinds of recognition based on the level of giving. Contributions from businesses and individuals who are not a part of the booster club form another important income resource. Concessions are another source of income and at large institutions become a significant part of the funding plan for the athletic program.

Television revenue has escalated rapidly and is now an important source of income for major athletic universities. Television revenue and other revenue from national tournaments is also used to support national tournament expenses for participants from all colleges and universities regardless of competitive level. To a much lesser extent, radio broadcasting fees are another source of income for some of the larger institutions.

Institutional appropriations remain an important source of income for most college and university athletic programs. The salaries of coaches and other personnel connected with athletics, as well as the expense of maintaining and operating athletic facilities, come from this source at all but a few universities. At nonscholarship institutions, the institutional appropriations often provide funding for at least part of the operating expenses such as equipment, travel, medical care, laundry, and officiating.

Student fees are used at many college and universities to support the athletic program. Most institutions require a student activity fee and from this fee a percentage is allocated for athletics. In some of the major athletic schools, the students must also purchase individual game tickets or a season ticket if they want to attend athletic contests.

Suffice it to say that most colleges and universities are faced with the challenge of finding ways to obtain money for athletic programs. In addition to the ways that have been mentioned, all types of innovative fundraisers are used for either general program support or for specialized needs such as financing a weight training facility.

It should be mentioned that there are still some colleges and universities that provide for the complete support of intercollegiate athletics in the general budget. All expenses are covered by appropriations. The athletic income is purely incidental and reverts to the institutional budget.

The Control of Finances

Presidents of universities are exerting more control over the finances of their athletic programs. This has become necessary as athletics have become big business and the public is demanding greater accountability. Specially trained people are employed to assume responsibility for athletic financial affairs. At institutions with smaller program budgets, the university treasurer or business officer becomes responsible for the athletic funds. This practice ensures that a well-qualified person is in charge and that acceptable financial practices are adhered to throughout the athletic program.

The athletic director is still ultimately responsible for the financial aspects of the athletic program even when the above procedures are followed. Financial control requires not only a good business sense but expertise in applying sound financial principles. This is why it is critical that the university have oversight of financial matters. Support staff with financial background is also needed if the athletic director is not skilled in financial management.

The Leisure and Health Promotion Industry Budget

Skill in financial management and budgeting procedures is especially important for those in the leisure and health promotion fields. They cannot depend on appropriations to keep operating and if finances are not handled appropriately they will soon cease to exist.

Sources of Income

The people who use the services provide the bulk of the income. Memberships and participant fees are the primary sources of funds for privately run organizations such as health clubs and racquetball and tennis centers. Special activities sponsored as part of the offerings and rental of facilities are other sources. Food, clothing, and equipment concessions bring in substantial revenue for well-run organizations.

Nonprofit organizations are more dependent on support from members of the organization and fundraising activities. Some fee income is usually available but great emphasis is put on private, corporate, and business contributions. Fundraising drives and activities designed to raise money form the basis for funding of many nonprofit groups.

Steps in Preparing a Budget

The first step is to decide on the type of budget to use. Most businesses use a form of the PPBES or ZBB budget. Planning for the next year must include consideration of different programs that can be used to meet the needs of the program participants and ways that the number of participants can be increased. Preparing this type of a budget is more difficult in many ways than preparing a physical education budget because personnel costs and facility costs, including mortgage or rental costs, renovation needs, and maintenance, must be factored into the equation. All sources of income must be estimated and balanced with the anticipated costs. In the business field, desired minimal profit levels must be considered when developing the budget. In physical education budgeting, the greatest effort must be devoted to the expense portion of the budget because money is appropriated for the income.

Control of Finances

The chief executive officer is responsible for controlling the finances in the leisure and health promotion industry. Financial responsibility is often delegated to managers and directors of programs in an organization or business. Solid business practices and accepted financial procedures must be followed. It is best to have policies in place that clearly spell out financial protocol so all employees know what is expected of them. In addition to written policies, an in-service orientation program that covers financial matters is vital for all employees.

Class Activities

Simulation 1

Situation   The budget for a high school health and physical education program is due in six weeks. The director of health and physical education is responsible for constructing the budget, which includes capital outlay, equipment, maintenance and repair, and operations.

Obtain the health and physical education budget for the current year from a local high school. In the class, form three groups of students who will function as budgetary committees for the director of health and physical education. Have each group construct a budget for the next fiscal year.

Group 1—Line-item budget

Group 2—PPBES budget

Group 3—Zero-based budget

Compare the budgets and have each group share the negative and positive features of their budget and explain the process they followed in constructing the budget.

Simulation 2

Situation   The athletic director of a high school has just been informed that she will be responsible for raising $15,000 to support the athletic program of her school for the following year. There are 1,400 students in the high school, located in a city with a population of 36,500. The school has eighteen sports, with six offered each season (fall, winter, and spring).

Members of the class will act as advisory committees for the athletic director and develop a plan or plans for raising the $15,000.

Performance Tasks

1. Obtain equipment inventory forms from five schools. Compare the forms and develop one of your own that makes use of the best qualities of the five you have examined.
2. Survey the athletic directors at three schools that have booster clubs and obtain their views on the values of booster clubs for fundraising.
3. Meet with the business administrator or a member of the business office at your university. Find out what steps are followed and what time frame is used in developing the university's budget.
4. Interview two athletic directors. Find out how they generate funds for their athletic programs and where money comes from for each of the following:

   a. Coaches' salaries
   b. Officials
   c. Equipment
   d. Travel
   e. Awards

5. Write a petty cash fund policy for an elementary school physical education department.
6. Determine the categories that should be included in a budget for a commercial health and fitness club. List the income categories and the expense categories.

References

Ambrosio, Joseph, "Funding the Athletic Departments' Capital Improvements: A Growing Dilemma." *Athletic Administration,* October 1993, 28:56–57.

Berrett, Tim, "Economics and the Pricing of Sport and Leisure." *Journal of Sport Management,* September 1993, 7:199–215.

Buttersby, Mark E., "Cash Flow Planning." *Dance Teacher Now,* February 1994, 16:45–50.

"The Fundamentals of Cultivation and Solicitation." *Parks and Recreation,* December 1993, 28:38–43.

Kelsey, Craig W., Howard R. Gray, and Daniel D. McLean, *The Budget Process in Parks and Recreation: A Case Study Manual.* Reston, VA: AAHPERD, 1993.

Maloy, Bernard, "Beyond the Balance Sheet." *Athletic Business,* January 1993, 17:29–31.

Schmid, Sue, "Alternative Revenue." *Athletic Business,* November 1993, 17:20.

Stier, William F., *Fundraising for Sport and Recreation.* Champaign, IL: Human Kinetics, 1994.

Wiggins, Jon, "Building a Budget." *Athletic Business,* December 1993, 17:53–55.

C h a p t e r

10

The Purchase, Care, and Security of Equipment

Importance

The purchase and care of equipment was not an important responsibility of those in charge of the first physical education programs, as very little equipment was used with mass calisthenic programs. As programs became more extensive and diversified and many companies started promoting the sale of physical education equipment, the equipment responsibilities of the physical education director became more and more important. Equipment was not a major problem for interscholastic and intercollegiate athletics during their developmental years either because the athletes furnished most of the equipment they used. Relatively little equipment was needed because the athletic program was limited to a few sports, the squads were small, and the players were not equipped as elaborately and completely as they are now. Furthermore, the cost of physical education and athletic equipment was considerably less than it is today.

Today, the purchase and care of equipment constitutes one of the director's most important responsibilities. It is the responsibility of physical education intramural and athletic

193

departments to provide high-quality equipment for every aspect of their programs. Desired educational outcomes cannot be attained when equipment is insufficient or inadequate. Safety of the participants is a prime consideration. Appropriate safety standards must guide selection of the kind and quality of equipment to be purchased. In addition to protecting the student, good equipment contributes to a better learning climate and increased pride in performance. Well-equipped, well-dressed athletic teams have the added advantage of appealing more to the public than unattractive teams do. Equipment expense has become one of the largest items in the physical education and athletic budgets and a great deal of money can be wasted unless equipment is purchased carefully and cared for properly. Many of the expense items in the budget do not lend themselves readily to reductions, but directors have found many ways to reduce the expense of equipment without sacrificing performance and appearance. It is essential that every director know equipment thoroughly and be acquainted with the policies, methods, and techniques by which equipment can be bought and cared for most economically.

Sport equipment has become a major industry throughout the world. Manufacturing, promotion of specific brands, multimillion-dollar media campaigns, vast wholesale and retail operations, and extensive research for more efficient and safer designs are just some of the parts of this large industry. The development of this industry has resulted in better and safer equipment but it has also resulted in more expensive equipment. The administrator is faced with the formidable task of distinguishing different quality levels, evaluating costs of items that appear to be the same, and comparing the safety, durability, and construction of different materials and products. Technological advances have spurred the development of increasingly sophisticated equipment and as the level of skill has improved in athletics, better equipment is needed to keep pace with the higher levels of performance that characterize athletic competition. Safety for participants is the most important consideration for the administrator when selecting and maintaining equipment. Performance, appearance, and all other equipment characteristics are secondary.

Interest in fitness has had a major impact on the development of the sport equipment industry. This interest has spurred people of all ages to become physically active, resulting in many different types of health promotion programs. Commercial health clubs, fitness and sport centers, and wellness programs are multiplying throughout North America to provide opportunities for people to participate in a variety of fitness activities. These programs usually use high-quality equipment to appeal to participants. Weight training and fitness equipment must not only look good, but meet the highest safety standards. The newest features, such as computerization to show work load and effect on the user, are found in the commercial fitness field. An administrator in this area is challenged to purchase equipment that appeals to clients, is safe and durable, improves fitness levels, and is easy to maintain. Equipment is a key component of a commercial fitness enterprise.

Provision of Equipment

In early physical education and athletic programs, students were expected to provide their own equipment. As they began to administer these programs, institutions gradually took more responsibility for the equipment that was used. The need for better and safer equipment, increasing costs of equipment, and the desire to make programs available to all students led schools to furnish most of the equipment. Because physical education instructional programs, intramural programs, and interschool athletic programs are all part of the educational program of the school, essential equipment should be furnished by the school. No student should be prevented from participating because of his or her inability to provide appropriate wearing apparel or equipment.

Physical Education

It is the responsibility of the schools to provide the equipment needed for the instructional program. Students generally furnish their own uniforms for classes. The courts have held that a specific uniform cannot be required unless the school furnishes it. Many schools provide clean towels for students for each class. If students must furnish their own towels, close monitoring is necessary to make sure wet and dirty towels are not left hanging in lockers and that students remember to bring clean towels. Schools should strive to provide all equipment, including uniforms and towels, for students. Students usually provide their own footwear.

Intramurals

All game equipment should be provided for intramurals. Students commonly provide their own personal equipment. For strenuous activities, a towel service is recommended.

Interschool Athletics

The school provides all items of equipment including uniforms and shoes. Practice and game uniforms should be available for participants to use. Students should not be required to provide any of the items of their uniform. Inevitably, some students will not be able to be on the team because they cannot afford the needed items. Practice and game footwear should be provided for the students, as well as clean towels after every practice.

Athletic equipment and uniforms that are handed down from the varsity to junior varsity or first-year team members must be in good condition and meet all safety standards. It is critically important that shoes and protective equipment fit properly for every participant.

Specialized and personal equipment such as golf clubs, softball and baseball gloves, and tennis racquets are normally provided by the athletes. However, each school should have some of these items available for students who are unable to purchase their own.

Leisure and Fitness

Commercial health clubs and fitness centers provide high-quality equipment for their clients. They also have towel service and toiletries available in the dressing rooms. Top-of-the-line equipment is one of the amenities of commercial facilities. The exclusiveness of the organization and the membership cost determine the scope of the individual equipment provided for those who use the facility. Community recreation programs are at the opposite end of the spectrum. They often provide the facilities but expect those who use the facilities to furnish their own personal equipment. For some sport leagues, teams are expected to furnish the game equipment. Employee programs sponsored by businesses traditionally provide equipment. Personal items such as racquets and footwear are normally furnished by the employee, but workout clothing and towels are provided by the employer.

Purchasing Equipment

Ordering Equipment

A budget must be approved before the administrator can order equipment. See Chapter 9 for details on making up a budget. Requests for equipment usually are initiated by the teacher or coach who will be using it. Requests go to the department head or athletic director for approval before being sent to the supplier. This approval is needed to ensure that all programs are considered, budget allocations are followed, and established priorities are honored. In some schools, all purchase orders are received by a central business office or a purchasing office. It is important that this office not make budgetary decisions but rather check orders for accuracy and handle the mechanics of submitting the order.

Three forms are commonly used during the ordering process. These forms are a requisition form, a purchase order, and a voucher or invoice.

Requisition Form   This form is used to initiate the purchase process and is sent to the administrator to request that equipment be purchased. This form must contain accurate and complete specifications. The brand name, number of items, description of items, color (if applicable), and any other qualities that are desired in the product should be stated.

Purchase Order   This form is sent to the vendor (company) from whom equipment is purchased. (It is sent after bids are received or a company has been selected on some other basis.) It contains the complete specifications that were included on the requisition form. It includes the number of items being ordered, the per-item price, and the total price for the order. Delivery date should be stated, together with the name and address of the responsible person and the purchaser (school or organization) who should be billed, and the shipping address. The vendor's name and address, conditions of payment, order and account numbers, the date, and the purchaser's signature are also on the purchase order. An agreed-on billing date might also be listed on the purchase order. Figure 10-1 is a sample of a purchase order.

Voucher   This is the form on which the purchaser is billed by the vendor. The voucher is sent to the vendor in duplicate as part of the purchase order and then one copy is returned by the vendor when the order is filled. It is common to use a combined form for the purchase order and the voucher. Using one form reduces the chances for errors because the same information about the equipment specifications and the purchase agreement appears on both the purchase order and the voucher. The form is composed of multiple pages of different colors so they can be distributed to the person who requisitioned the item, the administrator, the business office, and the vendor. Letter size, 8 ½" × 11", is the commonly used size for purchase orders. The vendor returns one voucher copy when the goods are shipped and the purchaser checks the voucher against a copy of the purchase order to confirm that all items have been shipped.

Purchase orders should be filed for easy reference pending receipt of ordered items. When the items are received, they should be checked with the purchase order to make sure all items have been sent. This procedure should precede the processing of payment.

Invoice   If a voucher system is not used, the vendor sends a company invoice. (Companies may send their own invoice even if a voucher is provided by the purchaser.) A company

PURCHASE ORDER

School/Organization
Name and Address

FISCAL YR	TRANSACTION	TRANSACTION CODE	P.O. NUMBER

ACCOUNT NO.	AMOUNT	ACCOUNT NO.	AMOUNT
ACCOUNT NO.	AMOUNT	ACCOUNT NO.	AMOUNT

INSTRUCTION TO VENDOR:
(1) SEND ALL INVOICES TO DEPARTMENT INDICATED IN BILL.
(2) SUBMIT SEPARATE INVOICES FOR ALL PARTIAL SHIPMENTS.
(3) ENCLOSE PACKING LIST WITH ALL SHIPMENTS.
(4) SHOW ACCOUNT NUMBER AND PURCHASE ORDER NUMBER
    ON ALL BILLS OF LADING, INVOICES, AND CORRESPONDENCE.

QUOTE NO.	CONTRACT NO.	VENDOR ID NUMBER	PURCHASING CONTACT	PHONE

VENDOR:

S
H
I
P

B
I
L
L

T
O

T
O

DELIVERY DATE: _____

COMMODITY CODE		VENDOR INVOICE NUMBER	TERMS	FINAL PAY INDIC.	BILLING DATE	PAYMENT DUE

ITEM NO	QUANTITY	UNIT	DELIVER THE FOLLOWING ITEMS F.O.B./DESTINATION DESCRIPTION	UNIT PRICE	AMOUNT

AUTHORIZED SIGNATURE _____ DATE _____ TOTAL AMOUNT _____

FIGURE 10-1. Equipment Purchase Order

Vendor Equipment Invoice

Date ——————————   Vendor Invoice Number ————

                          Purchase Order Number ————

Purchaser:

    Name ——————————————————————————————

    Delivery address ———————————————————————

                     ———————————————————————

                     ———————————————————————

    Billing address ———————————————————————

                     ———————————————————————

                     ———————————————————————

Send Payment to:

    Vendor's Name ————————————————————————

    Address ——————————————————————————————

            ——————————————————————————————

            ——————————————————————————————

Item(s) Purchased:

Description of Items	Catalog #	Quantity	Total Price

Terms ——————————————————————————————

Appropriation ————————   Approval ————————

Rec'd OK   ————————   Date   ————————

FIGURE 10-2. Vendor's Equipment Invoice

invoice is an itemized bill of all goods that have been purchased and is sent to the purchaser for payment. The invoice, in duplicate, is either sent with the shipment or mailed to the purchaser after the goods are shipped. Figure 10-2 is the type of invoice form used by companies when a voucher is not included with the purchase order. At the lower left-hand corner of the sample invoice, the word *Appropriation* appears. This space should be used for indicating the sport, department, or activity to which the goods will be charged. The line marked *Rec'd OK* is used when the order has been received; one copy of the invoice can then be sent to the appropriate office for payment. A second copy of the invoice should be filed with the purchase order to show that the items have been received and that payment has been initiated. Any shipping errors should be noted in the *Rec'd OK* space and the company notified. A similar procedure is used with vouchers.

There are sometimes emergency situations when orders are made verbally by telephone or in person. Letters might also be used. When this is the case, a follow-up purchase order should be sent with the notation that it is a confirming purchase order. It is poor policy to depend on verbal orders because they do not provide an adequate record of the transaction. When the merchandise arrives, it cannot be checked accurately, and in case of a dispute the buyer does not have documentation to show exactly what goods were ordered.

Physical Education

Physical education teachers should be consulted about the equipment to be purchased for their teaching specialties. They are conversant with the different kinds of equipment and know what materials and types of construction hold up the best and are most effective and safest. The physical education director uses the information obtained from the teachers as a guide when purchasing equipment. Individual requests must be weighed in light of the budget and needs of all areas of the physical education program.

The director should be permitted to make purchases without approval of other administrators as long as the budget is adhered to and the school's purchasing procedures are followed. The director is qualified to know what equipment is best for the program and to purchase the appropriate kind and amount of equipment for a high-quality physical education program.

Interschool Athletics

The coach and athletic director must work cooperatively when making purchases. The coaches are best qualified to purchase equipment for their squads because they have the practical experience and know what materials and product specifications are needed. The athletic director is responsible for seeing that the equipment requests are in line with the budget and that the amount and type of equipment ordered can be justified. If an institution has an equipment manager, this person may have this responsibility. Existing inventories must be reviewed, condition of equipment on hand evaluated, and anticipated needs of the program reviewed.

In some high schools, the principal, business manager, or the superintendent is responsible for approving athletic purchases. This should not be necessary if the athletic program operates within a budget that has been approved by the board of education.

Leisure and Fitness

The size and type of the organization determine the kind of purchasing plan to be followed. In some regional and national fitness centers and health clubs, a central purchasing format may be used. If the local group has autonomy, purchases go through the business manager of that organization. Purchasing principles followed for physical education and athletics are also applicable for leisure and fitness programs. Staff members should be consulted about their needs or they should initiate requests, which are then reviewed by the manager. Staff members as well as corporate administrators need to be involved in determining the equipment to be included in the budget each year.

The Inventory

An accurate, up-to-date inventory is an integral part of every purchasing plan. After program needs are determined, the next step is to compare the equipment that is available with the equipment that is needed. An itemized inventory of all equipment on hand is essential (see Chapter 9). The condition and quantity of each item must be included in order to create an accurate list of new items that are needed. Some directors can be rightly criticized for being unable to justify the amounts of equipment they purchase. An inventory is the best insurance against overbuying on some items and underbuying on others. Firsthand information on the amount and condition of the stock on hand should always be available and accurate information about equipment requirements for each program must be provided by teachers, coaches, staff members, administrators, and equipment managers.

Purchasing Policies

After the needs have been determined, the director is prepared to buy. The purchase of equipment involves much more than merely buying goods to the limit of the budget. Every director is anxious to obtain the best service and the longest life of equipment per dollar spent. In order to attain this objective, recognized policies of buying should be followed. Purchasing physical education, sport, and leisure equipment is a business activity and it should be conducted in a businesslike way. Certain procedures are recognized as sound in any business. Although each organization presents separate problems, certain fundamental principles of buying are effective in most situations.

Standardization of Equipment

Standardization of equipment is a common expression among those who are involved in purchasing equipment. By this they mean the adoption of a certain color, type, and style of equipment that is maintained over a period of years. There are advantages in buying consistent types of equipment, such as practice equipment and game uniforms that will be used over a period of years. It is easier and more economical to reorder; when replacement items are needed, it is not necessary to purchase an entire new set of uniforms. If a special size is needed after the initial purchase, this can also be done economically. When a type of equipment is used by several teams, it is cost-effective to have it standardized so that purchases can be made in large quantities. This also reduces the necessity of having a large inventory of equipment that is used only on a seasonal basis. Standardization makes it easier to obtain parts and replacement items and repairs can be made more successfully. It also alleviates inventory problems when one style of a piece of equipment is used.

High-Quality Merchandise

The best policy is to purchase high-quality equipment. Superior quality equipment provides longer use, more satisfactorily fulfills its designated use, fits better, looks better, and can be repaired more effectively than cheap items. The buyer should not confuse cost with quality. The most expensive equipment is not always the best, but it must be recognized that good material is more expensive than cheap material. The administrator is expected to recognize differences in quality and purchase only equipment that best meets user needs, provides good performance, and falls within the parameters of the equipment budget. A principle to keep in mind is that, in most cases, low-cost items are low-grade items. When in doubt, it is best to purchase from companies that have a reputation for selling high-quality equipment and to purchase brand-name items. Unless it is a new piece of equipment, it is also a good procedure to investigate to see how the equipment has served another school, health club, or recreation program. The practice of purchasing cheap merchandise for reserve or first-year teams or for physical education or intramural programs is not economical in the long run. It is better to pass down from the varsity team high-quality equipment in good repair than to provide a cheap grade of equipment that may last for one season but is not suitable for long-term use or for reconditioning.

Buy within Range of Ability to Pay

This is a sound policy in every business. Although schools, leisure programs, and athletics operate on a budget, it is easy to spend more for equipment than can be afforded. *Budgets should be adhered to with care.* Buying too much or too expensive equipment has plunged many into debt. Buying too much equipment is not as serious a mistake as buying too expensive equipment, unless this causes a serious cash flow problem, because surplus equipment can usually be used later. Many coaches and directors are overanxious to equip their teams with the best and go to extremes in their buying. Although high-quality merchandise is advocated, most secondary schools cannot afford to buy the same grade of equipment or as much specialized equipment as universities. When a director or manager overpurchases equipment, the operations of the entire department or organization may be curtailed and the ability of the administrator is questioned. Spurt buying also leads to difficulties. Consistent, regular buying is better in the long run.

Early Ordering

The director should not overlook the advantages of ordering equipment early. These advantages include the following:

Early delivery. This is an advantage because opportunity is still available to correct mistakes, make size adjustments, and order additional items as needed.

Better equipment management. When equipment is delivered early, ample time for marking and storing is available.

Better equipment. An early order is more likely to result in exact equipment carefully made to specifications by unhurried manufacturers.

Early buying also aids the manufacturer by providing a better estimate of the expected volume of business. Better materials can be produced at a better price if the labor is spread out over the entire year instead of being concentrated at certain intervals. In addition, the reputable manufacturer has the opportunity to replace materials that are defective or not up to standard.

Equipment dealers can provide information about ordering deadlines. These deadlines differ according to the type of equipment being purchased, the manufacturer, the geographic area of the country, and whether the item is a stock item or is to be custom-made. As a rule, equipment on hand should be inventoried and new equipment ordered as soon as the season is completed. The following schedule can be used as a guide for ordering equipment:

Fall sports—order by March 1

Winter sports—order by June 1

Spring sports—order by October 1

It is of paramount importance that the equipment be ready when it is needed. This is the most important reason why it should be ordered early. It might also be possible to save money, as sometimes discounts can be obtained for early orders. It is the policy in many schools to send in orders for all anticipated equipment once a year.

The Best Interests of the School Should Guide Purchasing Decisions

Many sporting goods dealers, in order to obtain a school's equipment business, offer gifts to the coach or administrator. A set of golf clubs, shoes, jacket, fishing tackle, or a tennis racket might be offered. Such inducements (bribes) should never be accepted; it is a violation of professional ethics to do so. Decisions about equipment purchases should be based on the best interests of the school rather than the personal gain of the person making the decision.

Purchase from Reputable Companies

It is essential to deal with companies that have a proven reputation for sound business policies. Reputable dealers properly serve all accounts. Service to a buyer is an integral part of the manufacturer's product. Reliable companies also guarantee the excellence of their products and this guarantee is worth paying for.

Few directors are accurate judges of textiles, leathers, and other materials used in the manufacture of sporting goods equipment. Cheaper grades of fabrics, fiber, padding, and leather can be made to look like better-grade materials. The integrity of equipment companies must be relied on unless the director knows equipment thoroughly. Administrators quickly discover that buying from reputable firms is more satisfactory and more economical as a long-term policy.

This does not mean that all goods should be bought from the same firm year after year. The tendency to form too strong an attachment for a particular manufacturer should be avoided. The quality and price of one company's goods may change to advantage or disadvantage. New materials and new processes may enable one firm to excel temporarily in certain items. It is better to keep an open mind regarding the products of different manufacturers.

Take Advantage of Legitimate Discounts

Many discounts that are offered to prospective buyers are, in reality, no discount at all. The amount of the discount is added to the original price so that it can be taken off to attract purchasers. However, "2 percent within 30 days" is a legitimate discount. Discounts of this type are offered by the seller for the advantage of being paid promptly, increasing the cash flow, and having the money to earn interest for a longer period of time. Considerable money can be saved if discounts of this type are available. When ordering early, a good procedure is to specify an acceptable billing date. This applies with or without a discount, so payment can be made as late as possible.

There are a number of other ways in which the director can secure legitimate discounts. Discounts are often offered on large orders, close-outs, overstocked items, promotional and new items, and on items that are classified as seconds. Seconds should be purchased only if the imperfection does not reduce the value of the equipment for its intended use.

Bids and Specifications

Directors must be aware of state statutes and local policies that determine the bid procedure that must be followed. Small purchases can usually be made without bids. This sum varies and might be $100 in one school district or wellness center and $250 in another. Informal bids may be telephone or written quotations and are required on more expensive purchases, such as those from $250 to $2,500. Formal bids are needed for anything over $2,500 and require public advertising and receipt of sealed bids that are opened at a public meeting. Bids are a valuable aid in getting the lowest possible price and they provide a fair method of determining which companies should supply the equipment. The usual practice is to require a minimum of three bids unless a piece of equipment is unique to one supplier or standardization policy requires a specific item.

There are problems with bids. It takes more time and one cannot always be certain that the low bidder will provide the best service. Some unethical companies submit bids on one item and deliver a cheaper item or attempt to have a poorer piece of equipment accepted. Because of this problem, it is critical that stringent, detailed specifications be written. This is particularly important when an or-equal clause is included on bid requests. It is the responsibility of the director to make certain an or-equal item is equivalent in all aspects to the requested item. There should be no hesitation in refusing an item even though the reason must be justified in detail. A company that provides inferior equipment or inadequate service should not be permitted to bid on future orders.

Some states now use a state contract system whereby vendors, including physical education suppliers, provide a standing bid on specified items for a six- or twelve-month period. State institutions then buy directly from the vendors who have been awarded a state contract based on their bids. School districts also have the option of buying from state contract sources at the bid prices.

Professional Relationship with Vendors

Be fair in all dealings with vendors and do not expect or solicit special favors. All dealers should be treated in the same manner and confidential information should not be shared with others. Keep them informed and give all vendors an equal opportunity to submit and amend bids. Communicate courteously and promptly during business dealings.

Official Equipment

Practically all games or sports have certain items of equipment that must be manufactured to specifications and are commonly marked *official*. The specifications may call for a definite weight, length, relative dimensions, certain types of material, or the exclusion of certain materials. Purchasers should be acquainted with such specifications or any changes that may occur from year to year or season to season. Cases have occurred where competitors have been ruled out of an athletic event or records have been refused on the grounds that the implements used were not official.

Local Dealers

It is a good policy to make purchases from local dealers if they provide the needed items of equipment at prices that are comparable to other dealers and the other dealers are treated honestly and fairly in the process. Ordinarily, the local dealer is in a position to provide better service within the community and this criterion should be considered in awarding non-bid contracts. (Service requirements should be stated as part of the bid process also.) Local businesses provide community support through taxes and other assistance they provide for schools and leisure programs in the community. These considerations justify dealing with local firms on a regular basis.

How to Buy

The best buyers study market conditions for good values. Equipment prices fluctuate and the director who knows when to buy and when to refrain from buying can save money. Although prices are fairly uniform among sporting goods suppliers, excellent values are often offered on certain items by the various companies. If the director or equipment manager records and files the prices of equipment of different firms, rapid comparisons can be made when preparing to order equipment and special discount purchase opportunities are readily noted.

The most effective way to discover how equipment stands up is to use it and check the results. Comprehensive records should be kept by the equipment manager or person serving in that role. Equipment should be marked and its condition checked periodically. Teachers, clients, students, athletes, and coaches who use the equipment should be asked for their impressions about the quality of the equipment and how satisfactory it was during use. The perpetual inventory (see Chapter 9) provides information that will help the administrator evaluate equipment durability.

Considerations in Selecting Equipment

Design and Style

Massive changes have taken place in the styling and design of equipment and clothing used for athletics and physical education. Uniforms for the various sports used to be the same from year to year and team to team. Baseball uniforms are a good example of how playing apparel style and design have changed. Now teams on all levels strive to outdo each other in coming up with eye-catching designs and styles. Part of this impetus has been provided by professional teams that employ fashion designers to outfit their teams. Although appearance and crowd appeal have been major factors in design changes, performance has not been forgotten. Uniforms are designed for comfort and ease of movement.

For competition, the rules for each sport must be followed when designing equipment. Practice and training equipment is often designed in innovative ways to improve performance. Equipment used in classes has undergone many styling and design changes to provide variety in classes, to enable participants of all ages to experience success, and to incorporate new and innovative games and activities into the curriculum.

In the leisure field, high priority is placed on specially styled and designed equipment that appeals to the user. For example, strength and cardiovascular development can be attained by using free weights and jogging on a track. However, health clubs know that attractive, state-of-the-art computerized machines are needed to bring in clients and motivate people to continue participating in an exercise program. The fitness boom has led to many styling and design changes in the equipment used in exercise programs in schools and commercial fitness centers. Changing styles and designs of equipment are excellent for motivation and research has improved all types of equipment used in physical education, leisure, and athletics.

Material

Each year, many new fabrics and materials, made from synthetics, different combinations of materials, and plastics, are introduced. The administrator is challenged to be informed about new materials and the qualities they have that can contribute to better programs. It is valuable to experiment with new materials and to learn from the experiences of others who use these materials. Research findings should be used to find out the positive and negative features of new materials that come on the market.

Utility of Equipment

Equipment should be purchased on the basis of utility; that is, it should meet specific game and safety needs. The purchase of equipment cannot be justified on the basis of appearance or innovative styling. It must be appropriate for the use for which it is purchased.

Maintenance

Equipment should be of such quality and construction that it is easy and inexpensive to maintain. In considering the cost of maintaining equipment, it is important to ask the following questions:

Are there ornamental attachments or other embellishments on the equipment that make it difficult to maintain?

Can the maintenance be handled by staff members?

Are there companies or skilled people available to provide maintenance?

Does the equipment have to be repaired and reconditioned after normal use?

Is the equipment easily maintained and will it retain an attractive appearance over several years?

Is the equipment excessively costly to maintain for effective use?

Color

A wide spectrum of colors and color combinations are used for wearing apparel and all types of equipment. Select for attractiveness, appeal to the user, and to fit into the color scheme of the school or leisure program.

Safety

No piece of equipment should even be considered if it is not safe to use! Safety should be the first criterion for purchasing equipment. When equipment meets this criterion, then other factors such as cost, maintenance, and material can be considered.

Quality

There is no substitute for quality in equipment. The construction and the material should meet high standards of quality if the equipment is to be satisfactory.

Good Supply Sources

It is important that sources of supply be readily accessible and that professional sales personnel, knowledgeable about the different features of equipment, be available for assistance.

Price

It is never wise to sacrifice quality for price. Don't experiment with untested low-cost equipment. Equipment should never be purchased on the basis of price alone.

Purchasing Specific Items

In this section, the discussion centers on some specific items of equipment and the features that purchasing agents should keep in mind when making selections.

Fabrics

A wide variety of fabrics are available for physical education, leisure, and athletic garments. There are natural fibers and synthetic fibers. Most of the fibers are synthetic, although cotton, a natural fiber, is used extensively and some wool is used. Commonly used synthetic fibers are nylon, rayon, polyester, and spandex. Fibers are combined to make many different fabric materials and this blending makes it possible to capture the advantages of each fiber that is used. Advanced technology in fabric manufacture has resulted in garments that are more durable yet lightweight, and can be designed for the specific needs of different sports. The purchaser must be aware of the advantages and disadvantages of the different types of fabrics and buy garments that are best for wear, comfort, appearance, weather, and sport or activity for which they will be used.

One of the problems encountered with fabrics is shrinkage. "Sanforized" garments have been tested for shrinkage in accordance with United States government-approved tests. They are guaranteed not to shrink more than 1% in width and length.

Colorfastness is another essential quality for fabrics. Because garments are subjected to sunlight, perspiration, and frequent washings, the best dyes and best coloring processes must be used to maintain colors and prevent fading and running of the colors.

Shoes

Shoes are important items of equipment. It is a sound principle to purchase the best shoes that the budget permits because, in the long run, it is most economical. Because so many different types of leather, tanning processes, and construction features are involved in the manufacture of shoes, it is particularly important to buy shoes from reputable manufacturers. The administrator should also be familiar with research findings that are reported in the trade journals about the strengths and weaknesses of different brands and grades of shoes.

The design of shoes change, as do materials that are used in their construction. The serviceability of shoes and their ability to withstand the stresses of each sport or activity must be considered when they are evaluated. Shoes are exposed to perspiration, sudden stops, quick starts, sharp turns, and abrasive surfaces. Shoes used outdoors must be able to withstand mud, water, high or freezing temperatures, damp grass, or snow. Shoes must keep their shape, give support, and maintain the characteristics that contribute to good performance and comfort.

A critical consideration in shoe selection is fit. Correct size is probably more important in shoes than in any other item of apparel. The consequences of improperly fitted shoes can be extremely serious for the athletes' performance and health.

Jerseys

Nylon and nylon mesh are the most common materials for jerseys. They are lightweight, feel good, wear well, launder easily, and are resilient. Lettering and numbering must be in accord with regulations established by the high school, college, or international organization under whose jurisdiction the team or individual competes.

Inflated Balls

Rubber balls of all types have been greatly improved in recent years and, because they are appreciably cheaper than leather balls, they have supplanted the latter in many instances. Rubber balls are used extensively in instructional classes and intramural activities. Some interscholastic and intercollegiate teams use them at times for practice. Rubber balls are durable, do not lose their shape, and do not pick up moisture. Because they resist moisture, rubber balls are especially valuable for football or soccer practices held in the rain or on a wet field. Rubber basketballs, volleyballs, and softballs are also available.

Governing bodies specify not only the dimensions of the balls that are used but also the material to be used in the manufacture of the ball. Some conferences adopt a specific brand and quality of ball to ensure uniformity from game to game. A better price can often be negotiated when a quantity purchase of this type is made.

Many different types of inflated balls are available for class use. The size and type of ball should vary according to the activity, the age of the children, where the ball is used, and the way that the ball is used in the activity.

Specialized Equipment

Every sport requires some specialized equipment. The list would be too extensive to be included here. Physical education directors, athletic directors, teachers, coaches, and leisure program managers must research the various types of materials and construction that are used in clothing and equipment specific to the different sports. Based on this information, intelligent equipment purchases can be made. New products are continually being made available. The director should evaluate the positive and negative features of new as well as extensively used products and use this information as a guide for spending equipment money as judiciously as possible.

National Operating Committee on Standards for Athletic Equipment

Safety in sports is the concern of a vast array of organizations, individuals, businesses, and agencies that are involved with sports and the well-being of those who participate in sports. In 1969, the National Operating Committee on Standards for Athletic Equipment (NOCSAE) was formed to commission research on injury reduction in sports. Organizations participating in the formation of this committee included the National Federation of State High School Associations, the National Athletic Trainers Association, the Athletic Goods Manufacturers Association, the American College Health Association, the National Collegiate Athletic Association, and the National Junior College Athletic Association. The NOCSAE organization is now made up of representatives from groups representing manufacturers, reconditioners, athletic trainers, coaches, equipment managers, and sports medicine and consumer groups.

The accomplishments of NOCSAE in commissioning research and establishing standards for protective athletic equipment are impressive. They're best known for their football helmet standard. Every player participating under either NCAA or National Federation football rules must wear a helmet on which the seal *Meets NOCSAE Standard* is permanently stamped on the outside rear portion of the helmet. NOCSAE has also established helmet standards for baseball batting helmets and for the lacrosse helmet and face mask. The research efforts of NOCSAE have also led to a better understanding of the mechanism and tolerance of head and neck injuries and more knowledge concerning the design and structure of football helmets, football face masks and attachments, baseball/softball batting helmets, and lacrosse protective headgear and face masks.

Care of Equipment

Equipment Manager

Most colleges and universities have equipment managers who are responsible for physical education and athletic equipment. In smaller institutions, this may be a dual responsibility; larger programs may have separate staffs for physical education and athletics. Secondary schools are also adding equipment managers to their staff as programs expand, equipment becomes more sophisticated and expensive, and liability concerns lead to the employment of equipment managers who are qualified to properly fit athletes with protective equipment for sports such as football and lacrosse. Fitness centers, health clubs, and other organizations involved in sport activities are also finding that it is important to have equipment managers.

The Athletic Equipment Managers Association has developed a certification program for equipment managers. This enables schools to employ people who are qualified to handle the multifaceted responsibilities of equipment management. Equipment managers are responsible for a number of duties. The exact responsibilities vary from institution to institution but the role of the equipment manager is expanding on all levels. Responsibilities are included in the following areas:

Purchasing of equipment

Fitting equipment and clothing

Maintenance of equipment, including repair

Organization and administration of the equipment room and the use of equipment (including developing policies and procedures for safe and efficient use of equipment)

Management and professional relations, including staff management skills and the ability to communicate and work with vendors, coaches, athletes, and administrators

Accountability for equipment, including the development of an effective issuing, control, security, and marking system for equipment

Equipment Room

A good equipment room is essential in the proper care of equipment. A carelessly kept supply room can take a greater toll on the life of equipment than many hours of hard service on the playing field because equipment spends most of its life in the equipment room. The equipment room should be conveniently located near the locker rooms or, in educational settings, near the training room. It should be large enough to store all of the equipment adequately and provide sufficient space for handling and repair. Proper lighting and heating are important. The equipment room must be well-ventilated, dry, free from sweaty walls and pipes, and protected from moths, roaches, mice, and other animals. The equipment room should be so constructed that shelves and bins can be built against the walls in order to hold articles readily accessible for issue. Deep shelves that will accommodate cartons and bulky articles are necessary. Narrower shelves for shoes and smaller articles are desirable. Enough shelves should be available so that nothing is dumped in the corners or on damp floors. Steel bins and shelves are recommended. A cage-door, sliding window with a counter is necessary.

Storage cabinets that can be locked should be provided for expensive and high-theft items. This is particularly important if the equipment room is not restricted to full-time equipment personnel. Out-of-season equipment should be placed in a locked compartment away from the issue area. Separate storage areas for each sport have been found to be the best procedure when individual coaches are responsible for their team's equipment.

Every athletic department needs a drying room in conjunction with the equipment room. Placing wet uniforms in a locker after practice or a game tends to rot the material and rust the lockers. An inexpensive drying room can be built in most gymnasiums if one is not available.

Equipment Room Management

An equipment room manager is indispensable to the teacher and coach who must be out on the field or court at the same time that students need to get equipment. It is best to have a full-time equipment manager. If this is not possible, a paraprofessional can be trained or a faculty member who does not coach can fill the function of the equipment manager for high school athletic programs. If a teacher or coach is responsible, students may be selected to manage the equipment room or team managers may have this as one of their responsibilities. The fitting of the equipment must then be done by the coach or another adult who has been trained to fit protective gear properly.

Student assistants may be used if the equipment room manager requires assistance. No other students should be permitted in the equipment room. When everyone has access to the equipment, the manager faces a hopeless task in preventing loss and preserving order.

Issuing Equipment Every piece of equipment issued should be accounted for. A very desirable method of keeping a record of equipment is through the card system. Each student signs a card on which is recorded the equipment issued. Every sport has a special card of a different color. For example, the football cards may be yellow and the basketball cards white. Cards are filed alphabetically by color. Each card lists the equipment items issued for that sport. Figure 10-3 is an example of a card that might be used.

At the beginning of the school year, the equipment manager should assign all lockers, issue equipment to the students on request of the director or coaches, and manage the towel service. In the course of a season, the equipment manager should inspect the playing equipment from time to time, taking out all equipment that is beginning to wear in order to protect athletes from possible injuries. The material that has been removed should be sent to the repair shop immediately. This means of checking and repairing often saves the department considerable money.

At the end of the playing season, the equipment manager and assistants check in all equipment. This can be done far better by clearing the lockers than by having the players check in their own equipment to the stockroom. There are always some players with more equipment than is charged against them, and this is the best method of securing it. Each piece of equipment, when checked in, should be tagged with its size and with the former player's name. This saves the manager time the following season in giving it out to returning players. Each article should be closely inspected and those needing cleaning and repair should be cared for at once. An inventory can be taken at this time in order to determine the equipment consumed during the season. A check can be made at the close of the season to see how the equipment has stood up in comparison with other makes during the previous years.

Some schools check each player's equipment into the equipment room daily. Every player is given a number, which appears on the locker to which the player is assigned. It is marked on each piece of equipment except the white equipment such as towels and socks. The number is also marked on the equipment rack above each player's hook in the equipment room, where the equipment is kept at all times. Only the white equipment is retained in the lockers. On reporting for practice, the player comes to the window of the equipment room and gives his or her number to the equipment manager, who goes to the rack and brings the player all the equipment placed under that number. At the close of practice every evening, the player returns the practice equipment to the window and the manager replaces it on the rack. The manager checks the equipment displayed under each number daily and, if any

Equipment Record Football

Name _____

Address _____

Date _____

Class _____

Practice	Out	In
Pants		
Shoulder pads		
Jersey		
Undershirt		
Sox–Inner		
Sox–Wool		
Supporter		
Stockings		
Shoes		
Special pads		
Towel		
Sweatshirt		
Game		
Pants–Rain		
Pants		
Jersey		
Shoes		
Shoes–Rain		
Sox		

Locker no. _____

Combination _____

Checked out by _____

Checked in by _____

FIGURE 10-3. Equipment Record

pieces are missing, tries to locate them. If any of the equipment needs repair, it is attended to immediately. The night before a game, the practice equipment is removed from the racks and temporarily stored. Game equipment is substituted in its place on the racks and the player follows the same routine for checking it out. This is an excellent system of handling athletic equipment and it is recommended if a large equipment room is available.

All equipment taken from the equipment room must be accounted for in some way. Instructors and coaches or their managers should sign for the equipment they use. Students who check out balls and other equipment for class and recreational use should sign for them.

Ordinarily, they are asked to return the equipment within a certain time and never to keep it overnight. The practice of students signing for equipment and then asking other students to return it later should be discouraged. This often results in lost equipment. In some schools, each student checking out an article exchanges it for an ID card, which is not returned until the borrowed items are returned. All equipment should be numbered and each student should then sign for a numbered item.

Use of Equipment   The development of the proper attitude among all students regarding equipment is the key to proper care of equipment. Much equipment is lost or damaged by carelessness or destructiveness. Often, varsity athletes do not feel an obligation to treat equipment carefully. Unless all students have respect for school property and a desire to care for their equipment, considerable damage and loss will be incurred. Students must appreciate the fact that equipment is lent, not given to them, and that they are responsible if it is lost. Petty thievery can best be combated by making each player accountable for everything he or she checks out.

Marking Equipment   All pieces of equipment should be marked in some way in order to identify them. The usual way of doing this is to stencil or stamp the name or initials of the school on the equipment. In addition, athletic clothing should have sizes clearly indicated. The identification of the school on athletic clothing does not suffice; the items issued to each player should be numbered and the numbers recorded in the equipment room. This is additional bookkeeping, but it helps to trace missing articles. When this system is known to all students in a school, it reduces the amount of stealing. Including the year of purchase in the marking system is a good procedure to use in determining the durability of equipment.

Cloth articles can be marked with a stencil and stencil paint or an India ink stamp. Leather goods can be stamped. In some institutions, initials are burned into leather goods, but unless this is done carefully, the leather will be damaged. Wooden items of equipment can be marked by burning initials at some convenient spot. Some items of equipment can be purchased already marked, usually for an additional fee.

Care of Specific Types of Equipment

It stands to reason that not all athletic equipment can be treated, cleaned, or stored in the same way. The materials from which the equipment is made—leather, rubber, fabric, wood, and so forth—require different methods of care. If the people using it are to get the maximum service from the equipment, they must know how to care for it.

Leather Balls   The vulnerable part of any leather ball is the stitching. The stitching can be protected by relieving the pressure inside the ball between seasons. Wiping off moisture and then slowly drying the ball when it is wet rather than forced drying also protects the stitching. When inflating a ball with a rubber core valve, always moisten the needle, preferably with glycerin. If the needle is moistened with the mouth, remove the moisture from the needle after using it. A rusty needle will injure the core of the valve. The needle should be inserted with a gentle; rotary motion. A pressure gauge should always be used to ensure correct inflation. A chart should be available next to the pump or on the wall to indicate the desirable air pressure for the different types of balls. Overinflation should be avoided because it strains the fabric lining and thus affects the shape and life of the ball.

A ball that has been used in the mud should be wiped clean with a damp cloth and dried at the normal room temperature. Leather balls should never be placed near a radiator or hot-air register. To clean a ball that has been discolored, commercial cleaners or saddle soap are recommended. When the leather of a ball has become harsh and rough because of repeated exposure to moisture, an application of a commercial leather dressing or a light mineral oil will prove helpful.

Leather balls should be partially deflated when stored between seasons. They should be stored in a cool, dry place without objects of appreciable weight on them.

Rubber Balls   The chief enemies of rubber are direct sunlight, heat, grease, and oil. Exposure to sunlight and heat should be avoided when possible. Grease and oil should be removed with soap and warm water. Dry-cleaning fluids should never be used on rubber goods. Rubber balls should be stored in a cool, dry bin, or box away from heat and sunlight.

Textiles   The manufacturer's instructions should be carefully followed to ensure maximum fabric life, prevent shrinkage, and maintain true colors. Equipment should be cleaned by trained and skilled operators. A good policy is to initially clean one item from a new group of garments to make certain the recommended cleaning instructions do not damage the garment. Water temperature, wet versus dry cleaning, the type of detergent, and the cleaning process should be determined by the manufacturer's recommendations.

After clothing is washed, it should be stored by size. Clothing not being used on a regular basis should be stored in closed containers or storage areas where dust does not collect, security is better, and clothing is protected from exposure to light and other atmospheric conditions.

Leather Goods   The most common sources of trouble with leather goods are high temperatures and excessive moisture. In order to prevent green mold rot, leather articles should be kept in a cool, dry place. When wet, leather equipment should be dried immediately, but the action should not be forced. The article should be dried at normal room temperature without the use of artificial heat. Sun drying and air streams or pressure drying should never be used.

Proper care of leather shoes is especially important. They are subject to dampness due to perspiration, rain, or snow. This moisture tends to remove the tanning oil from the leather, causing it to dry out and become misshapen. Dirt, mud, and other materials adhering to the shoes should first be removed. Warm water should be used if necessary. Leather oil should then be applied and worked into the leather. If the oil is warmed before application, it is more effective.

Before leather shoes are stored away after the season, they should be cleaned and oiled. They should be oiled again in the middle of the year. The toes should be stuffed with paper to help the shoe retain its shape. The shoes should be stored in special compartments to promote air circulation and to avoid crushing.

Wooden Equipment   Wooden equipment such as bats, hockey sticks, bows, and lacrosse sticks are built to last and will do so when properly handled. Moisture is the main source of damage, especially where the finish has worn away. Consequently, applications of warm linseed oil are recommended whenever the finish of the wood requires it. Equipment should be stored in such a way that prevents warping. Storage of wooden equipment in a cool, dry place is recommended.

Nets and Racquets   Top-quality nets should be purchased for both indoor and outdoor use. Top-grade nets are constructed to withstand the wear and tear of extensive use and weathering. The vinyl-coated headband and side and bottom tapes strengthen the net and extend its life significantly. This part of the net can be reconditioned.

It is good to have an equipment manager or an equipment staff member who is skilled at restringing racquets. A racquet should be restrung as soon as possible after a string breaks. Racquets have undergone rapid changes in the last few years. Equipment managers need to be familiar with construction of the racquet and the materials and string used in order to store them properly and provide appropriate care.

Archery   All bows should be unstrung when not in use. On the archery range, the bow should be hung on the ground quiver between rounds. When not in use, the arrows should be racked in a dry place. The rack should be so constructed that there are three pressure points on the arrow—two inches from either end and one in the middle—to prevent warping.

Mats   Mats should be washed daily with a mat disinfectant. Mats last longer if left flat rather than rolled. When mats must be rolled for storage, they should be rolled around a cylinder to minimize the pressure on the mat surface. Cuts, tears, and splits in the mats should be repaired immediately with the repair kit provided by the manufacturer. A clean surface under the mat will protect it from damage. Even after many years of use, mats can be recoated and restored to their original condition. Care must be taken when moving mats so they are not gouged or otherwise damaged. It is recommended that transporters be used for moving large wrestling mats.

Specialized Equipment   Different materials and a wide array of fabrics are used in the construction of physical education, athletic, and leisure equipment. The equipment manager, coaches, instructors, and program administrators need to be knowledgeable about the proper care for each item. Much of this information is received from the manufacturer who makes the item. Information should also be sought from those who use the equipment; it is often necessary to experiment with different ways of caring for new equipment just appearing on the market.

Cleaning Uniforms

Most uniforms used today are wash-and-wear and are designed to withstand heavy use. These two factors have been important in making it possible to keep uniforms clean and attractive even when they are worn frequently. There are three ways to wash school uniforms: commercial laundries or institutional laundries can be used or athletes can be held responsible for washing their own uniforms.

The school should be responsible for washing uniforms used for athletic contests. When the athletes are responsible for cleaning, the uniforms are not washed consistently, more damage occurs, and often they are not cleaned for the next contest. Explicit directions for the care of the uniform must be provided to athletes if they are expected to wash their uniforms.

Washing uniforms is a specialized type of work that requires trained personnel and proper facilities. The athletic director should seek a laundry that is capable of handling this specialized type of laundering. If the institution has its own laundry, the person who does the laundry should receive specialized training for washing uniforms. Sporting goods manufacturers recommend that the athletic director take a complete uniform to the laundry before the season to prepare the personnel for the type of cleaning it requires. If the staff at the laundry knows the fabric involved in all parts of the uniform, whether or not rubber is used, and the colorfastness of the garments, the fabric is much more likely to be cleaned properly. The staff at an institutional laundry should follow the same procedure.

Athletic uniforms are among the most difficult-to-clean garments. They are subjected to dirt, perspiration, rough use, and a variety of stains—grass, blood, resin, iodine, and adhesive tape. In addition, practically all pieces of the uniform consist of two or more fabrics, each of which may require specialized handling.

Excessive heat, whether in the wash water, rinse water, or in drying, will shrink the garment. Generally, lukewarm water (100°F) is recommended. In any case, the rinse water should be the same temperature as the wash water. Automatic tumble dryers and certain forced air methods are dangerous because of the heat.

White garments should always be washed alone. Different-colored garments should not be mixed. Colored garments are not adversely affected by lukewarm water, but high temperatures can be harmful. Any bleaching agent will have a serious effect on the colorfastness and therefore should be restricted to white or natural cotton garments.

Although few uniforms now require dry cleaning, the type of cleaning that is needed should be investigated before purchasing new uniforms. For certain fabrics, such as wool, dry cleaning is the only safe method. Any garment, such as two-way stretch football pants, that contains rubber yarn or elastic should never be dry cleaned as it will damage rubber threads. The same holds true for water-repellent garments.

Repairing Equipment

Physical education and athletic directors would profit by investigating thoroughly the possibilities of repairing their own equipment. The extent to which equipment should be repaired depends on the size of the school and amount of equipment handled. In some larger institutions, the stockrooms are so completely equipped that all equipment can be repaired. The practice in the majority of schools is to make simple repairs and to send the remainder to local or national reconditioning companies. Many schools could cut their equipment bills appreciably by enlarging their repairing facilities.

A sewing machine that can sew leather as well as textiles is indispensable in the equipment room. Such a sewing machine will more than pay for itself in a short time by mending the rips and tears that occur so often in all types of athletic materials.

Common sense must be used in repairing equipment. After a certain point, it is a waste of money to recondition athletic materials. Some directors make the mistake of repairing old equipment that will not give them enough service to pay for the repairs made. It is more advisable at times to sell old equipment to cleaning and reconditioning firms and use the money to buy new equipment.

In most schools, only minor repairs can be made on athletic equipment. The usual practice is to send all equipment in need of repair to special equipment reconditioning companies. Originally, many of these firms were not adequately prepared to do effective work, but most of those that have survived have developed the personnel, the specialized equipment, and the technical skill to do a superior job of reconditioning athletic equipment. Most directors find that in the long run it is more economical to turn over the bulk of the repair work to reputable companies of this type. Football helmets can be sent only to reconditioners that are authorized to recertify helmets.

Laundry

Today, many athletic programs, physical education departments, and health and fitness clubs are installing laundry equipment as a cost-saving device. The cost of sending out towels, game and practice uniforms, exercise attire, and other washable equipment has become a major expense. A significant amount of money is needed to install a laundry system, but it will pay for itself over a period of years. Convenience is probably as much of a factor as cost in stimulating this movement to institutionally run laundries. Clean clothing and equipment can be ready when they are needed. It isn't necessary to wait for the next delivery of clean laundry. Health clubs operate around the clock, teams play or practice at odd hours (during weekends and on holidays), and a rapid turnaround time is needed after apparel is used. There are some other advantages. A smaller inventory is needed and wet and dirty clothing isn't left rolled up until the next laundry pickup.

The work of laundering can be the responsibility of the equipment manager, someone who is employed to do the laundry, or student managers. Whoever is designated must be thoroughly trained for the work. It is important to be familiar with different fabrics and other materials and know the care each must have. As has been pointed out, athletic clothing and equipment receive hard use and it takes special knowledge to remove grass stains, heavy perspiration, and mud from a heavily soiled uniform or piece of equipment.

It is important that the washers, extractors, and dryers that are purchased have the capacity needed for the program. A system for transporting the dirty and clean laundry must be in place and the best laundry products provided for the laundry. The person running the laundry must also be skilled in operating the laundry equipment and know how to use it for maximum effectiveness.

Security of Equipment

Equipment is expensive and it is important to keep losses to a minimum. Having an equipment manager is the best way to minimize equipment loss. The effectiveness of an equipment manager in reducing equipment loss is one of the reasons more institutions are providing for this staff position. Several steps that can be followed to provide for security of equipment have been covered in this chapter. A summary of recommended procedures follows.

Attitude. It is important to establish a good relationship with those who use the equipment. There are fewer thefts and less vandalism when those who use the equipment have a positive feeling about the program and the benefits they receive by having equipment provided.

Careful recordkeeping. It is important to know who has equipment so if a loss occurs the person responsible is known. Careful recordkeeping is also a deterrent to carelessness on the part of those who use the equipment.

Checkout system. A good checkout system is needed. Exchanging an ID for an item of equipment for recreational use ensures that the equipment will be returned.

Firm policy on returning equipment. One person cannot check out equipment and another return the equipment. The equipment cannot be kept out overnight; it must be returned promptly.

Limited access to equipment room. Only authorized personnel should be permitted in the equipment room.

Issuing system. An efficient issuing system should be devised for athletic teams and individuals.

Storage areas. Equipment not being used regularly or seasonal equipment should be locked in a safe storage area.

Equipment for designated programs. It is impossible to keep proper control of equipment when several different programs use the same equipment. For example, if a community recreational program uses physical education equipment, it is difficult to determine who is responsible if equipment disappears.

Equipment manager. One person should be in charge and coordinate the operation of the equipment room.

Policies and procedures. Equipment policies and procedures should be developed and prominently posted.

Equipment room. The equipment room should be designed to limit access, provide for efficiently issuing equipment, and effectively secure equipment.

Lockers and locker rooms. The locker rooms should be well-supervised and lockers should be designed to prevent theft.

Class Activities

Simulation 1

Situation A significant amount of athletic equipment has been lost during the last few years at a mid-sized college that employs a full-time equipment person. The athletic business manager has told the equipment person that losses must be reduced by at least 50% during the next academic year.

Develop an equipment room security and control plan to decrease the amount of equipment that is stolen and lost through poor control and care of equipment.

Simulation 2

Situation It is the responsibility of the coach of each sport to order the equipment for his or her sport. The equipment must be ordered by submitting a purchase order to the athletic director.

Each student selects a sport to coach. Coaches then research equipment catalogs and complete a purchase order for their athletic director. Order the amount of equipment that would be needed to replace equipment worn out during an average season. Also, order one set of new uniforms for the varsity team.

Simulation 3

Situation The elementary school physical education department in a new school has been allocated $1,800 for equipment purchases. All equipment must be purchased through bids.

Select $1,800 worth of equipment and write bid specifications to make sure you will get the quality of equipment you want.

Performance Tasks

1. Design a program for the care, maintenance, and storage of physical education equipment.
2. Compare how the physical education equipment is issued and managed at the high school you attended with the procedure used at the high school of two other students in the class.
3. Meet with the athletic equipment manager at your university and review the procedure used for issuing practice and competition uniforms and equipment.
4. Design a storage area for the following:
   a. An elementary school physical education department
   b. A university physical education department
   c. A high school athletic program
5. Explain the importance of having an accurate equipment inventory.
6. Visit three sporting goods stores. Compare prices on four different items.
7. Contact three sporting goods vendors. Ask them to explain their policy for submitting bids to schools for physical education and athletic equipment.
8. Trace the process you would recommend be followed from the time a teacher determines that additional equipment will be needed the following year until the equipment is actually used in class.

References

Arbogast, Gary W., "Post-It: Use Physical Education Bulletin Boards." *Strategies,* January 1995, 8:9–11.

Athletic Equipment Managers Association, *Athletic Equipment Managers Certification Manual.* Berryville, VA: Health Care Forum, 1992.

Boos, Suzi, and Mary J. Jones, "Choosing Appropriate Equipment: Looking at the Child and the Task." *Teaching Elementary Physical Education,* October 1993, 4:8–9.

Brown, Susan C., "Selecting Safe Equipment—What Do We Really Know?" *Journal of Physical Education, Recreation and Dance,* February 1993, 64:33–35.

"The Rise of the Louisville Slugger in the Mass Market." *Sport Marketing Quarterly,* 1993, 2:9–16.

Seidler, Todd L., Edward T. Turner, and Larry Horine, "Promoting Active Lifestyles Through Facilities and Equipment—A Look at Children, Seniors, and People with Disabilities." *Journal of Physical Education, Recreation and Dance,* January 1993, 64:39–42.

The Sporting and Athletic Equipment Market. Commack, NY: Business Trend Analysts, 1990.

Walker, Marcia L., and Todd L. Seidler, *Sports Equipment Management.* Boston: Jones and Bartlett, 1993.

Werner, Peter H., and Richard Simmons, *Homemade Play Equipment for Children.* Reston, VA: AAHPERD, 1990.

Chapter

11

Evaluation

Evaluation Parameters

A separate chapter on evaluation is included in this book because evaluation is an integral part of the administrator's role in health promotion, athletics, physical education, and related fields. Evaluation is mentioned often in other chapters. The administrator must assess all aspects of the organization's operations and compare the results with valid criteria or standards. If this is not done, he or she will not know whether expectations have been met. More importantly, he or she will have no guidelines on which to base changes and chart future organizational directions.

The word *objective* is also often used in this text. Objectives are targets or desired results for the organization and various aspects of the organization. For example, there are student objectives for students who participate in a specific class or complete a comprehensive physical education or health education curriculum. Objectives are also established for adult participants in fitness programs and health promotion programs. A health promotion program on smoking cessation has stopping smoking as its major objective. An adult program on incorporating exercise into a person's lifestyle might have as its objective 30 minutes or more of moderate physical activity at least four days per week. Other facets of an administrator's responsibilities also entail setting objectives. Administrative objectives are set for public relations, staffing, and safety for each program.

Evaluation is the process of appraising how successful the individual or organization was in reaching its objectives. The results of the evaluative process are a foundation for the decision making that follows. These results indicate whether programs have been successful and provide guidance for revising or changing programs to better attain the desired objectives.

Importance of Evaluation

Evaluation is a major responsibility of the administrator and is required in every aspect of the position. The need for evaluation is present in any viable, dynamic organization. Only when results are measured against original objectives can the administrator judge progress. Of course, objectives must be realistic if they are to have value. There must be sufficient resources available to accomplish the objectives of the organization. The administrator is like the coach who constantly evaluates team strengths and weaknesses and tries to augment the strengths and eliminate the weaknesses.

The administrator's goal is to achieve the organization's objectives to the greatest extent possible. This requires the maximum contribution of all staff members. The administrator must evaluate the achievements of staff members individually and collectively to determine how successful they have been and how their future efforts can be improved.

The importance of evaluation cannot be overstated. An administrator must make time for evaluation. Only when the extent to which objectives have been reached is known can an administrator properly guide future actions. Evaluation gives direction for changes and the degree of emphasis to place on each objective. It is critical for informed decision making. In addition, evaluation is important because it makes it possible to diagnose strengths and weaknesses and to institute different approaches based on this information.

Accountability is important for every organization and every program. Education is placing more and more emphasis on accountability, commercial leisure programs must be accountable if they are to stay in business, and nonprofit organizations are accountable to the people, governmental units, and groups that provide support. Evaluation is the mechanism through which accountability is determined.

Aspects of Evaluation

Many different groups of people are involved in the evaluation of physical education, health education, leisure, and athletic programs. Some of these are evaluated formally. Administrators and staff members are formally evaluated and programs should be critically evaluated by those responsible for them. Educational administrative positions are evaluated by superiors and by staff members. Administrators in commercial and nonprofit organizations are evaluated by their superiors, who may include a board of directors. An administrator is evaluated and in turn evaluates the performance of staff members. Finally, all personnel should do a self-evaluation.

Informal evaluations in education include parents evaluating the effects of the program on their children, students evaluating their teachers and program, and other teachers evaluating the health education and the physical education programs. These evaluations are sometimes incorporated into a formal evaluation process but even when this is the case, this type of evaluation continues on an informal basis.

All of these aspects of evaluation are important in education but there is one that transcends all others. This is the evaluation of student achievement. Schools exist primarily for the education of students and their success or failure depends on how well this objective is accomplished. If student achievement meets expectations, the evaluations of physical education and health education departments by parents, students, other faculty, the school administration, and governing boards will probably be favorable. Also, an appropriate level of student achievement reflects excellent teacher performance. This, in turn, is a good indicator that the administrator is performing successfully.

Criteria and Standards

Objectives have little value if there are no criteria or standards with which to determine whether they have been attained. It is the responsibility of the administrator to know the standards programs should reach and to develop measurable criteria that can be used to evaluate program success. For example, if an administrator is to evaluate an intramural program, standards for an excellent program must be established. If an administrator is to evaluate an aerobics program in a fitness center, he or she must know what constitutes a successful program and design valid criteria that distinguish between a good and a poor program. Appraisal of the teaching effectiveness of a staff member should be based on the quality of teaching. Too often, poor programs fail to improve because administrators are unable to clearly define what constitutes superior teaching or an outstanding program. An administrator must be familiar with the standards that have evolved over the decades in such areas as facilities, equipment, public relations, instruction, and programs. Knowledge of these standards is indispensable to the administrator.

Purposes of Evaluation

For the administrator, the purposes of evaluation are as follows:

To determine the extent to which the objectives of the program have been accomplished

To demonstrate the worth and contributions of different parts of the program and the total program

To weigh the benefits received against the cost of producing these benefits

To determine how the programs compare with recommended standards

To ascertain the teaching effectiveness of each staff member

Where indicated, to encourage staff members to adjust and improve the teaching processes and methods

To obtain the basis for the periodic rating of staff members (used as a basis for recommendations for tenure, promotions, and merit salary increases in education)

To give guidance for program revision

To provide information for program accountability

To assist in decision making

To provide guidance for future action

In education, to use evaluative information as a basis for the awarding of students' grades

To determine whether all operations are proceeding according to plan

To correct weaknesses and inadequacies

To provide a check on personal administrative performance

It is important that everyone involved in a program be aware of the objectives that have been put in place and that they be knowledgeable about the evaluative methodology to be used.

Continuous Evaluation

For the administrator, evaluation is a continuous process. Decisions involving personnel or budget may be made only once a year but they are based on judgments that extend over many months. As administrators carry out their responsibilities, they constantly appraise every aspect of the operation. This is desirable because evaluations that are based on many impressions made over an extended period of time are sounder than those that are hastily made or based on only a few observations.

Feedback is an essential part of the continuous evaluation process. The teacher or the person responsible for an element of the program being evaluated should receive regular feedback. Weaknesses should be pinpointed at the earliest possible time to permit adjustments, changes, and improvements to occur. The reason for continuous evaluation is to obtain a true picture and to maximize the opportunity to use evaluation as an aid in revision and improvement.

Evaluation is used in many different ways by administrators in physical education, leisure, health promotion, and athletics. Four major evaluative categories are included in this chapter: student evaluation, staff evaluation, administrator evaluation, and program evaluation.

Student Evaluation

Student evaluation is a critical part of the instructional process. Too often, evaluation is equated with grading and the sole purpose of evaluation is considered to be a means of determining a grade. Instead, evaluation should be viewed as a way of determining how successful students are in achieving the instructional objectives on which each course and, in fact, the entire program is based. For example, in physical education evaluation is needed to determine the success of a student in attaining the desired outcomes that define a physically educated person in the cognitive, affective, and psychomotor domains. (These outcomes are explained in detail in Chapter 12.) The only way to know whether programs are meeting student objectives is by evaluating student progress. This reason for evaluation must never be overlooked when designing an evaluation program.

A second important reason for having a student evaluation program is to provide accountability for what takes place in the program. Accurate assessments are requisites for holding students accountable for what they are to know. The instructional objectives for individual classes are determined by the teacher and then students are evaluated to determine the degree to which they have reached these objectives. Student evaluations are also a basis for providing accountability to the educational system, the public, and parents and family. This type of accountability is receiving more and more of an emphasis in education. Physical education and health education programs must have evaluation programs that reveal program quality and accurately inform the many interested publics, including taxpayers, legislators, and educators.

Grading is a third important reason for having student evaluation. Evaluation determines whether the objectives of classes have been met; this information is used to arrive at a grade for the student. For the teacher, grading is probably the most important way in which student evaluation is used. A separate section is devoted to grading because it occupies so much of a teachers' time and it is one of the primary ways in which the results of evaluation are communicated to students and parents. Grading is also part of the way in which accountability is determined and proper grading gives an indication of the effectiveness of a program in reaching desired outcomes.

Although this section is titled "Student Evaluation," it is also pertinent for noneducational programs. It is just as important for a health club to evaluate or measure the achievement of its clients as it is for a school to evaluate its students. The difference is that only educational institutions use evaluations for determining grades. Nonprofit and commercial programs use client or participant evaluations to determine how well they have attained their objectives and for accountability purposes. Evaluations are also used for motivational purposes in educational and noneducational programs. Using a test to show that a student has reached a new level of performance is an excellent motivational technique in a school setting and providing regular evaluations of body fat, strength development, and cardiovascular fitness is a good motivational technique for health club members.

Grading Principles

This section is applicable for both physical education and health education. However, some principles are specific to physical education and the emphasis is on physical education grading because this subject has some unique characteristics and its grading procedures have come under harsh, and too often deserved, criticism. Health education grading does not pose the problems encountered in physical education grading because health education is a classroom subject that can be graded in the same manner as other classroom subjects.

Physical educators use a variety of methods for determining student grades. Many of these methods cannot be defended educationally, nor do they lend themselves to objectivity. Grades must reflect a student's performance in the class. Too often, grades are based on factors that have little relationship to the course objectives. They fail to inform either the student or parents about accomplishments in the course. Furthermore, when grades are based on factors such as effort, clean uniforms, and attendance, it sends a misleading message about the value and nature of physical education and results in a loss of respect from other members of the educational community. When the grading system fails to measure outcomes that have been established for physical education, it becomes difficult to defend physical education as an equal educational partner with other disciplines.

Grading principles for physical education include the following:

Achievement should be the primary basis for the grades awarded in physical education. Grades should be an accurate representation of how successful the student is in attaining the instructional objectives of the course.

Grading procedures should be clearly outlined and the students should be informed about the grading plan to be used at the beginning of the course.

Grades should indicate achievement and also be used as a basis for suggesting ways that a higher level of achievement can be attained.

The grading procedure should relate meaningful information to the student, parents, and administrators.

Improvement is an inadequate basis for determining a grade. The improvement potential of students varies with their initial skill. For example, a skilled badminton player has much less room for improvement than a beginning badminton player. To grade on improvement, pre- and posttests are needed. This requires an extensive amount of time to be taken away from class instruction. Also, many physical education courses are too short to provide an adequate amount of time for improvement to occur.

It is not appropriate to use effort in arriving at a student's grade. First of all, it is impossible for a teacher to accurately determine the effort level of every student in a class. Too often likes and dislikes enter into judgments about efforts. Even if effort could be measured, it would not be a legitimate way to arrive at a grade because it does not accurately indicate the level of success in reaching the objectives of the course.

Participation, cleanliness, and punctuality are too often used as a basis for grades in physical education. These and other standards of the course can certainly be required of a student but they should not be used in computing a grade.

Grades should not be used for disciplinary purposes. Punishment is not a proper function of grades and they should not be used as a mechanism for dealing with behaviors and attitudes.

Improper student conduct and other problems encountered in a class should be handled through administrative channels and procedures, not through the grading process. Disciplinary problems can be indicated on a school's report cards but these issues should be separate from achievement in physical education or any other subject.

A negative grading approach does not measure student achievement in physical education. Some grading plans for physical education begin by giving each student an A grade or a specified number of points and then deducting points throughout the course for disciplinary infractions. This negative grading procedure is a bookkeeping nightmare and it cannot be defended as a way of determining a student's grade.

The grade must reflect the student's final achievement in reaching course objectives.

Grading in physical education should be consistent with the grading procedures used in other disciplines.

Ability grouping of students should be incorporated into the physical education grading plan.

The units of instruction should be of sufficient duration to permit evaluation of student achievement.

Evaluation used to determine grades should be designed as part of the learning process in the course.

Evaluation techniques should be valid, reliable, and objective. Standardized tests should be used when they are available.

Grading Classifications

Psychomotor Domain   Many of the desired outcomes from a physical education class are in the psychomotor domain. Skill development and physical fitness are examples of instructional objectives included in physical education courses. Evaluating skill achievement in a course may require more than one test. A number of skill tests have been developed for physical education activities. Some of these tests may have limitations that preclude their use in a classroom setting. They may require too much equipment or time, norms may be lacking, or their reliability may be too low. Tests are also designed for different age and skill levels. Before a test is used it should be examined for appropriateness. The American Alliance for Health, Physical Education, Recreation and Dance (AAHPERD) has skill tests available for a number of sports and activities. Either a standardized test or teacher-designed instrument should be used to evaluate the degree to which a student has attained the course objectives.

If physical fitness is a desired outcome of a physical education course, a test or tests must be used to measure this objective. A test battery that measures physical fitness is commonly used for this purpose. The partnership between AAHPERD and the Cooper Institute for Aerobics Research (CIAR), which uses the educational component of the AAHPERD Physical Best program and the testing and assessment element of the Prudential Fitnessgram, is one physical fitness test used extensively in schools. Fitness testing can be time-consuming, so the test used should be applicable for school physical education settings. If cardiovascular fitness, strength, endurance, or some other component of physical fitness is the stated objective of a course, then tests specific to these components should be used for measuring students.

Physical fitness can be used as a departmental, yearly program objective rather than an objective for specific units. A physical fitness test is then used as a pretest and a posttest during the school year to measure both the degree to which each student has achieved physical fitness and the amount of physical fitness improvement, and the results of the tests are not included in the grade for a specific course. It is good to use physical fitness tests that have national norms so comparisons can be made with programs nationwide. This can be a helpful way of evaluating the effectiveness of the physical fitness component of a school's physical education program.

Cognitive Domain   Physical educators have used knowledge tests for many decades and it is commonly accepted that knowledge about the course content in physical education should be part of the final grade. These tests are usually objective. The tests may be constructed by the instructor or they may be published tests that have been statistically validated. The tests used differ according to the age and maturity of the student and the skill level of the course. Tests may include any or all of the following areas:

Knowledge of techniques to be used when performing a skill

Understanding the fundamentals and mechanics of movement

Rules and history

Strategy and activity patterns

Protective requirements

Effects of activity on health

Codes of etiquette appropriate to the activity

Understanding of effective movement patterns

Conditioning patterns

Factors affecting performance such as age, nutrition, tobacco, alcohol, other drugs, and fatigue

Knowledge tests are available for many physical education activities although most cognitive tests used at the secondary level are written by individual teachers and cover data included in written material that is given to the students and information that is incorporated into the teaching process.

Evaluating cognitive skills is an important component of the evaluation procedure in physical education.

Affective Domain   Affective skills encompass such categories as sporting behavior, effort, and attitude. It has been pointed out that accurate measurement in the affective area borders on impossible, certainly in the time available in a typical physical education class. This area is prone to bias, as it is highly subjective. Too often, items in the affective domain are used as a means of punishment or as a way of getting students to do what the teacher wants them to do.

The affective domain is certainly of concern to physical educators. However, grades based on factors such as attitude and effort are not valid and do not measure student achievement in a class. Grades should be based on achievement in the psychomotor and cognitive areas. The instructional objectives of the course determine the weight to be given to each category. For example, the cognitive testing might have a weight of 25 percent in determining the final grade and the psychomotor area might determine 75 percent of the grade. In the psychomotor and cognitive areas, weightings would be given for each part being evaluated. A rules test and a strategy test might be weighted differently. This depends on the emphasis in the course.

Grading Plans

The grading plan used for physical education should be consistent with the grading policy of the entire school. If 94% equals an A in an English course, then 94% should equal an A in physical education. Several different kinds of grading schemes are used. The most common are letter grades, with students receiving an A, B, C, D, or F depending on how well they meet course objectives. A pass–fail system is used in some schools. The O–S–U system is also used, with O representing outstanding work, S designating satisfactory work, and U indicating unsatisfactory work. There are variations of each of the above grading schemes.

In addition to some type of a letter or number grade, a comment section is found on many report cards. This provides the opportunity for the teacher to give more detailed information. It is also desirable if objective measurements can be included with a report. For example, a student's physical fitness scores can be given along with national norms that give the student and parent a basis for comparison.

The same grading procedure may not be used at all grade levels. The elementary grades, particularly the lower grades, may use a system that differs from the secondary classes. Whatever system is used should serve as an informational tool for students and parents and assist in motivating students.

Staff Evaluation

An important administrative task is to evaluate staff members. Whether the administrator is a department chairperson, an athletic director, or a health club manager, evaluation is one of his or her most important responsibilities. In an educational setting, the evaluation protocol is usually set by the governing board or by contract with the teachers. This protocol must be followed carefully.

The primary purpose of staff evaluation is to provide a basis for improving instruction. This should be a cooperative effort between the administrator and the teachers. There are two ways in which to evaluate the effectiveness of a teacher. One is through student performance and the other is by evaluating teaching skills demonstrated by the teacher. Formal evaluations by administrators are usually of the latter kind. Physical education is a unique discipline and the evaluation instrument used should be appropriate to evaluate a person teaching physical education.

Staff evaluation also provides a basis for administrative decisions about the retention of teachers before they receive tenure. In the commercial and nonprofit organizations, it is an ongoing reason for evaluating staff. Staff members determine the quality of the programs. This then becomes another extremely important aspect of evaluation. The goal is to improve instruction or the operation of some aspect of a program. This happens only when good people are in these roles and this highlights the importance of in-depth, regular staff evaluation.

Evaluation instruments used vary considerably. Some use a rating scale to indicate the degree to which each performance criterion is met, others consist of open-ended comments, some use a combination of these two approaches, and still others use a yes–no–NA approach. Evaluations are to be shared with the person being evaluated and an open and frank discussion of the evaluation should take place as soon after the evaluation has been completed as possible.

In education, the following categories are usually evaluated when observing a teacher:

Planning and preparation for learning

Teaching effectiveness, including classroom management

Instructional techniques and strategies

Student–teacher relationships

Knowledge of subject matter

Personal traits

Ability to motivate students

Consideration of individual differences

Student outcomes

Evaluations of coaches and nonteaching staff members are designed to evaluate the specific responsibilities of these positions. Figure 11-1 is a good example of a high school evaluation form used for head coaches.

Self-Evaluation

Staff also find it helpful to do self-assessments as an aid in analyzing strengths and weaknesses. Many teachers do not take time to stop and determine what teaching styles and methods they are using. Self-evaluation encourages an introspective look that gives insights into the difference between intent and what is actually occurring in the teaching situation. Self-evaluation can be used as a personal tool or the results can be shared with an administrator or peer for joint dialogue.

Peer Evaluation

Having peers evaluate teaching can be a frightening experience, but this technique is also an effective way to get feedback that helps to improve teaching skills. Peer evaluations designed exclusively for improvement, not for administrative decisions affecting the person being evaluated, are less threatening and are the most valuable in helping teachers improve their teaching performance.

Student Evaluation of Faculty

The evaluation of faculty members by students is more commonly used at colleges and universities than at the secondary or elementary level. These evaluations are valuable and give excellent insights into teaching effectiveness. They also provide information that pinpoints areas that need improvement and show where students perceive teaching strength. Student evaluations provide a good comparison between intended teaching style and methods and what is actually taking place in the classroom.

Administrator Evaluation

Administrators should evaluate their own leadership and performance. Too often this aspect of evaluation is neglected although organizational success is based to a large extent on the ability of the administrator. No one in an organization is more important. It is vital that administrators objectively appraise the manner in which they are administering the unit. Self-evaluation is as important for an administrator as it is for a teacher.

Criteria for Self-Evaluation

If the organization or the unit that a person administers is successful in reaching its objectives and the staff, facilities, and programs meet recommended standards, it is reasonable

PRINCETON REGIONAL SCHOOLS
EVALUATION REPORT FOR HEAD COACHES

Name of Coach ——————————————————— Date ———————————————

Sport ——————————————————————— Years in This Position ———————————

The following criteria represent the requirement for head coaches of Princeton High School athletic teams. They represent the spirit and regulations expressed in the Coaches' Handbook. A five rating indicates exceptional efficiency. A three rating indicates satisfactory performance. Less than a three indicates a definite need for improvement. The evaluation document reflects the major areas of responsibility.

1. An effort has been made to coach all members of the assigned team, allowing for the development of beginners as well as established team members.

5   4   3   2   1

2. The spirit of the no-cut policy has been met with opportunity for each member of the team to enter the competition of the game when the circumstances of the contest warrant participation.

5   4   3   2   1

3. Athletes are motivated in a positive manner, on a daily basis, in an effort to instill self-confidence and to reward players for individual contribution to the team effort.

5   4   3   2   1

4. Practices are planned thoroughly to make the fullest possible use of the time available and to provide each player with adequate instruction.

5   4   3   2   1

5. Drills, routines, and practice formats are designed to meet the skill level of the athletes and to provide a constant challenge for the players.

5   4   3   2   1

6. Meetings are held and written materials are provided to inform all players of the things they need to know in order to participate with the least possible distraction.

5   4   3   2   1

7. Standards of behavior are consistently applied and each player understands how he/she is expected to represent his/her school, parents and coaches.

5   4   3   2   1

8. Personal standards of behavior are set and situations that have the potential for negatively affecting team morale are addressed promptly.

5   4   3   2   1

9. There is evidence student-athletes have advanced their skill level in the sport, regardless of the win/loss record of the team.

5   4   3   2   1

10. The coach has a sound knowledge of the fundamentals of the sport and seeks through training and experience to improve coaching techniques and skills.

5   4   3   2   1

11. There is evidence of leadership by example and mutual respect between players and coach.

5   4   3   2   1

FIGURE 11-1. Evaluation Form for Head Coaches (Princeton Regional Schools—Princeton, New Jersey)

12. There is evidence that the rules and guidelines of the Athletic Department are enforced.

$$5 \quad 4 \quad 3 \quad 2 \quad 1$$

13. Public relations with parents, faculty, and the press are used to promote the team and players and represent the athletic program in a favorable light.

$$5 \quad 4 \quad 3 \quad 2 \quad 1$$

14. School equipment and uniforms and proper inventories are maintained both for closing the season and ordering in advance of the next season in cooperation with the equipment manager.

$$5 \quad 4 \quad 3 \quad 2 \quad 1$$

15. There is evidence contact is maintained with parents and guidance counselors to meet the requirements for students who seek athletic scholarships or who plan to participate in collegiate athletics.

$$5 \quad 4 \quad 3 \quad 2 \quad 1$$

16. There is an effort to attend on an ad hoc basis, school, parent, and conference meetings that relate to the sport.

$$5 \quad 4 \quad 3 \quad 2 \quad 1$$

17. Squad rosters are maintained to provide evidence of authorization for players with physicals and permission forms.

$$5 \quad 4 \quad 3 \quad 2 \quad 1$$

18. Buses and locker rooms are supervised and reasonable behavior of the players is enforced.

$$5 \quad 4 \quad 3 \quad 2 \quad 1$$

19. There is evidence of participation in clinics and professional organizations that emphasize developments in the coaching area.

$$5 \quad 4 \quad 3 \quad 2 \quad 1$$

20. Coach's end-of-season report has been submitted.

$$5 \quad 4 \quad 3 \quad 2 \quad 1$$

_____ Attach scores of all games
_____ Attach names of all letter winners and their grades
_____ Attach outstanding achievements of the team, individual\ players, and the coach
_____ Attach suggestions for improving the sport in the near and long-range future

Head Coach's Intent for Next School Year

_____ I would like to be reappointed for the next school year.

_____ I do not wish to be reappointed for the next school year.

_____ My plans are uncertain at this time.

Director of Athletics Recommendation

See attached comments

_____ Recommended for next school year

_____ Not recommended for next school year

Signature of Head Coach	Date

Signature of Athletic Director	Date

Signature of Principal	Date

White – Personnel Services   Canary – Director of Athletics   Pink – Coach

FIGURE 11-1. Continued

to believe that the administrator is effective. However, regardless of the success the administrator has enjoyed, there are invariably areas in which improvement can be made.

Important administrative criteria are listed below:

The administrator has been successful in eliciting strong effort from each member of the organization.

The administrator has secured sufficient budgetary support and other resources for the program.

High morale prevails among the staff.

The organization enjoys high respect from colleagues in the organization and the community.

Staff members are loyal to each other and to the organizational objectives.

The administrator is fair and impartial to all staff members.

The administrator personally sets an example that demonstrates the values for which the department stands.

Consistency characterizes the administrator's decisions and actions.

Regular, well-planned staff meetings are held.

The administrator follows the chain of command.

The administrator solicits and respects the opinions of staff members and students or clients.

Curriculum development is a cooperative process.

The program is respected both within and outside of the organization.

The organizational objectives are being accomplished.

Staff members feel free to express differences of opinion.

Channels of communication with staff and constituents are open.

All staff members participate in the development of departmental policies.

Changes of responsibility that are being considered are discussed with staff members.

Staff members are motivated to excel.

Recognition and praise are given to staff members for worthy achievements.

Confidential Evaluations

The members of an organization are in a strategic position to assess the performance of the administrator. However, it is difficult for an administrator to approach staff members directly and request their evaluation. There is an understandable reluctance for them to be frank, even if most of their evaluation is positive. A confidential evaluation has much more value for the administrator. Even a highly popular and successful administrator needs to know areas that need improving. This information will be more likely to be elicited by a confidential evaluation.

Confidential evaluations should be completed on a regular basis. This makes it possible to see whether suggested changes have been satisfactorily made and it helps to pick up new problems or issues that may be troubling staff members. The evaluation should cover the duties of the administrator and the important aspects of administration. It is designed to indicate how well the administrator is perceived to be functioning in carrying out his or her responsibilities.

Other Means of Evaluating an Administrator

Participants in a program can also evaluate the effectiveness of an administrator from their perspective. This can be students in an educational setting or clients at a health club in a noneducational setting. Their evaluations will be of the program in which they participate. Because the ultimate determination of the effectiveness of an administrator is the quality of the program, this is another good way to evaluate an administrator.

Program Evaluation

Programs should also be evaluated regularly. The first step is to state the objectives of the program. It is best to state these objectives in behavioral terms. It then becomes possible to evaluate outcomes and determine whether the objectives have been attained. For example, an objective in a 9th grade class may be for 80 percent of the students to make 6 out of 10 basketball shots from the free-throw line. An objective of a health club may be to increase membership by 6% within three months.

The program objectives should be based on accepted standards and be justifiable. It is good if outside consultants can be used to evaluate the program but in most cases teachers or staff members perform program evaluation. It is a good procedure to have an outside team or person evaluate programs periodically as it is sometimes difficult for a person who is involved in a program to be totally objective in carrying out the evaluation.

Program evaluation has the important function of providing information to be used as a guide for changes and modifications to strengthen the program. It is important to know how well program objectives are being met and to be able to compare existing programs with model programs. Properly used, program evaluation leads to staff development and can contribute to many different aspects of educational and noneducational programs. Evaluations not only show where improvements are needed but they are also important means of informing people of the high quality and value of existing programs.

Class Activities

Simulation 1

Situation   A new principal has been employed at the high school where you teach. One of the objectives that has been established for the year is to revise the current student evaluation form.

As the physical education department committee given the task of revising the evaluation form, design a student evaluation form to recommend to the principal. The form must clearly show the level of student achievement and provide meaningful information to the students, parents, and administrators.

Simulation 2

Situation   The state health, physical education, recreation, and dance association is having a panel on student grading at their annual conference.

Members of the class write a paper to present as part of the panel. Select any of the fourteen grading principles listed in this chapter as a basis for the paper.

Simulation 3

Situation   A large corporation in the community has a much-publicized wellness program for employees. New management has taken over the company and they are questioning use of corporation funds for this purpose.

Develop an evaluation instrument to measure the benefits of the program for the corporation.

Simulation 4

Situation   An irate parent of an 11th grade student has called the principal's office and demanded a meeting with the physical education teacher to discuss the basis for the poor grade his daughter received the last grading period. The physical education teacher has called the parent and scheduled a meeting.

Role play the meeting between the physical education teacher and the irate parent.

Performance Tasks

1. Collect teacher evaluation forms used in several schools. Highlight the similarities and the differences.
2. Set up a grading plan for the following:
   a. A health unit on nutrition
   b. A physical education unit on softball

3. Write a philosophical statement supporting the use of different grading systems at the secondary and elementary levels.
4. Develop an evaluation form for the administrator of a leisure or health promotion program.
5. Diagram criteria you would use to determine the physical education grades of students in grades K–4. Justify the weight you give to each criterion.
6. Explain how you would evaluate the following programs:
   a. A K–12 health education program
   b. A commercial fitness center
   c. A university athletic program

7. Develop a self-evaluation instrument for use at the end of one year by the director of a city recreation program.
8. Write a test to evaluate each of the following areas of a volleyball unit:
   a. Psychomotor domain
   b. Cognitive domain
   c. Affective domain

9. Interview two physical education teachers. Find out what objectives they have for their physical education classes and ask them how they measure the degree to which the students attain the objectives.

References

Barrow, Harold M., Rosemary McGee, and Kathleen A. Tritschler, et al., *Practical Measurement in Physical Education and Sport*, 4th ed. Malvern, PA: Lea and Febiger, 1989.

Baumgartner, Ted A., and Andrew S. Jackson, *Measurement for Evaluation in Physical Education and Exercise Science*, 4th ed.. Madison, WI: Brown and Benchmark, 1991.

Cusimano, Barbara Ewens, Paul W. Darst, and Hans van der Mars, "Improving Your Instruction Through Self-Evaluation: Part One: Getting Started." *Strategies,* October 1993, 7:26–29.

Darst, Paul W., Barbara Ewens Cusimano, and Hans van der Mars, "Improving Your Instruction Through Self-Evaluation Part Two: Using Class Time Effectively." *Strategies,* November/December 1993, 7:26–29.

Little, Sandra L., "Leisure Program Design and Evaluation." *Journal of Physical Education, Recreation and Dance,* October 1993, 64:26–29.

Lund, Jacalyn, "Assessment and Accountability in Secondary Physical Education." *Quest,* December 1992, 44:352–360.

Miller, David K., *Measurement by the Physical Educator.* Madison, WI: Brown and Benchmark, 1988.

Plewka, Mark, "Consider the Affective When Assessing Fitness." *Teaching Elementary Physical Education,* January 1994, 5:8–9.

Pultorak, Edward G., "Teacher Assessment: A Dimensional Change." *Journal of Physical Education, Recreation and Dance,* March 1994, 65:70–73.

Rauschenbach, James, "Checking for Student Understanding—Four Techniques." *Journal of Physical Education, Recreation and Dance,* April 1994, 65:60–63.

Sanders, James R., *Evaluating School Programs: An Educator's Guide.* Newbury Park, CA: Corwin Press, 1992.

van der Mars, Hans, Barbara Ewens Cusimano, and Paul W. Darst, "Improving Your Instruction Through Self-Evaluation: Part Four: Instructional and Behavioral Feedback." *Strategies,* February 1994, 7:26–29.

Wang, Philip and Richard L. Irwin, "An Assessment of Economic Impact Techniques for Small Sporting Events." *Sport Marketing Quarterly,* 1993, 2:33–37.

Wasem, Jim, "Pickleball: A Comprehensive Skills Test." *Strategies,* January 1994, 7:21–25.

III

Program Administration

C h a p t e r

12

School Physical Education Programs

Physical Education Defined

Physical education is the process by which positive changes in the individual are brought about through movement experiences. Physical education is concerned not only with physical development but with the education of the whole person through physical activity. It would be erroneous to believe that only physical responses are involved in physical education. The whole organism interacts in any experience; this includes mental, emotional, and social as well as physical reactions. Such behavior provides the physical educator with an exceptional opportunity to guide the responses of students so that valuable mental, emotional, social, and physical development accrues.

Whether the potentials of the students are realized depends on the teachers. Unfortunately, some physical educators concern themselves only with the physical outcomes and ignore these other valuable aspects of development. All of the results are important and should be constantly sought. If physical education is to make its maximum contribution to the development of the child, the physical educator must use *all* opportunities. For example, physical education can provide educational experience in thinking, reasoning, making quick decisions, and using long-term memory.

Physical education should be part of everyone's total education. Vigorous physical activity is a physiological necessity for optimum health and well-being, yet it is often poorly met in our sedentary society. Through physical education a person can learn the satisfaction of movement, exercise, and activity. The person can acquire adequate physical movement skills so that throughout life that person will seek physical activity and thus maintain muscle tone and cardiovascular efficiency. Physical education participation provides a means to maintain and extend endurance, strength, flexibility, and cardiorespiratory efficiency. Participation also allows a student to develop motor skills he or she will be use throughout life. It can be a physically beneficial, socially acceptable means to release tension; moreover, it provides a means for personal development and the opportunities to know oneself. An instructional program in physical education with opportunities for a wide variety of sports, dance, fitness, movement, outdoor, and leisure activities should be a part of the educational curriculum of every person.

Physical Education Objectives Derived from Educational Objectives

Physical education as part of the school curriculum must share the function of education. That function involves helping people develop and adjust to the problems of attaining personal happiness, achieving competent membership in the family, being a contributing citizen in a democracy, and understanding the ethical values that undergird our society.

In 1956, B. S. Bloom developed a taxonomy of objectives for education in which he established three domains: psychomotor, cognitive, and affective. In physical education, the psychomotor domain is a unique goal that is more specifically addressed than in other areas of education. It is included in all listings of physical education objectives as we consider general body coordination, fitness, and development of specific movement skills. The cognitive domain includes knowledge and understanding both of self and human movement, creativity, and game rules, strategies, and sporting behavior. The affective domain, including emotional and social development, is an objective that is shared with the rest of education. This area, sometimes called concomitant learnings, should include planned educational experiences where students can learn to adjust to the group and, perhaps even more important, to know and accept themselves as worthwhile and contributing people.

As a member of the educational family, physical education subscribes to educational objectives and endeavors to make its best contribution to them. The only justification for physical education—or any other subject in the school curriculum—is that it contributes in an important way to educational objectives. Every school subject or activity must be in harmony with educational goals. Physical education is not unique in the objectives it strives to attain but it is unique because students attain the educational objectives primarily through physical activities and games.

Objectives of Physical Education

It is easy to find lists of objectives of physical education. Through the years, authors have expressed the values they believed were inherent in physical education programs. Although the educational philosophy of the time and place exerts an influence on physical education objectives, it is amazing how consistent these statements have been. The wording changes and the objectives are structured in different ways, but physical educators continue to stress the way physical education programs meet the objectives of physical development, social and emotional development, and intellectual development.

The Physical Development Objective

This objective, which encompasses terms such as *physical fitness, motor skill development,* and *organic vigor,* is concerned with increasing the capacity of the body for movement and the health of the person. It is involved with such characteristics as strength, stamina, cardiorespiratory endurance, agility, flexibility, and body composition. Physical development has long been recognized as being important for health and for improving effectiveness in carrying out life's tasks. For example, military leaders have always been conversant with the role physical activity plays in improving the effectiveness of military personnel. Recently, businesses and industries have also come to this realization and started to develop worksite exercise programs designed to give employees the opportunity to improve their physical fitness. This objective continues to be a basic physical education objective.

Although the physical development objective has been highly regarded throughout history, the rapid development of automation and mechanization has enormously accentuated its importance. No longer do most people get the exercise they need from their work. Human physical effort continues to be replaced by technology. Even children are affected. They have been relieved of most of the exercise that at one time was required of children as they carried out chores. Also, the running and walking boys and girls have engaged in for generations has been greatly curtailed by our dependence on modern modes of transportation. Countless hours spent watching television and playing video games have further played havoc with the exercise practices of children and youth.

Modern technology, though providing many blessings, has had a disastrous effect on our physical fitness. Sedentary lifestyles have seriously deteriorated physical fitness and health levels because a fundamental biological principle is that disuse results in deterioration. What we do not use we lose. Thousands of years ago, Hippocrates said, "That which is used develops; that which is not used wastes away."

Motor Skills   Motor skill, an important part of the physical development objective, is the ability to move skillfully and effectively. The synonym—*neuromuscular skill*—is often used because the mechanisms of behavior involved are muscle–nerve structures.

Very early in life, the child begins to combine simple movements into a pattern for some purpose. This process of pattern forming is what is called motor skill learning. It continues in a sequential hierarchical development, with each skill made up of and built on the base of skills the person already possesses.

During the first few years of life, the child gradually acquires the skills of crawling, sitting, standing, and walking. Immediate problems are those of postural and balance control and space orientation. After many repetitions, these actions become automatic and the child is ready for the more difficult coordinations of running, jumping, kicking, bending, throwing, and climbing. These are all basic, fundamental movements on which complex motor skills are eventually built.

The degree of the development of motor skill depends on the variety, amount, and intensity of participation in motor activities during the years of growth. Nature gives the impulses for the proper amount of activity in the repetition of play. A child throws a ball many thousands of times in order to throw it effectively. So it is with each activity. Through infinite repetition, the harmonious coordination of the nervous and muscular systems is achieved and motor skill is the result.

At the beginning stages of learning motor skills, the child must give attention to detailed movements. With much practice, however, he or she can perform the skill automatically. This is of great advantage because the person can now devote attention to other considerations such as meeting the exigencies and contingencies of the game. Higher brain centers are now free to concentrate on relating personal efforts to those of teammates and on strategic maneuvers. Skilled performance would be impossible if the performer found it necessary to give conscious attention to detailed movements. Neuromuscular skill must be gained through regular activity during childhood and youth. It is difficult to gain after maturity.

Importance of Motor Skills   The attainment of the objectives of physical education depends to a large extent on the development of a wide variety of motor skills. We know that people will not continue to participate in sports, games, or dances unless they possess a reasonable measure of skill. People become frustrated and embarrassed when, after considerable practice and effort, their motor performance is still inept. There is no joy or satisfaction in participating in a physical activity if the result is always failure and defeat.

The attainment of the physical development objective depends heavily on participation in physical activities in out-of-school hours and throughout adult life. The limited time available in the physical education program pays much greater dividends if it is used to develop interest and skill in sports, dance, and other activities in which the person can participate after school. A strong correlation exists between the level of skill developed and future participation in that activity.

High among educational objectives is the development of desirable leisure-time activities. Unprecedented amounts of leisure at our disposal and the advent and rapid spread of technology mean that much more free time will become available to everyone. That this is not an automatic blessing is one of the lessons we have learned from experience. Because leisure has such great potential for enriching life, its proper use has become a major concern of society. As a consequence, recreation has assumed increasing significance as an educational goal.

The contributions physical education can make to wholesome recreation cannot be equaled by any other school subject. Participation in sports is a preferred form of recreation not only during youth but throughout adult life. Sports represent particularly desirable leisure activities because they are interesting, wholesome, healthful, adventurous, and truly re-creative. Inherently, youth desire physical activity, competition, cooperation, fellowship, and many of the other elements of physical education. It is well to note that adequate provision for the leisure time of adolescents is more important than preparation for their leisure time as adults.

For physical education to make a major contribution to recreational life, two conditions must prevail. In the first place, activities should be included in the program that have high potential for carrying over to present and future leisure. Secondly, at least a fair degree of skill in these activities must be developed. A strong correlation exists between the level of skill attained in a sport and the extent of recreational participation in that sport. Many physical educators adhere to the belief that physical education objectives are better served by teaching fewer activities but developing a higher level of skill in them than by offering twice as many activities that are learned only half as well.

Motor skills play an important role in the social adjustment of children and youth. In play, the good performer is the hero and the poor performer is pushed into the background. Much of child life is play life, and a large share of it deals with physical skills; only a small part of adult life is play, and good performance is not stressed as much. If an adult loses at golf or does poorly in a softball game at a picnic, it matters little, for success in those areas is not particularly vital; there are many other things that influence happiness much more. The child does not have these numerous other endeavors to which to turn for success if he or she fails in physical skills. The child who lacks skill loses status with peers and all too often retreats or vents discontent in unsocial behavior.

The Social and Emotional Development Objective

Students acquire social development when they become familiar with the ways of the group, become active members of it, adjust to its standards, accept its rules, and become accepted by the group. There is much for youth to experience, to learn and to incorporate as part of their behavior, before they become truly socialized. A variety of social habits, attitudes, and ideas must be acquired in order for the student to adjust to the family, peers, classmates, and to the wider social relationships in the community, state, nation, and world.

Character and personality are intrinsic aspects of the social objective. This is so because the behavior of an individual usually affects other people, who assess it as good or bad, moral or immoral, socially acceptable or unacceptable. The assessment by others of one's behavior reflects the character of an individual. Character, in turn, is the basis for personality. Because personality is the sum of an individual's responses to social situations it, likewise, has social implications.

Basic to the development of a strong character and desirable personality is a set of values that gives purpose, meaning, and direction to life. Everything we are and do and say reflects our basic values. Thus, character, personality, and values are all involved in social development. Likewise, citizenship, which is concerned with desirable attitudes and behavior toward organized society and its institutions, is a part of this objective. Specifically, it is socially desirable that the person act in a sporting manner, work for the common good, and respect the personalities of others. She or he enjoys, contributes to, and is at ease while participating in physical education activities with peers. The person learns to exercise self-control in activities that are mentally stimulating and often emotionally intense, to react quickly and wisely under pressure, and to be courageous and resourceful. She or he should be able to take defeat graciously and without rancor or alibi and victory with modesty and dignity. Students appreciate their obligations and responsibilities as leaders and followers in group situations. They have respect for the rules and for properly constituted authority.

In summary, the specific qualities of the social objective include sporting behavior, cooperation, teamwork, tolerance, loyalty, courtesy, justice, friendliness, service, unselfishness, integrity, dependability, helpfulness, and thoughtfulness.

Contribution of Physical Education to the Social and Emotional Development Objectives   Physical education is one phase of school work that lends itself to the development of character. Student interest prevails, activity is predominant, and relatively great authority and respect are accorded those in charge. The physical education class provides more than just a place to discuss character education theory; it furnishes a laboratory for actual practice. We develop character much more surely through experience than we do by hearing about what we should do or should not do. It is one matter to decide on the correct response to a tense situation when merely looking on, and an entirely different proposition to decide and act correctly in the midst of heated competition. One contestant may foul another, unnoticed by the official, near the end of a close game and thus prevent an opportunity to score. The player fouled cannot get advice about ensuing action and decide some time later what to do. One must decide at once and provide an immediate answer through action. This splendid educational laboratory demands actual responses to tense situations just as life in general does. The whole setup provides real rewards and punishments, which with proper guidance encourage sporting behavior, cooperation, sociability, self-control, leadership, and other qualities of character and citizenship.

The competitor is an active citizen, not a passive one. It is the acting citizen who receives training. There are laws or rules that must be obeyed as one pursues the ambition of winning the contest or performing well. Penalties are imposed immediately on any infraction of the law. Opportunities to give, take, obey, and cooperate are numerous. This is the ideal setting for developing the good citizen, the socially adjusted and ethical individual, provided that the situation is well-handled and well-regulated. In no school situation are these goals adequately attained if those in charge are incapable or indifferent.

The dominant drive for a winning team or good performance leads to the development of good habits. Responsible habits, such as abstinence from smoking and the use of other drugs, are steps in the direction of good health that can be prompted by physical activity. In order to be a better player, the student is encouraged to practice these and other habits of good citizenship. In the long run as well as the immediate situation, healthy living builds success. Habits of healthy living and good citizenship tend to carry on just as undesirable habits do. Enough good ones crowd out some bad ones. Our personality, with its basis of character, is the sum of our responses to the social situations in which we find ourselves. We establish characteristic reactions to familiar situations. Pursuit of interesting, desirable goals during the period of habit formation helps to develop desirable reaction patterns. Not all good traits carry over completely from one situation to another, but, if there are many, at least a few can be expected to carry over to similar situations. When all other phases of school life contribute to good citizenship and ethical character, *generalizations* of fairness, sporting behavior, and the like can be built up that have carry-over value. The identical elements involved should also carry over to similar home and community situations.

Much research data can be used to demonstrate the important contribution physical education makes to social development. The value of motor skills was shown. Studies provide convincing evidence that physical education under good leadership can make a major contribution to the education and socialization of the individual.

The fact that physical educators are able to develop such qualities as strength, endurance, agility, and a wide variety of physical skills imposes an obligation on them to develop in their students a sense of direction and a framework of values consistent with the purpose of the school. When a high level of physical fitness is developed in an individual, he or she is more effective for good or bad, depending on attitudes and ideals. It is just as easy to develop a more effective antisocial individual as it is to produce a person who uses superior physical endowments for social benefit. Accordingly, it is essential that physical educators stress the social and moral values of their activities as well as the physical.

The Intellectual Development Objective

The physical educator is concerned with teaching knowledge as well as skills. Although this objective does not ordinarily receive the emphasis and attention to which it is entitled, it is nevertheless a vital aspect of physical education.

One subject that is invariably taught in physical education is the knowledge of rules, techniques, and tactics. This content is indispensable. Much of it is presented in the form of outside reading assignments. There is a great deal of intellectual activity involved in physical education activities and successful performance is directly related to it.

A considerable body of related health information is taught in connection with physical education classes. Such health considerations as warmup, conditioning procedures, safety measures, and sanitary practices can be effectively covered. Students become acquainted with various physiological factors such as muscle soreness, hypertrophy, and second wind. A wide variety of exercise principles are naturally presented as a part of physical education instruction.

When the *why* of physical education is included in classes, such topics as the following are presented:

Physiological aspects of physical activity
Anatomical aspects of physical activity
Psychological aspects of physical activity
Physical fitness evaluation
Relationship of physical activity to physical and mental health
Meeting future physical activity needs
Importance of proper use of leisure
Sociological aspects of exercise and sports

Another type of knowledge that results from physical education is an understanding of other people. Although the physical education teacher does not formally present such materials to the students, the activities of physical education offer an exceptional opportunity to understand human nature. In the close, intimate, face-to-face contacts in physical activities, the real person is revealed. Particularly in competitive sports, students throw off self-consciousness, formality, artificiality, and restraints; their fundamental character and personality are displayed. Under the pressures, excitement, and emotional tension of competition, such qualities as honesty, loyalty, teamwork, determination, dependability, resourcefulness, and leadership can be observed. In ordinary relationships, in school or out, such insights are rarely possible.

Finally, a valuable part of the knowledge that comes through physical education is not easily expressed in words. Musicians and artists have called the sensory experiences associated with their disciplines nonverbal communication. In physical education, the sensory perceptions identified with kinesthesia are in the same category. Some of the most valued meanings in the lives of people come from the perceptions identified with movement.

The Physically Educated Person

The success of physical education programs in attaining their objectives determines the quality of the end product: the physically educated person. There is a strong movement in education to base program success on the outcomes attained. Responding to the need for a basis on which to judge the quality of physical education programs, the National Association for Sport and Physical Education (NASPE), an association of AAHPERD, has defined high-quality physical education programs in terms of a physically educated person in their nationally approved document "Outcomes of Quality Physical Education Programs" (Outcomes Committee, 1992). They present five characteristics of a physically educated person that result from a high-quality physical education program. These characteristics are the skills necessary to perform a variety of physical activities, physical fitness, regular participation in physical activity, knowledge of the implications of and the benefits from involvement in physical activities, and appreciation of physical activity and its contributions to a healthful lifestyle.

In addition to defining a physically educated person, the NASPE committee identified the outcomes that clarify and amplify this definition. Figure 12-1 shows the outcomes associated with each of the five parts of the definition. It should be pointed out that the five parts of the definition represent the important learning that is related to the major learning domains (psychomotor, cognitive, and affective) of physical education. The outcomes indicate the ways in which students change through participation in school physical education programs and become a physically educated person.

The outcome document also includes benchmarks that mark assessment targets and assessment times for different grade levels. Sample benchmark statements for grades K, 2, 4, 6, 8, 10, and 12 are included. These benchmarks are to be considered minimal levels of achievement and should be used as guidelines by teachers and curriculum developers. The outcomes committee was emphatic in stating that decisions about objectives, instructional activities, and assessment methods remain with local teachers, school district personnel, and state officials.

Physical Education: An Integral Part of Education

Physical education is the part of education performed by means of, or predominantly through, movement; it is not a separate, partially related field. This significant means of education furnishes one approach to educating the entire individual, who is composed of many interrelated functional units rather than of several distinctly compartmentalized faculties. The physical, mental, and social aspects must be considered together. Physical education, when well-taught, can contribute more to the goals of general education than can any other school subject; not more to each goal than any other subject but more to all goals than any other school subject. This is made possible, in part, by the fact that participation in physical activity is important to youngsters. The opportunity for meeting students' needs continually presents itself to the physical educator, making physical education one of the keenest-edged tools in the educational kit. With it the physical educator can sculpt beautiful figures or mutilate the already partially shaped raw material. In discussing contributions, it is assumed that a skilled teacher is in charge, for even the most perfect system or machine cannot function without competent direction.

Total Physical Education Program

The total physical education program consists of three aspects: instructional, intramural, and interscholastic programs. The traditional relationship of the three parts is shown in Figure

Definition and Outcomes of the Physically Educated Person

Approved by NASPE Association Delegate Assembly, April, 1990

A Physically Educated Person:

HAS learned skills necessary to perform a variety of physical activities

1.   ...moves using concepts of body awareness, space awareness, effort, and relationships.
2.   ...demonstrates competence in a variety of manipulative, locomotor, and nonlocomotor skills.
3.   ...demonstrates competence in combinations of manipulation, locomotor, and nonlocomotor skills performed individually and with others.
4.   ...demonstrates competence in many different forms of physical activity.
5.   ...demonstrates proficiency in a few forms of physical activity.
6.   ...has learned how to learn new skills.

IS physically fit

7.   ...assesses, achieves, and maintains physical fitness.
8.   ...designs safe personal fitness programs in accordance with principles of training and conditioning

DOES participate regularly in physical activity

9.   ...participates in health-enchancing physical activity at least three times a week.
10.   ...selects and regularly participates in lifetime physical activities.

KNOWS the implications of and the benefits from involvement in physical activities

11.   ...identifies the benefits, costs, and obligations associated with regular participation in physical activity.
12.   ...recognizes the risk and safety factors associated with regular participation in physical activity.
13.   ...applies concepts and principles to the development of motor skills.
14.   ...understands that wellness involves more than being physically fit.
15.   ...knows the rules, strategies, and appropriate behaviors for selected physical activities.
16.   ...recognizes that participation in physical activity can lead to multicultural and international understanding.
17.   ...understands that physical activity provides the opportunity for enjoyment, self-expression, and communication.

VALUES physical activity and its contributions to a healthful lifestyle

18.   ...appreciates the relationships with others that result from participation in physical activity.
19.   ...respects the role that regular physical activity plays in the pursuit of lifelong health and well-being.
20.   ...cherishes the feelings that result from regular participation in physical activity.

FIGURE 12-1. Outcomes of a Physically Educated Person

12-2. This triangle has a broad physical education instructional program as its base, which leads to participation by many students in the intramural program and ultimately to inter-scholastic participation by fewer students. The top two segments of the triangle are out-growths of the physical education instructional program. This triangle has little validity at

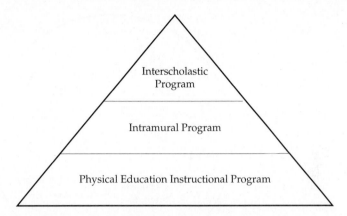

FIGURE 12-2. Traditional Physical Education Triangle

present, either philosophically or in terms of participation. In some schools, intramurals encompass a small program or do not exist and their activities do not necessarily reflect what is taught in the physical education program. The rapid expansion of interscholastic athletic programs with larger numbers participating, higher levels of skill needed to participate, and greater administrative sophistication required has resulted in a different relationship between the three components of a total physical education program. A circle can be used to show the relationship that now exists (see Figure 12-3). The three parts are still related to each other, perhaps administratively and certainly from the standpoint of facility use, goals of the programs, and the activities that are used in the programs. However, the size of each segment of the pie varies according to whether number of participants, extent of program, administrative control, or some other relationship is being portrayed.

Instructional, intramural, and interscholastic programs are all important and each should be present in a secondary school, with both instructional and intramural programs included at the elementary level. This chapter is devoted to a discussion of the instructional program and Chapters 13 and 14 present information about intramural and interschool programs.

Present-Day Instructional Programs

It is unfortunate when physical education practice lags behind current physical education philosophy. The curriculum must keep pace with modern programming. A good means of measuring the quality of the physical education program, which includes the curriculum, teaching, facilities, and community support provided, is to look at the outcomes. Are the students physically educated as measured by the NASPE outcomes document? There are many fine physical education programs throughout the country. The challenge of the physical education profession is to improve those that fail to meet standards of excellence.

Evidence of Inadequate Programs

Many studies show that the youth of our country have low levels of physical fitness. This is evident in reports describing the physical fitness and health of men who have been tested

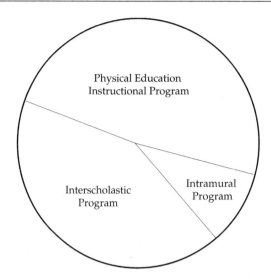

FIGURE 12-3. Current Relationship of Physical Education Instructional Program, Interscholastic Program, and Intramural Program

for military service. There is also concern over low fitness test scores for young people. The low level of health of school-age children is a national concern. Data have provided convincing evidence that our physical education programs have not met the physical development objective. Unquestionably, physical education programs have improved appreciably over the past several decades. Teachers are better prepared and facilities and equipment continue to improve. However, the need for physical education has been accentuated. Improvement in programs has not kept pace with the decrease in physical activity in our daily lives. In other words, the need for physical education has developed more rapidly than has program improvement.

Physical Fitness

Physical fitness is an important objective of physical education programs. A person who is physically fit is able to carry out daily activities with vigor and can enjoyably participate in many physical activities. People differ in their physical potential, so the same level of fitness is not possible for each person. The important factor is the well-being of individuals, as measured by the degree to which they have reached the level of fitness they need to live an enjoyable and productive life. Physical fitness is related to health and physically fit people have a lower risk of health problems associated with the lack of exercise. Stated another way, a physically fit person participates in an exercise program that alleviates health problems that result from insufficient exercise.

There are many components of physical fitness, but the ones of primary importance in a physical education program are aerobic capacity, body composition, flexibility, and muscular strength and endurance. These are classified as the health-related components of physical fitness and are the ones that must be emphasized if a physical education program is to have a significant impact on students' health.

School Programs to Promote Physical Fitness

The best way that schools can promote physical fitness is to have exemplary physical education programs from K through 12. Students will be physically fit and, more importantly, they will also value physical activity, understand how to attain a satisfactory level of physical fitness, and include physical activity as an integral part of their lifestyle. In addition, schools promote fitness by sponsoring fitness programs for the community, offering adult fitness classes, and communicating fitness information as part of their public relations program. Regularly scheduled parent–child workouts and elementary school family play nights are also effectively used.

Another activity that has been well-received in some communities is a series of programs on physical fitness presented by members of the physical education faculty. These programs are made available to service clubs and other community organizations. The programs include lectures, demonstrations, and participatory activities that highlight physical fitness and the school's role in promoting physical fitness.

Student–parent fitness clubs have been successfully implemented at a number of schools. This emphasis on entire families being involved in physical activities has been found to be a good way to promote fitness. A health day (evening) at the school, with the physical education faculty doing blood pressure screening and demonstrating skinfold measurements and other fitness testing, is a good way of motivating interest in fitness.

When new facilities are being built or renovations are being contemplated, provisions should be made to include facilities that can be used by the community. Schools that provide exercise rooms, swimming pools, and facilities for tennis, badminton, and racquetball not only promote physical fitness throughout the community, but also gain community support for the educational program.

Other ideas that have been successfully used by school districts include developing exercise trails on school grounds for community use and getting parental and community assistance to build community playgrounds that encourage physical activity by preschool as well as elementary-age children. Designating one day or evening as a walking day when everybody in the community is encouraged to go for a walk creates interest in physical fitness. Schools can use this as a way of relating exercise to good health by estimating the number of miles walked and computing the approximate number of calories expended. In some communities, the walking day has been expanded to become a fitness day with workshops on stress management, weight control, and nutrition. School districts can also sponsor a yearly community physical fitness symposium with an outstanding speaker giving a presentation on some aspect of physical fitness.

Many approaches can be used to promote physical fitness among students. Students are receptive to fitness clubs organized before or after school. Including fitness activities in the intramural program is also a good technique. Giving recognition to students who participate regularly in physical activity is another good motivator for physical fitness.

Causes of Inadequate Programs

Inadequate time allotment is a major factor that has made it difficult to accomplish the objectives of physical education. The objective of having daily physical education for all elementary, middle, and secondary school students is far from being attained even though AAHPERD is vigorously promoting this objective. *Healthy People 2000: National Health*

Promotion and Disease Prevention Objectives has as one of its objectives increasing to at least 50 percent the proportion of children and adolescents in grades 1–12 who participate in daily school physical education. When this objective was established, only 36 percent had daily physical education and only one state, Illinois, required daily physical education as part of the curriculum in grades K–12 (*Healthy People 2000,* 1990).

Another factor that has adversely affected physical education programs is inadequate facilities. Physical education activities require considerable space, which is expensive. In addition, activities such as swimming, racquetball, handball, and tennis require specialized facilities that are extremely costly. Because of their expense, many physical education facilities are often not provided or they are too small for program needs, and many worthwhile activities cannot be included in the program. Probably more than any other single factor, the limitations imposed by inadequate facilities restrict the type of program that can be offered.

Poor curriculum construction is a final reason why some programs are inferior. It is important to have a carefully planned curriculum based on the latest physical education curriculum principles. A good curriculum provides a framework within which teachers can use their special talents to provide a program that meets the specific objectives established for each grade level. Without a good curriculum progression, continuity and program breadth are likely to suffer. Also, some school administrators have a limited background in physical education. A strong curriculum provides a framework within which the administrator can evaluate and support the program.

Curriculum Development

In the past, too often the director or supervisor of physical education took primary responsibility for development of the physical education program. This administrator was presumed to be the expert on curriculum and the teachers were expected to follow the course of study the administrator planned. In some cases, particularly in large cities, the course of study was worked out in great detail, with each day's lesson prescribed, even to the sequence in which the activities were to be presented and the number of minutes to be spent on each. Teachers not only did not have any input into the curriculum but they were evaluated on the way they followed the detailed lessons written by the administrator.

Fortunately, curriculum construction and revision today are done in an entirely different way. All staff members are involved in the development of the curriculum and have ample opportunity to express their views. Modern curriculum development programs are postulated on the assumption that only as the teacher plays an active and intelligent role in the development of the course of study materials can the curriculum be effective. It is equally important that student input be received. When students and teachers join together to plan, select, evaluate, and revise the curriculum, the physical education program is more likely to meet the needs and interests of the participants and be geared for effective teaching.

There are other populations who can contribute to development of curriculum and who also should be consulted. The principal or a designated representative, curriculum specialists in the central office of the school district, school board members, and interested parents who have special qualifications also can be valuable contributors.

Citizen advisory groups are a must when constructing a modern physical education program. Program revision is often limited by facilities, equipment and supplies, staffing, and transportation. The citizens of the community can often help solve these problems, but they are less likely to be interested in trying to help if they are not represented in the development of the curriculum. On the other hand, when they are involved they can help to implement the seemingly impossible.

Many techniques should be used to implement curriculum construction and revision procedures. One that is very effective and widely used is a curriculum committee involving all populations who have a stake in the educational program. The curriculum committee should be ongoing and meet on a regular basis, not only to handle emergencies or write a new curriculum guide, but to plan for future needs.

The many populations (parents, students, and community) should be surveyed periodically to evaluate interest and needs. Evaluation of the present program by students, faculty, and parents provides important feedback in program construction.

Steps Involved in Curriculum Construction

A vast amount of literature on curriculum construction and revision has become available in recent years. Definite procedures should be followed in developing a school curriculum or a course of study. These steps usually involve the following:

Social Philosophy   Any consideration of the nature and purposes of physical education must inevitably be based on the social and educational philosophy of the time and place in which it operates. Physical educators often want to start the curriculum construction process with a consideration of the objectives of physical education and selection of activities that will attain the objectives. However, prior considerations are involved. Because physical education is a part of the entire system of education, its philosophy and objectives must be consistent with the philosophy that prevails in education. Educational philosophy in turn arises out of the social philosophy of the society in which it functions. Physical education does not exist in a vacuum. It obtains its direction and purpose from the society in which it exists and the educational system of which it is a part.

In the United States, our social philosophy is based on the belief that the total well-being of each person is a primary and controlling consideration. The basic tenets of a democracy include the following:

The belief that the individual and the society of which he or she is a part have common purposes: bringing about through effective cooperation the highest and fullest development of each individual

Belief in the equality of opportunity for the optimum development of each individual's potential

Reciprocal individual and group responsibility for promoting common concerns

Solution of common problems through the free play of intelligence rather than through force, appeal to authority, or uncritical acceptance of the value of any one group or individual

Educational Philosophy   The basic purpose of education during all periods of civilization has been to enable the person to become a better citizen of the society in which she or he lives. No society would tolerate for long a school system whose purposes were not in harmony with the welfare of that society. An educational program is successful only when in all of its aspects it contributes to the purposes of the society in which it exists. Thus, in the United States the aim of education is to assist each person to achieve optimum development in meeting the demands of living in a democratic society and in a closely interdependent world. Educational objectives implement educational philosophy.

Statement of Outcomes   Outcomes express needs as seen by the people who formulate them. Education, and therefore physical education, exists to meet the needs of children. These needs are of two types: individual and societal. Individual and societal needs blend into the outcomes the school establishes for the children.

The Nature of Children   Although the needs of children determine the direction of development for which the school strives, it is the nature of the child that determines what is appropriate for education at each stage of development. Having a productive, meaningful, satisfying life represents the goal toward which education must proceed, but the steps necessary in moving toward these goals are dictated by the makeup of the child's interests, capacities, and urges. Pangrazi and Dauer (1991) list the basic urges of children as the urge for movement, the urge for success and approval, the urge for peer acceptance and social competency, the urge to cooperate and compete, the urge for physical fitness and attractiveness, the urge for adventure, the urge for rhythmic expression, and the urge to know. It is evident that a thorough understanding of the nature of the child is essential for an educator building a program.

Selection of Activities   This is the most challenging aspect of curriculum construction. The activities that are of greatest value in meeting the needs of children obviously should be given priority. However, some are oriented more to one outcome than to another. It is therefore necessary to select varied activities. A balanced program enables the students to attain the broad spectrum of outcomes identified in the NASPE document described earlier in this chapter.

Evaluation of the Program   The program must be regularly evaluated to determine whether it is accomplishing the intended results. If it is not, the proper corrective steps should be taken. Evaluative procedures are considered in Chapter 11.

Principles for Selection of Activities

A number of factors determine the activities to be included in a physical education program. Facilities, equipment, and the specific skills of the teaching staff are factors that must be considered. It cannot be expected that each activity will contribute to every desired program outcome. However, a balanced program of activities makes it possible for each student to attain all the outcomes. The following are physiological, psychological, and sociological principles that should be used as guidelines for selecting physical education activities.

Physiological Principles
The program should provide ample opportunities for a wide range of movements involving the large muscles.

Facts about the growth and development of children should guide curriculum construction.

Provision should be made for the differences in physical capacities and abilities among students.

The physical fitness needs of students must be met by the program.

Psychological Principles
The program should consist predominantly of natural play activities.

The activities should be selected in the light of the psychological as well as physiological age characteristics of the child.

Activities that are valuable in arousing and expressing emotions should be chosen.

In the selection of activities, provision should be made for progression.

In the selection and placement of activities, sufficient time should be provided so that the skills can be learned well.

Activities should be selected that meet the seasonal drives of the students.

Sociological Principles
The curriculum should be rich in activities adaptable to use in leisure time.

Activities should be selected for their contributions to the youth's training for citizenship in a democracy, loyalty, leadership, fellowship, and teamwork.

The curriculum should be suited to the ideals and needs of the community.

Activities that are rich in possibilities for individual character training are especially desirable.

As these principles form the basis on which a successful program can be built, the following points concerning each should be noted:

Opportunities for a Wide Range of Large-Muscle Movements   Physical education is primarily concerned with big-muscle activities. The big muscles are those of the trunk, shoulders, hips, and neck and are used in running, jumping, throwing, striking, climbing, pushing, and pulling. The small muscles are those of the face, throat, fingers, and toes, which are used in writing, drawing, typing, piano playing, and similar activities. In human evolution, the big muscles are the older, fundamental muscles, and the small muscles are the newer, accessory ones. Most of the values attributed to physical education arise from the fact that the activities are big-muscle activities. For example, the development of health has already been mentioned as a prominent objective of physical education. Action of the smaller muscles contributes little to health because very little organic activity is involved. But when the big muscles of the body are used, they burn more energy, which results in a greatly increased functioning of the circulatory, respiratory, excretory, and heat-regulating mechanisms and, later, the digestive mechanism. This organic activity develops organic power, vigor, vitality, fatigue resistance, and health. The only known way to reach and develop the vital organs is through vigorous total body activities.

Facts About the Growth and Development of Children   In order to obtain the best educational results, educators should select activities that are best adapted to the strength, endurance, and coordination of each age group. From the standpoint of the readiness of the organism to assimilate physical education activities, there is a best time for each activity. There is also an optimum degree of exercise that is beneficial at the various stages of development.

Growth and development take place according to a definite and continuous pattern that depends on hereditary and environmental factors. Growth and development do not proceed evenly and do not occur in the same manner in both sexes. The growth spurt, the slow development of the heart, the physiological changes brought on by adolescence, and sex differences are a few of the factors that can affect the physical education program.

Differences in Physical Capacities and Abilities Among Students   Special provision must be made in the physical education program for the great physical differences among students. In order to avoid a program that makes excessive demands on any individual, it is necessary to know the students' physical capacities and abilities. Medical examinations reveal physical deficiencies that would partially or wholly prevent students from engaging in the regular program. For these students, other activities must be provided. These activities must be within the capacities of each person and selected with a view to remedying the deficiency, if possible.

There are also in every group those who are appreciably below normal in coordination, speed, strength, agility, and balance. Rather than requiring such students to participate exclusively in the regular activities, educators should arrange special programs to give special attention to their deficiencies. When these students have developed a suitable level of physical fitness, they should return to the regular program.

Physical Fitness Needs of Students   Automation, by drastically reducing the vigorous exercise involved in work of all types, has accentuated the importance of physical education's contribution to physical fitness. The physical aspects of each individual should be periodically assessed and proper activities to meet individual and group needs should be scheduled.

One aspect of physical fitness in which our youth is particularly lacking is strength of the arm and shoulder girdle. This deficiency hampers performance in many sports. Unfortunately, some of these sports are not particularly good developers of arm and shoulder girdle strength. For this reason, teachers must be alert to this situation and if a need exists they should provide appropriate activities. Among the better activities to develop strength in the upper extremities are wrestling, gymnastics, rope climbing, weight training, and selected conditioning exercises.

Natural Play Activities   Natural play activities are based on activities developed thousands of years ago in response to the situations that confronted primitive humans. They had to run, jump, throw, strike, chase, flee, pounce on, dodge, and climb to get food, provide goods, and avoid predators. From time immemorial, humans have performed these activities so that today there is a powerful inner drive to do these things. Twentieth-century life offers few opportunities for their expression except through physical education activities. All of our popular sports are popular largely because they are composed of natural activities. It might well be said that the most interesting activities are those that include most of these instinctive drives. Football is extremely popular because it satisfies so many urges, such as running, jumping, throwing, kicking, dodging, chasing, striking, and fleeing. Calisthenics and marching are unpopular because they include very few natural activities. Expression through natural play activities is inherently satisfying, for each individual is prepared by his or her nervous system to respond in the required way. The program, in order to use these inner drives to the fullest extent, should include a significant number of play activities based on them.

Psychological and Physiological Age Characteristics   This is one of the most important factors to be considered in constructing a physical education program. There are rather clearly defined age stratifications in regard to play interests and the content of the curriculum should be in harmony with them. As a general rule, children aged 9–12 have different play interests from those they had at ages 6–9. College students usually have different play interests from those in junior high school. Most men and women can readily recall their own changing interests in their youth. These changes do not appear and disappear at exactly the same time for all children, nor do all children express the same play interest in the same way. Individual differences do exist, but there is a striking similarity in the play interests children manifest at various ages. The good curriculum is guided by these natural tendencies.

The significance of this for the curriculum builder is that the programs should contain a variety of activities from which each individual can select those that interest him or her most. Of course, the activities of the program must be in harmony with the age level of the group. A wide variety of play activities should be presented in elementary school. It is important that students have exploratory experience before they are permitted to elect all of their activities. Unless they are familiar with the activities available, the privilege of election will be almost meaningless.

Activities that are Valuable in Arousing and Expressing Emotions   The development of intellectual capacities has so engrossed educators that they have devoted little thought and attention to the emotions that are the generative forces behind most conduct. Human behavior has sprung from emotions and instinct for so many thousands of years that we cannot expect our conduct today to be based entirely on intellect. What is needed in our schools, as much as anything else, is provision for the education of the emotions.

Physical education occupies a strategic position among the school subjects for guiding and modifying emotions. Biology, rhetoric, and mathematics do not offer the opportunities for emotional expression that physical education activities do. Humans crave sports and games that are dramatizations of situations that exercise instincts and emotions. If expression rather than repression were the rule, the mental health of our nation would be a much less serious problem. Emotional stability is achieved only through practice in controlling and modifying the feelings released. Physical education makes a substantial contribution to education by providing a laboratory setting in which emotional control is practiced. In view of this fact, physical education should include activities that are valuable in arousing and offering an outlet for emotional expression. Body-contact activities such as football, basketball, soccer, lacrosse, and wrestling are very effective in this respect because they exercise deeper, more powerful emotions than many noncontact activities. Contact sports benefit even spectators, who experience them vicariously and give expression to their aroused emotions by cheering.

Activities that Provide for Progression   The physical education program should show progression from grades K–12. This requires that physical education programs from elementary through senior high school be carefully integrated. Unfortunately, in many instances, the programs at these different school levels are completely unrelated. This results in over-lapping and duplication in certain areas and in complete neglect in others. A well-integrated program accomplishes significantly more results than one that is not.

Every school system should determine what outcomes it desires its high school graduates to gain from their experiences in physical education. These outcomes become the objectives of the entire school system and the program at the various grade levels should be developed to attain these objectives. All of the activities of the elementary and middle or junior high school should be planned with reference to the senior high school program.

Sufficient Time to Learn Skills Well   Far better results are secured from a physical education program that provides a few activities to be learned well than from one that offers many activities that are learned only partially. Everyone enjoys doing what he or she can do well. There is far more value in acquiring a fair degree of skill in several sports than in becoming a jack of all sports and a master of none.

Under this principle, more time is provided for more difficult skills. The backward handspring is a more complex skill than the forward roll, and the full gainer is more difficult to perform than a forward dive. If a skill is worth acquiring, it should be well-acquired. This does not necessarily mean that every skill must be thoroughly mastered by every student in the class. It suggests, rather, that sufficient time be allowed in order to enable students to perform each activity with a degree of skill that allows them to enjoy the activity.

Activities that Meet Students' Seasonal Drives   Students have a readiness for seasonal activities. When professional, college, and high school teams are playing football or soccer, students have a desire for these sports. When the football and soccer seasons are over, they anticipate basketball and other indoor activities. Spring is time for baseball, track and field, golf, and tennis. There is far more readiness for indoor activities in disagreeable weather than on warm, sunny days.

Activities Adaptable to Leisure Time   Schools are gradually devoting more attention to activities with which people occupy their leisure time. This concern is not solely with the leisure-time activities of adults, for children of all ages have been emancipated from many of the chores and duties that occupied their available time.

The increased emphasis on avocational activities in schools is of considerable significance to physical education. Young and old people spend countless leisure hours either playing or watching sports and games. Preparation for all these hours spent in the realm of sports is a major objective of physical education. The practice of postponing education in golf, tennis, handball, volleyball, swimming, racquetball, and other big-muscle play activities of adults does not produce satisfactory results. The vast number of graduates who have little or no skill in these sports, and will never develop any, is ample evidence of the weakness of the physical education program of the past. Moreover, in order to produce the most favorable educational results, some preparation for the leisure activities of children should be provided throughout their school life. It would be a mistake to select activities entirely on the basis of adult needs. One of the outstanding criticisms directed against education today is that the activities are too far removed from the student's present needs and interests and, therefore, are not significant to him or her. Although it is doubtful that this criticism would be true for play activities to the extent that it is true of some academic activities, nevertheless the program of physical education should be adaptable for leisure time.

Activities that Contribute to Youth's Training for Participation in a Democracy   One of the most fundamental objectives of our educational system is the development of the civic and social virtues desired in a democratic society. These virtues are best developed by practicing them in natural situations. This is possible in physical education activities. Team sports under capable leadership can develop cooperation, loyalty, leadership, sporting behavior, respect for the rights of others, and other qualities essential in the citizens of a democracy. In athletics, the dominating drive to win stimulates the development of these qualities, for youth soon finds out that they are necessary for success. Furthermore, provincialism, which is contrary to democratic principles, is reduced by team sports. Regardless of the diverse nationalities represented in a team, the players are teammates and all barriers between them cease to exist as they cooperate for a common purpose. In team competitions, the only measure of a person is what she or he does as a member of the team—race, creed, wealth, and class are all forgotten. No better training for citizenship in a democracy is available anywhere in the school system.

Curriculum Suited to the Ideals and Needs of the Community   What may be a perfect physical education program in one community might prove to be an utter failure in another. Social dancing is a physical education activity that is readily accepted in certain schools, but that in others would not be tolerated by the community. Preferences for particular sports are often determined by the ethnic makeup of the community. Thus, the ideals of the community are powerful factors to be considered in the selection of the content of the program. Likewise, the needs of the community must be reckoned with. In the northern states, winter outdoor activities can hold a prominent position on the program, but they may be utterly out of place in the south.

The physical educator who works in a community that is hostile to certain valuable activities should hold them in abeyance until public opinion has become favorable to them. Nothing is gained by attempting to force a physical education program on a community. The best procedure is to change gradually the attitude of the students and public in favor of the new activities.

Activities that Develop Individual Character   The development of character as an objective of physical education has already been discussed. Because physical education activities exercise the most fundamental emotions and instincts, they are powerful factors in developing good character. The skilled teacher, by teaching, suggestions, and example, uses the possibilities inherent in sports and games for developing desirable traits of character that operate in these activities and may even carry over into other life situations.

Multicultural Programs   An understanding of different cultures is important for gaining respect for the diversity of people who make up a geographical area, whether it be an individual school, a community, a state, a country, or the world. Acceptance of others and the views of others, together with an understanding of differences and similarities, is an important outcome of an educational program. The physical education program can easily incorporate a strong multicultural focus. This can be done through the use of games and sports of different cultures, the inclusion of words from different languages, using large outlines of country and world maps painted on playground surfaces for movement activities, developing an Olympic theme in classes to teach about other countries, participating in school cultural fairs, and correlating physical education activities with multicultural activities in the classroom in the elementary school, with art and music programs at all grade levels, and with subjects such as literature and history at the secondary level. Experiencing different cultures through physical education should be an integral part of every curriculum.

Curricula with an International Flavor   Students are extensively affected by international events and have more opportunities for international experiences than at any other time in history. This fact should be carefully considered as physical education programs are revised to have maximum pertinency for the students.

Coeducational Classes

By mandate of Title IX of the Educational Amendments of 1972, sex discrimination is prohibited in education in all programs and activities receiving or benefiting from federal financial assistance. Title IX states:

> No person . . . shall, on the basis of sex, be excluded from participation in, be denied the benefits of, or be subjected to discrimination under any education program or activity receiving Federal financial assistance.

A course that denies participation of either sex cannot be scheduled in school districts and postsecondary institutions as a result of the Title IX regulation. Elementary schools had to comply with the regulation by July 1976 and secondary and postsecondary level institutions had to comply by July 1978.

Most elementary school physical education classes were coeducational by the time Title IX went into effect, but it was common for secondary schools to hold single-sex classes. The mandating of coeducational classes has had far-reaching effects on physical education programs in the United States. There is a provision in Title IX that allows, but does not require, the separation of students by sex for contact sports such as wrestling, rugby, ice hockey, football, and basketball. A number of states have their own sex discrimination legislation that does not have this exclusion; in those states, all classes must be coeducational.

Physical education requirements and opportunities must be the same for males and females in physical education. This does not mean that all activities must be taught coeducationally. It is perfectly acceptable to group students by ability or to permit students to select the activity they want. This could result in a class being of predominantly one sex or the other. The key point is that students may not be grouped on the basis of sex.

Title IX also specifies that a single set of standards may be used to evaluate students in physical education unless one set of standards has an adverse effect on one sex or the other. In this case, an alternate set of standards is to be applied that does not adversely effect either sex; the schedule of classes may not be structured in a way that invariably results in single-sex classes.

Too many secondary school physical education programs fail to make use of ability grouping. The easy way out has been to make all classes elective without establishing standards for students to meet in order to enroll in the various classes. This too often results in recreational classes or such wide ranges of ability that effective teaching is impossible. It is also difficult to keep highly skilled students motivated when they are not challenged. Coeducational classes require physical educators to make extensive use of ability grouping, to develop appropriate evaluation procedures that are fair to both sexes, and structure the physical education program to be an enjoyable learning experience where in-depth teaching takes place.

Boys and girls must be treated equally in instruction, assignment of responsibilities, and disciplinary measures. There must also be equal locker rooms, equipment, and teaching aids. Additional information about Title IX is included in Chapter 2.

Time Allotment

The matter of time allotment is of great importance because no program can operate successfully unless a proper amount of time is allotted to it. Unfortunately, many states do not mandate enough time to meet the objective of daily physical education for all students. The minimum time requirement for the different states, based on a survey taken in 1994, is shown in Table 12-1.

There has been a trend to reduce the time required for physical education in many states. This is particularly noticeable at the secondary level.

Instead of having a time allotment, a number of states are moving in the direction of using outcomes as the basis for their physical education programs. Students in these states have certain minimum outcomes to achieve and it is up to the individual schools to provide the time needed in physical education in order to attain these outcomes. Time is no longer a factor but there is a series of performance-based outcomes for each grade level or at other designated points along a student's educational path and at graduation.

Whether a state uses an outcome approach or continues to use a time allotment, the decision still must be made as to what portion of the time available for physical education will be devoted to each of the activities in the program. The program should be systematically organized and evaluated so that the limited time is used to the best advantage. A variety of activities appropriate for the different grade levels and age groups should be selected in light of the desired student outcomes. It is not defensible to devote the bulk of time each year to the same activities. Variety is important in order to enable students to attain the broad spectrum of physical education outcomes. Even the best activity becomes less valuable when it is no longer challenging and the student repeats what was learned the year before. It is just as unjustifiable to offer the same students the same sport at the same level for three consecutive years as it is to offer the same students the same mathematics course three years in a row. Of course, more complex activities require more time than simpler ones. The first appearance of an activity in the program should call for instruction in the fundamentals; later appearances of the same activity call for instruction in more complicated skills and strategic maneuvers.

The Elementary School Program

In addition to the general objectives of education, each division of the school has a unique purpose. The unique function of the elementary school is to prepare the child in the tools of education or, as expressed in the seven cardinal principles, command of the fundamental processes. It is the place where the child acquires the basic knowledge, skills, habit, and the ideals of thought, feeling, and action that are essential for everyone.

TABLE 12-1. Time and Grade Requirements for Physical Education in Elementary and Secondary Schools—States and Possessions

State	Required by Law or Regulation	Time Requirement	Grade Requirement
Alabama	Yes	30 m/day 50 m/day	K–8 1 year in 9–12
Alaska	No	(Schools that offer P.E. must meet minimum requirements for issuing of credits)	
Arizona	No	Recommended only; 10% of day 14% of day Not specified	1–3 4–8 9–12
Arkansas	Yes	Required but no time specified 1 credit required	1–8 9–12
California	Yes	200 m / 2 wks 400 m / 2 wks	1–6 2 years in 9–12
Colorado	No	Not specified—local control by districts	Nonregulatory state
Connecticut	Yes	Recommendations only	Required by law in elementary and secondary schools; 1 credit required for high school graduation
Delaware	Yes	Suggested activity Must be offered 2 class periods per week for year or 5 days a week for semester 1 credit required during secondary school	1–6 7–8 9–12
District of Columbia	Yes	90 hours per year ½ unit 1 unit	7–8 9 10

TABLE 12-1. *Continued*

State	Required by Law or Regulation	Time Requirement	Grade Requirement
Florida	Yes	Regularly scheduled each year as determined by local school district	K–8
		½ credit in a fitness foundation course (personal fitness)	9–12
Georgia	Yes	60 hours per year	1–8
Hawaii	Yes	120 m / wk	K–3
		90 m / wk	4–6
		1 credit total	7–8
		1 credit total	9–12
Idaho	Yes	Required each year Recommended minimum of 90 / m per week	1–6
		One year required	7–9
		One year—equivalent to 140 clock hours	10–12
Illinois	Yes	Daily period equal in length to other subject periods	1–12
Indiana	No	105 m / wk minimum	1–3
		75 m / wk	4–6
		100 m / wk	7–8
		1 credit—2 semesters	9–12
Iowa	Yes	50 m / wk minimum	K–12
Kansas	Yes	No time requirements	Required to have P.E. program at elementary level
			Required one unit of P.E. for high school graduation
Kentucky	Yes	1 semester	9–12
Louisiana	Yes	150 m / wk	1–6
		250 m / wk (7 period day)	7–10
		275 m / wk (6 period day)	

TABLE 12-1. *Continued*

State	Required by Law or Regulation	Time Requirement	Grade Requirement
Maine	Yes	To be determined locally. Graduation requirement is 1 credit in physical education	1–12
Maryland	Yes	Required but no time specified ½ credit total	K–8 9–12
Massachusetts	Yes	30 clock hours 60 clock hours Prerogative of local school district	K 1–10 11–12
Michigan	Yes	Not specified	Not specified
Minnesota	Yes	45 m 2–3 times / wk 25 m per day 80 clock hour minimum each grade 60 clock hours minimum	K 1–6 7–9 10, 11, or 12
Mississippi	No	Recommended 20 to 30 m / day	Recommended 1–6
Missouri	Yes	Regular instruction 50 m per week 2 or 3 periods per week 1 unit of credit	K 1–6 Junior high school or Middle school 9–12
Montana	Yes	Daily 112 ½ m / wk	K–6 7–10
Nebraska	Yes	None by law; for accreditation— elementary: 150 m / wk; secondary: two 55-m periods / wk	Maintain accreditation for meeting indicated requirements
Nevada	Yes	Not specified 2 years of 5 daily periods / wk	1–8 9–12
New Hampshire	No	None	Recommended for elementary schools

TABLE 12-1. *Continued*

State	Required by Law or Regulation	Time Requirement	Grade Requirement
New Jersey	Yes	150 m / wk	1–12 (includes health, safety and physical education)
New Mexico	Yes	District decides— Usually 1 year 1 unit of credit	1–6 Middle school 9–12
New York	Yes	5 times per week for 120 m 3 times per week for 120 m 2 times per week for one semester and 3 times per week following semester	K–3 4–6 7–12
North Carolina	No	1 course unit of 150 hours	During high school
North Dakota	Yes	90 m / wk 80 m / wk 1 Carnegie unit	1–6 7–8 9–12
Ohio	Yes	200 m / wk for art, music, and physical education 80 m / wk ½ unit of credit	Elementary 7–8 High school
Oklahoma	No	None	None
Oregon	Yes	10% of school day 15% of school day 35–45 m / day 45–60 m / day Optional but strongly recommended	K–3 4–6 7–8 9–10 11–12
Pennsylvania	Yes	No time specified Outcomes to be achieved—no time specified	K–6 7–12
Rhode Island	Yes	Average of 20 m / day (combined with health)	1–12
South Carolina	Yes	75 m per week 2 or 3 periods / wk 1 credit (may apply 2 credits toward graduation)	1–6 7–8 9–12

TABLE 12-1.   *Continued*

State	Required by Law or Regulation	Time Requirement	Grade Requirement
South Dakota	Yes	No time specified (must be provided)	K–8
Tennessee	Yes	No time requirement 1 unit of wellness	K–8 9–12
Texas	Yes	Daily Weekly 1 ½ units 1 ½ units	K–4 5–6 6–8 9–12
Utah	Yes	30 m / day recommended 1 semester each year 1 semester in 2 of 3 grades	1–6 7–9 10–12
Vermont	Yes	2 times weekly 1 ½ credits	K–8 9–12
Virginia	Yes	No time specified 2 credits required of combined health and physical education	K–8 9–12
Washington	Yes	20 m / day 2 credits (2 years)	1–8 9–12
West Virginia	Yes	No time requirement	1–12
Wisconsin	Yes	3 times per week Weekly 1 ½ credits	1–6 7–8 9–12
Wyoming	No	Local control District requirements	
POSSESSIONS			
American Samoa	Yes	3 times per week for 45 m	K–10
Puerto Rico	Yes	150 m / wk 250 m / wk	K–6 7–12

Survey by Author, February–April 1994

Importance of Physical Education in Elementary Schools

Unquestionably, elementary school physical education is critically important in a child's development. This period is vital because this is when a strong foundation for physical and motor fitness must be established. The basis must be laid for the development of strength, endurance, agility, coordination, balance, flexibility, power, and skill in a wide variety of motor activities. In fact, if the proper beginnings are not made during this period, adequate adjustment may be almost impossible later. Unquestionably, the elementary school years represent the golden years from the standpoint of developing physical and motor potential.

The evidence concerning the alarming lack of physical fitness of North Americans and its impact on their effectiveness, health, and well-being has given rise to much speculation about what must be done to solve the problem. Many proposals have been made and it is almost unanimously agreed that improvement of elementary school physical education programs should receive high priority. Too many elementary programs need a more comprehensive curriculum and have inadequate resources in terms of time allotment, staffing, and facilities.

Time Allotment for Physical Education in Elementary Schools

The two most vulnerable aspects of elementary physical education are time allotment and leadership. Concerning time allotment, a daily period of 30 minutes is the minimum standard recommended by AAHPERD and many other professional organizations. Less than 30 minutes per day is insufficient in our highly mechanized, automated existence. The amount of physical activity children aged 6–12 partake in outside of school does not remotely compare to that which children 50 and even 25 years ago had. The physical work activities and chores that formerly provided for physical development have been virtually eliminated.

These changed living circumstances greatly accentuate the importance of physical education in our schools. We must now rely almost solely on school physical education programs to provide the physical activity that is essential to the well-being of our children. However, if physical education is to compensate for the effects of automation and technology and particularly the automobile and television, it must be at its best. More time and attention must be devoted to it. Elementary school physical education is incapable of meeting its greatly increased responsibilities with the traditional allocation of time. The time for physical education should be increased as the child moves from kindergarten through sixth grade.

Leadership for Physical Education in Elementary Schools

Classroom teachers are seldom capable of producing high-quality programs when teaching elementary school physical education classes. They have a very superficial professional preparation for such an assignment, if any. Furthermore, many of them are not interested in assuming the responsibility for this program. A major reason for their attitude is that they do not feel properly qualified for such teaching. Certainly, they cannot begin to approach the performance of a professionally prepared physical education teacher.

Professional performance is necessary in elementary school physical education programs. When life outside of school was meeting the exercise needs of children, the quality of leadership was not as crucial as it is today. We can no longer afford the myth that a nonprofessionally prepared teacher can do a professional job. Physical education has now become so important in our schools, it is so significantly related to the health, adjustment, happiness, and attitudes of children that it can no longer be relegated to untrained leaders.

It is an interesting fact that in most countries that have long-standing, well-established educational systems, specialists are used for the physical education program in elementary schools. For example, in most European countries it is considered so essential to get elementary school children started properly that specialists teach physical education. The attitude prevails that physical education in elementary school is even more important than it is in secondary school and it should be given high priority.

The Physical Education Program in the Primary Grades

Characteristics of Primary Grade Children   Before selecting activities for the physical education program in the primary grades, it is necessary to know the nature of the child physically, psychologically, and socially. The child is usually five or six years old when she or he starts elementary school. Preschool years have been spent mainly in getting control of the fundamental movements of the body and in familiarizing the child with his or her environment. Chief characteristics are as follows:

Physical Characteristics
(Ages 6–8)

Stature is in the period of slow but steady increase.

Weight is in the period of steady growth.

Susceptibility to disease is somewhat higher than it was before the child started school. The child does not have many antibodies in the blood when entering school because he or she has not come into daily contact with such large groups of other children.

Pulse rate is higher than in adults.

Blood pressure is lower than in adults.

Red blood cells are fewer in number; 4,000,000 per cc. of blood is normal for children of this age group and 4,500,000 to 5,000,000 per cc. is normal for adults.

The child can accumulate less oxygen debt than adults.

85 percent hemoglobin is normal for adults; 70 percent is normal for children of this age group.

Heart is smallest in comparison to body size of any age. The heart at age seven is one-third adult size, but it must supply a body that is nearly one-half adult size.

Endurance is poor, as would be expected from the red blood cell count, small heart, and hemoglobin content of blood.

Strength is not well-developed at this period. Arm and shoulder girdle strength are particularly lacking.

Eyes are not sufficiently developed to focus on fast-moving, small objects.

Child is just getting control of gross movements; not much skill in fine movements yet; kinesthetic control is improving.

Bones are soft and easily deformed. Postural emphasis is needed in the grades because it is difficult to remedy poor posture after bones have ossified.

Reaction time is not well-developed.

Much data are available to show that children of elementary school ages today are taller, heavier, and more mature than their counterparts of several decades ago. The accelerated rate of maturation of children is due to advances in medicine, nutrition, and control of our environment. Antibiotics and vaccines have eliminated or lessened many childhood diseases. Vitamin-fortified and balanced diets provide for more optimum growth.

Psychological Characteristics

Imitation is strongest characteristic.

The child has hunger and drive for exercise and activity.

Short interest span. The child needs a considerable number and variety of activities rather than a few.

The child is egocentric, not interested in team games.

Curiosity is a strong characteristic.

The child is very assertive.

Interest in activity is for its own sake rather than any future outcome of it. The child does not like to drill on a skill.

The child does not demonstrate leadership qualities.

Interest is chiefly in large-muscle rather than small-muscle activity.

Approval of adults is more important than that of peers.

Interest is great in stories, rhythms, swimming, chasing, being chased, hiding and finding, and search games.

Implications for the Physical Education Program in the Primary Grades   The elementary school program should provide the students with the opportunity to explore a great variety of movement activities, discover new and pleasurable movement patterns, and develop efficiency and control of their own bodies in structured activities. The elementary program must provide an environment in which the student can think, move, and learn while having an enjoyable experience. As with all other areas of the elementary school instructional program, the basis of future learnings, activities, thoughts, and attitudes are either nurtured or destroyed in the early formative years. Elementary physical education programs have received inadequate emphasis until recent years. Even now, far more is spent in most school districts on high school athletic programs than on the entire elementary instructional program.

Probably no single area of public school instruction has changed as much as elementary physical education in the last 20 years. It has become a thinking, moving, learning laboratory rather than an imitative sports skills program. The curriculum content and the methods of teaching have become more humanistic and individualized. With the development of the exploratory and active-learning approach to teaching, results have been more positive and future generations of adults should view physical education differently.

Although a daily period of 30 or more minutes of vigorous activity is recommended for all elementary school students, when teaching and learning are sacrificed to very large numbers in the learning laboratory five days a week, one must reassess this recommendation. When we find many children in third grade who still cannot perform basic locomotor activities because the teachers have had so many students in classes that it has been impossible to determine who can and who cannot skip, for example, we must reevaluate the daily period concept. This level is so critical to the student's present and future motor learning that the smallest size classes should be at this level so the teacher can do a good job of analyzing and assisting in correction of basic movement skills. If classes of over 25 students are necessary, they should be at the upper grade levels, but large classes are undesirable at any level if the teacher is expected to function effectively rather than simply acting as a traffic cop.

The elementary school teacher must have some unique qualities not necessarily required at the high school level. The teacher must be able to relate to young students on their own level and with a genuine and sincere manner of interest and concern. The teacher must present an enthusiasm that instills in students an anticipation and expectation of enjoyment. The teacher must also be able to effectively teach the curriculum to all of the ability levels within any given group of students. The effectiveness of the teacher to meet individual needs requires patient, dedicated involvement in the communication processes between student and teacher. The ability to organize and plan for the maximum amount of activity and learning during each class period is critical for providing a meaningful experience for students. The teacher must further be able to use both exploratory and analytical methods.

Planning the program of instruction for young students demands that the teacher understand the nature, interests, and abilities of the children involved as well as their physical growth and means of acquiring motor skills. If young students are to profit from their experiences in physical education, they must be exposed to a wide variety of activities. These experiences should be available to them on a vertical basis from simple to more complex, from low-organized games to modified or actual team games, from forward rolls to handsprings, and from creative movement activities to square-dance-type activities.

The process of programming begins with the teacher planning the general scope and sequence of instruction for the school year. Unit plans and specific lesson plans are developed during the school year as the time approaches when actual instruction is to occur.

Physical Education Program for the Primary Level (K–3)   The nature of the primary school child is one that can best be described by one word: *active,* mentally, physically, and socially. Although most children in this age group appear to be in a slow physical growth period, many are entering the accelerated growth spurt by the second and third grades. Most students evidencing acceleration in physical growth and changes in secondary sex characteristics are girls, but some boys may also be found to be growing rapidly.

Students at these ages are eager to learn when expectations are set within their individual challenge levels and not too far beyond their capabilities. Also, they are actively experimenting with acceptable and unacceptable behavior in their attempts to learn how to get along with others.

The physical education program should help these children learn to know their own bodies and what they can do with a reasonable amount of success. Body awareness and positive self-concepts should be basic competencies resulting from the physical education program (see Table 12-2).

Primary Level Program Content
1. Efficiency of movement

    Locomotor and nonlocomotor activities

    Posture and body mechanics

    Body awareness and self-concept activities

    Relaxation

2. Games and sports skills

    Ball-handling skills

Basic play skills

Beginning sports skills

Low-organized games with balls

Low-organized games without balls

3. Development activities

Playground apparatus

Stunts and beginning tumbling skills

Beginning gymnastics

4. Rhythms and dance

Expressive and creative activities

Singing games

Simple folk dance

Basic rhythm

5. Individual and dual activities

Rope-jumping activities

Playground games

Swimming

TABLE 12-2

Time Allotments Recommended for K–3	Percentage of Physical Education Instructional Time
Efficiency of movement	20
Games and sports skills:	
Ball-handling activities	10
Low organized games	20
Developmental activities	10–15
Rhythms and dance	30–35
Individual and dual activities	5

The Physical Education Program in the Upper Elementary Grades

These students are skill-hungry and their desire to participate in sports and games is dominant. When good leadership is available, they make extremely rapid progress. Students who do not have a good program during this period fall so far behind in their development that it is exceedingly difficult to catch up.

The consequences of children falling appreciably behind their group in strength, coordination, and skills in popular activities are serious. Play is the major concern of these students and repeated failure in this important realm produces social and emotional disturbances that often have detrimental and unfortunate results in later years. Children attach great importance to their peer group and if they do not perform well in physical activities, their peers often reject them. This can cause severe emotional and social consequences for the child who is not accepted by peers.

Characteristics of Upper Elementary Grade Children   The chief characteristics of students in these grades are indicated below. It is necessary to point out that children do not suddenly change when they reach a certain age; considerable individual differences exist in children at all school levels. In fourth grade, some students are as advanced as some sixth graders physically and psychologically. The converse is also true.

Physical Characteristics
(Ages 9–11)

There is a steady increase in height and weight.

The bones are still soft, but ossification is progressing.

Endurance is quite improved.

The child's heart is stronger and able to easily participate in strenuous activities.

Children's eyes can now focus better on fast-moving objects.

Many skills are now automatic. The child no longer needs to devote higher brain powers to body movements and can now think of the play and strategic measures he or she might use to effect activities.

Health is excellent, resistance to illness is high.

Strength is improved, but the child is still surprisingly weak, particularly in the upper extremities.

Reaction time is excellent.

Children have boundless energy. They are very active.

Psychological Characteristics

Child begins to develop gregarious spirit (teams, clubs).

Cooperation and teamwork are more developed.

The child is less individualistic and self-assertive.

Interest in competitive and combative activities is developing.

Interest span is gradually lengthening and fewer activities are needed to maintain interest.

There is love of excitement and adventure. The child likes to dare.

The child is interested in practicing to develop skills.

Children are ready to assume leadership responsibilities.

Interest remains high in rhythms if the teacher is skillful and a supportive learning environment is established.

In the latter part of this period, the standards and approval of the peer group become of paramount importance.

Children like to imitate sport heroes and heroines.

There is a marked interest in popular American sports.

Children from nine to eleven years of age are predominantly preadolescents. This stage of development is distinguished by two outstanding characteristics. The first is an emancipation of the child from primary identification with adults. Up to this time he or she has lived in submission and obedience to adults. The dependence on adults now gives way to a developing individuality with its normal desire for self-direction. The child in the latter part of this school level exhibits a growing independence and self-reliance. An attitude of hostility to parental and adult standards often develops. The child demands the right to make his or her own choices.

Secondly, as children begin to loosen ties with adults, they must turn elsewhere for the security that is so essential for healthy development. They find this in the peer group. This is a difficult but essential adjustment to make. This is where boys and girls learn important lessons in getting along with other people. This is also where they acquire another code of behavior: the peer code. Unfortunately, all too often this code is diametrically opposed to that of adult society. Adults must realize that the child is undergoing inner conflicts as a result of efforts to live up to the standards of both parents and peers.

The Middle School Program

Educators have experimented with almost every possible combination of grade and age levels between grades 4 and 9 in an effort to find some combination of groupings that function better than others. A commonly used combination has been to combine grades 4–6 as an intermediate grouping and grades 7–9 as a junior high school. The middle school concept continues to gain in popularity. The term *middle school* is applied to any combination of grades 4–9, the most common being grades 6–8. The inability of any of these groupings to be completely satisfactory undoubtedly stems from the tremendous ranges of individual differences found among these ages. At any one age level within these years, there is at least a five-year range of normal physical growth. Some students are well into the accelerated period, others have almost reached termination of this growth spurt, and still others have not yet begun. These broad ranges of development also apply to the mental and social development of students in these years.

The physical and psychological characteristics of the middle school student depends on the grade grouping used for the middle school. If lower grades (4–6) are included, the characteristics closely parallel those of the upper elementary grades. If grades 7–9 are included, then the characteristics are similar to those listed for the junior high school.

The Junior High School Program

This period is one in which all students are undergoing marked physical, psychological, and social change. At no other age level do such profound changes occur and such wide individual differences exist as during this period.

Characteristics of Junior High School Students

It is obvious that the physical education program for boys and girls of this age level must be geared to accommodate these radical adolescent changes. Before she or he can successfully set up a program adapted to the needs of these boys and girls, the curriculum planner must be familiar with their various physical and psychological characteristics.

Physical Characteristics (Ages 12–14)

Girls reach puberty one or two years before boys. A small percentage of girls have their first menstruation between 10 and 11 years of age; the typical girl starts at age 12; about 10 percent do not start until age 15 or later.

The union of the epiphyses of the metacarpal bones and phalanges of the female hand is completed at age 16. In the majority of boys this union occurs between 18 and 19, indicating a sex difference in anatomical age of two to three years.

Bones grow rapidly, especially the long bones of the arms and legs. This can contribute to poor posture unless prevention measures are taken.

The most rapid acceleration in rate of growth of height and weight is at the age of 12 for girls and 14.5 for boys. Prepubescent boys grow 1.8 inches and gain 7.6 pounds in one year. Postpubescent boys grow 3.3 inches and gain 16.6 pounds in one year. Great differences exist among pupils. Some are as much as five years apart physiologically.

Strength develops rapidly after puberty begins in boys. However, the greatest acceleration takes place *after* the rapid increase in height.

Motor ability continues to improve but at a slower rate. Some boys have a lower motor-ability score during the most rapid increase in growth. Awkwardness is more likely to accompany the rather sudden beginnings of growth than the later and more rapid growth.

The heart increases greatly in size and volume.

Psychological Characteristics

This is the age of loyalty, of teams and clubs.

The peer group assumes great importance.

Power of attention increases, interest narrows to fewer games.

Power of abstract reasoning is developing.

Desire for excitement and adventure is strong.

Hero worship and susceptibility to adult leadership are typical.

Fighting tendency is strong in boys.

Both sexes desire competitive activities.

Interest in personal appearance is high.

Self-confidence is often lacking.

Students tend to become moody and unstable.

Implications for the Physical Education Program for the Junior High School Level

The program of instruction for the junior high school level must be one in which the student can feel comfortable with a changing body and yet be exposed to types of activities different from those experienced in the early elementary program. The student must be allowed some opportunity for independent choice of activities.

The program at these levels should broaden the basic background of the student and build on the skills foundation established in the elementary program. The program should provide students with a greater repertoire from which to make choices as they progress into high school (see Table 12-3).

TABLE 12-3

Time Allotments Recommended	Percentage of Physical Education Instructional Time
Efficiency of movement	5
Games and sports skills:	25–30
Developmental activities	20–25
Rhythms and dance	25–30
Individual and dual activities	20–25

Middle and Junior High Program Content

1. Efficiency of movement

   Posture and body mechanics

   Integrate movement principle with skill instruction

2. Games and sports skills

   Specific sports skills (seasonal activities)

   Modified and actual team games

   Position play

   Team play (exposure)

   Strategy

   Low-organized active games

3. Development activities

   Tumbling

   Gymnastics, aerobics

   Track and field

   Wrestling

   Self-defense activities

4. Rhythms and dance

   Country western/line dancing

   Creative activities

   Native dance

        International folk dance

        Square dance

5. Individual and dual activities

        Outdoor education activities

        Boating, rock climbing

        Fishing, hiking

        Swimming

        Target games (bowling, golf, badminton, archery)

        Net games

        Skating

        Skiing

        Bicycling

The Senior High School Program

The senior high school years, grades 9 or 10 through 12, are those in which most students reach maturity. However, there is still a wide range in rate of maturation. Senior high school students continue to mature physically, mentally, emotionally, and socially. Their needs and concerns differ from those of junior high students. Many of the junior high student needs and concerns are accentuated; others lessened or eliminated at the senior high level. Peer behavior and performance standards are probably the most influential characteristics of this age.

Characteristics of Senior High School Students

Characteristics that influence the physical education program planned for the young people of this group are as follows:

Physical Characteristics

Girls have passed through the period of rapid growth. Their height remains comparatively constant, although they increase in weight. Some boys are pubescent and in the period of most rapid growth. Others are postpubescent and increase little in height. Boys increase rapidly in weight.

Strength increases greatly in boys during this period, although arm and shoulder girdle strength is deficient. The strength of girls reaches its peak at age 16.

Coordination shows gradual improvement.

Skeleton is well-calcified but posture is sometimes poor.

At age 16, the circulatory system is 82 percent of adult efficiency; at 17 it is 90 percent of adult efficiency; at 18 it is 98.5 percent of adult efficiency. The heart is capable of strenuous activities.

Endurance is better than at any previous age. With proper conditioning, endurance no longer represents a problem except in a few pubescents who are still in the stage of very rapid growth.

Reaction time is better than it has ever been.

Rate of motor learning increases, as does ability to handle the body. Pupils are eager to perfect skills.

Psychological Characteristics

Interests narrow and students move toward specialization.

This is still an age of loyalty and cooperation, but the desire to belong is tempered by consideration of personal interests and advantages. It is still an age of team games.

Self-confidence develops markedly.

Powers of attention and reasoning increase, as does ability to participate in group planning and problem solving.

Interest in grooming, personal appearance, and physical development is strong.

Hero and heroine worship is still a strong influence.

Fighting tendency is strong in boys. They are highly competitive.

There is a strong interest in the opposite sex.

There is increased interest and ability in leading.

Implications for the High School Physical Education Program

Students in senior high school need to be more involved in the decision-making process for planning their physical education curricula. If the programs in the elementary, middle, and junior high schools have been broad-based, the students are now ready for more selective programs. Provisions for selective physical education opportunities in team and individual sports, dance, and developmental activities are needed. The senior high school physical education program should provide the opportunity for students to elect many of their classes. Many high schools provide several alternatives from which the students may choose and the following are examples of the activities that may be included.

Senior High School
1. Dance

    Jazz, folk, social, square, country/western and line dance, modern

2. Development activities

    Gymnastics, aerobics

    Track and field

    Wrestling

    Self-defense activities

    Step aerobics

    Weight training

    Conditioning exercises

    Jogging and running

Power walking

Water aerobics

3. Team sports

Soccer and variations

Touch football and variations

Basketball

Lacrosse

Pickleball

Ice hockey

Field hockey

Speedball

Team handball

Softball and variations

4. Leisure-time activities

Bowling

Badminton

Tennis

Golf

Handball

Racquetball

Archery

Table tennis

Skiing (downhill, cross-country)

Adventure education activities

Mountaineering activities

Bicycling

Water skills

Hiking

The Physically Educated High School Graduate

Elementary and secondary school physical education programs should be designed to produce a physically educated graduate. The objective should be to attain to the maximum extent the desired outcomes of the program. The NASPE description of a physically educated person presented earlier in this chapter is recommended as a definition of a physically educated high school graduate. The outcomes that are part of the description of a physically educated person can well serve as standards to measure the success of the physical education program in graduating physically educated students.

The Block Program: Advanced Course Offerings

In junior and senior high school, the use of the block program of scheduling physical education activities is recommended. In the block program, the time allotment for an activity is concentrated rather than distributed. For example, if it were determined that 20 periods were to be allotted to basketball in the sophomore year, this entire period of time would be used in a block. Thus, if physical education were scheduled daily, basketball would be scheduled for four consecutive weeks before another activity were scheduled. The most popular block of time is four weeks. Blocks of three, five, and six weeks are also extensively used.

Some secondary schools schedule the same sport each year without change. In this type of program, students repeat in grades 11 and 12 what they had in grade 10. This procedure is defended on the basis that students have a readiness for seasonal activities and that they should have them when their interest is greatest. This is contrary to the block program, which is based on sequential learning. The only justification for a student to take the same sport or activity course more than once is if each course is progressively more advanced.

The use of the block system is preferred for several reasons. In the first place, there is no educational justification in repeating the same activities in the same way year after year. New material should be presented each class period (except, of course, an occasional period during which an examination is given or the previous material is reviewed), just as it is in the class meetings for every other subject. The expectation prevails that in an educational institution, children will grow in understanding, skills, and attitudes. The instructor is expected to start where the instruction ended in the previous period and to carry on from that point.

Secondly, the block program is favored because it facilitates learning. If the time allotment for an activity is spread out over a considerable period of time, with other activities intervening, students retain less of what they have been taught in previous lessons. Finally, students are better able to develop the skills and the physical condition for a particular activity when instruction is concentrated.

An advanced course in an activity is much to be desired if it is really advanced. The elementary course should definitely be a prerequisite to the advanced course. It is true that students want seasonal activities, but there are many of seasonal activities. Wrestling, gymnastics, badminton, racquetball, and volleyball are just as seasonal during the winter as basketball. When students want additional participation in a sport, intermediate and advanced courses should be offered or they may participate in the intramural program. For example, if a beginning unit on basketball were provided in grade 10, students could participate further in this sport in grades 11 and 12 by taking an advanced basketball class or by playing in the intramural program.

Modular Scheduling

By modular or flexible scheduling is meant that classes are of varying lengths and size and do not necessarily meet on a daily basis. Flexible scheduling is contrasted with the traditional set schedule in which all classes are of the same length and size and usually meet on a daily basis. This approach to scheduling is most applicable to secondary schools because elementary schools and colleges and universities have always had more variation and flexibility in the length, size, and number of periods per week.

The pattern of modular scheduling most often involves fewer periods per week but of greater length. For example, a school that previously had allotted a daily 45-minute period for physical education changed to two double periods and one single period per week. This really benefits physical education because more time is available for activity. Assuming that 20 minutes per period were needed for changing and showering, the daily period would provide 125 minutes per week for instruction and participation. Each double period would permit 70 minutes for physical education, so two double periods and one single period provide 165 minutes of actual class time, contrasted to 125 minutes in the daily program. If three double periods per week replaced the daily schedule—as is done in some schools—the advantage would be even greater.

Longer periods have an additional advantage. In many secondary schools, it is necessary to use facilities that are located at some distance from the school, such as athletic fields, swimming pools, tennis courts, bowling lanes, and golf courses. Double periods greatly facilitate the use of such facilities. In fact, double periods are advantageous for classes held at the school. Physical educators have complained for years about the difficulty of accomplishing their objectives in a 25- to 30-minute activity period. To have 70 or 80 minutes available for instruction, practice, and participation is much better.

In addition to varying the number and length of class meetings each week, modular scheduling also involves variations in class size. The students from three or four classes may be combined on regular occasions. Such an arrangement is advantageous when it is desired to present the same material to the students in several classes. It may be that the same lecture or film is planned. The economy of staff time under this system is apparent. Such an arrangement also facilitates the use of visiting speakers.

Modular scheduling is excellent for physical education programs and computer programs now make such scheduling feasible. It seems safe to predict that increasing numbers of schools will adopt some form of modular scheduling. What the ultimate effect will be on physical education programs is difficult to predict. At the present, there seems to be many advantages for physical education. The chief negative appears to be the reduction in number of class meetings per week. However, if this is offset by more minutes of activity per week and more efficient use of class time, this does not appear to be a serious disadvantage.

Substitutions for Physical Education

In some school systems, the substitution of band for physical education is permissible. This practice is based on the assumption that physical activity is involved in the marching band. It is immediately obvious that this is not a valid justification and that it should be resisted by the physical education administrator as strenuously as possible. A proper substitution occurs when the outcomes of the different programs are approximately identical. The results of band practice are worthwhile, but they are different from those of physical education. The exercise involved in this activity does not develop the flexibility, strength, endurance, and aerobic benefits that are received in physical education classes, nor does band practice develop neuromuscular skills achieved through physical education.

Still another type of substitution is found in many secondary schools. This involves the acceptance of participation on an interscholastic squad in lieu of participation in the instructional program. This practice is based on the assumption that the values of interschool athletics are the same as those of the instructional program. Proponents of this system point out that the physiological outcomes of athletics are greater than those found in the instructional program and that the social and character values are at least equivalent. In addition, it is argued that members of varsity squads, if they also participate in the required physical education program, get more physical activity than is good for them. Moreover, these athletes could make valuable use of the period normally devoted to physical education classes for study.

The opponents of this point of view argue that instruction in physical education is given in a wide variety of activities and that varsity squad members miss important units of activity if they are excused. It is clear that excusing those on the football team from instruction in swimming, lifesaving, tennis, dancing, golf, and adventure education deprives them of exceedingly valuable instruction. These opponents also stress that there is no evidence that participation in the instructional program overly fatigues varsity players. Having athletes return to physical education classes at the end of their season causes extensive logistical problems for the teacher whose unit has begun. Other students are held back while material is reviewed and previously learned skills are taught to the athletes. A different grading plan is needed for those who enter the class late. There is also the issue of liability when an athlete returns to a class after safety procedures and lead-up skills have been covered. For these reasons, the substitution of interscholastic athletic participation for instructional class activities is not recommended.

A middle ground is taken by those who recommend that interschool squad members be excused from the instructional program when that course is identical to or closely related to the varsity sport in which they are participating. Thus, members of the football squad might be excused from the instructional program when flag football is covered. They would not be excused from any other activity. Members of the basketball squad might be excused from participating in basketball instructional classes.

Preparation of Curriculum Syllabi

It is standard practice in secondary schools to require instructors of classroom subjects to prepare a syllabus for each course. This syllabus is ordinarily prepared in accordance with specifications that have been established by the school or the district. A copy of the syllabus is filed in the principal's or superintendent's office.

Such a practice is recommended for physical education also. The advantages of this procedure have been proven over the years, yet, in some schools, the physical educator is not required or expected to provide a syllabus. Relatively few school administrators have such syllabi from the physical education department on file. This is unfortunate and reflects poorly on the quality of the physical education program and the educational preparation and ability of the administrator.

Physical Education for the Disabled Child

The Education for all Handicapped Children Act of 1975 (Public Law 94-142) provides for an administrative and financial commitment on the part of the federal government to ensure that all disabled children have a "free appropriate public education." P.L. 94-142 emphasizes special programs and procedures designed to meet the unique needs of disabled children. Of particular importance is the fact that physical education is specifically identified in the law as a necessary and guaranteed course of study in the total curriculum for disabled students.

In 1990, Public Law 94-142 was amended by Public Law 101-476. P.L. 101-476 changed the name of the law to Individuals with Disabilities Education Act, reauthorizes many of the sections, and adds two categories of disability (autism and traumatic brain injury).

The law specifically stipulates that state educational agencies must guarantee that physical education is available to all disabled children as an integral part of their education. If possible, they should be in the regular physical education class.

There are two elements of this law with which the physical education teacher must be totally conversant. The one is encompassed by the term *the least restrictive environment* and the second is the Individualized Education Plan (IEP). The law requires that each disabled child be educated in the least restrictive environment. This is the setting that offers the best opportunity for educational advancement. The extent of the disability determines whether the least restrictive environment is the regular classroom or some other environment. For some children, placement in a school for disabled children with a specialist in adapted physical education might be the least restrictive environment.

The term *mainstreaming* is often used in physical education. This is the practice of integrating disabled children in classes with nondisabled peers. When the regular class is determined to be the least restrictive environment, children are placed in that class. Mainstreaming is a common practice in physical education; the goal is to move children with disabilities out of segregated special education classes and into regular physical education classes. Although controversy exists about mainstreaming, it has been found to be a valuable experience for both the disabled and nondisabled when the regular class is really the least restrictive environment for the disabled child and the teacher has a positive attitude and has the necessary teaching skills.

The physical education teacher should be extensively involved with the IEP prepared for each disabled child who is mainstreamed. Although the law does not specify that the physical education teacher be included on the committee that develops a child's IEP, it is preferable if a physical education teacher becomes a part of the committee. In any case, the physical educator should be involved in the assessment of the child to determine physical education capabilities and to recommend the least restrictive environment. Mainstreaming can be of different levels in that it might be only for certain activities, it might be with the support of an aide, the number of disabled students in a class might be restricted, or the disabled child might be completely mainstreamed. If the teacher is not involved in developing the IEP, he or she should study the IEP carefully before the student begins the class so the best possible physical education experience can be provided.

Most physical educators have disabled children mainstreamed in their classes. They need special skill in modifying regular instructional procedures to accommodate the disabled child and still provide a high-quality program for the nondisabled. In-service and expanded academic preparation is needed to prepare teachers to instruct classes with mainstreamed students. Preparation programs should also extend the scope of the practical experiences that are available for teaching children with special needs.

The College/University Program

When students enter a college or university in the United States, there are usually a number of courses that are required for graduation beyond the courses in their major discipline. These required courses are usually referred to as general education courses and are intended to provide a broad liberal arts background for all students. In many institutions, physical education activity classes are part of this requirement. These classes, sometimes referred to as service classes or nonmajor classes, are designed to meet physical education outcomes such as the ones described earlier in this chapter. The requirements differ from institution to institution. Usually there is a two-credit or a four-credit requirement and there may be a distribution requirement or a specific requirement such as swimming or the students might be free to select any course to fulfill the requirement.

When there is no college- or university-wide physical education requirement, individual departments or specific majors sometimes include physical education as part of the requirement for graduation. Again, the classes may be completely optional, specific courses may be required, or students may select from groupings such as team sports, individual sports, indoor activities, adventure activities, aquatics, and outdoor activities.

Most colleges and universities that do not have a physical education requirement do have physical education activity classes available for students. These courses normally satisfy part of the total hour requirement for graduation.

Should Physical Education Be Required?

This question is often asked of physical educators and is debated on college and university campuses. The arguments in favor of the requirement can be summarized as follows:

The health and well-being of the students depends on regular exercise. Regular exercise is universally recommended for health; a requirement ensures that university students continue to be physically active.

Unless physical education is required, those who need it the most will avoid it. Too often, students in poor physical condition who are poorly skilled do not engage in physical activities that are difficult for them.

Students need a requirement in order to motivate them to participate in physical education activities. Too many students do not register for an activity class unless it is required.

A certain amount of regular physical activity is necessary in a college or university to balance the time spent studying. A student is able to sustain intellectual efforts better after a period of vigorous, enjoyable physical activity.

College and university students also benefit from recreational activities. It is to their advantage to obtain recreation in wholesome activities such as sports and other physically challenging activities.

The physical education requirement does not limit students to a specific activity but gives them choice to select from a group of activities.

Universities require a certain number of hours for graduation. It is educationally sound to require some of these hours in the area of movement.

The common arguments against the requirement are as follows:

A requirement encourages poor teaching. The students are required to attend class, so the instructor finds little incentive to be a superior teacher.

College students are mature enough to do the things that are best for them. They will take physical education activity classes voluntarily if they need such activity or they will get their exercise by participating in the intramural program.

College students resent requirements, so they are not likely to continue participation after the requirement has been fulfilled.

The requirement is undemocratic. It provides a captive audience, which defeats the essence of an educational program.

The requiring of participation is the wrong approach to get people to participate voluntarily throughout adult life.

A required program stifles initiative in developing new and innovative programs to capture the interests of students.

In order for an elective program to be successful, the following essential conditions should prevail:

High school physical education programs should meet outcome objectives so students come to colleges and universities motivated and prepared to participate in physical education activity.

An adequate number of superior physical education teachers are available to teach the activity courses.

High-quality facilities and equipment should be provided for the program.

Students must be aware of the physical education activity courses available to them.

Faculty, staff, and administration must understand the physical education program, believe in its value, and encourage students to include activity courses in their schedules.

The physical education activity program must be included in a comprehensive physical education public relations program.

Proficiency Requirement

Some colleges and universities make extensive use of proficiency or achievement tests. By passing such a test, which is equivalent to the final examination in an activity course, the student completes one semester or one quarter of physical education credit. In other words, if he or she possesses the skill and knowledge that the average student possesses at the end of the activity course, part of the requirement is satisfied. No credit is granted. A skilled, versatile student might be able to pass enough achievement tests to complete the entire physical education activity requirement.

The Program of Activities

If the students entering a college or university have participated in high-quality physical education programs in their previous schooling, they are prepared to continue with activities in college that they have learned to enjoy and in which they have developed skill. They also have the movement base and confidence in their physical abilities that encourage them to try sports and activities that they did not experience previously. They are also likely to emphasize future leisure time recreational activities in their program. This preparation for leisure is in harmony with the purpose of college, which is to prepare students for their adult life. Students entering college are products of widely varying high school physical education programs. It is therefore necessary to have an extensive offering of courses at varying levels of skill.

It is desirable to stress recreational activities in the college instructional program. Provision should be made to ensure that each college student has some activities that can be used in later life. Activities such as golf, tennis, swimming, dancing, racquetball, handball, badminton, archery, skiing, and fly casting, which will provide recreation and enjoyment for many years to come, are essential to all college students.

The key to the success of both the required and elective physical education activity programs is to offer activities that appeal to the students and teach them expertly. Activities should change as students' interests change. Interest in physical fitness activities such as aerobics, weight training, step aerobics, jogging, power walking, and other conditioning activities has exploded across the country. These activities have been enthusiastically endorsed by college and university students. When programs change with the times and provide outcomes desired by the students, there is no problem in keeping the physical education activity (service) program vital on college and university campuses.

The list of activities in Table 12-4 is based on current interests of students. Beginning courses are an important part of the curriculum because they provide the opportunity for students who have limited background to learn to play a new sport. Advanced courses should be offered for those with a good skill background to advance further.

Class Activities

Simulation 1

Situation   Students in the high school where you are interviewing for the position as director of physical education are turned off by physical education. They consider it boring and dislike coming to class. All applicants for the position are asked what they would do to change this attitude on the part of the students.

Present your answer to the interview committee; be prepared to answer follow-up questions.

Simulation 2

Situation   The school where you are administrator has been found to be in violation of Title IX of the Education Amendments of 1972 because single-sex classes are offered in physical education.

Write a position paper to present to your principal explaining the changes you will make in your program to come into compliance. Support your changes from an educational and administrative standpoint.

Simulation 3

Situation   There are sharply differing viewpoints in your department on the extent to which students should be mainstreamed in physical education.

Table 12-4. Program for College Students

Adapted Area	Physical Fitness Area	Gymnastic Area
Adapted sports	Aerobics	Olympic gymnastics
Exercise program	Circuit training	Recreational gymnastics
Corrective program	Conditioning	Tumbling
Wheelchair sports	Jogging	
	Power walking	
	Step aerobics	
	Weight training	
	Yoga	

Outdoor Area	Team Area	Aquatic Area
Backpacking	Baseball	Diving—springboard
Bait/fly/spin casting	Basketball	Life saving
Bicycle touring	Field hockey	Water safety instruction
Cross-country skiing	Flag football	Water polo
Canoeing	Flickerball	Scuba diving
Camping	Ice hockey	Skin diving
Crew (rowing)	Lacrosse	Surfing
Downhill skiing	Rugby	Swimming—beg., int., adv.
Hiking	Softball	Synchronized swimming
Horseback riding	Soccer	
and jumping	Speedball	
Ice skating	Touch football	
Kayaking	Volleyball	
Mountaineering		
Orienteering		
River running		
Sailing		
Survival training		
Water skiing		
Winter mountaineering		
Trap and skeet		

Combatives Area	Dance Area	Recreational Area
Fencing	Ballet	Archery
Judo	Ballroom	Badminton
Karate	Clog and tap	Bowling
Self-defense	Country western	Golf
Wrestling	Folk	Handball
	Jazz	Horseshoes and quoits
	Line	Racquetball
	Modern	Squash
	Square	Table tennis
		Tennis

As chair of the physical education department, arrange for the two opposing views to be expressed in a debate held during a department meeting. You act as the moderator.

Simulation 4

Situation   As the administrator of physical education for your school district, you have been given four weeks during the summer to have your faculty join you in revising the district's physical education curriculum.

Divide your faculty into work groups and construct the following curricula:

Elementary (K–5)
Middle school (6–8)
Secondary (9–12)

Performance Tasks

1. Interview two people not in education and ask them what they think the two most important objectives of physical education are. Compare the replies received by members of the class.
2. Ask two educators in disciplines other than health and physical education what they think the two most important objectives of physical education are. Again, compare the results.
3. Analyze objectives of physical education for five school districts. What objectives are emphasized and do the objectives meet the needs of all ability groups?
4. Select two school districts and compare the way they articulate instructional, intramural, and interschool programs.
5. Survey three high schools and compare them in the following areas:
   a. What health and physical education courses are offered?
   b. What performance standard is required?
6. Brainstorm the following issue: What is the ideal way to schedule the equivalent of a daily class of physical education at the secondary level? (Daily blocks or larger blocks of time on fewer days?)
7. Design a program for children with disabilities attending school in your district.
8. Describe what you think are the strengths and inadequacies of current physical education programs at the following levels:
   a. Elementary
   b. Middle
   c. Secondary

   List changes that would improve inadequacies.
9. Map out several ways in which students can be grouped for physical education classes. Write a position paper supporting the grouping procedure you feel is best.
10. Write a position paper supporting or opposing the policy of substituting participation on athletic teams for physical education class.
11. Have each member of the class write her or his philosophy of education. Based on these philosophies, formulate in rank order the five most important objectives of physical education.

12. Physical education, when well-taught, can contribute more to the goals of general education than any other school subject. Debate this statement.

References

Auxter, David, Jean Pyfer, and Carol Huettig, *Principles and Methods of Adapted Physical Education and Recreation*, 7th ed. St. Louis: Mosby, 1993.

Block, Martin E., and E. W. Volger, "Inclusion in Regular Physical Education: The Research Base." *Journal of Physical Education, Recreation and Dance,* January 1994, 65:40–44.

Craft, Diane, "Inclusion: Physical Education for All." *Journal of Physical Education, Recreation and Dance,* January 1994, 65:22–23.

DePauw, Karen P., and Grace G. Karp, "Integrating Knowledge of Disability Throughout the Physical Education Curriculum: An Infusion Approach." *Adapted Physical Activity Quarterly,* January 1994, 11:3–13.

Dougherty, Neil J., IV (ed.), *Physical Activity and Sport for the Secondary School Student.* Reston, VA: AAHPERD, 1993.

Dummer, Gail M. (ed.), *Best Teaching Practices in Adapted Physical Education.* Madison, WI: Brown and Benchmark, 1994.

Dunn, John M., and Hollis Fait, *Special Physical Education: Adapted, Individualized, Developmental*, 6th ed. Madison, WI: Brown and Benchmark, 1989.

Eichstaedt, Carl B., and Leonard H. Kalakian, *Developmental-Adapted Physical Education: Making Ability Count*, 3rd ed. New York: Macmillan, 1993.

Healthy People 2000—National Health Promotion and Disease Prevention Objectives. Full report with commentary. Washington, DC: U.S. Department of Health and Human Services, 1990.

Heenan, Jill, "Inclusive Elementary and Secondary Physical Education." *Journal of Physical Education, Recreation and Dance,* January 1994, 65:48–50.

Hultstrand, Bonnie J., "Women in High School Physical Education Teaching Positions—Diminishing in Number." *Journal of Physical Education, Recreation and Dance,* November/December 1990, 61:19–21.

"An Inclusive Preschool Physical Education Program." *Journal of Physical Education, Recreation and Dance,* January 1994, 65:45–47.

Kelly, Luke E., "Adapted Physical Education National Standards." *Palaestra,* Fall 1993, 10:15–18.

Kelly, Luke E., "Preplanning For Successful Inclusive Schooling." *Journal of Physical Education, Recreation and Dance,* January 1994, 65:37–39.

Landy, Maxwell J., and Joanne Landy, *Ready-To-Use P.E. Activities.* West Nyack, NY: Parker Publishing, 1992.

Lirgg, Cathy D, "Effects of Same-Sex Versus Coeducational Physical Education on the Self-Perceptions of Middle and High School Students." *Research Quarterly for Exercise and Sport,* September 1993, 64:324–334.

Miller, Lori, Larry Fielding, and Brenda Pitts, "From the Field—The Impact of the Americans with Disabilities Act of 1990." *Clinical Kinesiology: Journal of American Kinesiotherapy Association,* Fall 1993, 47:63–70.

Miller, Sue E., "Inclusion of Children with Disabilities: Can We Meet the Challenge?" *Physical Educator,* Winter 1994, 51:47–52.

Mosston, Muska, and Sara Ashworth, *Teaching Physical Education*, 4th ed. New York: Macmillan, 1994.

Outcomes Committee of the National Association for Sport and Physical Education, *Outcomes of Quality Physical Education Programs.* Reston, VA: AAHPERD, 1992.

Pangrazi, Robert P., and Victor P. Dauer, *Dynamic Physical Education for Elementary School Children*, 10th ed. New York: Macmillan, 1991.

Rizzo, Terry L., Walter E. Davis, and Ron Toussaint, "Inclusion In Regular Classes: Breaking From Traditional Curricula." *Journal of Physical Education, Recreation and Dance,* January 1994, 65:24–26.

Sherrill, Claudine, Pilvikki Heikinaro-Johansson, and David Shininger, "Equal Status Relationships in the Gym." *Journal of Physical Education, Recreation and Dance,* January 1994, 65:27–31.

Siedentop, Daryl, *Developing Teaching Skills in Physical Education*, 3rd ed. Mountain View, CA: Mayfield Publishing, 1991.

13

Intramural Programs

History of Intramural Programs

Translated literally, *intramural* means "within the walls." Intramural programs, therefore, are defined as activities carried on within the walls of an institution. Intramurals appeared in the schools long before anyone even thought of physical education and interschool athletics. The desire to play is universal and some form of it has always existed. It seems inconceivable that this powerful urge could have been entirely suppressed in our first educational institutions. The beginnings of intramurals can undoubtedly be traced to the informal sports and games indulged in by our first students in their leisure moments. This type of play, within the confines of the institution, can properly be considered intramurals, although it does not exactly resemble our intramural programs of today.

There is ample evidence that boys participated in various sports in early American schools despite the obstacles in the form of hostile teachers and the Puritan philosophy of sinfulness and foolishness of play. As educational institutions multiplied and the school population increased, informal play activities among students expanded. The haphazard nature of these activities gradually gave way to better organization. In colleges and universities, competition was organized between societies, fraternities, dormitories, and classes. The students conducted their activities by themselves. The faculty was indifferent. In 1859, the Yale undergraduate body was divided into twelve intramural boating clubs of 20 men each. These contests continued for nine years before giving way to a system of interclass crews. Baseball was organized as an intramural sport at Princeton in 1864. Field days for track and field sports were conducted on an intramural basis at Yale and Princeton about this time.

As the intramural program developed, students looked beyond the confines of their own institutions for competition. It is interesting that interschool athletics arose from intramural sports, but the development of interschool athletics had no deleterious effect on intramurals. The students continued to play among themselves with no faculty guidance or interference. The fact that these activities continued with unabated interest in the face of the bitter interschool rivalries is ample testimony to the vitality of intramural athletics. Students who were not good enough to represent their school against other schools found an outlet for their natural desire for play and competition by competing with and against their schoolmates. Intramural athletics, discovered by students and promoted by students, continued to expand and develop.

About the beginning of the twentieth century, some progressive university physical educators began to take an interest in these intramural programs. They saw in these activities unusual opportunities to broaden the scope of physical education. From 1907 to 1912, it became increasingly apparent that some authorized individual was needed to control and regulate these expanding activities. The athletic associations at Michigan University and Ohio State University made provision for departments of intramural athletics in 1913. Other colleges and universities soon followed their example. World War I gave a tremendous impetus to intramural sports. Athletic departments were always favorably disposed because they saw in intramural athletics a training ground for varsity material. In high schools, the movement to include intramural activities was evident by 1925 and became firmly established in the 1930s. Intramural development was considerably slower in the secondary schools than in colleges and universities, where intramural athletics had a steady growth up to World War II. Because so many college men were drawn into the armed services, intramural programs were greatly curtailed during the war.

As the previous war had done, World War II exerted a profound effect on college and university intramural programs. The war clearly demonstrated the value of sports, and a general conviction prevailed that intramurals must be made available to all who were unable to make the institutional varsity teams. A determined effort was made to provide more intramural services to more students. Programs were expanded, chiefly by including additional activities. Although the ideal of athletics for all was not attained in most institutions, it was more nearly approximated than ever before.

Women's intramural programs did not experience the rapid growth that characterized programs for men even though many women in physical education strongly supported intramural programs rather than varsity competition. It was not until the 1960s that expanded intramural opportunities became available for girls and women on all educational levels. Women's programs were more likely to have a recreational approach, whereas men's programs had a heavy competitive emphasis. Competition in women's programs often took the form of play days or sport days because varsity athletic programs for women were in their infancy. On play days, several schools would come together at one location to compete in one or more sports but students from different schools made up the teams. On sport days, each school was represented by one or more teams in the competition. Intramurals provided competitive opportunities for girls and women until comprehensive varsity athletic programs became available at most secondary schools, colleges, and universities with the passage of Title IX of the Educational Amendments of 1972. Title IX also had a significant impact on the development of intramurals for girls and women. Equality in intramural programs was mandated in terms of scope of program, equipment, use of facilities, financial resources, and leadership. Intramural programs at both the secondary and higher education levels became similar for both genders. Coeducational activities became commonplace and increased opportunities became available for girls and women as the requirements of Title IX were implemented, sometimes immediately, but more commonly over a period of years.

Comprehensive intramural programs provide extensive programs for all students. At the elementary school level, coeducational activities predominate. At the secondary and higher education levels, many coeducational activities are offered along with female and male activities. Even single-sex activities are usually open to the opposite sex if similar activities are not offered in both programs or if a different level of competition is desired. The biggest changes since Title IX have been the development of strong coeducational programs and the change of emphasis in the women's programs to include more sports and a higher level of competition.

Intramurals at the university and secondary level existed many years before organized programs were offered to elementary school children. The benefits received by secondary-age students served as an impetus to expand programs to reach younger children in our schools also. A changing concept of intramurals was another factor. Initially, competition was the common characteristic of secondary school intramural programs, but programs were broadened to include recreational activities and it soon became obvious that these activities filled an important need of elementary school children.

Intramurals initially took the form of athletic competition. In the early years of intramurals, the programs were called intramural athletics. This term is no longer appropriate and the terms *intramural activities* or *recreational activities* more accurately describe the type of program that has developed in our schools. The word *intramurals* is used in this book to describe current programs. Although sports are an important component of intramural programs, a broad range of modified games and nonsport activities, both competitive and noncompetitive, is found in most intramural programs. Factors such as age, expressed interests of students, opportunity to participate on varsity teams, activities provided by community recreation programs, facilities, leadership, school and community support, financial resources, and geographical area of the country influence the type of activities available in intramural programs.

Philosophy of Intramural Programs

Physical educators initially viewed intramurals as an extension of the instructional physical education program. In some schools, this is still a legitimate philosophical position. Intramurals provide an opportunity for students to use skills learned in class and a close relationship between class work and intramurals can be of value to the total physical education program. However, the broadened concept of intramural programs requires a more comprehensive view of the objectives and values of intramural programs. To provide for all student needs, a program must be much more than merely an extension of a physical education instructional program.

Enjoyment should be a high-priority objective in every intramural program. The fun students have when participating in an event, activity, or contest is reason enough to establish an intramural program. Release of tension associated with the pressures of school life is another important objective and participation enhances mental and emotional health. Even the most intense competition can provide a means to relax from the physical and psychological stress of the school day. Intramural activities have an important carryover value. Interests and skills developed in these programs positively influence the future leisure activities of the students. Skill development is an important outcome for many participants. Through intramural activities, students can attain a higher level of skill that will be of value to them throughout their lives and assist them in enjoying activities more. They also have the opportunity to participate in activities that might not be available to them from any other source.

Vigorous activities assist students in attaining and maintaining satisfactory levels of physical fitness. There is increasing concern about the effect of sedentary activities such as watching TV and playing computer games on the health of students. Intramural activities can be used to break this pattern and to assist in establishing an active lifestyle. Vigorous activities can become part of a student's personal physical fitness program. Some intramural programs find that their fitness activities such as aerobic activities and weight training are popular among students. Intramurals also satisfy the desire of some students for competition. A good program provides noncompetitive as well as competitive experiences. However, intramural programs traditionally place a strong emphasis on competition for the senior high school student and above. This type of program is healthy if the program is properly administered.

Socialization and teamwork experiences are two additional goals that are reached through an intramural program. Students have the opportunity to meet and interact with other students in an enjoyable and meaningful manner. The lessened pressure on winning results in social experiences that are not possible in the highly competitive realm of interscholastic and intercollegiate athletics.

Intramural activities were once considered extracurricular because they were originally initiated and conducted by students and carried on outside of regular school hours on a voluntary, noncredit basis. However, when the concept of curriculum was broadened to encompass all the activities conducted under school auspices, intramurals came to be considered a legitimate curricular activity. Intramurals are an integral part of the educational program and justify the expenditures and attention given to them.

Intramurals should be available to everyone. This means that programs must provide for a wide range of abilities and interests. Interschool athletic programs are available for the superior athlete. However, many highly skilled athletes are unable to participate on school teams because the provision is made for only a small percentage of those who would profit from such an experience. Work demands and lack of interest in putting in the time and effort required of interschool athletic performers also creates a pool of skilled athletes who want to participate in intramurals. Specialization required of athletes makes it almost impossible for a student to participate in more than one sport even in many high schools. These highly skilled students often want to participate in competitive intramural programs in other sports when not in their season.

All levels of ability must be considered when administering an intramural program because competition against opponents of similar ability provides more educational value and more fun. The needs of students can best be met through a comprehensive, integrated physical education program including instructional, intramural, and interschool activities. Each of these phases of the total program should aid and supplement the others, but they each provide unique benefits for students. Therefore, intramurals should not be conducted as a training time for varsity athletics or to develop athletes for varsity teams. There can be no objection, however, if students develop skills through intramural programs that enable them to compete on varsity teams.

Organization of the Intramural Department

There are several different ways in which an intramural program can be organized. The educational level, size of the school, school philosophy, and emphasis placed on intramurals are all influencing factors. At elementary and secondary schools, most intramural programs are directed by the physical education department. At the college and university level, there are varied organizational relationships. Some intramural programs function as departments of schools or colleges of physical education. Others are organizationally attached to the office of the dean of students or vice-president of student affairs. In some colleges and universities, intramural programs operate as separate entities and may report to the provost, vice-president, or recreation coordinator. A few programs are still part of the athletic department, but this is usually for budgetary reasons or to gain student support for the athletic programs when student fees are distributed. Administratively this has been found to be an unsatisfactory arrangement for intramurals.

Figures 13-1 through 13-4 are examples of organizational charts for intramural activities in an elementary school, a small high school, a large high school, and a college or university.

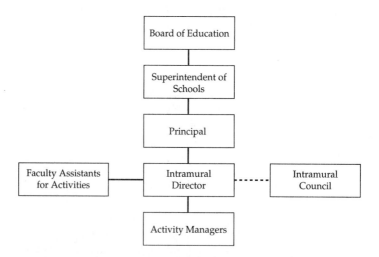

FIGURE 13-1. Organization of Intramural Programs for Elementary Schools

Elementary School Intramural Programs

Elementary school programs were slow to develop. This was due in part to the inadequate number of professionally prepared physical educators in the elementary schools. Recess

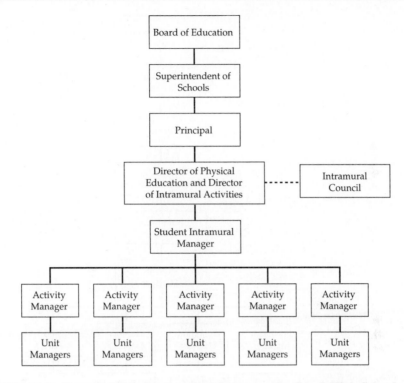

FIGURE 13-2. Organization of Intramural Programs for Small High Schools

activities and sporadically scheduled half days devoted to games were the most common examples of intramural programs in elementary schools. The improved quality and scope of elementary physical education programs has led to the implementation of strong intramural programs also. These programs provide an opportunity for the students to use and improve skills learned in class and to learn new sports and participate in innovative activities. A strong emphasis is placed on fun activities with a limited amount of stress placed on highly organized contests and league structure.

The Intramural Director

The intramural director should be a physical educator who is adequately compensated by the school district for administering the program. The director often uses the skills and competencies of other faculty members in the operation of the program. However, it is the director's responsibility to organize the overall program and to see that appropriate administrative procedures are followed.

Student Involvement in Administration

Students should be involved in as many leadership roles as possible. They can serve as recordkeepers, managers, scorekeepers, equipment supervisors, officials, and team captains.

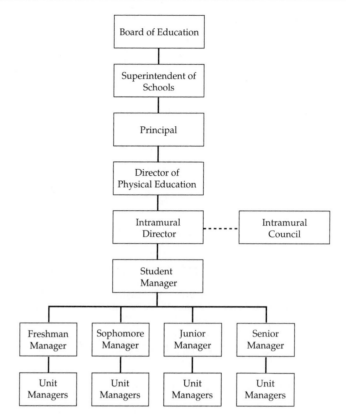

FIGURE 13-3. Organization of Intramural Programs for Large High Schools

Responsibilities should be rotated frequently to allow many students to gain this type of experience.

An intramural council should be formed to assist in planning and conducting the program. This is a valuable leadership development opportunity for the students and such a council assists the director in providing a program that is of interest to the students. The council is normally composed of representatives chosen by the classes or other units of competition. Additional representation can be obtained from the captains of the various teams.

Students are used as managers for each activity offered. They assist in preparing for an activity and cooperate with the director in administering and supervising the activity.

Finances

A relatively small amount of money is needed to operate an elementary school intramural program. The best procedure is to use physical education class equipment. This additional use must be considered when preparing the physical education equipment budget. Funds to cover administrative costs, salary of the director, publicity, awards, specialized equipment, and other expenses should be included in the school's operating budget.

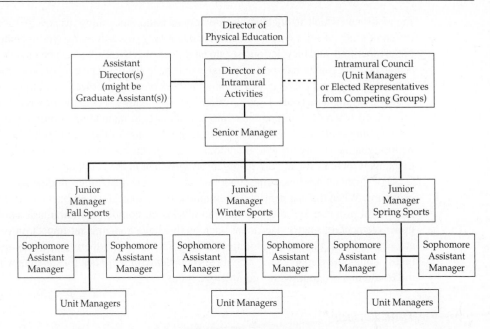

FIGURE 13-4. Organization of Intramural Programs for Colleges and Universities

Units of Competition

The groupings from which teams are organized are called units of competition. Good units of competition contribute a great deal to the success of the intramural program. Selection of competing units is not a problem in the individual sports because each individual is a separate unit. Strong units for team sports are necessary, however, because teams tend to break up after several defeats. This is not a major problem at the elementary level because less emphasis is placed on high-level team sport competition and the sport seasons are usually of a shorter duration.

The individual classroom has been found to be a good unit. Where appropriate, two teams can be organized from one classroom. This unit is particularly good when there are three or four classes in each grade level. Age can also be used as a basis for grouping. This grouping permits the teams to be equalized when there are participants of different ages. For some activities, it may be desirable to group on the basis of height and weight as well as age.

Some schools have found that the most effective way to group for teams is to have the intramural director or physical education teachers place students on teams in as equitable a manner as possible. Performance tests can also be used to make certain varying skill levels are present on all teams. In the interest of equal competition and encouraging all students to participate, the procedure of having students form their own teams is not recommended at this age.

Program of Activities

A program of activities as varied as the intramural director and the intramural council can devise should be provided. The activities taught in physical education classes form a foundation on which an imaginative director can build. Such things as novelty races, stunts, different kinds of relays and obstacle courses, hiking, rope-jumping, yo-yo contests, marble competition, and bicycle contests are examples of activities that can be included in addition to favorite games and sports. Special events have special appeal to this age group. Some schools introduce a sports day or a game day to complement the other activities included in the program. The type of sports offered in community recreation programs should be considered when determining the competitive sports to include in an intramural program. Overlapping sports have little chance of success because of the much higher level of competition that is usually present in community programs and there may not be enough participants if there is already a well-organized program in the community.

For financial reasons, some school districts have dropped their middle school athletic programs. When this happens in a community, provisions are often made to strengthen the intramural program and to place more emphasis on competitive intramural sports in the upper elementary grades. Decisions such as this have a significant impact on the type of activities offered through the intramural program. Although there may be an increase in highly competitive sports, there should still be plenty of activities for students who are not interested in a program with a competitive focus.

Time Periods

Finding a time can be the most difficult part of establishing an elementary school intramural program. If students are bused, logistic problems must be overcome when scheduling activities before or after school. These times are used successfully by many elementary schools. If the activities are appealing to the students, parents usually make arrangements for them to participate. School policy must be followed regarding approved transportation arrangements. Weekends and early evenings are also possibilities. Evenings work well for special events and for activities that include parents or other family members.

The ideal time to have intramurals in an elementary school is during a regularly scheduled activity period in the school day. It is possible to schedule intramural activities that are available to every student and there is no problem with transportation or conflicts with other nonschool activities. The lunch period can also be used for some types of intramurals. Use of the lunch period is limited if there is a short period of time allotted for lunch. Intramurals can be enjoyable and worthwhile to the students even if the activities are modified to fit into the available time frame. Time conflicts with community recreation sport leagues must be avoided if an intramural program is to be successful. If intramurals are scheduled outside of regular school hours, parental permission must be obtained.

Other Considerations for Elementary School Intramurals

Many of the problems associated with secondary and college intramural problems do not exist or are minimal at the elementary level. Eligibility rules are not needed, as every student should be permitted to participate unless the student is also playing that sport on a varsity team. School or family insurance should be required. Regular school physical examinations are sufficient for participation in intramurals unless students have a physical condition that requires medical approval for participation in some activities. Few officials are needed and physical education teachers and other faculty can usually handle the activities that require officials.

Publicity about activities can be distributed through physical education classes and the classroom teacher. Bulletin boards can also be used effectively. Awards are enjoyed by students at this level but they should have limited monetary value. Ribbons or homemade awards that provide desired recognition are satisfactory for elementary participants. A traveling trophy can also be used to promote intramurals when the classroom is the unit of competition.

Secondary School Intramural Programs

Intramural programs are not available in many secondary schools and programs that are provided vary considerably. Seldom do they have the support or interest that characterizes interscholastic athletic programs. Too often, programs are haphazardly organized and do not offer opportunities for all students. A comprehensive program should be the objective of each school and intramurals should be an integral part of the physical education program. Such a program can be considered a part of the school's educational program and should derive financial support from regular school funds.

The Intramural Director

The intramural program should be headed by one individual, known as the director or supervisor of intramural activities. The plan of placing one physical educator in full charge of intramurals is the most effective way of organizing and coordinating all activities. Some schools attempt to have different people responsible for different seasons of the year or for different sports. This procedure fails to provide for a comprehensive program and the lack of organizational and administrative uniformity often causes confusion and results in only a minimal program. The intramural director should not be a coach or have other administrative responsibilities and the salary should be consistent with that received by coaches or staff with similar administrative responsibilities and time demands.

An essential criterion of the intramural director is enthusiasm. Regardless of other desirable qualifications, the director cannot overcome the encountered difficulties and problems without dedication to the program. A low level of enthusiasm on the part of the director toward intramurals explains many weak programs.

The most readily available person is not always a successful director, nor can an intramural department function properly when the various coaches of the different sports combine to administer the program. Nothing does more harm to an intramural program than fluctuating leadership throughout the year. This is a weak administrative setup and should be avoided at all costs.

The custom of having coaches assist in the intramural department has been criticized on the grounds that the coaches may be primarily interested in developing candidates for their respective teams or providing additional experience for team members. If coaches have an adequate understanding of intramurals and support the concept of intramurals for all students, there should be little objection to their involvement. The intramural director requires assistance, and the coaches can be of great help in their various specialties or in their off seasons.

Intramural Councils

Most secondary school use intramural boards, councils, or committees to help administer the program. They are usually made up of the intramural director, student managers, representatives of the participating groups, a member from the student council, and perhaps interested faculty members. The functions of these boards include formulating policies, making eligibility rules, and modifying the rules of various sports to meet local conditions, acting on protests, deciding forfeits, and approving the budget.

Such a board is of great assistance to the intramural director. In addition, it provides an exceptional opportunity for students to gain experience in leadership roles. The democratic process also gives the program more vitality and appeal because the students are a part of it.

Student Managers

Student managers perform much of the work of the intramural department. They assist in making out schedules, notifying teams of their games and assignments, promoting activities, assembling data on contests, and providing general supervision of the program. Their many responsibilities and duties offer exceptional practical training in leadership and executive development.

Team Managers

Each unit participating in the intramural program should be represented by a manager. This person acts as the contact between the intramural department and the unit and usually acts in this capacity for the school year. Responsibilities include the submitting of entries, and eligibility lists, handling protests, and announcing scheduled contests. This person is also responsible for seeing that the team is in the proper place at the correct time. Some individual must assume the responsibility of the team when an intramural contest is being played. This may be the team manager, the coach, or the captain.

Intramural Finances

The per-pupil cost of intramurals is very low even when the salary of the director is included. Money is spent on awards, office supplies, equipment, intramural handbooks, and clerical and administrative salaries. Officials in high schools are rarely paid. Intramural departments, as a rule, require the players to supply their personal equipment. Footballs, basketballs, soccer balls, nets, bases, and other game equipment is generally provided. This equipment is usually part of the physical education department inventory. In some school districts, the intramural program pays a fee for use of this equipment to aid in cost accounting when planning budgets. Most intramural departments receive their funds from the physical education budget. It should not be necessary to resort to fundraising schemes to support intramural activities. The regular physical education facilities are used for most activities although money must be budgeted if community facilities are rented for some activities. The value of intramurals must be continually emphasized in order to obtain financial support in difficult economic times.

Units of Competition

Homerooms are a good basis for intramural competition. It is easy to reach the teams and communication difficulties are minimized. Physical education classes are also used, as are arbitrarily assigned teams. Interest groups, self-formed teams, clubs, and teams formed by random assignment of students who have signed up for the activity are other techniques used to form teams. Arbitrarily or randomly assigned teams sometimes lose the cohesiveness found when students compete with friends or as part of an ongoing group. Cohesive groups have better participation rates and fewer forfeits. Arbitrarily assigning groups does make it possible to better equalize the skill levels of the various teams.

The Program of Activities

Intramural programs naturally vary in different localities, just as physical education programs do. Winter sports are extremely popular in northern states, but may be impossible in the south. In varying localities, different sports predominate in popularity. For example, in some localities wrestling is more enthusiastically received than basketball. However, some activities seem to be in demand everywhere. Basketball, flag football, softball, volleyball, tennis, and track and field are almost invariably successful intramural activities. Nationwide, basketball is undoubtedly the most popular intramural activity. Practically all students are familiar with and enjoy the game. The number of players per team is small and can be readily assembled. Very little equipment is needed and the game does not consume an inordinate amount of time. Sports that are familiar, that do not need much time and equipment, and are free from long, arduous training periods are the most popular intramural activities. Students engage in intramural sports for the joy and recreation they receive and thus, for the most part, they are unwilling to undergo strenuous conditioning programs or the physical stress that accompanies participation in some physically demanding activities.

The range of activities naturally varies with the size of the school. Something for everyone all the time should be the objective of the intramural department. In order to provide for individual differences, several different activities should be available at all times. Sports in which little interest is demonstrated should be eliminated from the program after they have had a fair trial. There is a danger in having too many activities, but that is better than too few activities. The size of the school, the availability of facilities, and time determine the number of activities that can be offered concurrently.

Activities should be provided for all levels of ability. Special education students receive as much benefit and enjoyment from intramural participation as highly skilled athletes. Varying levels of competitive and noncompetitive recreational activities should be included in every intramural program so that low-skilled and inexperienced students want to participate and are not intimidated by highly skilled students. There should be a good combination of team, individual, and group activities. Activities should be offered for girls, for boys, and on a coeducational basis. Each student should have equal access to programs, facilities, and equipment.

Many physical education programs fail to satisfy the physical activity needs of students. This becomes more and more of a concern as states reduce physical education requirements and secondary schools provide fewer classes that keep students physically active. Intramural programs must be expanded and designed to help the physical education instructional program meet this need.

Eligibility for Intramural Competition

The opinion prevails that a student who is permitted to remain in school should be allowed to participate in intramurals, regardless of scholarship attainment. Little is gained by barring players from intramural competition because of scholastic deficiencies. The objective of intramurals is to encourage students to participate rather than setting up barriers to their participation. Eligibility rules usually specify participation on only one team in the same sport in the same season and do not permit switching of teams during the season. Interscholastic team members should be barred from intramural participation in their sport during the season.

Medical Examinations and Accident Insurance

Regular school medical examinations can be used as a basis for permitting intramural participation. For some strenuous activities, it is a good policy to require a medical examination prior to participation. Participants should be required to have either family or school accident insurance.

Preliminary Training Periods

In order to further safeguard the health of intramural contestants, preliminary training periods are advocated. The instances where students have participated in strenuous sports such as swimming, track, wrestling, speedball, soccer, basketball, and water polo without a day of preliminary practice are far too numerous. The intramural department should make it impossible for a participant to engage in strenuous activities without an adequate conditioning program.

Time Periods

The best time for intramural contests is in the afternoon after classes. Students prefer it, as do their parents. Faculty supervision is also easier to obtain at this time and transportation difficulties for the students are reduced and there are fewer conflicts for their time. For these reasons, intramural contests should be scheduled at this time if possible. The major problem is the conflict with interschool squads regarding the use of facilities. This is usually more acute during the indoor season than in the fall or spring. Several solutions to this problem are possible. The indoor intramural program can be scheduled in the fall and spring when the varsity program moves outside. It is also possible to schedule the intramural program on days when the varsity teams are playing away from home or not practicing, but this provides a limited amount of intramural time. The best solution is to have a period scheduled immediately after the end of the school day for intramurals and other activities. (Varsity players can use this time to study or participate in another activity and then begin their practice when the activity period is over.) Bus transportation for those who participate in intramurals is an important feature when this schedule is followed. The practice of scheduling intramural contests during regular physical education classes is not a satisfactory solution and cannot be condoned.

The noon hour is extensively used in high schools for individual activities. It is impossible to schedule team activities when there are multiple lunch periods. The time before classes begin in the morning is also used successfully for intramurals. A few schools also schedule activity periods during the day and when space, time, and staff resources permit, provision can be made for recreational activities during students' free periods.

Because of the lack of space, it is often necessary to schedule intramural activities at night. Care should be taken when scheduling so students have sufficient time to complete their homework. No more than one night per week should be scheduled for any student. There are some situations where more extensive scheduling works to the advantage of the students. In some locations, Saturdays are an excellent time for intramurals if facilities are not being used and students do not have other commitments. This varies from community to community. When outside facilities are used, their availability determines when the intramural activity can be scheduled.

Officials

Faculty members and varsity players commonly serve as officials in high schools. Volunteer students are also usually available. They should be closely supervised and trained to develop their officiating skills.

Protests and Forfeits

Policies should be established to handle protests and forfeits. Protests should be kept to an absolute minimum and the intramural director can alleviate many problems by settling disputes at the time of the contest.

Intramural Publicity

In order to arouse and maintain interest in the intramural program, the students should be kept informed constantly about its activities. Continuous publicity does much to encourage additional students to enter into activities and, at the same time, acts as an added incentive to those who have been participating. Good publicity also enables the intramural department to operate much more efficiently, as the students are better informed of playing dates, playing locations, changes in schedules, entry dates, league standings, playoffs, and other information.

The best source of intramural publicity is the student newspaper. Space is usually easy to obtain, and if the intramural director makes effective use of it, great interest can be stimulated in the program. Items of unusual interest, noteworthy achievements, unique program features, league standings, schedules, and daily results should be publicized. The local newspaper has also been found to be effective in publicizing the intramural program in small communities.

The bulletin board is an excellent means of informing the student body of the intramural program. Every intramural department should have at least one bulletin board. In some schools, several boards are used to good advantage. The bulletin board should be strategically located so that the greatest number of students see it. It should be well-lighted and well-maintained, with eye-catching, up-to-date announcements, posters, and schedules.

Announcements at student gatherings and in physical education classes are a commonly used method of conveying information to students. Homeroom announcements are very helpful. Mailing information bulletins to students is effectively used in some schools. A recommended procedure is to gather all new students together and explain the program to them. Such a meeting may well be a part of the orientation sessions that many schools provide for new students. At this occasion, intramural handbooks can be distributed and interest inventories obtained from all students.

Intramural handbooks should be available to all students if they can be afforded. Many departments furnish handbooks and feel that the expense is well-justified. Intramural handbooks give the student a clear picture of the intramural department, its organization, its administration, its rules and regulations, its leaders, the program of activities, and additional facts with which the students should be familiar. Intramural directors and managers find that handbooks save them many explanations and interpretations of the rules. Students discover that the handbook gives them a much clearer understanding of the operation of the intramural department and enables them to conduct their activities more intelligently.

Intramural Coaching

Coaching is usually done by team members. The intramural director, physical education staff, and coaches should be available as resource people to assist the students.

Intramural Awards

Awards are a good motivational tool for intramurals. The use of awards as incentives to intramural participation can be defended as long as they remain inexpensive and they are used as a basis of recognition of achievement and not as the exclusive objective for participating. Awards are prevalent in community athletic programs and interscholastic programs and there is an expectation that awards will be received for intramural participation also.

The winners of competition can be awarded medals, cups, school insignia, ribbons, or other items designed for the intramural program. Team trophies have little value unless the competitive units are homerooms. In this case, a traveling trophy might be appropriate. An intramural showcase displaying engraved traveling trophies, winners' plaques, and awards for the current year can also be a fine feature to highlight intramural activities.

Intramural Statistics

Records of intramural programming, participation, and results should be kept to evaluate the effectiveness of the program. Information of this type assists making changes and improvements to better meet the needs of the students. Computerized record keeping makes it much easier to keep comprehensive records and the information can be effectively used to evaluate all aspects of the program and make changes.

College and University Intramural Programs

College and university intramural programs fill an important role. More students are reached by intramurals than any other activity on most campuses. The values received in terms of enjoyment, group cohesiveness, and emotional and physical health make this program a high-priority item on every campus.

The Intramural Director

An intramural specialist is needed to administer and develop high-quality programs. Educational preparation in physical education or recreation and experience in working with intramurals are prime requisites for intramural staff. Many people develop an interest in intramurals and gain experience by assisting with their school's program as undergraduates. The director must be able to work effectively with many people and be proficient in record-keeping and administering a multifaceted program. Budgetary skills and the ability to use the talents of assistants (undergraduates, graduate assistants, and faculty members) are other attributes that a successful intramural director must have.

Supervision of activities is an important responsibility of an intramural director. Direct supervision is delegated to an assistant in large programs, but the ultimate responsibility rests with the director. Supervisory responsibilities include performing safety checks, following established first aid procedures, organizing activity sites, seeing that recordkeeping procedures are practiced, enforcing appropriate participant behavior, and providing for care and return of equipment. Graduate assistants and undergraduate intramural managers commonly serve as supervisors. Activities such as tennis and golf that have minimal potential problems are run by the participants themselves.

Developing a budget, publicizing intramurals and its many activities, and keeping meticulous records are examples of some duties of an intramural director. The detail work can be overwhelming in this position, even with a large staff. Computer literacy is an important attribute for every intramural director, as a computer system with extensive software is needed to properly operate a college or university intramural program.

Intramural Councils, Student Managers, and Team Managers

The well-run intramural program involves students in all aspects of the program, including organizing activities, establishing policies and procedures, budgeting, and allocating funds for the different facets of an intramural program. An effective intramural council composed of students representing the participants, student government, and students working in the intramural office together with faculty and staff members is critically important. A council is needed to formulate and gain support for administrative procedures and policies and to oversee implementation of the intramural program. The council is also responsible for enforcing regulations and rules, hearing and deciding on protests, approving team and officials' clinics, and generally overseeing the program. Many other tasks of intramurals are also done by students. They often organize officiating, see that the fields and courts are ready and playable, have equipment available when and where needed, and collect and record activity and game results.

Intramural Finances

The major expenditures are for awards, office supplies, postage, officiating, intramural handbooks, secretarial assistance, equipment, and salaries. Financial support comes from several sources at most colleges and universities. Student activity fees are a major source of funds. The institution often provides support in the form of salary, equipment, and facilities. Some intramural programs are supported as part of the physical education budget;

intercollegiate athletics provide support at other institutions. Entry fees are also used in some programs.

The intramural director is responsible for preparing and administering the budget, but should work through the intramural council.

Units of Competition

Sororities and fraternities are effective units for intramural competition. Residence halls are also strong units, particularly if they are not too large. Dividing students into smaller residence groups such as floors or wings makes good competitive units and provides a better opportunity for more students to participate. Sorority, fraternity, and residence hall students develop strong group solidarity, and they are easily organized for intramural competition.

In the past, smaller institutions organized competition by academic class. Interclass competition can still be successfully implemented in small colleges. Divisions within the college or university, such as natural science, social science, engineering, and education, are natural groups that can be used as the basis for competition. In larger institutions, the various colleges can be divided into their different departments, such as civil engineering and mechanical engineering and further subdivided into first-year, sophomore, junior, and senior engineering. Other competitive groups may be campus organizations, sport clubs, students in departmental major clubs and student groups.

The biggest problem of most intramural directors is to obtain participation by the unorganized, independent students. These students participate satisfactorily in individual sports, particularly if the activity is well-publicized and energetically promoted. The real difficulty is to secure participation in team sports. Students who are not a members of some campus group that participates in intramurals are difficult to organize for participation and they are hard to contact. The crucial factor is to find student leadership for these students. All methods of motivating and promoting participation must be consistently and effectively used to get a substantial percentage of these students into the program.

A number of schools have discovered that a good way to organize nonaffiliated students is to divide them into groups. The groups are carefully worked out so that each contains approximately the same number of students. Each group operates under the leadership of an intramural manager, who makes every effort to organize the students within the group for intramurals. It is preferable for these groups to compete among themselves with winners meeting sorority, fraternity, and residence hall winners for the overall championship of each sport.

Although seldom used now, one system that has been successfully used, usually in small institutions, is to assign all students by lot to an intramural group. New students are assigned to the group having the fewest members on its roster. Once assigned to a team, a student remains a member as long as he or she attends the college or university. This system can also be used on a temporary basis for entering students until they have a chance to affiliate with an organization that participates in intramurals.

Program of Activities

Activities that can be included in an intramural program are listed in Table 13-1. Many other events can be added to the list and will be successful if properly promoted.

TABLE 13-1.   Activities for Secondary and College Students

Archery	Floor hockey	Paddle ball
Backpacking	Fly or bait casting	Paddle tennis
Badminton	Free-throw shooting	Racquetball
Baseball	Golf	Rollerblading
Basketball	Gymnastics	Roller skating
Bowling	Handball	Scuba diving
Camping	Hiking	Skiing
Canoeing	Handball	Snowshoeing
Card games	Hiking	Soccer
Checkers	Horseback riding	Softball
Chess	Horseshoes	Speedball
Crafts	Ice hockey	Squash
Cross-country	Ice skating	Swimming
Curling	Indoor track	Table tennis
Cycling	Judo	Team handball
Dance (folk, line, modern,	Karate	Tennis
square, social)	Lacrosse	Track and field
Deck tennis	Mountaineering	Volleyball
Dramatics	Music activities	Water basketball
Fencing	Novelty events	Water polo
Field hockey	Open recreation	Weight training
Fishing	Orienteering	Wrestling
Flag football	Outings	

Eligibility for Intramural Competition

Scholastic requirements are not used as a basis for eligibility. Some of the common regulations are as follows:

> Varsity squad members are ineligible for all intramural activities during the varsity season. Any player who is dropped for ineligibility cannot compete in that sport in the intramural program.

> Letter winners are ineligible to compete for one season in the intramural sport in which they won their letter.

> Athletic team members cannot compete in intramural sports at the same time that they are on a first-year or junior varsity squad.

> A student who is barred from a school team because of professionalism is not permitted to compete in intramurals in the sport in which he or she is a professional.

> A student may play on only one team during a given season.

> After playing in one contest with a given team, a player cannot transfer to another team in that sport.

> A student taking less than half of a full-time academic schedule is ineligible for intramural competition. (Some programs are open to any student taking even one course.)

> Any student who is on probation for disciplinary reasons cannot participate in intramural activities.

> Any team using an ineligible player shall forfeit the contest or contests in which that player participated.

Any player who is guilty of unsporting conduct may be declared ineligible to compete in intramural sports.

Medical Examinations, Accident Insurance, and Preliminary Training Periods

Policies relating to these areas are covered in the secondary school section of this chapter.

Time Periods

Nights and late afternoons are the most common times for intramural activities. At universities and colleges with large resident populations, weekends are also effectively used for activities. Facilities for recreational use as well as informal activities should be scheduled throughout the day and at night. Many individual sport participants compete whenever they have free time if facilities are available. Challenge tournaments and some elimination tournaments can be run whenever two contestants are free to meet each other.

Students at many colleges and universities have used student fees to finance the construction of buildings that are used exclusively for recreation and intramurals. This makes it possible to schedule a broad range of activities day and night.

Officials

Specially attired and trained officials are an important ingredient in the success of an intramural program. Paying officials is a desirable practice and contributes to the quality of officiating.

High-quality intramural officiating is facilitated in colleges and universities that have a professional physical education program. Physical education majors make excellent officials. In some institutions, a course in officiating is offered and the laboratory part of the course consists of officiating in intramural contests.

Intramural officials' associations have proven effective in raising the standard of intramural officiating in many colleges and universities. The objectives of such associations are to promote a higher degree of sporting behavior and fair play in all intramural sports, to control serious injuries through competent officiating, and to make the games more interesting and enjoyable to both participant and spectator. Intramural officials' association should meet regularly throughout the season. Rating cards are sent to the association concerning each official's performance after each game. In many institutions, the intramural official's association conducts sports clinics for various intramural sports. Such clinics are scheduled before the competition and cover rules, interpretations, and discussion of ground rules. Sports clinics have the effect of improving officiating because participating teams have a better understanding of rules and officiating procedures.

Protests

The customary ruling in regard to protests is that they be made in writing within 24 hours after the contest in question, accompanied by a fee, which is returned if the protest is granted but kept if it is not. This gives the students time to cool off and reconsider their protest. Protests are reduced if the intramural department has someone available at the various games to settle disputes. The protests that are filed with the intramural department are usually acted on by the intramural council. No consideration should be given to protests that involve mistakes in judgment by the officials. Legitimate protests are those based on the question of ineligibility of players and mistakes involving interpretation of the rules.

Forfeits

Forfeits are the bane of the intramural director's existence. They present a problem for all intramural departments, although well-organized departments are less troubled in this respect than poorly organized ones. When students and organizations regard their intramural participation as a privilege, there are fewer forfeits. Some departments place a heavy penalty on forfeits, and this appears to reduce them. This penalty usually involves the loss of intramural points and the loss of any entry fee, although some departments deprive the forfeiting group of further participation, either for the season or for the remainder of the year. The cause of forfeits, in most cases, is discouragement following repeated defeats. If the competition is equalized to a reasonable extent, some of these forfeits can be prevented. The number of forfeits is appreciably diminished when weaker groups compete among themselves.

Intramural Publicity

Publicity techniques used in a secondary school are also applicable to colleges and universities. In addition, students often work with the intramural director or another staff member to develop and implement a comprehensive campuswide publicity program. All types of literature and promotional techniques should be used to reach students, inform them of intramural activities, and encourage them to get involved.

Intramural Awards

The winners of individual competition may be awarded medals, plaques, cups, souvenir items, intramural shirts, or some other wearing apparel. Group competition is usually divided into leagues comprising highly organized groups such as sororities, fraternities, and residence halls, and less-structured groups such as clubs, campus organizations, and groups that form just for the intramural competition. Winning teams of the highly organized groups are usually awarded pennants, shields, plaques, or cups. The other groups have little use for team trophies, so they are usually given emblems, medals, or some other personal item. A larger, more pretentious cup is awarded to the sorority, fraternity, or residence hall group with the best all-year performance. A similar award is given to the individual with the best all-year performance. Institutions should purchase the awards before the competition for them commences because it gives students the opportunity to see the awards for which they are competing and it ensures prompt distribution of the awards after they have been won. An award that is granted six months after it has been won has lost much of its value to the student.

Intramural Statistics

The intramural department should have careful records of student participation in the activities of the program. In order to have a true picture of the intramural participation, the director must discover the total number of students who have been reached by at least one activity, the average number of sports in which each student participated, and the average number of games played in each sport by each student or the participation hours of each student. The participation hours of every student in each activity is extremely valuable information, but is difficult to secure. The above statistics must be compiled every year. The values of these participation records are as follows:

> Gain or loss in intramural participation over the previous year can readily be ascertained.
>
> The proportion of the entire student body participating in intramural sports is discovered.
>
> Whether the students are taking advantage of the intramural program throughout the year or are only participating sporadically is disclosed.
>
> The popular and unpopular activities are discovered. The gain or loss in interest in the various activities from year to year is evident.
>
> The most successful units of competition can be ascertained.
>
> The statistics can be used to show the need for greater financial assistance.
>
> The success or failure of various administrative procedures can be checked.

Computerized recordkeeping has made it possible to keep more accurate and more comprehensive records. Even individual participation records are feasible and extensive yearly records are available for intramural use.

Point Systems

Intramural point systems are used to determine the group of individuals who performed most or best or both throughout the entire year. Such scoring plans are valuable in stimulating and maintaining interest in intramural activities for the entire year. Many organizations and individuals are inclined to enter only activities in which they are proficient. A point system, however, encourages them to engage in a wide variety of activities. The group influences all its members to participate and, incidentally, those who most need big-muscle play activity are persuaded to enter into various sports. Many students get their first experience with different activities in this manner. With individual and group point systems operating, the whole participation in the program becomes less haphazard and sporadic. Scoring plans function effectively in both college and high school intramurals.

Group Point Systems

There are different types of group scoring plans. Teams usually receive participation points and place points. Different activities have different point totals. The point totals are determined by the number of teams competing, the number of players on a team, the type of tournament that is used, and the length of the season. (See Appendix A for the many types of tournaments that are successfully used for intramural competition.) Additional points are sometimes awarded for each win.

Individual Point Systems

Individual point systems are similar to group scoring plans. Every student has the opportunity to compete for individual honors. The total points accumulated during the year are used to determine individual honors at the end of the final intramural event. Points are received for achievements in individual events and for participation and honors received from competing in team sports. The recordkeeping, particularly in programs that have large student participation, is extensive, but it is workable with appropriate computer programs. Recognition of the outstanding female and male intramural athlete of the year is an excellent tool for publicity and it generates extensive interest in intramural programs.

Characteristics of Intramural Programs

A wide variety of events, ranging from the highly competitive to informal recreational activities to outdoor education activities, are included in good programs. Many different sports are incorporated and programs are adjusted to meet changing student interests. Coeducational activities are an important part of intramural programs.

Many different clubs are included under the intramural umbrella at colleges and universities. These include sport clubs and special interest groups such as hiking, outing, and orienteering clubs.

Intramural directors also provide the opportunity for spontaneous informal athletic competition when facilities permit. There are always students who are anxious to play when the facilities and equipment are available. By setting facilities aside for such competition and publicizing the opportunity, schools involve many more students. Intramural departments can extend this program by providing a matchmaking service for all sports. The amount of participation and the number of participants justifies the effort of the intramural department to promote this informal competition.

Class Activities

Simulation 1

Situation   The middle schools in your community (grades 6–8) have decided to drop their athletic programs and substitute a comprehensive intramural program that includes a competitive experience for every student who wants to participate.

Design a model middle school intramural program for your community.

Simulation 2

Situation   The high school you attended wants to expand the existing intramural program or start a program if none exists.

Set up an intramural program that you would recommend to the school board in your district. Consider administration, program activities, policies, financing, scheduling, and awards.

Simulation 3

Situation   There are eight teams participating in a university novice intramural division. They compete in several different team sports.

Give each of the eight teams a name and make up a schedule for them using the following tournaments. (Refer to Appendix A.)

Round robin

Single elimination

Double elimination

Consolation elimination tournament

Seed four teams when seeding is appropriate.

Simulation 4

Situation   Community support is needed to expand an existing intramural program. Present the speech you would give to the parent–teacher organization in your community to gain its support for the intramural program or write an opinion column for your local newspaper pointing out the values of an intramural program.

Performance Tasks

1. Interview a university intramural director to find out how she or he feels a high school intramural program should differ from a university intramural program.
2. Establish an intramural council for an elementary school and a secondary school and develop guidelines for the operation of the council.
3. Debate the following issues:

   a. Awards should be given for winning intramurals.
   b. There should be no eligibility requirements in order to participate in intramurals.

4. Write a job description for a secondary school intramural director.
5. Write a job description for a university intramural director.
6. Conduct a survey of students in a high school or at your university to determine the activities they would like to have included in an intramural program.
7. Visit a school that has an established intramural program. Interview a school administrator and the intramural director to determine how they started the program and how they obtain support for the program.
8. Sketch an outline of an intramural handbook for a senior high school in your district.
9. Select an activity and design an intramural program for that activity in an elementary school.
10. Design a homeroom intramural coed lunch-hour volleyball league for a junior high school.

References

Bonnano, Diane (ed.), *Intramurals and Club Sports.* Reston, VA: AAHPERD, 1986.

Dexter, Robert H., and Jessanna T. Gartside, "Moving from Interscholastics to Intramurals." *Middle School Journal,* November 1992, 24(2):51–53.

Matthews, David O., *Managing Intramurals and Recreational Sports.* Champaign, IL: Stipes Publishing, 1984.

Miller, Thomas M. (ed.), *Organizational Management Administration for Athletic Programs*, 3rd ed. Dubuque, IA: Eddie Bowers, 1993.

14

Interschool Athletics

Intercollegiate Athletics

As far back as anthropologists can go in human history, they find evidence of participation in sports and games. Despite the fact that people have always wanted to play, and have played when possible, only recently have they ventured to play in the school. The traditional philosophy of education, with its emphasis on scholarship and intellectual development, could conceive of no place for play in an educational institution. Naturally, this powerful urge could not be entirely suppressed, and despite the unsympathetic and often hostile attitude of the faculty, the students indulged in various sports and games in their leisure time. It was not until the nineteenth century that students dared to form teams for interschool contests. Organized athletics appeared in England as early as 1822, when the first Eton–Harrow cricket match was played. Oxford and Cambridge met for the first time in 1827. In the United States, the first interschool contest was a rowing race between Yale and Harvard in 1852. In 1859, the first baseball game was played between Williams and Amherst; the first football game was played by Rutgers University and Princeton in 1869.

Despite sporadic contests before the Civil War, the real development came afterward. Up to this time, impromptu play on campus predominated. But the war, as all wars since have done, greatly simulated interest in sports. This fact, plus the greatly expanded enrollments, gave such impetus to athletics that the informal, intramural program developed a new facet: men's interinstitutional competition. The better teams in institutions began to challenge similar teams in nearby schools. This form of extramural competition proved immediately popular. Participants and student bodies were extremely enthusiastic and supported this new development wholeheartedly. Faculty members were undoubtedly aware of these student activities but took no action to control or curtail them.

At first, the captain was the coach of the team. As interest in intercollegiate athletics increased, it became obvious that more experienced leadership was needed. The practice developed of employing on a seasonal basis an alumnus who had been an outstanding performer. Alumni coaches eventually gave way to professional coaches. In the days before gate receipts, coaches were paid by the students, alumni, or friends of the institution. Because colleges and universities had no facilities for athletics, students had to obtain, prepare, and maintain the playing areas. Originally, all the playing equipment and uniforms were furnished by the players, but as the importance of the contests grew, parents, alumni, and friends contributed funds for their purchase.

For a number of years after the Civil War, this student-conducted program flourished. But as it grew, many problems developed. In the first place, the work became too much for students who were expected to carry a normal academic load. Second, the constantly changing student population prevented any stability in leadership and continuity in policy. Third, due to both of these factors many undesirable practices emerged. Business matters were not efficiently handled and financial irregularities resulted. A fierce struggle was waged within the institution when the different sports competed with each other for players, financial support, and facilities. Many questionable practices were used to recruit athletes. Eligibility rules were nonexistent; travel was unrestrained. Students with injuries did not receive proper medical care. Student leadership proved incapable of meeting the many problems that developed.

When it became clear that the leadership left much to be desired, college administrators concluded that the only way to conduct intercollegiate athletics along educational lines was to appoint a faculty member to administer them. The most logical person in the majority of institutions was the director of physical education or a staff member. These people were already concerned with the physical phase of the student's life. Many had participated in intercollegiate athletics and had coaching experience. When increasing numbers of these people received professional preparation in physical education, they were well-qualified to direct the athletic program. Along with this change in organizational setup, colleges and universities accepted financial responsibility for the program. The great majority of institutions provided and maintained the facilities and employed personnel from the institutional budgets. Generally, the intercollegiate program was expected to be self-supporting.

With these developments, athletics were accepted as an integral part of educational programs. Even though they were partially self-supporting and still included some type of athletic committee setup, they were organizationally and philosophically a legitimate phase of the educational life of the institution. There were exceptions, primarily among the larger institutions where the graduate-manager and student-athletic association type of organization persisted, but in the smaller colleges and universities and some of the larger ones, the athletic program had come to be regarded as part of the institutional curriculum.

Intercollegiate programs have been accepted as part of the educational program for many years and they are administered by college and university officials. However, the phenomenal development and expansion of athletic programs has placed new stresses on the relationship of athletic programs and the higher education institutions where they are located. In many institutions, they have become more powerful than any other aspect of the institution, including the academic programs. More than one university president has been replaced because he or she tried to rein in the athletic program and keep it within the academic mission of the institution. Too many athletic programs, unfortunately, are characterized by undesirable practices that are not too different from some of the practices that led college and universities to bring athletics under the educational umbrella in the first place. Athletics have become a big business, with millions of dollars being generated and spent. When vast sums of money are involved, added incentive is given to circumvent the rules and carry out practices that are inconsistent with educational goals. There has also been a significant change in the way intercollegiate contests are viewed. They are seen as entertainment rather than educational experiences for participants and the student spectators. Television makes extensive use of college sports programming; this not only contributes to the huge sums of money that universities receive, but also changes the public view of college and university athletics. The public often equates them with professional sports. Print media and radio sportscasters also contribute to this perspective of intercollegiate sports. When star athletes leave colleges and universities before finishing their academic program and sign multimillion-dollar contracts, it further strains the concept of athletics being part of the educational program. This is true even though only a small number of athletes have the option to sign multimillion-dollar contracts. The bottom line is that athletic program administrators, coaches, and athletes have gained so much power that universities and colleges have found it difficult to maintain an educational perspective in the administration and implementation of athletic programs.

It should be pointed out that in many institutions, athletic programs are an integral part of the school's educational program. Also, athletic governing bodies and university presidents are working diligently to ensure that athletic programs are run in a manner consistent with the educational objectives of institutions of higher education.

Interscholastic Athletics

The development of interscholastic athletics followed and paralleled that of intercollegiate athletics in many respects. It is quite likely that many features of high school athletics were copied from the intercollegiate patterns. The interscholastic movement began 10 or 15 years after the Civil War, when athletics in institutions of higher learning were already well underway. Like intercollegiate athletics, high school athletics were initiated by students without the support of school administrators and faculty. The students received more encouragement and assistance from the community than from the school. Early physical educators were uncooperative and, in many cases, hostile to the program because it was contrary to their philosophy and practice. Just as in colleges and universities, many problems and anti-educational practices developed under student sponsorship and leadership. When conditions became intolerable, school administrators were forced to assume control. This led eventually to the acceptance of interscholastic athletics as an essential part of the school curriculum.

Athletics are a strong force in schools throughout the United States. The importance of athletics has steadily increased in the lives of students. The number of participants each year surpasses 5 million students in the 50 states and the District of Columbia (*National Federation Handbook,* 1993). The level of athletic performance is as impressive as the number of participants. The quality of the coaching, equipment, facilities, and practice and game organization of the athletic programs provides safe, enjoyable, challenging, and healthful educational experiences. The variety of sports available to students has also expanded over the years. For example, the National Federation Handbook lists 24 different sports in which states determine state championships:

Archery	Golf
Badminton	Gymnastics
Baseball	Ice hockey
Basketball	Indoor track
Bowling	Skiing
Competitive cheerleading	Soccer
Cross country	Softball
Curling	Swimming
Decathlon/pentathlon	Tennis
Field hockey	Track
Fencing	Volleyball
Football	Wrestling

Competition is also offered in other sports for which state championships are not sponsored. These include water polo, weight lifting, judo, and equestrian.

It would be incorrect to say that all athletic practices are good or that there aren't problems in interscholastic athletics. Some of the same issues that confront intercollegiate athletics also face interscholastic athletics. These issues are examined in other parts of this chapter.

Athletics for Girls and Women

Historical Perspective

The most dramatic change that has taken place in intercollegiate and interscholastic athletics has been the expansion of programs to include girls and women. Until the 1960s, it was rare to find highly competitive interschool athletic programs for girls and women. Before that time, all such programs were for boys and men. With the passage of Title IX of the Education Amendments Act of 1972, programs for girls and women were given the legal base that resulted in widespread opportunities to participate in highly competitive sports on the secondary and collegiate level.

There were opportunities for women to compete in sports long before the 1960s. Until the late nineteenth century, women's sports and athletics consisted almost exclusively of gymnastic exercise. The trend toward sports participation became apparent as several colleges instituted physical training programs in tennis, crew, archery, croquet, bowling, track and field, and basketball. The formal beginning of athletic competition for girls and women in this country came near the turn of the century. At the 1899 Conference on Physical Training, a committee was appointed to make an extensive study of the many versions of basketball played by women. The committee published "girls' rules" for basketball, with special stress on standards safeguarding the health of the participants.

Basketball and field hockey were the principal sports in which intercollegiate competition was held before World War I. Field hockey was introduced to this country in 1901 by Constance Applebee, a player-coach from England. Individual and team merit were recognized with letters, chevrons, sweaters, and trophies.

A fear persisted during this time that women could not withstand the physical and mental rigors of sports competition. There was also concern about the possible negative effects of physical exertion on childbearing. Mabel Lee, one of the outstanding early leaders of the physical education profession, published the results of a 1930 survey of the advantages and disadvantages of intercollegiate athletics for women and listed 15 disadvantages including the following two:

> They would be apt to get more "physical straining than physical training," showing the most perhaps in nerve fatigue. . . . A question which should not be ignored is that raised by certain members of the medical profession as to the bad effect of intense athletic participation on child bearing. (Lee, 1931, pp. 96–97)

In 1923, the National Amateur Athletic Federation was formed to promote physical education in educational institutions, encourage standardization of rules, facilitate the participation of U.S. athletes in the Olympic Games, and foster the highest ideals of amateur sports. Herbert Hoover's wife, Lou Henry, assumed leadership in the girls and women's divisions of the federation. This women's division disapproved of highly intense specialized competition. Some of their reports included concerns that male scouts were "buying up" girls for teams and that girls were fainting in basketball games from heart attacks or overstrain. The mission of this well-organized group was to promote sports and games for girls and women and to ensure that sports and games were wisely chosen, promoted, and supervised.

There was virtually no championship competition for women in the schools in the early thirties. Lee (1932) further observed that, increasingly, the vast majority of physical education department directors, staff members, and women's athletic associations were opposed to interinstitutional competition.

Between 1930 and 1960, service and intramural programs predominated in the schools. Female physical educators used the term *extramural* for competition with other schools and organizations. Included in this category were play days and sports days, telegraphic meets, invitational meets, and interscholastic or intercollegiate meets. Play days and sports day were the type of athletic competition women developed as a substitute for intercollegiate and interscholastic sports. The women wanted to avoid the abuses and defects that characterized men's interschool competition.

A play day is defined as a day when students from several schools or colleges meet and play with, rather than against, each other. They come together at the invitation of one of the institutions. The players are divided into teams, each team representing not one school but a combination of all of the schools present. The emphasis is on sport for sport's sake and "play with us and not against us." The sports day is a variation of the play day. In this type of competition, several schools meet for the day, but the teams remain intact and the players are not interchanged. One or more sports may be included in the program. The advantages of these two types of events are obvious. They offer opportunities for social contacts and allow a large number of students to engage in a wide variety of recreational activities.

The question of interschool athletics for secondary school girls and college women was a controversial issue until well into the 1950s and, in fact, continued to generate heated views even after passage of Title IX of the Education Amendments of 1972. Until the 1960s, most female physical educators and women's professional organizations were united in their opposition to such competition.

In the late 1950s, it was common opinion among school administrators and people in general that the Division for Girls' and Women's Sports (DGWS) of the American Association for Health, Physical Education, and Recreation (the organization that preceded the formation of the American Alliance for Health, Physical Education, Recreation and Dance) was opposed to competition.

The 1958 revision of their standards made it clear that this was not true. Evidence suggested that the philosophy of the division had been misinterpreted and this had limited the development of programs for the highly skilled. Ley (1962, p. 10) stated, "[I]n an effort to do the greatest good for the greatest number, we have emphasized intramural competition but in the process we have not provided competition of sufficient quality and quantity to satisfy the highly skilled girl."

In 1962, the Executive Council of the Division for Girls' and Women's Sports committed itself to the position that highly skilled girls and women must have opportunities for competition that satisfy their desire to excel. Careful distinctions were made between the forms of competition that were intramural in nature and those that were extramural in nature. Standards were developed for the different kinds of competition for different grade levels. According to Clifton, it was at this time that competition for highly skilled girls and women was endorsed and wholeheartedly encouraged. She stated, "We have reached the point of 'no return'! Never again will our concept of girls sports be the same. Nor will it remain as we envision it today or tomorrow" (Clifton, 1964, p. 1).

In 1974, the Division for Girls' and Women's Sports became the National Association for Girls and Women in Sports. This professional association, along with its institutional membership organization, the Association for Intercollegiate Athletics for Women, and the National Federation of State High School Associations, provided the framework for competitive programs for school girls and college women. These groups developed standards and policies for competition and developed rules under which various sports were played.

Three major factors greatly affected the revolution of sports programs for girls and women during this era. The first was the realization that women were capable of strenuous exercise without adverse physical, mental, or emotional results. Research had refuted the claims that women could not withstand the strains of highly competitive athletics and physical achievements of women during this period established beyond question their ability to handle rigorous sporting endeavors. Secondly, the woman had been emancipated from her role of homemaker and mother. She was demanding freedom from stereotyped sex roles and equal opportunity in all avenues of endeavor, including sports. The fact that long-standing myths regarding harmful effects of physical exertion had been disproved and the fact that the women's liberation movement was in full swing caused an unprecedented change in the attitudes of men and women toward female participation in sports. However, the third and probably the most influential factor that fueled the revolution in girls and women's sports programs was federal legislation: Title IX of the Education Amendments Act of 1972. The basic provision of Title IX reads:

> No person in the United States shall, on the basis of sex, be excluded from participation, be denied the benefits of, or be subjected to discrimination under any education program or activity receiving federal financial assistance.

At this same time, many states also passed legislation that had the effect of prohibiting sexual discrimination in sports. Some of this legislation was even more stringent than Title IX.

Title IX has had dramatic effects on women's athletic programs throughout the United States. The number of female participants has increased significantly. The National Federation of State High School Associations reported that the number of girls participating increased from 294,015 in 1971 to 2,124,755 in the 1993–1994 academic year (Associated Press Release, *The Times,* Trenton, NJ, August 10, 1994). Similar increases were noted in the number of sports offered on the interscholastic and intercollegiate levels following Title IX. Huge gains have been noted in many other aspects of women's athletic programs. Coaching, equipment, medical care, facility use, financial support, and travel arrangements are examples of areas that have been significantly expanded or improved.

The euphoria about the gains that have occurred since Title IX became law is tempered by the realization that inequities still exist in athletics. Women are underrepresented as coaches, trainers, officials, and administrators. In fact, there has been a significant decrease in the percentage of women holding these positions since implementation of Title IX. Women's athletic programs often do not receive the media coverage that is afforded men's programs and too often female athletes are not viewed in the same light or given the same respect as male athletes.

Title IX requires that females and males have equal opportunity to compete in athletics. The first test is whether a female student has the same chance to participate in a sport as a male student. The identical sports do not have to be offered for both sexes, but the variety and number of sports that are offered must give the same opportunity for both female and male students. The caliber and support of programs must also be on the same level. The locker room, practice, and game facilities that are provided, the schedules, the travel arrangements, practice times, game times, equipment, medical care, and salaries for coaches and officials must be of the same magnitude and quality.

In some cases, institutions, male coaches, and male administrators have overtly as well as covertly prevented full implementation of Title IX. This has led to lawsuits that have had important ramifications. Litigation, with resulting monetary judgments and the threat of such judgments, has led universities to settle suits over Title IX out of court. Recourse to the courts has stepped up the pace of compliance.

The vast majority of educational institutions have increased the scope of their competitive athletic programs since the advent of Title IX. There has been a sincere effort in most institutions to provide equal opportunities for both sexes. A number of factors that have delayed the realization of this goal. One is that change is never easy. Another is that firmly entrenched male programs have felt threatened and the athletic leadership has reacted negatively to some of the steps that are necessary to bring about equity. A third factor is the financial issue; a finite amount of money must be extended to cover more sports and upgrade existing women's programs. This has led some schools to drop male sports and this has contributed to friction between those involved in men and women's athletic program and further delayed full compliance with Title IX.

Title IX has significantly changed the face of women's sports programs. Sports have become accepted as a positive experience for female as well as male students. The degree of skill exhibited in girls and women's sports has reached heights far exceeding performance levels before Title IX. However, there are still many obstacles to be overcome to meet the spirit as well as the legal requirements of Title IX. There is additional background information about Title IX in Chapter 2.

Jurisdiction over Girls' and Women's Athletics

The national Association for Intercollegiate Athletics for Women (AIAW) was formed to administer women's intercollegiate athletics in 1971. In many ways, it paralleled the NCAA and the NAIA, organizations that administered men's athletics on the national level. Their goal was to foster broad programs of intercollegiate athletics in accordance with the philosophy and standards of the DGWS. Initially, athletic scholarships were not permitted, but under threat of legal action the membership voted to permit scholarships, although there were some strong restrictions such as not allowing paid recruiters or subsidized visits of prospective athletes. Also, funds for books and tutoring services were not permitted. Every attempt was made by the organization to prevent undesirable practices in recruiting and performer exploitation that was causing so many problems for men's athletics.

AIAW established codes of conduct for players, coaches, administrators, officials, and spectators and had as its goal the enhancement of athletic competition for college women. They also sponsored national championships for women in a number of sports. This resulted in the need for a regional structure that acted as a means of qualifying for participation in national championships. Some of the regional organizations preceded the formation of the national organization but others were developed under the guidance of the AIAW.

A bitter battle ensued between the National Collegiate Athletic Association (NCAA) and the AIAW over control of intercollegiate athletics for women during this time. Many in the AIAW felt that their organization would maintain sanity in athletics and keep athletics in proper perspective in the educational scheme. On the other hand, there were many conflicts within universities and colleges over the different philosophies and procedures that were being followed by the women and the men's programs. Administratively, this caused many difficulties. A bigger issue was the financial one. University administrators felt that having all programs under one umbrella would be more cost-effective and that it would be possible to provide more equitable programs for both sexes if they operated under the same rules. The NCAA had much more money to sponsor national championships and other programs and had a strong financial base from revenue received from championship events and television revenue. These factors eventually led women's athletics to become part of the NCAA. Women's championships became part of the NCAA program in 1981–1982.

The AIAW made many impressive contributions to women's athletics from the time it was formed in 1971 until it ceased to offer programs and services in June 1982. By this time, the NCAA and the National Association for Intercollegiate Athletics (NAIA) had formally changed their structures to include women's athletics. At the time of its demise, AIAW offered 39 national championships in 17 sports to over 6,000 women's teams. At its peak, there were 960 member colleges and universities.

A similar struggle for control of girls' athletics occurred in many states after Title IX. Before this time, most competitive programs for secondary school girls were developed by female physical educators within the state, and were thus the concern of the state's physical education professional association and its Division for Girls and Women's sports. The state organization had committees to direct girls' sports programs. They followed existing guidelines developed by the AAHPERD Division of Girls and Women's Sports; however, the state group had little power to enforce guidelines or establish rules and regulations. In most states, the first state tournaments were completely under the direction of the Division of Girls and Women's Sports rather than the state high school athletic association.

The Division for Girls and Women's Sports at the state level did not have either the power, support, or organization that characterized AIAW. As a result, soon after passage of Title IX girls' athletics became part of the state athletic (or activities) association in most states. In some states, there was a brief struggle by the Division for Girls and Women's Sports to remain the organizational body for girls' competition. However, girls' athletic programs were soon administered by the state association along with the athletic programs for boys.

Middle School and Junior High School Athletics

At the middle school level, the main emphasis has been on intramural programs. Competition with other schools can be successfully implemented in middle schools where the program is tailored for the age of the students. The key consideration in the middle school is to be sure that sufficient resources are available to provide an extensive intramural program for all students.

At the junior high school level (grades 7–9), an extensive athletic program should be in place. The length of the season, practice schedule, and structure of the program can be less than at the high school level, but this is an age when students are ready to get extensively involved in organized sports. Most students at this age have already participated in organized sports in community leagues. Schools are better equipped to provide high-quality programs and good coaching than are community agencies that offer programs if the school doesn't. Plenty of opportunities should be provided for students not on the varsity teams to participate in sports through the intramural and instructional programs. Many students develop late or they have not had the chance to participate in youth programs. These students should have the opportunity to develop their athletic skills so that they can participate in junior or senior high school athletic programs later.

The Relationship of Athletics to Physical Education

While athletics were springing up without the encouragement or guidance of school authorities, physical education classwork was being increasingly emphasized in the schools. The growing number of students with mental and physical health problems finally forced school administrators to recognize that steps must be taken to safeguard the health of students. Confronted with this problem, educators turned to Europe again and borrowed the most popular system of physical education then in vogue, which, together with health (then called hygiene), was added to the curriculum to assist in the digestion of the already heavy intellectual diet. In colleges, physicians, because of their medical background, were placed in charge of the health and physical education classes. Physical education usually consisted of American modifications of German or Swedish formal gymnastics. This form of physical education was unpopular with students, who endured it only because it was required. At the same time, the students in their leisure time were vigorously promoting various sports and contests among themselves and with students of other schools.

When school administrators decided to accept interschool athletics and introduce it into the school curriculum, they logically located it in the physical education department. It proved to be an unwelcome guest. Physical educators viewed this foundling with suspicion and reluctantly accepted it as a necessary evil. A bitter struggle was waged for the leadership of the combined department. Little harmony and cooperation existed between athletics and physical education, and considerable jealousy and antagonism developed. This was to be expected because, at that time, the two areas were so far apart in philosophy, activities, and methods that they could not be harmoniously reconciled.

A new philosophy of education, emerging at the beginning of the twentieth century, had profound implications for physical education. This new philosophy exploded the ancient theory of the dualism of the mind and the body and accepted the concept of the unity of the human organism. It also conceived of the function of the school as directing children and youth in learning activities that contribute to socially acceptable conduct. No longer was the purpose of school limited to the development of the mental capacities. No longer was the classroom the brain factory and the gymnasium the muscle factory. The structural, analytical concept of education, which dismembered the child into mental, physical, social, and moral attributes and then attempted to develop each independently, was rejected. The school existed for the purpose of preparing each student for the finest kind of living he or she could achieve.

Out of this new philosophy of education, a new philosophy of physical education evolved gradually. It conceived of physical education as education by means of the physical rather than education of the physical. In other words, fine living became the aim of physical education just as it became the aim of every phase of school life. The emphasis shifted from the purely physical to the mental and the social as well. This new concept revolutionized traditional practices in physical education. In 1910, because of the influence of Wood, Hetherington, and other leading physical educators of the period, a new era of physical education began. They advocated the elimination of the formal systems of gymnastics and the substitution of natural play activities. This new movement gathered impetus, and today it is accepted as the American system of physical education. It has largely replaced the German and Swedish systems and their variations, which were not acceptable to American youth.

The broadened educational philosophy also gave athletics a new significance in the educational setup. Here was great potential for developing in youth desirable knowledge, skills, habits, and attitudes. It was found that athletics, under proper guidance and leadership, could become a powerful educational force, particularly in the development of social, moral, and physical qualities. The dramatic nature of interschool athletics made them even more valuable in some respects than the physical education activities of the curriculum. But the administration of interinstitutional athletics left much to be desired. Although the conduct of athletics has improved immeasurably since their first inclusion in the school program, certain practices still exist that can hardly be called educational.

Athletics and physical education have had a close relationship since interschool athletic programs became a part of the educational program. Because they were both based on physical activity and many of the sports in the physical education programs were also found in athletic programs, it was natural that they were grouped together. One person usually administered both programs and almost all of the coaching in the athletic programs was done by physical education teachers. Administrators and the public often viewed the two programs as being one and the same.

In addition to sharing staff, athletics and physical education also shared facilities and, to a lesser extent, equipment. They also shared many of the same objectives and used sports to reach these objectives. For these reasons, the two programs remained closely allied for many years.

The change in emphasis of college and university athletic programs began in the 1950s and by the 1970s most athletic programs were either totally separated from physical education or at least had much more autonomy. It should be pointed out that some colleges and universities still have closely related physical education and athletic programs where athletics are viewed as an integral part of the physical education program.

Numerous factors have led to the separation of athletic and physical education programs. The two major factors are the expansion of the athletic programs and the increased emphasis placed on winning. At many colleges and universities, winning became the overriding objective of programs; they were viewed more for their entertainment value than for their educational value. The administration of athletic programs became more sophisticated as athletics became big business, huge sums of money became necessary to run programs, recruiting became intense, and pressure increased to keep pace with programs at highly successful universities. Although only a small percentage of athletic programs actually are profitable, television money, national rankings, and the goal of participating in football bowl games and national championships were other influences that led athletics to be separated from physical education programs at colleges and universities. This separation was necessary in colleges and universities where athletics became big business. Athletic programs at small institutions also became autonomous as they increased recruiting, extended seasons, had longer practices, and improved the caliber of their programs. This development of highly organized, highly competitive athletic programs at all levels resulted in the need for them to be administered separately if they were to be effectively run. It also became extremely difficult for physical education teachers to teach and also coach. In addition, the increased number of sports included in athletic programs and the expanded coaching staffs made it impossible for physical education teachers to fill all the coaching positions that were available.

Although the separation hasn't been as pronounced, significant changes in the relationship of physical education and athletics have also taken place at the secondary level. One of the impacts of Title IX was a dramatic increase in the number of sports included in the athletic programs for girls. This, together with steadily increasing athletic performance levels, community pressure to have winning teams, and the patterning of high school programs after university programs, resulted in athletic programs being administered separately. The number of coaches needed for the boys' and girls' programs far outstripped the number of physical education teachers in the schools. Teachers of other disciplines and coaches from outside the school system were needed to coach; this further diminished the close relationship that had existed when almost all of the coaching was done by physical education teachers. There hasn't been as complete a break between athletics and physical education at the secondary level as at the college and university level, but philosophically as well as administratively, the two have come to have a very different relationship.

Differences of opinion remain as to what is the best relationship for physical education and athletics. Some feel that it is best for the two fields to be administratively linked. However, most educational administrators and athletic personnel feel that athletic programs should be autonomous. Many physical education professionals agree. Athletics are extremely popular and it is difficult for physical education programs to receive the attention and the emphasis they need when they are combined with athletic programs. This is clearly evident when coaches also teach physical education. In too many instances, most of the effort is put on coaching and the physical education teaching suffers.

Objectives of Athletics

Athletics has many of the same objectives as physical education. (Physical education objectives are discussed in Chapter 12.) Coaches of interschool teams have excellent opportunities to achieve physical education objectives. In many cases, coaches can help students attain these objectives better than can those who teach in the instructional program or run an intramural program. They have significant advantages in the greater time and intensity that characterize athletic programs. In addition, they work with a smaller group of students, most of whom are highly motivated. They have more time with these students than do physical education teachers, who teach many more students each day. Under these circumstances, participants in interschool competition attain a greater measure of physical fitness and motor skills than is possible in instructional and intramural programs. The potential for developing mental, emotional, and social objectives are greater in the interschool athletic program, but the extent to which these opportunities are realized depends on the caliber of coaches and administrative leadership. It is important that the program not be based on a win-at-any-cost philosophy. This philosophy negates the advantages of being part of a close-knit group and the exhilaration that comes from competition designed to bring about positive social and moral values.

Despite media and commercial pressures to overemphasize noneducational outcomes, people at all levels of education philosophically support the position that the only justification for interscholastic and intercollegiate athletics is their contribution to educational objectives. The great majority of school administrators and faculty members still evaluate athletics on this basis, although alumni, community groups, professional sports, and commercial organizations use their influence to emphasize other features of athletic programs.

Intercollegiate and interscholastic athletics have been conducted in America for well over 100 years. In this long period of time, many students have benefitted from the experience and many valuable lessons have been learned. Gradually, high standards for the conduct of athletics have evolved. Such standards have done much to improve interscholastic athletics. They represent ideal practices and policies that, if adhered to, will continue to raise the quality of athletic programs.

Control of Intercollegiate Athletics

When school administrators attempted to control and supervise athletics, they soon found that however well one school conducts its own program, other schools did not necessarily do likewise. The need for some organized body to direct and control intercollegiate athletic competition was soon felt, and this gave birth to our present athletic associations and conferences.

Another factor also promoted the development of athletic conferences. In the early days of intercollegiate athletics, administrators who wanted to raise standards found it very difficult to do so alone because of the pressures of alumni, students, supporters, and townspeople who did not always have the best interests of the institution and participants in mind. They found, however, that this objective was much easier to accomplish with a group of like-minded administrators. Pressure groups had difficulty in opposing the new standards because each institution in a league or conference had to comply or lose its natural rivals.

Control on the National Level

The two largest national athletic organizations in the United States are the NCAA, which has approximately 1,100 members, and the NAIA, which has over 400 members. Membership in both organizations is voluntary and is open to four-year colleges and universities in the United States. The National Junior College Athletic Association (NJCAA) is a similar organization that represents 540 junior colleges and strives to provide high-quality athletic opportunities to strengthen the collegiate learning experience of its students.

The national organizations strive to improve intercollegiate athletic programs. The NCAA has as its purposes the following:

To initiate, stimulate, and improve intercollegiate athletics programs for student-athletes and to promote and develop educational leadership, physical fitness, athletic excellence, and athletic participation as a recreational pursuit

To uphold the principle of institutional control of, and responsibility for, all intercollegiate sports in conformity with the constitution and bylaws of the association

To encourage its members to adopt eligibility rules to comply with satisfactory standards of scholarship, sporting behavior, and amateurism

To formulate, copyright, and publish rules of play governing intercollegiate athletics

To preserve intercollegiate athletic records

To supervise the conduct of, and to establish eligibility standards for, regional and national athletics events under the auspices of the association

To legislate, through bylaws or by resolutions of a convention, on any subject of general concern to the members related to the administration of intercollegiate athletics

To study all phases of competitive intercollegiate athletics and establish standards whereby colleges and universities can maintain their athletics programs on a high level

Each national body organizes and administers championships and has mechanisms to enforce rules that are passed by the members. They also assist institutions in taking steps to comply with the rules of the national organization.

College and university presidents have become more involved recently with the national athletic organizations. Academic standards for athletes, program costs, and the enforcement of rules and regulations are just some of the areas where they have become more active in the national organizations.

Regional Control of Intercollegiate Athletics

Athletic conferences have assumed much responsibility for controlling the athletic programs of member institutions. Most colleges and universities belong to some type of conference. Institutions of similar types, curriculum, philosophy, entrance requirements, size, and financial resources tend to join together in athletic conferences. Sometimes these institutions are all within one state, but often they are regional.

These conferences exist for the purpose of regulating athletic competition between like-minded institutions. The member institutions want to compete with schools that have similar standards. The national athletic associations necessarily must be general in their rules and regulations and allow the conferences to equalize competitive opportunities on a state or regional basis.

The athletic conferences are controlled by faculty representatives of member institutions. Athletic directors, coaches of various sports, and publicity directors have separate organizations of their own, which ordinarily meet at the same time as the faculty representatives. These different groups may make recommendations to the faculty representatives, but in the last analysis, the latter group establishes the policies, rules, and regulations of intercollegiate competition.

Larger athletic conferences employ a full-time commissioner who discharges stipulated duties in administering the conference affairs. The size of the supporting staff depends on the size of the conference and the level of competition. Administrative duties for personnel in an athletic conference organization involve the enforcement of the conference regulations, particularly those related to eligibility, subsidization, and recruiting. Institutions that violate conference regulations can be fined, lose television revenue, be prohibited from participating in national tournaments, be obliged to forfeit contests, be placed on probation, or be expelled from the conference.

The nature and scope of athletic conferences has changed dramatically with the advent of big television contracts for sporting events. One of the big challenges of conference commissioners is to keep their conferences intact or to entice new members to join to strengthen the conference and thereby increase their chances to get a bigger share of the television revenue. Conferences used to be relatively stable but even long-standing, prestigious conferences are adding or losing members as colleges and universities are motivated primarily by the financial returns of conference membership. With ever-bigger television contracts at stake, colleges and universities can be expected to continue to jockey for the conference affiliation that will result in the best financial return from their athletic programs. Easy access to all parts of the country via air travel has further resulted in conferences losing their local and even regional flavor.

Local Control of Intercollegiate Athletics

The final phase of controlling intercollegiate athletics resides within each institution. This control complements those of the national associations and the athletic conferences. Although each level of control is important and has its unique functions, the most important form of control is undoubtedly on the local level. No outside agency can adequately control an institution that uses devious practices to win games. The ideal in intercollegiate athletics is to have each individual college and university conduct its athletic affairs on such an ethical level that no outside regulation becomes necessary.

Over the years, the methods of administering athletics have gradually changed. When athletics was part of the overall physical education program, one person often administered both programs or at least was ultimately responsible for the athletic program. With most athletic programs now separate from physical education, administrators who specialize in athletic administration are usually responsible for the athletic programs. Sport management programs are found in many colleges and universities to prepare people to become athletic directors and to handle the specialized tasks included in athletic administration. A vast amount of information about the administration of athletics and experience working in an athletic office, handling coaching duties, and studying administration enable athletic administrators to acquire the techniques and understandings necessary to administer an athletic program.

Most institutions have athletic committees that serve in an advisory capacity to the athletic director. These committees are normally composed of faculty, students, administrators, and perhaps alumni. The committee makes recommendations to the athletic director and acts as a sounding board for ideas and changes being considered for the athletic programs. It is particularly important to keep faculty and students informed and to receive their input.

Responsibility for local control of athletics ultimately resides with the president and the board of trustees or board of regents of the university or college. The director of athletics has delegated responsibilities and may report directly to the president or to some other institutional officer. Concern about undesirable and unethical practices in athletics has led institutional presidents to take a more active role in overseeing athletic programs.

Control of Interscholastic Athletics

Interscholastic athletics, like intercollegiate athletics, are controlled on three different levels: national, state, and local. All of these different aspects of control are closely interrelated and complement each other. Each is discussed in turn here.

Control on the National Level

Interscholastic athletics are administered nationally by the National Federation of State High School Associations. This national organization was developed out of the state athletic associations in 1920, when representatives of five nearby state associations met in Chicago to discuss problems that had resulted from high school athletic contests organized by colleges and universities or other promoters. The need was evident for a national organization that could operate beyond the scope of the state athletic associations. In 1921, four states—Illinois, Iowa, Michigan, and Wisconsin—formally started the national organization. They were charter members, and the future development of the organization was due in large part to their leadership.

In 1922, representatives of eleven states attended the Chicago meeting. Since that time, the National Federation has grown rapidly. By 1940, a national office with a full-time executive staff was established. The national office is located in Kansas City, Missouri, and represents the 50 individual state high school athletic or activities associations and the association of the District of Columbia. Interscholastic organizations from other countries are also affiliated with the National Federation.

The purpose of the National Federation is included in its philosophy statement (*National Federation Handbook,* 1993, pp. 16–17). The philosophy together with two of the basic beliefs of the organization are as follows:

> The purpose of the National Federation of State High School Associations is to coordinate the efforts of its member state associations toward the ultimate objectives of interscholastic activities. It shall provide a means for state high school associations to cooperate in order to enhance and protect their interscholastic programs. In order to accomplish this, the National Federation is guided by a philosophy consistent with the accepted purposes of secondary education. Member state associations' programs must be administered in accordance with the following basic beliefs:
>
> Interscholastic activities shall be an integral part of the total secondary school educational program which has as its purpose to provide educational experiences not otherwise provided in the curriculum, which will develop learning outcomes in the areas of knowledge, skills and emotional patterns and will contribute to the development of better citizens. Emphasis shall be upon teaching "through" activities in addition to teaching the "skills" of activities.
>
> Interschool activities shall be primarily for the benefit of the high school students who participate directly and vicariously in them. The interscholastic activity program shall exist mainly for the value which it has for students and not for the benefit of the sponsoring institutions. The activities and contests involved shall be psychologically sound by being tailored to the physical, mental and emotional maturity levels of the youth participating in them.

Control of Interscholastic Athletics by State High School Associations

The history of interscholastic athletics is a story of a long, difficult struggle to place these activities on a sound educational basis. So many vicious, undesirable practices developed in high school athletic competition that school administrators were forced to take steps to control them in order to preserve their educational values. School superintendents and principals organized state high school athletic associations to control interscholastic athletics because they were unable to solve the problems individually. These organizations deserve most of the credit for the present high plane on which interscholastic athletics are conducted.

The first state high school athletic association was formed in Wisconsin in 1896. Indiana followed in 1903, and Ohio in 1904. Today, every state has an organization to administer interscholastic athletics. Membership in these associations is usually permitted to any accredited public high school, although in some states any high school that meets the standards for membership is permitted to belong. For each member school, the principal must be responsible.

It should be noted that some of these state organizations are known as school activities associations rather than athletic associations. This designation is used because in some of these state organizations responsibility for nonathletic activities come under their jurisdiction. Supervision of contests in musical, dramatic, speech, and other nonathletic activities is provided.

These associations are conducted by boards of control that range in size from state to state. Membership on the board of control is confined in most states to school administrators, but in some states teachers, coaches, school board members, and university professors are eligible for membership. The duties of the boards of control are usually to determine the general policies of the association, to decide the rules of eligibility, and to settle disputes referred to them by various districts or sections of the state into which the association is divided. Every state has an athletic commissioner or executive secretary who has full charge of the clerical, financial, and executive work of the association. The executive secretary conducts tournaments and meets, keeps detailed accounts of the competition, handles the finances, receives the scholastic records of the competing students, disseminates publicity, and performs other duties. The administrative authority, however, is usually vested in the board of control.

State athletic associations are classified into two types: voluntary, independent associations and associations affiliated with state departments of education. Approximately two-thirds of the associations are voluntary. In associations affiliated with state departments of education, control resides with the department of education. In voluntary associations, school administrators control the program. It is a common practice in these associations for the state director of physical education to be represented on the executive committee.

Functions of State Athletic Associations   State high school athletic associations vary in the functions they perform. The following functions are carried on by most state associations:

Establish academic standards for participation in athletics

Establish and enforce eligibility rules

Provide guidelines to protect students who participate in athletics

Develop policies and procedures to make athletic competition fair, educational, and enjoyable for participants

Establish standards and regulations for interscholastic athletics

Interpret playing rules

Interpret association rules and regulations

Conduct tournaments and meets

Establish contest regulations

Establish starting dates and length of practice and competitive seasons for each sport

Adjudicate disputes

Sponsor coaching clinics

Register and classify officials

Publish bulletins, newsletters, and other materials to keep the membership informed

Promote interscholastic activities

Arrange and supervise competition in various nonathletic activities

Financing State Athletic Associations   A variety of sources of income is available to support state athletic associations. Most states have annual membership dues, with some assessing the fee on the basis of school size. Receipts from the state tournaments and meets are the largest source of revenue in the great majority of states. Entry fees and fees for registration of officials are negligible from the standpoint of income production.

Local Control of Interscholastic Athletics

The activities of the national federation and the state athletic associations are translated to local high schools. The efforts of the state and national organizations are designed to come to fruition in each individual school. However, what happens in the local schools depends to a large extent on how the program is conducted. The standards that state and national associations endorse are strengthened by good local administration.

The Superintendent of Schools   The superintendent of schools is ultimately responsible for the type of athletic program in operation in the schools. Although the school board has the final responsibility for all that happens in the schools, it is the superintendent who recommends policies to them. The superintendent should take the initiative in establishing a desirable athletic policy for local schools.

The Principal   The principal is more directly concerned with the actual operation of the program and is held accountable by the superintendent for the conduct of interscholastic athletics in accord with the stipulated policies. In schools that have athletic committees, the principal is invariably a member, often the chairperson, and has veto power over the actions of the committee.

The relationship of school administrators to the interscholastic athletic program requires that they be prepared to cope with problems that develop. The principal and superintendent will make costly mistakes in their relationships to the athletic programs unless they are familiar with the philosophy, principles, policies, and standards that should prevail. Unfortunately, few school administrators ever receive sufficient professional preparation in this important area.

The Director of Athletics   The director of athletics administers the details of the athletic program and is responsible to the principal for the conduct of the athletic program in accord with the policies of the school and the state athletic association.

The Athletic Committee   Some schools organize athletic committees to provide input into the administration of athletic programs. The people generally serving on such committees are the principal, athletic director, coaches, faculty members, and students. The dean of students, superintendent of schools, and a member of the school board may also be members. The role of the high school athletic committee is similar to that of the university athletic committee.

Medical Supervision of Athletics

Protecting the Health of Athletes

In citing the values of athletics, coaches invariably mention the contribution it makes to health. There can be no doubt that athletics, if well-conducted, make a significant contribution to the health of the players. The medical care of students who participate in athletic programs is an important consideration for every school. Immense strides have been made at all levels to provide the best possible medical care for athletes.

The Medical Examination   The medical examination is the first and most important measure to be considered in the proper health supervision of athletes. All athletic aspirants should have a thorough examination to determine their physical fitness for participation in athletics in general. They should also be examined before each sport season and complete medical records should be maintained for each athlete. The examination should be made by a physician who has the time, facilities, and equipment to do the task properly. The physician should be attuned to the field of sport medicine.

Treatment of Athletic Injuries   The team physician is the key person in the treatment and care of the injured athletes. If only one physician is available, this person should have specialized training in orthopedics. Knowledge of sports medicine is another important prerequisite. It is valuable when the physician is interested in sports. Schools should employ only highly qualified physicians.

Colleges and universities have athletic training staffs who work closely with the team physician. They perform many valuable services, such as taping, bandaging, supervising the use of various therapeutic modalities, administering first aid, and supervising special exercises that have been prescribed by the physician. They also work closely with the coaching staff in developing injury prevention programs for the athletes. Increasing numbers of high schools are also employing trainers. This has been an important step forward in providing proper medical care for the high school age student. The National Athletic Trainers Association provides an excellent certification program for athletic trainers (see Chapter 17). They have also been instrumental in encouraging states to require the employment of certified athletic trainers for athletic programs.

The coach plays an important role in the reduction of injuries by emphasizing physical conditioning. Although state athletic associations require that athletes practice for a designated time before their first contest, players should be well-conditioned when they report for practice. More and more coaches are prescribing a conditioning program for all squad members before the opening practice. Many give a fitness test on the first day of practice to determine the fitness level of the players.

The use of weight training has grown not only for the purpose of improving performance but also for preventing injuries. Research has revealed that a properly designed and conducted weight-training program can reduce the incidence of injuries. Colleges and universities often have strength or fitness coaches for their athletes.

Coaches must exercise appropriate precautions to prevent heat cramps, heat exhaustion, and heat stroke. These conditions must be anticipated during practices in hot and humid weather.

Another cause of injuries is overmatching. A small institution with a limited squad should never schedule a football game with an institution that has a squad of a significantly greater size and strength. Likewise, individuals should not be matched against each other in contact sports if they vary appreciably in size, strength, ability, and experience. Courts have found coaches liable for negligence when injuries have occurred because of mismatching.

The coach should insist on equipment that provides a high degree of protection for the participants in body-contact sports. Much research has been done in order to develop equipment that reduces the incidence of injuries. As a result of this research, significant improvements have been made. The protection of the player should be of paramount concern in the purchase of equipment. Proper fitting of equipment is also an important consideration.

The many health implications of interschool athletics emphasize the importance of the professional preparation of the coach. The best preparation for coaching is found in the physical education curricula. The professional preparation of the physical education major is designed to prepare the individual to safeguard the health of the students. The coach whose preparation has been as an academic teacher does not have this background unless he or she has gone through a coaching certification program. States are increasingly requiring certification for coaches who do not have a physical education background. These certification programs include a sport science component that usually covers sport injuries, first-aid procedures, physiology of exercise, and appropriate ways to organize practices. Although certification programs differ in some of their requirements, each has as its goal the making of sport participation a safe and educationally valuable experience.

Drug Prevention Program   The use of drugs has become a major problem in sport programs at all levels. Testing programs are controversial but are being used by some universities to deter drug use. They are also used to test athletes during national championship competition. The use of performance-enhancing substances such as steroids is another area of medical concern. Strong educational programs designed to combat drug use have been implemented by intercollegiate and interscholastic governing bodies. They have also taken preventive measures such as banning the use of smokeless tobacco during baseball games. Individual institutions have counseling programs for drug users and provide programs to help athletes overcome addictions.

Athletic Accident Benefit Plans

Schools provide medical insurance for students who participate in athletic programs. Students are required to pay for the insurance in some schools; in others, the school assumes this expense. In some cases, the student's personal health insurance is used first and the amount not covered by this insurance is paid for by the school's insurance. State and national organizations usually insure contestants in tournament competition sponsored by these organizations. It has become a common practice for institutions to purchase catastrophe insurance to cover severe injuries. The NCAA provides this type of insurance for its member institutions.

Eligibility Requirements

Importance of Eligibility Requirements

Athletic associations and conferences have always been concerned with the eligibility requirements of those who take part in interschool competition. This problem was instrumental in the formation of these groups and is today one of their chief concerns. Standardization of eligibility requirements was necessary to equalize athletic competition. The entire structure of interschool athletics is based on uniform eligibility requirements. Equitable competition and educational outcomes would be impossible without common standards.

The Amateur Rule

The most frequently stipulated eligibility requirement is that each individual must be an amateur in order to compete against other schools. The problem is that the definition of an amateur changes over the years even at the college and high school level. For example, a college athlete who is a professional in one sport is now allowed to participate as an amateur in other sports. More recently, it was decided by the NCAA that an undergraduate athlete who came out for a professional draft would not lose amateur status if the student decided not to sign a professional contract. Considering the changes that have occurred in Olympic competition, where professionals are allowed to compete, who knows what will occur in the years ahead in high school and university athletics!

Many believe that the awarding of athletic scholarships is actually paying athletes and therefore the amateur rule in college and university athletics at this level is meaningless. Opponents of the rule also point out that the amateur rule does not operate for the other school subjects such as music, art, speech, or literature.

The National Federation of State High School Associations states that an amateur athlete is "one who engages in athletic competition solely for the physical, mental, social and pleasure benefits derived therefrom." The federation also states the ways in which an athlete forfeits amateur status in a sport (*National Federation Handbook,* 1993, p. 19).

1. Competing for money or other monetary compensation (allowable travel, meals and lodging expenses may be accepted).
2. Receiving any award or prize of monetary value which has not been approved by his or her state association.
3. Capitalizing on athletic fame by receiving money or gifts of monetary value (scholarships to institutions of higher learning are specifically exempted).
4. Signing a professional playing contract in that sport.

The NCAA defines an amateur student-athlete as "one who engages in a particular sport for the educational, physical, mental and social benefits derived therefrom and for whom participation in that sport is an avocation." They also specify that amateur standing will be lost if the student receives pay or promise of pay for using athletic skill, signs a professional contract, or competes on a professional team (*1993–1994 NCAA Manual,* 1993, pp. 63–64).

College and University Eligibility Regulations

The national associations (NCAA, NAIA, and NJCAA) have established minimum eligibility standards for students to participate in competitive athletics. Some conferences and individual institutions have set standards that are more stringent than those of the national organization.

The most controversial eligibility requirements for colleges and universities occur in the area of academic performance. Regulations apply to students as they enter a college or university and while they compete. Students must complete their participation within five consecutive years. Outside competition during the season on teams not representing the institution is uniformly prohibited. Financial aid is another heavily regulated area, as are recruiting procedures. There are many other standards and requirements that a college or university student must meet in order to remain eligible for competition.

High School Eligibility Regulations

In addition to the rule on amateurism, other eligibility regulations for interscholastic competition are as follows:

Age: The upper age limit is 19 for most states.

Enrollment/attendance: A student must be enrolled by a certain date and remain enrolled while competing.

Maximum participation: A commonly followed rule is that a student can compete for four consecutive years when entering high school in the ninth grade.

Transfer/residency: States establish rules for the time that is required before a student is eligible after transferring from another school; they also have rules about what constitutes residency in a school district.

Academic: Students are required to perform academically at a designated level to maintain eligibility.

Nonschool participation: There are restrictions on participating on nonschool teams and stipulations when a student can compete as an individual in competition outside the school athletic program.

Medical examination: Most states require a physician's certificate stating that the student is physically fit to participate in interscholastic athletics.

Recruiting/undue influence: States have regulations that declare a student ineligible if it is proven that undue influence has been used to get the student to enroll in a particular school.

Parents' consent: The national federation recommends that students have written permission from their parents each year to participate in interscholastic athletics.

Assumed name: Students become ineligible when playing under an assumed name.

Awards

The practice of granting awards to those who compete in intercollegiate and interscholastic athletics in found in practically all schools. This custom is in accord with the universal practice of honoring successful or outstanding performance. The types of awards that are given vary extensively. There are basically two types of awards athletes may receive. One award is a participation award given to students who meet designated criteria to earn a letter for the sport. The second type of award is given for special achievements such as being selected the most improved player, setting a school record, or being the most valuable player. At the college and university level, awards can also be given for special events such as bowl games and championships.

The type and cost of awards that may be given at the high school level are determined by the school, the conference, and the state athletic association. On the college and university level, the awards given must be approved by the institution, the conference, and the national organization to which the institution belongs. Schools and conferences cannot exceed the maximum cost levels established by the state associations and national organizations of which they are members. The awards commonly given in high schools are school letters, sweaters, and jackets. Plaques, trophies, and special certificates are examples of awards that are presented for special accomplishments. Similar awards, as well as blankets, are presented at colleges and universities. Championship rings and watches are also used for awards. Some schools give a different award for each year that a student participates in a sport.

The Athletic Director

The director of athletics administers the athletic program. In most institutions, this is a full-time position, although some athletic directors also have other responsibilities. Colleges and universities with large athletic programs usually hire associate and assistant athletic directors to share the administrative responsibilities. Athletic directors at large high schools may also have administrative assistants.

Responsibilities of the Athletic Director

The administrator of athletic programs is responsible for many different administrative duties. In large athletic programs, some duties are delegated to other staff members. Duties include the following:

Organize and supervise all aspects of the athletic program

Select, supervise, and evaluate coaching staff

Prepare budgets

Purchase and care for equipment

Prepare facilities

Administer public relations

Schedule contests

Prepare eligibility lists and eligibility procedures

Complete and sign game contracts

Oversee ticket sales

Manage finances

Administrate home athletic contests

Secure and contract officials

Arrange team travel

Arrange for scouting

Organize and supervise the student manager system

Arrange for appropriate medical care, medical examinations, and insurance

Develop and implement a long-range plan for the athletic program

A number of the above duties are considered in other chapters. The remainder are discussed below.

Scheduling   Responsibility for scheduling falls on the athletic director. In arranging schedules, close consultation with the head coaches of the various sports is necessary. Although it is not always possible to do so, the schedules should meet the approval of the coaching staff. In addition, the schedule should be approved by the athletic council or board. The school administrator—usually the principal, but in some schools the superintendent—gives final approval. In making schedules, the athletic director is guided by institutional policies and by league or conference regulations. The total number of games in each sport is determined in part by school policy and in part by conference or state athletic association regulations. Ordinarily, one-half of the contests are played at home. Ideally, the home games and games away from home are alternated. High school schedules are generally made a year in advance, but colleges and universities often arrange their schedules five or more years ahead. Schools that are in leagues or conferences have much of their schedules automatically filled. They may be able to play only a few outside teams in some sports.

Athletic directors are expected to arrange schedules that do not conflict appreciably with school work. For this reason, weekends are preferred. Care must be observed in arranging team trips so that absence from classes is minimized. The schedule should not conflict with important school events that are held regularly. It is advisable for the athletic director to consult with the school administrator and the student council because many major events such as homecoming, parents' day, and the like are built around the athletic schedule.

Game Contracts   The great majority of interscholastic and intercollegiate athletic contests are confirmed by means of contracts. Most state high school athletic associations have standard forms that the high schools in the state are expected or required to use. Each school has a signed copy of the contract that specifies the date, time, place, and financial arrangements for the contest. It may also state the manner in which officials will be selected. The principal and the athletic director sign the contracts for high school games.

Preparation of Eligibility Lists   A standard procedure in interscholastic athletics is for the competing schools to exchange eligibility lists before the game. This is required by most state associations. This list, which is certified by the principal, is usually exchanged about one week before the contest. The required data concerning each player varies from state to state. In some states, only the names of the eligible athletes are indicated. Others go into considerable detail and include such data as date of birth, year in school, number of semesters in athletics, and number of subjects passed the previous semester and passing the current semester. Most state athletic associations also require member institutions to submit an eligibility list to the association office.

Much the same procedure is followed in most colleges and universities. In some of the larger conferences, eligibility lists are sent to the conference commissioner, who checks the status of all players on the list.

Securing Officials   Poor officiating cannot be condoned. There are so many capable officials that there is no justification for hiring poor ones. The athletic director must carefully research information about officials and select the best. Players, coaches, and fans all benefit when good officials are obtained and good officiating improves the sport.

The usual practice in selecting officials is for the two schools to agree on certain individuals. The athletic director of the home institution initiates the matter by sending a list of approved officials to the athletic director of the visiting school. The athletic director of the visiting team deletes any names that are not acceptable and the home athletic director then sends a contract to the chosen officials who are available to officiate on the date of the contest. Such contracts usually specify the date, time, place, assignment, and financial arrangements. It is recommended that negotiations for officials begin early. Good officials are engaged many months to a year in advance. A reminder of the date and time should be sent to the official one week before the contest. In some conferences, a person is designated to assign officials. Officials' associations also assign officials for some leagues.

To promote uniformity in the interpretation of playing rules, as well as to ensure that only qualified people are in control of their contests, many states have established plans for the registration and classification of all who desire to become officials. Only officials who meet these standards are permitted to officiate in interschool competition. As a result, the players, schools, and spectators benefit from a more efficiently handled contest.

Some colleges and universities secure their officials through the office of the conference commissioner, who makes assignments from the list of approved officials. To get on the approved list, officials must pass rule examinations and demonstrate a satisfactory degree of competence in trial officiating. Larger conferences conduct rules interpretation meetings and carefully supervise the work of the officials. Many colleges submit a list of officials to the other institutions and decide on mutually satisfactory officials.

Arranging Team Travel   The athletic director must oversee a variety of details in connection with team trips and should consult with the head coach on important details such as the menu, the time of arrival and return, the hotel, and the like. Many directors permit the team managers to handle most of these details, but the responsibility still remains with the athletic director.

The squad should leave together, stay together after they arrive, and return home together. It is standard procedure not to permit players to return home with any people other than their parents. It goes without saying that the coach should always accompany the squad.

All details of the trip should be arranged in advance. All players should know who is on the traveling squad and the time and place of departure. The hotel, transportation, and eating arrangements should be prepared well ahead of time.

Money should not be given to the players for expenses. It is better for the coach or manager to handle the funds on trips. Sufficient cash should be available to meet all the expected expenses of the trip, and receipts should be saved for all funds expended. Ordinarily, hotel and transportation costs are billed to the school.

It is standard procedure for players to take responsibility for their personal equipment. Appropriate bags are usually provided for this purpose. The remaining equipment, such as balls, first-aid supplies, helmets, and blankets, is the responsibility of student managers. They also need to check the players carefully to see that they do not forget their personal equipment.

If the trip can be made in a few hours, it is preferable to make it on the day of the game. Not only is this policy less expensive but it is better for the players. They eat and sleep better at home and are more relaxed when they are in familiar surroundings.

Student Manager System   Student managers render invaluable services to athletic directors and coaches. Practically all high schools and colleges and universities use student managers. A good manager is a joy to both the coach and athletic director because the manager relieves the coach of many responsibilities.

The work of student managers is hard and time-consuming. In addition, it often appears to be thankless. However, the student stands to benefit from it in a variety of ways. In many schools, the head managership is considered one of the most coveted positions. The manager learns how to work with a variety of people and benefits from the responsibility and the lessons learned on the job.

The manager is generally appointed by the athletic director or coach of the sport concerned. Usually, the coach and athletic director agree on the candidate beforehand. Often, the selection is made on a merit basis. This last method is preferred in larger institutions where a number of candidates are available. In this system, there are a number of sophomore mangers from whom two junior managers are selected. One of the junior managers is then selected as senior manager. In smaller schools, the athletic director and coach consider themselves fortunate if they have any volunteers.

Student managers perform a wide variety of duties:

Recording daily attendance

Bringing all the equipment to and from the practice field

Caring for the equipment during practice

Keeping a list of the addresses, phone numbers, locker numbers and combinations, and class schedules for all squad members

Officiating practice games

Checking on players' eligibility

Arranging for trips, meals, and hotels

Rendering a report of all expenditures after a trip

Packing equipment for trips and making sure that the equipment is available

Checking that all players have their personal equipment on trips

Supervising the work of the assistants

Meeting visiting teams and rendering whatever assistance is needed

Meeting officials and taking care of their needs

Assisting the coaches and athletic director in any way they request

Arrangements for Scouting   Scouting of opposing teams is accepted today as an essential part of interschool football, basketball, and other sports. Scouting is an approved practice and follows procedures established by conferences or agreements between competing teams. Some conferences limit the number of games that may be scouted. The scout, often an assistant coach, calls for tickets at the athletic department office and makes her or his presence known to the team being scouted. The athletic director provides seats in the press box to the scout and extends every courtesy. The purpose of scouting is to analyze offensive and defensive team skills and game techniques. Scouts also rate the weaknesses and strength of individual players and observe game strategies that are used. In addition to personal scouting, game films are exchanged by teams in some sports. The athletic director makes arrangements for film exchanges and sees that films are sent and received at the agreed on time.

Supervision of Coaching Staff   The athletic director is responsible for conducting the athletic program in accordance with the policies of the institution and the regulations of the conference or league to which the school belongs. In addition, compliance with state and national athletic association regulations is required. The athletic director must be alert to the many policies and requirements and observe them in spirit as well as in letter. This involves, among other things, supervision of the coaching staff.

Only certified teachers used to be permitted to coach in secondary schools. There are now more coaching positions available in many schools than there are teachers who want to coach. This has necessitated employing nonteachers and teachers from other school districts for coaching positions. This has increased the supervision responsibilities of athletic directors. Additional provisions must be made to assist coaches who are not familiar with the school and who have contact with their athletes only when they come to the school for practice. It is important to provide special in-service programs to acclimate outside coaches to the school and the athletic program policies and procedures. Colleges and universities do not require that certified teachers be employed as coaches. Athletic directors must select coaches carefully, using criteria other than teaching certification.

The quality of the athletic program is determined more by the caliber of the coaches than by any other consideration. This fact makes their selection a vitally important matter. Unfortunately, coaches are too often chosen on the basis of their technical competence. The character and ideals of candidates receive too little attention. Ideally, the coach should understand the sport thoroughly and should understand boys and girls and be an effective leader. The coach must be a skilled teacher, with the ability to develop sound fundamentals and well-coordinated offensive and defensive team play. He or she must realize that athletics are a part of school experiences and they must therefore be conducted to achieve educational objectives. The coach must appreciate that sports exist for the education and development of students; students do not exist for the winning of games.

Administration of Athletic Contests   One of the most important responsibilities of many athletic directors is the management of home athletic contests. This task must be done well because the public, students, and visiting team will resent inefficient management. Poor administration of athletic contests eventually results in reduced income from gate receipts.

The efficient management of a home game depends on careful planning. Well-managed athletic contests do not happen accidentally; they are as efficiently managed as they are planned. The chief difficulty in the administration of contests is to handle the multitude of details involved. These details are well-known, but it is easy to forget or to overlook some of them. For this reason, some athletic directors use a checklist that includes all the details that must be handled in the management of a contest. After a detail has been discharged, a check is made to indicate the fact. Such a scheme should eliminate inefficiency in athletic contest management.

Problems of Intercollegiate Athletics

The popularity of intercollegiate athletics has reached heights that were not dreamed possible during the formative years. With this popularity have come many problems that confront educational institutions, athletic administrators, coaches, and student-athletes.

Education Versus Entertainment

Educational institutions are faced with the challenge of keeping athletics in proper perspective. Too often, they are viewed as entertainment rather than as part of the educational program. The success of athletics and the huge sums of money generated by the athletic programs at many large universities make it difficult to focus on the educational benefits students should receive from participating in athletics. There are many other issues that relate to this problem, but the major responsibility of colleges and universities is to maintain athletics as an educational function. Athletics should meet the goals of the institution, as stated in its mission statement.

Television

Television provides millions of dollars annually for intercollegiate athletics. This money is important for programs and has made it possible to expand and upgrade facilities, equipment, teams, and athletic management. The negative is that with money comes control. Television influences the way athletic programs are run, when games are scheduled, the length of seasons, and the behavior of athletes and coaches. Some universities and colleges have come to depend on television money for the future of their athletic programs. In this situation, the integrity of the athletic program as an educational experience is jeopardized.

Another major problem related to television is the maneuvering by conferences and individual institutions to get the best possible television deal for themselves. It has led universities to leave long-time conference affiliations to join conferences that provide more television money. The educational implications for the institution are seldom considered when a change of conference is made. There is a movement toward a few superconferences and independent institutions that will receive most of the television revenue. The impact on the institutions that are not in superconferences is a major problem for intercollegiate athletics.

Financial Problems

Athletics has become extremely expensive for colleges and universities that do not have high-powered athletic programs that benefit from television revenue and large gate receipts. How can small, low-key, nonscholarship programs continue to exist as costs continue to rise? This is a major problem for intercollegiate sports.

Academic Performance

Upholding academic standards for athletes and requiring the same level of performance required of other students is another important issue for intercollegiate athletics. Important steps have been taken by national governing bodies to require athletes to be students as well as athletes. Institutions must support these efforts and take their own initiative to be sure their athletes are qualified to enter college and maintain satisfactory levels of academic performance while competing. Taking steps to increase the graduation rate of athletes is important.

Player Conduct

Too often, college players are influenced by undesirable actions exhibited by professional players. This is another problem area.

Professional Leagues

Another ongoing problem is the issue of professional teams drafting undergraduate students.

Recruiting Issues

Recruiting high school athletes requires extensive attention. This continues to be one of the major problems in intercollegiate athletics. Consideration of the high school student must be paramount as recruiting regulations are added, changed, and enforced.

Scholarships

This continues to be a major problem area for college and universities. The needs of the student must be considered in light of costs to the institutions.

Equality in Women's Athletics

As has been pointed out earlier in this book, women's athletics have made tremendous strides since passage of Title IX. However, many inequities still exist and these must be addressed by intercollegiate athletics. Scholarship support, number of women coaches, inclusion of women administrators up to the highest levels, promotion of women's athletics, equitable salaries, scheduling of women's games, and budgets comparable with those for men's programs are just some examples of issues that must be faced.

Making Athletes Part of the Student Body

Too often, athletes are segregated from the rest of the student body, both literally and figuratively. Athletic residence halls are no longer permitted, but further measures are required to incorporate athletes into the student body.

Media Influence

The media have a tremendous influence on athletic programs. They glorify the star athlete and usually do not understand how a good athletic program fits into the educational program. They unduly influence the general public and overemphasize winning. Too often, their concern is with national championships, playoffs, and all-star games rather than with the value of athletics for the competitor and the student spectator. Often the media report on college and university sports as if they were professional sports. They also place excessive emphasis on point spreads and the encouragement that is provided for people to bet on college athletics.

Athletic Equipment Companies and Athletic Product Companies

These companies make huge sums of money from athletics. Their wealth gives them the power to have extensive influence on the way athletic programs are run. The free equipment and other supplies they provide to athletic teams and the lucrative contracts they give to college and university coaches for having their teams use their products have become major problem areas for intercollegiate athletics.

Alumni Groups and Booster Clubs

Successful programs generate extensive alumni and booster club support. In many instances, alumni and boosters have been involved in illegal activities to recruit players and to provide payments and other types of prohibited assistance to athletes. This remains a problem area for intercollegiate athletics. Firm procedures must be followed to keep total control of the athletic program within the institution.

Drug Abuse

Drug abuse is a grave problem in intercollegiate athletics. This problem requires united efforts by athletes, educational institutions, government agencies, and community organizations. The high visibility of college and university athletes puts this problem in the spotlight.

Problems of Interscholastic Athletics

A number of problems also confront interscholastic athletics. Some of the problems are similar to those found in intercollegiate athletics. For example, recruiting and scholarship programs can be viewed as joint problems. Player conduct, academic performance, including athletes in the high school mainstream of activities, and drug abuse are issues similar to those found in colleges and universities. Keeping athletics as an educational component and providing equal opportunities for girls' sports are other problem areas for interscholastic athletics. Some of the additional problem areas included in this section are also pertinent to the college and university scene.

Championships and Tournaments

For many years, there were strong forces opposing state championships and tournaments. There are several reasons why there is no a unified effort on the part of different groups to reform state championships at this time. State championships are highly popular and supported enthusiastically by the public. They have not caused the problems that were anticipated by those opposing such events. These contests have become so firmly entrenched in high school athletic programs that they are accepted as part of the program. They do raise significant amounts of money for state athletic and activities associations and the participating schools. It is also recognized that these contests benefit the athletes who compete and the students of the participating schools and members of the community. Social interaction, school spirit, and community interest and pride in the school's achievements are some of the benefits that accrue.

The most important reason for acceptance of the state championships and tournaments is because the state athletic and activities associations, together with school administrators, have organized the championships and tournaments in an educationally sound manner. A realistic number of games or individual events or matches are permitted and the contests are scheduled to have as little a negative impact on other parts of the school program as possible. The undesirable features of competition have been largely eliminated. Competition is usually arranged by school size to equalize competition and the amount of missed class time is kept to a minimum.

It is fortunate that the National Federation of High School Associations has taken a strong position against national championships. Although many groups, including the media, promote this concept, the federation does not sanction such events. It is the feeling of the federation that the states provide enough competition for the athletes. Students would be required to miss classes and their educational program would be otherwise disrupted.

The Coaching Shortage

This is a major problem for high schools. The days when there were enough physical education teachers to do all the coaching are gone. For many years, the issue of whether it was better to have an academic teacher or a physical education teacher do the coaching was debated. It was argued that if the physical educators teach classes, they would have less energy and enthusiasm for coaching. There was also concern that physical educators neglected their duties in the instructional program. Because of the pressure to win and the inordinate demand on their time, some physical educators who served as coaches became "ball tossers" in order to devote more time to preparation for their practices. This debate continues but the problem has been heightened by the fact that there aren't enough teachers in many schools to do all of the coaching and nonteachers are now being used.

The major advantage of having the physical education teacher as a coach is that he or she is specifically prepared for this responsibility. There are three separate aspects of this preparation. The physical education teacher can better appreciate the place and purposes of athletics in the total school program because of a background in the philosophy and objectives of physical education; he or she possesses the physiological, anatomical, and health background necessary to protect the health and welfare of the participants; and he or she has a much broader and more diversified preparation for the actual coaching.

The academic teacher and the nonteacher do have some advantages when it comes to coaching. Coaching is a change of pace from what they have been doing during the day. For the academic teacher, coaching makes it possible to relate to students in a different setting and perhaps for students and teacher to understand each other better. It is beneficial to the morale of the school to have a number of academic teachers interested in working with the students in athletics.

Nonphysical educators who coach usually do not have special preparation for this assignment. This makes the task of the athletic director more difficult and requires him or her to spend more time orienting and supervising these coaches. It is a special problem for the athletic director when out-of-school coaches are employed, as they are not available for consultation during the day and they have a much more difficult time staying in contact with the students because they are not present in the school.

The shortage of coaches is a severe problem and it requires that the athletic director join forces with other school administrators to employ teachers who are also good coaches. They must also search out the best possible people from outside the system to fill coaching positions that cannot be filled by teachers in the system.

Player and Crowd Control

Proper conduct on the part of players and people attending games is another problem area. High school sports have become highly competitive and continuing efforts must be made to keep this competition and the accompanying enthusiasm within bounds.

The following information, taken from an earlier edition of this book, shows how much high school athletics have changed and how different the philosophy of high school athletics are.

> On October 20, 1927, the Central Committee of the New York State Public School Athletic Association passed the famous "Regulation One," which was modified on December 27, 1927. In substance, this regulation recommended that after the contest began, the two coaches should sit together and permit the respective captains to direct the teams. The coach might attend to the physical injuries of the team, and could order the withdrawal of a player from the game; but that was the extent of his authority. When a player was withdrawn, that player was unable to reenter the game. A substitute was selected by the captain, who made substitutions as he or she chose. It was suggested that each coach send a representative to the other team's dressing room in order to prevent accusation of bad faith. The intention of the rule was to give every opportunity for the development of responsibility and resourcefulness on the part of the captain and of responsiveness to teammate control, true loyalty, and team play on the part of the players.

There immediately arose a storm of favorable and unfavorable criticism concerning this radical departure from the traditional method of conducting athletic contests. Those who endorsed this reform felt that it was in harmony with the best educational philosophy. Ability to solve problems is best attained by practice in problem solving; leadership is best attained by practicing it. The domination of the coach during the contests destroyed the richest educational values of leadership, responsibility, and resourcefulness. There were some who believed that the pressure on the coach to win would be reduced with the players themselves in control of the games. There is no doubt that the standard of performance would be lowered, but both teams would be equally affected.

The opposition to this proposal was very strong, particularly among the coaches. The opponents of the reform felt that it was idealist but impractical. They pointed to the early history of interschool sports when the faculty was forced to regulate these activities because of student mismanagement. Why abolish the coaches who have raised the standards of athletics from their poor position before the advent of the twentieth century? The coach is far better qualified to conduct athletics on a high plane than the coaches of the past have been. Another argument used against player control was that many schools, particularly the small high schools, had no student leaders who were qualified to handle this difficult assignment. Even with the coach on the bench, it is often difficult for the captain or team leader to control the team. Athletic contests are filled with intense emotional situations, and the responsibility on the captain in control would be tremendous. Mistakes would be magnified by team mates, and hard feelings would be sure to result. The captain would be accused of playing friends. It is doubtful whether the captain would be entrusted with the physical welfare of team mates, although the coach or a physician on the bench could manage this.

The sentiment in favor of "Regulation One" has practically disappeared. Few, if any, schools adhere to the recommendations of this regulation today. The unlimited substitution rule in college and high school football and the rule in basketball that permits the coach to talk to the players during a time out are steps in the opposite direction. However, even though present regulations increase coach control, good coaches will continue to make every attempt to develop leadership and resourcefulness in their athletes. There never was a good team without a good leader. By developing better leaders and thinkers, the good coach is building a better team. The coach is unable to dominate every situation that occurs during the game, and needs player initiative and leadership. Furthermore, the interval between halves presents the coach with a most favorable educational opportunity to inculcate the valuable lessons that can arise out of athletic competition.

Some of the information seems ridiculous in light of the coaching procedures followed now. It is important that change takes place in order for athletics to improve in the high schools but procedures to ensure the proper conduct of players must always have a high priority.

Cost of Athletic Programs

This is a real concern for many high schools. Programs have had to be reduced for budgetary reasons and in too many locations athletic directors and coaches find that their main task is to raise money. Athletics must be accepted as an integral part of the educational program and be funded in the same way. A balanced athletic program open to all students who want to participate is not possible when it is supported by cookie sales, talent shows, and VCR raffles.

This does not mean that athletic programs should be able to spend money indiscriminately. Sound business procedures should be followed in the operation of the athletic program and money should be carefully expended.

Liability

Liability issues constitute another significant problem area for interscholastic sports. This topic is covered in Chapter 7.

Pay to Play

This is one of the most disheartening and alarming happenings in athletic programs. In some schools, students are required to pay in order to play on the athletic teams. The implications for athletic programs are frightening. This practice reduces the number of students who try out for a team and sets athletics apart from the mainstream educational program. Some states have ruled that schools cannot implement the pay for play procedure, but in other states it is being used in more and more schools as they are faced with budget deficits.

Reducing Overemphasis

State athletic and activities associations have done a good job of providing rules and regulations to ensure that seasons are not too long and that schedules and competition are appropriate for the high school student. There are still instances in schools where athletics are overemphasized. It is the responsibility of athletic personnel and school officials to see that there isn't an overemphasis on winning, that athletes are treated the same as other members of the student body, and that there isn't undue pressure on coaches and athletes.

Public Pressures

It is important that schools administer their athletic programs and that they are not adversely influenced by groups in the community. Athletic departments should have a clear, concise statement of athletic philosophy and policy that guides the conduct of the program. Booster groups can be an important source of support for athletic programs but they must not become involved in developing policies or determining procedures to be followed in the athletic program.

Another important consideration is the selection of the right type of coach. Coaches who are selfishly interested in personal achievements use of pressure groups in unacceptable ways. This creates serious problems for the institution and athletic director by soliciting undesirable forms of assistance from outside groups. The preferred type of coach is one who is interested in the educational objectives of athletics and who subscribes completely to the athletic philosophy and policies of the school.

The athletic director and the educational administrator must stand behind the coach when criticisms come from pressure groups. Mistakes and defeats are inevitable but the solid support of the coach by his superiors not only maintains the morale of the players and the coaching staff but counters the undeserved judgments of critics.

The final measure to use in dealing with pressure groups is to take initiative in guiding their activities. They cannot be ignored. Rather than becoming involved in controversy, it is necessary to maintain good public relations with them. Meetings should be held and philosophy and policies explained. If proper rapport is established, such groups can become an asset rather than a liability to the athletic program.

Specialization

In many high schools, students are required to specialize in one sport. Each sport has become a year-round activity. Few students have the opportunity to participate in two or three sports in high school because too often coaches exert pressure on athletes to concentrate only on the sport they are coaching. Student-athletes should have the opportunity to compete in different sports at this age. Burnout is inevitable when a student spends 12 months out of the year practicing for and concentrating on one sport.

Desirable Trends in Athletics

Problems in athletics receive the most publicity and require an extensive amount of administrative time for athletic directors, coaches, and educational administrators. It is encouraging that many good things are happening in athletics and athletics continue to provide valuable educational experiences for high school, college, and university students. Some of the promising trends are included in this section.

Efforts of Athletic Associations and Conferences

State associations, national governing bodies, and individual conferences continue to take steps to improve the quality of competition, control undesirable practices, and uphold the integrity of athletics. These groups have become powerful forces for improving the standards of interschool athletics.

Coaching Certification Programs

This is one of the most important trends at the interscholastic level of competition. There are a number of national coaching programs available and many states have now established certification requirements for coaches who have not completed an approved undergraduate physical education program. With the need to employ coaches who do not have the educational background to prepare them for coaching responsibilities, certification programs have become more and more important. There is also a trend toward certification programs at the intercollegiate level. Canada is far ahead of the United States with their certification programs at this level.

Athletic Trainers

It is encouraging that there is a strong movement to have athletic trainers for all levels of athletics. College and university programs have had well-prepared athletic trainers for many years. Increasing numbers of high schools are also employing athletic trainers and well over half of the states now have certification, registration, licensure, or exemption regulations for athletic trainers (see Chapter 17). The trend to have athletic trainers at high schools is developing rapidly. It is anticipated that all states will soon have regulations for athletic trainers.

Expansion of Athletic Programs

Although economic conditions have forced some institutions to reduce the number of sports included in their athletic programs, overall there continues to be a trend to expand the scope of the sports that are offered. This has been particularly evident in girls' and women's sports, where this trend is continuing and must continue until all schools are in compliance with Title IX. Schools and conferences continue to offer new sports as they become popular in a region of the country and there are sufficient students and teams to offer the sports on the interscholastic or intercollegiate level.

Girls' and Women's Athletic Programs

Opportunities for girls and women to participate in athletics continue to increase. There was an explosion of opportunities following passage of Title IX and, although the rate with which opportunities for females to participate in athletics has slowed, new opportunities continue to become available. The programs are also becoming more challenging and the level of competition continues to raise in girls' and women's athletic programs.

Nutrition and Training Procedures

Research about nutrition for athletes and training procedures for athletic competition has resulted in much better information for coaches to use. Athletes are better informed about nutritional needs and the best diet for sport competition. Scientifically determined training procedures are increasingly used by coaches in high schools, colleges, and universities. The development of the field of sport medicine has been an important factor in improved performances and the application of scientifically determined training techniques.

Coaching

The quality of coaching found at all levels of athletics continues to improve. There is increased emphasis on preparing coaches and coaches attend clinics, workshops, and conferences to better prepare themselves. Coaching has become a specialized career field with many resources available to help a coach develop coaching techniques.

Salaries of Coaches

The salaries of coaches have improved significantly. With the continued emphasis on athletics in high schools, colleges, and universities, salaries can be expected to become even higher. Coaches' salaries in universities that have high-profile, income-producing programs are extremely high. In these institutions, coaching is one of the best-paying positions at the university. This trend could also be considered a problem in athletics! It is one of the factors that has caused athletics to lose its educational perspective on some university campuses.

Class Activities

Simulation 1

Situation   Student conduct at athletic contests in a number of communities has led to fights during contests and physical confrontations after the contests.

As athletic director, write guidelines for acceptable student conduct during athletic contests. Propose a program that will lead students to follow the student conduct guidelines you have written.

Simulation 2

Situation   Many coaching positions are filled by people who do not teach in the school district. This has caused problems when coaches are not aware of school policies and procedures.

Outline the topics you feel should be included in a coaches' manual used to inform all coaches of athletic department policy.

Simulation 3

Situation   The school board in a large school district (two high schools, four junior high schools, and twelve elementary schools) wants to provide a comprehensive athletic program for every student who wants to participate in athletics, with a no-cut policy.

Write the report to present to the school board explaining how you will implement such a program, even with financial constraints.

Simulation 4

Situation   As athletic director, you are responsible for planning a series of interscholastic tournaments each year.

Provide guidelines that you would follow to organize and direct a tournament for the following sports:

Tennis
Track and field
Wrestling
Basketball

Performance Tasks

1. Design an athletic director's handbook that could be used to guide a new athletic director in his or her responsibilities.
2. Compare the strengths and weaknesses of the girls' and boys' athletic programs in two or more high schools.
3. Conduct an anonymous survey of high school or university athletes to find out what they like least about competing in athletics and what they enjoy the most. Brainstorm ways that the information obtained in the survey could be used to improve athletic competition.

4. Interview an athletic director to obtain a list of responsibilities expected of a coach. Follow the same procedure with a coach. Compare the lists.
5. Write a position paper supporting the statement that interscholastic and intercollegiate athletics are educational.
6. Describe what you believe to be the major problems facing high school athletic programs.
7. Read the sport pages for seven consecutive days and clip out articles that contain information about problems in interscholastic and intercollegiate athletics. Compare these problems with problems discussed in this chapter.
8. Develop a code of ethics for high school athletes.
9. Set up a panel to highlight the different functions of a state high school athletic or activity association and the National Federation of State High School Associations.

References

Abney, Robertha, and Dorothy L. Richey, "Opportunities for Minority Women in Sport—The Impact of Title IX." *Journal of Physical Education, Recreation, and Dance,* March 1992, 63:56–59.

Acosta, Vivian, and Linda Jean Carpenter, "As the Years Go By—Coaching Opportunities in the 1990s." *Journal of Physical Education, Recreation and Dance,* March 1992, 63:36–41.

"Athletic Participation by Girls on the Increase." *Associated Press, The Times* (Trenton, NJ), August 10, 1994, D5.

Blinde, Elaine M., Diane E. Taub, and Han Lingling, "Sport as a Site for Women's Group and Societal Empowerment: Perspective from the College Athlete." *Sociology of Sport Journal,* March 1994, 11:51–59.

Bradley, Michael, "Controlling the Fanfare." *Athletic Management,* October/November 1993, 6:15.

Clifton, Marguerite, *Expanding Horizons in DGWS.* Paper presented at the Northwest Association for Health, Physical Education and Recreation Convention, March 1964, Spokane, WA.

Cohen, Andrew, "Thirteen Team Travel Tips: There Are Lots of Little Ways to Improve Your Travel Bottom Line." *Athletic Business,* December 1992, 16:63.

Cosby, Richard, *The Organization and Administration of Smaller College Athletics: A Handbook for Athletic Directors and Administrators.* Bessemer, AL: Colonial Press, 1990.

Danylchuk, Karen, *Managing Competitive School Sport Programs.* Champaign, IL: Stipes Publishing, 1993.

Dealy, Francis X., *Win at Any Cost: The Sell Out of College Athletics.* New York: Carol Publishing, 1990.

Duval, Doug, "ADs Need Clear Visions for Programs." *Interschool Athletic Administration,* Spring 1994, 20:29.

Fox, Connie, "Title IX at Twenty." *Journal of Physical Education, Recreation and Dance,* March 1992, 63:33–35.

Funk, Gary D., *Major Violation: The Unbalanced Priorities in Athletics and Academics.* Champaign, IL: Human Kinetics, 1991.

Hardy, David, "Fifteen Ways to Make Sportsmanship Happen." *Interscholastic Athletic Administration,* Spring 1994, 20:28.

Karlgaard, Dick, "Activity Programs: Cooperative Arrangements Provide More Chances for Kids to Compete." *Interscholastic Athletic Administration,* Winter 1993, 20:10–11.

Kinder, Thomas M. (ed.), *Organizational Management Administration for Athletic Programs.* Dubuque, IA: Eddie Bowers Publishing, 1993.

Kirk, Sarah, and Wyatt Kirk (eds.), *Student Athletes: Shattering the Myths and Sharing the Realities.* Alexandria, VA: American Counseling Association, 1992.

LeDrew, June E., and Corinne Zimmerman, "Moving Toward an Acceptance of Females in Coaching." *Physical Educator,* Winter 1994, 51:6–14.

Lee, Mabel, "The Case For and Against Intercollegiate Athletics for Women and the Situation Since 1923." *Research Quarterly,* May 1931.

Lehr, Robert E., "Sports Marketing: Schools Should Consider All Factors Before Enlisting Corporate Support." *Interscholastic Athletic Administration,* Spring 1994, 20:12–13.

Ley, Katherine, *Interscholastic Athletics for Girls.* Paper presented at the National Conference on Secondary School Athletic Administration, December 1962, Washington, DC.

Leyshon, Glynn, *The Coach and Sport Management.* Champaign, IL: Stipes Publishing, 1992.

Meier, Klaus, "Amateurism and the Nature of Sport." *Quest,* November 1993, 45:494–509.

Miller, Lori K., "Crowd Control." *Journal of Physical Education, Recreation and Dance,* February 1993, 64:31–32.

National Federation Handbook, Kansas City, MO: National Federation of State High School Associations, 1993.

NCAA, *1993–94 NCAA Manual.* Overland Park, KS: National Collegiate Athletic Association, March 1993.

Olson, John, Elroy Hirsch, Otto Breitenbach, and Kit Saunders, *Administration of High School and Collegiate Athletic Programs.* Philadelphia: Saunders College Publishing, 1987.

Olson, John R., "Role of Booster Club Should be Defined." *Interscholastic Athletic Administration,* Fall 1993, 20:24–25.

Pelino, Mario, Brian Fitzgerald, and Angela Hickey, "Does Your School Have a Specific Program for Dialoguing with Athletes on Such Subjects as Sportsmanship, Dealing with the Press, Improving Team, Player, Coach Rapport, Etc.?" *Scholastic Coach,* April 1994, 63:17.

Sawyer, Tom, "Coaching Education in North America." *Journal of Physical Education, Recreation and Dance,* September 1992, 63:33.

Schmid, Sue, "Pay for Play." *Athletic Business,* May 1993, 17:55–57.

Slaughter, John, and Richard Lapchick (eds.), *The Rules of the Game: Ethics in College Sport* (ACE-Macmillan Series on Higher Education), Washington, DC: American Council on Education, 1989.

Wolohan, John W., "Scholarship Athletes: Are They Employees or Students of the University—The Debate Continues." *Journal of Legal Aspects of Sport,* Spring 1994, 4:46–58.

15

Student Leaders in Physical Education, Intramurals, and Athletics

Educational Values

Student leader programs become an extension of the traditional educational programs in physical education classes, intramurals, and athletics. Students have the opportunity to gain experiences that contribute to their personal development. In addition, they expand their interpersonal skills by interacting with peers, faculty, and administrators. Finally, they learn to organize groups and activities, moderate differences of opinion, demonstrate physical skills to individuals and to a group, and develop their teaching skills.

Leadership Development

In a democratic society, everyone is granted the right to be a leader in any line of endeavor for which she or he can adequately prepare. Certain classes of people are not selected as the ruling or leading groups and other people are arbitrarily relegated to nonleadership roles. It is believed that there should be give and take and in some aspects of life, a person may follow and in other situations may lead. Educational institutions have a responsibility to develop the self-confidence and life skills that enable students to function effectively in both leadership and follower roles. Student leader positions in physical education, athletics, and intramurals provide ideal laboratories in which students can get practical leadership experience that they can apply in other situations, both in school and after graduation.

The best way to develop leadership ability is to have the opportunity to experience leadership. This opportunity enables students to develop poise and self-assurance. They can acquire a sense of responsibility and initiative. The ability to take charge of a group of peers and to accomplish the purposes of the program is a valuable educational experience. Tact, sensitivity to the interests and needs of others, and thoughtfulness are valuable attributes many students gain through such experiences.

Student Opportunities Through Leadership Programs

Modern educational philosophy accepts and sponsors the proposition that we learn best by doing; that is, by actually practicing or living out an experience we acquire more knowledge of it than by just hearing or reading about it. If schools are to prepare students to live enriched lives, many opportunities must be provided for practice of the elements of successful living. One of these elements certainly is leadership, around which can be developed cooperation, loyalty, sociability, and many other desirable social qualities. Few other school subjects provide the number of leadership opportunities found in physical education, intramurals, and athletics. The instructor who does not take advantage of these outstanding opportunities is not making the most of the talents that have been entrusted to the school by the community.

Ordinarily, student leaders are highly motivated to improve their own performance in the activities of the program. Being a student leader is a motivation to competently perform the skills being learned in class and to capably demonstrate different sport skills. This desire to be a good role model extends to personal appearance and physical fitness. In every way, student leaders strive to excel, and they are willing to spend extra time practicing to reach this goal.

Another advantage of a student-leader program is that it encourages participants to consider a career in physical education, intramurals, or athletics. The experience provides a realistic introduction to these fields and the interest generated by student leader programs has led some to become physical education teachers or coaches. This experience of teaching has also stimulated students to select teaching careers in other disciplines.

Benefits to Professional Staffs

The use of student leaders does not provide an opportunity for the teacher, coach, or intramural director to rest while the students do the work. In fact, it takes careful planning, time, and special efforts on the part of the professional person to organize a leaders' program and direct it in a manner that benefits the student and the school. A student leader program augments a student's educational program by permitting the student to share in various aspects of leadership, which the instructor directs.

In addition to providing invaluable opportunities to develop leadership, a student-leader program can also contribute to the improvement of physical education, intramural, and athletic programs. The help that student leaders can give to each of these programs is appreciable. They can assist with countless administrative details, thus enabling the teacher and coach to devote more time to their primary teaching and coaching tasks. Most important of all, student progress in a physical education class is facilitated. More individual attention is available and the level of accomplishment of the entire class is raised.

Physical education teachers carry a heavy load. Often, they have too many students in a class to provide the individual attention students need. Their responsibilities involve a multitude of details. To accomplish their objectives, they urgently need assistance. When additional faculty members are not available, a solution to the dilemma is to use student leaders. They can be an invaluable asset if used properly. The astonishing fact is that many secondary schools fail to capitalize on this resource. What makes this more surprising is that countless schools have had great success with student-leader programs. Out of these experiences have come models that can be used to implement new programs. The benefits of such programs to student leaders and to schools should provide the incentive for more schools to implement the program.

Student Leaders in Physical Education

Two types of leadership programs are found in physical education departments. One is a highly structured program organized as a club. The second is a loosely developed program designed to give as many students as possible the opportunity to assume a leadership role, even if for only a brief period of time. The first type of leadership program requires much more planning and must be a departmentwide program with full support from all physical educators. The second format is readily available to an individual teacher, and should be incorporated into every teacher's methodology.

Leaders' Club

Schools that have a well-established leaders' club are fortunate. This is a prestige organization that is highly respected throughout the school. The members represent an elite group in the school and membership is highly prized—in fact, it may be considered one of the highest honors in the school. Students strive to meet the standards that are required to become members and club members are respected by other students.

Standards for membership are high. The following criteria are commonly established: excellence in physical education activities, a level of physical fitness that is appreciably above the average, superior academic achievement, leadership ability, good citizenship, and interest and enthusiasm in physical education.

In senior high schools, a common practice is to select only seniors for the leaders' club. They have the advantage of greater maturity and more physical education experience. Ordinarily, the selection is made in the spring of the year when the students are juniors. Their training sessions start soon after they are selected so they are prepared to begin when the fall semester begins. It has also been found to be helpful to have the students serve an internship with the current leaders' club members for at least a few weeks.

New members are selected by the entire physical education faculty. They base their selection on the criteria listed for membership in the club. Some schools have found it helpful to have interested students submit an application. However, in schools where this program is firmly established, almost every student who is selected considers it an honor and becomes a member of the leaders' club.

Members of the club usually wear a distinctive uniform and may be given a whistle or clipboard that further identifies them as members of the leaders' club. In some schools, they may wear a jacket or insignia that designates them as members.

The duty of the members of the leaders' club is to assist the teacher in physical education classes. To render more valuable assistance, they usually go through one or more training sessions per week with the instructor. The extra meetings are held at times when students have free periods or before classes begin in the morning. The purpose of such sessions is to provide the student leaders with a thorough understanding of the next lesson and the manner in which they will perform their role. In addition, they have the opportunity to perfect their own skills.

Leaders' club members relieve teachers of many administrative details so they can focus on their teaching responsibilities. They take attendance, assist in testing, secure the necessary equipment, prepare the teaching stations, officiate, and return equipment to the proper locations at the end of class. It should be pointed out, however, that the members of the leaders' club are equipped to do much more than handle administrative tasks. Their maturity, careful selection, previous experience, and specialized preparation enable them to make an invaluable contribution to the teaching program. They assist with demonstrations, serve as spotters, provide individualized help to students needing special attention, and serve as role models to motivate other students in the class.

The most successful leaders' clubs are formally organized with officers, a constitution, and bylaws. Regular meetings are held and a carefully prepared agenda is followed. The induction of new members is formally executed with a dignified ceremony in the presence of all club members. High standards of performance must be maintained for continued membership in the organization. The aims and objectives of the program are carefully explained to inductees. The contributions of the members are publicized in appropriate ways and recognition is given to the members in the school and in the community.

Other Leadership Opportunities

Because most students in the school take physical education classes for at least a part of their school career, regular class work offers an opportunity to provide leadership experience for a large percentage of the students. The principles and procedures are essentially the same in the middle or junior high school, senior high school, and college. They can be applied below these grade levels, but this involves more adjustments. Some minor modifications must be made at the various age levels and for different types of activities.

A number of schools have developed programs in which older students assist teachers who are teaching younger students. These programs have been highly successful in individualizing instruction. It is a wonderful experience for older students and they have proven to be great motivators.

These leadership opportunities can be incorporated into a leaders' club program or they can be effectively implemented in schools without such programs. Individual teachers can also provide these leadership opportunities in their classes.

Presenting the Leadership Plan   This should be done at the first meeting of the class. (Information about the plan should also be included in the student handbook.) The different types of leadership opportunities should be explained. Some time might well be spent pointing out the values of these opportunities for class members. The general setup and procedure of the plan should be explained, and in this connection the authority and responsibility of a leader should be clearly designated. To overcome the possible objection that one student should not have the right to tell another what to do, it should be explained that there can be no leaders unless there are followers; in order to have followers when one's turn comes to lead, it is only fair to serve as a follower for the other person's leadership.

Opportunities to Lead   There are enough different activities in a physical education class so that each student should be able to find something in which he or she can lead reasonably well. Some of these opportunities are listed and discussed in brief:

Leader of squad or class group: There can be four or five such leaders in a class. This is one of the better leadership possibilities, for students in this position take charge of their group, under the instructor's direction, for many activities.

Activity leader: Student leaders can be of invaluable assistance to the instructor by demonstrating activities in which they are competent and by helping students to master skills that have been presented.

Individual assistant to students with special needs: There will probably be students who need assistance to catch up with the class. They may have been absent or they may have difficulty with a particular skill. One-to-one guidance is needed for such students to achieve satisfactory progress.

Leader of warmup exercises: This duty should be passed around so that several class members have the chance to lead the group. These leaders must display enthusiasm and assurance tempered with friendliness.

Spotters: Spotters are necessary in gymnastics. Students selected for this purpose should be among the most highly skilled in the group.

Officials: A class should provide its own officials for the games that are played. Some of the more skilled students can act as chief officials and those less experienced as assistants. These boys and girls should be granted the customary authority due officials of the game.

Member of the equipment and grounds inspection committee: The activity area should be in proper condition to use, but it must be checked by someone to be sure that it is. From a liability standpoint, the equipment and the area being used for the activity should be checked thoroughly on a daily basis and before each class. Members of this committee should be trained to inspect equipment and grounds for safety. They serve an important function in assisting teachers in completing safety checks.

Facility and equipment preparation: Courts and fields must be prepared for class use. In softball, the bases must be placed and taken up later; in volleyball, the nets must be put up; and in practically every sport the equipment must be brought out before class and returned after class.

Leader for games of lower organization: Every student in the class should have a turn at presenting a game of this type and directing the class during the playing of it.

Assistant in the production of special programs such as demonstrations, exhibitions, and clinics.

Assistant in the testing program: Students can time and measure performance and check and record test results.

Assist in maintaining the bulletin board.

Assist in the supervision of the locker and shower rooms.

Assist in administering a before-school or noon-hour recreation program.

Assistant to the instructor in planning the physical education program: Input from the students is valuable.

Methods of Selecting Leaders   In most cases, the advantages of participation are distributed more evenly and the whole plan works more smoothly if the instructor appoints leaders and thus apportions opportunities. This is particularly true concerning officials, committee members, leaders for warmup exercises and for games of lower organization.

Group leaders can also be appointed by the instructor. This is important if every student is to have the chance to serve in this leadership role. This procedure entails more preparation time on the part of the instructor. It also shows confidence that each student is capable of developing the leadership skills a group leader needs. This entails managing a group during a large part of the class time.

A second procedure is to have students select their group leader. They can vote for as many leaders as are needed and the students with the highest number of votes can act as leaders for a designated period of time until the next leaders are selected. Those who advocate this procedure feel that students know each other and will elect those who have the best leadership qualities. Having the most qualified students serving as group leaders makes it easier for the instructor. The negative feature of this procedure is that fewer students have the opportunity to function in this leadership capacity.

Methods of Guiding Leaders   This can be done in part by means of general instructions to all concerning the responsibilities and techniques of leadership, but it is done chiefly through leaders' conferences with the instructor. These may be group or individual conferences. For new leaders, there should be group conferences at which the specific duties to be performed are discussed, additional suggestions are made, and questions are answered. As the leaders gain experience, the conferences should become less frequent and more individual in nature. A definite effort must be made to help the leader who needs help, but those who are having no difficulties need not be included in the later conferences.

Method of Selecting the Group   It is recommended that each leader have the opportunity to choose his or her group. This must not be done in the presence of the rest of the class. Because the purpose is to develop leadership and not inferiority complexes, the poorer performers must be spared the embarrassment of being chosen last. They need to have their confidence built up, not destroyed by being told that they are the least desirable candidates. (This principle applies whenever teams are selected in a class.) The following method of selection is recommended. All class members' names except those choosing are written on the board. The right to choose first, second, third, and fourth (assuming four leaders) is determined by lot. On the second round, the order is reversed and the leader who chose fourth gets the chance to choose fifth, the person who chose third chooses sixth, the one who chose second chooses seventh, and the one who chose first chooses eighth and ninth. This method is followed in order to provide for more equal competition. The choices granted each leader

TABLE 15-1

First	1	8	9	16	17	24	25	32	33	40	41	
Second	2	7	10	15	18	23	26	31	34	39	42	
Third	3	6	11	14	19	22	27	30	35	38	43	
Fourth	4	5	12	13	20	21	28	29	36	37	44	45

are given in Table 15-1. As a student is chosen, that name is marked off the board and placed on the list of the leader who chose that individual. The teams should be posted on the bulletin board with the names arranged in alphabetical order; then none will be shown to have been chosen last or next to last.

Each new group of leaders chooses their squads from the class roll. This tends to place the students each leader wants on his or her squad and give each class member a chance to become better acquainted with a larger percentage of the class.

Class Control Under Leaders   Class control does not ordinarily present a problem because of the presence of the teacher. If a problem arises for a student leader, the instructor should, if possible, permit the leader to handle the situation. Only in extreme cases should the instructor step in and take charge of a group for control purposes; for when the teacher does, the confidence of the leader and the respect of the group for their leader is diminished. The instructor should provide control assistance, but it should be indirect.

Control problems usually involve failure to comply with the group leader's requests, objecting to officials' decisions, not following prescribed procedures, speaking out of turn in rules meeting, and any other acts that provide evidence of not being willing to accept the authority of those in charge. Individual conferences with the chronic offender and with the leader who has control difficulties are often helpful in improving control. Simply talking it over with the offending student in private conference may clear up the matter. In the case of the leader, helpful suggestions and confidence building are important. In some cases, the plan of making anyone who objects to an official's decision the new official helps to maintain high standards of officiating.

Student Leaders in Intramurals

Historically, intramural activities have furnished outstanding opportunities for students to obtain leadership experience. This still remains a particularly favorable area of operation for student leaders under faculty guidance.

Secondary Schools

Student leaders are used in several ways. They serve as assistants to the intramural director. In these positions, they assist with all administrative aspects of the program. With guidance, they can set up tournaments and leagues, keep records, handle publicity, and serve as members of the intramural council, which formulates policy and administers the rules and regulations. Some intramural programs have activity managers who are responsible for designated activities in the intramural program. For example, one activity manager may be responsible for organizing and directing the basketball program and another activity manager has the same role with the volleyball tournament.

Student leaders serve as team managers. They are responsible for all administrative tasks relating to the team's participation in the intramural program. Students also serve as coaches and officials.

Colleges and Universities

Students are given even more responsibilities in college and university intramural programs. They are assistant directors, team managers, activity managers, officials, site supervisors, equipment coordinators, and coaches. Students have primary responsibility for the running of intramural programs in colleges and universities.

See Chapter 13 for more information about student leadership opportunities in intramural programs.

Student Leaders in Varsity Athletics

Interscholastic and intercollegiate athletics provide two distinct types of student leadership opportunities: those delegated to the students selected to direct their respective teams and those provided for managers, assistant managers, and assistant athletic trainers. Captains of the various teams and other specific team leaders, such as the quarterback in football, the catcher in baseball, the point guard in basketball, and the coxswain in crew, are leaders of the first type. The captains may be elected by the letter winners of the previous year or the current year team members, or be appointed by the coach for a season or single game. If the practice of having a different captain or captains for each contest prevails, the coach almost always appoints the captains. Specific team leaders, other than captains, are selected by the coach to fit the requirements of these positions.

These positions of leadership in varsity athletics are some of the most desired and most valuable in the entire school. Students have the opportunity to gain this experience under the leadership of a coach or coaches, most of whom have a wealth of leadership training and experience themselves. The athletic arena provides an ideal setting for the development of leadership skills by all participants. A skillful coach sees that each member of the team has the opportunity fill the role of a leader.

See Chapter 14, on interschool athletics, for the leadership opportunities available for managers in varsity athletics.

Class Activities

Simulation 1

Situation   The community high school where you teach is asking each department to provide leadership opportunities for students.

Write a position paper to present at a department meeting outlining your ideas for increasing leadership experiences for students in physical education.

Simulation 2

Situation   The school district where your university is located has decided to implement a K–12 intramural program. The director of physical education in the school district has come to the physical education major's club at your university and offered to contribute $1,000 to the club in return for assistance with the intramural program.

Draft a proposal from the club indicating the assistance members would provide for the $1,000 contribution. Develop the proposal to provide leadership opportunities for university students as well as a comprehensive program for the participants.

Performance Tasks

1. Devise ways teachers can use student leaders in their classes to give students more activity time.
2. Design a training program for student leaders in physical education.
3. Establish a plan for instituting a leader's group in the physical education department at the high school you attended.
4. Survey your university and list all the leadership opportunities you find in the physical education program, intramurals, and athletics.

16

School Health Education Programs

State of Health Education in Our Schools

Why is health education included in a book devoted to the administration of physical education and leisure sports? This is a legitimate question and requires a look at both the historical and current relationship of physical education and health education. The terms *physical education* and *hygiene* were used interchangeably during much of the nineteenth century. The emphasis was on health issues and the first leaders in colleges and universities were medical doctors. The focus on health remained well into the twentieth century for both health education and physical education and continues to be an important common educational objective. This is one reason why a chapter in this administration book is devoted to health education. Both disciplines have the common objective of improving the health of students and important benefits are received by the students when health education and physical education combine efforts to attain this objective.

The second reason for including a chapter on health education is the close relationship between health education and physical education in our elementary, secondary, and higher education institutions. Although they are distinct disciplines with their unique bodies of knowledge, administratively they are almost always joined at the elementary and secondary levels and often at colleges and universities. It is imperative that students preparing for administrative tasks have background in both health education and physical education.

Finally, although health education and physical education are separate disciplines, many students will teach in both areas. It would be better if health education specialists taught health education and physical education specialists taught physical education. This is usually the case in colleges and universities but, for several reasons, at the elementary and secondary levels teachers are often expected to teach both health and physical education. Significant progress has occurred in having health specialists in the schools, but progress has been slow. A drop in student enrollments and economic pressures have made it difficult for many school districts to employ health education specialists because there are not sufficient financial resources to employ additional teachers specifically for health education. School administrators are also in a quandary. Although they may philosophically believe that specialists should be employed, administratively it becomes much more difficult to schedule classes for both physical education and health education if teachers only teach in one area. This is particularly true in small schools, where there may be too few health classes for one person or when there aren't sufficient classes to fill up a teaching load for all the health education specialists who are employed. It is much easier to schedule teaching loads if the teacher can teach both health education and physical education. This also increases the flexibility a principal has when scheduling lunch periods and preparation periods for staff members.

The primary obstacle that slows the employment of health education specialists is that most states certify students to teach both health education and physical education rather than one or the other. The solution to this problem is for state departments of education to provide teaching certification in health education and in physical education and not have dual certification. Until this occurs, teachers will continue to teach both health and physical education and administratively the two disciplines will stay linked together. The advantage of this arrangement is that joint efforts for the benefit of the students are easily carried out. The disadvantage is that administrators, parents, members of the community, and even students consider health education and physical education to be synonymous and it is more difficult for each discipline to make its unique contributions to the education of the students.

Health education and physical education are separate and distinct, though closely related, fields. These fields were recognized as unique in 1974, when the national professional organization encompassing both fields changed from an association that included health education and physical education to an alliance (the American Alliance for Health, Physical Education, Recreation, and Dance) that includes a separate health education association. Health education comprises experiences that contribute to understandings, attitudes, and behaviors relating to an individual's health. Physical education is the phase of education that includes physical activity, usually vigorous, to bring about positive changes in the psychomotor, cognitive, and affective domains. It is clear that there are many similarities but also differences in teaching methods, subject matter, and specific outcomes.

Health education and physical education have important contributions to make to one another. It is important that health educators and physical educators work together. Unfortunately, conflicts do occur and some educators demonstrate a lack of respect for the other profession. This weakens both health education and physical education and fails to take into consideration the strength that comes from a close working relationship of these two fields. Many of the principles that are covered in a health class, such as ways of handling stress and understanding the different rates of human growth, are better understood through physical education experiences. In a similar way, the principles of exercise covered in a physical education class can be explained in more depth in a health class. However, a health class project investigating misleading consumer advertising is not physical education, nor can learning wrestling moves in a physical education class be considered health education.

Specialists in Health Education

The days when a person with a general physical education degree could adequately teach health education are gone. It takes a specialist to teach health education because of the extent of the program and also because of the sensitive nature of many of the topics covered. A typical health education program includes how to handle emotions, human growth and development, nutrition, physical fitness, substance abuse, diseases, family life, environmental health, safety and accidents, consumer health, and community health issues. In addition, a health educator must be able to present these topics to a wide variety of ages, ability levels, and socioeconomic groupings.

It has been pointed out that most states provide for dual certification to teach health education and physical education. It is therefore imperative that teacher preparation programs give equal emphasis to health education and physical education. In addition, students who plan to teach health education must take every opportunity to expand their knowledge of health education topics by obtaining related certifications such as CPR, taking additional courses, attending pertinent workshops and conferences, and reading current literature in the health field. Advanced study in health education is important for anyone who teaches health education. This applies equally to the person who teaches both health and physical education and to the teacher who becomes a health education specialist after completing a combined health and physical education certification program.

Schools still need physical educators who are well-qualified in health education to teach in health education programs. It is essential that physical educators who have this responsibility be enthusiastic about this teaching role and be committed to the importance of health instruction for students.

It is also important that the physical educators strive to understand health education principles and coordinate their efforts with the health educators. Many health principles are covered in physical education classes and a physical education teacher has a golden opportunity to reinforce proper health attitudes, encourage good health practices, and share accurate health information.

Health instruction in elementary school is often left to the classroom teacher. The teacher should be as well-prepared for this task as for teaching reading, social sciences, mathematics, or any other subject. This is rarely the case. Unfortunately, state certification requirements for the classroom teacher to teach health education are often minimal. It is encouraging to note that an increasing number of school districts are employing health education specialists. When this is not done, every effort should be made to have the specialist available to provide assistance to the classroom teachers and to organize and supervise the elementary school health education program for the school district.

The same person often administers both the health education and physical education programs in elementary and secondary schools. This person must be thoroughly familiar with health education because she or he is responsible for implementing what should be a model health education program. It is obvious that anyone involved in teaching or administering a health education program must be a specialist in the field.

The Health Educator

Students learn of health through many classes in a school and because health is a major educational objective, health education can be considered to be the responsibility of the entire faculty. Unfortunately, the incidental teaching of health has been found to be totally inadequate. Students need a carefully planned health curriculum with health education teachers available to teach the courses if a school's health objectives are to be attained.

Health educators form the backbone of a good health education program. It is important for health educators to have exemplary personal characteristics, excellent teaching skills, and an academic background that prepares them to teach health education courses competently. Personal characteristics of physical educators that are presented in Chapter 4 also apply to health educators. These characteristics include strong personality attributes such as emotional stability, honesty, communication skills, satisfactory health and physical fitness, high level of intellectual ability, creativity, flexibility, enthusiasm for teaching and the discipline of health education, acceptance of students with varying abilities, and leadership ability.

It is important for the health teacher to have strong teaching skills. Creativity is an important component of a teaching style if the subject matter is to come alive for the students. The key is to have the students involved in the learning process. This means that the teacher must have many different ways of presenting the material to the students. Lecturing skills and effective use of audiovisuals and guest speakers are all valuable teaching tools, but the main emphasis should be on student activities. Students learn best by doing and the ability to have them become active participants in the learning process is the mark of a successful health educator. The health educator should have a wide repertoire of games, simulations, and activities that makes learning come alive.

The academic preparation of a health teacher should include the general education and professional education components, which are discussed in Chapter 4. A student preparing to teach health needs a strong foundation in the social and natural sciences. The major courses should include in-depth study of subject matter areas included in health education curricula. Courses should encompass stress management, drug dependencies, family life, environmental health, physical fitness, nutrition, anatomy, physiology, HIV-AIDS education, community health, and other topics included in the programs the student will be certified to teach.

The health educator's influence extends far beyond the school into the community. Because health issues involve many different segments of society, the health educator has a wonderful opportunity to serve as a bridge between the school, family, and community. Leadership opportunities abound for health educators who are willing to mobilize students and community groups in the fight to solve local health problems and to make these citizens part of state, regional, and national efforts to alleviate health-related suffering and improve the health and well-being of people throughout the world.

Healthy People—The Goal

Good health has always been desired by humans and this motivating factor has made health education an important part of the educational system. Health education was initially called physical education and the emphasis was on exercise and physical fitness. The scope of health education programs has broadened significantly to include the broad range of courses and student health care present in schools today.

Health, as the term is used today, encompasses most areas of a student's life and is considered to be one of the most important objectives of education. There are many definitions of *health,* but they all revolve around positive aspects of a healthy lifestyle. The World Health Organization was instrumental in developing this concept with its definition of health as complete physical, mental, and social well-being, not merely the absence of disease. In order to promote good health, the school health program must encompass all aspects of the school. This is an awesome challenge for the health education profession.

Health has long been recognized as being an important goal of the schools. For instance, The Commission on the Reorganization of Secondary Education listed health as the first objective for the schools in its list of Cardinal Principles of Secondary Education, published in 1918. This should not imply that after that date comprehensive health education programs suddenly appeared. Credibility was given to including student health as a concern of the schools. Unfortunately, it took wars to raise the consciousness of the schools and the public to the poor state of health of our young people. The selective service medical examinations revealed all too clearly that insufficient attention had been given to health. This aroused public opinion and had the effect of getting support that enabled schools to better respond to the challenge of meeting the health needs of students.

The many health problems in our society have been the most important factor in generating support for health education programs in schools. Concern about drug use, the AIDS (HIV) epidemic, the high teenage pregnancy rate, poor nutrition, child abuse, obesity, youth suicide, and unhealthy living conditions are just some of the health problems that have sparked the development of current school health education programs designed to deal with these issues. Although these are societal problems, schools are expected to assume a key role in the struggle for good health for all citizens. It is realized that individual and family initiatives are inadequate by themselves and government efforts and programs also require the involvement of the schools.

Health programs in the schools are important in dealing with societal health problems. Health is essential for optimal learning to take place and is a prime factor for success, effective citizenship, and productive living. Current health programs must be designed to respond to these complex health needs for all ages. This is a formidable task but gives a good indication of the status health education now has in schools.

Healthy People 2000

Too often, health initiatives arise in response to crises in some aspect of health. The U.S. Department of Health and Human Services document *Healthy People 2000—National Health Promotion and Disease Prevention Objectives,* issued in 1990, is particularly important because it sets health goals that call for a concerted effort to improve the health levels of all citizens and places a strong emphasis on preventive techniques that lead to improved

Health Promotion
1. Physical activity and fitness
2. Nutrition
3. Tobacco
4. Alcohol and other drugs
5. Family planning
6. Mental health and mental disorders
7. Violent and abusive behavior
8. Educational and community-based programs

Health Protection
9. Unintentional injuries
10. Occupational safety and health
11. Environmental health
12. Food and drug safety
13. Oral health

Preventive Services
14. Maternal and infant health
15. Heart disease and stroke
16. Cancer
17. Diabetes and chronic disabling conditions
18. HIV infection
19. Sexually transmitted diseases
20. Immunization and infectious diseases
21. Clinical preventive services

Surveillance and Data Systems
22. Surveillance and data systems

Age-Related Objectives
Children
Adolescents and young adults
Adults
Older adults

FIGURE 16-1. Priority Areas
Source: Healthy People 2000, 1990, p. 7.

health. It carries a strong health message and has as its purpose the attainment of three broad goals designed to help U.S. citizens reach their full potential (*Healthy People,* 1990). These goals are to increase the span of healthy life, reduce health disparities, and achieve access to preventive services for all Americans.

The means of achieving these goals are described by 300 measurable objectives grouped into 22 priority areas (Figure 16-1). The first 21 areas are grouped into three broad categories: health promotion, health protection, and preventive services. Health promotion strategies are those that relate to individual lifestyle—personal choices made in a social context—that can have a powerful influence over one's health prospects. Priorities included are physical activity and fitness, nutrition, tobacco, alcohol and other drugs, family planning, mental health and mental disorders, and violent and abusive behavior. Educational and community-based programs can be more effective when they jointly address these lifestyle issues.

Health protection strategies are those related to environmental or regulatory measures that confer protection on large population groups. These strategies address issues such as unintentional injuries, occupational safety and health, environmental health, food and drug safety, and oral health. Preventive services include counseling, screening, immunization, and chemoprophylactic interventions in clinical settings. Strategies for preventive services focus on maternal and infant health, heart disease and stroke, cancer, diabetes and chronic disabling conditions, HIV infection, sexually transmitted diseases, immunization and infectious diseases, and clinical preventive services. Because the issues and paths to work with these issues vary by age, *Healthy People 2000* has grouped some objectives by four age groups: children, adolescents and young adults, adults, and older adults.

School health organizations were prominently involved in the consortium of nearly 300 national membership organizations and all the state and territorial health departments that joined the Public Health Service to support the development of the year 2000 objectives. This was appropriate because health education has an important role to play in attaining the objectives developed. These objectives are for the 1990s, but should have an influence on health education programs far beyond the year 2000.

Many of the objectives are related to school health. For instance, McGinnis and DeGraw state that more than one-third of the objectives for the year 2000 can be either directly attained by schools or influenced in important ways by schools (McGinnis and DeGraw, 1991). One of the most important objectives for health education programs in the schools is objective 8.4:

> Increase to at least 75 percent the proportion of the Nation's elementary and secondary schools that provide planned and sequential kindergarten through 12th grade quality school health education. (*Healthy People 2000,* 1990, p. 255)

Other objectives relate directly to topics included in comprehensive school health education programs. These include nutrition, tobacco, alcohol and other drugs, physical activity and fitness, communicable diseases, family life, environmental health, HIV infection, and sexually transmitted diseases.

McGinnis and DeGraw capsulize the importance of school health education programs in attaining *Healthy People 2000* objectives in the following statement (McGinnis and DeGraw, 1991, p. 294):

> Successful school health programs represent a key to attaining the year 2000 objectives. Planned and sequential health education in the school setting is crucial for helping children and youth develop the increasingly complex knowledge and skills to avoid health risks of childhood and adolescence. But school health programs have the potential to yield an even greater impact. The knowledge, attitudes, behavior, and skills developed as a result of effective school health programs enable individuals to make informed choices about behavior that will affect their own health throughout their lives, as well as the health of the families for which they are responsible, and the health of the communities in which they live.

Organization of the School Health Program

It is important that supervision and control of the school health program be centered in the board of education for public schools. It is also important that schools work closely with community health organizations and government agencies that have programs seeking to better the health of the community. There must be cooperation among all local groups concerned with health. Only then will they be able to meet their health objectives. *Healthy People 2000* objectives clearly recognize the important role schools have to play in the health of students as well as parents, siblings, and others in the community. The educational health program must be an integral part of the school organization, with the superintendent, principal, and health education director delegated responsibility from the board of education to administer the school health program.

A community health council is an excellent way of coordinating community and school health efforts in matters relating to the health of the school population. This council should be made up of representatives of the schools, the local board of health, medical and dental associations, community health organizations and agencies, local government, and other groups concerned with health issues. Student representatives should be on the council, as should the director of the health education program and a health education teacher. The council endeavors to set policy to effectively deal with health issues and problems and gives needed direction to attack community health problems and to cooperatively work on health issues. The community council can be a valuable aid in mobilizing the resources of the community to support school health programs.

A health committee should be organized, where possible, in each school. The function of the health committee is to give guidance and leadership to the health education program in the school and to cooperate with the community health council. The health committee should include the principal, the nurse, the person who coordinates the health program, a representative from the child study team, the health coordinator, a counselor, teachers, and student and parent representatives.

Every school must have a physician who functions as a school medical advisor. It is essential that schools have a physician to advise them about the many health problems that require medical judgment. School policy on medical matters should be formulated with the advice of the school physician and this person is consulted when health problems develop in a school or school system. A school physician is also needed for physical examinations for interscholastic athletic participation.

There must be someone in each school who has overall responsibility for the school health program. This person may have the title of director, coordinator, or supervisor in larger schools. In smaller schools, the principal might serve in this role, with some of the responsibility delegated to a person who teaches health.

The School Health Program Administrator

A common administrative plan is for one person to be responsible for the health program in all the schools in the community. This person should have a strong educational background in health education, preferably with an advanced degree in the field. In many districts, a person has administrative responsibility for both health education and physical education. This procedure is acceptable only if the person is qualified in both fields. Unless a physical educator is well-prepared for health education, there is no justification for placing that person in charge of the health education program, even though both fields may have similar objectives.

The success of the district school health program depends to a great extent on the administrator in charge. This person may have the title of district director, chairperson, coordinator, or supervisor. This person should have the following qualifications and training:

A master's degree or its equivalent in health education

A strong science background, including physics, chemistry, biology, physiology, and bacteriology

Extensive preparation in education, including educational psychology, multicultural education, teaching methodology, curriculum construction, evaluation in education, and principles of education

Thorough preparation in the field of health, with academic courses or in-service study covering the topics included in the district's health education curriculum

An understanding of the purpose and functions of all the health agencies in the community, particularly the local public health organizations and government agencies

An understanding of all facets of the school health program

An appreciation of the interrelatedness of the school health program with other subject matter fields and other phases of school life

Administrative skills that are required to develop and sustain an exemplary health education program, including competencies in public relations, curriculum development, valuative techniques, budget construction, and knowledge of teaching procedures and materials that are effective in health education

The school health administrator has responsibilities covering a wide range of activities. Some of the duties of the position can be delegated to other health personnel, but the administrator has ultimate responsibility to see that they are satisfactorily handled. For example, the usual procedure would be for the school nurse to follow up on medical and dental examinations, but it is the responsibility of the administrator to see that this task is completed appropriately. Duties of the school health administrator include the following:

Assume the responsibility for developing and supervising the total school health program

Coordinate the school health program with all pertinent agencies and individuals, including parents, public health agencies, physicians, and the local medical and dental societies

Have interpreted for teachers the results of the physical, medical, dental, and psychological examinations of their students

Assume responsibility for the follow-up of medical and dental examinations

Ascertain that the school physician's and group study team's health recommendations for special programs for students are implemented

Help secure the most effective use of the school physician's time

See that students needing special medical attention are referred to the school physician

Assist teachers and counselors who have students with health problems

Determine appropriate cocurricular activities for students with health problems

Supervise students who return to school after illness or injury and assist with their reentry to school programs

Assume responsibility for checking the cleanliness of the school environment

Analyze the health factors involved in truancy and excessive absence and take appropriate action

Maintain all health records of the students

Make arrangements early in the year for screening tests for vision, hearing, and posture

Secure publicity for the school health program

See that all staff members are aware of the services available to them

Give leadership to the health instruction program, including participation in curriculum revision; preparation of syllabi; selection of textbooks; assistance in obtaining videos, reference books, and other instructional materials; provision for in-service training and staff attendance at workshops, conferences, and conventions; and coordination of health instruction with other subjects

Attend meetings that relate to the school health program

Work with staff to plan and implement special programs on health awareness topics for students

Arrange for preparing student teachers, school aides, and peer instructors to assume their role in the health education program

Organize an ongoing in-service program to strengthen the school's health education program

Establish detailed procedures to be followed when accidents occur and see that these procedures are implemented

Assume responsibility for the school safety program

Set up valuative procedures for the school health program and complete the procedures as scheduled

Other Personnel

The instructional program is an important component of a successful school health program, but health education is not something that happens just during the time a student is in a health class. Actually, a health-conscious staff is the most essential ingredient of a successful school health program. The entire staff (administrators, faculty, clerical, custodial) must project, promote, and disseminate health concepts and principles every day if students are to have an optimal health education.

Schools' health personnel vary with the size of the school, the comprehensiveness of the program, and financial and community support. In addition to the health educators and teachers of other subjects, all of whom are involved with different aspects of the school health program, other health specialists are employed by the district, usually on a part-time basis. These include physicians, dentists, psychologists, psychiatrists, nurses, ophthalmologists, nutritionists, and visiting teachers for the homebound student. The school athletic trainer is another important member of the health staff at the secondary school. Some states require an athletic trainer and an increasing number of states have certification requirements for this role. See Chapter 17 for additional information about the athletic trainer.

The Comprehensive School Health Program

Total health promotion is increasingly being accepted as the responsibility of the school health program. This extended role challenges schools to find the resources, staffing, and appropriate policies and procedures to meet the challenges posed by their expanded role in health. *Healthy People 2000* recognizes the key role schools play in attaining the health objectives that have been established for the year 2000.

School health programs for many years have been composed of three parts: health instruction, healthful school living, and health services. The broader view of the program now includes eight elements, each of which has responsibility for promoting the health of students. The five additional components are physical education, student assistance and counseling, nutrition and food services, staff wellness, and the joining of school, community, and family resources for student health.

All of these components must be correlated to maximize their impact on the health of the students. Health promotion and wellness are the key objectives of the comprehensive school health program. Such a program contributes significantly to academic success and personal well-being.

School Health Instruction

Meaning and Purpose of Health Instruction

Health instruction forms the foundation of the school health education program. Students learn a great deal about health promotion and wellness from the other seven components of the program, but health instruction has the best opportunity to advance the understanding of health and to cultivate desirable health practices. Effective health instruction programs bring about positive changes in behavior that result in a healthier person. The fundamental purpose of health instruction is to equip the students with sufficient knowledge about health to enable them to attain and maintain, both in attitude and practice, the highest possible level of wellness.

Importance of Health Instruction

Health instruction is an important means of bringing about healthful behavior among all people. None of the other school health program components taken by themselves can solve all health problems. Every individual must make countless decisions that affect not only personal wellness but also the wellness of others. Health instruction serves a key function in preparing students to make wise decisions and to put these decisions into practice.

Many health objectives depend on the understanding and cooperation of others for successful implementation. Thus, every person should attempt intelligent self-direction in matters related to personal and community health. Instructional programs are geared to making this a possibility by providing an information base on which to act. As far as possible, everyone should have a scientific attitude toward wellness; personal conduct can then be in accordance with recognized scientific knowledge.

Ignorance, indifference, and prejudice must be combated as vigorously as sickness and disease. The outstanding problem in disease prevention at present is not the accumulation of more knowledge about disease but the putting into practice the available knowledge of disease prevention and control. The failure of many people to have themselves immunized is an example. Many physical defects developing during childhood, such as those involving hearing, sight, posture, nutrition, and dental decay, could be prevented in large part by intelligent health behavior. A scientific understanding of health is needed to break down superstitions and fads to counteract misleading advertisements and erroneous information relating to health.

There is no doubt that health education instruction in schools is a critical part of every student's education. It enables them to think critically about factors that influence their wellness and strengthens positive behaviors that improve their level of health. Schools provide a perfect means of disseminating health information and establishing practices contributing to good health. The importance of health instruction is clearly demonstrated by the leading role given to the schools in attaining the health objectives of *Healthy People 2000*.

Time Allotment

In the first three grades, the teaching of health is generally carried out largely through a correlation of health with other subjects in the curriculum. The classroom teacher usually has this responsibility. It is encouraging that a number of school districts are employing health specialist to teach health education starting with kindergarten. The specialist is also able assist the classroom teacher in extending health instruction throughout the curriculum. It is recommended that at least two class periods per week be devoted to exclusively to health instruction. The amount of time devoted specifically to health instruction should be increased as the child moves into the upper elementary grades. Specific health units should be required in secondary school, with daily periods devoted to health for the length of the unit. The number of units is determined by the comprehensiveness of the program. At least one unit of six or more weeks in length should be included each year. The amount of time devoted to health instruction in colleges and universities should be at least one course of two or three semester hours included in each student's degree program. Such a course is often required either for all students at a college and university or by specific departments or academic areas in the institutions.

Many schools do not give proper emphasis to health instruction. One of the most pernicious practices is to use part of the time allotted to physical education for health instruction. This is sometimes done when inclement weather prevents outdoor physical education activities. In some schools, one period per week of the physical education time is given over to health instruction. Other schools do not have a specific time allotment but attempt to teach this subject entirely through the use of special speakers. The speakers used are mostly physicians, dentists, nurses, or public health personnel. Although these talks have value, health instruction, if it is to take its rightful place in the school program, should be made part of the regular curriculum with a health educator in charge.

Basic Principles of Health Instruction

The emphasis of health instruction is on health promotion and wellness. Students are concerned about their health and the challenge for health instruction is to develop courses that reach out to the students in a nonthreatening, nonjudgmental, supportive manner. Health instruction should begin the first day of school and should not end until the last day. This means that there must be a carefully planned instructional program extending throughout the school years. The focus is on developing a healthy lifestyle.

Relevancy is the code word for successful health teaching. No subject in the curriculum is more relevant to children, particularly during the preadolescent and adolescent years. They are struggling for peer acceptance and they are faced with a long list of health issues daily. Health instruction is relevant when the topics are of current concern to the students and the teaching approach actively involves the students in investigating the topics and searching for solutions.

Health instruction is effective when the students are participants in the learning process, not simply receivers of information. It is important to have games and activities that make the concepts of health come alive and help the students to learn by simulating health situations that affect their lives. The book *How to Survive Teaching Health* (Tillman and Toner, 1990) is a good example of the effective application of this principle.

Health instruction is the foundation of the school health education program. This instruction should be integrated with all facets of the life of students that have an impact on their health. Provisions should be made for incidental teaching of health to take place on the sports field, during counseling sessions, as an outcome of student meetings, while working on the school newspaper, and during many other parts of a student's school experiences. Correlating health teaching with other subjects is another facet of health instruction that must be planned if it is to be maximally effective in influencing students to give wellness a high priority.

The school does not exist in a vacuum. Students' health and attitudes toward health are formulated outside of school as well as inside. The home molds a student's views of health and has far-reaching effects, good and bad, on the health of every student in school. The community is another agent that envelops children of all ages as they struggle for identity and acceptance and influences their perception of health. The goal of the health instruction program is to become the synthesizing medium for wellness and the promotion of good health.

Scope of the Health Instruction Program

The health instruction programs should not be limited to the formal health course. Two other aspects of health instruction are recognized as important. These are incidental instruction and correlated teaching. Incidental health instruction is that which arises naturally in various contacts with students. In such associations, situations develop that enable the instructor to give guidance in health matters. The student may come to the teacher with a personal health problem and solicit advice. As a result of close, informal relationships with students, teachers often discover students who need health advice. A review of each student's medical examination by the nurse provides an exceptionally good opportunity for incidental health instruction.

Interest can be aroused and health habits motivated by the ways in which health is taught. In addition to being taught in a course devoted to the subject, health can be presented in many other school subjects. The practice of teaching various aspects of health in other school subjects has long been advocated by leaders in health education. If the faculty member directly responsible for the health program is well-trained and is given proper cooperation by the entire teaching staff, health concepts, and acceptable health knowledge can be presented through other subjects in the curriculum. Health instruction is to be looked on not as a responsibility of the health teachers alone but as a joint responsibility of the entire faculty. Too many times, no practical application to the field of health is made by the other teachers. The health educator is usually responsible for direct instruction, and the health program administrator for the integration of health with the other subjects in the curriculum. The administrator should be able to show the other members of the faculty how they can integrate health instruction with their subject in a natural way, and the program should be worked out so that duplication of factual material is minimized.

The Health Course   In junior and senior high schools and in colleges and universities, formal courses in health are essential. Although some health can be effectively taught through incidental and correlated instruction, invariably important areas are omitted. In addition, such courses are needed to provide students with a unified, integrated presentation of health materials related to their needs.

Health Instruction in Elementary Schools   In the elementary grades, health instruction is often the responsibility of the classroom teacher. In the primary grades, a daily period of health instruction is not essential, but a minimal time allotment would be two 30-minute periods per week. In the intermediate grades, three periods of substantial length are needed. It should be stressed that incidental and correlated instruction, of which there is a good deal in the elementary grades, should not be counted in this time allotment. Another important consideration is that when teachable moments arise, the teacher should spend considerably more time on health instruction.

In the elementary grades, emphasis is placed on the development of desirable habits and attitudes toward healthful living. The scientific facts on which habits and attitudes are based should not be stressed. Instruction should be informal and should grow out of the daily experiences of the children. In the upper elementary grades, the development of health practices and attitudes should continue, but the children need to know reasons for acceptable health behavior. They are interested in factual information and are eager to discover answers for themselves.

The major health emphasis in the elementary grades should be based on the interest and needs of children at each grade level. The same topics may be covered from grade to grade but they are structured to relate to health issues and concerns of the students at each grade level. It is apparent that health topics must be covered in a sequential fashion. For example, family life education must begin when a child enters school and continue each year. Likewise, appropriate exercise patterns and attitudes must be a part of life from birth and it is not logical to wait until third or fourth grade to include exercise in the curriculum. Studies have found that the major emphasis in the early elementary grades should be given to developing habits of personal cleanliness, caring for teeth, ears, eyes, and nose, proper eating habits and choice of foods, developing proper attitudes toward physical and dental examinations, preventing colds and other illnesses, skin disease and other infections, wearing appropriate clothing, and acquiring safety habits. In the upper elementary grades, instruction can be continued on many of the above items but on a more advanced level. Other aspects that may be covered at both levels with different approaches and depth include nutrition, fire prevention, traffic safety, safety measures in school, home, and playground, rest, getting along with adults, simple first aid procedures, responsible drug consumption, stress reduction, and family life.

The health administrator is particularly needed in elementary schools because the classroom teachers are not generally as well-prepared for their health education responsibilities as specialists are in secondary schools. Someone must plan a program with sequential, progressive learning experiences at each succeeding grade. Teachers need assistance in coordinating what they teach with what has been taught before and with what will be taught later. In planning what is to be taught in the separate health class, the health content that has been taught through other subjects and incidental teaching must be taken into consideration. Without such coordination, the elementary school health education program will be conducted on a hit-or-miss basis that will inevitably result in needless repetition of content and omission of essential material.

Health Instruction in Secondary Schools   In secondary schools, an increasing emphasis should be given to health knowledge, although the goal of instruction is still to affect behavior. Experience has clearly shown that the relationship between health knowledge and health behavior is not high. Most people with unhealthy lifestyles really know better. The problem is one of proper attitudes. The study of feelings and emotions and learning how to use feelings and emotions in a healthy fashion must be as much a part of the instructional program as is factual material. Both mental and physical health should be integrated into the health instruction program. The development of proper health habits, attitudes, and knowledge should proceed concurrently. Of course, the health education program as well as the physical education program is concerned with all three domains (cognitive, affective, and psychomotor).

Four important considerations involved in determining the content of the secondary school health instruction program are health interests of students, strengths and weaknesses in health content areas, needs of students as revealed by research, and current health issues and problems of national concern. Community mores differ, but we know that children are maturing earlier than in the past and this results in the need to change the emphasis on different health topics at each grade level.

Many topics must be included in the health curriculum in the secondary schools. Among these are the following:

Feelings, emotions, and other aspects of mental health

Physical fitness

Nutrition

Personal health

Consumer health

Substance use and abuse

The body systems

Diseases and disorders

Safety and accident prevention

Human growth and development (including family life education)

Environmental health

Death education

The Conceptual Approach

This approach to the health education curriculum grew out of the School Health Education Study (*Health Education: A Conceptual Approach,* 1965). The conceptual approach was designed to solve such problems as the needless repetition of subject matter and memorization of facts, the failure to produce behavioral change, and the difficulty of selecting what to teach from the extraordinary amount of knowledge that has developed in recent years. The conceptual approach emphasizes concepts or generalizations about related data rather than facts. This approach is used in many curriculum areas.

Health education really has no alternative but to use the conceptual approach. The accumulation of facts about the physical, mental, and social dimensions of health is so enormous and changes so rapidly that it would be virtually impossible for students to absorb and retain this information. With the conceptual approach, students acquire generalizations about related data rather than try to master the vast number of specific items of information. The teacher of health education would do well to use the conceptual approach because no other method has a chance for success.

The conceptual approach involves setting up a framework for health education from kindergarten through the twelfth grade. This framework includes the following:

1. Three key concepts are the unifying threads that characterize the process underlying health:
   a. Growing and developing
   b. Interacting
   c. Decision making
2. Ten concepts emerge from the key concepts and are the major organizing elements of the curriculum or indicators for the direction of the learning experience:
   a. Growth and development influences and is influenced by the structure and functioning of the individual.
   b. Growing and developing follows a predictable sequence, yet is unique for each individual.
   c. Protection and promotion of health is an individual, community, and international responsibility.
   d. The potential for hazards and accidents exists in every environment.
   e. There are reciprocal relationships between humans, disease, and the environment.
   f. The family perpetuates the human race and fulfills certain health needs.
   g. Personal heath practices are affected by a variety of forces, often conflicting.
   h. Use of health information, products, and services is guided by values and perceptions.
   i. Use of substances that modify mood and behavior arises from many different motivations.
   j. Food selection and eating patterns are determined by physical, social, mental, economic, and cultural factors.

3. Thirty-one substantive elements act as guides to select and order the substances of health education in its physical, mental, and social dimensions.

4. A set of long-range student objectives is categorized under three domains (cognitive, affective, and psychomotor). (Health Education: A Conceptual Approach to Curriculum Design, 1967)

There have been dramatic changes in health issues since the School Health Study was completed. However, the model that came out of the study continues to be a framework within which health teaching can effectively occur. New learning theory can be easily applied and current health concerns for all ages incorporated into the model.

Sensitive Subjects

A number of sensitive and controversial topics are included in health curricula. Communities differ widely in their acceptance of course content in areas such as family life education. Lack of information, scare tactics by people who are against teaching about some topics in the schools, misinformation, and new health problems that face society are all factors that affect the health education coverage of sensitive issues. It is also interesting to note the difference time makes. A sensitive issue five years ago gradually becomes an acceptable part of the school health curriculum as a result of better understanding of the issue.

Several approaches should be used by schools and health education professionals when dealing with sensitive issues. The most important consideration is the manner in which the material is presented. It should be part of a comprehensive health education program, not a special area set apart. After all, health issues and programs are interrelated and the health curriculum must be an all-inclusive approach to the health of the students.

Good public relations are of paramount importance. Many problems can be defused simply by openly and honestly addressing them and making certain parents and members of the community are informed. Rumors and erroneous information can have disastrous effects on even the best health education curriculum. The public must be kept informed and become supporters of a comprehensive health education program that includes all health issues. This occurs only when an effective public relations program is in place.

Another critically important consideration is the qualifications of the health education instructors. Competent teachers know how to approach even the most sensitive topics in a way that avoids sensationalism and public opposition. Teachers should also seek the support and involvement of parent groups, community organizations, and health professionals. They should also gain the support and assistance of all teachers in presenting health topics so the students realize that health, even aspects that the community might view as sensitive, is an integral part of all aspects of their lives.

Methods of Teaching Health

One of the most common criticisms of health teaching is that the subject lacks interest. This criticism has been made by elementary and junior and senior high school groups as well as college students. This problem is due largely to insufficient preparation of the health instructor and too much duplication of teaching material. Some school principals, superintendents, and other faculty members still think of health in terms of washing the hands before eating, brushing the teeth three times a day, and drinking six or eight glasses of water daily.

Although these facts have value, one can hardly expect interest if they are taught in the elementary grades and again in junior and senior high school and college. If the health course is to appeal to students, their interests and needs must be considered in the selection of subject matter. These needs and interests are constantly changing; and unless the health instruction is modified and adapted to them at the different school levels, this subject proves distasteful and uninteresting. There is also the tendency to base the instruction predominantly on adult needs and interests. Although these are important, it is extremely difficult to interest students in health problems that are thirty to forty years away. The best procedure is to follow the middle path and to consider both present and future needs and interests.

There has been a dramatic change in the approach to teaching health during the past decade. With the better preparation of teachers, the stereotyped health teacher who lectures by reading out of the book and varies the class by showing films, many of them outdated and irrelevant to the topic, is in the past. Typical health classes today are exciting, with a wide variety of teaching methods used. The key is that students are actively involved in the learning process. There is still a time for lecturing, but the focus is on experiential activities for the students. This is what makes learning come alive and results in behavioral changes that are less likely to occur if factual information is the focus of health teaching. It is desirable to have up-to-date health textbooks each year. There are excellent health education textbooks that are correlated for the different grade levels. The rapidly changing field of health requires that the teacher use current materials in conjunction with the textbook that has been adopted.

Learning occurs when students are involved in the learning process. Games and activities give meaning to the health principles covered in class. The goal is to positively affect behavior, not to simply learn facts. Students also get involved when they have the opportunity to discuss the health issues that are presented in class through games, activities, audiovisuals, lectures, and textbook information.

Numerous commercially produced teaching aids are effective for use in health classes. The innovative health educator also constructs and improvises teaching materials that give greater relevance to the health topics as they are covered in class. Through the use of well-selected instructional materials such as health videos, slides, posters, and hands-on classroom equipment relating to different topics such as exercise, nutrition, drugs, sex education, AIDS, and self-esteem, a health course will be interesting and have relevance for the students. An extensive number of health videos are available for all ages in elementary through senior high school. These videos present material in an interesting way and include material that might be impossible or at least very difficult to present by other class methods. Health videos and other health instructional materials should be looked on as aids, not as a teaching method. Most state boards of health have extensive video libraries, where videos can be rented for a nominal cost. Slides and films are also available from these sources as well as from other rental agencies. The low cost of videos has made it possible for schools to purchase new videos as older materials become dated. It is also possible for the teacher or the school's media department to produce audiovisual materials that are appropriate for class use. Posters and many other materials are also available from many national associations such as the National Safety Council, the National Society to Prevent Blindness, the National Diary Council, American Diabetes Association, American Council on Alcoholism, and the National Mental Health Association. The materials from such associations are usually free or available for a nominal cost and they contain the most current information available.

Class demonstrations are a very effective means of presenting health facts. The teacher should have received sufficient training in health to carry out simple experiments. The growth requirements of bacteria, their wide distribution, the effects of drying, sunlight, boiling, and pasteurization on them can be easily demonstrated. A comparison can be made of the bacterial count of raw milk with that of pasteurized milk or of river water with tap water. The size and the shape of various types of bacteria can be shown easily by staining these organisms and using a microscope. Simple feeding experiments carried out as a class project would be an interesting and worthwhile method of presenting certain facts in this field. Many other simple, inexpensive demonstrations can be made. Various health workbooks and laboratory guides include many ideas and suggestions for class demonstrations.

In every community, class trips can be taken that add interest and increase the value of health instruction for the students. A visit to the sewage-disposal and water plants creates more interest in municipal health programs than does ordinary classroom instruction. A visit to a dairy to observe modern sanitary methods of processing milk and to a fruit orchard or a vegetable farm to learn about nutrition are excellent field trips that enhance classroom experiences. The health teacher should take advantage of facilities outside the school whenever feasible.

Graphic materials such as wall charts are great aids in teaching health. Some universities and colleges use human cadavers and specimens to facilitate instruction. Many departments use health habit inventory charts as a means of bringing desirable and undesirable habits before the students. In junior and senior high schools, an excellent practice is to put on a health exhibit.

Television is also an effective teaching aid. Programs that relate to health units can be incorporated into the classrooms. Cable television is a resource that is just beginning to be tapped for use in the health curriculum. It is also possible to get permission to tape television shows and use the tapes for classroom instruction. All copyright regulations must be carefully followed and permission obtained before taping programs to use in class. Public television is a particularly rich resource for programs that are pertinent for use in the health classroom.

The emphasis in health instruction is on outcomes. Each school should establish program outcomes for each grade level. Desired behaviors, pertinent knowledge, and the application of appropriate health concepts in a person's lifestyle are important outcomes. The instructional health program plays a significant role in the strategy for improving the health of all citizens. In the United States, this strategy is clearly spelled out in the publication *Healthy People 2000.*

Health education teachers have a variety of teaching methods at their disposal. The considerable research that has been done to evaluate the different procedures indicates that there is no one method that is best for all teachers in all situations. A variety of methods is preferable to the exclusive use of one method. The teacher must consider the age and background of the students, class size, student interests and goals, and the nature of the subject matter in selecting methods.

Healthful School Living

Meaning

Healthful school living refers to the entire environment that surrounds the pupil. It involves not only safe and sanitary facilities but also careful planning of the school day for study, play, and rest. Because teachers are also part of the school environment, healthful teacher–pupil relationships are an important aspect of healthful school living.

Wholesome School Environment

Every school is obligated to surround its students with a physically, socially, and emotionally healthful environment. Intelligently planned, healthfully arranged, well-equipped school plants kept in a sanitary and safe condition are essential in the development and protection of child health. Construction and maintenance of the school building should be in accordance with standards established by law and by official building and health regulations and codes. Adequate and well-arranged lighting and seating, properly functioning heating and ventilating systems, reliable equipment for fire protection, approved plumbing, suitable acoustics, adequate toilet facilities, and sanitary drinking fountains are some commonly recognized requirements for a healthful school environment. Furthermore, adequate hand-washing facilities, hot and cold water, liquid or powder soap, and paper towels are all necessary for pupils and teachers.

Standards for school facilities are established in building codes of state education departments and sanitary regulations of state health departments. These standards were determined by experts and, if they are up to date and adhered to in a school, they ensure the proper physical environment for children. The responsibility for sanitary inspections may be handled by the school nurse, school physician, health officer, sanitary inspector, principal, or superintendent. In smaller schools, the health administrator or superintendent may make the inspections.

The Organization of a Healthful School Day

The health educator, together with other school officials, has more control over the organization of a healthful school day than over the environmental conditions of the children. Any organization of the school day must be considered unacceptable if it overtaxes students mentally or physically. Some of the factors that must be considered are these:

The length of the school day

The number and length of the periods

The student academic load

The number and kind of study periods

The placement of the activities

The amount and kind of homework and the importance attached to it

The number, length, and kind of rest and relaxation periods

Extracurricular activities

More high school and college students have had their health affected adversely by poor organization of the school day and unsatisfactory teacher–pupil relationships than by unclean surroundings. High school and college students need guidance in the scholastic load they are carrying. They often undertake heavy extracurricular loads and other outside work. Some supervision is necessary to prevent them from undertaking too much. Extracurricular participation may be restricted, the scholastic schedule may be lightened, or, if possible, the outside work may be reduced if the student demonstrates that he or she is carrying too great a load.

The daily schedules of high school and college students should enable them to establish a regular program of work and sufficient time for meals, sleep, rest, exercise, and recreation. College scholastic work should be limited to approximately eight hours per day or forty hours per week. The high school scholastic load should be about six hours per day.

Teacher–Pupil Relationships

Every teacher in the school has a contribution to make to the health of the pupil. In addition to instructing and supervising the health of the students, the teacher can do much to promote health by using student-friendly teaching methods. These methods are particularly important from the standpoint of mental wellness. Too much stress should not be placed on term examinations as a basis for promotion or final grades. The policy of rewards and punishments should be considered carefully. Imprudent disciplinary measures can have serious emotional implications. The instructor should not use fear to motivate desirable attitudes and conduct. Classes should be conducted so that fear of failure, ridicule, sarcasm, or embarrassment do not result. It must be recognized that constant failure invariably causes poor mental health. The instructor is confronted with many different personalities and cannot treat them all alike. Teachers who understand the principles contributing to positive mental and emotional health and apply these principles make an indispensable contribution to the health education program.

The Teacher's Health

The highest attainable health of the body, mind, and the personality of every school child is the aim of the health education program. There is a strong relationship between the health of the teaching staff and the health of students. Teachers are role models and their attitudes toward health have a powerful influence on students. Teachers are able to carry out their teaching and nonteaching responsibilities with vigor and enjoyment when they are healthy themselves. A teacher who is physically fit is able to meet the challenges of teaching, enjoy a life outside of teaching, and motivate students through their lifestyle to be physically active. Teaching is a demanding profession. It is important that teachers be physically fit if they are to handle the stress of teaching and maintain good mental and emotional health. Teachers vary in the level of health they are able to attain, but it is important that they strive to reach a level of personal well-being that in turn contributes to a healthy learning environment.

The school also has an important role to play in the health of teachers. The teaching situation must be conducive to good health and support teachers in carrying out their responsibilities. This means that both the physical surroundings and the psychological milieu in which the teacher works must promote good health. A pleasant classroom with high-quality lighting and appropriate heating and ventilation systems is essential. Recognition for personal and student achievements and encouragement to be innovative contribute significantly to emotional health. Administrative support in all aspects of a teacher's work, ranging from student disciplinary situations to instituting a new teaching approach, continually ranks as one of the most important needs of teachers. A satisfactory teaching load, good instructional materials, and supportive colleagues are other important factors that contribute to the health of teachers.

The teacher's health can be promoted and safeguarded in a number of other ways. The following are recommended procedures for maintaining and improving teacher health:

Health standards for new teachers

Periodic health examination, including a tuberculin test and a chest x-ray for positive reactors

An appropriate teaching load, considering numbers of students, number of classes, and different preparations

Time for relaxation during the day

Comfortable teachers' lounge and eating area

Satisfactory compensation and fringe benefits

Clean and healthful teaching environment

Comprehensive health promotion program for teachers

Smoking cessation, weight control, stress reduction, and exercise programs

Recreational opportunities

Stimulating in-service workshops

Opportunity for attendance at conferences and conventions

School Health Services

Nature and Scope of Health Services

This service program embraces the protective measures taken by the school to conserve and improve the health of students. The highest attainable physical, mental, and emotional health of every school child is the goal of the school health services program. The health services vary considerably in different institutions, but the essentials of a good program include the following activities:

1. Health appraisal:
   a. The periodic medical examination
   b. The periodic dental examination
   c. Psychological examinations
   d. Screening tests
   e. Teacher–nurse observations
2. The follow-up program
3. Communicable disease control
4. Emergency care procedure
5. Health supervision of school personnel
6. Student excuses

The scope of the school health services is limited in the curative and remedial field because of legislation limiting the schools' jurisdiction and limited money and time.

Health Appraisal

The total assessment of the health status of the school child is called *health appraisal*. Health appraisal is the process of determining the health status of a child through such means as health histories, teacher, nurse, and staff observations, screening tests such as hearing, vision, and postural tests, and medical, dental, and psychological examinations. Not only do the physician, dentist, and nurse play a part in the health appraisal but the parent, teacher, psychologist, and child study team are also involved. The term *health appraisal* is broader and more comprehensive than *physical examination, health examination,* and *medical examination.*

The Periodic Medical Examination   The medical examination is the phase of health appraisal performed by the physician. A periodic medical examination is the very foundation of the entire health program, as health protection, health instruction, and health promotion all depend on it. The medical examination can be used as the basis on which to plan students' curricular and extracurricular activities or as a yardstick to measure improvement in health and to guard against health impairment. Cases of communicable disease must be discovered so that their transmission may be checked and treatment obtained.

The ideal program is one in which the examination is done by the family physician and the results reported to the school. The parents and pupil thus have strengthened the concept that medical care and supervision are personal responsibilities. In addition, the family physician is better acquainted with the pupil, and more time is available for a thorough examination. If any therapy is needed, it can be done immediately. The family physician's examination should encompass all the examinations the school system requires.

Students who do not have regular examinations by their family physicians should receive one from the physician serving the school. If a school physician is not available, there are usually local agencies, such as a welfare or health department clinic, that can take care of children who are unable to afford satisfactory medical care.

The recommended standard for the number of medical examinations includes one before entrance to kindergarten or first grade, one in the intermediate grades, one in junior high school, and one before leaving school. Additional examinations should be arranged whenever there are indications of a medical problem. Previously, the recommended standard was an annual examination. Experience has shown that this standard was impractical. Schools that attempted to meet this standard often provided such superficial examinations as to invalidate the procedure. Less frequent but more thorough examinations produce better results.

When examinations are given at school, qualified physicians and nurses should give them, although the faculty and reliable students can assist in some of the routine details, such as weighing and measuring. The physician's time should be devoted as much as possible to aspects of the examination that cannot be done by anyone else. A satisfactory examination requires 20 to 30 minutes for each student. A minimum of 15 to 20 minutes of the physician's time should be given to each student. The child should be stripped to the waist or clothed in a slipover. Privacy is essential to ensure optimum physical and emotional comfort of the student.

Before the examination, all available health records of the student should be brought up to date and reviewed. Each pupil should have a cumulative health record throughout his or her school career. Excellent forms have been developed for this purpose. In addition to the data from the periodic medical and dental examinations, the cumulative record should include the family health history, the health history of the individual, health habits and complaints, symptoms and signs of health disturbances he or she reports, teachers' and nurses' observations of health, attendance record, and the results of all psychological tests.

The medical examination should be complete. If a blood test or urinalysis is indicated, it should be done privately because these tests are too expensive for most schools to provide routinely. Some provision should be made for detecting tuberculosis. Many schools require the tuberculin test and x-ray the positive reactors. Schools can obtain specialized assistance from local, state, and national organizations devoted to tuberculosis control.

Participation in interscholastic and intercollegiate athletics should be contingent on passing an adequate medical examination. The recommended standard is an examination of the participants before the beginning of the sport season. The minimum standard is an examination once each year, with a reexamination for those who have had a disabling injury or illness. The general examination that is ordinarily given to students is not thorough enough for athletes. The medical examination of athletes should include an examination of the heart, pulse, and blood pressure before and after exercise, the lungs, bones, joints, and the inguinal and umbilical region for hernia. A urinalysis is strongly recommended.

The Periodic Dental Examination   The periodic dental examination is another essential aspect of the health appraisal program. The fact that dental decay is the most prevalent physical defect among schoolchildren emphasizes the necessity of providing such a program. The great majority of schoolchildren experience some dental decay, which could readily be prevented by the application of proper procedures.

An annual visit to the dentist for an examination and correction of defects that are found is essential. This procedure enables the dentist to discover and correct conditions before they become serious.

The school's responsibility for dental health involves the encouragement of children and their parents to see a dentist at regular intervals. Every parent should be made aware of the child's dental defects and the possible consequences if not corrected. It also includes, in many communities, the conduct of dental inspections. A dental inspection is not as complete as a regular dental examination in the dentist's office, but it does reveal dental conditions that require correction. Some schools routinely provide dental inspections, but many do not. Dental hygienists often administer the dental inspections. The trend is definitely to place the responsibility for dental treatment on the parents. Special arrangements are usually possible for the children of families in economic need.

Psychological Examinations   Another important aspect of health appraisals is related to mental and emotional health of the pupils. This is a significant aspect of health and must not be neglected. Tests of intelligence, reading, social adjustment, personality, and attitudes toward school and other children are very helpful in assessing the health of children. In addition, the classroom teacher is able to report anecdotes, particularly of children who deviate from the normal. The school administrator, psychologist (if one is available), counselor, guidance teacher, social worker, health educator, physician, and nurse may have valuable data to add to the cumulative health record in regard to mental and emotional health.

The mental health program is concerned with the discovery and prevention of mental and emotional illness. In the discovery of such conditions, the classroom teacher plays a vital role. Close association with students throughout the school year gives the teacher an exceptional opportunity to understand them. The teacher who has a good preparation in child growth and development and understands child behavior can identify children who deviate from the norm. A knowledge of the factors that lead to mental and emotional illness is important in the prevention program. One of the most important considerations is that the child experience some success in school activities. Constant failure is damaging to mental and emotional health. Providing an opportunity for each pupil to be creative in ways natural to that child is another important factor. Satisfying relationships with classmates are also indispensable for the well-adjusted child.

Screening Tests   Screening tests are so called because they "screen out" pupils who may need further examination and diagnosis by specialized health service personnel. Such tests are used particularly for height, weight, vision, and hearing. The screening process is often done by the classroom teacher or nonmedical personnel.

The classroom teacher should measure the height and weight of pupils at stipulated intervals, preferably at the beginning, middle, and end of each school year. Weighing and measuring should be done under constant conditions. Children who lose weight, show no gain, or gain excessively over a period of three months should be examined by a physician to determine the reason.

The Snellen test is the most extensively used screening test for vision in the schools. Whichever test is used, it should be administered by the classroom teacher. It should be given annually to all elementary and secondary school pupils and more often when visual defects are suspected. A screening test for color deficiency should also be administered once in the upper elementary grades.

The screening test for hearing should be administered annually in elementary schools and every two years in secondary schools. The audiometer is used for this test. It should be administered by a technician, nurse, or classroom teacher. The teacher who does it should have special training.

Teacher–Nurse Observations   Teacher–nurse observations are also an important part of health appraisal. The teacher, particularly, has constant contact with the students and can readily observe changes in their behavior and appearance. Often, teachers are not qualified to detect deviations that may be significant but they can easily be taught to do this by the school nurse, health administrator, or physician.

Teachers should be aware of any abnormalities in students or changes in their normal appearance or actions. Eyes, ears, nose, throat, scalp, skin, teeth, and mouth are easily observed and should be watched for deviations from the norm for children of similar age. Growth patterns can give indications of the health status of students and physical condition and appearance provide clues that the observant teacher finds useful. Many children have postural and muscular problems that may become noticeable or increase in severity after screening tests. The teacher has an important role in spotting these abnormalities.

A student's behavior is one area where the teacher can obtain health information that is not observed on most screening tests. Psychological and emotional problems often manifest themselves in changes in the student's behavior that can range from withdrawing from other students to overly aggressive actions. Careful observation of a student's actions creates the opportunity for the teacher to gain insight into possible health problems and bring them to the attention of parents and the school medical team.

If the teacher observes signs of disease or health defect, the student should be taken to the school physician, the school nurse, or the principal. Every school should have some individual who can make a more thorough examination of the suspected cases and authorize a more comprehensive review by the appropriate medical person. The teacher should never be expected to make the decision of whether the pupil should be excluded from class. The parents should be informed immediately when a medical problem is suspected. They should be urged to secure medical attention and the school should be informed of any action taken.

When the student is able to return to school, a certificate to that effect should be brought from the doctor. It is recommended that the students be examined by the nurse before being readmitted to class. The control of communicable disease is made more difficult in schools where undue emphasis is placed on perfect attendance. Students should be encouraged to protect classmates by staying home when not well.

The Follow-Up Program

The value of a medical examination depends in large measure on the follow-up program. In too many institutions, the results of the examinations are recorded, filed, and forgotten. The number of defects that are corrected after the examination is far more important than the number of defects discovered by the examination. Concerning the correction of defects, two principles must be recognized: No school health service should take away the fundamental responsibility of the parent and any corrective work must be made an educational procedure.

The school is an educational institution, not a hospital or clinic. The school is not prepared for extensive curative or remedial services. The responsibility for the treatment of defects and disease rests on the family. The school staff should render first aid in emergencies and then call the family physician if further attention is needed. The primary corrective work to be undertaken by the school should be educational in nature. Adapted or corrective physical education falls into this category. The department of physical education provides corrective classes in which students with physical defects and organic disturbances that are amenable to correction by physical modalities are given certain exercises or activities. Instruction and practice in appropriate recreative activities are also given.

If the parents are unable to be present at the medical and dental examinations, they should be notified by letter of the findings, and suggestions should be made concerning future examinations, treatment, and care. It is advisable to invite the parents to visit the school and confer with the school physician or nurse on the examination result. Instead of sending a letter, the school nurse may visit the home and report and interpret the results of the examination and the recommendations of the examiner if there is a problem. At school, the results should be interpreted to the students and their individual needs pointed out.

The teachers should be informed of the health status of their pupils, insofar as the law permits, and steps should be taken to remedy any defects. Teacher–nurse conferences should be regularly scheduled. They are usually most valuable if part of the time is devoted to discussing the general health of the class and then reviewing and exchanging information regarding specific children who seem to need medical care, follow-up, or special study. The fully informed teacher can be helpful in adjusting the classroom program to the student's needs and influencing the student and parents to correct the remediable conditions, as recommended by the family or school physician.

The correction of all remediable defects found on the medical and dental examinations is the chief purpose of the follow-up program. When the family does not take responsibility for correcting the defects, the school should bring this fact to the attention of public health authorities and social agencies. All agencies contributing to child health should coordinate their efforts, and their services should be brought to the attention of families unable to afford appropriate medical care. The school nurse or the visiting teacher is usually in the best position to make the arrangements between the family and social organization.

Communicable Disease Control

The local health officer is the legal representative of the state board of health, which has full power in the control of communicable disease. The health officer consults with the private physician when the illness affects the community or school and informs the schools concerning the current rules, regulations, and policies for the control of communicable disease. The health officer also plans jointly with the school administrator for the immunization and testing program, in cooperation with private physicians, and advises school officials concerning the exclusion from school of pupils or teachers because of exposure to or presence of communicable disease.

The superintendent or principal is responsible for giving the school staff adequate interpretation of the most recent public health practices and for developing procedures based on these practices. Written and printed instructions on the teacher's role in communicable disease control should given to every teacher in the school. The school administrator collaborates with private physicians and public health officials in formulating plans for the schools and should also keep parents informed about the school's policies and procedures, usually by letter and group meetings.

One of the most important considerations in communicable disease control is immunization. It is recognized that immunization through vaccination is highly effective against smallpox, diphtheria, tetanus, measles, whooping cough, and polio. Despite this fact, too many schoolchildren are unprotected against all of these diseases and most states find it necessary to require immunization before students can attend school.

Parents should be encouraged by every means possible to have their children immunized by their family physician in their preschool years. It is recommended that the smallpox vaccination be administered to children before their first birthday. The diphtheria, whooping cough, and tetanus immunization is recommended for children from three to six months of age. This can be done at one time by means of the triple antigen, which provides protection against all three diseases simultaneously.

These protective procedures should be performed before the children enter elementary school. The public must be educated on the value of immunization and the necessity to have it done early. The real facts should be placed before the public through newspapers, school publications, letters, visits by the school nurse, and parent–teacher meetings. Carelessness and ignorance are the chief foes. Religious objections must be handled according to state and federal law and school policy. Schools should cooperate with the public health program in promoting immunization.

As children enter elementary school, their needs for immunization should be determined. The necessary information is obtained from the family physician on a form that is sent to the parents. Some children will not have had an immunization. The children who have been immunized will require booster injections. Whatever the needs of children, follow-up procedures are necessary to ensure proper immunization. Parents are expected to assume this responsibility through their family physician and documentation of immunization is required for each student's medical file. When the family cannot afford this expense, public health or social agencies are available to handle it. Some colleges and universities give vaccinations as part of the service for the student health fee. Others make no charge for it and vaccinate those who need it as part of the entrance examination. During epidemics, public health agencies or schools usually furnish emergency inoculations.

The Common Cold   The common cold is a communicable disease that presents special problems. No difficulty is presented when the student actually has a severe cold. Such a student should be excluded from school. Also, when it becomes clear that a severe cold is impending, the student should be discouraged from coming to or remaining in school. However, it would not be feasible to exclude from school all students who manifest symptoms of a cold. Often, the student has an allergy rather than a cold. Probably the best procedure is to delay action until the evidence confirms the onset of a cold. The nurse should establish a procedure for the school to follow.

Emergency Care Procedures

All schools should be prepared to render first-aid treatment in emergency situations. The school doctor should prepare detailed instructions with emergency procedures. The nurse should administer first aid if it is needed. If the nurse is not available, first aid should be given by some qualified member of the teaching staff. Teachers of physical education, health, driver education, and safety education classes should be certified in CPR and Red Cross first aid. All other teachers should have in-service opportunities to become certified. In the event of a serious accident, the school doctor or other physician should be called immediately. The emergency plan should be posted prominently throughout the school with emergency numbers. The names, addresses, and telephone numbers of physicians who can be called in emergencies should be posted in the principal's office.

After first aid has been given, the parents should be tactfully notified of the child's accident. The parent should pick up the child unless it is a serious accident and an ambulance has been called. The parents should be kept fully informed about the procedures being followed. A sick or injured child should never be sent home alone. If the parents cannot be reached, there should be, on file, the name of a friend or relative who is authorized to make decisions in emergencies. There should also be on file in the school the name of each pupil's family physician, whose notification in case of an emergency has been authorized by the child's parent. A well-qualified person, usually the nurse, should be available to help an uncertain parent decide what is to be done next for the child. All school personnel should clearly understand that they should not go beyond first-aid treatment of a student who has been injured or is ill. They should not diagnose or administer medication of any kind unless prescribed by a physician. All teachers should be familiar with the school's approved emergency plan.

Excuses

The problem of excuses arises chiefly in connection with physical education classes. A written excuse by a physician should be the customary method of excusing students from classes. Whenever possible, the school physician should be the only person authorized to grant excuses. Many unjustifiable excuses are requested by family physicians. In order to reduce unwarranted excuses to a minimum, the family physician should be asked to write out the reasons why the students should be excused. The school physician should then review the validity of the excuse and in case of doubt request justification by the family physician. When family physicians know that their excuses are subject to the approval of the school physician, they hesitate to grant unjustifiable excuses. Whenever excuses are granted, their duration should be indicated.

When the problem of excuses develops, the cause may be that the program is so poor that it does not deserve the support of the physician. Another reason may be that many physicians do not understand the nature and purposes of the program. In this situation, program administrators should reach out to the medical profession with a comprehensive public relations thrust. Physicians can also be approached through the local medical society. Close cooperation should exist between the school physician and other physicians in the community.

Physical Education

Chapter 12 describes a comprehensive physical education program. It is obvious that physical education programs make significant contributions to the mental and emotional health as well as the physical health of children.

Student Assistance and Counseling

Many programs in the schools are geared to helping students in their psychological and emotional development. Examples include special assistance for abused children, children of alcoholic parents, and children who need help in coping with other life situations. Some children have low self-esteem or a poor self-image and need help in these areas if they are to capitalize fully on their educational opportunities. It is also realized that all children from elementary through the secondary grades profit from a counseling system that gives them someone to assist with normal concerns as well as with personal and educational problems. This type of health support system often makes the difference between educational success and failure for many children.

Nutrition and Food Services

Good nutrition makes a valuable contribution to the ability of a student to achieve in school. The program has two objectives: to improve the health of children through nutritious, well-balanced meals priced within the reach of all students and to use meal time as an educational experience, whether it is a before-school breakfast or a lunch. The food service staff has the important function of preparing nutritious meals that appeal to the students. They must be properly trained and be part of the school's effort to provide nutritious meals and to help students incorporate good nutrition into their lifestyles.

Staff Wellness

A comprehensive health promotion program should be in place for staff. Their health has far-reaching effects on the children they teach. Programs can be developed to meet a variety of health needs, ranging from exercise classes to coping skills and stress reduction. Improved staff morale and the ability to teach without wearing out by the end of the day are just two of the outcomes of a staff health promotion program.

Joining of School, Community, and Family Resources for Health

Health resources for children include, first of all, their family. However, the school and community are also heavily involved in the health of students. A student has the best chance for good health when all three of these components work together. Each has its own unique responsibilities and its own unique contributions. However, the only way the child can maximally benefit is when the family, school, and community cooperate. The school must work closely with the family in all matters relating to health and join forces with the community to use all available resources to promote student health.

Administrative Practices for the School Health Program

An administrator must assume a number of responsibilities to operate a high-quality school health program in all areas of the school. The aim of the school health program is the development of optimal physical, mental, emotional, and social health among all students. A checklist of administrative practices that can guide the administrator in the accomplishment of this aim is outlined by Creswell and Newman (1993):

Recognize health as a basic objective of education and reflect this priority in the school's written administrative practices and policies.

Secure and budget adequate funds for health programs.

Regularly keep parents informed of the health program.

Establish an appropriate cooperative relationship with community health agencies.

Maintain communication with community organizations.

Employ qualified school health service personnel.

Become informed about health problems of the school-age group.

Arrange the school day in accord with sound health practice.

Establish an effective system for keeping health records.

Establish a policy on school health examinations.

Provide for health observations by the teachers.

Establish a systematic referral program.

Promote measures to ensure services for every child in need of such services.

Institute program policies aimed at control of injuries and communicable diseases.

Procure necessary materials, time, facilities, and equipment for health instruction.

Appoint only qualified teachers for health instruction.

Provide a healthful and safe physical environment.

Ensure adequate food services.

Provide facilities, personnel, and an established plan to meet emergencies.

Provide health services for professional personnel.

Provide in-service health education for teachers.

Provide adequate faculty sick leave.

Enable communication between school counselors and the teachers and the school nurse.

Provide health promotion activities for teachers and staff.

Class Activities

Simulation 1

Situation   Your school district has decided to have teachers teach only health or physical education.

Write an advertisement to be placed in newspapers and professional journals to attract highly qualified applicants to teach in your district health education program.

Simulation 2

Situation   The school health program in your high school has been based on health instruction, healthful school living, and health services. The health education teachers feel that the program should be expanded to include the five additional components described in this chapter.

Call a meeting of the health educators in your school and write a paper for your principal explaining the advantages of emphasizing the five additional components.

Simulation 3

Situation   The district curriculum coordinator wants to have the health curriculum updated in light of current research in the field.

Form curriculum subcommittees and write a new health education curriculum guide for grades K–12.

Simulation 4

Situation   At a department meeting, the health educators indicated that the students were receptive to an activity approach to teaching health. More activities were needed for some topics. It was decided to construct additional games and activities for class use.

Schedule a workshop to construct a game or activity for each of the following topics:

Nutrition

Consumer health

Human growth and development

Feelings and emotions

Substance use and abuse

Indicate the appropriate grade level for each activity.

Performance Tasks

1. Survey high school students to find out what health topics are most important to them.
2. Design a questionnaire to give to classmates to determine attitudes toward drinking.
3. Visit a community health organization and determine whether its activities correlate with the health education program in the schools.
4. Make a transparency for each of the eight components of a health education program. On the transparency, outline what is encompassed by each component.
5. Interview a school nurse to find out what health services are offered for students in the school.
6. Describe the role of the health education specialist at the elementary level.
7. Give examples of how incidental health instruction can occur during an athletic contest or in a counseling session.
8. Write a newspaper article advocating increased emphasis on health education programs in schools to reach the health objectives of *Healthy People 2000.*
9. Debate this question: Should a health educator or a school nurse teach the topic of sex education?
10. Have half of the class present the case for having a health specialist serve as the school health coordinator and the other half support the position that it is better to have one person serve as the coordinator of both health education and physical education.
11. Have students write a paragraph describing what they see as the relationship of health education and physical education. Categorize the results and discuss.

References

Anspaugh, David J., and Gene Ezell, *Teaching Today's Health in Middle and Secondary Schools.* New York: Merrill Publishing, 1994.

Creswell, William H. Jr., and Ian M. Newman, *School Health Practice.* St. Louis: Mosby Yearbook, 1993.

Elders, M. Joycelyn, "Schools and Health: A Natural Partnership." *Journal of School Health,* September 1993, 63:312–315.

Feingold, Ronald S., "Health and Fitness in the Third Millennium." *International Journal of Physical Education,* 1993, 30:10–18.

Hahn, Dale B., and Wayne A. Payne, *Focus on Health.* St. Louis: Mosby, 1994.

Healthy People 2000-National Health Promotion and Disease Prevention Objectives. Full Report with Commentary. Washington, DC: U.S. Department of Health and Human Services, 1990.

Jones, Chester S., G. Greg Wojtiwicz, and Min Qi Wang, "School Health Education Curricula: The Case for Grade Level Differences." *Wellness Perspectives: Research, Theory and Practice,* Winter 1994, 10:70–75.

Kingery, Paul M., B. E. Pruitt, and Robert S. Hurley, "Adolescent Exposure to School Health Education: Factors and Consequences." *Journal of Health Education,* November/December 1993 Supplement, 24:42–46.

McGinnis, J. M., and Christopher DeGraw, "Healthy Schools 2000: Creating Partnerships for the Decade." *Journal of School Health,* September 1991, 61(7):292–296.

Pollock, Marion, and Kathleen Middleton, *School Health Instruction: The Elementary and Middle School Years.* St. Louis: Mosby, 1994.

School Health Education Study, *Health Education: A Conceptual Approach.* Washington, DC: School Health Study, 1965.

School Health Education Study, *Health Education: A Conceptual Approach to Curriculum Design.* Washington, DC: 3M Education Press, 1967.

Smith, Dennis, Laura K. McCormick, Allan B. Steckler, and Kenneth R.. McLeroy, "Teachers' Use of Health Curricula: Implementation of Growing Healthy, Project Smart, and the Teenage Health Teaching Modules." *Journal of School Health,* October 1993, 63:349–354.

Tillman, Kenneth G., and Patricia Rizzo Toner, *How to Survive Teaching Health.* West Nyack, NY: Parker Publishing, 1990.

Wiley, David, and Danny J. Ballard, "How Can Schools Help Children from Homeless Families?" *Journal of School Health,* September 1993, 63:291–293.

17

Leisure and Health Promotion Programs

Nonteaching Careers in Physical Education

A student studying movement and areas related to this domain has many career choices. No longer do all students who major in physical education plan to be physical education teachers. It is common for physical education departments to offer nonteaching tracks or majors as part of their program. This permits students to specialize in a program geared to working in many different, though related, fields. Nonteaching programs have expanded the offerings available in physical education and have increased the number of jobs and careers available for students who major in physical education.

Closely related to this trend is a change in the designation of the physical education department at many colleges and universities to reflect the broadened scope of the program. Terms such as *leisure studies, human performance, exercise science, health science, human kinetics, sport science, kinesiology, wellness,* and *health promotion* are all used to designate departments or other units that used to be labeled physical education. These departments include separate majors or distinct tracks within a major for students preparing for nonteaching career options.

Specialized components are included in nonteaching programs (majors or tracks) at colleges and universities. Although some of the foundation courses apply to all physical education majors, special physical education courses and supporting courses from outside the major form the curriculum for programs that prepare students for nonteaching careers. Health, physical education, and recreation are commonly grouped together in a department or school with specialists in each area. A similar situation has developed with the different nonteaching emphases found in physical education departments. A distinct curriculum with faculty who have expertise in the career field being studied are incorporated into the physical education department.

Students who have majored in physical education move into many different career positions. It is beyond the scope of this chapter to mention every conceivable position a physical education major is qualified to assume. For example, there are many highly specialized positions such as a nutrition consultant for a professional athletic team that are held by only a few people. This chapter covers leisure and health promotion programs that prepare students for a wide variety of positions in the following fields:

The fitness industry

Sport medicine

Recreation

Special programs

Sports

Dance

Challenge programs

Fitness Industry

The fitness industry has exploded on the scene throughout the world and it seems unlikely that its growth will slow. Chapter 16 points out the emphasis being placed on wellness in the United States. People want to feel good and look good and the fitness industry has responded with many types of programs and facilities that wouldn't have been thought possible even a decade ago. The desire for good health and escalating health costs are two factors that have contributed to rapid expansion of the fitness industry. Businesses provide fitness programs for their employees because they know good health increases productivity, reduces medical costs, and contributes to good staff morale. People join health and fitness clubs not only for the enjoyment they provide but also because they are seeking to improve or maintain their level of fitness. Organizations such as the YMCA, YWCA, Jewish Community Centers, and private clubs have increased the number of fitness programs they offer. *Prevention* has become a key word and as a result the medical profession, including hospitals, supports fitness programs of all types and in many cases even develops programs designed to prevent the onset of health problems.

The fitness industry has opened up many career possibilities for students. There are different types of fitness careers available in different settings. The fast-growing commercial field includes health clubs and fitness centers and the corporate or business field includes programs that are provided for employees in the private sector. Many community programs are provided by organizations in the community. This includes community recreation department programs as well as fitness programs offered by organizations such as Jewish Community Centers. Government units are also becoming more active in providing fitness programs for their employees. It is obvious that there is a wide range of settings in which fitness careers are possible. Several of the more prominent careers in the fitness industry follow.

Health Promotion

People have never been more conscious of their health. For this reason, career opportunities abound in the area of health promotion. Health promotion is a broad field that has several objectives. One of these is the imparting of information about wellness. Another is to assist people to understand the principles that underlie positive health and to help them adjust their lifestyles to incorporate these principles. The final step is to provide the environment, support, and programming that is conducive to behavior modification for improved health.

Many different types of positions are available in the health promotion field. Management, marketing, and public relations positions are found in all aspects of health promotion. In addition, there are many other jobs in the industry. A major one is the organization, development, and operation of physical fitness programs of many types. Rehabilitation programs are becoming another important facet of the health promotion field. Health promotion programs include opportunities to be involved with all aspects of wellness, including nutrition, smoking cessation, stress management, drug addiction, mental health, and behavior modification. Health education is an essential component of health promotion. The information in Chapter 16 is pertinent to careers in health promotion and covers other topics of health promotion. It can be said that the health promotion field covers any organized activity that is designed to upgrade personal and public health. The job possibilities are extensive.

Not only are there many career opportunities in health promotion but these careers are available in the private, government, and public sectors. Many of the positions are available in educational settings, both higher education and elementary and secondary. Corporate settings, private fitness centers, and health clubs all have experienced rapid growth and place a high priority on many different kinds of health promotion programs. Hospitals, recreation agencies, community organizations such as the YMCA, medical clinics, and health-related organizations such as the Diabetes Association all have programs designed for people with a broad background in health promotion or those who are specialists in one or two aspects of health promotion. Local, state, and federal government units are also expanding their health promotion programs. Jobs in the health promotion field are varied, as are locations and organizations where these jobs are available.

Health and Fitness Clubs

These privately run operations are called health clubs, fitness clubs, or fitness centers. Some are owned by individuals and some are part of a regional or national chain of clubs that specialize in physical fitness programs and include other programs geared to reaching a variety of health objectives for the clients.

Physical activity usually is the base for these clubs. Weight training facilities, aerobic activities, and sports such as tennis and racquetball are often offered as part of the fitness program at these clubs. A full range of responsibilities, ranging from budget to concessions to fitness measurement and evaluation to presenting classes, is included in these clubs. The size of the club determines the scope of a person's duties and how the duties are assigned to the different personnel. A large club may employ full-time specialists in exercise physiology whereas a small club may use consultants to fill this role. These clubs have been successful in presenting excellent fitness programs that attain the health objectives for their members. The programs must be good because the clubs are depend primarily on membership fees for continued existence.

Many large hotels and resort centers have also formed health and fitness clubs that use the available facilities such as swimming pools and exercise rooms. These clubs have a twofold purpose. One purpose is strictly financial: They are designed to make money for the hotel or resort. The second purpose is to make the hotel or resort more attractive to guests. Of course, the second purpose is also financial in nature but the health club does not have to generate as much money from the fees and other income of its operation. Programs provided for temporary users of the facilities differ from those offered to full-time club members. The number of professionals employed in these club programs is determined by the same factors that determine the number and type of health promotion personnel employed by private health and fitness clubs. Available facilities, extent of the program, and financial resources are some of the determining factors.

Corporate Fitness

Corporate fitness programs basically duplicate the programs of health and fitness clubs but they are sponsored by businesses for employees. Available positions are the same as those in health and fitness clubs although the fitness program may be organized around employee schedules and interests. Large companies are more likely to have diverse programs similar to those found in commercial health clubs. A corporate fitness program is designed to show support for employees and to provide activities that increase staff morale and productivity. The major goal of many corporate fitness programs is to reduce employee health costs. This means that they have a heavy emphasis on exercise programs, smoking cessation programs, weight control, stress management, and nutrition education, all of which can significantly improve the health of the participants.

Corporate fitness programs and health and fitness club programs are characterized by sophisticated assessment tools and individualized plans for participants. Modern exercise equipment placed in attractive facilities are important for success. The corporate fitness field has many career opportunities as it continues to expand both to new companies and within existing ones.

Management

There are many management roles to fill in the fitness industry. Management principles covered in Chapters 1 and 2 are particularly pertinent to management responsibilities in the fitness industry. Management encompasses the administrative planning and the implementation to reach the objectives of the organization, whether it be in a government, commercial, corporate, or community program. Program and facility management are two of the primary management categories.

Program   The top management person in many fitness settings is called a program manager. This person has overall responsibility for the fitness program of the corporation, medical facility, or community organization. Management tasks include setting up programs, supervising the operation of the programs, handling personnel matters, and arranging for or assuming responsibility for all the supportive activities needed to carry out these program responsibilities. These activities include office operations, staff supervision, budgeting, developing and carrying out promotional activities, maintaining facilities, scheduling activities, and purchasing supplies and equipment. Specifics involved in carrying out these many responsibilities are included in earlier chapters of this book.

Facility   In the commercial fitness field, the person who has administrative responsibility for all aspects of programming and operation of the facility commonly is called the facility manager. Duties include developing programs that appeal to the public and then carefully supervising these programs. Staffing, public relations, supervision, budgeting, developing staff training programs, and purchasing equipment are just some of the tasks that confront a facility manager. Because commercial fitness centers must make money to remain in business, a significant part of the facility manager's time and effort is spent on designing and implementing marketing and sales strategies. Facility managers are charged with controlling costs and increasing revenue. This becomes their overriding responsibility and all other administrative tasks are keyed to this charge. Facilities require constant attention. They must be attractive in order to appeal to the participants. They must also be safe and carefully maintained. One serious injury because of unsafe or poorly maintained equipment can have disastrous financial consequences for the fitness center or club. It is also critically important that the manager stay informed about new trends in facility design and facility construction. New materials come on the market regularly, as do other new products and designs used in facility construction. Renovations add another challenge for the facility manager. It is obvious that it takes special skills to manage a commercial fitness center. This is an extremely important role in this industry.

Health Fitness Instructors

These instructors teach the many health promotion courses offered in the different fitness programs described in this chapter. They may specialize in one or two areas or in smaller fitness centers they may need to be prepared to teach many different fitness activities. Examples of the activities that may be included are aerobics, yoga, nutrition courses, weight training, back care, and swimming. Any program that is offered must have highly qualified instructors. Not only must the instructors be skilled and knowledgeable in each area that is taught, but they must be able to design individual programs and use sophisticated assessment and evaluation tools if outcomes are to be determined accurately and the participants kept motivated.

Sport Medicine

The sport medicine field is assuming more and more importance as competitive intensity increases, more people participate in sport activities, liability concerns intensify, and serious sport injuries continue to occur. The prevention and treatment of sport injuries and the study of the functioning of the human body during and after physical exertion are key elements of the field of sport medicine. Students in the physical education track need in-depth study and practical experience to move to this career path.

Athletic Training

During the early years of interschool athletics, all athletic training was handled by coaches. This was not a satisfactory arrangement for several reasons. Coaching responsibilities interfered with the time that was needed to properly care for injuries. In many cases, insufficient attention was paid to prevention of athletic injuries. An added concern was the lack of preparation of many coaches to properly handle athletic training responsibilities. The athletic training field developed in response to the obvious need for well-prepared people who could devote their full attention to the prevention, evaluation, and care of injuries.

Athletic trainers have been an integral part of college and university athletic programs for many years. Secondary schools have just as great a need for qualified trainers and it is encouraging to note that the number of secondary schools that have qualified athletic trainers is increasing every year. The National Athletic Trainers' Association (NATA) has been instrumental in advancing the athletic training profession. The work of this organization has been the most important factor in promoting the employment of athletic trainers in secondary schools. At present, more than half of the states have some type of regulation for athletic trainers. These regulations are in the form of registration, exemption, licensure, or certification.

In 1991, the American Medical Association (AMA) officially recognized athletic training as an allied health profession. As a result, all entry-level athletic training education programs depend on the AMA's Committee on Allied Health Education and Accreditation for approval. This recognition by the AMA was an important step forward by the athletic training profession.

The National Athletic Trainers' Association has assumed an important leadership role in establishing standards for certification as an athletic trainer. The general requirements include the following:

A high school diploma and then directly supervised clinical hours that are required for certification

A baccalaureate degree from an accredited college or university in the United States

Proof of current American Red Cross Standard First Aid Certification and current basic CPR or equivalent

Verification that at least 25 percent of credited athletic training experience hours were fulfilled in actual (on location) practice or game coverage with one or more of the following sports: football, soccer, hockey, wrestling, basketball, gymnastics, lacrosse, volleyball, or rugby

Endorsement of certification application by an NATA Certified Athletic Trainer

Passing the certification examination, which includes written, oral practical, and written simulation sections. Competency is tested in prevention of injury, first aid and emergency care, rehabilitation and reconditioning, organization and administration, and education and counseling

Approved clinical experience can be attained either by successfully completing an NATA-approved athletic training program from a college or university or through satisfactory fulfillment of an internship program. An internship candidate must present documentation of at least 1,500 hours of athletic training experience under the direct supervision of an NATA-certified athletic trainer over a minimum of two and a maximum of five calendar years. At least 1,000 hours must have been attained in a traditional athletic setting.

Most athletic training positions in the past were in college and university athletic programs. Professional sports also employ athletic trainers and job opportunities are increasing in secondary school athletic programs. A recent growth area has been in sports medicine clinics. Job opportunities are also expanding in industrial settings, where the athletic trainer supervises fitness and injury rehabilitation programs for employees.

Physical Therapy

Physical therapists are part of the health care team. They test and measure functions of the musculoskeletal, neurological, pulmonary, and cardiovascular systems and treat physical problems caused by illness, injury, or birth defect. They work closely with other members of the health care team such as physicians, rehabilitation nurses, psychologists, occupational therapists, and social workers.

Physical therapy techniques include therapeutic exercises, cleaning of wounds, relaxation exercises, joint mobilization and range-of-motion movements, cardiovascular endurance training, biofeedback, therapeutic massage, pulmonary physical therapy, and ambulation training. Various modalities, including ultrasound, diathermy, traction, cryotherapy, hydrotherapy, electrotherapy, and laser therapy are used during treatment. There is an opportunity to specialize in various areas. The American Board of Physical Therapy Specialties recognizes seven specialty areas: cardiopulmonary, clinical electrophysiology, geriatrics, neurology, orthopaedics, pediatrics, and sports.

Physical therapy is a rapidly growing field and over 130 colleges and universities offer physical therapy entry-level education programs in the United States. The American Physical Therapy Association encourages students to enter the profession with a post-baccalaureate degree and, as a result, the majority of colleges and universities are changing their programs from a bachelor's degree to a post-baccalaureate degree program. Students need courses in psychology, biology, physics, chemistry, statistics, English, professional writing, and the humanities to enter a physical therapy education program. Prospective students should request materials from the school to which they plan to apply. They will then know the courses that are required for entrance and can include them in their undergraduate program.

To be licensed to practice, a physical therapist must graduate from an approved physical therapy program and secure a license by successfully completing the national licensure examination. In addition, the person must comply with all the legal requirements for the practice of physical therapy in the state or other jurisdiction where he or she intends to practice.

Exercise Specialist/Exercise Physiologist

Exercise specialists must have a strong scientific background. Careers for a person with this kind of a background used to be found primarily in college and university professional preparation programs. The fitness industry has opened up many additional career opportunities for the exercise specialist. Fitness clubs and fitness centers have exercise specialists who are responsible for exercise testing, assessment, and establishing protocols for individual exercise plans. This person serves as a fitness adviser for participants and evaluates progress and keeps clients motivated to remain on their exercise program and attain the goals they have set. The exercise specialist must also be able to lead exercise programs and be skilled in organizing groups.

There are advancement opportunities for the exercise specialist to move into management positions. Graduate study is important, as are advanced certifications in the exercise and fitness field. The American College of Sports Medicine (ACSM) has a number of highly respected programs that certify the exercise specialist for increasingly higher levels of responsibility. The ACSM certification requirements are in two tracks. One is the clinical track for the professional working in the preventive and rehabilitative exercise programs for people with cardiovascular, pulmonary, and metabolic diseases. The other is the health and fitness track, which is for professionals working in a health and fitness program for apparently healthy people who have no history of disease or who have controlled disease.

Clinical Track
ACSM exercise test technologist

ACSM exercise specialist

ACSM program director

Health and Fitness Track
ACSM exercise leader

ACSM health/fitness instructor

ACSM health/fitness director

Exercise Rehabilitation

Some exercise specialists emphasize rehabilitation techniques. These people work closely with physicians who provide exercise prescriptions for participants to follow. The exercise specialist designs programs based on the prescription and works closely with the person participating in the rehabilitation program. Clients range from those who are rehabilitating after open-heart surgery to those who have muscular weaknesses or postural deviations that are causing health problems.

Recreation

The field of recreation has a close relationship with physical education. Skills learned in physical education are used in all forms of recreation and the attitudinal and social objectives of both fields are complementary. Early in the development of the recreation profession, most recreation professionals entered the field with physical education backgrounds. Recreation is now a separate discipline that provides viable career opportunities for students who are not entering the teaching profession. Recreation is sometimes included in the administrative unit that includes physical education or it may be in a separate unit or allied with other disciplines. In any event, recreation has career opportunities encompassing skills closely associated with those required for teaching physical education or working in the fitness field. Movement is a core part of recreation and the person in recreation needs strong organizational skills and the ability to lead and interact with other people.

Students prepared in a traditional physical education program can find satisfying careers in different aspects of the recreation field. For example, a community recreation program has positions for people responsible for organizing and administering the sport activities that usually form an important part of a community recreation program. A physical educator who is an exercise specialist might develop exercise programs for older adults or direct an aquatic program for community organizations that provide recreational services. Many classifications of recreation use physical education competencies. Each of these classifications has career opportunities.

Community

Different community recreation programs use movement skills. Exercise and sport programs for all ages constitute an integral part of most recreational offerings. Leadership skills developed through physical education and leisure curricula also prepare students to enter the community recreation field.

Industrial

The emphasis in industrial recreation is now on fitness programs. An earlier section of this chapter covered corporate fitness programs that provide jobs in exercise and management positions. Businesses and industrial companies also employ people to organize and run sport programs and other types of activities for employees.

Commercial

Programs of fitness centers and health clubs were discussed earlier. There are also sport clubs and facilities such as tennis centers, golf driving ranges, ice rinks, and aquatic centers that open up career possibilities for students studying in the leisure and physical education curricula.

Institutional

Hospitals, youth correctional institutions, prisons, and psychiatric units are just some of the institutions that have nonteaching recreational positions available. Students with strong movement, sport skill, and leadership backgrounds are well-qualified to be part of recreational programs in these settings.

College and University

Careers in intramural and campus recreational programs are expanding. Intramurals are covered in Chapter 13. In many cases, intramurals have broadened their scope to encompass all campus recreational services or there is a separate office or administrative unit for broad-based recreation programs for students, faculty, staff, and administration. These programs normally have a strong fitness component to accompany other facets of the program such as sports, drama, music, and interest groups that cover an extensive array of subjects.

Programs Targeted for Select Groups

Unique recreational opportunities are available in the fields of therapeutic and urban recreation. The number of programs designed for disabled children and adults and for older adults is also expanding. Students who major in physical education or leisure studies are prepared to assume a variety of duties in these recreational spheres.

Public School and Community Cooperation

Professionals in the public schools have the opportunity to be involved in community recreation programs. They also have opportunities to focus career objectives on the recreational programs that evolve from cooperative efforts of the public school and the community.

One integral aspect of the community school concept is a joint endeavor by the school and community to provide recreational opportunities for community residents. Combined efforts to provide recreational activities have traditionally been present in communities even when other cooperative phases of a community school such as educational and social services have received only minimal attention. A major advantage of this approach is the reduction of program and administrative overlap and duplication. Better use is made of facilities because school facilities can be used for community recreation during times when they would otherwise be idle. The tax dollar can be stretched further to provide better recreational services for the community.

Improved facilities for both school and community use are possible because construction funds can be allocated where they are most needed and will not be spent for facilities that duplicate services. More effective use of available facilities is also a strength of school/community recreation programs.

School/community recreation can provide broad recreational programs that will be more comprehensive than would be possible if the community recreation department operates as a separate entity. Better use is made of staff and administrative resources and concentration can be placed on developing superior physical education and recreation programs that support and complement each other.

Whether the community's recreation program is administered separately or as part of a school board's responsibility, a close working agreement should be established to mutually benefit both the recreation department and the school system. Milwaukee, Wisconsin is an outstanding example of the latter administrative arrangement. The Division of Municipal Recreation and Adult Education is responsible to the Board of Education. This recreation program has gained worldwide recognition and provides ample evidence that school/community recreation programs can be an important factor in improving the quality of life of the members of the community.

Special Programs

Physical education relates closely to many other disciplines. For example, joint efforts with teachers of other subjects by physical educators have proven to be mutually beneficial. Motor development is an important ingredient in reading and writing readiness. Mathematical and spelling skills can be taught through movement education. Significant learning experiences occur when combining movement with music activities. Multicultural opportunities abound in physical education; for example, dances from different cultures can be used in history and social studies units covering these cultures. A biology unit on body systems can be effectively related to what occurs in a physical education class. There are also activity-oriented programs in some schools that are part of the physical education instructional program or private entities that contract with schools to provide programs, usually in the form of a mini unit for a week or perhaps a weekend. These programs are also offered on a private basis during weekends or vacation periods or after school. Most of the programs are designed for youth, although some provide programming for adults. This is a great career choice for students interested in working outdoors in a part of the leisure field that embraces personal challenges for the participants.

Outdoor Education

Outdoor education is not a separate discipline. It is a vehicle for learning. Through outdoor settings and experiences, children learn better than when they are limited to the indoors. Outdoor education makes use of the natural environment to assist in learning and emphasizes first-hand experiences. Outdoor education does not supplant classroom experiences, but cultivates and complements the indoor educational experiences. Certain aspects of every subject can be taught more effectively by using the outdoors.

Outdoor education takes many forms. One form is available to almost every teacher: the outdoors that exists just outside the school door. Good teachers make use of the school yard, a nearby park, or other recreational area on a regular basis to enrich the lessons they teach. An outdoor setting can provide a laboratory situation for most curricular areas and is ideally suited for the study of natural sciences and social studies. School sites should be designed with outdoor education in mind. A well-designed school site is pictured in Figure 17-1. It should be remembered that components of this excellent outdoor education setting are present or can be developed on many existing school sites.

> *Possible Uses of the Outdoor Education School Site Diagrammed in Figure 17-1*
> School building: basic schoolwork, laboratories, places to store materials found and used in the outdoors
>
> Water areas, including a pond and wetlands: acquaint students with water life and pollution and teach swimming and boating skills
>
> Camping area and picnic sites: overnight camping experiences to learn the art of outdoor cooking and living
>
> Athletics fields: crafts, sports, and recreational activities
>
> Horticultural areas (gardens, lawns, vegetation and shrubs): develop skills and knowledge related to home gardens, soil problems, seeds, fertilization, plants, and plant families
>
> Wooded areas: study principles of tree growth, identification of trees, animals, birds, and insects (a wildlife habitat and bird sanctuary), survival techniques, edible foods and plants, compass and map work
>
> Brook: provide information about origin, flow, and problems of rivers and plant and animal life found in streams
>
> Weather station: study weather, atmosphere, wind direction, temperature, and astronomy
>
> Rock garden: identification of rocks and minerals

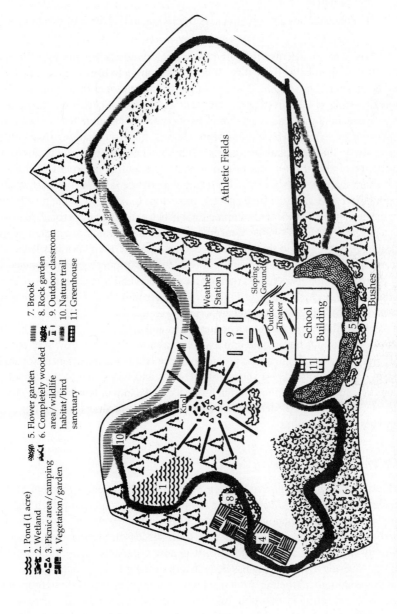

Legend:
1. Pond (1 acre)
2. Wetland
3. Picnic area/camping
4. Vegetation/garden
5. Flower garden
6. Completely wooded
   area/wildlife
   habitat/bird
   sanctuary
7. Brook
8. Rock garden
9. Outdoor classroom
10. Nature trail
11. Greenhouse

Athletic Fields

Weather Station

Sloping Ground

Outdoor Theater

School Building

Bushes

Knoll

FIGURE 17-1. School Site Designed for Outdoor Education
Designed by Elizabeth Wishna and Joyce Lykes

401

Outdoor classroom: study of outdoors as related to classroom activities

Outdoor theater

Nature trail throughout the entire site: observe and develop an appreciation for the wonders of nature

Greenhouse: observe seedlings, germination, and growth of plants inside

Day trips are also used effectively for outdoor education purposes. In some communities, these might be walking trips. It is more common to use buses to travel to a site related to the subject being taught. The site might be a geological formation, a forest area, a historical setting, a waterfront or any area that will make the classroom instruction come alive.

Residential camping is another form of outdoor education that has been enthusiastically endorsed by schools where it has been integrated into a comprehensive outdoor education program. In the typical residential camp, children have the opportunity to live for an extended period of time (usually one or two weeks) in an outdoor environment. Students and teachers share learning experiences. The camp experience is a focal point for school activities both before and after the time spent at the camp. In addition to the results directly related to the curriculum, residential camping establishes a significant personal relationship between teacher and pupil. Valuable concepts and understandings associated with our natural resources and living in the outdoors become a part of the children's lives. The incidental learnings are as important a feature of residential camping as is the planned instruction.

Some school districts own their own camps and children are sent to the camp on a rotating basis throughout the year. Failure to own a camp should not prevent a school district from implementing a residential camping program. Many federal, state, and regional facilities are available to schools at a nominal cost and private camp facilities can be rented. Private organizations have come into existence as a result of the growth of outdoor education programs. These organizations provide outdoor education experiences for students on a fee basis. They usually have a variety of offerings and will come to the school or provide an outdoor education experience through a residential camp or tent camping. The length of time devoted to these experiences depends on the desired outcomes and the types of experiences provided for the students.

Orienteering

This activity had its origin in Sweden, where there are many permanent trails used for orienteering. The activity starts in the early grades and continues through high school. There are specified days when the entire school goes orienteering and during the winter months participants use cross-country skis. Due to its success in Sweden, it soon became a favorite activity in Norway and Finland also. It is now popular in many European countries and North America. Orienteering has been incorporated into some outdoor education programs on this continent, particularly the residential camping aspect of these programs. The potential for orienteering is enormous and it is expected to dramatically increase in popularity.

Orienteering was started to encourage young people to make use of forests for physical and mental enjoyment. The intent was to use the natural environment to stimulate youth to do more running. Courses were established through whatever terrain was available and by the use of a map and compass, participants traversed the course.

Orienteering has become very competitive and yet it provides an opportunity for all ages and all levels of ability. The length of the course and the choice of terrain can be changed to provide a challenging activity for everyone, regardless of their competence. Age group competition and divisions based on skill equalize competition in orienteering events. There is a personal challenge present that allows a person to enjoy orienteering even though the individual times of competitors might vary considerably.

Orienteering puts a premium on map and compass reading. There are usually six to ten control points that must be passed in a designated order. In addition to the challenge of correctly determining the location of the control points, the competitors search out the best route to reach the control points. Sometimes this is a direct route; other times, a detour to miss obstacles such as a swamp or a steep hill is best. The route to follow differs from person to person. A fast runner might choose a longer path that has more open area in which to run whereas a slower contestant might use a more direct route that allows better use of other talents such as the ability to negotiate rock outcroppings.

Orienteering provides a mental as well as a physical challenge. Its adaptability to all ages and skill levels has made it a very popular activity. An important added dimension is the premium it places on map reading and compass skills.

Outward Bound

The first Outward Bound school was established in Wales in 1941. Since that time, it has expanded to other countries and has found acceptance by people from many walks of life. The emphasis of this program is on character training and is based on the premise that putting a person in a challenging situation brings out positive reactions to subsequent situations that are encountered. Each Outward Bound school in the United States provides a unique type of physical challenge. Some aspect of the environment, whether it be a climatic condition or geography of the area, is used to provide a challenge to the participants. Emphasis is placed on such skills as mountaineering, rock climbing, whitewater canoeing, and snow camping.

Several programs patterned after Outward Bound have come into existence. Their aims are similar. Participants are expected to gain a greater understanding of themselves by experiencing challenging situations that they must overcome individually or as a member of a group. Group work and problem solving are heavily emphasized. The intent is to develop not only personal skills but a spirit of cooperativeness with others. Many problems that are presented can be solved only by joint efforts.

Personal development and social awareness are additional objectives of these programs. Participants find that they are capable of doing much more than they thought they could do. Increased self-confidence and the ability to relate positively to others are important outcomes.

Adventure Education

Many of the elements of Outward Bound are contained in adventure education programs that are being enthusiastically received by students. In more and more schools, outdoor adventure education is being incorporated into the physical education program. Challenge activities form an integral part of adventure education and ropes, cables, and wooden structures are commonly used to provide challenges. Overcoming fears and developing self-confidence are key outcomes of adventure programs.

Physical challenges form the core of adventure education experiences. Rock climbing, scaling walls, climbing trees, and caving are just some of the activities that are successfully used for this purpose. Learning new skills such as winter camping, canoeing, cross-country skiing, and backpacking open up exciting new vistas for students. Educational goals remain the same for students participating in adventure programs but the means by which these goals are attained are different. Unique learning opportunities are provided by the physically challenging activities that make up adventure education.

The physically challenging activities are just one part of an adventure education program. Students also interact with each other in activities that are as mentally challenging as walking on a cable strung between two trees 50 feet above the ground is physically and emotionally challenging. Students learn to trust each other and the skills of problem solving, cooperation, teamwork, and communication unfold as students work together to complete the challenges that are presented.

Personal development is an easily observed outcome of adventure education programs. Social skills evolve and greater understanding of the self and others comes from this type of experience. Adventure situations offer ideal settings for teacher–student interaction. Teachable opportunities in all domains—psychomotor, affective, and cognitive—abound.

Special preparation is required for those who teach adventure education programs. A teacher must be able to demonstrate and participate in physically strenuous activities. Just as important are the skills needed to use outdoor adventure settings for instruction. Finally, finely tuned interpersonal skills are needed to relate to students as individuals and within group settings to nurture desired social skills and self-esteem.

There are also adventure programs found outside the education field. Many recreation agencies, youth organizations, resorts, and hospitals also sponsor these programs. In addition, a number of privately run commercial programs offer adventure experiences for schools, colleges, universities, troubled youth, businesses, organizations, families, and even individuals. Businesses have found that a program such as this develops teamwork and is a good group-building process. Educational institutions have used adventure experiences for incoming students to build friendships, overcome personal fears about beginning a new experience, and develop self-confidence. Adventure programs are valuable for both individuals and groups.

Dance

Students interested in dance who want to make a career in this field usually intend to teach in an educational setting. However, there are several other career possibilities in dance. Dance therapy requires a special kind of expertise combining dance with medical and psychological preparation. Dance is used as a treatment for various types of disorders. This is not a large field but is a challenging career for those who choose to move in this direction.

Private dance schools provide another career path for a person interested in dance. Teaching, directing of performances, choreography, and management roles are possible in these schools. For select few, a career as a dance performer is possible. For most, people combining performance with work in a dance school or giving private lessons is a more likely scenario.

Sport

Highly competitive but expanding career opportunities are available for those who do not want to teach but want to be involved with sport in some capacity. Many of the positions that are available are part-time or even seasonal in nature. The field is growing with educational programs that prepare students to move into full-time sport careers.

Sport Management

As in any industry, management positions are available in all levels of the sport industry. These positions range from local programs for amateur sports to professional sports on the national level. There are management positions with amateur sport organizations. Most amateur sports are represented by national organizations and for some sports there are also state or regional organizations. There are private clubs such as gymnastic, tennis, and golf clubs and commercial entities such as ski resorts, ice skating rinks, and aquatic centers. Sport management opportunities are found in community recreation departments, social agencies, and some corporations and companies. There are also a number of positions available in college and university athletic departments and with professional sports teams. Professional teams are established on many levels, with minor leagues supporting the major leagues in sports such as basketball, baseball, and ice hockey. Sport occupies an important niche in North American countries and this has led to the formation of semiprofessional as well as professional teams in many different sports. All of these teams need people with sport management skills. Management skills and responsibilities are covered in Chapters 1 and 2 and the role of program and facility managers in the fitness industry covered earlier in this chapter is also pertinent for sport managers.

Sport Marketing and Promotion

These are management responsibilities but they are listed separately because these positions have a high priority in the sport industry. Money must be generated not only for a successful operation but even for continued existence of an existing organization, team, or program. Marketing and promotion are key factors in attaining success with a sport franchise, a sport facility, or any other sport business.

Sport Journalists

This career can move in different directions. There are careers in the print media, television, and radio. In smaller communities, some of the positions in the sport media field begin as part-time positions. Specialized preparation is particularly needed to break into television reporting. Most colleges and universities also have sport journalists who publicize the athletic programs at the institution, develop team brochures, keep statistics and records, and provide information requested by the media. The sport information director (SID) has a challenging, highly important role and in large programs numerous staff members are needed to carry out the SID functions. Although a different term such as *publicist* or *public relations director* might be used, professional teams also place heavy reliance on an information director and staff.

Sport Facility Management

Communities, private groups, colleges and universities, and professional teams all have facilities that must be managed. This has become a highly specialized aspect of sport management and larger complexes require large staffs of people with specialized skills to manage their facilities. There are also positions with private management groups that are hired to manage facilities. All management skills that have been discussed previously are required of a facility manager. Adeptness in interacting with the public, a strong financial background, negotiating skills, and the ability to organize and direct a variety of activities are especially important skills for a sport facility manager.

Sport Organizations

Positions with groups such as Special Olympics and youth sport organizations such as Babe Ruth and Little League are also viable career avenues.

Sport Clubs and Camps

Tennis, racquetball, swimming, ski, and golf clubs employ people for a variety of teaching and management positions. This is a fast-growing field with many career opportunities in an extensive number of sports. The type of sport clubs found in a community varies with community interests, geographical area, socioeconomic situation, and government and private support and promotion. Sport camps are an important phenomenon on the sport scene. They are often seasonal. During the summer, many positions are available at private sport camps and at camps operated by colleges and universities. Some private camps have their own facilities but there are more and more private groups that organize the programs and rent facilities for their camps.

Sport Equipment

The sporting goods industry is a huge business with many careers opportunities. Retail sales positions are entry-level means of moving into management positions. There are also opportunities in the manufacturing, safety, and design of equipment. Sport equipment repair and maintenance is another subfield of the sport equipment industry.

Coaching

Apart from the higher levels of amateur sports or coaching on the professional level, most coaching positions are either on a part-time basis or are with college and university programs. Some coaching positions at smaller colleges and universities include teaching or other responsibilities, whereas larger athletic programs have full-time coaching positions. Coaching positions are also available with swimming clubs, gymnastic clubs, soccer clubs, and other sport clubs. Many coaching positions with community programs are volunteer positions but they do provide experience that will assist in obtaining a part-time or even a full-time coaching position. Most of the coaching positions are for specific sports but there are some strength coaching positions available with sport teams and at the higher levels of competition, sport psychologists are also employed.

Officiating

Having a full-time officiating position is a remote possibility. There are a limited number of such positions, primarily in professional baseball, basketball, and ice hockey. The road to these positions is long, arduous, and highly competitive. There are many opportunities to officiate on a part-time basis at the recreational, high school, university, and semiprofessional levels of competition.

Summary

The leisure, health promotion, and sport fields offer numerous career opportunities for students. This chapter has covered a number of professions that are available in the sport, leisure, and health promotion sphere but it is not an all-inclusive list. As the fields keep expanding, it can be assumed that an increasing number of career opportunities will present themselves. The diversity of jobs is also expected to increase as new frontiers are opened.

People are concerned about their health and health issues demand attention at all government levels and at the personal level. There will be even more emphasis on health promotion in the future. Closely allied to health promotion are other leisure programs that have been presented in this chapter. These programs will also continue to be viable career paths.

The public love of sport shows no sign of diminishing. Sport at all levels continues to develop and offers exciting career possibilities.

The administrative principles covered earlier in this book apply to the duties of administrators in the leisure, health promotion, and sport fields as well as those in health education, intramurals, and physical education. Facilities, liability, budgeting, evaluation, purchasing of equipment, public relations, and office management are examples of areas of concern that demand close attention and skillful application of administrative techniques. Although each program has its own uniqueness, there is a shared commonality in management procedures.

Class Activities

Simulation 1

Situation   A large corporation in your community is planning to initiate a health promotion program. They will employ a professional in the health promotion field to start and administer the program.

Write a proposal to the president of the corporation outlining the health promotion program you would recommend for the corporation. Describe the program and the way you would administer it for the first year.

Simulation 2

Situation   A high school has decided to include a six-week adventure education program as part of its ninth-grade physical education program.

Research adventure education programs by sending for literature and obtaining course outlines from physical education programs that have programs in place. From this information, develop a model six-week adventure program.

Simulation 3

Situation   There are several senior citizen groups in your community that meet on a regular basis. They have many trips, play cards, attend concerts, and participate in nonphysical activities.

Option 1: Design an exercise program for the senior citizen groups. Present your first day exercise routine to another class or group of students and have a follow-up critique.

Option 2: Contact the director of the senior citizen groups and arrange to run a pilot exercise program with one of the groups.

Simulation 4

Situation   A facility manager must be sure that equipment is attractive and in safe working order.

Option 1: Inspect the physical education or athletic facilities and equipment at your university. Write a report with recommendations to improve safety and attractiveness of the facilities and equipment.

Option 2: Visit a commercial health, fitness, or recreational facility. Note appealing features of the facility and its equipment. Compile a list of the features that can guide facility managers for all types of sport facilities. Note: This simulation can also be used for Chapters 7 and 8.

Performance Tasks

1. Observe an athletic trainer for several days and during one athletic contest. Describe the special skills that are required of an athletic trainer.
2. Visit an adventure program and participate in the program.
3. Contact the recreation directors in four communities. Find out what relationship their programs have to the public schools in the community.
4. Plan an outdoor education program for your elementary school.
5. Interview two high school athletic trainers and summarize their duties.
6. Design an orienteering program for a school or recreation program.
7. Organize a panel discussion for all interested students on the topic of careers in the leisure and health promotion field. Invite guest speakers to represent different careers.
8. Develop a manual on job opportunities in the fitness industry in your community. Visit hotels, businesses, health and fitness clubs and other organizations that have fitness programs to gather the information.
9. Collect information from the American College on Sports Medicine (ACSM) on their certification programs. Make a poster showing certification requirements and job responsibilities for each certification.

10. Members of the class meet with professionals in career fields covered in this chapter and report back to the class on job responsibilities and suggested procedures for entry into the profession.

References

Anderson, Marcia K., "Women in Athletic Training." *Journal of Physical Education, Recreation and Dance,* March 1992, 63:42–44.

Arnheim, Daniel D., *Modern Principles of Athletic Training,* 8th ed. St. Louis: Mosby, 1992.

Association for Fitness in Business, *Guidelines for Employee Health Promotion Programs.* Champaign, IL: Human Kinetics, 1992.

Bryan, Jean M., Gary D. Geroy, and Susan J. Isernhagen, "Nonclinical Competencies for Physical Therapists Consulting with Business and Industry." *The Journal of Orthopaedic and Sports Physical Therapy,* December 1993, 18:673–681.

Casey, Ann, "Title IX and Women Officials—How Have They Been Affected?" *Journal of Physical Education, Recreation and Dance,* March 1992, 63:45–47.

Catlin, Sherry, "Bringing Dollars in the Door." *Ideas Today,* February 1993, 11:23–26.

Clark, Dawn, "Voices of Women Dance Educators: Considering Issues of Hegemony and the Educator, Performer Identity." *Impulse,* April 1994, 2:122–130.

Fisher, A. Craig, Kent C. Scriber, Michael L. Matheny, Mark H. Alderman, and Laurie A. Bitting, "Enhancing Athletic Injury Rehabilitation Adherence." *Journal of Athletic Training,* Winter 1993, 28:312–318.

Fisher, Shirley P., and Charles E. Hill, "Development and Implementation of a Pilot Wellness Program in a College Setting." *The Reporter,* Spring 1992, 65:16–18.

Gass, Michael A., and Ted Williamson, "Accreditation for Adventure Programs." *Journal of Physical Education, Recreation, and Dance,* January 1995, 66:22–27.

Gerson, Richard, *Marketing Health/Fitness Services.* Champaign, IL: Human Kinetics, 1989.

Hill, Charles E., and Shirley P. Fisher, "Professional Preparation in Health Promotion." *Journal of Physical Education, Recreation and Dance,* November/December 1992, 63:58–62.

Hooper, Jacqueline, and Louis Veneziano, "A University Employee Physical Activity Incentive Program: Initial Participation Results." *Wellness Perspectives: Research, Theory, and Practice,* Spring 1994, 10:45–53.

Jenkins, Richard D., "Where the Jobs Are Today." *Dance Magazine,* January 1994, 68:58–59.

Kraus, Richard, "Tomorrow's Leisure: Meeting the Challenges." *Journal of Physical Education, Recreation and Dance,* April 1994, 65:42–47.

Luckner, John, "Effective Skills Instruction in Outdoor Adventure Education." *Journal of Physical Education, Recreation and Dance,* January 1994, 65:57–61.

Minkler, Meredith, "Challenges for Health Promotion in the 1990s: Social Inequities, Empowerment, Negative Consequences, and the Common Good." *American Journal of Health Promotion,* July/August 1994, 8:403–412.

Opatz, Joseph, *Economic Impact of Worksite Health Promotion.* Champaign, IL: Human Kinetics, 1994.

Parkhouse, Bonnie L., *The Management of Sport: Its Foundation and Application.* St. Louis: Mosby, 1991.

Parks, Janet B., and Beverly R.K. Zanger (eds.), *Sport and Fitness Management.* Champaign, IL: Human Kinetics, 1990.

Patton, Robert W.,William C. Grantham, Richard F. Gerson, and Larry R. Gettman., *Developing and Managing Health/Fitness Facilities.* Champaign, IL: Human Kinetics, 1989.

Pelletier, Kenneth R., "Getting Your Money's Worth: The Strategic Planning Program of the Stanford Corporate Health Program." *American Journal of Health Promotion,* May/June 1994, 8:323–327.

Wankel, Leonard M., "Health and Leisure: Inextricably Linked." *Journal of Physical Education, Recreation and Dance,* April 1994, 65:28–31.

Wilson, Bradley R. A., and Timothy E. Glaws, *Managing Health Promotion Programs.* Champaign, IL: Human Kinetics, 1994.

Wissen, Bill, "Administration of a Comprehensive Sports Medicine Program." *Texas Coach,* September 1993, 38:46–47.

Methods of Organizing Competition

The kind of tournament to be used is determined by a number of factors. The type of activity, the amount of time, the facilities and equipment that are available, the purpose of the competition, the age of the participants, the number of entries, and the availability of officials must all be considered when selecting a tournament. The criteria for a tournament to be used in a class situation differ from the criteria for an intramural tournament, which in turn differ from standards used to choose a tournament for interscholastic or intercollegiate competition. All types of tournaments have strong and weak points; some serve one purpose well and others serve another.

For interscholastic and intercollegiate competition, the rules governing play for each sport should be consulted for additional scheduling and tournament regulations and information.

Elimination Tournaments

This type of tournament involves the elimination of all competitors until only one winner remains. There are basically five types of elimination tournaments.

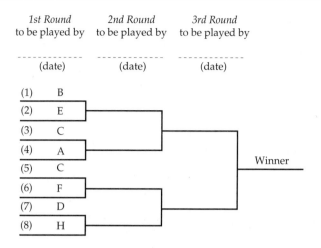

FIGURE A-1. Single Elimination Tournament

Single Elimination

The single elimination tournament is the least desirable because it emphasizes the *elimination* of teams and players. For example, in this type of tournament one half of the competitors are eliminated after their first contest. Furthermore, because a single defeat eliminates a contender, the eventual winner often is not the best team or player, nor is the defeated finalist necessarily the second-best team or player because one of the teams or players in the other half of the bracket may be superior. However, despite these disadvantages, there is a place for the single elimination tournament. It is short and selects a winner quickly. It is interesting to watch and can be conducted with limited facilities and a large number of entries. The use of the single elimination tournament is justified when the time available is limited.

The first step in arranging a single elimination tournament is to draw for positions. The positions in the brackets are numbered, and each team or player takes the position indicated by the number drawn, as in Figure A–1. In the tournament shown, the location of each team was determined by the number drawn. Thus, the captain or representative of Team B drew #1; the representative of Team A drew #4, and so forth.

When the number of entrants is not an even power of two (that is, 2, 4, 8, 16, 32, etc.) "byes" must be arranged so as to avoid having an uneven number of teams or players left to compete in future rounds. *All the byes must be placed in the first round.* The competition is less intense in the first round, and a rest before play does not provide the same advantage as a rest after a game or two. The number of byes must be sufficient to ensure a number of contestants for the second and each succeeding round that is an even power of two. This is accomplished by subtracting the total number of entrants from the next higher power of two. For example, with eleven entrants, subtract 11 from the next higher power of two, which is 16. This leaves 5, which is the number of byes. The total number of entrants (eleven) minus the five byes leaves six contestants to play each other in the first round. Three will lose, leaving eight contestants in the second round. As 8 is an even power of two, only two teams will now meet in the final round. The byes should be distributed as evenly as possible between the upper and lower brackets. If there are an uneven number of byes, the extra bye is usually placed in the lower half of the bracket. Figure A-2 shows a sample bracket for thirteen teams.

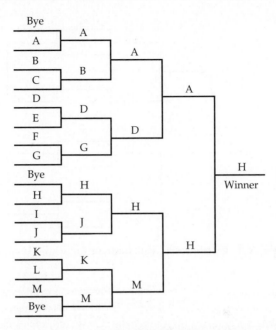

FIGURE A-2. Single Elimination Bracket for Thirteen Teams

Seeding is a process used to place the competitors who are considered superior, by virtue of previous performance, current record, or reputation, in separate brackets or as far apart as possible in the same bracket in order to ensure that they do not meet in the early rounds. With two seeded entries, one should be placed at the top of the upper bracket and the other at the bottom of the lower bracket. If four entrants are to be seeded, the third should be placed at the top of the lower bracket and the fourth at the bottom of the upper bracket. If there are byes, the seeded players get them in the order of their ranking. Thus, number one gets the first bye, number two the second, and so on. No team or player ever receives more than one bye. Seeding should be used only when the previous record of the teams or players justifies it.

The number of games in a single elimination tournament is always one less than the number of entries. Thus, with thirteen teams entered, 12 games would be required to complete the tournament. The number of rounds required is equal to the power to which two must be raised to equal or exceed the number of entries. With 13 entrants, 4 rounds are necessary to complete the competition.

Consolation Elimination Tournament

This type of tournament is superior to the single elimination in that it permits each team to play at least twice. A good team that has been eliminated by the champion in the first round may continue to play, with a chance to win secondary honors. More games are involved, and greater player interest is engendered.

There are two general types of consolation elimination tournaments. In the first type, all the losers in the first round (or those who lose in the second round after drawing a bye in the first round) play another single-elimination tournament. The winner of this second

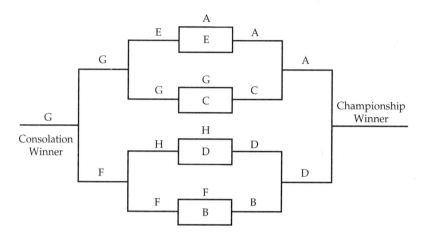

FIGURE A-3. Consolation Tournament for Eight Teams (First Type)

tournament is the consolation winner. Figure A-3 is an example of the manner in which a consolation tournament of this type with no byes is arranged. Figure A-4 illustrates the manner in which a consolation tournament that includes byes can be arranged.

A second type of consolation tournament provides an opportunity for any loser to win the consolation championship, regardless of the round in which the loss was sustained. Figure A-5 is an example of this second type of consolation tournament.

Double-Elimination Tournament

This is a tournament in which a player or a team must be beaten twice to be eliminated; the play continues until all but one have been twice defeated. The double-elimination tournament is a step in the direction of a round-robin tournament and selects a more adequate winner. It provides for at least twice as much play as in a single-elimination tournament and maintains maximum interest. A double-elimination tournament of eight teams will involve either 14 or 15 games (Figure A-6). The formula for determining the minimum number of games in a double-elimination tournament is $2(n - 1)$ and the formula for the maximum number is $2(n - 1) + 1$.

Bagnall–Wild Elimination Tournament

This is a modified form of the elimination type of tournament. Its strong point is the selection of true second- and third-place winners; its weakness is the delay following the first round before those who are to try for second or third places can be matched. It should be used when second and third places are of particular significance or when a point system is in operation and points are awarded for these places.

First place is determined by means of straight elimination play. To determine second place, all the competitors defeated by the two finalists compete against each other in a consolation elimination tournament, the winner of which plays the defeated finalist for second place. In Figure A-7, K defeats A and so is the second-place winner. If A had defeated H in the championship contest, no further competition would have been necessary because H

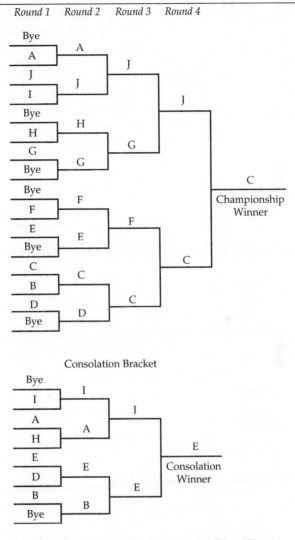

Round 1   Round 2   Round 3   Round 4

FIGURE A-4. Consolation Tournament for Ten Teams (First Type)

had already defeated K. Competitor H would be the second-place finisher and K the third-place finisher.

The playoffs for second and third place should not await the playing of the finals match. As soon as it is determined that Teams A and H are to be the finalists, the elimination competition should begin. Thus, before the finals, Teams B and F and G and I should play matches. This reduces the amount of play after the winning finalist has been determined.

In a more complex form of the Bagnall–Wild tournament, second- and third-place winners are not determined until the semifinal loser to the first-place winner has defeated the winners of the consolation competition shown in Figure A-8.

If the defeated finalist (Team A) loses in the match for second place, Team K becomes second-place winner. This automatically leaves Team A the third-place winner.

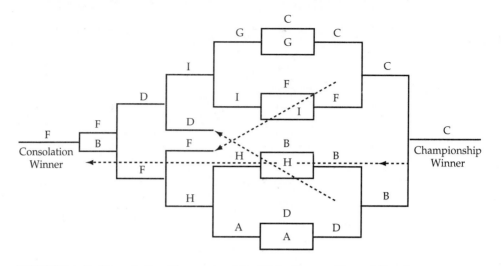

FIGURE A-5. Consolation Tournament for Eight Teams (Second Type)

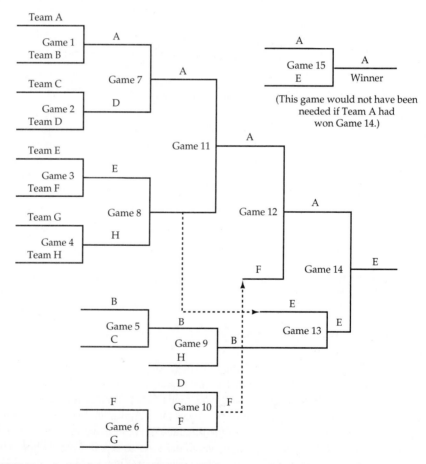

FIGURE A-6. Double-Elimination Tournament for Eight Teams

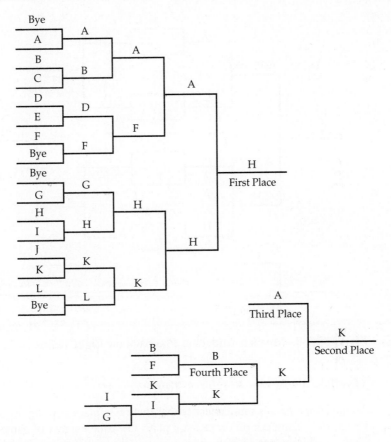

FIGURE A-7. Bagnall–Wild Tournament for Twelve Teams

A variation of the Bagnall–Wild tournament is commonly used for wrestling tournaments. If six places are to be awarded, consolation rounds start among all contestants defeated by the winner of each quarterfinal round. At the conclusion of the championship semifinals, the losers are cross-bracketed into the consolation semifinals so they do not meet a wrestler they wrestled earlier.

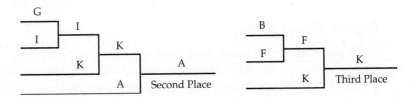

FIGURE A-8. Bagnall–Wild Alternate Method of Determining Second and Third Places

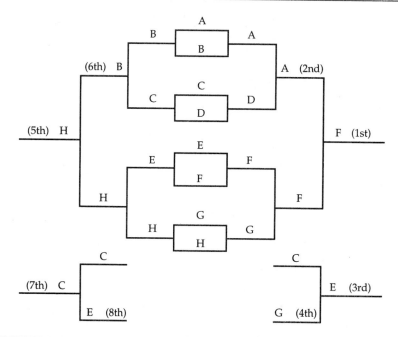

FIGURE A-9. Mueller–Anderson Playback for Eight Teams

Mueller–Anderson Playback Tournament

An advantage of this tournament is that there is a place ranking for all entries. Another advantage is that each player or team plays the same number of games. This tournament requires a longer period of time to complete than does a single-elimination tournament. Although there might be some loss of interest on the part of losing teams, enthusiasm remains high as there is motivation to finish the tournament with as high a ranking as possible. Figure A-9 illustrates an eight-team tournament with a place ranking of each team.

Round-Robin Tournaments

If sufficient time and facilities are available, the round-robin tournament is the best type of tournament to use. It produces a true winner, ranks the other competitors, permits all participants to continue play until the end, and does not require one contestant to wait until others have played the next round.

Regular Round Robin

In the round-robin tournament, each team or player plays each other competitor in the league. In a single round robin, one game is played with each other team or player; in a double round robin, two games are played with each of the opponents.

The positions of the teams at the end of a round-robin tournament are determined by percentages. Each team's percentage is obtained by dividing the number of games won by the total games played. For example, if a team played eight games and won seven, its percentage

TABLE A-1

Round 1	Round 2	Round 3	Round 4	Round 5	Round 6	Round 7
⬅ 1 vs. 8 ⬆	1 vs. 7	1 vs. 6	1 vs. 5	1 vs. 4	1 vs. 3	1 vs. 2
2 vs. 7	8 vs. 6	7 vs. 5	6 vs. 4	5 vs. 3	4 vs. 2	3 vs. 8
3 vs. 6	2 vs. 5	8 vs. 4	7 vs. 3	6 vs. 2	5 vs. 8	4 vs. 7
⬇ 4 vs. 5 ➡	3 vs. 4	2 vs. 3	8 vs. 2	7 vs. 8	6 vs. 7	5 vs. 6

would be .875. In cases of tie games, the customary procedure is not to count such contests as games played when the percentages are computed. A better plan is to count a tie as half a victory and half a defeat. Thus, a team that wins seven games, loses four, and ties one would have a percentage of .625 (7.5 ÷ 12).

The British and Canadian systems of determining team standings in round-robin tournaments are somewhat different. In the Canadian system, two points are awarded for each victory and one point for each tie. Thus, if a team wins twelve games, loses three, and ties one, its total points would be 25. The team with the greatest point total is the winner. The British carry this one step further. They determine points as in the Canadian system, but the point total obtained is then divided by the total possible points (total games played multiplied by two). In the example just given, the team's percentage would be .781 (25 ÷ 32).

The formula for determining the total number of games to be played in a round-robin tournament is $n(n-1)/2$, with n representing the number of teams in the tournament. Substituting for n in an 8-team league, the formula is $8(8-1)/2$, or 28 games. Because 8 teams are involved, 8 is used; because each team plays every team but itself, 8 minus 1 is used; and because it takes two teams to play one game, it is necessary to divide by two.

To draw up a round-robin schedule, place as many numbers as there are teams in two vertical columns. The numbers should be arranged consecutively down the first column and up the second. With each number representing a team, this arrangement provides the pairing for the first round. Thus, Team #1 plays Team #8; Team #2 plays #7; Team #3 plays #6, and Team #4 plays #5 in the first round. To obtain pairings for subsequent rounds, rotate the numbers *counterclockwise* around one of the numbers that remains fixed. In the example given in Table A-1, number 1 is fixed, with the other numbers rotated around it.

When an uneven number of teams is entered, the same plan is used. However, in this case the bye should be placed in one of the positions and the other numbers rotated about it. The number opposite the bye signifies the team that receives the bye in that particular round. In the example given in Table A-2, the bye is placed in the upper left-hand corner and the other numbers are rotated *counterclockwise* around it. Another method of drawing up a round robin tournament is illustrated in Figure A-10. Schedules for even numbers of teams follow one general plan; those for odd numbers of teams do likewise except that the schedule is drawn for the next greater even number and the last vertical column to the right represents the byes.

The letters in Figure A-10 represent teams, and the numbers playing days. Numbers at the intersections of the vertical and horizontal columns indicate that the team represented in the columns concerned play on the playing day indicated by the number. That is, 7 on vertical F and horizontal C means F plays C on the seventh playing day; likewise, E plays

TABLE A-2

Round 1	Round 2	Round 3	Round 4	Round 5	Round 6	Round 7
Bye 7	Bye 6	Bye 5	Bye 4	Bye 3	Bye 2	Bye 1
1 vs. 6	7 vs. 5	6 vs. 4	5 vs. 3	4 vs. 2	3 vs. 1	2 vs. 7
2 vs. 5	1 vs. 4	7 vs. 3	6 vs. 2	5 vs. 1	4 vs. 7	3 vs. 6
3 vs. 4	2 vs. 3	1 vs. 2	7 vs. 1	6 vs. 7	5 vs. 6	4 vs. 5

B on the fifth playing day. These relationships can be noted in the arrangement of the numbers in the schedule. All numbers are in regular order except those in the last column to the right (1 following 7 is in regular order when 7 is the largest number). The last column to the right starts with the largest odd number, then goes to the smallest even number and on up through the even numbers in order, then starts with the smallest odd number and continues through the remaining odds in order. The numbers in this last vertical column, except the first and last, are always one less than the first number in the horizontal column.

The Lombard Round Robin

The Lombard tournament is a unique form of round-robin competition in which the entire tournament is completed in a day or several hours. This is accomplished by playing abbreviated contests. This type of tournament should not be thought of as a substitute for regular round-robin competition. Rather, it is a special type of tournament that can be used effectively under certain conditions.

Assuming a tournament of 17 basketball teams and a playing time of 32 minutes, which is the customary length of high school basketball games, the tournament works as follows. Each team meets every other team and plays 16 short games. Therefore, divide 32 by 16 to give the length of time of these abbreviated games, which is exactly two minutes. Eight courts and sufficient officials to conduct eight games at a time are desirable but teams can play on a rotating basis if fewer courts are available. Each team is assigned a scorer, who keeps a record of its scores for all games in one column and scores of all opponents in another. If possible, all teams start play at one time, play two minutes, and shift to another court to play another opponent until a complete round robin tournament of two-minute games is played. The scores for each team are totaled for the 16 games. The opponents' score is then subtracted from each team's own score to determine place winners. In some Lombard tournaments, the two teams with the best record play a regulation game for the championship. Another variation is to have the four teams with the largest positive scores play a regular round-robin tournament at some future date. In the event of a tie for fourth place after the first round robin of two-minute periods, the tying teams play for the right to enter the final tournament.

During World War II, the Lombard tournament, used somewhat differently from that indicated above, was extensively and effectively used in the army. Its great value lay in the fact that an entire round-robin tournament could be completed within several hours. For example, a Lombard round-robin tournament in basketball in a league of 12 teams (66 games) can be completed in less than 4 hours if two courts are available and 6-minute games are played. If more courts are available, the time can be further reduced. The Lombard tournament works successfully with 6–12 teams playing on two or three courts. In this way, teams alternate playing and players have a chance to rest. For this reason, it is an excellent

Eight-Team Schedule

	A	B	C	D	E	F	G	H
A		1	2	3	4	5	6	7
B			3	4	5	6	7	2
C				5	6	7	1	4
D					7	1	2	6
E						2	3	1
F							4	3
G								5
H								

Nine-Team Schedule

	A	B	C	D	E	F	G	H	I	Bye
A		1	2	3	4	5	6	7	8	9
B			3	4	5	6	7	8	9	2
C				5	6	7	8	9	1	4
D					7	8	9	1	2	6
E						9	1	2	3	8
F							2	3	4	1
G								4	5	3
H									6	5
I										7
Bye										

FIGURE A-10. Round-Robin Schedules

TABLE A-3

	#1	#2	#3	Games #4	#5	#6	#7	Total	Score
Team #1	−5								
Team #2	+6								
Team #3	−6								
Team #4	+5								
Team #5									
Team #6									
Team #7									
Team #8									

tournament for players who are not yet in condition to play full-length games. The best length of basketball games is 5–6 minutes.

To assist in scoring the Lombard tournament, a scoreboard as diagramed above has been found helpful. For each game played, two scores must be recorded, one for each team. A team's scores are recorded and added *horizontally*. If Team #4 defeated Team #1 by a score of 10 to 5, Team #4's score would be +5 and Team #1's score would be -5. If Team #2 defeated Team #3 by a score of 6 to 0, its score would be +6 and Team #3's score would be -6 points. These scores are recorded as shown in Table A-3. The Lombard type of tournament can also be used effectively for volleyball, speedball, soccer, touch football, cage ball, handball, badminton, squash, and tennis. When it is used for volleyball, handball, squash, badminton, and tennis, only one game or set should be played against each opponent or a time limit can be used. This type of tournament is excellent for class competition and for one-day intramural tournaments.

Combination Tournaments

An excellent tournament for intramural purposes should provide for even or well-matched competition, be neither too long nor too short, exclude none from competition after a game or two, require few or no competitors to play a great many more games than other participants, and select a true champion. There are several forms of combined elimination and round-robin tournaments that meet these requirements reasonably well.

For purposes of illustration, a combination elimination round-robin tournament is presented for 20 basketball teams in Figure A-11. Two rounds of a double-elimination tournament are played first to classify the competitors into four leagues. To do this, seed teams as well as possible and play the first round, then have winners play winners and losers play losers. Place those who won twice in the first league; those who won one and then lost one in the second league; those who lost one and then won one in the third league; and those who lost two in the last league.

Now that the teams are classified, play a round-robin schedule for each league. Each team will then have played six games, two in classifying and four in its league. Place the first- and second-place winners of leagues one and two and the first-place winners in leagues three and four in the final championship tournament. This will discourage the practice of losing in the classifying rounds in order to gain a place in a weaker league. A double-elimination

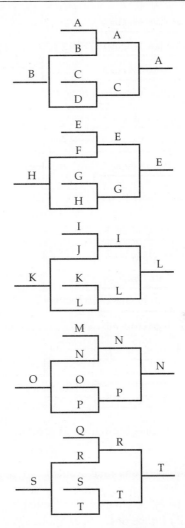

FIGURE A-11. Elimination Bracket (for a Combination Elimination Round-Robin Tournament

tournament is recommended for these six teams, but if time is short, a straight elimination may be necessary. A round-robin tournament may be used but it is not recommended because most of the teams are already eliminated, and the remaining six would need to play much more than the other teams.

An interesting method of providing even more participation is to group the place winners in leagues together in single-elimination tournaments. For example, put all first-place winners together; do likewise with the second-place teams in each league. Similar tournaments are drawn up for the teams in third, fourth, fifth, sixth, seventh, and eighth place. Figure A-12 shows the procedure when there are eight leagues. If there are fewer leagues, fewer games would be required to determine a champion. Byes would be used if the number of leagues isn't a perfect power of two.

FIGURE A-12. Single-Elimination Tournament for Finalist

At times, the space and time available are inadequate to permit even an elimination tournament for a large number of entries. When this occurs in certain sports, the number of participants can be quickly reduced by holding a qualifying round in which only the best performers qualify for the finals. Such sports as track and field, swimming, golf, bowling, and foul shooting are well-suited for the use of qualifying rounds. For example, in a golf tournament all the contestants may play a qualifying round and the 16 players with the best scores play a single-elimination tournament for the championship. To simplify tournament play, the number of entries that qualify is usually a power of two.

Challenge Tournaments

This form of tournament is desirable when the activity is such that is can be carried on by the players independently without formal schedules. It is used for single or dual competition rather than team sports. Tennis, golf, handball, squash, badminton, racquetball, horseshoes, and archery are the activities for which this type of competition is most commonly used.

A challenge tournament affords competition with contestants of near-equal ability. It provides an opportunity for all competitors to continue play because none are eliminated. It is entered into with more zest when all the players know each other. This type of tournament is useful in selecting team members in individual sports. When it is used this way, the players at the top of the ladder represent the institution in interschool competition. The ladder tournament is widely used by wrestling coaches to select the competitors in each weight each week.

There are two common types of challenge tournaments: the ladder and the pyramid (see Figure A-13). Contestants' names are written on cards that can either be placed in slots or hung on hooks. Placing the players on the ladder or in the pyramid in the order in which they sign up furnishes an incentive for all who are interested to sign up quickly. Positions can also be determined by the various players drawing numbers from a hat. Only if the time is short is seeding to be recommended.

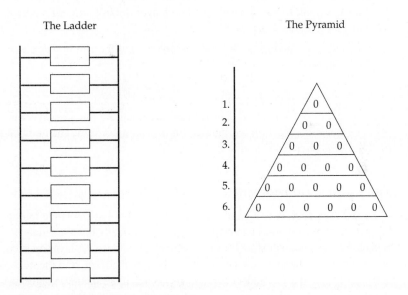

FIGURE A-13. Challenge Tournament

Rules governing play for the various forms differ somewhat, and local factors also modify them, but in general the following rules, with minor modifications, suffice.

It must be definitely stated what constitutes a win.

Players may advance by challenging and defeating, or by gaining default from defending player (player challenged).

In the ladder form, a player may challenge two players above him or her; that is, C may challenge A or B.

If the challenger wins, only players involved change places; if the defender wins, positions remain as before and the defeated challenger may not challenge the same player again for a week.

Challenges must be met in the order that they are made.

After two contestants have played, they cannot play each other again until each has played once with another contestant.

In some pyramid challenge tournaments, the rule exists that a player must defeat someone in her or his own horizontal row before he or she can challenge someone in the row above.

A defender must play within three days after receiving a challenge.

There is no acceptable excuse, except inclement weather, for failure to play within three days; if defender cannot play within a set limit, a forfeit is awarded.

In case of difficulty concerning challenging and acceptance of challenges, set up a challenge board or require all challenges to be dated and handed to tournament manager, who will then post them.

In the pyramid form, a player can challenge any player in the rank above; that is, any player in rank five may challenge any player in rank four, who may in turn challenge any player in rank three, and so on.

The player at the top of the ladder or pyramid at the end of a specified period of time is the winner.

An extension of the pyramid tournament has been found to be successful in intramural competition. A completion date is designated and the top 15 players in ranks 1–5 then play in a single-elimination tournament for the championship. The number-1 person on the pyramid gets a bye the first round.

The Funnel Tournament

The funnel tournament is a combination of the ladder and challenge tournaments. It works best with activities such as handball, badminton, racquetball, table tennis, and horseshoes. It is played off in a manner similar to a challenge tournament. A player must defeat someone in her or his own horizontal row before she or he can challenge into the next row. The top-six positions are played as a ladder tournament. When more than 20 contestants are entered in the tournament, the additional participants are placed on the bottom row (see Figure A-14).

The Tombstone Tournament

This is not a widely known tournament, yet it has been used very effectively for group and individual competition. It involves a cumulative score, and the person or team that accumulates the best record over a specified period of time or achieves a predetermined goal in the shortest time is the winner. For example, in swimming, each entrant indicates on a chart the distance swum each day. At the end of the stipulated period of time, the contestant who has swum the greatest distance is the winner. If the distance is established, such as 100 miles, the winner would be the person who first swam this distance. A chart such as that shown in Figure A-15 should be used to record the performance in this type of tournament.

The above procedure may be used for competitions in hiking, chinning (one trial per day), pushups, situps, distance running, long jumping, shot-putting, football punt for distance, and many similar events. For example, in basketball free throwing, it could be specified that each person was to make 25 throws each day. At the end of a month (or some other specified period) the player who has made the greatest number of baskets is the winner. In horseshoes, each player might play three games every day and record the total ringers made.

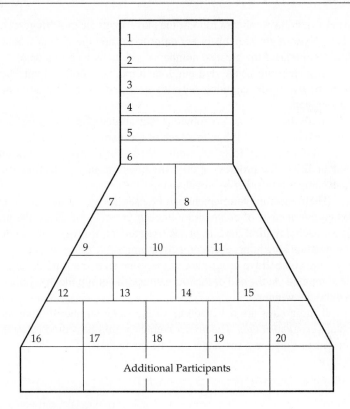

FIGURE A-14. Funnel Tournament

	June 1		June 2		June 3		June 4		June 5		
Entries	Daily Record	Total Score	Daily Record	Total Score	Daily Record	Total Score	Daily Record	Total Score	Daily Record	Total Score	
Jones, H.	44	5068	66	5134	22	5156					
Henry, B.	60	4896	60	4956	88	5044					
Brown. W.											
Marsh, M.											

FIGURE A-15. 100-Mile Swim (8,800 Pool Lengths)

After a definite number of rounds, the player with the most ringers is the winner. In archery, each player might keep his or her daily score, and the winner would be the contestant who had accumulated the greatest number of points by a certain date.

In such events as the shot put, long jump, and football punt, each player may be given three or five trials, counting only the best performance. Additional practice each day is encouraged.

In all these events, it is obvious that all competitors should compete under the same rules and conditions. When this type of tournament is conducted among widely separated units, it is necessary to select events that are little affected by varying weather conditions and facilities. The progress of the tournament in such a situation is made known to the various competitors either by telephone, post or e-mail.

The tombstone tournament can be used for group as well as individual competition. When the number of competitors in each group is the same, the group total can be computed each day until the end of the tournament. For example, to determine the winner in the standing long jump, each competitor jumps five times each day and counts the best jump. If all the competitive groups are of the same size, the total distance jumped each day can be computed. At the end of the tournament, the group that has jumped the greatest distance will be the winner.

If the groups are not made up of the same number of contestants, it is necessary to obtain group averages. The group average would be scored every day, and the group with the greatest total at a set date would be the winner.

B

Athletic Field and Court Layouts *

---

* Permission to reprint granted by Little League Baseball Incorporated, the National Federation of State High School Associations, and The National Collegiate Athletic Association.   Diagrams are subject to annual review and change.

5. Football

    a. Interscholastic
    b. Intercollegiate

6. Horseshoes
7. Ice Hockey
8. Lacrosse
9. Paddle Tennis
10. Pickle Ball
11. Racquetball/Handball
12. Soccer
13. Softball
14. Squash
15. Table Tennis
16. Tennis
17. Track

    a. 400-Meter Track
    b. Field Events

18. Volleyball
19. Wrestling

    a. Interscholastic
    b. Intercollegiate

It is beyond the scope of this appendix to include every detail of field and court dimensions or to show differences for all levels of competition. There are some differences between female and male competition in the same sport. Current rules of each sport should be consulted for detailed field and court information and for rule changes that affect court and field dimensions.

Badminton

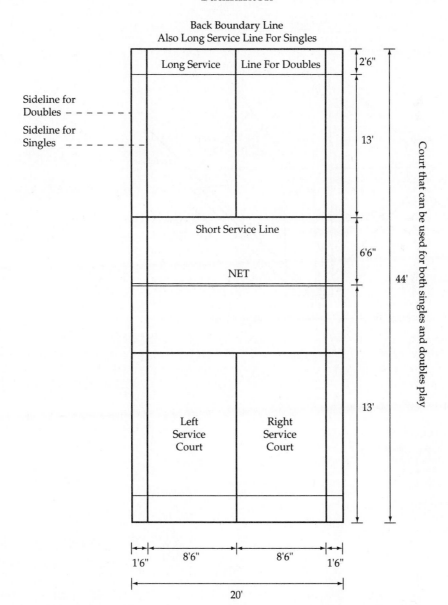

Back Boundary Line
Also Long Service Line For Singles

Long Service | Line For Doubles

2'6"

Sideline for
Doubles

Sideline for
Singles

13'

Short Service Line

NET

6'6"

44'

Court that can be used for both singles and doubles play

13'

Left
Service
Court

Right
Service
Court

1'6" 8'6" 8'6" 1'6"

20'

All marking stripes lie entirely within the court areas which their outer edges delineate, except the center line stripe, which is shared equally by its adjacent court. All marking stripes should be 1½" wide.

Baseball Diamond
(Regulation)

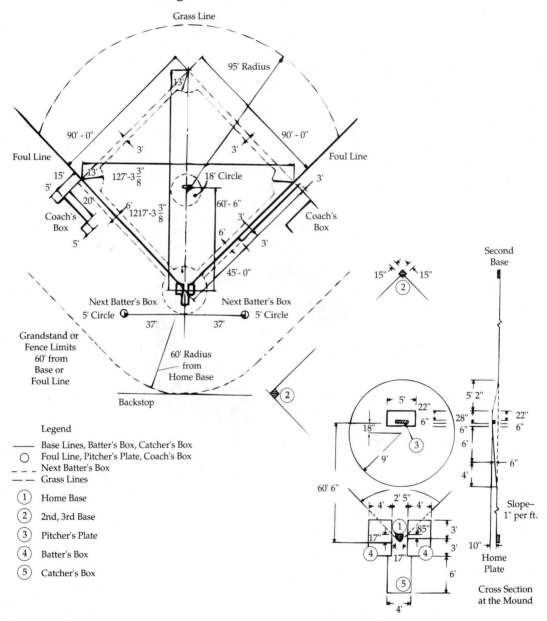

Grass Line

13'

95' Radius

90' - 0"

90' - 0"

Foul Line

Foul Line

15'

13'

127'-3 3/8"

18' Circle

3'

5'

20'

60'- 6"

6'

1217'-3 3/8"

3'

Coach's
Box

6'

Coach's
Box

5'

45' - 0"

Next Batter's Box

Next Batter's Box

5' Circle

5' Circle

37'

37'

Second
Base

15"

15"

2

Grandstand or
Fence Limits
60' from
Base or
Foul Line

60' Radius
from
Home Base

2

Backstop

5' 2"

5'

22"

28"

22"

18"

6"

6"

3

6'

9'

6"

60' 6"

4'

Legend

Base Lines, Batter's Box, Catcher's Box
○ Foul Line, Pitcher's Plate, Coach's Box
- - - Next Batter's Box
— — Grass Lines

① Home Base

② 2nd, 3rd Base

③ Pitcher's Plate

④ Batter's Box

⑤ Catcher's Box

2' 5"

4'

4'

3'

17"

85"

4

1

4

3'

17"

6'

5

4'

Slope–
1" per ft.

10"

Home
Plate

Cross Section
at the Mound

Baseball *
(Little League)

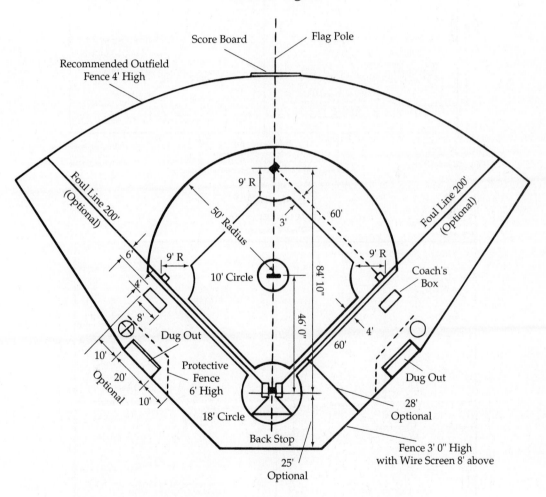

Score Board

Flag Pole

Recommended Outfield
Fence 4' High

Foul Line 200'
(Optional)

9' R

50' Radius

60'

3'

Foul Line 200'
(Optional)

6'

9' R

9' R

Coach's
Box

4'

84' 10"

10' Circle

46' 0"

4'

8'

Dug Out

60'

10'

Optional

20'

Protective
Fence
6' High

Dug Out

10'

28'
Optional

18' Circle

Back Stop

Fence 3' 0" High
with Wire Screen 8' above

25'
Optional

*Reprinted by permission of Little League Baseball Incorporated.

Basketball*
(Interscholastic)
Basketball Court Diagram

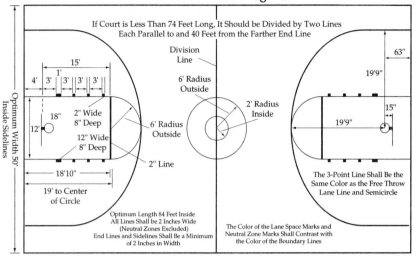

If Court is Less Than 74 Feet Long, It Should be Divided by Two Lines
Each Parallel to and 40 Feet from the Farther End Line

Division Line

6' Radius Outside

2' Radius Inside

63"

19'9"

15"

19'9"

Optimum Width 50' Inside Sidelines

15'

1'

4' 3' 3' 3' 3'

18"

2" Wide 8" Deep

12' 12" Wide 8" Deep

6' Radius Outside

2" Line

18'10"

19' to Center of Circle

The 3-Point Line Shall Be the Same Color as the Free Throw Lane Line and Semicircle

Optimum Length 84 Feet Inside
All Lines Shall be 2 Inches Wide
(Neutral Zones Excluded)
End Lines and Sidelines Shall Be a Minimum of 2 Inches in Width

The Color of the Lane Space Marks and Neutral Zone Marks Shall Contrast with the Color of the Boundary Lines

Left End Shows
Rectangular Backboard
72 Inches Wide

Minimum of 3 Feet
Preferably 10 feet of unobstructed space outside. If impossible to provide 3 feet, a narrow broken 1 inch line should be marked inside the court parallel with and 3 feet inside the boundary

Left End Shows
Fan Backboard
54 Inches Wide

Basketball**
(Intercollegiate)
The Court

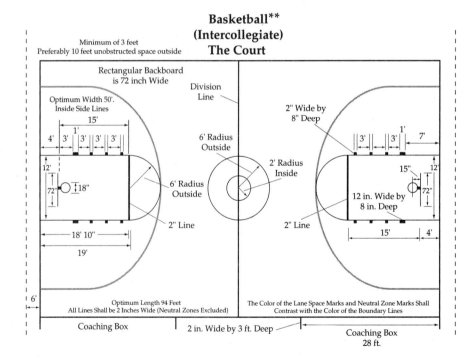

Minimum of 3 feet
Preferably 10 feet unobstructed space outside

Rectangular Backboard
is 72 inch Wide

Division Line

2" Wide by 8" Deep

Optimum Width 50'.
Inside Side Lines

15'

1'

4' 3' 3' 3' 3'

12'

72' 18"

6' Radius Outside

6' Radius Outside

6' Radius Outside

2' Radius Inside

2" Line

18' 10"

19'

1'

3' 3' 7'

15" 12'

72'

12 in. Wide by 8 in. Deep

2" Line

15' 4'

6'

Optimum Length 94 Feet
All Lines Shall be 2 Inches Wide (Neutral Zones Excluded)

The Color of the Lane Space Marks and Neutral Zone Marks Shall Contrast with the Color of the Boundary Lines

Coaching Box

2 in. Wide by 3 ft. Deep

Coaching Box
28 ft.

---

*   Reprinted with permission of the National Federation of State High School Associations.

**   Permission to reprint granted by the National Collegiate Athletic Association. This diagram is subject to annual review and change.

434

Field Hockey*

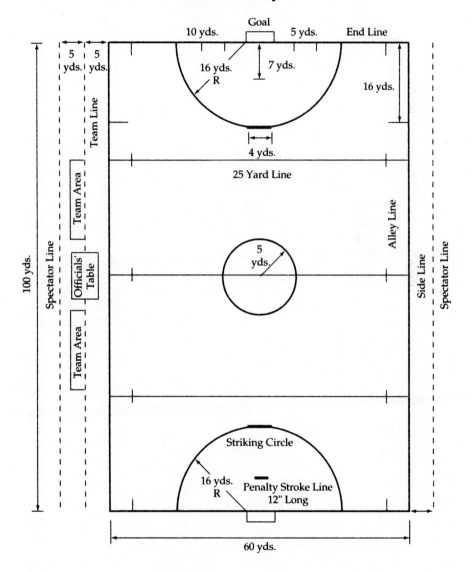

*   Reprinted with permission of the National Federation of State High School Associations.

435

Football*
(Interscholastic)

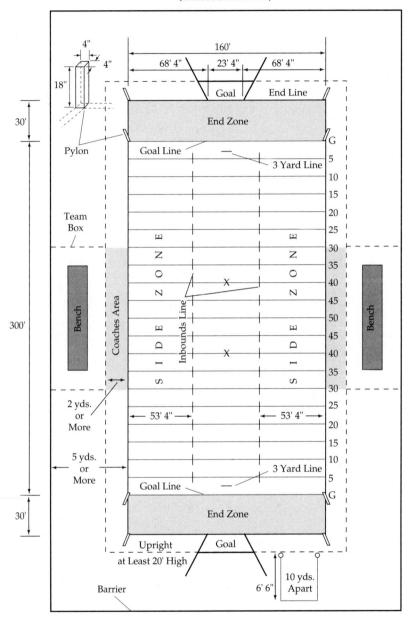

Note: Both team boxes may be on one side between the two 45- and 20-yard lines. End lines and sidelines should be at least 4 inches wide. Other field dimentions should be 4 inches wide.

Note: Recommend the area between team boxes and sidelines be solid white or marked with diagonal lines.

Note: Inbounds lines should be 24" long and 4" wide.

Note Recommend the field slope from center to each sideline at ¼-inch per foot.

Note: A 4-inch wide broken restraining line may be put around the entire field, 2 or more yards from the boundaries.

---

* Reprinted with permission of the National Federation of State High School Associations.

Football *
(Intercollegiate)

Diagram of Field

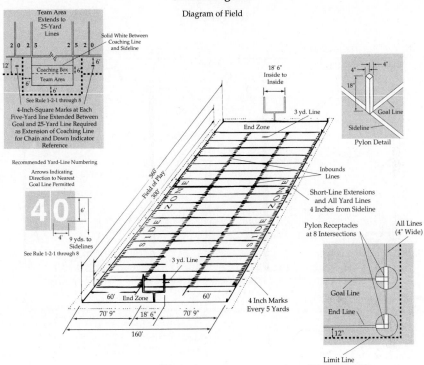

Team Area Extends to 25-Yard Lines

Solid White Between Coaching Line and Sideline

Coaching Box
Team Area

See Rule 1-2-1 through 8

4-Inch-Square Marks at Each Five-Yard line Extended Between Goal and 25-Yard Line Required as Extension of Coaching Line for Chain and Down Indicator Reference

Recommended Yard-Line Numbering

Arrows Indicating Direction to Nearest Goal Line Permitted

40

9 yds. to Sidelines
See Rule 1-2-1 through 8

18' 6" Inside to Inside

3 yd. Line
End Zone

Inbounds Lines

Short-Line Extensions and All Yard Lines 4 Inches from Sideline

Pylon Receptacles at 8 Intersections

All Lines (4" Wide)

3 yd. Line

60'   End Zone   60'

70' 9"   18' 6"   70' 9"

160'

4 Inch Marks Every 5 Yards

Goal Line
Sideline
Pylon Detail

Goal Line
End Line

12"

Limit Line
(12" at 24" Intervals)

Horseshoes

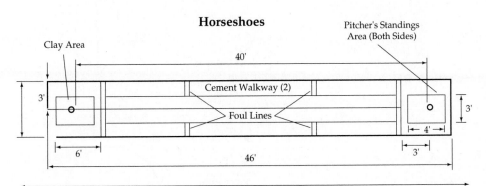

Clay Area

Pitcher's Standings Area (Both Sides)

40'

3'

Cement Walkway (2)

Foul Lines

3'

6'

4'

46'

3'

50' Total Court Length

1" x 3' stakes extended 14" above ground and incline 3" toward each other. Stakes 30' apart for women and boys under 16 years.

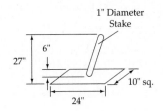

1" Diameter Stake

6"

27"

10" sq.

24"

*   Permission to reprint granted by the National Collegiate Athletic Association. This diagram is subject to annual review and change.

Ice Hockey

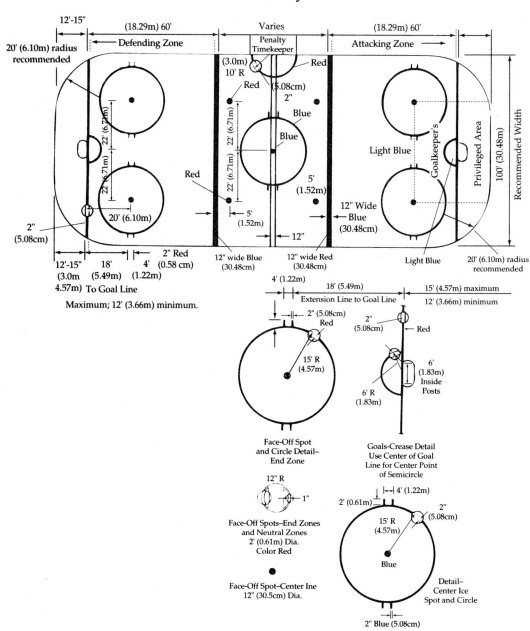

12'-15"

(18.29m) 60'

Varies

(18.29m) 60'

Defending Zone

Penalty
Timekeeper

Attacking Zone

20' (6.10m) radius
recommended

(3.0m)
10' R

Red

Red

(5.08cm)
2"

Blue

Blue

Red

Light Blue

Goalkeeper's

Privileged Area

Recommended Width

22' (6.71m)

22' (6.71m)

22' (6.71m)

22' (6.71m)

100' (30.48m)

2"
(5.08cm)

20' (6.10m)

5'
(1.52m)

12" Wide
Blue
(30.48cm)

5'
(1.52m)

12"

Light Blue

20' (6.10m) radius
recommended

2" Red
(0.58 cm)

12'-15"
(3.0m
4.57m)

18'
(5.49m)

4'
(1.22m)

To Goal Line

12" wide Blue
(30.48cm)

12" wide Red
(30.48cm)

Maximum; 12' (3.66m) minimum.

4' (1.22m)

18' (5.49m)

15' (4.57m) maximum

Extension Line to Goal Line

12' (3.66m) minimum

2" (5.08cm)
Red

2"
(5.08cm)

Red

15' R
(4.57m)

6'
(1.83m)
Inside
Posts

6' R
(1.83m)

**Face-Off Spot
and Circle Detail–
End Zone**

12" R

1"

**Face-Off Spots–End Zones
and Neutral Zones
2' (0.61m) Dia.
Color Red**

**Face-Off Spot–Center Ine
12" (30.5cm) Dia.**

**Goals-Crease Detail
Use Center of Goal
Line for Center Point
of Semicircle**

2' (0.61m)

4' (1.22m)

2"
(5.08cm)

15' R
(4.57m)

Blue

**Detail–
Center Ice
Spot and Circle**

2" Blue (5.08cm)

Lacrosse *

The Lacrosse Field of Play

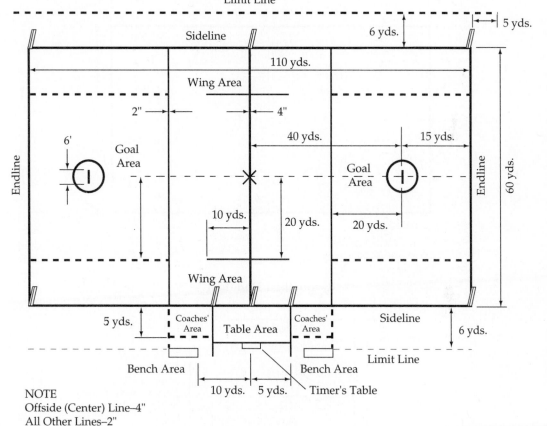

Limit Line

Sideline

6 yds.

5 yds.

110 yds.

Wing Area

2" — 4"

40 yds.

15 yds.

6'

Goal Area

Goal Area

Endline

Endline

60 yds.

10 yds.

20 yds.

20 yds.

Wing Area

5 yds.

Coaches' Area

Table Area

Coaches' Area

Sideline

6 yds.

Limit Line

Bench Area

Bench Area

10 yds. 5 yds. Timer's Table

NOTE
Offside (Center) Line–4"
All Other Lines–2"

Paddle Tennis

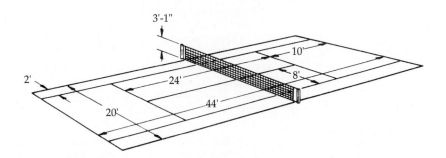

3'-1"

10'

2'

24'

8'

20'

44'

*   Permission to reprint granted by the National Collegiate Athletic Association. This diagram is subject to annual review and change.

Pickle Ball

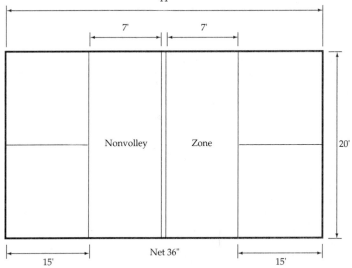

Racquetball/Handball

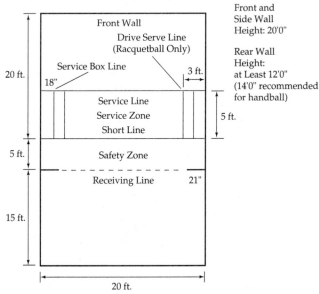

Handball One-Wall

The dimensions for a standard one-wall handball court are: the wall shall be 20 feet from the outside edge of one side line to the outside edge of the other side line, and 16 feet high, including any top line.

Handball Three-Wall

The dimensions for a standard three-wall handball court are: 20 feet wide, 20 feet high and 40 feet long, with side walls recommended length of 44 feet.

Soccer *

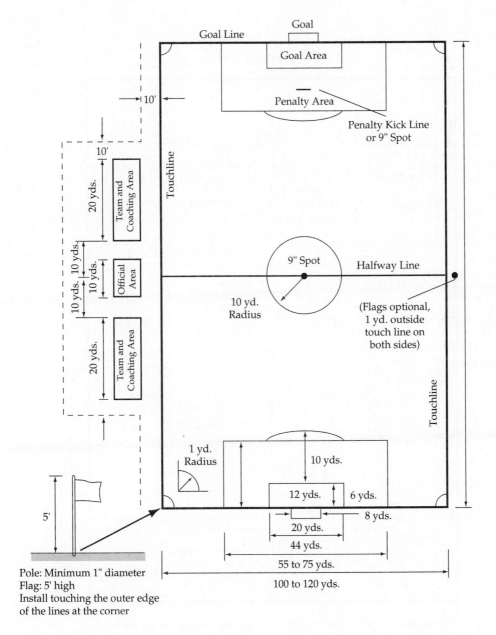

Pole: Minimum 1" diameter
Flag: 5' high
Install touching the outer edge
of the lines at the corner

* Permission to reprint granted by the National Collegiate Athletic Association. This diagram is subject to annual review and change.

Softball

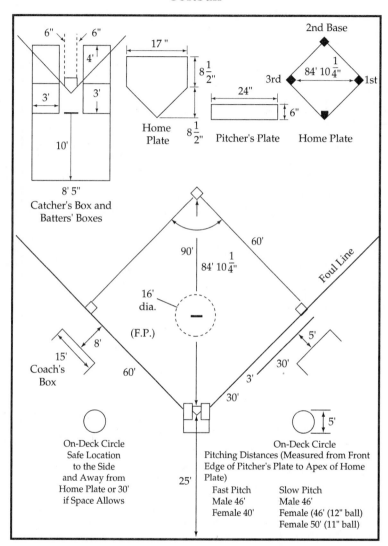

The minimum and maximum distances for the outfield fences vary with the age of competitors and level of competition.

Squash

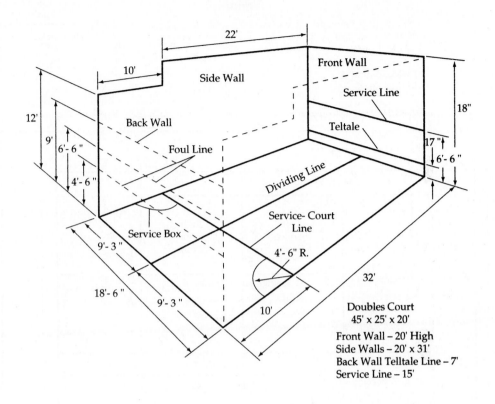

22'

10'

Side Wall

Front Wall

Service Line

18"

12'

Back Wall

9'

6'- 6 "

Foul Line

Teltale

17 "

6'- 6 "

4'- 6 "

Dividing Line

Service Box

Service- Court
Line

9'- 3 "

4'- 6" R.

32'

18'- 6 "

9'- 3 "

10'

Doubles Court
45' x 25' x 20'

Front Wall – 20' High
Side Walls – 20' x 31'
Back Wall Telltale Line – 7'
Service Line – 15'

Table Tennis

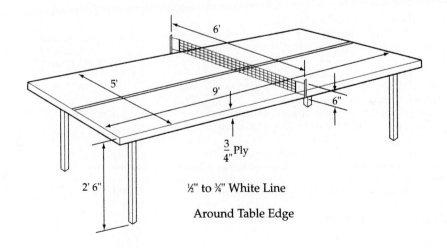

6'

5'

9'

6"

$\frac{3}{4}$" Ply

2' 6"

½" to ¾" White Line

Around Table Edge

Tennis

True Plane Slope Requirements:
1" in 20' 0" to 1" in 30' 0"
Fast Dry Courts

1% Maximum
Hard Courts

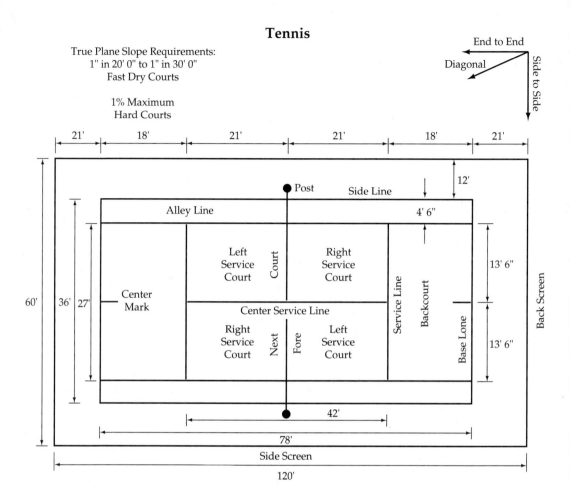

HOW TO LAY OUT A TENNIS COURT

First spot place for net posts, 42 feet apart. Measure in on each side 7½ feet and plant stakes 27 feet apart at points A and B in diagram

Then take two tape measures and attach to each peg—one tape 47 feet 5¼ inches, the other 39 feet. Pull both taut in such directions that at these distances they meet at point C. This gives one corner of the court. Interchange the tapes and again measure to get point D and measure 18 feet toward net and put in pegs to denote service lines.

Proceed in same way for the other half of court and add center line from service line to service line—distance 42 feet. Then add 4½ feet on each side for alleys. Alleys should then be 2 feet inside posts on each side. Put in permanent pegs to mark all corners.

Measure to outside edge of boundary lines.

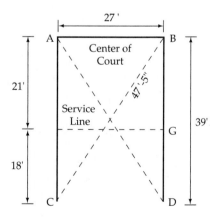

Track*
(400 Meter)

400 Meter Event Markings Layout

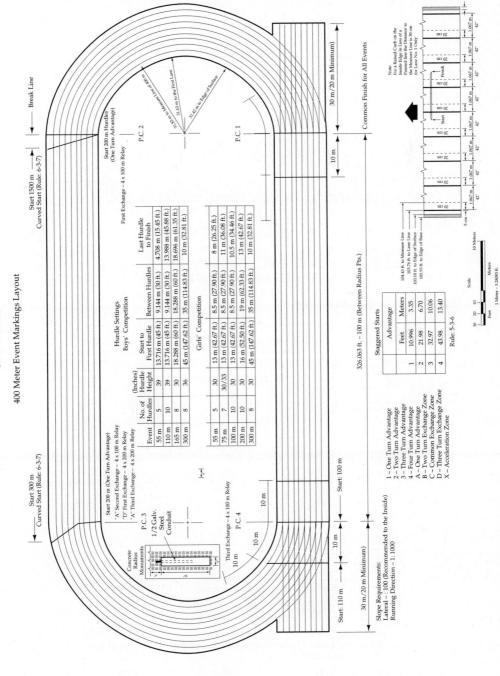

Hurdle Settings

Boys' Competition

Event	No. of Hurdles	Hurdle Height (Inches)	Start to First Hurdle	Between Hurdles	Last Hurdle to Finish
55 m	5	39	13.716 m (45 ft.)	9.144 m (30 ft.)	4.708 m (15.45 ft.)
110 m	10	39	13.716 m (45 ft.)	9.144 m (30 ft.)	13.988 m (45.88 ft.)
165 m	8	36	18.288 m (60 ft.)	18.288 m (60 ft.)	18.696 m (61.35 ft.)
300 m	8	36	45 m (147.62 ft.)	35 m (114.83 ft.)	10 m (32.81 ft.)

Girls' Competition

Event	No. of Hurdles	Hurdle Height (Inches)	Start to First Hurdle	Between Hurdles	Last Hurdle to Finish
55 m	5	30	13 m (42.67 ft.)	8.5 m (27.90 ft.)	8 m (26.25 ft.)
75 m	7	30/33	13 m (42.67 ft.)	8.5 m (27.90 ft.)	11 m (36.08 ft.)
100 m	10	30	13 m (42.67 ft.)	8.5 m (27.90 ft.)	10.5 m (34.46 ft.)
200 m	10	30	16 m (52.50 ft.)	19 m (62.33 ft.)	13 m (42.67 ft.)
300 m	8	30	45 m (147.62 ft.)	35 m (114.83 ft.)	10 m (32.81 ft.)

Staggered Starts

	Advantage	
	Feet	Meters
1	10.996	3.35
2	21.98	6.70
3	32.97	10.06
4	43.98	13.40

Rule: 5-3-6

1 – One Turn Advantage
2 – Two Turn Advantage
3 – Three Turn Advantage
4 – Four Turn Advantage
A – One Turn Advantage
B – Two Turn Exchange Zone
C – Common Exchange Zone
D – Three Turn Exchange Zone
X – Acceleration Zone

Slope Requirements:
Lateral – :100 (Recommended to the Inside)
Running Direction – 1:1000

Start 300 m
Curved Start (Rule: 6-3-7)

Start 1500 m
Curved Start (Rule: 6-3-7)

Break Line

Start 200 m (One Turn Advantage)
"A" Second Exchange – 4 x 100 m Relay
"D" First Exchange – 4 x 200 m Relay
"A" Third Exchange – 4 x 200 m Relay

Start 200 m Hurdles
(One Turn Advantage)

First Exchange – 4 x 100 m Relay

P.C. 2

P.C. 1

P.C. 3

P.C. 4

Concrete Radius Monuments

1/2 Galv. Steel Conduit

Third Exchange – 4 x 100 m Relay

Common Finish for All Events

30 m/20 m (Minimum)

10 m

30 m/20 m (Minimum)

Start: 100 m

Start: 110 m

326.063 ft. – 100 m (Between Radius Pts.)

10 m

10 m

10 m

Note:
For a Raised Curb on the Inside Edge in Lieu of a Painted line the Distance to the Measure Line is 30 cm for Lane No. 1 Only.

104.43 ft. to Measure Line
103.76 ft. to Lane Line
103.10 ft. to Edge of Surface
102.93 ft. to Edge of Base

Scale

Meters
Feet

1 Meter – 3.2808 ft.

*   Permission to reprint granted by the National Collegiate Athletic Association. This diagram is subject to annual review and change.

Track *
(Field Events)

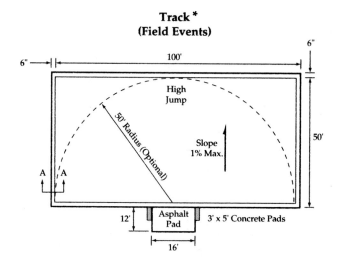

Long Jump and Triple Jump *

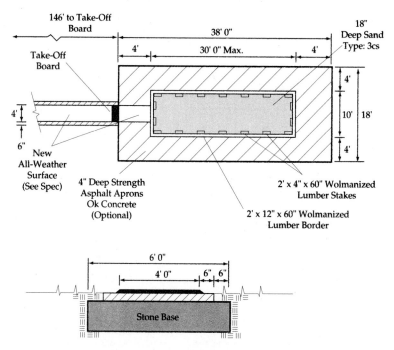

The scratch line shall be located by measuring from the nearer edge of the landing pit a distance of approximately:

	Boys	Girls
Long Jump	12 feet	8 feet
Triple Jump	32 feet	24 feet

---

* Permission to reprint granted by the National Collegiate Athletic Association. This diagram is subject to annual review and change.

Pole Vault*

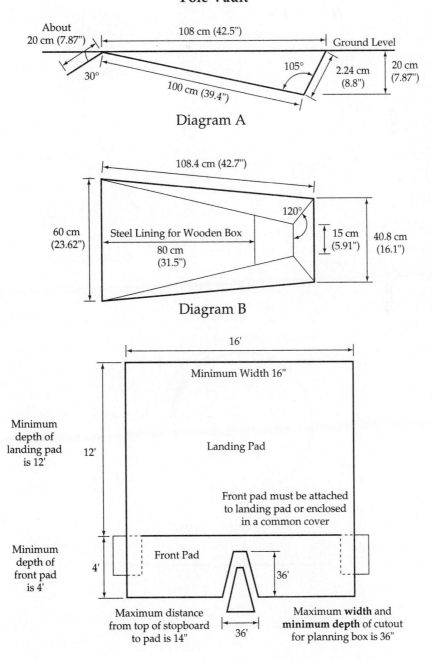

About
20 cm (7.87")

108 cm (42.5")

Ground Level

30°

100 cm (39.4")

105°

2.24 cm
(8.8")

20 cm
(7.87")

Diagram A

108.4 cm (42.7")

60 cm
(23.62")

Steel Lining for Wooden Box

80 cm
(31.5")

120°

15 cm
(5.91")

40.8 cm
(16.1")

Diagram B

16'

Minimum Width 16"

Minimum
depth of
landing pad
is 12'

12'

Landing Pad

Front pad must be attached
to landing pad or enclosed
in a common cover

Minimum
depth of
front pad
is 4'

4'

Front Pad

36'

Maximum distance
from top of stopboard
to pad is 14"

36'

Maximum **width** and
minimum depth of cutout
for planning box is 36"

*   Reprinted with permission of the National Federation of State High School Associations.

Discus*

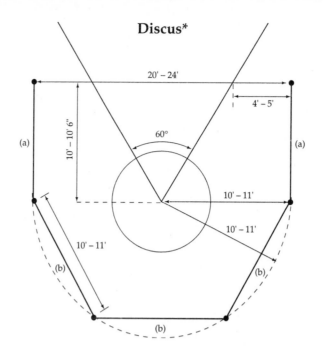

Shot Put*

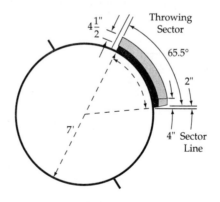

Javelin Throw*

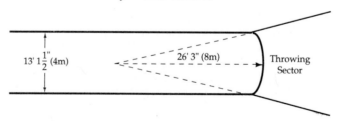

*   Permission to reprint granted by the National Collegiate Athletic Association. This diagram is subject to annual review and change.

Volleyball*

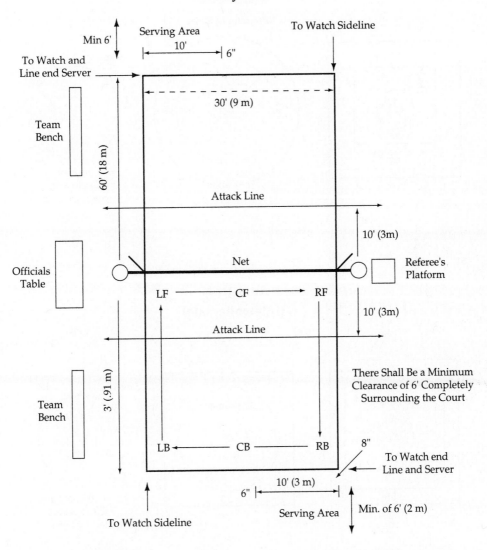

It is recommended that the area above the court be clear of any obstructions at least 30 feet high.

---

*   Reprinted with permission of the National Federation of State High School Associations.

Wrestling*
(Interscholastic)

Minimum Mat Size

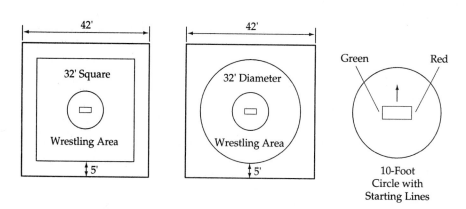

10-Foot
Circle with
Starting Lines

Wrestling
(Intercollegiate)

10-Foot
Circle with
Starting Lines

* Reprinted with permission of the National Federation of State High School Associations.

C

Curriculum Guidelines

Sample Curriculum Guide for Elementary Physical Education (Grades 1–5)

The program will be based on the mission statement, philosophy, and objectives of each school district.

Mission Statement of the School District

Mission Statement of the School

Philosophy of Physical Education

Objectives of the Physical Education Program for Each Grade as Formulated by the School's Curriculum Committee

Kindergarten Objectives

Grade 1 Objectives

Grade 2 Objectives

Grade 3 Objectives

Grade 4 Objectives

Grade 5 Objectives

Sample Scope and Sequence Program Content (Determined by Grade Objectives)

K–3

Movement Activities	8 weeks
Basic Play Skills and Ball-Handling Skills	4 weeks
Low Organized Games	8 weeks
Gymnastics and Tumbling	3 weeks
Basic Rhythms, Expressive and Creative Activities	10 weeks
Rope Jumping and other Playground Games	3 weeks

Grades 4–5

Physical Fitness Activities	4 weeks
Games (some modified) and Sports Skills	16 weeks

Soccer	Basketball
Football	Track and Field
Floor Hockey	Softball

Tumbling and Gymnastics	5 weeks
Folk Dance and Rhythms	5 weeks
Individual and Dual Activities	6 weeks

Skills of Bowling, Paddleball, and Racquet Use
Modified Individual Games

Sample Curriculum Guide for Middle School Physical Education (Grades 6–8)

The program will be based on the mission statement, philosophy, and objectives of each school district.

Educational Goals of the School District

Educational Philosophy of the School District

Physical Education Philosophy

Objectives of the Physical Education Program for Each Grade as Formulated by the Curriculum Committee

Grade 6 Objectives

Grade 7 Objectives

Grade 8 Objectives

Sample Scope and Sequence Program Content (Determined by Grade Objectives)

Grades 6–7

Body Mechanics	2 weeks
Physical Fitness Activities	4 weeks
Team Games and Sports Skills	16 weeks

Soccer	Basketball
Flag Football	Floor Hockey
Field Hockey	Softball

Rhythm and Dance	4 weeks

Square Dance
Line Dances
International Folk Dances

Developmental Activities   6 weeks

Track and Field
Wrestling
Tumbling and Gymnastics

Individual and Dual Activities   4 weeks

Tennis, Bowling, Golf

Grade 8

Physical Fitness	4 weeks
Team Games	14 weeks

Soccer	Basketball
Field Hockey	Flag Football
Softball	Speedball

Rhythms and Dance   5 weeks

Square Dance
Line Dance
Country Dance
International Folk Dance

Developmental Activities   5 weeks

Track and Field
Wrestling
Self-Defense

Individual and Dual   8 weeks

Swimming	Golf	Bicycling
Tennis	Skating	Adventure Education Skills

Sample Curriculum Guide for Senior High School Physical Education (Grades 9–12)

The program will be based on the mission statement, philosophy, and objectives of each school district.

Mission Statement of School District

Mission Statement of the High School

Physical Education Philosophy

Objectives of the Physical Education Program for Each Grade as Formulated by the Curriculum Committee

Grade 9 Objectives

Grade 10 Objectives

Grade 11 Objectives

Grade 12 Objectives

Sample Scope and Sequence Program Content (Determined by Grade Objectives)

Grades 9–10

Dance	6 weeks

Jazz	Line
Folk	Country
Social	

Developmental Activities	12 weeks

Tumbling and Gymnastics
Track and Field
Wrestling
Self-Defense Activities
Weight Training

Team Sports	12 weeks

Soccer	Volleyball
Touch Football	Softball
Flickerball	Field Hockey
Basketball	Lacrosse
Team Handball	

Leisure Time Activities	6 weeks

Handball	Tennis
Racquetball	Pickleball
Table Tennis	Adventure Education

Grades 11–12

Dance	6 weeks

Jazz	Line
Folk	Country
Social	Modern

Developmental Activities	10 weeks

Aerobics	Wrestling
Weight Training	Track and Field
Jogging	Self-Defense
Power Walking	Physical Conditioning
Stress Management Techniques	

Team Sports	8 weeks

Ice Hockey	Volleyball
Basketball	Ice Hockey
Floor Hockey	Team Handball

Leisure Time Activities	12 weeks

Badminton	Golf
Archery	Swimming
Bowling	Downhill Skiing
Orienteering	Mountaineering
Cross-Country Skiing	

Sample Curriculum Guide for Senior High School Health Education (Grades 9–12)

The program will be based on the mission statement, philosophy, and objectives of each school district.

Statement of Educational Beliefs of the School District

Philosophy for Health Education in the Education of Students

Role of Health Education in the Curriculum

Coping and Decision-Making Skills

Objectives of the Health Education Program for Each Grade as Formulated by the Curriculum Committee

Grade 9 Objectives

Grade 10 Objectives

Grade 11 Objectives

Grade 12 Objectives

**Sample Scope and Sequence Program Content
(Determined by Grade Objectives)**

Grade 9

Concept of Wellness and Personal Health   9 weeks
Substance Use and Abuse   9 weeks
Human Growth and Development (Family Life Education)   9 weeks
The Body Systems   9 weeks

Grade 10

Human Growth and Development (Family Life Education)   9 weeks
Physical Fitness and Nutrition   9 weeks
Safety and Accident Prevention   9 weeks
Mental Health   9 weeks

Grade 11

Diseases and Disorders—Coping with Disease   9 weeks
Consumer Health   9 weeks
Substance Use and Abuse   9 weeks
Human Growth and Development   9 weeks

Grade 12

Environmental Health   9 weeks
Death Education   9 weeks
Mental and Physical Wellness and Health Care Systems   9 weeks
Safety and First Aid   9 weeks

Index

458